# BANJO

# EYES

# BANJO

# EYES

*Eddie Cantor and the Birth of Modern Stardom*

HERBERT G. GOLDMAN

*New York Oxford*
*Oxford University Press*
*1997*

Oxford University Press

Oxford   New York
Athens   Aukland   Bangkok   Bogotá   Bombay
Buenos Aires   Calcutta   Cape Town   Dar es Salaam
Delhi   Florence   Hong Kong   Istanbul   Karachi
Kuala Lumpur   Madras   Madrid   Melbourne
Mexico City   Nairobi   Paris   Singapore
Taipei   Tokyo   Toronto   Warsaw

and associated companies in
Berlin   Ibadan

Published by Oxford University Press
198 Madison Avenue, New York, New York 10016

Oxford is a registered trademark of Oxford University Press

Library of Congress Cataloging-in-Publication Data
Goldman, Herbert G.
Banjo eyes : Eddie Cantor and the birth
of modern stardom / Herbert G. Goldman.
p.   cm.   Discography: p.   Filmography: p.
Includes bibliographical references and index.
ISBN 0-19-507402-5
1. Cantor, Eddie, 1892–1964. 2. Entertainers—United States—
Biography. I. Title
PN2287.C36G66   1997   791'.092—dc21   [B]   97-8254

1 3 5 7 9 8 6 4 2

Printed in the United States of America
on acid-free paper

*To*
*Randi Heather, Jordan, Daniel, and Kevin*
*My niece and nephews*

# CONTENTS

*Acknowledgments*                                          i x

*Prologue*    MORE THAN MEETS
              THE EYES                                     xi

*Chapter*  1  THE *BUBBA* AND HER
              ITCHIK                                        3

*Chapter*  2  THE TURNING                                  2 0

*Chapter*  3  THE CLIMB                                    3 6

*Chapter*  4  THE *FOLLIES*                                5 7

*Chapter*  5  OF EQUITY AND
              SHUBERTS                                     7 5

*Chapter*  6  *KID BOOTS*                                  9 4

*Chapter*  7  *WHOOPEE*                                   1 1 6

*Chapter*  8  EYES ON THE MEDIUM   1 3 5

*Chapter*  9  THE PEAK                                    1 5 8

*Chapter* 10  ''BEFORE I'M A
              PERFORMER . . .''                          1 8 3

*Chapter* 11  ''WE'RE HAVING A
              BABY''                                      2 1 2

*Chapter* 12  THE OTHER MADONNA   2 2 9

*Chapter 13*   COLGATE COMEDY
                        HOUR                                256
*Chapter 14*   "... AND YOU HAVE TO
                        GIVE IT ALL BACK"           282
*Epilogue*       "OLD PERFORMERS
                        NEVER DIE..."                   308

*Notes*                                                         313
*Bibliography*                                             316
*Stageography*                                          317
*Filmography*                                             356
*Radiography*                                             370
*Televisionography*                                   377
*Discography*                                             381
*Index*                                                         395

# ACKNOWLEDGMENTS

Constance Moore, Sheila Rogers, Jane Kesner Ardmore, Arthur Penn, Ernest Lehman, the late Harry Fender, Barney McNulty, the late Winnie Branley Hanson, Lee Newman and other members of the Eddie Cantor family, Eddie Kafafian, Eddie Fisher, Doris Eaton, Thelma Carpenter, Irving Cahane, Dr. William L. Brooks, Joe Breeden, Miles M. Kreuger of the Institute of the American Musical, Joe Franklin, Fayard Nicholas, Amanda Gari, Judy McHugh, the late Henry Morgan, the staff of Surprise Lake Camp, Cold Spring, N.Y., Phyllis Rosenteur, David Brown, Jean Vanderpyle, Henry Tobias, Donald Kahn, Gloria Stuart, Robert Feldman, Henny Youngman, Budd Schulberg, Arthur Tracy, Virginia Mayo, and Elliott J. Novak are hereby thanked for their time and cooperation.

Several photographs are from the private collection of Elliott J. Novak.

*Prologue*

# MORE THAN MEETS
# THE EYES

Eddie Cantor has been dead for more than thirty years. In view of the high level of stardom he enjoyed, the length of time he held it, and the different media in which he was important, he has become the most forgotten star of the twentieth century.

Cantor made no films that are either enjoyed as classics, like Frank Capra's It's a Wonderful Life, or analyzed obsessively by students of the cinema, like *The Cabinet of Dr. Caligari*. He did not star in TV shows that have remained in syndication. He is also not—and never was—a darling of the intelligentsia.

Cantor, his individual talents aside, was essentially a musical comedy performer. Musical comedy—its comedy as important as its music—ruled the Broadway stage during the '20s, survived well past the establishment of "integrated musicals" in the 1940s, and did not die until the mid-1960s, when the musical theatre took new directions ranging from theatrical (*Man of La Mancha*) to cynical (*Sweet Charity*) to experimental rock 'n' roll (*Hair*). By the early '70s, musical comedy, and indeed, musical theatre as, primarily, an *entertainment* medium was a rarity, presented as "nostalgia."

Indeed, musical comedy, arguably the purest form of *entertainment*, is often viewed as something of a jester-lackey to the culture of pre-1965—a culture now seen, frankly, as repressive. Nor can old Broadway musicals be viewed as abstract art, as can silent films, which seem a world unto themselves due to their very nature. Cantor was so much a part of this now largely despised "show biz"—the very mention of which causes discomfort to many and which is often thought as "better left forgotten"—that his name has, since the '70s, been greeted with disdain, or with blank stares from those who do not understand his importance, style of performance art, or talent.

His films do not "wear well." *Whoopee*, a decided triumph when it premiered back in 1930, has been called a "film fiasco," as indeed it is—when seen on home TV. Cantor's subsequent UA-Sam Goldwyn pictures fare only slightly better on television.

Cantor's highly theatrical style seems antiquated, not only because the advent of twenty-four-hour television replaced our taste for entertainment with a need for pacifing diversion or because the stage no longer serves as mainstream entertainment. The influence of rock 'n' roll, in which the performer is largely the catalyst for a group experience as opposed to the performer-audience experience of traditional stage entertainment, has tended to make presentation-style performing of the sort practiced by Cantor seem pretentious. His style with a song does not seem much in keeping with the rather joyless spirit of the post-Watergate era. He is not an icon, like Marilyn Monroe, or an antihero, like James Dean. Nor is he saved by anarchy, as are the Marx Brothers.

Cantor was an "antic" as opposed to a "skill" performer. His performance persona is very Jewish, pushy as opposed to merely upwardly mobile, a character with whom the "average man" (c. 1920) could either (as a Jew) readily identify or (as a non-Jew) recognize and readily accept. Nor does Cantor's frequent use of blackface make him any more politically correct.

Shows like *Whoopee* and *Kid Boots*, filled with topical humor, geared to certain stars and decked out with long-forgotten stage conventions that seem bizarre in surviving films, were looked upon as old-fashioned in the 1950s. By the 1980s, they seemed scarcely real, not merely primitive "old" shows but archaic relics from a long-forgotten era that had been not merely eclipsed but totally supplanted by new entertainments. "Stagey" became a term of contempt with the growth of film study in the 1970s. Broadway shows became increasingly abstract, often bloodless imitations of the cinema, striving vainly to compete with film on film's own terms. If shows like *Whoopee* and *Kid Boots* seem not just old but hopeless to us now, it is primarily because we have lost our taste for not only musical comedy (which seemed sinfully indulgent for a faulted culture during and after Vietnam) but for stage show business itself.

Performers of Eddie Cantor's genre are seen, in general, as vaguely reactionary—the result, largely, of George Jessel's hawkish image during Vietnam and Walter Winchell's pro-McCarthy rantings after World War II. Nostalgia for the '20s, common from the '50s to the mid-1960s, is viewed in much the same way. Cantor, in a sense, was the "inventor" of nostalgia— the first still established media star to reminisce and lionize "the old days."

Nor does Cantor's later image, from the '30s on, as the father of five daughters, strike responsive chords in a society in the process of rethinking old ideals of family and parenthood.

Why then, do a book on Eddie Cantor?

That he was a talent at one point becomes apparent to those who seriously study his career and take into consideration his best recordings (made in the late '20s and the early '30s), his two silent films (the first of which reveals his great talent as a pantomimist and physical comedian), and his early sound films (when viewed in a theatre). Cantor did not leave us a great body of work. There is, however, enough to suggest (and, at times, to display) the great performer he was at his peak in the mid-'20s.

Cantor was the first great performer-"humanitarian." He founded the March of Dimes, which still functions as one of the world's leading money raisers for good causes. He was an early, vociferous, and quite effective supporter of the State of Israel and raised, all told, more than a billion dollars for various charities within a span of less than forty years. All this, of course, is temporal. The March of Dimes, like other charities of its ilk, is today taken for granted, and philanthropy seems old hat and meaningless within the context of the modern welfare state.

Cantor's importance lies in how he, singlehandedly and consciously, changed the very nature of stardom.

Stars, before the 1930s, were, quite simply, actors of a certain rank, performers who had reached the top rung of an insular and curious profession, not potential role models for public behavior or people whose public and private lives were interchangeable—and fair game for paparazzi.

Eddie Cantor came into an unexploited, largely unexplored medium called commercial radio and used it to redefine stardom. Through his repeated references to his wife, Ida, and to their five daughters (Marjorie, Natalie, Edna, Marilyn, and Janet), he made himself a "member of the family" to millions of Americans in a way that no performer had ever sought to be. This star—Eddie Cantor—cared, ostensibly (and really), about politics, the kids who might be killed by careless drivers, and the lives of all the "ladies and gentlemen" who listened to his weekly broadcasts, which invariably concluded with his singing one chorus of "I Love to Spend Each Sunday with You." Listening to Cantor was a family experience, and Eddie seemed both more and less than a performer. He was "one of the family" and yet a public figure only slightly less revered than Franklin D. Roosevelt.

Eddie Cantor's use of his own family as radio props—allowing him to share his own private life with millions of Americans—made his private life a public one as well. Through Cantor's influence, the line between "celebrity" and "actor" became gradually blurred, and stars were finally perceived not as simply top-of-the-line actors but as public figures.

This is the story of "Banjo Eyes," the Jew who rose from truly abject poverty to become the best-known and most highly paid performer of the mid-1930s, a man who conquered all the media but whose star has proved to be the most ephemeral of any of the "superstars," an entertainer who demanded more than "just" show business and in so doing redefined the nature of his calling.

# BANJO
# EYES

# Chapter 1

# THE *BUBBA* AND
# HER ITCHIK

*"I grew up on the sidewalks of New York,
with an occasional fall into the gutter."*

There are myths about Eddie Cantor, the perpetually young Jew with the big, rolling eyes, joyous, clapping hands, and chatty East Side manner who became the first multimedia superstar and a "member of the family" in countless homes during the 1930s. He was born in New York City, supposedly on January 31, 1892, and was orphaned at the age of two.

These myths, like others about Cantor, are untrue. He was not born on January 31, 1892. Nor was he, apparently, an orphan.

The Cantor saga begins in Belarus, in 1834, the year a daughter was born to Javel Lazarowitz and his wife, Mindel Abramowitz. They named her Esther, and, like most girls of that time, she married early. Her husband, a cigar maker named Abraham Kantrowitz, doubtless gave her many children. Only four survived, however—three sons and a daughter. Life expectancy was not high in Belarus, and Abe died, a victim of the tobacco and nicotine fumes of his trade, around the age of forty, leaving his still young wife to support four children with a small cigar business.

Esther rolled cigars, ran the business, kept her house, and raised four children, saving a few rubles on the side but never purchasing a license. Dragged before a magistrate on more than one occasion, she made funny faces, danced, and made him think that she was totally insane.

She continued rolling her cigars, which grew steadily in local reputation, until nihilist revolutionaries assassinated Czar Nicholas II in March 1881. Anti-Semitic pogroms and the so-called "May laws" followed. The lot of the Jews in the czar's empire, never enviable, steadily grew worse, and Esther used part of her savings to get her two elder sons, now both in their twenties, to America.

Esther's main concern, at this point, was her daughter, Meta—in her

3

early twenties and in love with Mechel Iskowitz, a young local ne'er-do-well and dreamer who spent most of his time playing the violin. Esther blessed their marriage, but she worried for their future. Mechel could not seem to make a living.

Her two sons in America were both supporting families. So were many other Jewish immigrants. Opportunities in the United States seemed limitless compared to those in Belarus, especially, she hoped, for dreamy Mechel.

Esther gave her daughter and her new son-in-law the money to emigrate, helped them through the czar's red tape in Mintz, and wished God's blessings on them as they left for what would be a two-week journey overland, by ship across the Baltic Sea to England, and from there to New York City. The year was 1890.

New York City in the early 1890s—known, somewhat ironically, as the "Gay '90s"—consisted of a cauldron of immigrants crowded into its southern end, growing businesses as one went north to midtown, and fine private residential homes beginning in the Fifties (recalled by Clarence Day in *Life With Father*). The theatre district was "everywhere," with theatres in the Bowery, along Fourteenth Street, and the most prestigious houses along Herald Square [Thirty-fourth Street]. More than a cauldron, however, New York was then a cacophony of sounds—a dozen accents ricocheting off surrounding buildings as immigrant mothers called their children home for supper, noon whistles blowing, vendors hawking their wares on the streets, children shouting, horses whinnying, and people yelling. America, the land of opportunity for many, was, for Mechel, a big noisy, senseless world he never made—a nightmare he would never understand.

What, if anything, he did to gain employment is uncertain. He played the violin but probably did not read music well enough to play in corner cafes, much less symphony orchestras. At times, he found jobs, but they never lasted. To top it all off, Meta became pregnant after a year and a half. With the baby due about September, Meta and her helpless husband turned to the only stable influence their lives had ever known—to Meta's mother, Esther.

Esther sold her business for a fraction of the price she might otherwise have gotten, said good-bye to her youngest son, now also in his twenties, and left for America as quickly as she could. She arrived to find her pregnant daughter all but starved and Mechel unemployed and hopeless, the two of them living in a two-room tenement apartment above a Russian tea room on Eldridge Street in the dreariest section of the East Side ghetto.

Esther moved in quickly, doling out money to Mechel to buy food and pay the rent and preparing for the birth of her new grandson.

Israel Iskowitz was born on Rosh Hashanah, the Jewish New Year, in September 1892. He was dark, resembling his father, with large eyes and a deceptively strong body that showed signs of the malnutrition Meta had experienced in the months prior to Esther's arrival.

In later years, the wife of this same Israel would ask his grandmother what it was like on the day he was born. "Hot" was Esther's answer. Hot and, it might well be added, hopeless.

Esther's savings dwindled as the baby grew, forcing the family to move to even cheaper rooms at 39 Jackson Street. When Israel was a year old, Meta came down with a lung disease, phthisis pulmonolis, and the rest of Esther's money went for medicines and, as things worsened, doctors.

Meta Kantrowitz Iskowitz died, age twenty-seven, on July 26, 1894. Mechel was completely numbed, but Esther, through her grief, found strength enough to arrange for a funeral and to continue caring for her grandson.

Esther had no money left to bury her young daughter. The Hebrew Free Burial Society deposited her body in an unmarked grave in Silver Lake Cemetery, Staten Island.

Eddie Cantor's various memoirs say that his father died a year after his mother, a victim of pneumonia. These same accounts say that Meta died in childbirth.

In point of fact, it was his mother, Meta, not his father, who died of a lung disease. Meta's death certificate confirms this. One might expect the doctor who attended Meta to have attended her husband a year later. Many births went unreported in New York until the City of Greater New York (comprising the five boroughs of Manhattan, the Bronx, Brooklyn, Queens, and Richmond) was incorporated in 1898. (There is no birth certificate for Israel Iskowitz.) Comparatively few deaths, though, went unreported.

Yet there is no death certificate for Mechel Iskowitz. Indications are he simply left his young son in his mother-in-law's care and left to start a new life with his violin. He may have changed his name, remarried, and started a new family. One thing, though, is almost certain: Israel Iskowitz, later known as Eddie Cantor, *thought* he was an orphan.

Or did he? About 1950, Eddie told his new son-in-law, Roberto Gari, that the worst thing a man could do was to desert his children. He said it with an angry passion, as if he either knew—or sensed—the truth of his own background.

He did not learn it from Esther. The God-fearing Jewess simply looked after her grandson and, in time, told him he was an orphan. It was easier that way. As far as Esther was concerned, her ne'er-do-well son-in-law was dead indeed—free to start a new life without Itchik, as she called her grandson. An orthodox Jew, Esther may have covered up the mirrors in the tiny rooms on Jackson Street, the same way she had done when Meta died a year before.

Izzy never saw his mother's unmarked grave on Staten Island—probably so that he would not ask why his father's grave was not there alongside it. His parents would remain a closed book to the boy. He seldom asked about them, and his grandmother volunteered very little information, discouraging his inquiries with quick and rather nebulous responses.

What became of Mechel, when and where he died, and whether he lived to see the son he had abandoned become rich and famous is unknown. All that remains is a photograph of Mechel, well dressed and looking deceptively prosperous. He is seated in a chair, his handlebar mustache and dreamy eyes the chief distinction between him and his well-known, saucer-eyed son. There is no indication when, or why, the photograph was taken— only the conspicuous absence of his young wife, Meta. Whether it was taken before or after her death—or his own presumed disappearance—is a matter of conjecture. Suffice to say that his son possessed it in the 1920s, had it published in his first, ghost-written, book, and never seemed to mention it again.

Itchik replaced Meta in his grandmother's affections. From this point on, her grandson and her grandson alone, became the recipient of her incessant, selfless devotion.

Esther, who was sixty-one, appealed to one of her sons, now living in New York with his wife and three small children, to take her and Itchik in until such time as she could figure out another course of action. It did not work out, due largely to her daughter-in-law's resentment but partly also because of the hyperactive Itchik. The boy was either beating his two female cousins, Minnie and Annie, or being beaten by his male cousin, Irwin. When his uncle's wife found Itchik dropping forks and spoons over the railing from the fifth floor to the foyer, she made him go to bed without his supper. Esther, the indulgent grandma, brought him chicken and cookies and kissed and soothed him.

Esther had gone into business, of a sort, by peddling such things as candles, threads, and other bric-a-brac from a basket, becoming known to other Jewish women in the neighborhood. Increasingly, she was expected to supply the food for Itchik. If his aunt prepared a special dish, he was summarily informed that it was for "the family"—not for him. The situation worsened, until Esther thought the time had come to take the boy and raise him on her own.

Esther Lazarowitz Kantrowitz and her maternal grandson, Israel Iskowitz, moved into the basement apartment at 47 Henry Street in or around 1897. Next door, at 49, was Henry Hall, the scene of innumerable Jewish wedding receptions. The neighborhood was Jewish, with the buildings getting better as one walked a few blocks north.

They had three rooms—a living room, a bedroom, and a kitchen, with a bathtub in the kitchen. "From here, there's only one place to go  up," Esther told Itchik in Yiddish. She also spoke Russian and Polish but was just beginning to learn English. Speaking Polish, though, is what enabled her to live and support Itchik.

Esther now had businesses besides her basket vending. One was sewing—almost as a sideline, since most housewives still did their own mending. Another one was running an unlicensed employment agency for servant girls straight off the boat. The girls were generally Polish, and Esther soon established a small network by which they were contacted, still in Poland, via other girls for whom she'd found employment or who lived with her and Itchik in the basement flat on Henry until she could find them positions. Six or seven Polish girls might occupy the living room on any given night. Occasional inspectors were informed that they were young Itchik's cousins or sisters.

Employment for servants was then plentiful; middle-class people, as well as the rich, generally could afford two or three servants due to the low cost of living. A housewife would come to the basement apartment and tell Esther what she wanted in a servant: someone who could cook well, clean well, care for a baby like its own mother, with a good disposition—all for the lowest possible salary. The minute she would leave, Esther would take a couple of small, mincing steps and imitate her client with a Yiddish accent: "Cook vell, clean vell, care for de babee. . . ." Esther never lost the inborn talent for theatrics that had let her run her cigar-rolling business with no license.

Esther would select one of the girls from the next room, carry her trunk (on her own sturdy, sixty-year-old back) to the address, and collect a dollar as her finder's fee. Such was the Kantrowitz unofficial, unlicensed employment agency.

Another source of Esther's income was her work as a *shadchen*—a matchmaker. Most of the young women were immigrants, and Esther's matchmaking fee was twenty-five dollars—if the couple married.

Then she would attend the wedding, go to the reception at Henry Hall, wrap all sorts of delicacies in napkins, and stuff them in the long pocket of her skirts. Arriving back in the apartment late at night, she'd waken Itchik from a sound sleep and give him chicken, meat balls, lox, and wedding cake. She was concerned about her grandson's wan appearance. "So skinny," she would say in Yiddish, "such a plucked little owl." She'd rub the back of Itchik's neck and murmur, "Itchik, Itchik, we build this up, make it strong, yes?"

She hoped the boy would live to his Bar Mitzvah.

The woman did the best she could raising the "orphaned" boy. In the fall of 1898, she dressed him up and took him to Public School 126 at 80 Catherine Street, near Henry. When the registrar asked "Name?" she mistakenly gave her own, Kantrowitz. The registrar wrote down "Kantrowitz," and the school, ever anxious to accelerate "Americanization," shortened it to "Kanter."

More confusion followed. At one point, Itchik had to know his birthday. *Bubba* (Yiddish for "grandmother"), as he always called Esther, told him he was born on "New Year's" and the boy, thinking she meant the "American" New Year, wrote "January 1st." This somehow became corrupted into January 31st. The latter date was celebrated as his official birthday for the remainder of his life, making Itchik think he was seven and a half months older than he really was.

As a boy without a father, Itchik had one real goal as soon as he reached seven, or "the age of reason": to see just how much he could get away with.

Itchik—Izzy on the outside—was quickly initiated into the world of the street. There were gang wars—Henry Street against Division Street, Cherry against Catherine, Market against Oliver. If boys on Division found a boy from Henry on their turf, they'd back him up against a corner, threatening to kill him. Itchik suffered beatings on a number of occasions. Sometimes, he would get away by pleading, "Go ahead, hit me. I've got no one to protect me, no father, no mother. . . ." He had found a way to turn his "orphan" status to advantage.

He stole . . . because he was hungry, because it was the thing to do among the neighborhood boys, because it gave him status and made him "one of the gang"—a kid no one would pick on. He stole because he wanted things he didn't have, because he had no parents and wanted to see how far he could go before the law, or *Bubba*, or some other, unseen force would stop him.

His first thefts were from pushcarts, groceries, and delicatessens. Esther left a nickel on the kitchen sink each morning for him to buy lunch with—four cents' worth of salami and a penny's worth of bread. But the hungry boy would augment this with fruits swiped from pushcarts—plums, bananas, anything he could grab while the vendor was distracted.

Isidore (as he was called by his teachers) Kanter's enrollment at P.S. 126 did not last long, probably because the school found out that he should have gone to P.S. 2 or P.S. 1 on Henry Street. His stay at P.S. 2, his next stop, at 112 Henry, lasted scarcely longer. They expected him to do homework, pass tests, and know the answers to questions in class.

Izzy had heard of anti-Semitism, though he seldom experienced any on New York's East Side; even the various street gangs at war with one another were all largely Jewish. The concept, nonetheless, was both inviting and convenient, as much a crutch for him as Jews would be scapegoats for others. The teachers at this new school, he told *Bubba*, hated Jews.

They were certainly not soft on children. "My father, Sam Levy, was a friend of his at that time," Ted Levy recalls. Sam, the leader of a street gang, got "an A in work, a D in conduct" while attending P.S. 2. "One time, he misbehaved, and the teacher walked toward him to hit him with a ruler. Kanter, who was seated near him, laughed, so the teacher forgot about my father, turned around and whacked Kanter, who started to cry."

Izzy soon left P.S. 2 for P.S. 1.

Nostalgic though he was in later years, Eddie Cantor never romanticized his youth on New York's Lower East Side as an easy existence. He would, however, dramatize his childhood, making it sound as if some mysterious hand had guided him into show business while Lefty Louie went to the electric chair for the Rosenthal murder—the implication being that a handful of God-favored kids, like him, were "rescued," while the rest went on to lives as either criminals or beggars. Sidney Kingsley couldn't have written it any better.

In fact, most of Eddie's peers—Ira Atkins, Jonah Goldstein, Sammy Levy—wound up owning and/or working in small businesses. Others studied and fought their way into professions such as medicine or law. East Side residents did not see themselves as victims, and if immigrant Jews like Esther Kantrowitz were forced to spend their lives in poverty, their children could—and usually did—better. America was the land of the possible. In the meantime, there were candles to be sold and steamer trunks to be hauled up five flights of stairs by seventy-year-old women.

The people of the East Side had little concern for fresh air. In truth, there was no fresh air on the East Side at the time. Each and every neighborhood had its distinctive odor—of cheese (Orchard Street), garlic (the Italian quarter), herring (Jewish), or fish (the area under the Williamsburg Bridge). Nor did people object to these smells; each was simply part of the neighborhood. If New York seemed like a cacophony of sounds to Mechel Iskowitz, it seemed like a mélange of smells to his son, Izzy.

There was no air conditioning, and most kids thought that summer was the roughest season, weatherwise, in the city. To Izzy, though, the winters were the toughest. In November, seeking to keep out the cold air, he and Esther nailed all the windows shut in their basement apartment. "We'd go to sleep literally drugged from lack of oxygen," he later recalled, "the servant girls on the floor and *Bubba* and me in the big feather bed, and all about us in the tenements, other people struggling similarly for survival and a breath of air."

Izzy's first attempts at comedy date from this time. Seeking to relieve the humdrum poverty of his existence and to win the approval of his schoolmates and the tougher kids who made up the street gangs, he'd imitate his *bubba*'s imitations of the customers who called on her for servants, do other imitations of the Polish girls who slept in the apartment, pretend that he was choking, and pop his big eyes when all else failed. After a short time, he was accepted as a "neighborhood character" who made the other boys laugh. He was soon considered valuable, worthy of protection by the toughest of the street gangs.

This bent for entertaining carried over to his schooling. Turn-of-the-century school curriculums were oriented toward reading, memorization, and, to some extent, reciting; Izzy soon distinguished himself with two "classic" monologues, "The Traitor's Deathbed" and "The Soul of the Violin." The former concerned Benedict Arnold, while the latter was a rather overwrought soliloquy about a starving violinist, forced to sell his violin, remembering a long-ago performance in Vienna. "It has come at last, old comrade," he now tells his violin. "It has come at last, the time when you and I must say good-bye." Miss Walker, his first-grade teacher, was so impressed with his heartfelt rendition that she had him recite it at graduation exercises, overlooking undone homework, failed tests, and lack of concrete answers to the questions asked in classroom in the process.

Part of Izzy's inattention may have been due to hyperactivity. Also to blame were his hunger, his lack of a father figure, and the fact that, in the winter, he was cold. "Our clothes were so thin," he later recalled. "I never had an overcoat, and no matter how many old vests, ragged sweaters, or shirts I piled on—*Bubba* was always bringing home some rag for extra padding—the wind from the East River sliced through to the bone. You'd sit in school all day in snow-damp clothes, your shoes stuffed pulpy with wet cardboard."

In December 1900 he wrote to Santa care of the Children's Column of the New York *Evening Journal*: "Dear Santa, I am an orphan. I have no mother or father." It was the way he started everything. He asked for a warm overcoat, a pair of boots, some mittens, and a sled.

On Christmas Day, he sat on the stoop of 47 Henry, a sodden heap of wet clothes watching other children bellyflop down the street on their sleds, cursing the New York *Evening Journal* and its owner, William Randolph Hearst, whose name was on its masthead. *Bubba* urged him to come in for tea, but he just sat there all day, sad, silent, and angry, until the end of the day when, suddenly, a New York *Evening Journal* truck pulled up to 47 and the driver asked the kids for "Isidore Kanter."

He ran up excitedly, received the package, and opened it out on the street, his friends clustered around. Inside were all the presents he had asked for in his letter.

He wept tears of relieved anger and depression. *Bubba* also wept, but for a different reason. She, like him, had never received anything before.

One year later, he received a different present. Using the cover of a boiler as a shield over his arm in a street gang battle, he squared off against another kid who came waving a rock. Izzy shielded his body, but the kid cracked him on the forehead.

Izzy went to the local drugstore—as close to an M.D. as East Side people liked to get—and had the pharmacist sew up his cut. The next morning, he awoke to find his forehead looking as if a baseball were imbedded in the skin. *Bubba* took him to the Good Samaritan Dispensary on Essex Street, where a doctor took him to an operating room, reopened his forehead, cleaned the wound, and sewed it up again.

Predictably, he was left with a scar. In later years, the onstage Eddie Cantor always covered it with makeup. It was a souvenir of childhood, a childhood so filled with misery that he could not disguise it.

One of the earliest reform movements aimed at life on New York's storied but wretched Lower East Side was the Educational Alliance, with its Community House at 197 East Broadway. Izzy was introduced to its pleasures, which included a warm place to spend some hours on cold winter Sundays, by his best friend, Dan Lipsky. Dan was smart and serious, forever calculating, and not disposed to emotion. He didn't fight, he did his homework, and he was a "nice Jewish boy" who used his brain to aid the other boys around Henry and Orchard. As was the case with Izzy, Danny's talents won him acceptance, and he was not generally bothered by the larger, rougher kids who ran the street gangs.

The street gangs in the neighborhood were practically all Jewish. So too were the shopkeepers, pushcart vendors, and the Educational Alliance. Indeed, the only non-Jews in young Izzy Kanter's world were a few landlords and the teachers—a sharp contrast to New York as it would later be. Izzy thus saw non-Jews as the "haves." They had the education, the position, and, presumably, the money and the power and—in Izzy Kanter's own subconscious—the parents. *They* were the people that the Jews would have to show.

Izzy, poorer than his friends and schoolmates, was also much more conscious of his Jewishness and lack of power. Not all of this was due to *Bubba*'s tales of White Russia. Izzy actually admired the non-Jewish world and people, but the sword was double-edged. The non-Jews were a mountain to be climbed, a ruling class to be not only emulated but brought down, on occasion, to the level of "the poor," the "tenants," and, of course, "the Jews," who would, in Izzy's mind, be poor forever. It seemed that much a part of being Jewish.

In the early 1900s, three leaders of the Educational Alliance created a new program through which East Side kids were sent out to the country for fresh air, good food, exercise, and a "wholesome" environment markedly different from the crowded City of New York. So was born the Alliance Camp in Cold Spring, Putnam County, New York, forty-five miles north of New York City.

July 1903 saw Izzy Kanter and Dan Lipsky among the boys sent to Cold Spring for two weeks of canoeing, swimming, baseball, and fresh air. The nominal fee of three dollars included transportation via the New York Central Railroad to a small station called Storm King, just a little north of Cold Spring and the camp. From the station, the campers, carrying their baggage, hiked three and a half miles on the stony Breakneck Road until they reached the camp.

To Izzy, it seemed like a different world—land without end, innumerable trees, no tenements, few buildings, very little noise, aside from that made by him and the other campers, and a large (man-made) body of water, ideal for swimming and canoeing, known as Surprise Lake. The land on which the camp lay had been bought from William O. and Catherine Jaycox for $2,125 only a few weeks before the boys' arrival. The camp then had six tents, which housed twenty-five campers and five counselors.

Kanter would idealize the camp in later years, but indications are that it was far from ideal, especially for ten-and eleven-year-old kids away from home for the first time. Mr. Moses, a club leader at the Educational Alliance, ran the camp, with Leonard Bloomer as general handyman and Mrs. Bloomer as the cook. The counselors were all in their late teens and did not hesitate to use physical discipline on their young charges.

According to some people who had been there in the early days, Izzy ran away after a counselor had hit him and hid out, alone, in the woods. He came back at the end of day and was befriended by the Bloomers.

He, along with other kids, broke windows with rocks—"for the hell of it"—wherever they could find them. Cold at night while sleeping in a tent, Izzy stole the blankets of other boys as they lay sleeping.

He fought, he played, he slept, and, most important, he ate. He still detested getting up in the cold mornings and was often late for breakfast. Camp rules forbade the serving of latecomers after the last bell, but Mrs. Bloomer never let a kid go hungry—especially her pet, the scrawny little orphan Izzy Kanter.

He signed up to entertain at the big campfire on Saturday night, reciting both "The Traitor's Deathbed" and "The Soul of the Violin" with such vehemence that he got laughs instead of tears and the directors complimented him on his "parodies." Hailed as the camp's "comedian," he broke into his imitations of the Polish girls and, wrapping a kerchief around his head, posed as a grand and haughty servant girl interviewing and cross-examining her miserable mistress. He also sang—on key, and well enough to earn the admiration of his audience of perhaps thirty people.

In the days that followed, Izzy tied a tin can on his head to imitate "Happy Hooligan" of the comic strips. He became known as "Happy Kanter" and, much to his great joy, was told that he could stay on for another two weeks to entertain new campers. Then those two weeks ended, and he was put back on the train to a hot August in New York and the meager diet he had known since birth.

The closest things approaching hearty meals for him in New York were the *Shabbos* dinners Esther made for Friday evenings—usually a stew prepared from the tough cuts of meat she could afford to buy from the cheap butchers. Izzy swallowed most of it unchewed and tried to sneak out of the house right after dinner. If Esther caught him, he would have to wash his face and go to *shul* with her. Usually, he managed to evade her and get on the streets to prowl, joke for other kids, and sometimes get himself in trouble.

At the age of eleven, Izzy got his teeth knocked out. How or why it happened is unknown. He may have been dashed to the pavement by a larger kid, been punched in the mouth by an irate shopkeeper who discovered he'd been swiping produce from his market, been smashed by a cop, or taken another rock in a street battle. At any rate, a photo taken when he was about thirteen shows him, mouth ajar and toothless, with his cousins Jack and Murray. He is wearing big and awful-looking shoes and looks, to all intents and purposes, like a gangly, adolescent bum.

Esther had been paying nine dollars a month rent for the basement apartment at 47 Henry Street. Late in 1903, the rent was raised to twelve dollars, and Esther hunted for new lodgings. She found them in the backyard of a tenement house at 11 Market Street, which contained a cheaper building that housed sixteen families. These "backyard" houses were one-building slums, even by the lowest standards of the early 1900s. There was no fire escape at 11 Market, and the only toilet was out in the yard, but the rent was only seven dollars a month. There was little room for Polish girls to stretch out on the floor, but Esther took the apartment and moved in with Izzy. She tried to make up for the blow to her employment business by selling more bric-a-brac and taking in more sewing, but it was a losing battle. These were the really bleak times, and Izzy always went to bed a little hungry. Sometimes a lot.

He got a job as a delivery boy at a delicatessen next door at 13 Market Street. The deli sold Isaac Gellis meat products, and Izzy's job consisted principally of picking up corned beef, pastrami, salami, and frankfurters from the Gellis factory at 37 Essex and carrying them to the deli in a basket. He got three cents a trip—or two sandwiches, whichever he preferred. He always took the sandwiches. "Salami," he remembered. "I was all salami. When I walked down the street, I was a sausage with eyes." The arrangement lasted until the rent at Henry Street dropped back down to nine dollars. He and *Bubba* moved back to their old basement apartment, with its ample room for Polish girls to bed down on the floor.

He went back to the Alliance Camp—now known, increasingly, as Surprise Lake Camp—in the summer of 1904. This time, he fit in with camp life from the start and formed a "Camp Club" with Dan Lipsky and several other kids from the East Side. He also became friendly with Jack Holman, back for his second year as one of the counselors, a friendship that would last sixty years and work to the great benefit of Surprise Lake.

In the city, he continued to run wild, all the more so since, at going on thirteen, he was old enough to run with tougher street gangs. He remained the darling of P.S. 1 and of teachers like Miss Craig, Miss Luddy, and Miss Fuller, but even his free passes in the world of academics were to end in 1905.

His teacher at this time was the redheaded and red-mustached Thomas W. Clark, a no-nonsense educator who called Izzy to his desk and told him he did not care how well he could recite; he would not get promoted until he got passing grades.

A short time later, Izzy asked permission to leave the room. He left, and never returned.

Izzy did not tell Esther he had dropped out of school. He spent his days wandering around the city, sometimes playing games with his companions, swiping fruit and vegetables from vendors. When, in due course, a truant officer called at 47 Henry while Esther was out peddling her wares from door to door, Izzy told him he had quit school because he was the "sole support" of his poor old grandmother. The official looked at the apartment, nodded, left, and never came again.

He went away to Surprise Lake for the third time that summer and managed to stay there for the entire eight-week season. Surprise Lake Camp had become one place where he belonged—the star of every campfire entertainment, the camp "ham" and comedian, and one who lent a hand to younger campers.

That fall, at thirteen, he was Bar Mitzvah, the official confirmation ceremony for Jewish boys. Esther paid a dollar and a half a week for him to take the lessons that would enable him to read from the Torah in perfect Hebrew, with a little *haftorah* (later books of the Old Testament) thrown in. He pretended to go for the lessons but spent his time on the street until a few days before his Bar Mitzvah. Then he spoke to the rabbi, who gave him a short bit to learn in order not to disgrace Esther Kanter.

Izzy added a few lines to his Bar Mitzvah speech. Looking at his *bubba*, seated in the upstairs of the Pike Street Synagogue, he said, "There sits my grandmother. She has been my father and my mother."

It was, he later claimed, the closest that she ever came to seeing him onstage.

Esther had put enough money aside to get Izzy a watch for his Bar Mitzvah. By the time the service ended, and he left the Pike Street Synagogue, the watch was missing. He was sure the *shamos* had stolen it.

From that point on, he went from bad to worse, joining with a gang that robbed Applebaum's Bicycle Shop in the neighborhood. Raised up on the shoulders of two older boys, Izzy crawled in through the transom and unlocked the door. The boys then rode three bikes to Harlem, where they sold them to another shop—whose owner asked no questions—for fifteen dollars. The two big kids split most of the money, leaving Izzy little more than carfare to get home. Crime, at thirteen, did not pay—well.

In June 1906 Izzy bummed around the playground of P.S. 177 and watched a vivacious girl in a basketball game. She was the star of the team—athletic, vivacious, and exciting—things he was unused to seeing in the poor girls who, half-starved, fearful, and miserable, lay down to sleep in the "living room" of *Bubba*'s Henry Street apartment.

Seeking to impress her, he began to do his pantomimes, stomping around like the various vaudeville comedians, doing imitations and parodies of popular songs. The athletic director, Mrs. Ray Schwartz, sought to throw him out, but the athletic girl asked her to let him stay.

He implored Mrs. Schwartz to let him sing with the brass band, and she at last relented. Izzy sang "My Mariucca Take A Steamboat," a popular Italian dialect number of the day, and watched as the girl looked at him with a curious mixture of love, pity, and admiration.

The girl, Ida Tobias, was a few days short of her fourteenth birthday. Her father, David, was a businessman who made a good enough living to support his son, Milton, his six daughters, Anna, Jenny, Minnie, Ida, Clara, and Nettie, and his wife, the former Rachel Slotzki, a religious fanatic who made her apartment home to every starving rabbi in the city.

"The apartment always stank from them," Ida later recalled. Rachel's other prominent characteristics were frugality—many considered her the stingiest woman on New York's East Side—and a steadfast refusal to learn English.

The Tobias home, located at 123 Henry Street, a couple of blocks north of Esther Kanter's place at 47, was noted for the female figures on either side of its main entrance—busts with exposed bosoms. The building—and the busts—remain there to this day.

Izzy started, more and more, to hang around the Recreation Center at P.S. 177—entertaining with his bits and trying to make Ida laugh. He invited her to the Educational Alliance where, after the meeting, the other boys would go for a soda. Izzy tried to hustle up a dime, but the only time sodas materialized was when Ida fixed it so that he would earn a dime running an errand. It was always, he later found out, her own dime.

"For Ida," he would later recall, "summer nights when the kids were sitting on the curbs, I'd hang myself from the street lamp, sing, crack jokes, stand on my head. Anything for an exhibition." One of Ida's friends was going with a boy named Eddie. Ida thought the name was "cute" and that it suited Izzy.

If Ida liked it, Izzy loved it. "Eddie" soon became his name.

He went away to Surprise Lake Camp for the fourth time in July and wrote letters to *Bubba* and Ida. He was going on fourteen, and deep into puberty. Ida gave him something to hang on to, a focus, a sense of self-worth at one of the most difficult periods in any boy's life.

In August, just returned from Surprise Lake, he found that Ida had been seeing another boy, a budding postal clerk named Louis Rosner. Ida's family did not approve of Eddie Kanter. He was a bum, her father said, who had dropped out of school, could never hold a job, and ran around with wild kids and stole things. Hearing this from Ida, as he did, was sobering. He wanted her and the good things she represented, and he knew he had to change. For the moment, all he felt was alienation.

He never had the money to go to the theatre, but one play related to his juvenile interest in the Wild West—young Joseph Santley in *Billy the Kid*. The play, based on the exploits of the twelve-year-old killer of the 1880s, played the Thalia Theatre late that summer. Eddie wanted desperately to see it.

A young girl, a recent immigrant still living with them in the basement flat on Henry Street, had saved twelve dollars—and had been naive enough to let young Eddie know it. He stole her purse while the girl was washing her face, used the twelve dollars to see *Billy the Kid* every night for a week, and, fearing Esther's wrath, stayed at a Bowery flophouse for twenty-five cents a night. For once, he dreaded going home.

Finally, his money gone, he went to face the music at the old basement apartment, proclaiming that he "didn't do it" as his *bubba* cried and hugged him. She had given the girl back her twelve dollars and, having learned that Itchik had dropped out of school, now insisted that he get a job.

It was September 1906, and Eddie got a job mailing out letters at an insurance company on William Street. That meant he was in charge of stamps. "I'd slip twenty twos in my pocket and sell them for a quarter. With this I'd go to Tony Pastor's. One day, these snide people tricked me; they counted the stamps." He was fired.

He did not, at this point, get another job. Having his grandmother to supply a roof over his head, as well as skimpy meals, he was free to do just what he liked—which included hanging around pool rooms, loafing with "the gang," and going to shows.

Eddie Kanter did what many starving theatre buffs have done since the beginnings of intermissions—"second act" a show. He'd wait, from a safe distance, until he saw the audience file out of the theatre at intermission; then he would mingle with them and then go in to catch the remainder of the play, undetected by the manager and ushers as anyone other than a person who had paid for a seat and seen the first act. "I never saw the first act of anything," he later said. Many times, he did not get to see the second act, either. An usher might suspect the boy in ragamuffin clothes and ask to see his ticket stub. Sometimes, Eddie was tossed out by an irate house manager. Once or twice, he barely escaped arrest.

One may wonder why, given Eddie's flair for dramatics, love of the theatre, and singing ability, he did not go into show business in his early teens. Work was surely plentiful, given the hundreds of theatres, acting companies, and vaudeville bills that dotted the country. Environment provides the answer.

There was no television to bring actors into homes on a twenty-four-hour basis. Neither was there radio or full-length motion pictures. There was only the live theatre, a huge, commercial business—not a vehicle for educating poor youths of the ghetto. Neither were there public high schools offering programs in drama or colleges giving degrees in theatre. (In fact, few children got more than an eighth-grade education.)

The theatre, to poor boys like Eddie Kanter, was a magical, intimidating place. Actors on the stage invariably looked and dressed well and had beautiful voices that boomed out to the galleries in clear, crisp, rounded tones. Eddie had no decent clothes, presumably did not yet speak well enough, and would not have known how to present himself had he been given the proper entrée. He was a scrawny, horrible-looking Jewish kid with broken teeth and a scar down his forehead that made him look much tougher than he was. In short, he lacked the looks, the background, and, as yet, the nerve.

Politics, however, was a part of his own world. Ward heelers were very active on the East Side of the day, "fixing" things for recent immigrants in exchange for votes the next election day. The plural, "votes," is purposely used. Many voted more than once, ensuring that "Big Jim" Something-or-Other would be "your next assemblyman."

Eddie saw tough men with common speech and common, often unpressed suits get up and speak on behalf of local candidates. The best-liked, most legitimate, and most concerned of all these East Side politicians was Assemblyman Al Smith.

Smith embodied all the East Side virtues, along with few, if any, of its vices. He was caring, warm, and human, "one of the boys," worldly-wise, with seemingly true wisdom. Smith was also on the side of the tenant, rather than the landlord.

Elected to the New York State Assembly for the first time in 1903, Smith would often take men and boys into saloons for drinks. The men—eighteen or over—were bought beer; the kids got sarsaparillas (root beers). Eddie felt at home in this environment, and, blending his flair for dramatics with his fondness for Al Smith, he began to make street speeches for the beloved assemblyman.

Soon, he began speaking for—or against—whomever at the time happened to strike his fancy. Beginning to get cocky, he sometimes praised a candidate on one day and destroyed him on the next. One time, he attacked a candidate he had extolled the previous day, for which he was beat up by some thugs in the service of the politician. He never again attacked a Democrat.

His best friend was still Dan Lipsky, bright and studious and, for the moment, much more enterprising than the poor, pathetic-looking Kanter. It was Lipsky who suggested they team up to entertain.

For a while, they played club dates, weddings, and Bar Mitzvahs, most of them at Henry Hall next door to *Bubba*'s. When their act was over, Eddie often tried to organize a crap game, sometimes winning more than he and Lipsky had been paid.

The act was simple. "Dan did comedy bits and I recited the tear-jerkers," Kanter would later recall. "But I couldn't resist some of the wisecracks I'd heard in vaudeville; I glued on a beard and opened with Joe Welsh's line, 'If I had my life to live over, I wouldn't be born.' Next night at the Educational Alliance, I'd play Little Lord Fauntleroy in a blond wig, no teeth, and an East Side accent, 'Does the *oil* want to see me?' When Dan and I stood on a real stage for the first time at the Clinton Music Hall, our beard-and-joke act fell flat—we spoke in English, not knowing we were in a Yiddish theatre."

They did their act in Yiddish for the remainder of the week and never got another booking in a theatre. The act broke up a short time later when Dan Lipsky got a job. Eddie simply went back to his aimless street existence, living with *Bubba* in the basement apartment, bumming money, and making kids—and sometimes cops—laugh at his antics on the street.

Ida Tobias was not Izzy's only audience, or his most overtly appreciative. One of the girls who lived in *Bubba*'s basement was named Fania, a sad-eyed nineteen-year-old Jew whose family had suffered in the Russian pogroms. "In her native town, nobody had ever laughed, except the Cossacks," recalled Eddie.

> She had learned to associate laughter with bloodshed. So to her my comedy was not a joke, but, as she said, "It was a new world, a revelation." I should have become suspicious right then and there, but I didn't. I asked her to tell me more. I liked it.
>
> She said, "I long to be always in the presence of your warm, pure humor. It's a new kind of sunlight."
>
> She became jealous when I made the other girls laugh. She tried to save me and my jokes all for herself. It was the first time anybody had made a fuss over me and I fell headlong, like down a flight of stairs. But when she finally managed to be alone in the house with me and gave me those earnest, longing glances, I began to feel uneasy. Being a Russian, she took even comedy seriously.

When Esther caught them petting and ordered the girl from her "house," Izzy rose to her defense. "If she goes, I go." Fania packed her bags and left, practically half-dragging Eddie with her.

Fania, who was working, took Izzy to an apartment on Cherry Street, put down a week's rent, and set up what amounted to a love nest with the fifteen-year-old Kanter.

A panicked Esther spoke to Danny Lipsky, who soon tracked them down. Esther went over immediately and tried to force her grandson to come home. Eddie refused, but finally relented after tears, threats, dire predictions, and the promise of meat balls for dinner. He went home for dinner but later returned to Fania.

He had become, after a fashion, a poor "gentleman of leisure," supported by a woman of nineteen, four years his senior. He presumably had his first sexual experience at this time, Fania guiding him through the awkward moments, investing him with confidence and, finally, with polish.

Esther tried to persuade him to come home again, but this time he refused. He was almost sixteen now, and, Esther realized, fully initiated into the mysteries of sex. She wept and left him, and, devout Jew that she was, prayed that he would not end up a *bumika* like his father.

During the days, while Fania worked, Eddie continued to roam the streets and make his political "speeches." One gang, to which he had attached himself, encouraged his speechmaking, since the crowd that gathered was a pickpocket's paradise.

He claimed, in later years, not to have known just what his "friends" were doing. Possibly he knew, but didn't care—or dare—to ask or to stop his speeches. He knew what it was to take a beating.

He still tried to see Ida, but his liaison with Fania was now news on Henry Street, and Ida was reluctant to be seen with or even talk to a fifteen-year-old boy who was living with an "older woman" and who neither worked nor went to school. He needed something special to persuade Ida to see him and found the answer when Fania got a raise at her job. It was April 1908.

To celebrate, she gave Eddie four dollars and instructed him to purchase two tickets to see Victor Moore in *The Talk of New York* at Springer's Grand Opera House at Twenty-third Street and Eighth Avenue. The thirty-two-year-old Moore had scored a major hit in George M. Cohan's *Forty-Five Minutes from Broadway*, and this show, a sequel to the earlier one, with Moore back in his character as "Kid Burns," had elevated him to stardom at the Knickerbocker Theatre several months earlier. It was a success, and seeing it was an event for poor young people like Eddie and Fania.

Eddie bought the tickets—and asked Ida to go with him. Then he put on his best act and told Fania that he had lost the money. "Then we can't go," the girl said philosophically. She had been through too much in her life to weep at such a loss.

Eddie and Ida enjoyed the show and exited the theatre to what they both thought would be a pleasant spring walk down to Henry Street. What they found was Fania, waiting outside the theatre with the largest hat pin Eddie had ever seen.

Ida looked on, horrified, as Fania chased him down the street and out of sight.

That night, for the first time in his life, Eddie slept on a park bench, knowing he could not return to Fania's place on Cherry Street but too proud—and uncertain—to go back to *Bubba*. After one more night, spent sleeping on a rooftop, he returned to Esther. Predictably, she took him in again.

Itchik was a bum, she now thought, like his father. There was nothing she could do but feed him. "The angels watch over the children," she once said to him, in Yiddish, "but God Himself looks after orphans."

She could only hope that it was true.

Chapter 2

# THE TURNING

*"In my neighborhood, a boy was hung. Why—or how—I escaped the
same fate, I still don't know."*

Eddie was back in his grandmother's apartment but not in her good graces.
She said he had to get a job, and stop fooling around.

Esther gave her grandson a scant breakfast and some dinner but no
money to buy lunch. He took to bumming off his friends in the two weeks
that followed his return to *Bubba*'s basement—friends who soon grew tired
of his mooching and, like her, told him to "get a job."

"Ah, I'm an actor," he would whine. "I'm looking."

History seemed to be repeating itself. He was an actor in the same way
his father had been a violinist. Major population centers like New York
needed performers in those days before the advent of the mass media, but
Eddie, like his father, merely whined and asked for help.

His friends—other East Side kids in their teens—were predictably un-
sympathetic. If he was an actor, they maintained, he could go on amateur
night at Miner's Bowery Theatre. Even if he got "the hook" that dragged
unsuccessful performers off the stage before the audience could pelt them
with rotten fruit, he still would earn a dollar. Eddie pointed to his torn
pants, but one of the gang, Herman Walker, offered to lend him his trousers—in return for half the dollar he would earn.

That evening, Eddie Kanter stood in the wings at Miner's Bowery Theatre, shivering in Herman Walker's pants as seasoned amateurs—some of
whom made livings off their winnings on these nights—were jeered and
hooted and finally got the hook. Nor was Kanter helped by the announcer's
introduction: "Next, Mr. Edward Kanter. He says he's an impersonator."

The rougher element in the gallery, there to jeer the amateur performers, echoed "Ed-ward" in tones that suggested the name was effeminate and greeted Kanter's entrance with a storm of noisy catcalls.

Suddenly, inspired by the moment, Eddie held his hand up to subdue the din, stamped his foot, and exclaimed, "Oh, dat makes me so mad!" in imitation of comedian Sam Sidman. The audience roared and let him go on with his act.

Kanter had never seen most of the veteran vaudeville comedy stars he imitated—Cliff Gordon, the "German Congressman," spicing his opinions with ridiculous analogies; Harry Thompson, the Irish "Mayor of the Bowery," dismissing of his cases in the Essex Market Court with one-line witticisms and double entendres; and Junie McCree, "Sappho in Chinatown," a drug addict who spoke with a soft, tired drawl.

"I'm so broke, that if they were selling steamboats for a nickel, I couldn't buy an echo of the whistle. . . . If I had a million dollars, I'd buy a half a million of hop and a half a million of room rent and leave word not to be disturbed."

There were still some jeers ("Lay down, you're dead" and "Stick to it, kid, you're lousy"), but Kanter, who had gained a solid foothold, persevered and soon won the audience's acceptance. Coins pelted the stage at the end of his act. Eddie quickly picked them up, with help from the emcee, and left the stage.

Kanter won first prize—ten dollars—in addition to the two dollars he had picked up off the floor.

Eddie treated Herman and the other boys to chow mein on Doyer Street in Chinatown, went home, and gave his grandmother five dollars. *Bubba* began to change her mind about "ectors" and, beginning at the London Theatre, Eddie entered every amateur night in New York over the next few weeks. He did not always win, but the experience he gained proved much more valuable, in the long run, than any money he collected. He learned how to deal with tough audiences, how to get over with weak material, how to get on and off stage with something that might pass for professionalism, and how to deal with stage managers and other "theatricals."

When the well of amateur nights ran dry, he played an Elks Lodge date for seventy-five cents. Gradually, he got to know other performers, most of them amateurs, but some with modest ties to the world of professional entertainment. In October, he got his first job in commercial show business playing four different parts in a third-rate burlesque show called *Indian Maidens*, produced by Frank B. Carr.

Frank B. Carr was then fifty-three years old. An eccentric, he wore a full-dress waistcoat at all times and displayed diamonds that rivaled those of Diamond Jim Brady for sheer brilliance, if not worth. *Carr's Thunderbolts* had been one of the most popular shows on the Western Burlesque Wheel at one time, and Carr once had several companies on tour in addition to owning his own theatre in Brooklyn. By 1908, however, his fortunes had slipped.

*Indian Maidens* was a poor show, and the only scene that impressed Eddie was the one in which he played one of a row of bootblacks shining the shoes of a row of attractive young women wearing very short skirts. Looking up at the shapely legs, the bootblacks sang out, as a chorus, "It's a shame to take the money!" Eddie also played, in other scenes, a Jew, a waiter, and a tramp. His weekly salary of fifteen dollars was more than he had ever earned before.

The big-time burlesque companies, none of which yet featured the strip tease, played set routes of close to forty weeks, appearing in major cities serviced by the Columbia Amusement Company, later known as the Columbia "Wheel." Frank B. Carr's *Indian Maidens* was, by contrast, strictly small time, playing one-night engagements in places like Carbondale, Pennsylvania, and Hendricks, West Virginia, for six weeks beginning Christmas Day before Carr's company manager ran out with the payroll after an engagement at the Masonic Opera House in Hinton, West Virginia, on February 6, 1909. Eddie had, presumably, been spending his salary on food, hotel bills, and a few "good times" with local prostitutes, sending a small portion home to *Bubba*. Now he wired her to send ten dollars; he was stranded and had to get home.

Frank B. Carr's own fate was much worse. In June 1910, after several additional failures, he threw himself into the northern end of New York's East River and drowned.

Having had his first job in show business, Kanter now felt justified in calling himself an actor—just returned from touring and "At Liberty" (the contemporary term for theatrical unemployment) to accept other engagements. His only pressing problem was a total lack of money.

He had not seen Ida since the debacle at the Grand Opera House the preceding April. He was now persona non grata, not only to her family, but to Ida herself. When her sister Jennie got married that spring, he found himself looking at the wedding party as they exited the *shul* from a doorway across the street. Ida saw him and was sorry. But she made no move to go across the street. She was being courted, once again, by Louis Rosner, and her days with Eddie were long over.

Kanter felt a sense of loss—a rather unfamiliar feeling, since he knew nothing but the poverty in which he had been raised and thus had little to lose. Young Eddie rarely thought of anything except in terms of what he could get away with. He had no goals, only rather vague ambitions about being an "actor." He lacked focus; Ida gave it to him.

He was in love with this girl, Ida—with her laughter, her shy but admiring glances, and the cleaner, better life she represented. For the first time, he was now willing to go out and look for jobs, to push himself (and others, if need be) to get ahead.

Early in June, he and his friend, Joe Malitz, another show biz aspirant with a good singing voice, went out to Coney Island to get summer jobs as singers at Carey Walsh's saloon; next to Roseben's Pavilion and across from Diamond Tony's.

Joe and Eddie sang three numbers each for Carey Walsh, Eddie's being

"Put Both Hands Up," "Wild Cherries" (a ragtime song by Irving Berlin and Ted Snyder), and "When I'm Alone I'm Lonesome." Walsh, whose locomotor ataxia kept him confined to a wheelchair, hired them on the spot. "It wasn't hard to get jobs like these," Eddie recalled years later. "The boss had nothing to lose. The singers who hung around a saloon worked for twenty dollars a week and tips."

The pianist at Carey Walsh's was Jimmy Durante, then a homely kid of sixteen with a passion for ragtime and a great ability to fake and vamp his way through any song or music. The latter skill was a clear necessity at Carey Walsh's in the summer of 1909.

"On Friday, Saturday, and Sunday," Eddie would remember, "you'd sing a hundred and fifty to two hundred songs; the more you sang the more you were likely to make." Eager to make all the money that he could that summer, Eddie never turned down a song request, whether or not he knew the song in question. "Say a guy asked for 'Springtime in Kalamazoo,' which neither of us even heard of," Durante later remembered. "I'd fake a melody and Eddie'd turn to the customer and sing 'Oh, it's springtime in Kalamazoo,' then turn away and double-talk softly, 'My thoughts go wanderin' back to you, I'll never ever be nothin' but blue, . . . ' All the time I'd be pounding away *fortissimo*, then Eddie'd swing back to the customer and moider 'em with '*When it's springtime in Kalamazoooo.*' Sometimes the guy was so drunk he wouldn't notice." Other times, the customer would complain that the song that Eddie sang was not the song that he had asked for. "You mean there are *two* songs with that title?" was the perfect answer, and the customer might tip the singer simply for having enlightened him as to the existence of the *other* "Springtime in Kalamazoo."

Such measures were rarely necessary; Kanter and Durante made sure they knew practically every popular song of the past twenty years. They made an interesting, slightly improbable team: a Jewish comic singer with big eyes and an Italian ragtime pianist with a large nose. Their hours at Carey Walsh's did not start until nine at night, meaning that Eddie could sleep in the mornings and spend afternoons at various Tin Pan Alley music publishers. Sometimes, he would find unpublished songs there, sing them at Carey Walsh's and soon find that singers at other Coney Island establishments, like Diamond Tony's, had begun to sing them, too. In a few weeks, the songs were published.

Before the end of his first week at Carey Walsh's, Eddie found that the waiters made more money than the singers. Joe Malitz quit, but Eddie, eager to make money, soon became a waiter, purchasing five dollars' worth of checks for drinks for four and a half dollars every evening and thus making fifty cents—plus tips—for every five dollars of drinks he sold. Sometimes, another waiter would take over his table as he did a song. Sometimes, too, a patron did not tip; and Eddie would spit in his beer. In the main, however, he combined both jobs successfully and made real money for the first time in his life.

He and Jimmy would get to Coney Island around seven o'clock and

spend the next two hours exploring the various concession stands and ar-
cades in the area. Eddie soon became a "shillaber," working as a "come-
on" for concessionaires. He would walk past a shooting gallery, pick up a
gun, shoot, and hit the bell. Other men would soon step up, lay down their
cash, and shoot. They would invariably miss, not knowing that the gun and
the target had been switched from "on" to "off" right after Eddie's turn.
Eddie had no qualms about the ruse, as his East Side mentality let him
take keen delight in outsmarting "suckers." He and Jimmy would then put
in their night's work and take the Brooklyn "El" back home to the East
Side after Walsh's closed around 4:30 in the morning.

Eddie was now seventeen—a young man in the New York of the early
1900s. *Bubba* thanked God that he had a good, honest job, and Eddie told
Ida he was making good money managing a restaurant. Ida asked her
friends, found out he was working at Carey Walsh's, and persuaded her
new brother-in-law to take her and Jenny to Coney Island. Eddie was horrified when he saw them walk in. Quickly, he snatched off his apron, started
barking orders to his startled fellow waiters, told the new arrivals it was his
night off, and arranged to meet them outside and show them the sights.
Two weeks later, Eddie was invited to the wedding of Ida's sister, Minnie,
scheduled for early in October.

By Labor Day, when Carey Walsh's place closed for the season, Eddie
had saved between three and four hundred dollars. Determined to impress
David Tobias with his new-found "wealth," he attended Minnie's wedding
dressed in the finest tuxedo he could rent, bought shiny patent leather
shoes that buttoned on the side, got a high silk hat, and rented an automobile for the night. He tipped everyone at the reception, ordered champagne for the entire crowd, and disregarded David Tobias's admonitions to
save his money, saying there was "more where" it had come from.

One week later, a more sober Eddie Kanter wished he had been more
conservative that night. Ida had been proud of him, but his hard-earned
four-hundred-dollar bankroll had been cut in half. He tried to call on Ida
but found himself talking to her father.

Asked just what his prospects were, Eddie said that he was going back
to acting now that Carey Walsh's had closed for the summer. He could not
have said anything more wrong.

Like Esther Kantrowitz, David Tobias was an immigrant, and actors, to
Russian-Jewish immigrants, were bums. No daughter of his was going to
go around with an actor. Eddie would have to get a responsible position if
he wanted to see Ida.

Eddie acquiesced.

Eddie Cantor's reminiscences have him sticking with show business from
the moment he won first prize at Miner's Bowery in May 1908. "Giving up
the business" is and remains a painful experience for any performer to
undergo, and one that is shameful to admit. But giving up show business
is what Eddie Kanter did late in 1909. It was either that or not see Ida.

"He gave up the stage for me, and got a series of jobs—including one in a garment house," Ida would recall years later. "As long as I live I shall always remember that I was more important to my Eddie even than his career."

The garment house was not the first in the "series of jobs." The New York census of 1910 has "Edward Kanter" living with his grandmother at 47 Henry, working as a runner in a brokerage house. Herman Walker, who had loaned Eddie his trousers a year and a half earlier, had a job as a runner at J. C. Weir & Co. at 25 Broad Street and had gotten Eddie a similar position at five dollars a week. The pay may have been low, but the work—delivering stock certificates from one brokerage house to another—was easy and did not tie Kanter down inside a room. Friday afternoon, after the market had closed, when the Weir staff got out a market news-letter recommending certain stocks, was the only time he had to really work.

John Campbell Weir himself was in charge of the letter. Then in his mid-forties, Weir later recalled Kanter as "a bright boy" but one "always up to pranks, making the others in the office laugh. I caught them soldiering on the job. One day, I had to tell him he was fired.

"He said, 'My God, I can't be. I have to take that five dollars home to my grandmother.' It was so pathetic that I took him back." One Friday afternoon, Weir had to leave the office early and instructed Kanter and the other boys to finish the letter. Eddie took the opportunity to grab a girl's muff from the hatrack, jump onto a table, and imitate Anna Held singing "I Can't Make My Eyes Behave." In the middle of the song, the laughter stopped. J. C. had returned.

Quickly, he pulled Eddie off the desk and threw him out the door. Kanter did not even get his cap.

Decades later, then age eighty, Weir claimed to have "softened" by the following Monday. Kanter, though, did not return.

Eddie's next job was in the "garment center"; he worked as a stock clerk at the National Cloak and Suit Company for seven dollars a week. Louis Rosner was still courting Ida, but most of the candy that he brought her wound up in Eddie Kanter's stomach. It was at this time, in fact, that Ida became "Eddie's girl."

They spent all of their spare time together, going for sodas and taking long walks up to Proctor's 58th Street Theatre, one of New York's finest vaudeville houses. Their reciprocal playfulness made theirs a classic "young love" of the Edwardian Age: Eddie meeting Ida at her doorstep to take her to work, Eddie with his singing, jokes, and imitations. He was cute and charming, and Ida, the former "Belle of Henry Street," was now, to him, the Belle of Brooklyn. Her laughter was both girlish and hearty, and it seemed the most pleasant sound in the world to Eddie Kanter.

Ida's sartorial efforts were mostly lost on Eddie, who was color-blind. Sometimes, his indifference to fashion—and to what Ida was wearing—went much further. Once, she bought a new hat with beautiful flower ornamentation and wore it when he took her up to Proctor's. They ran into a rainstorm, and the distressed Ida left her ruined hat behind when she and Eddie left the theatre.

Eddie never even noticed it was missing.

Kanter had his stock clerk job for more than six months before he either quit or was discharged around the end of 1910. The boss, a Mr. Rosenbaum, had caught him entertaining other workers on at least one unpropitious occasion. But the loss of the job mattered little. Kanter, age eighteen, was now a "working man" with a history of almost steady employment for the past two years—as an actor in a burlesque show, a singer-waiter at Coney Island, a runner in a brokerage house, and a clerk in a garment house. The only job at which he'd made good money was the one in Coney Island. Singing was, or could be, much more lucrative than stock work.

There were also more personal considerations. Eddie needed money to continue seeing Ida, but his constant desire to perform made him a less than valued employee. The desire could not be satisfied by nighttime work in amateur contests or similar theatricals. Cantor was by nature a performer, and his endeavors in that line had given him the only meaningful positive feedback he had ever known—save for that from his grandmother, Esther. Even Ida had been won by Kanter the comedian.

Making steady money had improved his looks and his confidence. Eddie was not the awful-looking kid with broken teeth he had been five years earlier but an aware and focused youth with talent, drive, and energy. In 1911, that was frequently enough.

The nerve was born of ego. "I liked myself pretty well," Eddie confessed late in life. The ego had been cultured by his *bubba*, Esther. It was further nourished by Ida Tobias.

Ida had a built-in talent for appraising people, and she understood her future husband's need to entertain. "I didn't want my man to turn himself into a drudge—a tame, husbandly, clerkly person—even for me," was the way she would explain her having sanctioned Eddie's return to the stage. It was Ida's support that allowed Eddie to make his first serious attempt at cracking "the show business."

Eddie and Ida were the perfect "mastermind" or "partners for success"—not mentally, but emotionally. She was Eddie's rock of strength, confessor, rabbi, alter ego, and, of course, girlfriend.

It has been said that people of ability need someone—a parent, authority figure, close friend, or professional benefactor—to give them *permission* to succeed. Stories of performers who attain success despite their families' unanimous disapproval and constant disparagement are largely mythic. Talent and ambition can, indeed, be squelched, as children tend to mold themselves to others' expectations. Thanks to Esther and to Ida, Eddie needed only to make a conscious effort to succeed. Ida was the perfect audience, and her encouragement of Eddie's stage ambitions—totally against her father's will—brought them together as "conspirators." Ida's reassurance gave Eddie the strength and extra confidence he needed to surmount all obstacles—to "batter down the doors" that stood in his way.

Determined to make a concentrated and sustained effort at breaking into show business, he spent twenty-five dollars for his first new suit (a natty gray striped outfit), had cards printed—"Eddie Cantor, dialectician"—and began to make the rounds of booking agents and producers. It was the first time he spelled his name "Cantor"—a rendering that seemed at once more commercial and yet more proudly Jewish than the mundane, faintly "greenhorn"-smelling "Kanter."

Breaking into vaudeville was not easy, even with his new clothes, cards, and talent. Eddie's confidence and charm seemed almost commonplace to people in the forefront of the entertainment business, and the bookers did not care even to see his alleged "act."

At this point, he knew no one in show business. Frank B. Carr was dead, and even the contacts with borderline professional performers he had made while playing amateur shows two and a half years earlier had evaporated. After a few weeks, however, Eddie began talking to small-time vaudevillians who suggested he stop wasting his time hounding major bookers and seek out the small-time agents like Joe Wood.

Joe Wood was, indeed, king of the small-time agents, supplying small-time theatres from Manhattan to Albany with alleged talent ranging from pseudo-opera singers to Dutch dialect comedians. Like his big-time collegues, he had never heard of Cantor, was not impressed by Eddie's experience in a Frank B. Carr burlesque show, and did not want to see his act.

Eddie hung around Wood's office part of every day beginning in late January. "This is a business for professionals," Wood told him repeatedly. "No one's born a professional" was Cantor's reply. After two weeks, Wood told his secretary to tell Cantor, at all times, that he was out. Eddie's response was to wait around for hours. Finally, Wood gave in and told Cantor to go through his act.

Cantor's act did not impress Joe Wood, who shook his head and stopped him halfway through. Amazingly, however, he gave Eddie his card and told him to be at Gain's Manhattan Theatre, Thirty-fourth Street and Sixth Avenue, the following Monday morning.

The action was probably meant more to dispose of Cantor once and for all than to start him on his way to a career in show business. Three or four agents would send house manager Gain four or five acts for the weekly bill. Gain would put on all twenty for the first show, choose seven to stay for the balance of the week, and send the rest home with no money. Cantor, Joe Wood reasoned, would be one of those rejected and give up all thoughts of making it in vaudeville.

Cantor was no more successful at that first show—the Monday matinee—than he had been in Wood's office. But Eddie, to his own surprise, was among the seven acts Gain retained for the week. Gain told Wood that Cantor had not made good but was "different . . . I think you ought to come down and see him."

Cantor vindicated both himself and Gain by getting laugh after laugh that evening at the seven o'clock show. Joe Wood came down to catch his act the following day. Eddie flopped again, but Wood told him he was "okay. . . . You have a good act. Don't worry about an agent; you've got one."

During the months of February, March, and April 1911, Joe Wood booked Cantor into small-time theatres in upstate New York burgs such as Troy, Schenectady, Mechanicville, and Utica, where he, Gertrude Dudley & Co., and the Manson Sisters constituted the entire bill, along with one-and two-reel films and "illustrated songs"—sterioptican slides with lyrics for the audience to sing along with. "Eddie Cantor, a comedian, had some good talk and some good songs which he handled so well that there was not a dull moment in the fifteen minutes he used," is how the Utica *Daily Press* reviewed his act. The review belies Cantor's later claim that he did not sing at this time, as does contemporary sheet music for "That Mysterious Rag" by Irving Berlin and Ted Snyder. Featured on the cover is a photo of a sinfully young Cantor, looking like a refugee from grammar school and labeled "Eddy Canton." He was in the "small time," totally unknown.

He was making only a little money—about twenty dollars a week, minus expenses—two dollars for agent Joe Wood's commission, fourteen dollars for room and board, and three dollars for railroad fare—leaving him a dollar at the end of every week. His only consolation, besides the applause and an occasional good notice, was that he was working—earning his own way as a professional performer.

Most New York theatres of that time had "Sacred Concerts"—vaudeville shows performed in street clothing to get around the sabbath "blue laws" that made theatrical entertainments illegal on Sundays. Wood accordingly booked Cantor into the West End Theatre, a Harlem movie house that featured acts of vaudeville on Sundays under this guise, in the month of April. At the first performance, a man walked backstage and gave Eddie a card that identified him as Joseph M. Schenck of the People's Vaudeville Company, a fledgling minor small-time chain whose other officers included Nicholas Schenck, Adolph Zukor, and Marcus Loew—all future moguls of the movie business.

Schenck booked Cantor for two weeks in small-time vaudeville—half weeks at the Lyric in Hoboken, the New Lyceum in Elizabeth, the Royal and the Lyric in Brooklyn, and a Sunday Concert at the Amphion in New York.

Eddie was successful with these undemanding audiences, and Schenck told Eddie he would book him for immediate return dates in the same theatres if he had another act. Cantor lost no time in telling Joe Schenck that he had one.

He had nothing but the one act he had built up since 1907. To give the appearance of a "different" act, he dressed as a "Dutch comic"—a little chinpiece with a pillow in the front and all the other tricks of costume that would make him look like Joe Weber of the famed "knockabout" "Dutch" comedy act of Weber and Fields.

With this "new" character, he did the same act as before—but all in German dialect. The little Italian in the subway now became a Dutchman in the subway. Harry, the Mayor of the Bowery holding court, was now Harry with a German or "Dutch" accent.

Cantor claimed he played the four-theatre People's Vaudeville Company circuit for another two weeks as a "Dutchman," followed by another tour of the same houses as a "Hebrew" or "Jew" comic. "The fourth time around," he told Jane Kesner Ardmore, "I was really stumped. I sat down with a piece of charcoal to put a few lines on my face. The lines only made me look haggard. I tried to wipe off the marks, they spread. Blackface! I quickly rubbed cork over my cheeks, neck, ears."

And he played the circuit a fourth time. The story seems quite fanciful, nor can it be validated by contemporary sources. No advertisements in the *Hudson Dispatch*, which covered the Lyric Theatre in Hoboken, list "Eddie Cantor," although many of the ads list only that week's headliner. Cantor once recalled having used a different name on each of his four tours. This seems likely, but no reviews exist either to deny or to confirm it.

It is also possible, as George Jessel recalled, that Cantor played the Imperial Theatre in Manhattan, doing imitations one week, a monologue in Yiddish the next, and a blackface act the third week. There is little doubt that Cantor first used blackface at this time, but the story as to how he "stumbled" on the makeup is sorely lacking in credibility.

Blackface had been a staple of show business for more than eighty years by the time Eddie Cantor donned burnt cork, presumably at the Lyric Theatre in Hoboken, around June 1911. Its roots go back to Pittsburgh around 1830, when Thomas Rice (later known as "Daddy," the progenitor of all nineteenth-century blackface performers) introduced the song "Jump Jim Crow," based on the singing of a black lorry driver he had heard in Cincinnati.

Blackface soon became commonplace on the American stage, chiefly in the "olios" of vaudeville routines presented between acts of plays in northern cities. The first blackface "minstrel" organization, the Virginia Minstrels, made its debut at the Bowery Amphitheatre in New York on February 6, 1843, inspiring many imitations.

Minstrelsy, which flourished over the next quarter of a century, wore out its welcome by the mid-1870s, as "plantation" life lost its believability with the passing of slavery. It found a new life ten years later, with elaborate stage settings and blacks portrayed in more "modern" surroundings in the major cities. By 1905, however, these big shows (e.g., Dockstader's, Haverly's) were on the wane, due not to racism but to sexism. The minstrel shows, being all-male aggregations, could not compete with the developing musical comedies, extravaganzas, and revues that featured music, a half-hearted story, and beautiful women. The comedians were the most important ingredient in many, if not most, of these primitive musicals. After 1910, that comedian was sometimes found in blackface, sounding the deathknell of minstrel shows.

Cantor, with his lithe build and his large eyes, was well suited to blackface, a modern incarnation of the harlequin tradition. The costume he adopted consisted of big, white-rimmed glasses, a straw hat, and street clothes a size or two too small so as to increase the impression of slightness. In contrast to the rural characters that dominated blackface comedy in the 1800s, Cantor presented a blackface character who was intellectual, effete, and something of a physical coward.

Cantor's final two weeks on the People's Vaudeville Company circuit meant that he had worked eight weeks in a row. Ida was proud of him. *Bubba* did not fully comprehend; she knew only that he was without work when the eight weeks ended.

Eddie went to see Gus Edwards, composer of the famous "School Days" song and producer of kids' vaudeville acts, at this point and was hired to play the part of a tramp in an act called "Benches in The Park," along with a thirteen-year-old named George Jessel. Jessel later remembered Cantor's "inventive mind," which was always working on ideas: "He suggested that I play a baby in a carriage. He would come along and flirt with my nurse and, to make a hit with her, he would do all his imitations. He then invented some lines for me to say. He taught me how to sock the point over." The act was never mounted, and mid-summer found Eddie still out of work, waiting for the new season to start and with no immediate prospects.

The boys of Henry Street, however, championed him as someone who had "made good," especially when the boys of Jefferson Street paraded their own famous son, Roy Arthur, of the big-time act Bedini & Arthur, on a Sunday afternoon in August. The Henry Streeters insisted that Cantor do his act, and Eddie responded with his usual imitations of Junie McCree and Walter C. Kelly. "The crowd applauded," Eddie recalled, "but that didn't matter; what mattered was this man from another world, the world of top-line theatres. He didn't burst into cheers, but he did say, 'Drop around sometime next week and look me up at Hammerstein's.' "

Hammerstein's Victoria, at Forty-second Street and Seventh Avenue, was the Mecca of vaudeville, a position it would lose soon after the Palace opened its doors in March 1913. Managed by William Hammerstein, the son of Oscar Hammerstein I and the father of the lyricist Oscar II, it featured, like all big-time theatres, eight acts on a bill and two shows daily. The greatest vaudeville stars in the world played Hammerstein's (pronounced Hammer*stene's* by most vaudevillians), although manager Willie, ever the great showman, also featured "sensational" acts like acquitted murderers and other notorious celebrities who told their stories—anticipating the talk shows of many decades later.

Roy Arthur, then in his late thirties, was the comedy end of Bedini & Arthur, an act built largely around Jean Bedini, a master juggler whose outdoor publicity stunts included catching a turnip thrown from a height of 180 feet on a fork held in his mouth. Arthur always worked in blackface, often in drag in parodies of other acts that preceded Bedini & Arthur on the various bills they played on major circuits. Arthur did not speak, relying on outrageous facial expressions and physical comedy to complement the calm, assured perfection of his partner.

Bedini was originally Jean Pefsner, son of Leon Pefsner, allegedly a court magician during the reign of Czar Nicholas I of Russia. Bedini owned the act, which meant that Arthur worked for him. From time to time, the act also employed "stooges"—assistants to Roy Arthur's comedy, especially in travesties of popular stage hits like *Madame X*.

Cantor showed up at the stage door of Hammerstein's the day after Roy Arthur's invitation. Bedini thought that Cantor's imitations and other bits were funny, but he did not think there was a place for him in the act. Roy suggested that Eddie hang around. Bedini & Arthur remained at Hammerstein's for four consecutive weeks, during which Cantor became Jean Bedini's "go-for"—going out for laundry, food, and anything else needed for the sometimes elaborate Bedini & Arthur stage act. Arthur, in the meantime, pushed Eddie's case before Bedini to the point that, at the end of the team's run at Hammerstein's, the nineteen-year-old Cantor was hired at thirty-five dollars a week.

Joe Wood had not gotten Cantor this job, so Eddie, anxious to make and save as much money as possible, did not pay him any commission. Wood, from this point, ceased to be his manager, which bothered Cantor little. He was in the "big time" now, making thirty-five dollars a week clear and, he sensed, advancing in his field.

At first, his only assigned onstage job was to walk on, hand a plate to Jean Bedini, and walk off. It was nothing too impressive, and a step down in prestige from the act he had been doing for Joe Wood in small-time theatres. But the increased pay allowed him to save money and, increasingly, help *Bubba*. Eddie did his assigned stage task but added a flourish.

He came on stage, took time polishing the plate, looked leisurely at Bedini and Arthur in turn, and then gazed loftily at the audience while both his partners exchanged amazed glances at his "cheek." Then he finally, rather condescendingly, handed the plate to Bedini and took his exit—to both laughter and applause. Bedini, ever the stage artist and eager to improve his act, congratulated Cantor on his efforts when the act was over and made plans to use him more extensively as time went on. In the meantime, he gave Cantor a good bit to do with him and Arthur in the closing. Eddie lost no time in telling Ida, who showed up at Hammerstein's the following Saturday afternoon with her friends from Levi Simpson's, where she worked, designing jabots. The act, however, had been cut on Friday evening, so all Cantor had to do on Saturday was come out and give Jean

Bedini props. He did not call on Ida until the middle of the following week and had to explain—for the umpteenth time—why he had failed to live up to her best expectations.

In the meantime, he continued learning. Bedini showed him how to roll a hat down the length of his arm and catch it as it dropped. After Cantor mastered that, he showed him how to do the same thing with a plate. "I devoted every spare minute to juggling so that I could be in the act," Cantor recalled. "We worked out a routine. After Bedini slid the plate off his arm and caught it, Arthur would try clumsily to do the same thing, and he'd smash it. Then I'd take another plate, slide it down my arm with ease, and snap my fingers scornfully at Arthur. Arthur'd chase me with a hammer, and I'd scream, 'He means to do me bodily harm!' "

Arthur and Cantor soon developed a sissy-bully routine, with Roy the boor and Eddie the cultured, effeminate, slight, blackfaced man with spectacles. In the spirit of *commedia del l'arte*, the men played their roles quite deftly. Neither Arthur nor Bedini ever spoke on stage, but Jean allowed Eddie to say whatever he thought might get a laugh or advance the onstage situation. After a time, he was allowed to come onstage whenever he wished, provided he had something to contribute, and Bedini told the orchestra to drop to *pianissimo* whenever Cantor entered.

Bedini and Arthur played the Midwest in October, staying at the best hotels and playing two shows a day in first-class theatres like the Orpheum in Des Moines, the Majestic in Chicago, the Lyric in Dayton, and Keith's in Indianapolis. Cantor, for the first time, lived "the good life," wondered at the opulence of major cities in pre-World War I America, and marveled that he had been transported to this "better world" by "somebody" who cared. "Somebody," in this case, meant Arthur and his boss, Bedini.

Eddie's value to the act increased as time wore on. On one train journey through Minnesota in December, Arthur noticed Cantor shivering and threw his coat around him. "You're gonna be a great star some day," Roy told him. Eddie never forgot.

They changed the act from week to week, parodying many of the top stars on the bills, including Molasso, who introduced the *apache* dance to the United States in his act, *Paris By Night*. Bedini & Arthur followed immediately, using Molasso's set and "seriously" imitating the highlights of the dance. Dancers were the usual subjects of their largely pantomimic satire, including Ruth St. Denis, Mlle. Dazie, and Gertrude Hoffman. Cantor played "Salome" ("The Dance of the Seven Veils" was then done in vaudeville by women ranging from Maud Allen and Ruth St. Denis to Eva Tanguay), still in blackface, dancing to Mendelssohn's "Spring Song" in a dress. Once, he accidentally lost the dress, and the audience screamed. From then on, he lost the dress at every performance—sometimes twice; if the act was not getting over, Bedini often signaled him to "drop the dress." It never failed to get a huge laugh.

Seriously, looking spiritual and wan, Cantor would recite:

> Twinkle, twinkle, little star
> How I wonder what you are!
> Up above the world so high
> What care I?
> What care I?

Then he would run off stage. "It was the contrast of nonsense and earnest delivery that was funny," he remembered. "And the impromptu mode of play was wonderful discipline. It quickened your wits."

By April 1912, when Bedini & Arthur played Shea's Theatre in Buffalo, Eddie Cantor had been with the act for more than seven months. Cantor had been trying to get Bedini to let him sing in the act, but Jean saw no place in the act for songs of any kind.

The song that Eddie planned to do—as soon as the occasion came—was Irving Berlin's "Ragtime Violin." The occasion came in Buffalo, where Bedini & Arthur were put next to closing, which meant they had to close "in one" (in front of the curtain) while the rest of the stage was prepared for the "full stage" act that closed the program.

Since Bedini & Arthur never closed "in one," the solution was for Cantor to sing "Ragtime Violin." It was the first time Eddie had sung in a first-class theatre, and he was extremely nervous at the Monday matinee. Cantor came out with a big violin case, opened it with a huge flourish, and got a big laugh when he took out a small dime store toy fiddle. He scratched a few awful-sounding chords, took out a can, oiled the fiddle, and began to sing. "I was so nervous," he remembered, "I walked quickly up and down, clapping my hands as I sang, rolling my eyes, and bobbing like the red, red robin. The audience went crazy. After three encores I started adding catch lines so they'd bring me back. By Wednesday, the song was running close to seven minutes."

Arthur and Cantor shared the same dressing room, divided by a thin partition from Bedini's. Arriving back in the dressing room after the Thursday night performance, Eddie overheard Mike Shea say to Bedini that he'd "get rid of you and Arthur" if "that little guy in blackface could do five more minutes."

When Shea walked out, Cantor walked in and told Bedini he would "have to have a raise." Bedini might have been offended at the young man's impudence, but he had been getting seventy-five dollars more for the act since he had hired Cantor. Moreover, he liked Eddie's nerve and appreciated young performers eager to work hard and "go the extra mile"—as Cantor certainly was—to reach the top. Eddie's resulting five-dollar raise pushed his weekly salary to forty dollars.

He shared hotel rooms with Roy Arthur, spent no more than ten dollars a week, mailed *Bubba* ten, and sent the rest to Ida. She and Eddie had talked about getting married but had set no date. In the meantime, she saved all the money he sent in a bank account.

The Tobias family was now living in Brooklyn. David Tobias still did not approve of one of his daughters having a suitor who worked on the stage. Eddie was, however, making money, and David was persuaded to give the boy time to put aside a nest egg, presumably to buy himself a respectable business. Nothing was ever spelled out, but that was the understanding. In the meantime, Ida waited, worked, and saved.

Bedini & Arthur played the Savoy Theatre in Atlantic City in July. Another act on the bill was Gus Edwards's troupe, which featured the teen-age performers Lila (Cuddles) Lee, Eddie Buzzell, and George Jessel.

Edwards, a German immigrant originally named Gustav Simon, had written "School Days" for a legitimate production in 1905. He went on to produce a number of "kid acts" in vaudeville, notably "School Boys and Girls," an act whose many imitators included the Three Marx Brothers (Adolph, Julius, and Milton at the time) in "Fun In Hi Skul." Edwards also wrote "By the Light of the Silvery Moon," "In My Merry Oldsmobile," "If I Was a Millionaire," along with several other big successes. Time—and Cantor—would eventually dub him the "Columbus of Show Business," "discovering" (or giving early employment) to such all-time greats as Groucho Marx, the Duncan Sisters, Jessel, Hildegarde, Phil Silvers, Ray Bolger, and Eddie Cantor.

Cantor now renewed his acquaintance with Jessel (an "old boy" who thought and acted much the same as most vaudevillians in their thirties), who got him invited to a midnight party at the Chelsea Yacht Club.

The "party" was a free performance. "Gus was the original benefit fellow," recalled Jessel. "He would go anywhere, no matter what the cause. He was particularly the fall guy in each town for one or two rich men, who would always tell Gus they would back him in any proposition. 'But you must come up to the house tonight and bring your show with you.' He came through, but they never did." This party at the Chelsea was a stag affair, and the men, who had been drinking, were in no mood for Edwards songs like "By the Light of the Silvery Moon." Jessel said they became "uncontrollably noisy."

Eddie saved the evening, telling two or three off-color stories and imitating (Joe) Smith and (Charley) Dale in "The New Teacher" with Jessel. They had framed this up on the ride to the yacht club. Eddie, as the German teacher, hit George with a bamboo stick, at which Jessel skipped up and down. ("Hit me again, teacher, I'm seeing diamonds!") They dirtied up the act in spots, making it a big hit at the Chelsea.

Edwards liked the way that Cantor worked with Jessel and thought there was a part for him in a new act planned for the next season. He understood when Cantor said that he was under contract to Bedini but told Eddie to call him "if anything" happened.

Eddie knew that he had gone as far as he could go with Jean Bedini. He conferred with Ida when the act hit New York two weeks later and decided to get "fired" out of his contract.

He behaved obnoxiously toward his boss during their engagement at the Fifth Avenue Theatre. Finally, his patience broken, Bedini told Cantor he would fire him if Cantor said another word.

"You wouldn't dare," Cantor replied.

That did it. Less than fifteen minutes after he was fired by Bedini, Cantor phoned Gus Edwards at Morrison's Music Hall in Rockaway and told him he was free.

Cantor and Edwards met again the following Monday—August 5, 1912—and signed a two-year contract that gave Eddie seventy-five dollars a week to play the part of Jefferson, the butler, in a new act called "Kid Kabaret."

Seventy-five dollars would have paid a year's rent down on Henry Street. He rushed home to tell *Bubba*, and the old woman looked at him, uncomprehendingly. She was seventy-eight years old, and Itchik's new success meant that she was free at last.

In the years that followed, Esther's health declined. Increasingly, she lapsed into senility, her work, at last, complete.

Chapter 3

# THE CLIMB

*"There's No Business Like Show Business"*
*—Irving Berlin*

Vaudeville was born of variety acts presented in saloons and beer gardens in the nineteenth century. When it died, after almost half a century (1881–1928), its acts returned to those saloons, now called "nightclubs," shedding the wholesome cloak that vaudeville had given them and signaling the start of a new, harsher era.

At its peak (1900–19), vaudeville employed close to ten thousand people as dramatic actors, sketch artists, monologists, singers, dancers, animal trainers, acrobats, musicians, and magicians. Thousands more were employed as stagehands, ushers, concession sellers, washroom attendants, and house managers. The institution, like the jobs, is gone. Even the nightclubs have passed into history.

A vaudeville act might consist of one person, or two dozen. It might consist of anything and qualify as vaudeville, providing that it entertained and did not offend popular mores. Vaudeville was entertainment for the masses—the genteel middle class, as opposed to the "rough element" after men like Pastor, Proctor, and Keith brought it up from its beer garden roots. Drinking was prohibited, civility encouraged. Vaudeville, in essence, was a "wholesome" marriage between theatre and cafe-saloon entertainment—a grease-paint icon of America between the Spanish-American War and the start of the Jazz Age. The new morals, a demand for faster living, and the outlooks of the '20s caused a new generation to leave it for the smarter world of jazz records and for shows with scores by Gershwin, Richard Rodgers, and other "sophisticates" of the new Broadway. The librettos of these shows incorporated sexual and other mores that the world of vaudeville would have deemed "offensive" to its audiences. Vaudeville waned during the Jazz Age and was dead before the age of swing.

"Don't say 'damn' or 'hully gee' in this theatre," read a sign backstage at all Keith vaudeville houses. Stars like Eva Tanguay nothwithstanding, "vulgarity," sex, and religion were officially taboo in vaudeville. Ethnicity and race were not. Dutch (i.e., German), "Jew," Irish, and "blackface" comics formed the backbone of vaudeville at the turn of the century.

Gus Edwards's "Kid Kabaret," like many vaudeville acts, was built around a theme, if not a full-fledged plot: The parents of Carlton Terrace Jr. (Eddie Buzzel, later a Hollywood director) have gone to a cabaret with several other couples. All the children have been left under the charge of Jefferson, butler at the Terrace home, where they decide to put on their own cabaret show.

"Jefferson," the only adult role, was played by Eddie Cantor in blackface, at twenty the senior member of a cast of teen-aged "children" that included Enid Morel (as Annette, Carlton Jr.'s sweetheart), Lillian Lipman (Millie Bon Bon), Al Hinston (Chauncey Pickadilly "from dear London"), Ruthie Francis (Rosie, a flower girl), Betty Washington ("The Little Violinist"), Evelyn McVey (Annabella O'Hara, a "Kid-Kut-Up"), and several others, including Jessel as Mutky, programmed, with typical understatement, as a "Little Bit Yiddish."

"Kid Kabaret" opened at Hammerstein's Victoria on Labor Day 1912, an ambitious booking for the start of the new season and premature for a new act with young performers. "There is a signal absence of comedy on the bill, undoubtedly due to the lack of it in the thirty-seven minute 'Kid Kabaret' turn" was how Josh Lowe dismissed them in *Variety*. Most of the other reviewers were of similar opinion, but the lack of good reviews did not vex most of the performers. "They don't care a jot about losing their positions, lack of professional advancement, or anything else," Edwards described it at the time. Edwards, however, did not travel with "Kid Kabaret," as he was then heading yet another of his "kid" acts, titled "Gus Edwards' Song Revue." Harry Little, programmed as "Mr. Edwards' Representative," was the official company manager of "Kid Kabaret," but Cantor, as the only performer past his teen-age years, was soon made his unofficial assistant, introducing Jessel, whom he roomed with, to such niceties as regular bathing (which he himself had first experienced with Bedini & Arthur one year earlier) and "watching out" for the attractive girls. He was somewhat derelict in that last duty, as one of the girls soon became pregnant. Cantor notified Gus Edwards, and the girl, although replaced onstage, was kept traveling with the company until things could be properly "worked out."

Such things were fairly common in show business, where constant travel, uninhibited socializing, and staying in hotel rooms was the norm. Eddie may have had a "girl friend" in the company, but he never had second thoughts about marrying Ida. His masculine interests while on the road in vaudeville had no more to do with his projected life with her than his boyhood street activities had to do with *Bubba*. Ida, like his grandmother, was "home." Show biz, like the streets, was the "outside." Each had different codes of behavior.

His courting of Ida continued when "Kid Kabaret" played in or close to Brooklyn. Twenty-year-old Ida was indeed cute and vivacious by the standards of New York's East Side. Eddie's feeling were obvious, and Ida "was really starry-eyed about him," in the words of one of Eddie's daughters. The starriness increased as Eddie became more successful, polished, and romantic. Escorting her to work each morning was a problem, given his late hours as an actor and the fact she lived in Brooklyn, not Manhattan, but Eddie did it on a number of occasions. He also took her out on Sunday evenings, when legitimate and vaudeville theatres were closed but the Winter Garden's lights blazed brightly for its "Sunday Evening Concerts" with performers like the Dolly Sisters, Harry Fox, and the magical Al Jolson, whose electric joy and thunderous vitality captivated the young couple. Jolson's sexual humor—implying an awareness and, indeed, an acceptance of sexual norms that fell just shy of actual endorsement—and his forays into insult humor were an important influence on Eddie, as was Jolson's use of his eyes and body in handling up-tempo, frequently suggestive songs. Before too long, something of Jolson found its way into the character of "Jefferson" in "Kid Kabaret", and an imitation of Jolson by Jefferson was put into a segment of the act titled "Mimic Land."

On St. Valentine's Day 1913, as "Kid Kabaret" was in the midst of an engagement at Harlem's Alhambra Theatre, Eddie Cantor proposed to Ida Tobias. She readily accepted, but no wedding date was set; the couple simply firmed their plans to marry in two years. In the meantime, they would continue saving money—Eddie's money—and hope that he continued to advance in his career.

Cantor was not a typical vaudevillian, one who felt "at home" traveling and seldom looked beyond his more or less comfortable niche aside from vaguely dreaming about "headline" status. He was sojourning in vaudeville—in it, but not of it, ever conscious of his goals in the "civilian" world. Having "got ambition" in the sense that other people "got religion," Eddie planned ahead. He sent Ida fifty dollars a week for the bank account and stayed within his budget by getting invited to dinner, along with Georgie Jessel, by admiring vaudeville fans wherever the act played. Eddie, who avoided pork and shellfish, preferred Jewish homes; in 1913, they were certain to be kosher.

Cantor did not plan to stay with Edwards more than the two seasons called for in his contract. After that, he might go back to working single— but on the big time. The important thing was to work constantly—on new gags, a new act, and new contacts.

Cantor and Jessel had bought a box camera, and a host of early "snapshot" photographs survives to document their travels on the Orpheum Circuit. Eddie and Georgie, who always identified with the world of his elders, met and became friendly with a host of older vaudeville performers, such as the singer Helen Trix, the Dolce Sisters, and Will Rogers, the part-Cherokee cowboy who would become an American institution.

The Orpheum Circuit was a carefully strung-out system of theatres stretching from Winnipeg through the Pacific Northwest, down to Los Angeles and through to New Orleans. Will was on the bill with Eddie, Georgie, and "Kid Kabaret" in Winnipeg, Spokane, Seattle, and Portland in succession, traveling on the same trains with them between engagements. A bit of an enigma in the polyglot world of vaudeville, the thirty-three-year-old Rogers carried both a man and a horse with him in his roping act and was still developing as a topical monologuist. (Cantor would remember that he did not speak at all.) Eddie was intrigued by what seemed like Will's "foreign" culture, his genuine love for his wife, Betty, and his easygoing manner—a contrast to his own nervous demeanor.

Rogers taught Cantor a few roping trips, talked about his Indian background, and became, in large part, Eddie's mentor. Rogers even recommended Cantor to his agent in New York, Max Hart, possibly the best and most powerful "artist's representative" in vaudeville. Hart also handled Fanny Brice and Frank Tinney, considered the greatest "natural" comedian in the world and the inspiration for the Chaplin classic *Limelight*.

The Orpheum Circuit was the "class" circuit of vaudeville, its theatre orchestras equipped with harps, its theatre auditoriums lavish celebrations of early-twentieth-century popular culture. The cast, aside from Cantor, was on a sliding scale of ages; they were allegedly nine-year-old children on the stage, at least sixteen (which many were not) to combat the feared Gerry Society, and twelve or under to ride half-fare on the trains. To that end, Eddie had the boys wear knickers and the girls wear short skirts. In that era before printed forms of identification were common, train conductors mostly looked the other way when confronted with the need to resolve questions of age. The only trouble came en route from Portland, Oregon, to San Francisco in July 1913, when a conductor saw the "half-fare" Jessel smoking a cigar in the club car, wearing a derby and amusing fellow passengers with off-color stories.

The segment of "Kid Kabaret" programmed as "Mimic Land" had Jessel imitating David Warfield (best known as star of *The Music Master*), Ruthie Francis doing Raymond Hitchcock (a top musical comedy star of the pre–World War I era), and the blackfaced Cantor as Al Jolson. Jolson, then in his late twenties and already well known as "the (New York) Winter Garden comedian," had made his first reputation at the National Theatre in San Francisco in 1906–07. He was still married to his first wife, the Oakland-born Henrietta Keller, and spent most of his summers in the San Francisco Bay area.

Waldemar Young of the San Francisco *Chronicle* thought no more of "Kid Kabaret" than did other critics when the act opened a two-week engagement at the 'Frisco Orpheum on Sunday, July 27, 1913.

> Ever since the success of his "School Boys and Girls," [Gus] Edwards has found it profitable to employ adolescent talent. In his own

"Song Revue," seen here recently, the kids were "kute and clever"—
you know the patter. Now comes along another flock of them, featuring slim and little youths who endeavor to be comic after the
fashion of adults and who, insofar as the male section is concerned,
greatly overdo it.

The girls, on the other hand, quite attractively act like girls, and
young girls, too, which they are. That is the only possible way in
which a stage child can be appealing. Simulating sophistication is
inevitably sad. That is why it is that the girls in the "Kid Kabaret"
are immeasurably better than the boys, although a word of high
praise should be said for Eddie Cantor, who plays the colored servant. His is youthful ebullience, slapped across naturally. Of the
girls, Enid Morel pleases daintily with a song and Betty Washington
scores an individual hit with a violin solo. The others are youthfully
charming.

Jolson doubtless read the review and heard that Cantor, like a growing
number of vaudevillians, did a Jolson imitation. Even their stage characters
had similarities—the impudence, lack of broad southern accents, Cantor's
"sissyisms" and Jolson's occasional forays into tongue-in-cheek homosexuality. Cantor and Jessel, who both admired Jolson, spent time in his well-
known haunts without, however, running into "Jolie." Then, on Thursday,
following their matinee performance, someone knocked on their dressing
room door and said Al Jolson was waiting to see them.

Cantor thought it was a joke of Jessel's and said to "let him wait." Jessel
echoed the sentiments. They dressed and were amazed to find Al Jolson
waiting for them.

Jolson told them they were "a couple of talented kids." Eddie still kept
moderately kosher, so Al took them to a Jewish restaurant on Turk Street.
Eddie and George sat in stupefied and worshipful silence as Jolson gabbed
away about his life in show business. The two youngsters listened and
learned.

Playing big-time vaudeville was opening doors. Will Rogers and Al Jolson
both influenced Cantor, but Rogers would prove the more fruitful contact.

Work on the Interstate Circuit, with theatres throughout Texas, followed.
Eddie, who now had increased freedom to interpolate new songs as he saw
fit, reportedly introduced "Ballin' the Jack" in the act at the Majestic Theatre in Houston. The increased singing, on top of the fact that Cantor never
had a vocal lesson, made him strain his voice; he had laryngitis by the time
"Kid Kabaret" opened at Keith's Theatre in Knoxville, Tennessee, and was
sent to a local doctor, who sprayed his tonsils, gave him a gargle, and told
him he had to learn to use his voice. But Eddie, like most performers of
the time, was far too busy working to take lessons. Continued misuse of
his vocal chords would cost Cantor his high notes before he reached the
age of fifty-five.

Through all the talks with more established vaudevillians, dinners at the homes of theatregoers, crap games, traveling, and—twice a day—performing, Cantor kept his ears and his huge eyes open for ways to make more money and advance in his profession. He and Jessel never missed an opportunity to play late-night parties for clubs, lodges, or private groups, using the same "blue" material they'd used at the Chelsea Yacht Club in New Jersey.

Ida saw "Kid Kabaret" when the act reached New York in March and played the fabled Palace. Critics threw their darts again. (*Mark* of *Variety* said that some "of those East Side homes depleted to produce the 'Kabaret' turn could easily have the old hearthstone happiness restored by returning the kids, as they are about the most obstreperous, untalented bunch offered in many a day," and Walt Hill of *The Billboard* noted that "Gus Edwards' 'Kid Kabaret' closed the show, getting started at just five o'clock and lasting until nearly everybody in the audience had gone home.") Eddie, though, was thinking far beyond his job with Edwards. He had wired Max Hart on Will Rogers's recommendation and gone to see the powerful agent in the Palace Theatre building. Hart, like most, was unimpressed with "Kid Kabaret," but he conceded that Eddie was a possibility and recommended that he get a partner. Eddie first approached Lew Brice, Fanny's younger brother, a notorious gambler and ne'er-do-well despite his talent for dancing, but Brice turned him down, ostensibly because he thought they did not "have a chance" but more likely because he preferred working with female partners. Eddie's second choice among those then available was an unknown named Sammy Kessler, who had contacts for a tour of England. An act was written and rehearsed over the next three weeks—topical and up-to-date, the kind of act the bookers most preferred.

Eddie's and Ida's joint account contained more than $2,500. Ida would turn twenty-two on May 15, and Eddie's bookings in English music halls with Kessler would give them a paid overseas honeymoon. The time had come to marry.

If Ida had any trepidation about marrying a working vaudevillian who was guaranteed to spend half of the year away from home, she was also thrilled about finally marrying Eddie. He was growing handsomer, more polished, and more personable, not to mention more successful, each year. The only trouble came from Ida's father, who now practically demanded that Eddie use the $2,500 he had saved to buy a haberdashery.

"He asked me what I'd be making on the stage in England," Eddie recalled. "So I told him. He said, 'Clear?' I said, 'Well, I have to provide my own makeup.' He said, 'See, always a catch.'"

Eddie bluffed his way through in fine fashion. "A man as big as David Tobias should have a son-in-law with only one store?!? It should be three, minimum—one in Manhattan, one in Brooklyn, and one in the Bronx. Let me make enough for two more stores." David remained skeptical but made plans for the wedding.

"Kid Kabaret" played seven more weeks on the road, closing at Keith's

Theatre in Atlantic City on May 30, 1914. Cantor had another meeting with Max Hart the following Monday and spent the remainder of that week preparing for his wedding and his working honeymoon in England.

Eddie Cantor and Ida Tobias were married at the Tobias home, 67 Ames Street, Brooklyn, on Tuesday, June 9, with two of Ida's brothers-in-law as witnesses. George Jessel attended, and Eddie solemnly invited everyone to attend their twenty-fifth wedding anniversary in 1939.

Eighty-year-old Esther Kantrowitz, her health failing, could not attend the wedding. Eddie had arranged to have her moved to Cherry Street, where she could receive proper care. Esther loved Ida but could only send her blessings.

Eddie and Ida spent their wedding night in an apartment Eddie rented at 109 South Third Street in Brooklyn. Despite his sexual experience, Eddie was quite shy and hesitant on that first night with the girl he had worshipped, so much so that she, a virgin, wound up the aggressor—a real-life enactment of what might have one day been a classic Cantor stage scene. The marriage was nonetheless consummated in fine fashion, and the newly married couple sailed on the *Aquitania* with Sammy Kessler before the end of the week. They arrived in England several days prior to the act's slated debut at the Oxford on Monday, June 22.

Cantor & Kessler were not a success. Eddie later blamed the material, the topicality of which was lost on English ears. The act was badly written and, it seems, naively planned, Eddie imitating stars the English had neither seen nor heard of. Cantor & Kessler played out the week at the Oxford, but the rest of their English bookings were abruptly canceled.

Cantor, with a bride to care for, wired Max Hart in New York asking for help. Hart acted quickly, putting him in touch with Andre Charlot, then a young producer of music hall revues, who added Eddie to the cast of his show *Not Likely* at London's Alhambra Theatre.

Cantor wisely did not try his imitations. Borrowing what he had learned from Jean Bedini and Roy Arthur, he kidded the other acts on the bill, including a burlesque of *Kismet*, which had a tattered beggar asking alms.

"Ladies and gentlemen," he said, "don't be fooled by this beggar. I know for a fact that he backs Andre Charlot. He owns several apartment buildings, and his chauffeur picks him up after the show." Then he sang a song titled "To the Ladies," which was well suited to his bouncy, effervescent delivery; the song gave him opportunity to score with telling punch lines and won him encores. After a few nights, he found that members of the audience knew all the words and sang the song right along with him. The London press soon gave him notice.

The Cantors nonetheless remained on a strict budget. Ida did their laundry in the basin of the cheap hotel they stayed in, and she climbed the stairs to the balcony to watch his act for two shillings every night. They were, however, on their honeymoon and went to the chic Lyons' Corner

House for tea on one occasion. The waitress brought a beautiful tray of pastries, which, they were informed, cost the equivalent of twelve and a half cents in American money. Eddie and Ida forced themselves to eat every last crumb before learning that the pastries were twelve and a half cents *apiece*. The Cantors had to pay the equivalent of $1.25; Eddie was still wincing more than forty years later.

Eddie Cantor may have been the most security-conscious variety performer in the history of American show business. He had starved as a kid, had learned the value of money, and was determined that he would make the same kind of living in the entertainment field that his father-in-law had made in business—better, if possible. In a profession never known for economic faithfulness, he pursued security for himself and his loved ones with the zeal of a missionary. ("Jesus saves, but not like Cantor," Jessel later quipped.) He was determined to enjoy the home life he had never known.

The family he wanted would begin arriving shortly. The money, in sums that would cause Eddie to stop worrying—a little—would take longer.

Eddie left *Not Likely* after two weeks, and the Cantors sailed back home on the U.S.S. *St. Paul*, arriving in New York on July 29, 1914. Eddie sent his bride in a taxi to 631 East 168th Street in the Bronx, where they had arranged to rent a single room from Ida's sister, Jenny, and her husband, Sam Rosenthal. Cantor himself went to the Palace Building to see Hart.

Hart liked the notices Cantor had received while in *Not Likely* but felt he still needed a partner. Hart provided one himself in Al Lee, only two years Eddie's senior but a seasoned pro. Born Albert Lee Cunningham, he had worked as straight man for Ed Wynn a few years earlier; he sang well and would provide the perfect foil for the Cantor energy and insult humor.

The result was "Master and Man," written largely by Cantor with assistance on the jokes from *Judge* and several other "humor" magazines. Lee was the "Master" in whiteface, Cantor his "Man" servant in black. The big news of the moment was the European war, and Cantor and Lee spoofed it in the opening segment of their seventeen-minute act.

CANTOR: You'll have to let me go.
LEE:     Why?
CANTOR: To fight in the war, to fight for my mother country, Russia.
LEE:     Russia?
CANTOR: *Darkest* Russia.
LEE:     I didn't know you were Russian.
CANTOR: Oh, yes. My relatives are all in the war. My father's General Petrovitch, my uncle's General Ivanovitch. Then there's eczema—another itch. . . .

Lee then sang a ballad, "Carolina," interspersed with offbeat comments from the blackfaced Cantor, who proceeded to sing three songs in succession: "They Turn on the Victrola and Go Dancing Around the Floor," "Poor Pauline" (spoofing Pearl White's *Perils of Pauline* silent-movie serial), and

"The War in Snyder's Grocery Store," trivializing the war raging in Europe. Cantor played his part sans "Negro" dialect (southern or otherwise) and wore plain clothes two or three sizes too tight in order to increase the impression of slightness—a trick he would make more extensive use of as a star on Broadway.

They rehearsed in August and tried out the act at the Star Theatre at 107th Street and Lexington Avenue in New York in September. Max Hart was not particularly impressed; he said Cantor & Lee needed better material but that he'd keep them working till they got it.

Cantor went back to the joke books and, with Lee, worked at switching jokes around and sharpening the act in all respects. "Master and Man" opened its first regular engagement at the Bushwick Theatre, Brooklyn, on October 12, 1914, and continued playing big-time theatres in the east and the midwest, its bookings made considerably easier by the fact that it played "in one," before the curtain, and did not require scenery.

Ida, in the fifth month of pregnancy, saw "Master and Man" often, joining Eddie on the road in Baltimore and in other eastern cities. One of the acts on the bill with "Master and Man" featured a Boston bulldog named "Poonelo" with big eyes—like Eddie's. Ida fell in love with the dog and called Eddie "Poonelo" ever after.

The name, to her, meant "schnook"—naive, lovable, and helpless. It signified the Eddie she had met, fallen in love with, and nurtured on the East Side eight years earlier. As time went on, Ida would sigh "Poonelo" when Eddie made a naive business deal, wasted time and money in an effort to save both, or made rash promises he could not keep. The use of the name "Poonelo" was maternal—filled with both endearment and reproach.

"Master and Man," which depended largely on Cantor, got good notices; the anonymous critic for the Indianapolis News said Eddie was "one of the most refreshing blackfaces seen here in a long while. While having quite different methods, he is rather a reminder of and just about as good as Jack Wilson. When he has restrained the ultra-feminine slap-me-on-the-wrist imitation just a trifle there will be hardly anything in his act that will not deserve the highest praise. He is a singer and actor and he is well assisted by Al Lee."

They were in the "big time": a good "number four" act on most eight-act bills in the Keith theatres that then graced the nation's leading eastern and midwestern cities. They were not, however, "headliners," such as Eva Tanguay, Nora Bayes, Elsie Janis, Sophie Tucker, or other great names (mostly female) who went on in the "next to closing" spot and made as much as three thousand dollars a week. (They later learned that Max Hart was using them as "throw-ins" when he booked his bigger "name" acts on the same circuits.) Their salaries, while good, were not terrific. There was no pay for "open" weeks or for those reserved for travel, and each man's share was rather small after paying commission and deducting traveling expenses. Cantor lived quite frugally, avoiding the costlier hotels, and sent home all he could. Ida was expecting the baby around the end of March.

A last-minute booking at the Palace Music Hall in Chicago, one of the nation's leading vaudeville theatres, got Cantor & Lee reviewed in the "New Acts" section of *Variety*: "Carries a good quota of laughs. . . . Cantor does some travesties on pictures that are laughable. Cantor also pulls a lot of 'cissy' stuff, which is unusual in blackface. Act ends with a brisk duet. Went so well at the Palace that Cantor had to make a speech. Good comedy act, and out of the beaten rut."

Al, while in Chicago, married Lilyan Tashman, a beauty in Gus Ed-wards's "Song Revue." Their marital happiness stood in sharp contrast to the act's *blasé* reception at the Majestic Theatre in Milwaukee, following three other acts that, like them, worked "in one." Cantor blamed this place-ment for the poor response that "Master and Man" received at the opening show: "no laughs, no applause." The stage manager rearranged the bill before the evening show; Cantor & Lee now opened the program.

Opening acts, which often performed when audiences were still settling into their seats, were usually acrobats or "animal" acts featuring trained seals, dogs, or something like "Swayne's Rats and Cats," which did not rely on dialogue. Cantor & Lee did not get one laugh all week.

The worst was yet to come. James Higler, manager of the Majestic The-atre, called Cantor into his office before the end of the week. Higler was then forty-one and had been involved in show business for eighteen years, starting as financial manager for the investor Herman Fehr. He had "seen all the great ones" but had never been a stage performer.

"You're a nice young man, Eddie," he began, "personable, easygoing, and you're taking your failure here this week with good grace. That's why I want to give you a piece of advice. In this business there are those who have it and those who haven't. You just haven't got it. You're a married man; get out of show business and into something else where you can possibly be a big success. Believe me, I've been in this business for years; I know what it takes to make it, and you haven't got it. Take my advice and get out as quickly as you can."

Cantor stood there, taking it all in. He thanked Higler for the advice, left his office, went out to the street, and wept.

He had never before known despair. In his adolescence, Cantor had been desperately poor. But poverty had acted as a shield. With no posses-sions, wife, or family and no real hopes or dreams, there had been nothing to lose. Now he had the wife, a child on the way, and a career he had worked years to build. Show business had become his passport to happi-ness: meaningful work, hope for the future, and, by giving him the means to marry Ida, reciprocal love. Now he cared almost too deeply. For a min-ute, on the street in Milwaukee after listening to Higler, Eddie wished a truck would run him over—"one big Milwaukee beer truck."

The following Monday, Cantor & Lee were on the bill at the Columbia

Theatre in St. Louis. The sting and pain of Higler's speech grew less intense with every good performance.

In March 1915, with the baby's arrival three weeks away, Cantor & Lee played the Temple Theatre in Rochester. Trying to earn extra money, they accepted a late-night date at a firemen's stag party, and Cantor did the same "blue" routine he had done at the Chelsea Yacht Club in Atlantic City. Lee served as the "feed." After they were finished, having scored a major hit with the all-male audience, Cantor removed his blackface makeup and went back to his hotel, where he found the revelers from the stag getting their keys and talking about the funny guy in blackface with the "filthy mind."

He got his key and slunk back to his room, vowing never to tell "dirty" jokes again. He would, in fact, be criticized for using suggestive material on radio in later years. Never again, though, would he resort to outright "blue" jokes or use vulgar humor—partially because he would be playing to well-heeled, comparatively genteel audiences. Cantor would play private parties at swank homes during his Broadway days, but he never played a stag after that night in Rochester.

Marjorie Cantor was born in the Bronx on March 31, 1915. Ida, not yet twenty-three, was strong and healthy and saw no reason to enter a hospital to have her baby. Cantor & Lee were playing the Orpheum Theatre in Brooklyn at the time, and Eddie spent every available moment at the Rosenthal apartment, waiting and rejoicing at the birth of his first daughter.

Marjorie was named after his mother, Meta, the anglicization of the name in keeping with Eddie's penchant for Americanization without abandoning his Jewish heritage. The Cantors' one room in the Rosenthals' apartment gave them little space after the addition of the cradle. In reality, though, they had the run of the entire flat. Ida and Jenny split the household chores between them, and Jenny did the cooking. (Ida never learned to cook, in contrast to her daughters, almost all of whom turned into culinary experts.) Ida's responsibilities included taking Jenny's two children to Van Cortlandt Park for walks. Now she proudly took her baby daughter in a carriage with them, as proud of her position as a mother as her husband was of his as a vaudevillian. (The former had more prestige in most circles at the time.)

Cantor & Lee continued playing eastern dates that spring, including one at Keith's in Boston. Eddie was the dinner guest of Max Tobias, his father-in-law's brother, in nearby Worcester. Max, a tailor, had been living in Worcester for twelve years with his wife and their four sons, Henry, Charley, Nathan, and Harry, the youngest, who remembered Eddie knocking at the front door, "only used in those days for special events like weddings and special visitors":

Eddie was always the life of the party and was always "on," as they say in show biz. He didn't need a stage or lights; any audience of any given number and he started making with the jokes and songs.

Mom had her precious antique dishes hanging on the wall of the parlor. We were always warned never to touch or go near them for fear we would break them. Eddie—we never knew he was a professional juggler—immediately grabbed two of the most precious possessions and started juggling. I'll never forget his one trick. He placed the plate on his straight bent elbow and let go. Just as it was about to smash on the floor to bits, he grabbed it—while Mom screamed.

Those first months with his new daughter were golden to young Cantor. He struggled to save money, but he loved the baby, not only as a proud young father but in much the way that *Bubba* had loved him. He wanted to indulge her but had not, as yet, the means to do it.

Nor would he be there to raise the child. In mid-November, Cantor & Lee left to play Keith's theatres in the Midwest and, finally, the Orpheum Circuit. Ida was pregnant again, with the new baby due in April. That winter, to make things even harder, the ten-month-old Marjorie had an earache that was diagnosed as an infection of the mastoids. Ida, supremely self-reliant when occasion warranted, inquired for the best doctor in New York, wrapped Marjorie in blankets, and took her downtown for the necessary operation. She called Eddie, long distance, as soon as it was over.

Aside from that, they kept in touch by post. Eddie made his letters short and entertaining, seldom bothering to add more than a line or two about the different audiences, let alone the difficult stage managers, the act encountered.

Cantor & Lee opened a two-week engagement at the Orpheum Theatre in Los Angeles on Monday, February 28, 1916. The theatre was known for its "professional" audience—silent-screen stars and directors, producers of both films and stage shows. Many influential people in show business saw Cantor & Lee at the Los Angeles Orpheum. But the one who made a difference was the songwriter Earl Carroll.

Earl, a Pittsburgh native and the same age as Eddie, had written "Dreams of Long Ago" to music by the famous tenor Enrico Caruso a couple of years earlier. "Women and Light," another Carroll lyric, had been used in one of J. J. Shubert's New York Winter Garden shows. During the preceding year, he had written lyrics for two shows produced by Oliver Morosco: *Pretty Miss Smith*, starring Fritzi Scheff, and *So Long Letty*, starring Charlotte Greenwood. He knew Eddie Cantor slightly, having met him in New York, but the two men were hardly friends. Carroll was, however, quite impressed with Cantor's work in "Master and Man" and thought he would be great playing a chauffeur in *Canary Cottage*, a new show Carroll was writing for Morosco. With Al Goodman, the producer's musical director, Carroll came backstage and told Cantor that Morosco wanted to see him.

Cantor reported to Morosco's office early the next afternoon and found the producer to be "an impeccably groomed man who wore all the assurance of his own success." Born Oliver Mitchell, he had risen to become the most important producer on the West Coast in a day in which the live stage was still all-important. Acting on Carroll's recommendation, he offered Cantor a role in *Canary Cottage* at a salary not much greater than Eddie was getting in vaudeville. Morosco had no part for Al Lee.

Eddie turned him down because he did not want to desert Lee and because he was reluctant to leave a big-time vaudeville act that had fed both himself and his growing family for well over a year. The first objection was overcome when Al Lee voiced no objections to Cantor's breaking up the act: "I wouldn't be tied up in a town like this at any price. I'm Broadway."

Eddie weighed the options. "Master and Man" would never be a headline act, and he did not want Ida living in one room with him and two (or more) children for years to come. It was necessary, therefore, to take chances and explore new fields. Broadway was Cantor's ultimate goal, and Broadway meant the theatre. *Canary Cottage* would provide Eddie's first experience in real musical comedy.

He went back to Morosco and accepted.

Rehearsals would not start until May 1, which meant that he and Lee could tour for an additional six weeks. They played Salt Lake City, Denver, Des Moines, Kansas City, and Omaha, closing in St. Paul on April 29, two days after Ida gave birth to her second child, Natalie, in Jenny's apartment in the Bronx.

The birth was mercifully easy. Nor was Eddie's absence Ida's major problem. Shortly after Natalie was born, Ida was given an alcohol rub by a practical nurse. The woman smoked as she rubbed, and Ida's back was set on fire by a stray ash. The nurse screamed and ran out of the room as Ida cried for help. Jenny then ran in and put the fire out by turning Ida over smothering the flames.

Ida had beautiful skin—silky, almost satiny, much like her daughter Natalie's in later years. The accident, however, scarred her back with surface pock marks that resembled lunar craters. She was young, however, only twenty-four, and out of bed within a week. The scars eventually faded.

Eddie wanted to return home, but he was needed for rehearsals of *Canary Cottage*. He returned to Los Angeles from St. Paul; Al Lee headed for New York. Lee was fated to be on Broadway, but not as a performer. In the 1940s he wound up a house manager on Broadway.

Cantor's role in *Canary Cottage* was not, he quickly saw, very important. As "Sam" Beverly Moon, he was the chauffeur of Blanche Moss, the starring role, played by the rotund Trixie Friganza. (Others in the cast included the future movie actor Charles Ruggles in the part of Jerry Summerfield.)

Carroll's score contained two songs for Cantor: "It Ruined Marc Antony" in Act I and "I'll Marry No Explorer" in Act II. With no acting training to inhibit or restrain him, Cantor started to ad-lib lines at rehearsals, breaking up not only Carroll but the librettist, Elmer Harris. When he would repeat the same lines and/or business the next day, he would be told "That's out" by Frank Stammers, the director. Stammers was obeying the instructions of the star, Trixie Friganza, who, with considerable justification, saw *Canary Cottage* as a vehicle for her. No "amateur," as she referred to Cantor, would upstage her.

Former stage star Raymond Griffith, who had turned to film acting after losing his voice, had become a friend of Cantor's when "Master and Man" played the Los Angeles Orpheum. Eddie, with no legitimate stage experience, asked Griffith to sit in on some rehearsals. The advice Griffith gave him was completely practical, if devoid of the respect for craft and discipline taught in good acting schools.

"Don't be a fool," he croaked in his hoarse voice. "Everything you try at rehearsal, she'll have cut. Just make notes of what you want to do and save it for opening night."

Cantor took Griffith's advice. When *Canary Cottage* opened at the Empress Theatre, San Diego, on May 18, 1916, the big news was the presence in the chorus of one Lily Carr, a young woman with a remarkable resemblance to Anna Held, the one-time common-law wife of the Broadway producer Florenz Ziegfeld. Reporters who spoke to Carr received the startling news that she was, indeed, the daughter of the celebrated Anna, best known for her "milk baths" (a publicity stunt of Ziegfeld's) and for the song "I Can't Make My Eyes Behave." The resulting publicity infuriated Trixie Friganza, who demanded that Carr (whose real name was Liane Carrera) be fired. Carr was dismissed before *Canary Cottage* opened at the Mason Opera House in Los Angeles on May 21.

The opening, before the leading West Coast critics, showed that Friganza had misdirected both her jealousies and her fears. Eddie Cantor literally pulled the stops out, placing his ad-libs at the strategic places he had mapped out at rehearsal. When Trixie made her exit, Eddie looked at her and exclaimed, "God, a milk wagon!" When she said, "Bring the car around," he grabbed three oranges off the fruit bowl and juggled. He picked a yellow shawl from the piano and danced off in it, added extra choruses to his songs (Goodman and the musicians, accustomed to stars giving extra choruses, just followed), and made his small part into the comedy feature of *Canary Cottage*.

Friganza raged after the show, but Eddie simply took his makeup off and left, without a word, to meet his friend Ray Griffith. Ray took Eddie to his apartment for a glass of champagne, and Cantor talked about his fears of being fired. "So maybe you'll be fired," Griffith said. "Tomorrow, there'll be a hundred jobs waiting."

The headline of Guy Price's review for the Hearst newspapers, "Vaude-villian Romps Home with *Canary Cottage*," vindicated Cantor's talent, if not Griffith's wisdom. Cantor was told to report to Morosco when he arrived at the theatre the next afternoon. Morosco's office was seven minutes away from the Mason Opera House, and Eddie walked there, certain that he would be fired.

Morosco came right to the point. "Eddie Cantor, what you did last night is the most unforgivable thing that can happen in the theatre. Now you go back to the matinee and do everything you did last night, exactly the same way."

Friganza had her own speech prepared for that afternoon's rehearsal, threatening to give in her two weeks' notice if "this amateur" was not dis-missed. But Morosco, sitting in the third row with Earl Carroll and Elmer Harris, never flinched. "We intend to keep Eddie Cantor for the run of the play," he told his star. Friganza might have quit and gone back into vaude-ville; however, she was still the star and reluctant to have the profession know that an unknown had caused her to depart from her own starring show—with her producer's blessing.

Cantor's victory did not get him more money. He sent home all but twenty-five dollars, lived above a Pig 'n' Whistle coffee shop for a dollar a night, and used the remaining eighteen dollars for food, laundry, and other expenses. No coffee drinker, he treated himself to a chocolate ice cream soda every other night. Again, unlike most actors, he watched every penny, always planning for the future. His big dream at this point was to give Ida, himself, and their babies an apartment of their own.

The conflict with Friganza had made Cantor yet another ally. Liane Carrera, delighted at how Eddie had upstaged Friganza, now approached him and said that her "stepfather" (the great Ziegfeld) could do him "a lot of good." Cantor made no protest when Carrera wrote Ziegfeld a letter, telling him about the "wonderful new comedian" who was handled by Max Hart.

Ziegfeld's familiarity with Max's name had grown into a sharp awareness since Will Rogers, still Hart's client, had made his Broadway debut in the 1915 *Follies*. The 1916 *Follies* had opened in June, but Ziegfeld was already giving thought to a new edition of his *Midnight Frolic*, the after-theatre revue he presented on the "roof garden" of the New Amsterdam Theatre. A letter to Max Hart from Eddie moved the matter further.

*Canary Cottage* ran for eight weeks in Los Angeles and moved to the Cort Theatre in San Francisco. In the meantime, Max Hart spoke to Zieg-feld. By Labor Day, he had closed a deal whereby Eddie Cantor would appear in the new edition of the Ziegfeld *Midnight Frolic*, due to open on October 2. All Eddie had to do was get a release from Morosco.

Cantor wrote to Ida, telling her to instruct Jenny's husband to send him a telegram—a masterpiece of tear-jerking malarkey that said Ida was so heartsick over not seeing her husband for ten months that she could not eat, sleep, or take care of her children. Eddie had to "come at once." He showed the telegram to Oliver Morosco, wept crocodile tears, and got his release after the show closed its run in San Francisco on September 6. His understudy, Lew Cooper, took over as Sam Beverly Moon when *Canary Cottage* reopened in Los Angeles, with the understanding Cantor would return.

Eddie had not seen his wife since early in November, and he had not seen his new daughter, Natalie, at all. Margie, now one and a half, saw her father for what seemed like the first time. To Ida, he was the conquering hero, the breadwinner returned after a successful campaign in the western provinces and practically assured of a triumphant debut for the emperor, Florenz Ziegfeld. "We've no more worries," Eddie told her. "Max says Ziegfeld is crazy about me. I'll probably go from the *Frolic* to the *Follies*."

He was, in fact, assured of nothing.

Max Hart had not told Cantor that Ziegfeld had not offered him a contract. The engagement was, effectively, a tryout, and Cantor reported for rehearsals with supreme confidence—a confidence born out of naivete.

He arrived at the Roof Theatre in September 1916 to find Ford Dabney, one of the first black conductors to work for a white Broadway producer, playing the piano, beautiful young Ziegfeld dancers rehearsing in abbreviated costumes, and a seeming madhouse of technicians, carpenters, and assorted personnel engaged in wiring, hammering, and otherwise assembling the various aspects of a first-class show. In the midst of it, but somehow towering above it all, in Cantor's big brown eyes, was Ziegfeld, himself.

Florenz Ziegfeld Jr. was then forty-nine years old, his grey hair making him look more distinguished and handsome than he had been when he captivated Anna Held in Europe twenty years earlier. Wearing a blue shirt and working jacketless, he rapidly took in the works around him as his righthand man, writer, lyricist, and virtual prime minister, Gene Buck, talked about performers, material, and other details. On Broadway, Florenz Ziegfeld was a monarch, and he looked the part.

Cantor went right up and introduced himself with all the confidence of a young performer grown accustomed to success.

"Mr. Ziegfeld, I'm Eddie Cantor."

Ziegfeld looked at him blandly. "Eddie Cantor," Eddie said again. "Max Hart . . . my agent, spoke to you, and. . . ."

Gene Buck intervened. "Oh yes, Max Hart," he said. "He spoke to me about you. Just what do you do?"

"Oh, I'm marvelous."

"Well, that may be," said Ziegfeld. "But what do you do?"

"Mr. Ziegfeld! Do I ask you what *you* do?"

Ziegfeld smiled slightly, and Buck laughed, nudging "Zieggy." Cantor had the audacity of someone who belonged.

But Ziegfeld did not stay to see whatever Cantor did. The most believable accounts say that he mumbled something to Gene Buck and walked out to a luncheon date.

Eddie sang for Buck, giving his lead sheet of "Oh, How She Could Yacki Hacki Wicki Wacki Woo" to Ford Dabney, and followed up with some quick jokes told in his emphatic, knowingly Jewish, and exuberant manner.

He told Buck about his "character": "a colored comedian with white bone-rimmed glasses who is refined and slightly effeminate." Ziegfeld's righthand man was satisfied; Cantor was in the *Midnight Frolic* unless "Mr. Ziegfeld" said otherwise.

Eddie was hired—for the opening. There was still no guarantee of anything more.

He rushed back to the Bronx by subway to tell Ida the good news, exaggerating Ziegfeld's personal response and telling her that their worries were "over." Two weeks of rehearsals followed, with Ford Dabney and his musicians working out the orchestrations while Cantor polished the ten minutes of material he had written on the train from California.

For the dress rehearsal, he brought down his alpaca suit, straw hat, white glasses, gloves, and burnt cork and went to the dressing room to which stage manager Kiraly had assigned him. *Miss Springtime*, the show that introduced America to P. G. Wodehouse lyrics, was playing the New Amsterdam, and Cantor spent the hours preceding the *Frolic* watching the swank cars pull up in front of the theatre. Broadway musical comedy audiences of that day were composed of native New Yorkers rather than tourists from "middle America." The New Yorkers were, in general, the rich and the upper middle class whose names were counted among the "Four Hundred"—Diamond Jim Brady, the Harrimans, the Astors, the DuPonts, and others of the city's—and the country's—famous families. Broadway had been their home before the theatre district had moved uptown to Times Square in the 1890s. They would desert neither the district nor the theatre for some years to come.

Cantor, who had never been in any Broadway show, let alone a Ziegfeld musical, sized them up wisely. Billed as "A New Nut" (probably at Buck's suggestion), he came on for his *Frolic* "turn" around 12:45 A.M., Tuesday, October 3, 1916. Following the stuttering comedian Joe Frisco, W. C. Fields, and Lillian Lorraine, Cantor presented a good "Broadway" blend of Ziegfeld theatricality and "parlor" entertainment that endeared him to the audience.

"Ladies and gentlemen, I'm not a regular actor. I work for a plumber in Hastings and yesterday something went wrong with the plumbing in Mr. Ziegfeld's house. He heard me singing in the bathroom and thought this would be a good gag. So it doesn't matter if you applaud or not. Tomorrow I go back to plumbing."

The slight, young entertainer thus endeared himself to New York's *crème de la crème*. Theatre statisticians class the *Midnight Frolics* as "nightclub," rather than "theatre," and omit the shows from Broadway reference works. Their argument is that *Frolic* audiences were seated at tables; in many other respects, Ziegfeld's *Midnight Frolics* were "roof" versions of the *Ziegfeld Follies*. There were the (smaller) production numbers, star comedians, songs, an orchestra, and programs. Missing were the *tableaux* and the topical sketches. The *Frolic* was a tabloid *Follies* produced by the original master and transplanted to a rooftop nightclub. The menus were printed on silk, and a five-dollar cover charge (equivalent to about one hundred dollars in 1997 money) guaranteed a well-heeled and genteel audience. Cantor knew what he was facing. "Here was cafe society, blasé and *intime*, deigning to be amused; here were Mr. Ziegfeld and Billie Burke sitting at a table with friends. I'd have died to amuse them. But it had to be just right—intimate but not offensive and, my God, not common!"

He whipped out a deck of cards, shuffled them like a good sleight-of-hand artist (a trick he had perfected under Jean Bedini), and, with an air of complete seriousness, approached three "guests" to help him with his act—William Randolph Hearst, Diamond Jim Brady, and Charles B. Dillingham, a rival producer. They were to stand and hold the cards high over their heads so that the audience could see them. As they held the cards, Cantor, ignoring them completely, did the same routine he'd done for Ziegfeld at rehearsals, singing "Oh, How She Could Yacki Hacki Wicki Wacki Woo" and "Hawaii, America Loves You." (Both songs were then in keeping with a craze, then current, for "Hawaiian" numbers.) As he went on energetically, oblivious to his three well-known "stooges," the audience began to howl, egged on by the smiling, exasperated looks of Hearst, Brady, and Dillingham. Cantor now pulled out a three-stringed banjo and strummed aimlessly. ("Two weeks ago," he said, "I couldn't play this thing at all.") When Eddie finished singing, he collected the cards and thanked the gentlemen for their assistance with mock gravity. The applause was heartfelt, warm, indicative of both approval and acceptance.

Holding up his hand for quiet, Eddie addressed the audience: "I may not go back to plumbing after all. Still, it might be good to have two jobs. Mother needs me now that Dad's gone." He looked sad. "With good behavior, he may be out in ten years. You know how it was with Dad. When you work in a bank, you just can't take home samples."

Eddie took the subway home about 2:00 A.M., told Ida of his triumph, and slept for the remainder of the morning. When he awoke, there was a telegram from Ziegfeld: "Enjoyed your act. You'll be here a long time."

He took the telegram to Max Hart's office. Within the hour, Hart got Ziegfeld on the phone and okayed a deal. Eddie Cantor would receive two hundred dollars a week—an amount comparable to two thousand dollars a week in the mid-1990s—as long as he remained in the current edition of the Ziegfeld *Midnight Frolic*.

Cantor raced home and celebrated. A review of the *Frolic* in the New York *Evening Telegram* that night said he combined "the spontaneity of Will Rogers with the humor of Frank Tinney"—both of whom, ironically, were clients of Max Hart. Most of the other reviews spotlighted Frances White, although the New York *Herald* reported that Cantor "strolled among the audience and proved himself to be a regular humorist, with a quaint line of blackface comedy." The New York *American* merely said that he, Peggy Brooks, and Lawrence Haynes were "truly additions."

Cantor was still young—just twenty-four—with a wife and children and a blossoming career. On Saturday, he received his first salary from Ziegfeld—two hundred dollars in cash—and went downtown to show *Bubba*.

The old woman, then living on Cherry Street under a nurse's care, looked uncomprehendingly at the money and her grandson and said, in Yiddish, "Honest, Itchik? No stealing."

Eddie laughed, hugged *Bubba*, and assured her. Her days were numbered, but he did not want to admit it. He had earned his triumph and his happiness. No thoughts of doom would penetrate his teeming brain just now.

Eddie and Ida got their own apartment late that month—a six-room deluxe flat in the same building as the Rosenthals', and hired their first regular household servant, a maid who lived in their apartment in her own small room and was paid sixty dollars a month. The Cantors were arriving.

Eddie saw many of the same faces in the *Frolic* audience from night to night. The tourist trade was comparatively small in New York, which meant that Broadway audiences, especially for Ziegfeld's *Midnight Frolic*, were made up largely of repeaters—town playboys, rich couples, major politicians, and sundry celebrities—"theatre habitués and sons of habitués," as William Hammerstein had dubbed them. Cantor therefore tried to vary his routine and songs each night. His popularity with Ziegfeld's elite patrons grew as a result, and the *Midnight Frolic* became so successful that Ziegfeld had to find space for an extra row of tables around the Roof, increasing the room's capacity by some two hundred people.

Cantor's ambition never remained dormant long; he soon wanted more money. Since Ziegfeld would not give him an immediate raise, Eddie decided to moonlight, accepting vaudeville dates arranged by Max Hart through the United Booking Office, the official arm of the Keith theatres. He was scheduled to open at the Colonial Theatre on Monday afternoon, November 27, until the matter came to Florenz Ziegfeld's attention. Their contract granted Ziegfeld exclusive rights to Eddie Cantor's stage work, and the fact that Eddie had not asked his permission to do vaudeville galled him, not that Ziegfeld would have given it. Cantor had to withdraw from the Colonial Theatre booking after one performance, and the incident left bad feelings between Ziegfeld and the U.B.O.

Cantor, like Bedini and Roy Arthur, found a source of new material in spoofing other acts. Claudius and Scarlet had a singing turn called "The Call of the (18)60s," in which they sang old songs, the lyrics of which went up on a sheet so that the audience could join in on the choruses. Their routine resembled the "illustrated song" acts, in which scenes from each number were shown on steriopticon slides.

One night, Cantor did a burlesque of an "illustrated song" act, wearing blackface and using comedy picture slides loaned to him by Tom Smith of Smith & Austin. Cantor went on before Claudius and Scarlet. Dane Claudius, who thought the burlesque ruined their act, told Eddie to cut the bit. When Cantor repeated it the next night, Claudius went to his dressing room and punched him.

Ironically, Ziegfeld had asked Cantor to withdraw the number after that night's performance, claiming that the show was running long. Cantor, in the meantime, sued Dane Claudius for two thousand dollars.

Cantor was expected to rejoin *Canary Cottage* when that show opened on Broadway. His two-year contract with Ziegfeld, then in negotiation, ruled that out by late December, and Hart had to square affairs with Oliver Morosco. *Canary Cottage*, without Cantor, enjoyed only a brief run in New York.

On Monday, January 29, 1917, Esther Kantrowitz died at the age of eighty-two.

Eddie and Ida went to her apartment on Cherry Street following the orthodox funeral at the synagogue on Pike Street. They found a hundred dollars in a bureau drawer along with a note, "For my funeral, please."

*Bubba* had wanted "nothing from no one."

In an era when paid stage work was relatively common—and not held in particularly high repute—professional performers, with extremely rare exceptions, were not thought of as celebrities. Their families (except for those in high social stations) were nonetheless proud of them. But Esther, never having understood the theatre or its import in America, could neither gauge nor comprehend her grandson's mounting stage success. She only knew he made a living and that he was married. An ector? This was good, no? Esther never was quite sure.

Despite his calculating attitude about show business, his desire for the home life he had missed in childhood, and his great devotion to his wife and daughters, Cantor was an entertainer, with a strong need to perform. It was what had led him to amuse his friends on Henry Street, to hang suspended from the lamp post and do imitations. It was the reason he had chosen to become an entertainer and, despite her wholehearted support, to risk losing Ida.

But Esther's lack of comprehension of his stage success had made that success feel strangely pyrrhic. The knowledge that his triumphs as an entertainer made no difference to his grandmother—and that now they never would—would haunt him for the rest of his career. Success on stage would never be enough.

Esther was buried in Mt. Zion Cemetery in Maspeth, Queens, New York. Eddie soon erected an impressive granite headstone, calling her a "loving mother and devoted grandmother."

Two days after *Bubba*'s death, Eddie signed a two-year contract with Flo Ziegfeld that gave him four hundred dollars a week. Cantor's years of struggle were now over—but not his insecurities, his drive, or burning hunger.

## Chapter 4

# THE FOLLIES

*"Do you know what aristocrats are? We were aristocrats
in the* Follies, *mister."*

ddie Cantor was a feature of the *Midnight Frolic* for twenty-seven consecutive weeks, his act changing almost nightly, his popularity with Ziegfeld "regulars" increasing to the point where it soon rivaled his
self-confidence.

His stage persona was unmistakably Jewish—pushy, slightly nebishy, but
without the intellectual neuroses that would distinguish Woody Allen in
the 1960s. His impudence—always a large part of his onstage character—
seemed balanced by a readiness to do his very best, and his seeming lack
of awe for the money, names, and personages in the audience allowed him
to be entertaining without being ingratiating. Cantor had an air of familiarity coupled with the naivete of a young virgin out to "see the girls," one
who gets pulled in too deeply and has second thoughts.

Eddie's willingness to please his almost exclusively non-Jewish audience,
composed of such names as Harriman and Vanderbilt, made it seem that
he genuinely *liked* them, while admiring their breeding, class, and wealth.
In short, he was a "white Jew"—acceptable to Ziegfeld's "uptown" audience,
a little man with banjo eyes whom they could take to heart and, perhaps,
home, to treat to the finer things in life he would appreciate, if only for a
brief and fleeting instant.

His determination and inventiveness were also quite endearing, making
him seem like the underdog who succeeds by sheer will, persistence, and
native intelligence. Above all else, he seemed the weakling, a role he sometimes carried to extremes by playing an extremely effeminate character that
suggested, sometimes bordered, on homosexuality while leaving little doubt
that he was "playing" at the part. He had done this with Bedini & Arthur

and had played the same role at one time or another with Al Lee, in *Canary Cottage* (as "Sam" Beverly Moon), and now in the *Frolic*.

Such characterizations were part and parcel of the stage, whether done in drag (à la the flaming Bert Savoy), in character (like Cantor), or as parts of stand-up monologues (like Frank Fay and other "straight" monologuists of the late '20s). Truly gay men (aside from such outrageous types as Savoy) would not have dared employ such mannerisms. Cantor, in his stage work, seemed to play both ends against the middle, suggesting a borderline homosexual at one moment and rolling his eyes in genuine appreciation of the Ziegfeld beauties in the next. His character's effeminacy seemed part of a presexual youth's sexual awakening—a young man uncertain of his sexual orientation but with a definite susceptibility to the charms of beautiful women. The later Eddie Cantor, who rolled his eyes and boasted of his sexual prowess in siring five daughters, seemed almost the completion of this cycle.

The Cantor of 1917, more boy than father on the stage, was nonetheless a young man on the rise in private life. He was not immediately spoiled by success, remaining frugal and departing straight for home, by subway, when his nightly *Frolic* stint was over at 1:30 in the morning. Ida would be waiting with hot chocolate and cookies.

He slept till noon and spent the rest of the day eating, going through the mail, and entertaining visitors—friends from the old neighborhood, acquaintances from vaudeville, and song pluggers hoping to get their publishers' latest numbers in the Ziegfeld *Midnight Frolic*.

Cantor's song delivery had improved greatly since the night he had sung "Ragtime Violin" at Shea's Theatre in Buffalo while with Bedini & Arthur. He sang his songs while prancing joyously up and down the length of the stage, interpolating light and rapid clapping of his hands, rolling his big, brown bug-eyes, and exiting at the close of each number with a wave of his breastpocket handkerchief.

Cantor was not yet one of the top "plugs" for any song—Nora Bayes and Jolson topped the list—but he never lacked for new songs to sing in the *Midnight Frolic*. He supplied his own material at this point, most of it topical, much of it knowingly directed at the society "swells" who loved, within obvious reason, to see and hear themselves lampooned. Part Al Smith Democrat (perhaps slightly to the left of Smith), part aspiring plutocrat, he neither loved nor despised the millionaires who came to see the *Frolic*. Success was all that mattered to him now, and Eddie, like other performers, did not think of success in terms of potential sociopolitical influence. Certainly not yet.

He would soon discover different ways to augment his income, including coauthoring new songs, making recordings, performing at private parties, and collaborating with experienced sketch writers on vaudeville acts. (Trixie Friganza, his one-time enemy, now paid him two hundred dollars for material.) Energy and ambition were the trademarks of the young and now successful Eddie Cantor.

The Fourth Edition of the Ziegfeld *Midnight Frolic* closed on April 7, 1917. Within a week, Cantor and Max Hart met with Ziegfeld to discuss Eddie's part in the new *Follies*.

The sketches he appeared in, Ziegfeld said, would be provided by Gene Buck and other writers. The great Bert Williams's presence meant that Cantor would not be the only blackface comedian in the *Follies*, and plans were being made to have the two men work together in a sketch. Eddie would be responsible only for his own "specialty," including two new songs. Rehearsals for the *Follies* would begin on May 7.

The *Ziegfeld Follies* of 1917 was the eleventh annual edition of a series started back in 1907, when Ziegfeld was forty. The series, uniformly well produced, was nonetheless uneven in its inclusion of first-rate material, top songs, and even top performers. A breakthrough was achieved in the 1915 edition with the scenery of Josef Urban, Europe's finest scene designer, which lent the show breathtaking elegance when combined with Ziegfeld's own chic use of color, lighting, and beautiful young women. Working in conjunction with Urban and Buck, Ziegfeld had finally succeeded in creating the artistic masterpieces he had always desired.

Eddie was confident but nervous, full of anxious energy when he reported for rehearsals. Except for Trixie Friganza, he had never worked with any major star. Now he would be a colleague of established Broadway and vaudeville favorites like Fanny Brice and W. C. Fields and share the stage with the imcomparable Bert Williams.

Egbert Austin (Bert) Williams was considered the greatest stage comedian of his day, a master of timing, pantomime, gesture, facial expression, and line shading who could get the most out of any scene, song, or bit of business he either created or had assigned to him. (A number of acoustic phonograph recordings and a couple of brief silent films support this reputation. Williams's recording of "My Landlady" is a classic.) Of African-Dutch ancestry, he was born in the West Indies in 1874 and moved, with his family, to California in childhood. Having become an entertainer to earn money for tuition after his first year in college, he soon teamed with George Walker to form one of the greatest comedy teams on the American stage. Walker's failing health—he died in 1911—forced Williams to work as a single. Williams's appearance in the *Follies* of 1910 had marked the first time a black performer had appeared on Broadway in a major role.

Williams, although black, performed in blackface, using the stylized "mask" to its fullest effect in comic expression, including his famous "mournful" look when playing against Walker, the "dandy" of their act. Modern writers may have exaggerated his resentment of the blackface medium. Interviews suggest that he accepted blackface as a part of the theatrical profession, a remnant of the stylized makeups popular in nine-teenth-century show business.

There had been some resentment among members of the cast when Williams joined the *Follies* in 1910. Quick action by Ziegfeld, and Williams's own dignified demeanor, stamped it out almost at once, and there was no further trouble when Williams appeared in the *Follies* of 1911. Cantor had no compunctions about working with a black man. His only apprehension was that Williams would resent another blackface comedian in the *Follies*.

His fears, as it turned out, were groundless. Williams, eighteen years his senior, acted as his mentor in their scene, in which Bert, as "Murgatroyd Jones," brags to his fellow porters at the "Information Bureau" about his son, Abner, due from college on the train. "He's on the football team," he tells them, "like his dad." When "Abner" arrives, it's Cantor, a boyish, slight, effete young man who embarrasses his father with his immature behavior ("Look, dad. I carry matches!").

Williams told Cantor he could "afford to underplay this scene somewhat because the situation almost carries itself." Williams was not the only one of Cantor's senior players in the *Follies* to notice Eddie's tendency to over-play his comedy. "Don't *bang* that line over, boy" was the advice of W. C. Fields. "When you're on stage with Bert Williams, there's only two places for the audience to look when you deliver your line—at Bert or at you." Cantor's desperate, frequently exaggerated style was born partially of his experience in vaudeville, in which one had to "grab" indifferent audiences within the first two minutes of an act or run the risk of being canceled. *Follies* audiences were more sophisticated, and much more attentive. They were, as Cantor would discover, the best, and possibly the easiest, audience of all.

Eddie was amazed at the camaraderie and lack of jealousy among the more established *Follies* names. Each one was a solid and well-seasoned "pro," including Will Rogers, still a fellow client of Max Hart's, a friendly and familiar face to talk to at rehearsals. W. C. Fields seemed slightly intimidating; he and Cantor would not come to know each other well until the *Follies* went on tour. Fanny Brice, the other Ziegfeld comic star, regarded Eddie as a younger brother who needed advice. "I was young and brash," remembered Cantor. "Fanny set me straight. She didn't want me to get slapped down."

Fanny, a satirist whose forte was doing comic songs in Yiddish dialect, was the only other Jew among the *Follies* principals. If the male comedians found him an amusing "stooge" or student, she felt an affinity with Eddie, partly because of their common ethnicity and partly because she felt the same kind of maternal instinct Ida had, an instinct that, in Ida's case, had blossomed into love.

Fanny, who had made her Broadway debut in the *Follies of 1910*, had come into her own in the 1916 edition and was then regarded as the top comedienne in the United States. When she suggested Cantor do a number with her, he jumped at the chance.

"She asked me if I could dance. I lied, of course I could, but I kept stalling when she wanted to rehearse." Finally, the day before the cast left for the tryout in Atlantic City, Fanny dragged him on the stage. "I hoped I could follow her and get away with it, just a simple soft-shoe dance; but after a dozen steps she turned her head sideways, muttering as she danced, 'You sonofabitch, you can't dance a lick!' " Fanny had the veteran Ned Wayburn teach Eddie a simple time step he used throughout the number. It was the first dance training he had ever received.

The *Ziegfeld Follies* of 1917 had its pre-Broadway tryout at Nixon's Apollo Theatre in Atlantic City, a resort area attracting thousands of well-to-do vacationers but beyond the comfortable reach of New York reviewers. The Broadway opening, at the New Amsterdam Theatre on Tuesday night, June 12, 1917, was a gala event attended by top politicians, business people, all the New York critics, and the "Four Hundred" of society.

They were not disappointed. The 1917 *Follies* was the richest, most sumptuous show ever seen on Broadway, eclipsing all previous editions in scenery, production values, comedians, and beautiful women. Bert Williams, Will Rogers, W. C. Fields, Walter Catlett, Fanny Brice, and Eddie Cantor constituted the greatest array of comic talent and names ever assembled in one Broadway show.

The first scene showed Irving Fisher as a prospective son-in-law betting his future father (Gus Minton) that he could show him more in three hours around New York than ever was written in the *Arabian Nights*. This "plot" was then forgotten, but a New York locale was maintained for most of the remaining scenes.

Sime Silverman, founding owner, publisher, and editor of *Variety*, said that Eddie Cantor was "liked" in the scene he had with Williams, though he also charged that the sketch "badly dragged," a statement strangely out of step with Cantor's later claims. Eddie's first act solo scene, "The Episode of the Eddie-cantor" had him do what was referred to as a "semi-monologue"—several one-and two-line jokes with light banter—and two songs: "The Modern Maiden's Prayer" and "That's the Kind of a Baby for Me." The former was a tongue-in-cheek recitation of the "modern" woman's prayers—for "millionaires," a "bathing suit so folks will say I'm cute," and ("in case my marriage proves to be phoney") "lots of alimony"—a type of girl all too familiar to the *Follies* audience. The other number was a "show song" that allowed Eddie to prance up and down and clap his hands with joy on the assorted punch lines. "The other evening in a cabaret we spent. And when I saw the check I thought it was the rent. But when the waiter came, she simply signed her name. That's the kind of a baby for me." He was the "boy" delighting in the liberated woman who practically supported him, a reminder of the days when he, a teenaged "innocent," was "kept" by the sad Fania. He rolled his big eyes joyously beneath his large white glasses and waved his handkerchief behind him for what Sime described as a "riotous finish to his act."

Brice and Cantor were singled out for special praise by most of the reviewers, leaving the artistic comedy of Bert Williams and Fields, along with Rogers's witticisms, among the also-rans.

The New York *Evening Telegram*:

Mr. Cantor . . . is new to the *Follies*, and won the warmest welcome of the evening in clever singing patter and dancing.

The New York *World*:

A comparatively new singing comedian, Eddie Cantor, who descended from the *Frolic* on the roof, made one of the hits of the night with the song, "That's the Kind of a Baby for Me."

The New York *Tribune*:

Cantor is a blackface comedian who possesses the comic spirit and knows what to do with a song. He runs considerably ahead of the dependable Bert Williams in the new show, although the latter, with a Ring Lardner song and a cinnamon bear stunt as his principal contributions, is funnier than he has been in the several preceding *Follies*.

The New York *Herald*:

Eddie Cantor . . . sings and talks in an intimate way about everybody, like Frank Tinney, only faster. He, too, made a hit.

Comparisons with Bert Williams and Frank Tinney, considered the two greatest comedians on Broadway, represented more success than Cantor had dared hope for. Eddie was not the runaway hit of the show ("The star of the production was the chorus," said the caustic New York *World*), but his success was large enough to gain him permanent acceptance by the audience, the critics, Ziegfeld, and his colleagues—Rogers, Fields, and Bert Williams. He now "belonged" in the same way he had pretended to belong at his first meeting with Ziegfeld.

Ida was present at the opening, and she rejoiced at a party afterward in company with Ziegfeld, Abraham L. Erlanger, the Harrimans, the Vanderbilts, and several other multimillionaires. Eddie could not afford to have her family attend—Ziegfeld had auctioned off the opening night tickets—but arranged to have them at the next day's matinee. They were waiting at the stage door with a friend after the show. "Meet-my-son-in-law-makes-four-hundred-dollars-a-week" was how David Tobias introduced Eddie Cantor.

Eddie recorded his two *Follies* songs for Victor one month after the show opened. He was a success, a fact not lost on his friends from Henry Street. Saturday night, when he received his pay, in cash, a line formed to greet him at the stage door. Kids were sick, food was needed, rent had to be paid and debts made good for what seemed like every Jew on the East Side. Eddie seldom turned them down and sometimes found his pay cut by a quarter by the time he reached 168th Street.

He and Ida lived in style—still in the apartment, as they had no real savings, but with a maid, cook, a car, and a chauffeur, who doubled as his boss's dresser. Ida often called for Eddie on the matinee days, sitting in the back seat of the car as other *Follies* players either arrived at or left the New Amsterdam Theatre—W. C. Fields, Walter Catlett, and Fanny Brice, slim, elegant, and chic in her riding habit. Ida longed to get to know her but remained in the back seat, somehow sensing she did not belong. In truth, she lacked the feel of show business—the fine speech, the poise, and, especially for the past year, the figure.

Ida, barely five foot two, had ballooned to one hundred and eighty-five pounds since the birth of Natalie some sixteen months before. She did not carry the weight well and looked far older than her boyish husband. The fact that Eddie was surrounded by the world's most beautiful young women only made her feel worse.

Eddie was the model family man that summer, taking Ida, two-year-old Margie, and one-year-old Natalie out to Van Cortlandt Park on Sundays, the chauffeur's day off, in the Maxwell. With them would come Harry Ruby (composer of "The Dixie Volunteers" and other songs featured by Cantor) and his only child, his daughter, Toby. Harry, possibly the biggest baseball fan in the United States, would toss a ball with Eddie while the kids ran on the grass until the time came to eat the box lunch Ida had brought with her. The Cantors were a young and happy married couple with two children, an enviable income, and a future that seemed brighter every week.

The *Follies* concluded its Broadway run on September 15, 1917, and opened its annual tour at the Colonial Theatre in Boston the following Monday evening. W. C. Fields, knowing Cantor wanted to save money, suggested that they share accommodations.

Fields lived well, if not ostentatiously, sending fifty dollars to his wife each week out of the seven hundred and fifty Ziegfeld paid him and banking whatever else he did not spend on his mistress, Bessie Poole (whom he never spoiled), personal and professional necessities, liquor, and books.

It was liquor that he first shared with Cantor. To celebrate the show's successful opening in Boston, Fields had three buckets of champagne in the living room of their suite at the Touraine Hotel. "We kept drinking to my health until we damned near ruined it," said Cantor. "By 3 A.M. I was the sickest owl you ever saw." The champagne had no great effect on Fields, although his continued drinking would gradually extinguish his great jug-gling ability, destroy his health, and finally lead to his death.

Cantor would insist, later in life, that he, Will Rogers, and Bill Fields had been like the Three Musketeers in that year's *Follies*. To Will and Bill, however, Eddie was a guileless and sometimes brash young kid, an almost perfect butt for practical jokes. When Cantor won some money on that year's World Series, Fields and Rogers said he was "expected" to share his winnings by throwing a party for the company. Eddie, ever credulous and still wanting to please his older colleagues, threw the party. It cost almost all his winnings.

Fields traveled with large theatrical trunks under the care of his valet, Shorty, a rather dwarfish, cross-eyed individual whose obvious deformities made Ziegfeld, the purveyor of bodily perfection, extremely uncomfortable—to Fields's own delight. Two of the trunks, as Cantor soon discovered, were loaded, not with liquor, but with books—works by Dickens, Dumas, Hugo, Eliot, and other classic nineteenth-century authors. Fields, whom Cantor knew as a "man of the world," was a highly intelligent individual who spent most of his offstage hours working on material or reading. He inspired Eddie to read, telling him that books were the key to another world.

"W. C. Fields helped educate me," Cantor told the author Bob Thomas a few months before his death. "He read the *New York Times* every day, along with other papers. Each night, he would get out the dictionary and pick out three words that he made me use in sentences." Eddie soon had what he later called a "pretty good vocabulary."

Cantor lived in two worlds now. There was his mundane but nonetheless rewarding home life. Eddie spent as many weekends as he could with Ida and the girls, catching midnight trains to New York after Saturday night performances at the Forrest Theatre in Philadelphia and staying home till Monday. (On Monday afternoon, November 5, in New York, he recorded six songs for Aeolian-Vocalian, a company whose vertically cut disks could be played only on special machines, having spent that Sunday in the Bronx.) The show's next bookings, in Baltimore and Washington, prevented Eddie from arriving home until noon on Sunday. On one occasion, two-and-a-half-year-old Margie discovered Eddie in the sitting room and ran to tell her mother that "that man is here again."

Then there was his "other" world—the public one. In Washington, Will Rogers introduced Cantor to Assistant Secretary of the Navy Franklin De-lano Roosevelt at a dinner at the Mayflower Hotel. "You know Little Kosher here," said Rogers. Roosevelt was then thirty-five, handsome, genial, and urbane. Eddie met him again a few nights later at a benefit at Walter Reed Hospital and was floored by the man's breeding and impressive Harvard education. He sat, transfixed, as Will spoke at the dinner, kidding the high politicians. This, he thought, not Broadway, was the world that mattered most. For him, a Jew from Henry Street, to be accepted here would be the ultimate success.

If Cantor's eye-on-the-next-season, send-the-money-home mentality differed from that of most vaudevillians, exceedingly few actors shared his attitudes regarding politics. The very idea that actors and politicians were in seriously related fields would have been ridiculed by almost all performers, and most stars, when Cantor first appeared on Broadway.

Performers of that era regarded acting not so much as an art as a profession, closely knit, with certain expectations, modes of conduct, unwritten rules, and camaraderie that cut across ethnicity and sex, in theory if not practice. The lives, the aspirations of its members were concerned with the stage only—to "make good" in vaudeville, play the greatest Lear, and carry on the great traditions of The Theatre. One expected—or one hoped—to make a decent living in the theatre and gain the respect of one's colleagues. The love of audiences around the country was the ultimate achievement, the ideal. To have influence in politics, let alone to serve as a serious "role model" for the lives and mores of the public, was outside the ken.

The absence of mass media maintained this rather, to us, quaint perspective. A "star," by definition, was an actor billed above the title of a play, and any actor not so billed, no matter how familiar to the theatre-going public, was, by definition, not a star. Lives of stars consisted, in the main, of working in plays on Broadway for a few months and spending, on average, the next two years touring the United States and Canada—a life of almost constant travel, gracious living in the larger cities, and little or no contact with the public except for frequent talks with young stage aspirants.

Publicity was limited and achieved solely through the press if one excepts the handbills posted by "advance men." A star's arrival in a new play would be heralded by a few lines in the theatrical sections of the local press and might be followed, the day after his (or, more usually, her) arrival by a brief interview: "I really enjoy touring for Mr. Dillingham, and the public's response to the new play has been most heartening. I'm from Easton, Pennsylvania, you know, and broke into the theatre with a local stock company. When I'm not on the stage, I spend most of my time knitting." That was the sum total of the public's knowledge of the offstage lives of stars. Few people would remember even that much a day later.

A star, in essence, was a working actor of a certain rank whose life was not much different from that of his fellow, nonstar actors. For almost all, the theatre was an insular profession. Nothing outside "the business" seemed important to their lives.

Major stars, like Eddie Foy or Lillian Russell, might be photographed at a ball game with a batting champion, at a prize fight, or on the White House lawn with the president, and feel that each event was but a part of his (very limited) "offstage public life." No part was more important than any other, and an actor would no more think of influencing (let alone entering) politics than of stepping into the ring with world heavyweight boxing champion Jess Willard.

Those, however, were not Eddie Cantor's feelings. Strongly influenced by Al Smith and his own youthful excursions into political rabble rousing, by his poor Jewish background and the spirit of social responsibility that had sent him to Surprise Lake Camp, and, perhaps, on a much deeper level, by his grandmother's inability to appreciate his early stage achievements, he felt that success within the theatre "was just not enough." In time, and further influenced by Will Rogers's political humor and his own broadened horizons, he would transform the very nature of stardom.

W. C. Fields usually drove between engagements in his touring car, sending "Shorty" on the train with the big trunks but keeping a complete of line of camping equipment for his car. Eddie often rode along with Fields's entourage, including Bessie Poole, Fanny Brice, and even, on occasion, Fanny's husband, Nick Arnstein.

Cantor, who could not drink, was also quite susceptible, as Fields found, to cold. As Fields drove on, heated from within and remarking, in his highly individualistic way, upon the wonders of nature, Eddie's pronounced ears turned blue, his knees began to knock, and he would ask Bill to turn the top down. Fields's response was to offer Cantor some "libation" and suggest that he take fragments of the paper he'd been reading and use them for insulation.

The former world middleweight boxing title claimant Jack (Twin) Sullivan, a friend of Fields, threw a party for the cast when the *Follies* played Buffalo. The supper dish was pork chops, and Cantor, who did not eat *trafe* (non-kosher food), ignored Fields's call to "dig in," admitting that he did not eat "pork chops." Another dish was prepared "just for Eddie"—ham and eggs. Cantor, famished, said he wasn't hungry.

Fields said, "Let the boy starve."

Bert Williams came to Cantor's rescue. Having overheard Bill Fields's plans, he'd brought a steak for Eddie. Forty-three years old, a great artist, and a star of the first rank, Williams nonetheless proceeded to prepare the steak himself.

Less than three weeks later, the 1917 edition of the *Ziegfeld Follies* closed in Montreal. With it ended Cantor's "freshman" Broadway year. Despite what might be viewed as the anti-Semitic tone of the episode at Sullivan's party, Eddie was merely the victim of a ritual hazing very similar to those handed first-year students at leading colleges. His youthful appearance and manner, alternately brash and awestruck, invited this treatment, and his Jewishness served merely as a peg on which to hang some gags in that pre-Hitler era.

The tour, perhaps more than the run on Broadway, had been a learning experience for Cantor. He had opened in the *Follies* as a rather impudent, naive young man determined to make good. Now, no longer a rookie but a recognized and valuable performer, a more aware and self-assured young Eddie would go into the new *Follies*.

Eddie was not idle in the weeks before rehearsals. He appeared in the new Seventh Edition of the Ziegfeld *Midnight Frolic*, in which he and Will Rogers did what Louis Sherwin of the New York *Globe* called "a series of ludicrous" imitations: Rogers as Gene Buck, Cantor as Ned Wayburn; Will as Charles Dillingham, Eddie as Ziegfeld in a very funny bit about the two producers losing money on their joint venture at the Century Theatre. Sherwin reported Rogers as "not quite so happy when he worked alone. He explained that he had not had time to read the papers, and expected to be considerably funnier by the end of the week." Eddie made "That's the Kind of a Baby for Me" the backbone of his solo turn, saving his new songs and other material for the *Follies*.

Before rehearsals started, he received a call from his boyhood friend and one-time partner Danny Lipsky. The two had corresponded through the years but had not seen each other since Danny's marriage to Eddie's cousin, Annie Kantrowitz. Dan, who never went to college, mastered Pittman shorthand as a six-dollar-a-week office boy and got a job at the New York Bureau of Licenses. Three years later, he became confidential secretary to Brooklyn Borough President Edward Riegelmann. World War I—and an election—brought a downward turn to Lipsky's fortunes. He was a stenographer at Manufacturers Hanover Trust, making fifty bucks a week, when he contacted Cantor.

Danny got a quick, ingenuous report in answer to his queries about Eddie's finances. The car, the chauffeur, the cook, and the maid, along with rent on the six-room apartment, handouts, the cost of caring for a wife and two small children, less than frugal spending since the start of his two-year contract with Ziegfeld, and investments in two worthless stocks had left Eddie just enough to live on until the new *Follies* opened. He and Ida hoped to have their own home, but the day seemed far away.

Lipsky guaranteed that Cantor would own his own home in two years if Eddie would make him his financial manager at ten dollars a week. Eddie agreed. The only bright spot in Cantor's financial picture, outside of his growing popularity and his contract with Ziegfeld, was that he was not in debt. Lipsky's idea was to *put* Cantor in debt—to Manufacturers Hanover Trust, which would finance his purchase of ten thousand dollars' worth of Victory Bonds. Eddie would pay back the bank in forty weeks in two hundred and fifty dollar weekly installments.

Lipsky arranged a meeting between Cantor and Nathan S. Jonas, president of Manufacturers Hanover Trust and a former insurance agent who won Cantor over with his understanding manner. Cantor, who agreed to Lipsky's plan, adopted Jonas as a father figure. The meeting also served to elevate Dan Lipsky, who became Jonas's private secretary less than six months later.

Ida, a terrific judge of character, neither liked nor trusted Dan beyond a certain point. When she asked tough questions about money—questions at which Eddie would stare blankly—or probed into Lipsky's own position, Dan became evasive, sometimes even bordering on hostile. Ida, Danny well knew, was potential trouble in his efforts to use Eddie's name and money to advance his own career and build a large financial nest egg. A private, undeclared war between Mrs. Cantor and Dan Lipsky soon begun.

Cantor's onstage role was also changing. He had been advised to pressure Ziegfeld for sketch roles in whiteface, under the assumption, later proved correct, that abandoning "the cork" would open the gates to stardom in "book" musical comedies, as opposed to featured spots in revues. (Jolson was the only man ever to star successfully in Broadway shows in blackface.) Blackface, though lending accent to broader facial expressions, was often said to inhibit the rendering of subtler emotions.

Eddie had a scene prepared in which he played "Percival Johnson," a ludicrous weakling applying for admission to the Aviator Corps, who undergoes a grueling physical examination at the hands of recruiting officer Frank Carter (Marilyn Miller's boyfriend, whose defection from the Shuberts had led Marilyn herself to sign with Ziegfeld). Max Hart got Ziegfeld to okay the sketch, as well as Cantor's playing it in whiteface.

The show tried out in Atlantic City under the watchful eyes of not just Ziegfeld but of Abe Erlanger as well. The active boss of the Theatrical Syndicate, which controlled almost all the leading houses and attractions in America before the emergence of the Shuberts, Erlanger was one of the most powerful men in the American theatre. More important, the Syndicate backed Ziegfeld with its theatres (which the Follies played in New York and en tour) and its money.

Erlanger ordered the sketch cut before the first performance, arbitrarily deciding that there was "no room for it" in the show. The next day, Cantor met with Erlanger and Ziegfeld, asking that he be allowed to quit the Follies if the scene was not restored. Erlanger stormed and threatened but agreed to give the sketch a "trial."

The scene turned out to be the biggest hit of the show ("Good, rollicking, belly-shaking slapstick that recalled the palmy days of Weber and Fields," according to the New York Globe), vindicating Eddie's faith in himself as a performer and a judge of material. Cantor's improvement, his growing skill and even subtlety in pantomime, was due mostly to his work with the great Williams and to his observations of both Williams and Bill Fields.

Cantor's pantomime involved not so much action as reaction. Physical discomfort became, not pain, but a bewildering, incomprehensible assault. The same approach was evident in Eddie's work with dialogue. His incredulous, bug-eyed stare and his style of raising an eyebrow made a simple line like "Really?" into a profound satiric comment. Cantor (or "the little fellow," as he called his onstage character) was the interested innocent who stumbled on something fascinating—and found himself rendered totally vulnerable as a result. Not completely guiltless (much like his real self), he was an easy victim for ambitious women, musclemen, and sharpsters. He was the slightly larcenous, essentially benign young man, upended temporarily, who triumphs by revealing his true and better nature—and maturing in the process.

The Twelfth Edition of the *Ziegfeld Follies* opened at the New Amsterdam on Tuesday evening, June 18, 1918. Bert Williams and Fanny Brice were gone, but Fields and Rogers remained, along with Cantor. Dimple-kneed Ann Pennington was back after a two-year absence, Lillian Lorraine, a one-time Ziegfeld paramour, returned for her last *Follies*, and the nineteen-year-old Marilyn Miller, wooed away from Lee and J. J. Shubert, lent her beauty, charm, grace, and modest dancing ability.

In Cantor's first onstage appearance, he played Clarence, an anemic-looking office boy in the employ of a patent attorney named Bunkus Munyan, played by W. C. Fields. The aviator sketch was in the second act, with Cantor's solo spot as Scene 22, near the end of the evening. Working, once again, in blackface, Eddie joked and introduced "But After the Ball Is Over," a comic ballad based on the old song.

The *Ziegfeld Follies* of 1918 established Cantor as one of Broadway's top comedians. Now known as "The Apostle of Pep" and increasingly secure among the other *Follies* players, he began to play "the star," according to Doris Eaton, then a teen-age *Follies* chorine. "He became aware of his status, and began to make his presence felt as an authority backstage." A pecking order then existed in the theatre (despite the often close-knit camaraderie), and Cantor was quick to assume the mantle that went with his new position. He grew more and more "upstage," less "one of the fellows"— "running" scenes that he was in and, increasingly, referring to himself in the third person. Even when he dealt with scenes in which he was just "Eddie Cantor," telling jokes and singing songs, he would tell stagehands, "Okay, he enters here and does the business" or (in scenes), "the little fellow comes in here and says 'hello.' " In time, he would begin to call himself by name in arguments. ("What's your name? John Smith? Eddie Cantor thinks you're a jerk.") This was something quite beyond an understandable desire to protect his hard-won new position; it was as if he viewed not only Eddie the performer but Cantor the star as entirely separate persons from Eddie Kanter of Henry Street.

This detachment was, of course, a by-product of Cantor's late entry into show business and his identification of himself as more than a performer. It would, in turn, lead him to transcend being a performer and finally to integrate show business socially with the larger world.

Marilyn Miller, Ann Pennington, and Lillian Lorraine lent the 1918 *Follies* an air of backstage romance that made up for the show's paucity of comic talent compared with the 1917 edition. Miller's mother did not like Frank

Carter (ten years Marilyn's senior), but their love affair continued, Cantor serving as a "beard." Mrs. Miller had no objections to Marilyn's having dinner with safe, Jewish, married-with-two-children Eddie Cantor—"and he makes her laugh to boot." After the show, Eddie would put on his dinner jacket and take Marilyn—to Frank. Then he would go to a delicatessen and *kibitz* with "the boys" until it was time to take Marilyn back to her mother.

Ann Pennington—called "Penny," never "Ann"—was a likable, petite (4 foot 10 inch) novelty dancer who had a sign reading "For Men Only" on her dressing room door. Her fondness for sex was well known backstage, but Penny did not try for many conquests. She liked Eddie, but her boyfriend was George White, the dancer who would produce his first *Scandals* a year later and become a rival to Flo Ziegfeld.

Lillian Lorraine was a different matter. She, like Cantor and Will Rogers, had come to the 1918 *Follies* directly from the Seventh *Midnight Frolic*. Two years Eddie's senior, she had had her first affair at the age of thirteen, with a man who paid her father for the privilege of sleeping with her. In 1908 she replaced Anna Held as Ziegfeld's mistress. Lillian was, thought Billie Burke, the only one among the Ziegfeld beauties that her husband really loved. Lillian's unchecked promiscuity was soon legendary. She broke up Fanny Brice's romance with the wealthy young Fred Gresheimer in 1911 and almost drove Ziegfeld insane by marrying that worthless playboy. The marriage was, predictably, short-lived.

"Will Rogers was the only man I ever knew who I would swear did not cheat on his wife," Fanny once said. Rogers did not enjoy Lorraine's favors, though they almost certainly were offered. Other men, from reports that have come down over the decades, did.

Most famous people in show business have been rumored to have had extramarital affairs, Cantor being no exception. The close proximity of Ziegfeld's beauties would certainly have tempted many men. Eddie loved his wife but tended to compartmentalize his life into "backstage," "onstage," "home," and so on—despite the fact that he would later integrate all parts of his life for the benefit of radio audiences. Conquests of non-Jewish women may have seemed to him, in part, like conquests of the whole non-Jewish world—the world he wanted to impress and from which he longed to gain acceptance.

The *Follies* closed its Broadway run on September 14 and began its annual tour at the Colonial in Boston the following Monday evening. The show outdrew all other attractions in the city through Thursday night, September 27, when the Spanish Influenza epidemic forced the closing of all Boston theatres. The *Follies* shut down for a week, with Cantor, Lillian Lorraine, Ann Pennington, and Bee Palmer sent back to New York and added to the *Midnight Frolic* on the New Amsterdam Roof. *The Follies* itself reopened at New York's Globe Theatre for three weeks beginning Monday night, October 7.

While New York theatres remained open, straddling their curtain times to avoid mass congestion, the influenza scare brought on what *Billboard* called a "theatrical depression worse than probably ever before in the history of the American stage," causing all productions to run at a loss. Tickets for the *Follies* were offered to brokers near the Globe for half price, with "few takers," according to *Variety*. Cancelations for all shows piled in at all hours, and one agency lost a thousand dollars on tickets over two days in October. The huge number of agencies, and the fact that orchestra seats could be purchased for one (nonmusicals) to four (the *Follies*) dollars apiece, give a clear indication of the suddenly desperate state of business in the theatre.

The United States had been in World War I for almost six months. Eddie, whose position as a husband and the father of two children exempted him from military service, joined the ranks of entertainers who "did their bit" for the war effort. At 7:00 P.M., October 17, he, Coleman Goetz, and Harry Ruby went to entertain the wounded soldiers at a hospital in Brooklyn, expecting to return in time for Cantor's first scene in the *Follies*. After Eddie performed, he looked at his watch and saw that it was 8:30, a mere twenty minutes before he was due on stage at the Globe Theatre. The hospital's head doctor solved the trouble with an ambulance that delivered Cantor and his friends to the Globe Theatre five minutes prior to his entrance.

The *Follies* closed again when Philadelphia theatres were not allowed to reopen on schedule, canceling its two weeks at that city's Forrest Theatre. Cantor, Rogers, Lorraine, Palmer, Pennington, and several other members of the *Follies* cast were again added to the *Frolic* in New York. "The valiant aid lent the performer by the intimate atmosphere of the roof garden," said the *New York Times*, "was demonstrated anew at the performance of the Ziegfeld *Midnight Frolic* on Monday night, when Eddie Cantor, Ann Pennington, and Will Rogers, in their various specialties, scored far more decisively than is their customary wont in the *Follies*." Philadelphia theatres reopened Thursday evening, October 31, and the *Follies* played nine evenings at the Forrest. The "panic" calmed before Thanksgiving, ending almost three months of horror for the nation and absolute terror for the professional theatre.

Eddie's East Side politics—Democratic, for the tenant and the working man—had led him to join Actors' Equity Association, the actors' union. He attended every meeting that he could and was elected to the union's council to complete the term of Edwin Arden, who died in October. Working for Equity was almost intrinsic for a man who championed the working man, identified (to a degree) with actors, and admired politicians. Cantor still remembered being stranded with the *Indian Maidens* Burlesquers. And, slave driver though he'd often be to both actors and writers, Eddie truly empathized with the chorines who worked endless hours learning steps under a roaring dance director. Cantor's involvement with Actors' Equity combined professional responsibility—of which he, a consummate professional, had plenty—with union involvement and civic affairs. Equity was the Lambs' Club with a purpose. It seemed almost made for Cantor.

Eddie Cantor had become a respected figure in the show world, a man whose formal countenance adorned the frontispiece of sheet music. "Would You Rather Be a Colonel with an Eagle on Your Shoulder or a Private with a Chicken on Your Knee?" was one of Eddie's topical song interpolations in the *Follies*. The song was dropped when the war ended on November 11, the night the show opened its annual six-day engagement at Baltimore's Academy of Music.

He was also writing lyrics. "I'm Making a Study of Beautiful Girls and I'm Still in My A.B.C.s," with music by Al Piantadosi and Jack Glogau, was published before the end of the year. While not a huge commercial hit, it nonetheless made Cantor needed money. Ida was pregnant again.

Touring with the *Follies*, which kept Eddie from his family a good part of the year, nonetheless established him in all the major cities. His undisguised Jewishness did not prevent him being a hit everywhere the show played, although his greatest popularity was always in New York—or, to judge by weekly grosses, in nearby Newark.

The 1918 *Follies* closed its tour on May 10, 1919, at the end of a two-week return Boston engagement. Cantor had become, increasingly, the backbone of the show, and Ziegfeld promptly signed him to another two-year contract. Cantor would make six hundred dollars a week while appearing in the *Ziegfeld Follies* of 1919 and eight hundred dollars the year after, with the verbal promise of a starring show.

Irving Berlin wrote most of the score for the new 1919 *Follies*, including "Sweet Sixteen," "You Cannot Make Your Shimmy Shake on Tea" (sung by the returning Bert Williams in a scene on prohibition), "A Pretty Girl Is Like a Melody" (introduced by John Steele to a parade of Ziegfeld Girls as "Humoresque," "Spring Song," "Elegy," "Barcarolle," "Serenade," and "Traumeri"), "You'd Be Surprised," and "Mandy."

"Mandy" was the climax of "The *Follies* Minstrels," preceded by Johnny Dooley's singing of "I Love a Minstrel Show" and featuring Cantor as "Tambo," Bert Williams as "Bones," and George LeMaire as the "Middle Man" or Interlocutor.

Cantor also figured in three sketches—as a taxi driver in "The Popular Pests," a waiter in a (Prohibition) "Saloon of the Future," and "Percival Fingersnapper" in "At the Osteopath's," his major scene, with George LeMaire as "Dr. Cheeseboro Simpson" and Eddie as his patient.

It was LeMaire's debut in the *Follies*. Physically robust, with a vibrant voice and a strident manner, he proved a major asset, not only to Cantor but also to Bert Williams in the latter's scene, "He Seldom Misses." Cantor called LeMaire "the best straight man the theatre has ever known," and the two began a friendship that would soon include George's brother, Rufus. Both LeMaires would figure in Eddie's career in the near future.

In early June, the week before the *Follies* opened in Atlantic City, Cantor, LeMaire, Kathryn Perry (who later married Owen Moore, the former husband of Mary Pickford), and Hazel Washburn tried out "At the Osteopath" at a small Bronx theatre, billed as "Kathryn Perry & Co." to avoid the critics. Cantor took the opportunity to introduce "You'd Be Surprised," inviting Ziegfeld and Berlin for the final three performances. Cantor listened when Berlin suggested that he sing the song while standing still, relying on his gestures, rolling eyes, and shocked expressions. At the song's conclusion (sometimes sung "You'd Be Surprised" and sometimes as "You'd Be Amazed"), he would turn abruptly, shocked and rather frightened of the secrets he had disclosed, and run off the stage.

The *Follies* opened in Atlantic City for its usual pre-Broadway warmup on June 10, 1919. Shortly before curtain time, Eddie received a telegram from Ida in the Bronx: ANOTHER GIRL EXCUSE IT PLEASE. The baby was named Edna June, the Edna an Anglicization of Esther. At Lipsky's suggestion, Eddie started "thrift" accounts for all three children at this point— accounts that later grew into trust funds.

"From the angle of sheer amusement," Cantor wrote in later years, "the 1919 production [of the *Follies*] was Zieggy's masterpiece. It was one of those happy blendings that bespoke the last word in stage generalship and a perfect harmony existed between actor and material. Everyone in the cast clicked. Each specialty, no matter what its character, was performed by the acknowledged master of that field." There were Johnny and Rae Dooley in a rough-and-tumble dance routine, Bert Williams, John Steele for ballads, Marilyn Miller, and Ann Pennington—not as strong in comic names as the 1917 edition, but with a smoothness to the show that made the 1919 *Follies* flow with the liquidity of an integrated "book show."

Advance reports from Atlantic City were confirmed when the show opened in New York to nearly unanimous raves. (Sime Silverman, the founder of *Variety*, was a dissenter; he thought the comedy was weak but singled out "The Osteopath" for special mention.) The three standouts in the show, it was conceded by most critics, were John Steele, Marilyn Miller, and Eddie Cantor, programmed as "The Apostle of Pep" in his Act One solo scene. "Presidents may come and presidents may go," said Eddie, "but Wilson does both."

"Cantor is developing a personality," said the New York *Globe*, "which means a rival to Mr. Jolson." The New York *Evening Sun* lauded all the comedy but called "At The Osteopath's" the "most amusing scene" in the show, surpassing Eddie's "Aviator" sketch in the previous year's *Follies*.

The training he had received from Bert Williams helped to make "The Osteopath" one of the most popular scenes in *Follies* history and Eddie one of the top sketch comedians on Broadway. His earnest attitude in pantomime—his struggling but seeming haplessness, his apparent slightness, and his portrayal of ruptured human dignity—made Cantor's work in physical comedy stand out above his verbal humor. It would later find regrettably short-lived expression in his silent movies.

Cantor's position as a top plugger of up-tempo and comic stage songs, an important part of the commercial music business, led to offers to record for both Pathe and Emerson. (Neither company demanded an exclusive, allowing Cantor to record the same numbers for both. The extra money complemented his stage income and was promptly given over to Dan Lipsky.) His *Follies* solo scene allowed him to interpolate new songs as they were written, a necessity to entertain "repeaters." "You Don't Need the Wine to Have a Wonderful Time (While They Still Make Those Beautiful Girls)," a prohibition number introduced by Cantor in the *Follies*, was also sung by Lou Holtz in George White's *Scandals* (probably the best of all the shows that emulated the *Follies*), prompting Ziegfeld to consider seeking an injunction.

Cantor interpolated new songs almost every week. At four o'clock one afternoon in late July, he heard a new Berlin song called "I've Got My Captain Working for Me Now." Eddie got the lyrics, read the song to Ziegfeld, and was asked to sing the number in the *Follies* that same evening. Cantor promptly got the orchestrations, memorized the lyrics, rehearsed with the orchestra, and introduced the song, as requested, that very night. Few worked as hard—and none, it seemed, as constantly—as Cantor.

Ziegfeld, a German-American Protestant, increasingly regarded Eddie as a type of son despite their different backgrounds. He "adopted" him in much the same way that his moneyed, gentile audiences had adopted Eddie in the *Midnight Frolic*.

But the growing symbiotic relationship between Ziegfeld and Cantor would be severely strained before the summer ended. The result would be hurt feelings, recriminations, charges of alleged betrayal, and a wedge between the two men that would last four years.

*Chapter 5*

# OF EQUITY AND
# SHUBERTS

*"Money makes the world go around."*

orld War I, the first "modern" war, gave birth to new hopes, new ideals, and a feeling that the postwar world had somehow to be "different," with new values that would give credence to the description of the conflict as "the war to end all wars." (Warren G. Harding's "Return to Normalcy" was the other side of this coin.) The country began to look more favorably on unions, and Actors' Equity Association, formed in 1913, attracted many members as the war drew to a close.

On Thursday, August 7, 1919, Actors' Equity, claiming the Producing Managers' Association had stalled, if not reneged, on a promise to negotiate, called a strike of Broadway shows produced by members of the P.M.A. Frank Bacon, father of motion picture director Lloyd Bacon, immortalized himself as the first star to strike on Equity's behalf, and *Lightnin'* became the first play closed by A.E.A. As a member of Equity's Council, and as a leading player in the *Ziegfeld Follies*, Cantor was thrust center stage.

Some expected Cantor to walk out of the *Follies* the same night Bacon took his stand. The *Follies*, though, played that night according to the program—with Cantor. It was "explained" that Cantor was not reached in time. In fact, he had thought better of such drastic action. He admired Ziegfeld, was at the beginning of a promising career, and had a wife and three small daughters to support. Forced to balance forthrightness with prudence, Cantor determined not to strike the *Follies* until he had spoken with Ziegfeld.

Cantor spent the next afternoon out on Broadway, recruiting new members for Equity, declaring that the *Follies* would not open that evening, and mentioning Bert Williams, Eddie Dowling, and Johnny and Rae Dooley as fellow strikers in the show.

The *Follies* went on that night, although Cantor did not appear until late in Act II. Cantor's sudden return surprised many Equity members until Eddie explained that he had learned Ziegfeld was not a member of the P.M.A. and therefore was exempt from strike action. Once he had Ziegfeld's assurance, Cantor explained, he went on.

Ziegfeld was not a member at the time, but pressure from other producers, exerted through Erlanger, forced him to capitulate and join the P.M.A within a week. At the same time, Ziegfeld secured an injunction to prevent the *Follies* cast from striking. To Equity, this was a gesture of supreme defiance.

Cantor arrived at the New Amsterdam Theatre on Wednesday night, August 13, met with Ziegfeld, went to the box office, drew out $230—the amount due him, on a per performance basis, for the current week—and gave it to the Equity strike fund. Johnny and Rae Dooley followed Eddie's lead and struck the show.

Given Cantor's concern for security and his need to make money to support his growing family, he might have been expected to spend this time playing vaudeville. Eddie's feelings for "the Equity" were strong, however, and he spent his time recruiting for the union and giving pep talks to his fellow strikers.

On Saturday night, August 16, he spoke to some reporters while getting a facial massage in the Strand Barber Shop. "I am with the Equity Association and will go back to the cloak-and-suit trade if they lose in their fight against the managers." He even signed a written statement.

Cantor now saw the strike as a matter of principle—Ziegfeld had joined the P.M.A.—and of loyalty to his fellow Equity members; it placed the workers in direct opposition to management. Eddie, as a poor kid from the East Side who had seen poor families tossed out on the bare street with all their furniture, had no doubts as to where he stood.

The *Follies*, minus Cantor and the Dooleys, played for one more week before the lights went out on Broadway. Equity having joined the American Federation of Labor, the International Association of Theatrical Stagehands and Employees walked out in sympathy on Monday, August 25.

Marilyn Miller, of all Ziegfeld's players, felt that she could not support the strike. Like George M. Cohan, she had spent her childhood in vaudeville and been raised to think the theatre was a sort of shrine, with its own rules and regulations that could not subscribe to "civilian" notions like unionism. Marilyn, accordingly, reported to the theatre every evening, ostensibly prepared to perform in the *Follies*. Ironically, she was angry with Ziegfeld, who'd reacted to her marriage to Frank Carter by firing the bridegroom from the *Follies* during rehearsals and promising that Frank would never work for him again. Frank was promptly signed up by the Shuberts, his former employers, and put into a new show titled *See Saw*.

Ziegfeld tried to have his striking *Follies* cast enjoined, but Equity stood by its members, primed to go to court. The strike was settled on Monday,

September 15, 1919, with Equity acknowledged as the Broadway actors' union. The strikers had won.

The *Follies* resumed its run at the New Amsterdam that evening, Cantor back performing with his customary vigor. But his father-son relationship with Ziegfeld had been broken. From this point, it was strictly business; Ziegfeld did not speak to Cantor for the remaining twelve weeks of the *Follies'* run on Broadway.

The *Follies* jumped out to Detroit to start its tour on December 8, 1919, and was in the second week of its annual engagement at the Colonial Theatre in Chicago for New Year's. Ida was back in the Bronx with Margie, Natalie, and Edna. Eddie had spent the last two New Year's Eves in the same place—Chicago—with Will Rogers and Bill Fields. He wanted to spend this one with Bert Williams.

Bert had many friends within the black communities of every city the show played in, but he accepted Eddie's invitation to a late supper with wine in his hotel suite. "I'll come up the back elevator and meet you there," he told Cantor. Williams, the only African American in the company, insisted on using the back elevator in every hotel the show stayed in, avoiding the humiliation of being told he *had* to use it—or of being told he could not stay at that hotel. Always, he remained the gentleman—composed, well spoken, courteous, and dignified. Rarely did he let his pain, and rarer still his anger, show itself to whites.

On this occasion, though, he turned back to the younger man and said, "It wouldn't hurt so much, you know, if the applause wasn't still ringing in my ears."

Cantor always insisted that there had not been race prejudice on the East Side during his childhood. He had, however, grown up in an almost exclusively Jewish neighborhood. Now, at twenty-seven, he knew few black people well. Bert Williams had given him a tiny glimpse of what being a black man might entail. Cantor would remember Williams's words. More, perhaps, than even Rogers, Williams had awakened in Cantor a recognition of others' pain and suffering, a suffering that went beyond the physical poverty of his own childhood.

Ziegfeld had promised Cantor he would have an author for his promised book show by March 1, 1920. When that date passed with no further word from Ziegfeld, Cantor became suspicious. His pre-Equity contract with Ziegfeld contained no iron-clad guarantees about a starring vehicle. Indeed, the only guarantee was money—eight hundred dollars a week for the season of 1919–20 and one thousand dollars weekly for 1920–21. Cantor figured Ziegfeld was procrastinating on the starring show in order to use him in the 1920 *Follies*—and then drop him when his contract expired the following May.

Ziegfeld was complaining, via telegram, about everything from royalties

(Eddie was listed as coauthor of the aviation scene) to running times to Cantor's new recordings. The latter had become a very sore point.

Emerson, having shared Cantor's recording services with Pathe for the previous six months, had signed him to a new exclusive contract after New Year's. The contract, which guaranteed Cantor $220,000 over five years, was the most lucrative of its type ever offered.

Emerson made the most of Cantor's appearances in the *Follies*, conducting an intensive publicity campaign when the show played a week at the American Theatre in St. Louis after closing in Chicago. Emerson claimed that the Famous-Barr Company, a major St. Louis department store, reported a big sale of its Cantor records and that other "Emerson stores in the Missouri city" reported big demands for Cantor disks as well.

Similar campaigns were launched in Indianapolis, Cleveland, and other cities where the *Follies* played en tour. Ziegfeld objected vehemently, citing his "exclusive" rights to Cantor's services, Emerson's exploitation of Eddie's appearances in the *Follies*, and the inferior quality of the recordings, which, he felt, reflected poorly on the show. (The pre-1925 acoustic recording process gave Cantor's voice a "whiney" quality it did not really have.)

The *Follies* played two weeks in Philadelphia that spring. At the close of the first week, Frank Carter closed his tour in *See Saw* in Wheeling, West Virginia, and drove to Philadelphia in the new customized Packard touring car he'd bought as a surprise first anniversary present for Marilyn. Carter never made it, crashing into an embankment outside Grantsville, Maryland, on Sunday, May 9.

If Eddie had been cross at Marilyn for not supporting the Equity strike, his resentment vanished when he saw her, only twenty-one years old, disconsolate and broken-hearted. Frank Carter was the love of her life and would remain so until she died sixteen years later.

With Cantor's help, and that of Van and Schenck, Marilyn came back to the *Follies* after missing only one performance. For the balance of the season, she did her usual work onstage in the *Follies*. At other times, the girl wept uncontrollably. When Cantor took her back to her hotel suite after one performance at the Colonial Theatre in Boston, where the *Follies* spent the final two weeks of its tour, he saw three or four photographs of Carter in the living room. "She went around the room," Eddie remembered, "looking into Frank's face and crying hysterically. I had to get a doctor to give her a shot and put her to bed."

Cantor, Gus Van, and Joe Schenck did all they could to help Marilyn momentarily forget her pain. Said Cantor, "We couldn't make her laugh, but we could keep her from sobbing herself sick. One night, I put on a pair of shorts and a tam-o'-shanter, took my golf clubs, and about 2 A.M. went out into the hall. I sent Van and Schenck to tell Marilyn to come right out. She came.

" 'Eddie, what are you *doing?*'

" 'Well, Marilyn, I want to get out on the golf course before it gets crowded.'

"Marilyn laughed and laughed until she was tired enough to sleep."

Nothing is more illustrative of the camaraderie existing in the theatre— or of the humanity of Cantor.

When the *Follies* closed on May 29, Cantor returned to New York to find his Bronx apartment up "To Let." Ida, Margie, Natalie, baby Edna, and the servants were gone. Shocked and worried, he called Danny Lipsky and was told his family had gone up to Mount Vernon "for a rest." Lipsky picked him up within the hour, and the two men drove up to a country home at 101 Park Avenue, Mount Vernon. The area made Eddie think of his days at Surprise Lake Camp, although the white-facaded home was a far cry from the tents he had known at Cold Spring.

Before they went inside, Lipsky informed him that the house was his. "Ida and he" had picked it out, and Nathan S. Jonas of Manufacturers Hanover Trust had sent up an appraiser to make sure they were getting the right value for their money. Eddie was astonished when Dan handed him the deed.

The house had been bought outright with no mortgage—a huge relief to Cantor, whose future in the theatre seemed uncertain at this point. Eddie weighed his options. Lipsky assured him he could get his money back if he was forced to sell the house. If Ziegfeld stalled on the new book show or did not renew his contract in a year, he could go back to vaudeville as a single, star in shows for other top producers, or, if need be, go to Europe.

Cantor, true to Ziegfeld's word, was not included in the book for the new *Follies*, which opened in Atlantic City to a less than enthusiastic response on June 15, 1920. Lack of decent comedy and songs—two crucial areas in revue— was cited, and Ziegfeld programmed Scene Twelve of Act Two as ?-?-?-?-?-? when the show opened at the New Amsterdam on June 22, promising a "surprise" to the audience and critics.

The "surprise" was Cantor, who had agreed to fill a bad stage wait near the finale. Cantor actually dragged Ziegfeld onstage with him, but Flo slipped away, leaving Cantor to do his act solo. It consisted of two songs and some jokes, including one about the Hotel Claridge, where you could "get a room, bath, and house detective for five dollars."

Cantor continued in his "turn" for the remainder of the week, bowing out, with Ziegfeld's grudging acquiescence, ostensibly because he felt the need for more special material. In truth, he was still waiting for a book for his projected starring show, and he feared Ziegfeld would go right on stalling if he remained in the *Follies*.

By mid-August, Ziegfeld claimed he was still "hunting" for a story for the new show starring Cantor, refusing, in the interval, to grant Eddie permission to play vaudeville. Ziegfeld had allegedly commissioned Aaron Hoffman to write the libretto that summer, but nothing had been written or agreed upon by Labor Day; the original agreement called for the show to be produced by the third week in September. At one point, they discussed the possibility of Cantor's playing a big featured role in *Sally*, the new musical Ziegfeld was preparing for Marilyn Miller. Cantor wavered; he would have liked to work with and help Marilyn but did not want to give up the starring vehicle. Finally, the offer was withdrawn.

The situation blew up in the middle of September. Ziegfeld, Cantor alleged, was not living up to his promise and had violated the terms of their contract. Ziegfeld called the Emerson recordings a similar breach, and the two men finally agreed to disagree. Their contract, which had five more months to run, was torn up by mutual consent.

News of the break traveled around Broadway quickly, as did the news that Max Hart had placed Cantor with the Shuberts.

Sam and Lee Shubert founded what would later be described as the Shubert empire in Syracuse, New York, in 1900. Through incredibly long hours of hard work, strategic alliances, pragmatism, great attention to every detail of their various enterprises, and a consciousness of money quite the opposite of Ziegfeld's, they soon began to rival and eventually supplant the Theatrical Syndicate as the dominant force in the American theatrical business.

The Shuberts owned or controlled hundreds of theatres, productions, top stars, and millions of dollars by the early 1920s. Lee Shubert undoubtedly made—and kept—more money from the theatre than any other man in history. A survey of the richest showmen in the world in 1924 found the circus magnate John Ringling at the top with sixty million dollars, the realty and opera impresario Henry W. Savage next with forty million, the motion picture moguls Adolph Zukor and Marcus Loew in the next slots with thirty-nine and thirty-five million, respectively, and Lee Shubert next with thirty million. Lee and Sam, unlike Savage, had started in the theatre with nothing.

Sam had died, age thirty, in a 1905 train wreck, as a younger Shubert brother, Jacob (known as J. J.) rose to prominence. J. J., however, never replaced Sam in the affections of their older brother, Lee. "Sam S. and Lee Shubert" remained the name of the firm, leaving Jake to carve out his own career as a producer of big musicals at the New York Winter Garden under the producing title "Messrs. Shubert." Not until the 1930s would a show officially be produced by "J. J. Shubert."

Lee hated Ziegfeld, a Syndicate producer and therefore the "opposition" to begin with, due to an old breach of contract involving Ziegfeld's common-law wife, Anna Held. Jake, in time, would come to hate him even more. The *Follies* got the good reviews, while *The Passing Show*, the summer revue he had begun in 1912, was received coldly by the critics.

In 1917 Ziegfeld had added further injury to insult by stealing away Marilyn Miller, who had signed with the Shuberts while only fifteen years of age. J. J. therefore looked upon the strained relations between Ziegfeld and Cantor with interest, almost with glee. He had been speaking to Max Hart about Eddie for months before the final, inevitable break came in September.

Hart had found the United Booking Office reluctant to give Cantor more than eight hundred dollars a week to appear in vaudeville. Cantor, it was explained, had not played the big time as a single and had never, in fact, starred in any show. Anything above eight hundred for him, they maintained, was undeserved and risky. That figure, furthermore, was what he had been getting from Ziegfeld.

Nor was Cantor anxious to play vaudeville. He had had a taste of the legitimate, wanted Broadway stardom, and, much like the U.B.O., did not think he could get top money in the world of vaudeville unless he achieved stardom first. His career had to be built.

The Shuberts had the answers. They recognized in Cantor a performer who could shoulder the star duties of a full-scale production, a bright and willing young man they could deal with and use to seek revenge on Flo Ziegfeld. To them, it was a matter of honor, principle, and money—not necessarily in that order.

The Shuberts seldom wasted time. They would take *The Midnight Rounders*, a show then playing on the roof of the uptown Century Theatre, rewrite it as a vehicle for Cantor, and send it on the road with Eddie starred above the title. While it toured, they would construct a show to star Cantor on Broadway. The efficiency resembled that of Henry Ford's assembly plant. The trouble was that Cantor had been used to Ziegfeld's Cadillacs.

Cantor went into another show until *The Midnight Rounders* was made ready. George LeMaire, wishing to be more than "just" the world's top straight man, was producing a show, with Shubert backing, titled *Broadway Brevities* and featuring Bert Williams. Eddie was more than agreeable to working with both men while waiting for his starring vehicle.

Eddie, bearing sketches from the latest *Ziegfeld Follies*, arrived in Philadelphia on Monday, September 13, 1920, to witness the show's opening at the Lyric Theatre. Three days of extensive rewrites and rehearsals of both old and new material commenced on Tuesday morning. Cantor joined the cast beginning Thursday night, by which time *Broadway Brevities* resembled more the 1919 *Follies* than the show of the same title that had opened three nights earlier, including a one-scene minstrel show with Eddie and Bert Williams and a sketch titled "The Dentist's Office"—"The Osteopath's Office" with a minimum of alteration.

The show played Philadelphia for ten more days before opening at the New York Winter Garden on Wednesday evening, September 29. Ziegfeld, outraged at the lifting of material, threatened LeMaire with an injunction if "The Dentist's Office" was not excised from the *Brevities* within a week.

LeMaire complied, knowing Ziegfeld could do nothing about the minstrel scene. Cantor, in the meantime, found and brought in songs like "I Wish That I'd Been Born in Borneo" and, in November, "Margie."

The lyricist Benny Davis had written the song for his wife, Margie, with music by Con Conrad and further contributions from J. Russel Robinson. Cantor had introduced Robinson and Conrad's "(Lena Is the Queen of) Palesteena" one month earlier and was, they knew, the father of a five-year-old named Margie. Having him sing "Margie" was a natural.

Eddie's first public performance of "Margie" took place in a Winter Garden Sunday Evening Concert. He pranced up and down, not with the bouncy verve he had displayed in other songs but with a joyous love he seemed to reserve for his daughter. He, along with other writers, including, very notably, Bert Williams, wrote several encore choruses, including:

> Margie, I'd even cut out liquor.
> Margie, one kiss and I get sicker—
> You are like a doctor to me.
> When I'm nervous, you just put me back in service.
> Margie, you're my idea of a perfect dream come true.
> Come and sit right by my side.
> Let your conscience be your guide.
> Oh, Margie, Margie, it's you.

The five-and-a-half-year-old Margie, brought to see the show with Natalie and the year-old Edna, was probably both charmed and dumbstruck. She saw her father as a magic knight, magnificent in black armor, joyously proclaiming his love for her as he pranced, with perfect rhythm, up and down the stage of Broadway's grandest theatre before more than fifteen hundred admiring people. He had been, up to that point, a mysterious figure, seemingly appearing out of nowhere to smother her with sincere hugs and kisses and then having to leave. Now the love she had desired from this mystery figure was being proclaimed in the most thrilling and spellbinding of all settings.

Cantor's friendship with George LeMaire strengthened during the run of the *Brevities*. George gave Eddie quite an education on the Shubert ways of doing business. They were, as LeMaire saw it, simple chiselers, who demanded unfair terms from other producers (like himself) who used their theatres, squeezed independent theatre owners who played host to Shubert shows, painted over and then reused ancient sets, and stripped their shows of small parts and replaced their casts with cheaper actors before sending them on highly profitable tours. LeMaire congratulated Cantor on his new and lucrative contract with the Shuberts but guaranteed him that the Shuberts would make money—lots of money—on the deal.

Cantor, as a product of the New York streets, was a strange blend of innocence and cynicism. Listening to George LeMaire was, at first, disillusioning. Eddie's Shubert contract now seemed almost tainted. Lee and J. J. seemed but little better than the Lower East Side pickpockets who'd urged him to make speeches.

Soon, however, disillusionment gave way to increased cynicism. If that was how the Shuberts (and the rest of the world) played, so be it. Cantor would play the game as well—and make sure that the Shuberts paid for having him star in their shows.

Eddie spent the days on which there were no matinees of *Broadway Brevities* rehearsing for his starring tour. The Eddie Cantor version of *the Midnight Rounders* was a new production that bore virtually no resemblance to the show of the same title that had played the Century since July 12. "Eddie Cantor in *The Midnight Rounders*" opened at the Shubert Theatre in Philadelphia on Monday evening, November 29, 1920. It marked the first time Cantor had starred in a show, with his name above the title. He proved more than equal to the task of carrying a three-hour revue.

The Philadelphia *Inquirer*:

> Eddie Cantor, in whiteface, was the principal comedian, and he was decidedly amusing in his various stage characters. No less comic was Harry Kelly, in his famous Deacon Flood impersonation, while Lew Hearn was a good foil for Kelly, especially in the cafe scene, wherein the diminutive Lew was somewhat roughly treated by Joe Opp as the cafe proprietor, who objected to sandwiches and "hooche" being brought into his place. Muriel DeForrest did some nimble dancing, and there were others who also contributed to the gayety of the piece. Helen Bolton joined the company at short notice, and did remarkably well, not only in acting, but singing the few numbers which fell to her lot.

The rest of the reviews had a similar tone—no rhapsodies, but acknowledging the fledgling star as "decidedly amusing" and capable. It would require several months of touring before Eddie felt secure enough to energize his performance, carrying the show in his own wake and thus "arriving" at the total stardom he desired.

Cantor's contract with the Shuberts, not typed out and signed till New Year's, guaranteed him $1,250 a week against ten percent of gross receipts—at least $450 more than Eddie had been getting under Ziegfeld and several hundred more than he would probably have gotten from the U.B.O. Cantor, though, was far from satisfied. Accustomed to the high production values, taste, and quality of the Ziegfeld productions, Eddie bridled at the cheap, quick ways in which the Shuberts produced shows. Wrongfully equating J. J. Shubert's position with that of Ziegfeld (who generally produced only one show at a time), he bristled at the former's lack of personal attention to all aspects of production. (In truth, if one may judge from the surviving correspondence, J. J. gave each one of his productions much more personal involvement than do today's Broadway producers, who rely exclusively on award-winning experts to handle each phase of production.) Where Ziegfeld had bombarded him with ceaseless telegrams, Cantor now bombarded J. J.'s office with complaints about everything from poor advertising to the chorus girls.

Eddie said the Shuberts had "a lot of the worst girls in the world traveling with the show" and that, when the Shuberts succeeded in getting rid of them, someone in New York sent them right back.

One Hartford paper described the girls as "easy pickin' " and claimed that "many a gay, all-night party was staged during the week" the show played in New Haven—with young men from Yale:

> Practically all musical comedy choruses figure in their share of clandestine gatherings, of course, but the *Midnight Rounders* more than lived up to their name.
>
> One of the parties in question that was staged at a roadhouse, not so many miles away, didn't conclude until the sun was well up over the eastern hills the following morning. The waiter who served this party upon going to their room, after they had left, found mute evidence of the celebration in the form of a pair of corsets, a pair of silk stockings, and 'certain things' somewhat essential to feminine adornment.
>
> Then again, a bevy of the girls one night endeavored to smuggle a number of student friends to their rooms in the Taft Hotel. But the house detective was on his job, halted their advance, and told them that it "wasn't that kind of a hotel." They remonstrated with him, but to no avail.
>
> One of the mild complaints revolved about the girls who stayed at the Avon Hotel, it being claimed that they undressed in their rooms without regard for convention in the matter of drawing curtains or window shades.

If such stories whetted the appetites—or the imaginations—of prospective ticket buyers, they did not harm Shubert business. A news report in the Hartford *Union* was potentially more damaging: "Lillian Washburn, 22, of Sylvan Beach, New York, a chorus girl in the cast of *The Midnight Rounders*, was taken into custody last Saturday night on a charge of theft by Detective John F. Shea."

Eddie did not trust the Shuberts to be honest with him about the box office grosses and sent a handwritten letter to introduce J. J. to Daniel Lipsky, described as Cantor's "personal attorney and financial representative." It was Lipsky, and not Hart, who made sure the box office figures were available to Cantor at the end of every week and who acted as Cantor's liaison with Shubert in New York. At first, J. J. resented Lipsky, but gradually he came to see him as a young but levelheaded businessman, who was easier to deal with than Cantor.

Nor was Eddie easier for Lee, Jake's older brother. "Spoke to Max Hart," he wired Cantor on March 16. "Does not think you should ask more than five hundred dollars for [March 20] Sunday Night [Concert at] Century Theatre. Will you kindly wire me that you will accept this so we can bill you?"

"Regret that I cannot play next Sunday," Cantor wired back. "Must rest my voice for Newark. Best wishes."

The grosses were impressive in the cities Cantor had played with the *Follies*, disappointing elsewhere. "My various managers," Jake wrote Eddie in mid-April, "tell me the only reason we do not do capacity at every performance is that the show lacks a New York reputation. Therefore, I think it would enhance the show's value if we have a New York run. We can cancel the bookings from now on so you can have one two weeks' rest, opening in New York for the summer season, and reopening in Chicago on Labor Day." Cantor also refused this, citing a general business slump and noting that the *Follies* was playing to empty seats. In truth, he was reluctant to oppose the *Ziegfeld Follies* and George White's *Scandals* with what he regarded as a slipshod show. Following a talk with Danny Lipsky, Cantor sent a wire to Max Hart in which he claimed that "a very good physician" said he "would be taking a terrible chance" if he did not take a long summer vacation. Hart then spoke to Shubert, who gave in to his new star.

"Eddie Cantor in *The Midnight Rounders*" closed for the summer at the Globe, Atlantic City, on June 4, 1921. Cantor took part in the *Friars' Frolic* at the Manhattan Opera House on Sunday night, June 12, and spent the next two weeks squaring accounts with Lipsky, Max Hart, and the Shuberts, recording one more song for Emerson, and seeing Broadway shows. On Thursday night, June 23, he was raised to the (Third) Degree of Master Mason in Munn Lodge No. 203, Free & Accepted Masons, at Masonic Hall in New York City.

Little has been written of the bond between the theatre and freemasonry before the Great Depression, when one-ninth of all adult American males were members of the masonic fraternity. The affinity had its roots in the eighteenth century, when few churches would bury actors and few inns accepted them as guests. Masons conducted their own funeral services and, if need be, welcomed fellow masons into their own homes. Edwin Booth, his career greatly damaged by his brother's assassination of President Abraham Lincoln in 1865, relied on fellow masons for lodging while en tour from that time up to the 1880s. Touring remained the lifeblood of the American theatre until after World War I, and masonic membership among performers peaked from the 1890s to the 1920s.

Roughly 90 percent of all major male stars on the English speaking stage prior to 1930 were freemasons. David Garrick, Sir Henry Irving, Edmund Kean, Sir Herbert Beerbohm Tree, George M. Cohan, Al Jolson, Sir Donald

Wolfit (model for "Sir" in the hit play *The Dresser*), Ralph Reader, and many other stars were members of the masonic fraternity, as were many of Cantor's colleagues in the *Ziegfeld Follies*, including Bert Williams, Will Rogers, W. C. Fields, Leon Errol, Ed Wynn, and Ziegfeld himself.

Cantor had been initiated into the masonic order under Irving Berlin's sponsorship in 1919. He would eventually become a thirty-second degree mason and, through that rank, a Shriner.

In late June, Eddie took his family for a month's vacation in Luzerne, a resort area in the Adirondacks. "God alone knows how much I needed this rest," he wrote to J. J. "I feel like a new man already. By the time August arrives, I will be able to play in the show, usher the people in, give out programs, and do the bill posting. This is the most ideal spot in all the Adirondacks and I wish you could spend a week or so with me." Shubert was more interested in Cantor's health and fitness for performing than his own, although he made one quick trip there with the writer Harold Atteridge.

The rest helped Ida, too. Six months pregnant by the time they got to Luzerne, she delivered in Mount Vernon on September 16, twelve days after the reopened *Midnight Rounders* had begun a long engagement at the huge Apollo Theatre in Chicago. MY WIFE PRESENTED ME WITH FOURTH DAUGHTER FEEL GREAT, Eddie wired J. J. CONGRATULATIONS, Shubert wired back. YOU WILL YET BE THE FATHER OF YOUR COUNTRY.

The baby was named Marilyn, among the first of untold thousands of baby girls named after Marilyn Miller since the opening of *Sally* the previous December. (Cantor, who still kept kosher, reached the heights of ecumenicalism by naming Miller, a non-Jew, the child's godmother.) Born with minor respiratory trouble, Marilyn would be the only one of Eddie's daughters to essay a stage career. Fittingly, she was the first—and for a time, the only—daughter Eddie used to promote his career.

Phony telegrams to and from J. J. Shubert had Eddie threatening to "leave for New York" if means were not devised for him to see his new baby. "Will send your wife and baby out to you next Thursday," read the sham response, "if I have to charter a special train and hire a regiment of nurses." The publicity stunt worked. Eddie was there with a bevy of reporters when Ida, Margie, Natalie, Edna, and the two-week old Marilyn arrived in Chicago on the last day in September.

The baby's respiratory trouble abated after a few months, but not her painful sinuses. Childhood would be a prolonged battle for Cantor's fourth daughter.

There were battles vis-à-vis *The Midnight Rounders*, too. Green & Blyler missed several performances at the Apollo, and Jake Shubert thought— perhaps quite rightly—that they were trying to break their contract. "I am not going to let them do so," he wrote Cantor. "Let them stay out as long as they want. We can get along without them until such time as we can use them to our own convenience, but I am not going to let them put anything over on us if I can help it."

Jane Green and Jimmy Blyler, her husband and accompanist, had been put into the show at Cantor's own insistence. Discoveries of the *Follies* comedian Leon Errol, they had first come to Cantor's attention in Ziegfeld's *Nine O'Clock Revue* and *Midnight Frolic* in 1918. Jane Green was an incredible "blues" singer, with a musicality beyond the reach of most vaudevillians. Cantor had secured her a Pathe recording date while *The Midnight Rounders* was still in the East; at the same time, he recorded one of Jane's own songs, "I Never Knew I Could Love Anybody (Honey, Like I'm Lovin' You)" for Emerson. An accident in 1927 would diminish her great singing ability and lead to her untimely death in 1931.

One of the show's best sketches was "Joe's Blue Front" (also known as "Belt in the Back"), about a tailor, his pushy Jewish assistant (played by Eddie), and an older Jewish customer ("I vant you should make me a suit, I should look like a college boy"). Cantor had bought the sketch from Lew Hearn and hired him to play the customer. Joe Opp—another Max Hart client, foisted on the Shuberts—received four hundred dollars a week for playing the proprietor and for appearing in two other scenes.

Opp, whose background was burlesque, reacted to his ill-deserved success with what was known as the "small-timer's mentality." Secure with what he saw as Cantor's backing, he told other members of the show he'd "make the Shuberts pay" for what they got. J. J., who had spies in every company, was incensed, especially when he received a letter from Opp in September saying that Jake would have to "see my agent, Max Hart," if he wanted to renew his contract.

J. J., who despised Opp's "loud, boisterous and objectionable personality to start with," did not feel like "chasing around" for his manager, whether Hart or anybody else. "Anyone can fill [Opp's] place at $125 to $150, and at least be a gentleman about it," he declared in one letter to Eddie. Cantor's wires on Opp's behalf served to annoy Shubert further. "PLEASE GIVE OPP FIFTY DOLLAR RAISE, read one. "AM ALMOST SURE I CAN GET HIM TO STAY." J. J. finally raised Opp twenty-five dollars in order to keep Cantor happy. "As long as I don't have to see Mr. Opp it is a matter of indifference to me, but to have to sit through a performance of his would be far from my desire, if I could spend an evening elsewhere."

What J. J. might or might not have realized—but appears quite likely, given Cantor's later "double dipping" (an accepted show biz practice) as an employer and agent for performers—was that Eddie got a cut of Joe Opp's salary. Four hundred dollars a week for an unimportant actor was unheard of in the early 1920s. And yet Cantor, though no friend of Opp's, insisted he receive it. Opp would certainly have signed for less than half that figure and (no matter what his claims) been glad to get the work.

Cantor was, indeed, the one who "made the Shuberts pay." Others like them would pay in the future. Stage and film producers, corporate sponsors of radio programs, agents, and fellow performers would find Eddie Cantor shrewd about the show world. George LeMaire, Jake Shubert, and years of experience, as well as his own street background, taught Eddie very well.

When *The Midnight Rounders* did less than great business in four weeks at the Apollo, it was shifted to the older Garrick Theatre. Cantor blamed lack of publicity. "We fell down $3,000 on our last week [at the Apollo]," he wrote J. J. on October 3. "I am surprised that we got away with the money that we did because we are receiving no help at all from either Mr. Gerson or Mr. Garrity or Mrs. Couthoui. I know for a fact that she is forcing other shows and giving us the worst of it. I hope you will give this matter your immediate attention as it means a great deal to both of us." Cantor also remonstrated when the show's top ticket price was put at $3.50 at the Garrick. "I can stay here for twelve more weeks with a three thirty," he wired J. J. "Please do not allow Garrity and outsiders to influence you. I am positively right in this matter."

Eddie's belief that the chorines were "the worst girls in the world" did not apply to one sweet seventeen-year-old, who wound up getting pregnant. "She . . . expects to give birth in the next five months or so," he wrote to J. J. "I actually believe that it is noticeable and feel that we ought to have her replaced in the show, or maybe we can put her in one or two numbers in the show and keep her until it is absolutely necessary that she leave." The girl in question later married a well-known stage and film actor.

After only three weeks at the Garrick, J. J. moved the show to the Great Northern, a comparatively small, out-of-the-way Chicago theatre, over Cantor's—and, claimed Eddie, the whole cast's—objections.

*The Midnight Rounders* played four weeks at the Great Northern, left Chicago, and played major midwestern cities before closing in Detroit on January 14. A chorus call, reputedly the largest in history, for *Kiss Me*, the working title of the new show Harold Atteridge had been preparing as Cantor's first starring Broadway vehicle, was held at New York's Century Theatre the following Monday.

*Kiss Me*, soon retitled *Make It Snappy*, was not the book show Cantor had desired. It was a revue, similar to *The Midnight Rounders* in tone, scenes, and personnel. It smelled of cheap recycling, the kind of Shubert approach to the theatre Cantor had come to despise. He did, however, work with Atteridge on his own scenes for *Make It Snappy*, interpolating "Joe's Blue Front" from *The Midnight Rounders*. The songs, while undistinguished, included an ensemble number called "Doin' the Eddie Cantor," about a supposed Cantor mania sweeping the country. (The song was cut before the New York opening.) Regardless of what faults Eddie had found, the Shuberts were committed to promoting him as a major star.

*Make It Snappy* opened at the Baltimore Auditorium on Tuesday evening, February 14. Its Broadway opening, eight weeks later at the Winter Garden, marked that theatre's return to "legit" after more than six months as the flagship of the Shuberts' 1921–22 foray into vaudeville, a doomed enterprise whose acts included The Four Marx Brothers & Co. (Cantor had demanded a prohibitive 25 percent of the gross to play a week in "Shubert Advanced Vaudeville.") "Theoretically, vaudeville disappeared from the Winter Garden last night," wrote Kenneth MacGowan in the New York *Globe*. "Actually, it was very much in evidence. There were dancers like Georgie Hale, Carlos and Inez, and the marvelous Arab tumblers who now call themselves 'The Eight Blue Devils.' And there were Nan Halperin and Lillian Fitzgerald, two typical examples of instinctive talent cheapened by the easy standards of vaudeville."

> But in spite of this, the thing that the Winter Garden offers is one of those arrangements of girls and songs and comic skits, clothes and spectacle and ballet, which are regularly reviewed under the heading 'The New Play.'
> A large part of *Make It Snappy*—the largest part, in fact—has a perfectly good claim to be treated as legitimate dramatic entertainment. This part is Eddie Cantor. Not because of the fact that he is beginning to look like Ben-Ami, but because of what he does when he looks most like the distinguished tragedian. He is funniest then and at the same time he makes you believe that he couldn't stop from being a mighty good serious actor if he put his mind to it.

Cantor played himself at the stage door of the theatre, an applicant for the police force, a sheik, a taxi driver, and "Moe, the Tailor" in "Joe's Blue Front." In between, he talked and sang new songs: "I'm Hungry for Beautiful Girls," "I Love Her—She Loves Me," and others, some of which were cowritten by him.

"The Sheik," a parody on the then current craze for Rudolph Valentino in the movie of that title, saw Eddie at what Kenneth MacGowan called his "funniest," acting the part with tongue-in-cheek severity before singing "The Sheik of Araby." The comedy high-water mark, however, was "Step in My Taxi," in which Eddie played a caustic taxi driver who explained that his cab went ninety miles an hour since he fed it the glands of a Packard. This taxi driver character would be revived in 1950 as "Maxie the Taxi" on the NBC television show *Colgate Comedy Hour*.

*Make It Snappy* marked Cantor's first appearance—name above the title—as a star in New York City. Eddie nonetheless felt that his popularity had not grown far beyond the level he'd enjoyed in the *Follies* three years earlier. He was probably right. He was just another star among the many then on Broadway.

By the time that *Make It Snappy* closed on July 1, after less than twelve weeks at the Winter Garden, Cantor was completely disillusioned. He was making much more money than before, but the thrill of being in a Ziegfeld show was gone. "Working for the Shuberts," Cantor later wrote, "was just show business." Working for—and, sometimes, practically against—them, had left Cantor feeling both jaded and empty.

He was again recording, having severed his relationship with the bankrupt Emerson to begin a three-year tenure with the Columbia Graphophone Company, the longest continuous relationship of Cantor's usually sporadic wax career. After recording two songs in July, Eddie took his family to The Breakers, a kosher hotel in Atlantic City popular among Jews in show business. Eddie, while not keeping strictly kosher, still avoided things like pork and shellfish.

J. J. Shubert was a normally pugnacious man with little patience for performers, less for people on his staff, and none for those who went against his will. But J. J.'s biggest star, Al Jolson, was thinking of deserting the Shuberts when his contract expired the following September. This, above all things, made J. J. anxious to keep Cantor. When Eddie wanted to play vaudeville at Atlantic City's Garden Pier in August, J. J. gave his permission. Jolson himself had been denied permission to play vaudeville in the past.

But nothing could make Cantor enjoy working for the Shuberts. In September, he incorporated Eddie Cantor Theatrical Enterprises for $50,000 to engage in "general theatrical producing." The shareholders were Eddie, Ida, and, predictably, Dan Lipsky. No productions were announced, but Lipsky said that a musical was being "considered."

The company, and the possibility he would produce his own shows, might have given Cantor added leverage in contract negotiations with producers. No shows, in fact, were ever planned, and Eddie Cantor Theatrical Enterprises was dissolved within a year.

*Make It Snappy*, its cast reassembled after Labor Day, opened for its season's tour at the Majestic Theatre in Brooklyn on September 18, 1922. "There is plenty of color in the show, but not a vast amount of humor," said the Brooklyn *Eagle*.

> Cantor provides most of what comedy there is, Lew Hearn providing the rest. The best of the lot is one in which Cantor appears as a bootlegging taxi driver with Hearn a thirsty rural visitor. Cantor sings a number of songs in his usual manner.
>
> Last night's performance was somewhat ragged—so much so that Cantor felt it necessary to explain that the show was just starting on the road. The chorus, seemingly well trained in some numbers, was decidedly nervous in others, and seemingly unaware of what was coming next. One chorus number ended with the girls scampering off the stage as best they could. Some of the chorus, by the way, were good to look at. There were some, however, whose beauty was hardly up to the traditional Winter Garden standards.

Cantor had already resolved not to re-sign with the Shuberts when his contract ran out on June 1. Dan Lipsky tried to change his mind, citing the investment the Shuberts had made in him and saying they might be prepared to offer him more money. But Cantor remained adamant. He had already asked Max Hart to get him work in vaudeville and other Broadway shows, especially for Dillingham or Ziegfeld. Erlanger made a fine offer, but Hart, at Cantor's own insistence, put out feelers to Ziegfeld. There was no warm response. The Great Glorifier was no longer interested in Eddie Cantor.

*Make It Snappy* opened at the Apollo Theatre in Chicago on January 7, 1923, on the heels of Al Jolson's sixteen-week engagement at that same theatre in *Bombo*. Eddie's reviews, generally good or better despite his paltry vehicle, were capped, in his own mind, by a line in Sheppard Butler's critique for the *Chicago Tribune*: "Eddie Cantor at $3.30 is keen competition to *Sally* at $4.40."

Ida brought the girls out to Chicago after a few weeks and Eddie told his wife—again—of his desire to return to Ziegfeld. Cantor's nerve and shrewdness, not his considerable talent, finally did the job.

In March, as *Make It Snappy* neared the end of its run in Chicago, Cantor took a full-page advertisement in *Variety*, reprinting Butler's line from the *Tribune* review. The ad ran in the issue dated Thursday, March 15, when *Make It Snappy* was at the Hartman Theatre in Columbus. Eddie told Ida that Ziegfeld, who was in Palm Beach, would call "on Tuesday, the latest," after seeing the ad.

*Make It Snappy* was in Cincinnati on Tuesday, March 20. The phone rang at noon in the Cantors' hotel suit: Mr. Ziegfeld from Palm Beach.

Ziegfeld met with Cantor in St. Louis a week later. Negotiations between Ziegfeld and Hart followed and, on May 14, Ziegfeld's office announced that Eddie Cantor had signed a "long-term" contract and would replace Will Rogers (who was leaving for film work in California) in the *Follies* on June 4. The contract also stipulated that Cantor would star in a Broadway book show by the end of the year.

*Make It Snappy* closed its tour at the Chestnut Street Opera House in Philadelphia on May 26, 1923. Cantor's contract with the Shuberts ran out six days later.

J. J. fumed, but he had no recourse. Eddie opened up a week's vaudeville engagement at the Orpheum in Brooklyn the following Monday afternoon and opened in the *Follies* that same evening. "Eddie Cantor is an entertainer with a capital 'E,'" *Variety* reported. "He is value received for vaudeville."

Cantor spent the next two weeks "doubling" between the *Follies* and the Palace Theatre, singing songs like "How Ya Gonna Keep Your Mind on Dancing (When You're Dancing with Someone You Love)?," "Oh, Gee! Oh, Gosh! Oh, Golly! I'm in Love," "Yes, We Have No Bananas," and spicing up his act with comments about the Shuberts' penny-pinching—comments quickly relayed back to J. J.

The younger Shubert fired off a letter to Dan Lipsky:

> While I was not greatly surprised at Mr. Cantor's attitude—not looking for much gratitude in that direction—I at least thought he would have the common decency not to openly insult us from the stage of the *Ziegfeld Follies* and the Palace vaudeville stage. I know you would not countenance anything of this sort, and I can only credit it to his ignorance and stupidity. When you take into consideration the fact that we have done more for this man than anybody else has ever done for him, it is hard to understand. We took him when he was offered $800 a week by the Keith Office and made him a big star. . . . He benefitted to the extent of from $200,000 to $250,000 . . . [while we] show a loss of $50,000. . . . I don't care what he does, nor how he does it, as long as he leaves us alone. I don't want to go to extremes, but as you know, no man can go upon the stage and openly insult us as he has done repeatedly since he closed with us. What hurts me more than anything else, however, is that a man could be so unappreciative—to accept everything and then in return insult us in order to get a laugh at the expense of his benefactors. If that is the only way he can get laughs, he certainly is lacking in material.

Lipsky responded immediately, saying he was "not aware that Eddie was making references to you or your brother from the stage, but assure you that so far as it lies within my power, he will discontinue any remarks. . . . Cantor does not mean anything personal by his remarks—using them solely for laughs, but he shouldn't do it under any circumstances, and I will see him tomorrow and talk it over with him, feeling sure he will see it my way." Cantor cut the gags, but he never changed his mind about the Shuberts.

A revised edition of the *Follies*, with Cantor's part expanded, opened Monday evening, June 25, with Ziegfeld charging the unprecedented price of twenty-two dollars a seat. Before the overture, Cantor began banging at an orchestra seat equipped with hammer, wrench, and saw. "Let me alone," he told an "interfering" usher, "I paid twenty-two dollars for this seat and I'm taking it home."

Eddie sang six songs in this production, appeared with Andrew Tombes in a special parody version of "Mister Gallagher and Mister Shean," and played Ann Pennington's little brother, "Cicero," in a sketch with banjoist Brooke Johns that "stopped the show." The show received the usual Ziegfeld raves from reviewers, with the New York *Herald* calling Cantor "another shining light, especially when his black make-up began to glisten. . . . He sang some new and amusing songs, told stories, capered irrepressibly, and engaged in a fairly diverting skit on the arrest of a speeder, called 'Getting a Ticket,' which seemed to be enjoyed by a distinguished audience, most of whom owned cars."

Cantor spent his matineeless days golfing in Van Cortland Park with friends like the lyricist Joseph McCarthy, who thought Eddie looked funny in the cap and knickers that were the standard outfit for golfers in the twenties. McCarthy finally concocted an idea for a show in which Cantor played a bootlegging caddy master at a country club who could not be fired because he had a "line" on every member of the club.

Cantor brought the idea to Ziegfeld, who commissioned William Anthony McGuire to write the book, McCarthy to do the lyrics, and Harry Tierney to compose the score. Eddie, in the meantime, left the *Follies* on August 4, played a week of vaudeville at the Globe Theatre, Atlantic City, took a needed five-week rest, and returned for three more weeks of vaudeville in September.

When, by the end of September, the alcoholic McGuire had fallen hopelessly behind schedule, Ziegfeld brought in the veteran Otto Harbach as his collaborator. In four more weeks, the book was ready. Rehearsals for *Kid Boots*, the show that would make Cantor one of the world's biggest stars, began on Monday, October 29, 1923.

# Chapter 6

# KID BOOTS

*"He could dynamite a song like a masculine Bayes."*
—*Douglas Gilbert*, American Vaudeville

The American craze for golf, heretofore a sport for Britishers and pluto-crats, began in 1913, when two outstanding British pros were beaten by the American amateur Francis Ouimet in the U.S. Open. Within three years, there were hundreds of golf courses around the country, catering largely to middle-class businessmen. Golf became a major sport and pas-time after World War I, a reflection of the leisure and prosperity America enjoyed during the fabled 1920s.

If golf was not big business, "bootlegging" was. The Eighteenth Amend-ment, prohibiting the distribution and sale of alcoholic beverages, took ef-fect on January 16, 1920, the beginning of the "Roaring '20s." Enforcement of the Volstead Act, the Amendment's criminal-law teeth, was initially put in the hands of the Department of the Treasury, whose officials proved so easily corruptible that two hundred thousand speakeasies sprang up across the country. In New York City alone, fifteen thousand legal saloons were replaced in quick order by more than twice the same number of speakeas-ies. Although widely damned for sparking the enfranchisement of "organ-ized crime," Prohibition did succeed in lessening the alcohol and beer consumption of the poor and working classes, its primary aim. As the mild recession of the early 1920s gave way to prosperity, however, more people had the money to buy bootlegged whiskey. By 1923, Prohibition was a national joke, a fit and frequent subject for the humor of comedians in vaudeville. *Kid Boots* could not have been more timely.

Its premise was more daring than those of *Irene* or *Sally*, the "Cinder-ella" musicals that were the big hit shows of the postwar era. Boots (Cantor) is the less than honest caddy master at a golf club, using crooked balls to trick the patrons into taking lessons, selling bootlegged liquor on the side, and blackmailing anyone who threatens his position. His best friend, Tom Sterling (Harry Fender), the club champion, loses a big tournament while inadvertently using one of Boots's trick balls. Tom, however, wins his love, the wealthy Polly Pendleton (Mary Eaton), when Boots confesses his tricks and redeems himself at the same time. Boots's own love interest is the diminutive Jane Martin (Marie Callahan), who swallows her two-hundred-dollar engagement ring early in the show.

The show's strength was its comedy, especially the scenes between Boots and Dr. Josephine Fitch, the club osteopath, played by the imposing Jobyna Howland. One scene had her catch Boots in the ladies' locker room, searching for liquor.

FITCH: Boots, what are you doing here?
BOOTS: I'm sick.
FITCH: Where?
BOOTS: In the ladies' locker room.
FITCH: Get on the table.

Dr. Fitch proceeds to take Kid Boots apart with a massage bordering on mayhem. Cantor's subtle, alternately pained and detached reactions would prove to be the high point of the show, rivaling or topping his work in the 1918 and '19 *Follies*.

Cantor believed in *Kid Boots*—his first starring "book" show—to the point of sheer fanaticism, overcoming any and all obstacles against it with the same brand of energy and pushiness that had marked his career since 1911. Mary Eaton, Marilyn Miller's original understudy in *Sally*, seemed headed for stardom after receiving critical plaudits in two *Follies*, and her father insisted she be costarred in *Kid Boots*. Cantor categorically refused but finally consented to Eaton's being featured. The final billing read:

EDDIE CANTOR
IN
*KID BOOTS*
WITH
MARY EATON

Eaton later starred in *The Five O'Clock Girl* (1927). She is today remembered, if at all, as the romantic lead in the Marx Brothers' first sound film, *The Cocoanuts*.

Ziegfeld had a streak of pessimism rare in a producer, a trait born of the same sensitivity that enabled him to mount his great and beautiful revues. Again and again, throughout the twenties, he privately insisted that the shows he was producing were all certain failures. *Kid Boots* was no exception. After three weeks of rehearsals, Ziegfeld became convinced that the show was a mistake, a guaranteed flop that would forever soil the great

Ziegfeld reputation. Explaining that he wanted to cut his losses before costly sets were built, Ziegfeld proposed to Cantor that *Kid Boots* be scrapped in favor of some—any—other vehicle.

Eddie argued, acting out the show's funniest scenes for his producer with a vibrancy usually reserved for opening nights. He jumped on sofas, rolled on the floor, and cried as Boots would cry, frantically and mournfully, in the scene where the golf pro, his friend, loses the match. By the time he finished, Ziegfeld was still unconvinced, but he was willing to take a chance.

Ziegfeld had, in fact, good reason to be skeptical. Unlike *Sally*, Ziegfeld's previous successful "book" show, *Kid Boots* starred a male comedian and featured a beautiful young woman. (*Sally*, quite the reverse, starred the girl and featured the comic, Leon Errol.) Also unlike *Sally*, *Kid Boots* boasted no great hits in its score. (Cantor and Marie Callahan had one charming number called "Let's Do and Say We Didn't, Let's Don't and Say We Did.") *Kid Boots* rested on a strong, funny libretto, a popular, multitalented star comedian, a good supporting cast, and topicality—one of the key elements in shows and sketches before Rodgers and Hammerstein sent musical theatre around the globe in search of subjects. *Kid Boots* did not approach the smooth sophistication of Gershwin's *Lady, Be Good!*; nor did it integrate its songs to the extent that *Oklahoma!* would twenty years later. But it was musical comedy in its purest sense—with the accent on comedy—a perfect vehicle for its star, Eddie Cantor.

Despite Ziegfeld's fears, *Kid Boots* was in near perfect shape by the time it opened at the New Detroit Theatre on Monday night, December 3, 1923. The first-act curtain fell to cheers, and Cantor, Ziegfeld, and director Edward Royce actually came out on the stage, joined hands, and danced "ring-around-a-rosy" like three children. The second act, as Cantor later claimed, was "better than the first. Usually an opening night runs till midnight; then the work starts: the cutting, realigning, smoothing the thing into final tempo. But that night in Detroit, *Kid Boots* ran like a dream. The curtain rang down at eleven twenty-five. Two encore dances were to be cut, that was all; a perfect show."

Talent was one thing; judgment was another. Eddie's passionate conviction in the show's worth had earned Florenz Ziegfeld's respect. From that night on, he was no longer "Mr. Ziegfeld" to the still young Eddie Cantor; he was "Flo" or "Zieggy."

Cantor's later reminiscences portray Ziegfeld as a sort of father figure to him and imply the two had an extremely close relationship from this time on, except for a brief period in 1928. In point of fact, their relationship remained that of a top-flight producer and his treasured, streetwise, sometimes petulant star. Cantor, still the product of Al Smith's East Side, saw producers as "management," the enemy with whom one might exchange nice pleasantries amid an undeclared "cold war" that might erupt into open fire at the drop of a contract. Ziegfeld, in the eyes of Cantor, was no great exception to this rule, despite his admiration for Flo's quality producing. Zieggy may have been a father figure to Eddie (as was Nathan Jonas at Manufacturers Hanover), but he was a father who, in Cantor's view, was there to dole out money—and suffer condemnation during periods of crisis. Flo was like a modern government in human form to Eddie—not so much a father as "Big Brother."

Orchestra seats for the Broadway opening of *Kid Boots* at the Earl Carroll Theatre were priced at $16.50—the equivalent of more than $200 in 1997— and were occupied by New York society leaders, well-known politicians, leading figures in the show world, and the city's first-string theatre critics.

*Kid Boots* was called Ziegfeld's greatest triumph since the opening of *Sally* three years earlier. Mary Eaton and the rest of the supporting cast were given nods of general approval by New York reviewers, but the bulk of the raves went to Eddie Cantor. His personal notices were actually better than those received by the show.

H. Z. Torres in the *New York Commercial*:

It is a whale of a musical comedy which F. Ziegfeld is presenting at the Earl Carroll Theatre, and it is Eddie Cantor who is the "whole show." This notwithstanding that *Kid Boots* has dainty Mary Eaton for its prima donna, and that Mr. Ziegfeld has surpassed himself in the taste and beauty of settings and costumes. There is an unusually good cast, and a bevy of pretty choristers adorn the piece. William Anthony McGuire and Otto Harbach have provided a super excellent book.

And yet, with intelligence—and talent far in excess of the average musical comedy, the sum of the success of *Kid Boots* is Eddie Cantor: Eddie Cantor as an irrepressible, excruciatingly funny caddy and bootlegger. Eddie Cantor in songs and dances, and Eddie Cantor in blackface. A real hit.

The *New York Times*:

For it is Eddie Cantor, seeming a bit more fervent and wide-eyed than he ever has before, who makes *Kid Boots* what it is. He is the most intense of the comedians—the light blazes in his eye and communicates itself to his audience, convincing them of his passionate sincerity. In *Kid Boots*, he even strikes a respectable serious note now and then, and he imparts an unexpected sublety to several scenes designed as broad comedy.

Eddie's only scene in blackface came at the show's end, when he appeared as himself, "Eddie Cantor of the *Ziegfeld Follies*," at "The Cocoanut

Ball," singing songs, exposing a cheating golfer, and bringing the hero and heroine together in a love clinch. In this, Cantor's only chance to sing songs not in Harry Tierney's score, he was accompanied, not by the pit orchestra, but by George Olsen's band, which Fanny Brice had heard in Portland, Oregon, and recommended to Ziegfeld. Olsen's vibrant, quick, and upbeat tempos were perfect for Cantor's joyous, almost sexually frenzied singing, and they proved to be the musical highlight of the show. Eddie sounded better than he ever had before.

Cantor was already a star; *Kid Boots* made him a celebrity, one whose doings were now duly noted by the daily press, which, caught up in the arts excitement of the '20s and influenced by Hollywood's growing power, began paying more attention to the major film and stage stars of the day. The *New York Times* printed Eddie's portrait in its Sunday Arts & Leisure section less than two weeks after *Kid Boots* opened at the Carroll, a sure sign of his arrival at the head of his profession.

His dressing room at the Earl Carroll soon became the capital of the nation's show business empire. Governor Al Smith, Marcus Loew, Adolph Zukor, Paul Block, Commander Robert Byrd, Harold Lloyd, Jesse Lasky, and Mayor James J. Walker were visitors at one time or another, as were the expected greats of show business: his friend Will Rogers, Marilyn Miller, George Jessel (inevitably), and many others he'd known from his early days in vaudeville. Then there were the "newsboys, gunmen, sick and destitute, old acquaintances from the East Side—all anxious for a helping hand, making this little room the center of their world and hoping for anything from an autograph to a new start in life."

"Backstage," Eddie recalled just a few years later, "I now carried on a complete and separate life from the comic caddie in the golf club. And after every exit I had to pick up the thread where I had left it for my cue. I had to answer a great deal of fan mail, I dictated articles, thought up skits for revues, concerned myself with welfare work."

The beginnings of this "welfare work" was the Eddie Cantor Surprise Lake Camp Committee, founded by Cantor, Danny Lipsky, Benny Schulberg, and Jack Holman. Eddie had emceed the Committee's first All-Star Vaudeville Benefit Show while still working for the Shuberts a year earlier. Now, with help from the Committee, and with Flo Ziegfeld's acquiescence, he made plans for a larger show with major Broadway names. These yearly shows continued, ever more successfully, until 1930.

Motion pictures entered Eddie's life by way of Dr. Lee DeForrest, inventor of the audion vacuum tube, who hired Eddie to joke and sing two songs on Phonofilm, a primitive sound-on-film process developed with the aid of Case and Sponable of Rochester. Phonofilm went nowhere, but Marion Davies's Cosmopolitan Pictures soon offered Cantor a "week or two" in a costume vehicle called *Janice Meredith*. Eddie reportedly asked for too

much money, and W. C. Fields wound up appearing in one hastily interpolated sequence as a British army sergeant.

Cantor's weekly income was about $3,400 (10 percent of *Kid Boots*'s
gross), plus money from recordings and other sources that pushed the total
close to $4,000. Max Hart was still his agent, collecting 10 percent of
Cantor's salary from Ziegfeld and, increasingly, in need of every penny.

Hart, who controlled seventy acts, had been excluded from the Keith
Vaudeville Exchange in 1920, his clients leaving, one by one, to place their
fates—and their commissions—in the hands of the Exchange itself. His
income now restricted to commissions from clients in "legit" shows, Hart
launched an unprecedented $5,250,000 antitrust suit against the Keith
Exchange.

Cantor, testifying on Hart's behalf on Wednesday, January 23, 1924,
said that his earning capacity had increased from $275 to $3,500 in ten
years and that he did not hesitate to give Max Hart "full credit" for his
present earning power.

Cantor said that musical comedies were "*garnished* with girls" when
asked the difference between a revue and a musical comedy. On cross-
examination, Cantor was asked if he was "still clowning."

"Oh, no," he said. "I'm getting to be quite a legitimate actor." Asked if
his talent was not "natural," Cantor admitted that he had natural talent but
added that Hart had developed it.

Hart lost the final round of his suit when the federal court decided the
Keith-Albee empire was not in interstate commerce, despite its having theatres in almost every state. The massive legal fees, plus his costly battles
with his former wife, Madge Fox (the "Flip-Flop Girl" of vaudeville), finally
left Hart broke and destitute.

Cantor, his income rising with little or no help from Hart, did not renew
when their final contract expired in 1928. He did, however, put the agent
on his personal payroll and kept him there until Hart died in 1950.

Cantor, as Jake Shubert had discovered, could be difficult—stubbornly
uncompromising and demanding with producers, surprisingly impatient
with his own supporting players. But Eddie did not forget his early bene-
factors. Indeed, the sentimentalism Cantor showed for his boyhood and, of
course, his grandmother was extended to include those who had helped
him toward success. Max Hart was the first recipient of Eddie's beyond-
the-call-of-duty personal generosity. There would be many others.

The *Kid Boots* years saw Cantor flower—almost literally. Having spent his
childhood in filth, despite his grandmother's best efforts, he now reveled
in the joys of frequent bathing—not merely in hot water, but water laced
with Chanel No. 5.

From this time on, the smell of Chanel heralded an Eddie Cantor entrance. ("You smelled it a few seconds before he came into a room," to

quote many who met Cantor over the next forty years.) With Eddie's "arrival" as a full-fledged Ziegfeld star, he also began patronizing the finest Broadway tailors. He liked the new soft collars and expensive wing-tipped shoes and became one of New York's best-dressed men despite his color-blindness.

Eddie was always "on the go," and male visitors to his dressing room at the Carroll often found him shadowboxing with them. If Eddie was around the theatre district with no business to attend to, he would sneak into a special movie house that showed nothing but newsreels. Every waking minute of his life was filled with show business, good causes, politics, social activities, or family.

Harry Fender, who played Tom Sterling, the romantic lead in *Kid Boots*, was Cantor's best friend in the company. Their relationship, in fact, seemed to mirror the one between "Kid Boots" and "Tom" onstage—the small, wise, manipulative character and his tall, good-looking friend. But Cantor's backstage dictatorship and hounding of lesser players about everything from late entrances to excessive backstage noise often made him seem like half star, half stage manager. The latter role, as producer's rep and backstage "warden," was seldom popular, and Mary Eaton, whom Eddie later painted as "completely light-hearted," frequently told her mother and sister that "he started up again" after one of Cantor's backstage tirades.

One scene in the show had Kid Boots, to avoid detection, hurriedly stick a huge loving cup over his head and pose, for a full minute, like a statue as the chase goes on around him. One evening, Eddie stuck the cup over his head to find that it was partly filled with Limburger cheese. Forced to hold his pose for what seemed an eternity of torture, Eddie did not find the practical joke funny. When the scene mercifully ended and his mask of agony was finally removed, Cantor raged and threatened to "fire the entire cast."

His position, at that point, was such that he could probably have done it. By the next day, however, he had chosen to forgive and forget. No one ever claimed responsibility for Cantor's "stinking prison," although several stagehands were suspected.

There was no question of Cantor's popularity with the public, especially with Jews, to whom he seemed a paragon of *Yiddishkite*—a Jew of humble origins, triumphant in mainstream American show business, who openly proclaimed his Jewishness in jokes and Yiddish ad-libs on the stage. His name was recognizably Jewish, he looked Jewish, and he spoke, not with a Yiddish accent, but with Jewish inflections, interpolated as the moment struck him. When the New York *Telegram-Mail* sponsored a contest to elect the first "Mayor of Broadway" in April, Eddie won with 19,441 votes, beating out the nightclub talent impresario Nils T. Granlund (17,446 votes), the publicist Walter J. Kingsley (5,972), and *Vaudeville News* columnist Walter Winchell (4,825). The "title," as such, was honorary (despite Cantor's announced intention to "clean up" [the litter] on Broadway), but Eddie took a stand in real politics a short time later.

"I am going to form a [Governor Alfred E.] Smith for President Theatrical League," Cantor announced at the Earl Carroll Theatre on May 6. "The organization will take in all branches of the stage and motion picture industries, actors, stage hands, ushers and usherettes and all persons connected with motion pictures. When we get organized we will have a big mass meeting, which will be addressed by speakers from the theatrical world and in all walks of life.

"I think, personally, that Governor Smith is the only Democrat who can and will be elected President, there being no doubt that he will get the nomination. I have a strong regard for Governor Smith because we both come from the East Side. I used to live on Catherine Street, while 'Al' lived just around the corner." (Eddie, of course, never lived on Catherine Street.)

Cantor, already a member of the Roosevelt Commitee, had an appointment with F.D.R., now paralyzed with polio, the next day to discuss the league's formation. Nor did Smith's failure to secure the nomination sour Cantor, who became president of the Davis and Bryan Theatrical League "to carry on a campaign for the Democratic ticket among members of the stage." Coolidge and Dawes won despite his efforts.

*Kid Boots* thus marked Cantor's debut as a "public figure," raising untold dollars for Surprise Lake Camp and other worthwhile causes while throwing his support to Democratic champions of "the poor" and the "working classes." (One of his most touching and worthwhile efforts came on Saturday, May 10, when he and Ida, their three elder daughters in tow, played host to twenty-five blind girls at a luncheon given at the Concourse Plaza. Eddie entertained with songs and banter until he had to leave for that day's matinee.) The show's year-long run also meant that he could live at home— Park Avenue, Mount Vernon—the whole year through and take an active part in the raising of his daughters.

Ida had raised Margie, Natalie, and Edna by herself. The girls were well behaved, though Natalie remembered Ida coming after them with phrases like "You're gonna get it" as they ran around the dining room table. Margie was a serious child, and not even Natalie, her closest sibling, who became her best friend as the years went by, would ever really understand her.

Margie was an "old" girl, mature far beyond her years and comfortable with people of all ages. She and Natalie, so close in age, inevitably had their fights and quarrels. On one occasion, Natalie bit Margie, who informed their father. Eddie never spoke to Natalie about it but subsequently introduced her to a distinguished-looking guest by saying, "This is my daughter, Natalie. She *bites*." The mortified girl never bit again.

Margie was eight and a half, Natalie eleven months her junior, at the time *Kid Boots* opened. They saw the show many times, usually on weekends, almost always from backstage. "The theatre was his medium," said Natalie. "He had magic on stage, great vitality, timing, and an endearing quality. No matter how long a show ran, he was still giving his all, building scenes, improving, always working at it." *Kid Boots* was a physically demanding vehicle, and Eddie, in the "ball" scene near the show's conclusion, bounced around while singing interpolated numbers such as "Oh, Gee! Georgie," "If You Do What You Do," "The Dumber They Come, The Better I Like 'Em," and a dozen others that were changed from week to week. On one occasion, between encore bows, Eddie ran offstage to his two daughters, standing in the wings, and pressed their palms upon his heart. "See how hard your daddy works?" he told them before dashing off to yet another round of applause. Natalie looked on with wonder. Margie became terror-stricken; it seemed as if her father, the mysterious crusading knight who reappeared and disappeared as need arose, might, she now feared, fall "in battle" on the stage.

It is no exaggeration to say that Marjorie Cantor was absolutely fascinated by her father. She would, in years to come, devote her life exclusively to him.

Articles on Cantor now appeared in mainstream magazines. The first was the autobiographical "We All Like the Medicine 'Doctor' Eddie Cantor Gives," in *The American Magazine*, the result of an extensive interview given to Mary B. Mullett in Mount Vernon.

> "Let me tell you something: If you've seen me pretty often on the stage, you must know that I work hard. You don't know how hard I work *off* the stage; but I can honestly say that I don't have many idle moments in the course of the day—and it's a long day, too! Sometimes, after two performances at the theatre, I go on at a benefit or a dinner or banquet. Even on Sundays, I often appear at two or three benefits for charity. And I'm always working up new scenes and new lines to put into our regular performance, not only for myself but for other members of the company. I work hard now, and I have worked hard for years."

It was all true. And with *Kid Boots* running smoothly, despite the constant changes and interpolated numbers, Cantor branched out further. He produced two new plays (*Restless Jim Mallon* by J. C. Nugent and *Engaged to Be Married* by Caesar Dunn), neither of which made it to Broadway. And he started managing new talent.

"I met Cantor through George Jessel," says Arthur Tracy. "He had me come to the theatre and audition. Then he put me under contract, and I never heard from him again. Finally, I had to tell him our agreement was over. I could never even get to see him."

Cantor soon abandoned talent management. He would try again in seven years, when radio enabled him to give his clients work on his own program and thus develop the art of double dipping in show biz to new heights.

Kid Boots ran for more than a year on Broadway, one of the few musicals to do so before 1927—a testament to the show's popularity as well as to the rising costs of shows throughout the '20s. Kid Boots was probably the most expensive show done to that time, and Ziegfeld's original calculation that he would lose "only" $1,200 if the show sold out every performance proved accurate, especially when he tossed out the revised Act I finale shortly after the Broadway opening and replaced it at a cost of almost twenty thousand dollars.

Ticket prices could be raised no further; the only way Kid Boots could make money was to move it to a larger house. Accordingly, the show was moved to the more spacious Selwyn Theatre on Forty-Second Street on Monday, September 1, 1924.

There were those who maintained, to their deaths, that both New York and Broadway reached their zeniths in the fall of 1924. No fewer than nine Broadway musicals (including Rudolf Friml's then new Rose Marie) opened that September, followed by three in October, three more in November, and six (including George Gershwin's ground breaking Lady, Be Good! and The Student Prince by Sigmund Romberg) in December. Sidney Howard's Pulitzer Prize-winning They Knew What They Wanted led the nonmusicals, which included Eugene O'Neill's Desire Under the Elms, George S. Kaufman and Edna Ferber's Minick, and the antiwar What Price Glory? by Maxwell Anderson and Laurence Stallings. It was three months of magic, with Kid Boots—and Cantor—up among the leaders in both grosses and prestige.

Cantor had been wise in pushing Ziegfeld for a book show. Despite the increasingly long Broadway runs of Ziegfeld's Follies in the early 1920s, musical comedies, not plotless revues, were the rising tide. Lady, Be Good!, first of the great Gershwin-Astaire musicals, was ushering in a new Broadway era with the emphasis on dancing, sophisticated numbers like "Young Man of Manhattan," and smart, witty dialogue, rather than the satirical sketches found in most revues.

Nineteen twenty-four was, indeed, a landmark year for musicals. Composers, through the American Society of Composers Authors and Publishers, won the right to control scores. Gone forever was the practice of augmenting scores with songs by composers other than the nominal score-rewriter so that the show became little more than a three-hour crazy quilt with music. Performers like Cantor and Jolson would continue their magnificent performing and song interpolations with the blessings of both ASCAP and songwriters. But they were the exceptions, no longer the rule.

The '20s were indeed a patchwork of the older, prewar stars like Jolson and the younger element, made up of the Astaires and English imports like Bea Lillie and Gertrude Lawrence. Old stars, new stars, writers and producers, town "wits," and intellectuals—everyone seemed to travel in circles. Harpo Marx became the darling of the Algonquin set, a group of literary lights who often lunched together at a big round table in the Algonquin Hotel. An older circle moved around George M. Cohan; a younger set moved around F. Scott Fitzgerald, whose wife, Zelda, once astounded a dinner companion by asking, "Don't you think Al Jolson is greater than Christ?"

Cantor, despite his interest in politics and causes, was not, and would never be, a darling of the intellectuals. Like Chico Marx, his stage character was ethnic, streetwise, and concerned with making his own way within the system by means either fair or foul. He represented and appealed to the masses.

Nor did Eddie epitomize what would be called the "roaring '20s." He was not a drinker, and his identification with the East Side of his youth did not allow him to adopt the whimsical callousness of the generation born between 1900 and 1910. Cantor, practical jokes aside, was a serious person who seemed more at home discussing social problems, like the revived Ku Klux Klan, than whooping it up at wild parties.

The middle '20s marked the beginning of the "big boom" years, and a spirit of unbridled optimism kept New Yorkers moving at the briskest pace in history. Never before—or again—would New York reign so forcefully as the world's greatest city. There were rich and poor, and the rich, their numbers growing, gloried in their wealth, flaunting rather than hoarding their money and spreading it around in a good-natured spirit of "what the hell" that would have done Diamond Jim Brady and other prewar millionaires proud. "The idea," said Ruth Gordon, "was to wear, not one, but two or more bracelets—*good ones*—on your wrist. You wanted to be *extravagant*; that was the way."

Cantor was simply too much of a worrier, and much too ethnically Jewish, for that kind of moneyed, devil-may-care, liquor-soaked, and distinctly non-Jewish culture.

On Sunday night, January 11, 1925, one week after his all-star benefit show for Surprise Lake Camp at the Hotel Commodore, Cantor, accompanied by George Olsen's orchestra, sang a few songs during halftime at a Celtics-Washington basketball game at Madison Square Garden. The game itself was a benefit to raise additional money for Surprise Lake, but Eddie was served with a summons for violating the Sunday "blue law" by Police Sergeant Patrick F. Ryan of the East Twenty-second Street Station. Two ticket takers and a ticket seller were also served.

"It's a fine state of affairs," said Cantor, "when a man who works every day and night during the week and gives up his only night off to try to raise money for the benefit of those in less fortunate circumstances than himself finds himself called to court as a consequence."

The case came before Magistrate Vitale in Yorkville Court on Thursday, January 22. Sergeant Ryan told of going to the Garden (then located at Madison Avenue and Twenty-sixth Street), watching the game, and hearing Cantor sing.

"What song was he singing?" asked the magistrate.

"I don't know the name or whether it was in Hebrew or Greek. But he was making a noise." The magistrate asked Cantor if he was a basketball player. "No, Your Honor," replied Eddie. "I'm a singer."

"Are you willing to sing?"

"Sure, if you'll sell tickets."

The magistrate dismissed the case.

Cantor dismissed someone else a few weeks later, shortly after a lingering cold forced him to miss a Wednesday night performance on February 11. Jobyna Howland, who played Dr. Fitch, was a top comedienne who had been prominently featured in Avery Hopwood's original play *The Gold Diggers* in 1919 and starred in *The Texas Nightingale* prior to appearing in *Kid Boots*. Eddie claimed that Jobyna's status as a star made her resentful of her role in *Kid Boots* and that she turned the show into "a tug of war. . . . Every time I had a line that was funny, she'd fan herself furiously with a large feather fan—old and cheap stuff, an attention distractor, and it went on week after week until I told her, 'I don't mind competition, Jobyna, but that fan's too much for me.' She stopped making like a fan dancer but she got even. In the osteopathic scene she had a chance to rough me up and she did. She'd actually come out with tufts of my hair in her hand, when all she had to do was let me move slightly and it would look as though she was pulling my hair."

Cantor later claimed that Howland left *Kid Boots* for a vacation. In fact, he had her fired one week prior to the show's closing on Broadway. Cecil Cunningham, an equally statuesque comedienne who later lent her talents to films like *The Awful Truth* with Irene Dunne, took over Howland's part and, according to Cantor, "never lost a laugh." *Kid Boots* closed at the Selwyn on February 21, 1925, and opened what would prove to be a seven-week run at Boston's Colonial Theatre the following Monday.

"All through the play," wrote Philip Hale in the Boston *Herald*, "Mr. Cantor pops in and out, cracking jokes—a few of them weak, for even he cannot be uproariously funny for three hours—indulging in philosophical remarks, delighting in non sequiturs from absurd premises, speaking volumes by popping eyes and quick facial changes, singing and dancing, and incidentally doing his best in bringing together Tom and Polly."

Cantor was the guest of honor at the Harvard Union's special luncheon on March 10. Having learned that many of the two to three hundred undergraduates at the luncheon wanted to make the stage their careers, he suggested that they enter the chorus of some Broadway musical comedy and drill on regular song-and-dance work for about a year as part of their

training. Such a statement would seem puzzling today, when chorus jobs
are scarce and require extensive dance training. But Cantor's words at Harvard just brought laughter—for different reasons.

"I'm serious," continued Cantor. "Regular men are going in for chorus
work now. Ever since the war, when a lot of soldiers and sailors found for
the first time that they could dance or sing in Y.M.C.A. and Salvation Army
shows, regular men have been going into the chorus. There are several
shows in New York that have got half a dozen ex-servicemen in the chorus.

"It's the same way with you men at college. A lot of you have found that
you could do pretty well in amateur productions like the Hasty Pudding
shows. And if you are thinking of continuing with stage work, the best way
to begin is in the chorus." How many took the advice is impossible to gauge.

Pluggers from song publishers continued to seek audience with Cantor, in
New York or on the road. Shortly after Jolson's illness closed *Big Boy* on
March 14, a representative of Shapiro-Bernstein persuaded Cantor to sing
"If You Knew Susie," introduced and tossed aside by Jolson shortly after
*Big Boy* opened.

"If You Knew Susie," with its sly sexual allusions, double entendres, and
half-spoken "punch lines," fit the Cantor style perfectly. As time went on,
Eddie lent more accent to the "ohs" in "Oh, Oh, Oh (What a Girl)" until
he'd wrenched out all that it would yield in suggestiveness and shocked
innocence. Jolson's "Susie" was half horse (the show, *Big Boy*, had a racing
background), half woman, known and liked by Jolson for her roguish and
aggressive ways. Eddie Cantor made her a seductress, introducing him, an
innocent, to the world of sex—a world forbidden, but, as he joyously proclaimed (with just a touch of shyness), totally delightful. His prancing in
the number exemplified both his running from the girl and his dancing with
delight at her forbidden fruits of love. His eyes, rolling on the punchlines,
symbolized the climax of their relationship, when "Susie" cornered her reluctant "Eddie" and introduced him to life's finer pleasures. Cantor's high-
pitched tenor, almost quivering on every "Oh," added to the picture of the
shy but eager innocent about to cross the threshold into manhood.

The song, quite justifiably, became Eddie's trademark number. Few remembered that Jolson had introduced "If You Knew Susie" or that Willie
Howard, Jay C. Flippen, and Jack Rose had featured it in other Broadway
shows that year. The song belonged to Cantor from the first time that he
sang it.

*Kid Boots* played a six-day week at the Shubert Theatre in Newark after
Boston, breaking all local records with a gross of $37,221 for nine perform-
ances. A week at Werba's Brooklyn and four more in Philadelphia closed
out both the season and the show's year-and-a-half continuous run.

Friday night, June 5, 1925, was "Eddie Cantor Night" at the *Ziegfeld
Follies*. Will Rogers made a speech on behalf of Florenz Ziegfeld and pre-

sented Cantor with a platinum watch commemorating the one thousandth performance of *Kid Boots*. George Olsen's orchestra provided the music, and Cantor was dragged from his seat—on cue—to perform several numbers. A buffet supper followed, with an informal "Eddie Cantor" program.

Eddie and Ida sailed for Paris the next day, their first vacation since their London honeymoon eleven years earlier. In Paris, they met Mrs. Schwartz, who'd been in charge of the playground at P.S. 177 where Eddie and Ida had met in 1906. In Barcelona, Eddie satisfied a long-standing curiosity and saw a real bullfight. "I would not have missed it for a million dollars," Cantor later said, "and I would not give a nickel to see one again. It has got every spectacle on the stage in any part of the world beaten to a frazzle for excitement, blood, and fire."

There was no need for penny-pinching on this trip, no repetition of the night they'd forced themselves to eat a tray of pastries in London, and few or no worries for the future. When the Cantors arrived back in New York harbor on the *Rotterdam* on August 7, they were met at Quarantine by a tugboat with two dozen chorus girls. George Olsen's orchestra played "The Gang's All Here" as soon as they saw Eddie leaning over the ship's railing. Ethel Shutta then led the chorus in "Eddie (Steady)," and Cantor was met in the lounge of the *Rotterdam* with an elaborate reception, complete with a microphone to broadcast the speeches over radio. There were photographers, plum cake, and pineapple juice—a tongue-in-cheek deference to Prohibition that made little or no difference to the nondrinking Cantor.

Like most good times, it seemed "the norm," an era that would last forever.

Cantor went back into rehearsals two weeks later, and *Kid Boots* began the season with a two-week engagement at Cleveland's Ohio Theatre—really just a warm-up for a long, indefinite run at the Woods Theatre in Chicago. "Eddie Cantor's premiere week was a riot of excitement," wrote the Chicago correspondent for *Variety*. "Sharp figuring predicts that the Cantor show is good for twenty weeks of capacity business."

Cantor's relationship with Ziegfeld was closer than ever, but the telegrams continued unabated. While the show was at the Woods, Flo sent a twelve-page telegram with suggestions about changing certain lines and scenes and cutting songs, along with complaints about actors who were muffing their lines. Eddie, long accustomed to the telegrams and knowing that a response would be helpless, merely wired back: YES.

An even longer telegram came back from Ziegfeld: WHAT DO YOU MEAN YES? DO YOU MEAN YES YOU WILL TAKE OUT THE SONG OR YES YOU WILL PUT IN THE LINES OR YES YOU WILL FIX THAT SCENE OR YES YOU HAVE TALKED TO THOSE ACTORS?

Cantor wired back NO.

What many—including Cantor—did not know was that Ziegfeld had a yearly contract with Western Union that allowed him a million words a year at a fixed rate. Ziegfeld had little respect for money, but he used the million words.

*Kid Boots* was Chicago's highest-grossing show, despite the limited capacity of the Woods Theatre and Ziegfeld's public vilification of ticket "scalpers," which boomeranged and actually hurt sales in November. The weekly gross was usually around $31,500, about a thousand dollars below capacity, with heavy advance sales.

The *Follies* opened at the Illinois Theatre on December 20, followed by Jolson in *Big Boy* at the Apollo on Christmas night. These two shows—and *Kid Boots*—did great business during the week of December 27; Jolson, aided by the Apollo's huge "floor" (bottom-level) capacity, shattered all existing records with a gross of $60,400.

*Kid Boots* had been running in Chicago for three months. Its slip to third place among the city's highest-grossing shows was therefore understandable. Neither Cantor nor Jolson seemed disturbed about what others called a "rivalry." Each knew there was room for both of them at the top of the profession; each appreciated the other's talent. They sometimes supped together after their respective shows.

The two men's similarities were obvious. They were Broadway musical comedy stars, Jewish and dark, comedians, and singers of comedy songs, and both performed in blackface. Both elicited support from audiences, but with different forms of appeal. Jolson was mysterious, a knowing, supernatural being, seemingly above the goings-on (despite a tendency to cow or shed facetious tears) and sharing his own private joke with members of the audience. There was a life-affirming message to Al Jolson's work, a feeling that the human soul was not only magnificent but unassailable and, finally, immortal as well.

Eddie Cantor's appeal was of this world—that of the boy on the threshold of young manhood, the young man making his way who isn't above petty dishonesty to get there. He was the innocent "Peck's Bad Boy" who finally redeems himself from his minor misdeeds, conquers his initial cowardice (or hypochondria), becomes a full-fledged member of the "real" world, gets married, and, presumably, has children. (Cantor's own life as the father of five girls would complement that final phase in the years to follow, as he grew too old to play "the boy" and publicized his real life along the nation's airwaves.)

The two men shared a common enemy—the cold. Jolson, who had a "bad spot" on his left lung, the result of a bout with tuberculosis in his mid-teens, now developed a bad throat infection. Cantor was soon battling pleurisy, a lung ailment similar to the one that had killed his mother more than thirty years before.

Cantor later claimed that Al concealed his own illness, trying to bluff Eddie into closing *Kid Boots* first. According to Ray O'Brien, the pit pianist in Jolson's show, the two stars made a playful bet regarding which one would fold sooner.

There was a minor epidemic in Chicago at the time. Mary Eaton was in the hospital with pneumonia (also diagnosed as pleurisy) by January 7, her role in *Kid Boots* taken by the lesser-known Louise Brown. Jolson and Cantor were both in agony by the third week of the month. Eddie's pain was so bad that he could hardly breathe. "The doctor strapped me with adhesive tape and the show went on. *Kid Boots* was a rough show. I bounced all over the place, and it got to the point where I could barely bounce through a performance. The doctor wanted to drain the fluid, but I wouldn't let him. Ida begged me to close the show."

The vast majority of tickets for performances through the beginning of February had been sold, but Cantor virtually collapsed between acts on Sunday night, January 24, and the show was closed after four months of great business in Chicago.

Jolson bought Cantor a warm jacket for the train ride back home to New York. Arriving in Grand Central Station on Wednesday, Eddie got a copy of The *New York Times* and saw, on page sixteen, the story "Jolson Ill, Closes *Big Boy*." Al had waited for Eddie to close *Kid Boots* and leave town before closing his show. Cantor was the younger star, had been playing in Chicago three months longer, and Al Jolson was . . . Al Jolson, with his well-known ego.

Ziegfeld, wintering in Palm Beach, Florida, invited Cantor down there to recover. Eddie was nursed back to health in time for *Kid Boots* to reopen in Indianapolis on Monday night, February 8.

*Kid Boots* continued on tour for three months, playing major midwest and northeastern cities—St. Louis, Kansas City, Milwaukee, Detroit, and Pittsburgh, where song plugger Harry Akst played Eddie a new song by Irving Berlin, a song that Cantor thought was frankly "awful."

Akst then came back to the William Penn Hotel with Cantor for a quick snack before he caught the late train home to New York City. While there, he played a new song he had written titled "Dinah." Cantor liked the number, arranged for Akst to spend the night, and called Berlin to say that he was using Harry's song in his show instead of Irving's. "Okay, Eddie," Cantor claimed Berlin replied. "If you think the song's that good, we'll publish it."

That, at least, was how Cantor chose to remember it, long after he had assumed Gus Edwards's mantle as the entertainment world's discoverer of talent. In point of fact, Berlin had published "Dinah" six months earlier, along with "Hot Footin' (We're Gonna Have Fun)," another song by Akst with lyrics by Sam Lewis and Joe Young. Akst and Young had placed both numbers in a revue at the New Plantations Club in New York, where the young Ethel Waters scored a notable success. Cantor interpolated "Dinah" into *Kid Boots*, and the song became a part of his permanent repertoire. But he neither introduced the song nor got it published. Nor did he "discover" Harry Akst, a well-known accompanist with a resume of published songs that extended back five years.

Cantor nonetheless made "Dinah" a huge popular success. It was not the typical up-tempo Cantor number but a song Eddie could bounce his way through, waving his hand knowingly on lines like "because my *Dinah* might change her mind about me."

The sheer number of songs Cantor introduced and sang to popularity is astounding, considering the fact that he generally stayed away from ballads. His use of accents, slurring, and phrasing was, in fact, remarkable for someone who was more a comedian than a popular singer. But it was Cantor's attitude that generally sold his numbers. He injected just a hint of joyful naughtiness into the most innocent of numbers. When that tinge of naughtiness was finally extinguished by advancing years that forced him to abandon his "boy virgin" character, a crucial part of Cantor the performer ceased to be.

Cantor's daughters never felt their father was away for any length of time. He kept in touch by telephone or, much more often in these early days, with letters. Scarcely a day passed without his writing one of them a brief letter, laced with humor and gentle admonitions. Eddie's letters to his wife were tender, often filled with funny little poems that expressed his love.

*Kid Boots* closed in Hartford on May 8, 1926. It had been one of the highest-grossing, most successful musicals in history, despite the absence of a hit song in its score (the major reason it has never been revived). Paramount had bought the film rights from Ziegfeld for $75,000, a huge sum for the period, especially since films were silent and *Kid Boots* was a musical, and signed Cantor to play the lead. The picture would be shot during the summer so as not to interfere with Cantor's stage work. Such was the importance of the theatre at the time.

Eddie, Ida, and their four daughters, Margie, now eleven, Natalie, ten, Edna, seven, and Marilyn, four and a half, boarded a train for Los Angeles at Grand Central Station on Tuesday night, June 1. William Morris, Walter J. Kingsley, Trini, Harry Hershfield, Sophie Tucker, and Walter Huston were there to see them off, and Georgie Jessel, who was going to make his first film (*Private Izzy Murphy*) at Warner Bros., traveled with the Cantors, who appreciated his wit around card tables as much as they disdained him as a person.

Jessel, notwithstanding his later reputation as a quoter of gentle poetry and a bastion of sadly laughable patriotism during the Vietnam era, was in many ways a vulgar man. He regularly shocked Ida with his "girlfriends" (quasi-prostitutes), obvious philandering (one would never know Georgie was married), and frequently off-color stories. Ida did not want her daughters to hear any of the latter, no matter how hilarious. The girls, as they grew older, saw more of Jessel's vulgarity and his huge ego and pomposity. He stood in strong contrast to their father.

This first trip to the West Coast was generally not pleasant for the Cantor girls. The train ride was uncomfortable for all of them, especially for

Ida, who had only one nurse to help her deal with four-and-a-half-year-old Marilyn. Ida, true to form, never complained.

Cantor's boyhood friend from the East Side, Ben Schulberg, was now head of production at Paramount. Benny, or B.P., as he was now called, assigned his best director, Frank Tuttle, to *Kid Boots*, the screenplay of which bore scant resemblance to the stage show. Boots was no longer a caddy, no longer a bootlegger, and the character of Polly Potter was now almost a bit role. Golf was not the subject, and even the country club came in as little more than a backdrop in the middle of the film.

Jane Martin, the character that Marie Callahan had played on Broadway, was built into a costarring role. To play it, Benny gave Eddie the hottest star in films, twenty-year-old Clara Bow.

From Clara and Frank Tuttle, Eddie learned that spontaneity onscreen was as essential as rehearsals in the theatre. Silent films, he found, did not require much rehearsal. ("Talkers," when they did arrive, would get on Bow's nerves and drive her into retirement.)

Many thought that Clara taught Eddie things off camera as well. But Clara, not withstanding her voracious sexual appetite, had scruples about married men, and Eddie spent his off-screen hours resting or with Ida and their daughters. Clara planned to marry Gilbert Roland at this juncture but found the time to fool around with Lawrence Gray, who played Tom Sterling.

Work began on June 14. This silent movie, more than any Cantor talkies, still delights today. Cantor's timing, takes, expressions, sense of character, and, above all, pantomime give ample testimony to his skill as one of his profession's most skillful physical comedians. One marvels at the opening scene, where he receives an unflattering caricature of himself captioned "To My Valentine—Don't Look In The Mirror, The Glass May Break" and nods, knowingly, resigned to what he perceives as his mournful fate. One looks on, amazedly, at the scene in which he makes use of a restaurant partition to make Clara think he's with another woman. He bares his left arm, powders it, crooks it back, and carries on a conversation with a presumed woman, who strokes his face aggressively. He chastises her, protests at her flattering, and carries out the story of what might be a year's romance with his own left arm with subtle takes, reactions, and lightning-quick changes of mood and direction that might rival those of Chaplin, Decroux, or Marceau.

*Kid Boots*, whatever one's misgivings about losing a filmed record of McGuire's stage show, was well scripted for the screen and well paced by director Tuttle. Its only major defect is the way it drags when Cantor is offscreen. Happily, those moments are comparatively few.

Eddie stayed in Hollywood with Ida and the girls for two weeks after filming was completed on July 24. Cantor delighted in explaining the "in things" of Hollywood to his four daughters as they went out driving through the sunny land of palm trees. In Hollywood, he said, the stars honked their horns when they saw one another on the road. As if to prove his point, he honked when he saw Greta Garbo passing in her chauffeured limousine. Garbo turned, stared at the Cantors haughtily, and promptly pulled the shade as Eddie looked on in stunned silence. Finally, he turned and resumed driving, totally abashed.

Cantor and his family arrived back in New York on August 18. Plans for a series of personal appearances with the film—really full-fledged vaudeville turns with jokes, songs, and stories—were finalized with Famous Players' New York office by the time Margie, Natalie, and Edna returned to Lincoln School. Cantor, accompanied by George Olsen and his orchestra, opened with the picture on October 9, 1926.

Police had to be called out to keep the crowds lined up outside the Rialto Theatre at the Saturday premiere. Cantor's first live appearance (in a sketch titled "Me, Too") was at 7:00 P.M. to a house completely bought out by the Merchants Trust Company. The second show, at 9:00 P.M., was a benefit for Surprise Lake Camp, and the third, at midnight, was a gala at $5.50 a ticket. Eddie gave four shows a day beginning Sunday.

"I would like to bring out one thing about this four-a-day we have heard so much about," he said. "That is that the total time I'll spend appearing four times daily at the Rialto is less than the actual time I had to be on the stage in the first act of *Kid Boots*."

*Kid Boots*, trimmed from nine reels to six shortly before the premiere, was a success with critics and audiences alike. Mordaunt Hall of The *New York Times* said Cantor screened well and appeared "to be just as much at home before the camera as he is on the stage," a fair statement. Fred Schader of *Variety* said Eddie was a " 'natural' in more ways than one, as far as the screen is concerned. In fact, he has such a sense of natural comedy that those working with him were often broken up and hard put to it as Eddie would improvise a piece of business that was not in the script. As far as pictures are concerned, Eddie need not worry as to his future. He is set if ever a comedian was, and with his first effort." Schader said that the scene in which Cantor makes love to his own powdered arm would "go down in screen history as a classic."

Cantor, scheduled to play four weeks at the Rialto, left abruptly after two at the request of Adolph Zukor and Jesse Lasky, who wanted him to serve as toastmaster at the Paramount convention banquet in French Lick, Indiana. Weekly receipts at the Rialto promptly dove from $23,000 to $17,500, and all plans for more appearances were scuttled.

Cantor had already accepted a $2,000 offer to appear on WEAF radio's *Eveready Hour* on Tuesday night, November 2, for what added up to twenty minutes, telling gags and working in plugs for both *Kid Boots* and his next picture, *Special Delivery*. ("One hundred dollars a minute on radio," quipped Eddie. "Did I tell my gags s-l-o-w.")

Eddie's appearance on the *Eveready Hour* provided a banner headline for *Variety*, marking, as it did, the first time a performer of his stature had appeared throughout a whole one-hour prime-time show. Cantor claimed to have received an incredible twenty thousand requests for autographed photos in the weeks that followed. Far more important was the program's impact on radio, which found that it could no longer afford what Joe Laurie Jr. later called the "small-time approach. . . . Half-baked entertainers who exchanged their services for 'publicity' had to make way for paid talent." NBC, the medium's first network, began regular broadcasts four weeks after Cantor's appearance on *Eveready*, and Socony signed Van & Schenck to a thirteen-week contract for a daily quarter-hour show at two thousand dollars a week. Commercial radio on a major scale had begun.

Eddie left for Hollywood a week after his broadcast, arriving on November 14. *Special Delivery* was his own story, originally called *Love Letters*, about a conscientious, if blundering, mailman in love with a waitress (played by Jo-byna Ralston), who becomes engaged to Harold Jones, a get-rich-quick promoter Eddie finally exposes as a swindler. (A title says that Eddie's ancestors have been in the Postal Secret Service since the day the Scarlet Letter was mailed. The audience, however, gets no clue as to the nature of the "Postal Secret Service," and Eddie seems to spend more time delivering letters than pursuing Harold Jones, played by William Powell.) The picture was directed by "William Goodrich," alias Roscoe (Fatty) Arbuckle, surviving with behind-the-camera jobs since the scandal that had ended his career five years earlier.

On December 23, while at work on the new film, Cantor announced he was quitting the stage in favor of motion pictures "to get better acquainted with his wife and family."

"I don't want my children to get into the habit of saying when I come home, 'Mama, that man's here again,'" Eddie told a reporter from the Associated Press, repeating Margie's own words of a few years earlier. "I must spend more time with my family than the stage permits me; otherwise all I would be living for would be to leave them a lot of money."

Cantor now expected to remain in pictures for at least a year. (Ziegfeld had already leased the rights of *Kid Boots* to George Nicolai and Joseph DeMilt, who opened their own touring version of the show starring Eddie Nelson, a tour that folded after five weeks due to competition from the Cantor film.) Ida brought the girls out from Mount Vernon toward the end of January, and the Cantors were soon esconced in a fourteen-room house in Beverly Hills.

*Special Delivery* seemed jinxed almost from the start. Cantor seemed lethargic, had trouble swallowing food, and held production up for days when Arbuckle could no longer shoot around him. A tonsilectomy—not quite a routine operation at the time—was postponed until shooting was completed. Cantor got through his remaining scenes, but further problems arose before editing began. Paul Kelly, who played one of the detectives in the film, was convicted of killing Ray Raymond, the husband of the stage actress Dorothy Mackaye. Work on *Special Delivery* had already gone over the schedule; refilming was impossible. Kelly's part, accordingly, was all but excised in the cutting room, making *Special Delivery* look more like a flow of gags than the story Cantor had written.

Eddie's next screen vehicle still had not been selected; possibilities included *Service Station*, in which he would play a gas station attendant; a film version of Rodgers and Hart's show *The Girl Friend*; and a story Cantor had been toying with about the valet of a Spanish toreador. Eddie, who planned a vacation from films until early May, returned to New York in time to emcee another all-star benefit for Surprise Lake Camp at the Casino Theatre on March 20. He underwent a tonsillectomy the following Wednesday at the New York Eye and Ear Infirmary, after Nathan S. Jonas, his financial savior, had him reexamined by Jonas's personal physician.

Cantor now regarded Jonas and his wife as foster parents of a kind, seemingly unaware he was their fair-haired boy only so long as he kept bringing in the money and his name was useful for the bank's public relations. Eddie Cantor, to quote several old-timers, was a master at making money in show business. When it came to investing, he was a Jewish *Candide*, a real-life version of the well-meaning innocent he would portray on screen during the next decade.

Cantor spent the next few days after his operation recovering in his suite at the Roosevelt Hotel, with Ida acting as a practical no-nonsense nurse who served him plenty of ice cream and tried to keep him quiet. The latter was a difficult assignment, given Eddie's energy and gregarious personality, plus the fact that everyone on Broadway seemed to telephone or visit him in person. Among them was Flo Ziegfeld, who wanted Cantor for new shows.

Eddie, with his wife, returned to the West Coast in April, stopping off en route for a special engagement in St. Louis. (The children were left in care of the servants in a rented house in Great Neck, the new favorite spot of Broadwayites who wanted their own homes.) No decision had been reached concerning the next Cantor picture, but *The Girl Friend* seemed to be Lasky's first choice; he had paid top dollar for the film rights.

On April 23, several days after the Cantors' arrival in Hollywood, *Special Delivery* was premiered at the Paramount in New York. Reviews were very mixed, some papers saying it put Cantor with the screen's top comics, others, like Sime's son, Sid Silverman, proclaiming that there was "too much Cantor," scoring the film's isolated "gags," and saying Eddie could not handle love scenes. Mordaunt Hall, screen critic for the *New York Times*, called *Special Delivery* "a fractious, windy affair furnished with old and new gags."

Lasky and Schulberg now decided on *The Girl Friend* as Cantor's next picture; Eddie felt the story was not strong enough. *Special Delivery* was doing only mediocre business in New York and Boston, and Paramount chief Adolph Zukor, ever the hard-headed businessman, began to wonder if Eddie Cantor had the makings of a true screen star. Preproduction work on Cantor in *The Girl Friend* nonetheless proceeded, with production scheduled to start on June 2.

The disagreements and uncertainties about his next film caused Cantor, ever nervous about inactivity and lack of work, to have Frank Vincent book him for one-week engagements at the Orpheum theatres in San Francisco and Los Angeles. Eddie sang Irving Berlin's "You've Got to Have 'It' in Hollywood" and presented a series of blackouts featuring Chain & Archer, the veteran song plugger Tubby Garon, twenty-three-year-old Sally Rand, and George Sofranski, a Loew's vaudeville agent since leaving Bedini & Arthur in 1911.

Theatre economics of the time enabled Broadway to compete with Hollywood in bidding for top stars, and Cantor, still unhappy with the script for *The Girl Friend*, was ready to listen when Ziegfeld guaranteed him $4,500 weekly to return to stage work. He was getting "only" $4,000 a week at Paramount.

Zukor and Lasky were amenable, mainly due to the disappointing receipts on *Special Delivery*. Plans for Eddie Cantor in *The Girl Friend* were forgotten, and the Ziegfeld office announced Cantor's return to its fold on May 17, 1927.

## Chapter 7

# *WHOOPEE*

*"Another bride, another June . . ."*

"**S**tardom" has had many different meanings in the ever changing world of entertainment—always, though, connoting some performer of distinction. Prior to the television era, a star was one whose name was billed above the title of a show, play, film, or other vehicle. "*Oh, Joy!* with Harry Smith" meant that Harry Smith was merely "featured."

The *Ziegfeld Follies* was a special case. Ziegfeld guarded jealously the prestige of his annual revue, and no one was accorded even featured billing—except Eddie Cantor, who received it by *starring* in the *Follies* of 1927—in fact if not in name.

What had started as a yearly summer revue had evolved into an opulent, expensive show that generally ran for more than a year on Broadway. Legal action by Abe Erlanger's partner, Marc Klaw, kept the title *Ziegfeld Follies* in litigation in 1926, and that year's *Follies* was produced under aliases ranging from the *Ziegfeld Palm Beach Girl* (in tryouts) to *No Foolin'* (on Broadway). Only when the show had completed its run at the Globe and gone on tour was the title out of litigation and the show properly billed as the Twentieth Annual Edition of the *Ziegfeld Follies*.

So much tradition had been either bent or broken that Ziegfeld had few qualms about according Eddie featured billing in the '27 *Follies*. Ziegfeld would not suffer giving Cantor any more; nor would Eddie accept less.

"The *Ziegfeld Follies* with Eddie Cantor" was a two-and-a-half hour revue with Cantor onstage for more than an hour and three quarters. He was "the Lover" in a scene called "The Star's Double," "Gregory" in "The Trans-Atlantic Flight," and "Eddie" in "It Won't Be Long Now—A Taxi Ride," and he had a solo spot—all in Act One. In Act Two, he was Mayor James J. Walker in "At The City Hall Steps," "The Husband" of Irene Delroy in

"A Ballet Master's Idea of the Spoken Drama," "Eddie" in "The Dog Shop," and himself, Eddie Cantor, in the show's finale.

Cantor wanted to play two weeks of vaudeville at the Albee in Brooklyn and Loew's Hillside in Jamaica before starting rehearsals for the *Follies*. But the Keith-Albee office planned an elaborate exploitation campaign for the Brooklyn appearance, and Ziegfeld thought Cantor's appearing in vaudeville would lessen his commercial effectiveness in the *Follies*, especially since Eddie wanted to try out material earmarked for the show. Cantor was resentful, but he obeyed the Ziegfeld edict.

Cantor and Irving Berlin stayed at the Ritz-Carlton in Boston during tryouts, where Irving wrote "It All Belongs to Me," a song for Eddie that he thought would rival "Ain't She Sweet?" Berlin wrote seven encore choruses before the song was ever introduced. None were ever needed; "It All Belongs to Me" turned out to be the worst song in the score. "You've Got to Have 'It' in Hollywood" went over well before Ziegfeld ordered it cut. The Great Glorifier did not want Broadway audiences thinking about the glamour of Hollywood while they watched his *Follies*.

The show, especially the second act, was in rough shape in Boston. Critics ruffled Ziegfeld's ego by mentioning "the use of first-act costumes over again in the second act" and Cliff Edwards's use of the months-old "Me and My Shadow" in his solo scene. Ziegfeld and his people went to work; the *Follies* that opened in New York on August 16 was a polished, smart production, sensually tasteful in "Glorifying the American Girl" and relying on Eddie Cantor for almost every laugh.

The 1927 *Follies* was large on beauty, taste, production excellence, and talent but short on good sketches and songs. The former, by Harold Atteridge (the long-time Shubert hack who'd written *Make It Snappy*) "and Eddie Cantor," lacked the sharp wit necessary for the times and seemed paltry in the context of the great Ziegfeld production. But if the work of Atteridge and Berlin (then beginning a long drought that would not end until the middle '30s) faltered, that of Ziegfeld, Cantor, and the cast displayed a luminescence equaled in few shows that season. "In this year of its coming of age," wrote Brooks Atkinson, "the *Ziegfeld Follies* merely outdoes itself in extravagance of beauty, grace of movement and style of theatrical producing—'glorifying the American girl,' as the old ballyhoo slogan still insists, by every imaginative device of the hippodromic stage. . . . To see [Cantor] in blackface again, clapping his white hands and strutting breathlessly across the stage, or to see him in his [Jewish] racial vein of selling maladroit dogs to amazed customers, cracking his straw hat in sheer vexation at an unwilling purchaser, is to see the Eddie Cantor who is justly famous."

The closest thing to a hit song was "Shaking the Blues Away," sung by Ruth Etting and what seemed like forty chorines. "Ruthie," thirty, had been married to "Colonel" Moe (The Gimp) Snyder for five years. "The Colonel," a quasi-gangster with good contacts in Chicago, had managed to get Ruth extensive work in the Loop night clubs. Once her career went past the local level, however, Snyder's eccentric behavior and strong-arm, threatening tactics hindered more than helped.

His "baby's" success in the *Follies* made "The Gimp" extremely happy. He went around backstage, sticking his finger in a different actor's back each night and saying "bang." Even the show's dog shop skit, which failed "to warrant the time allotted," was funnier than that.

The scene, in which Eddie tried to palm off a sorry-looking mutt named Morris to prospective buyers as everything from a French poodle to a German shepherd, had Eddie turn to the dog after every failed sale and say, "Morris, we'll get rid of you yet." The line became a staple in the Cantor household for the next ten years, usually denoting any leftovers the cook tried to recreate as a new dish the following night.

By far the best scenes were "The Taxi Cab," with Eddie as a modest boy-man being taken home by an aggressive young woman (played by Frances Upton, one of Broadway's top comediennes), and "City Hall," in which he portrayed New York's playboy mayor, James J. Walker.

Upton, as a "bold, bad lady," flirted with the shy, resistant Cantor until she exclaimed in disgust, "You're the coldest proposition."

"I'm sorry," he indignantly retorted. "I'm sorry we're not the same temperature."

He was finally invited to walk the remaining ten miles—"or else" agree to be mauled with affection.

"I guess I'll 'else,' " he wailed, crawling back into his seat. Frances, of course, played what amounted to a 1920s version of Fania, Eddie's "older woman" girlfriend of the early 1900s. It is interesting to note that Eddie later claimed that Fania, "happily married," always came to see his openings on Broadway. One can only guess at her reaction to "The Taxi Cab." She may not have recognized herself in Frances Upton, but Eddie as the shy "boy-man" was unmistakably the same boy she had known, and introduced to love, some twenty years before.

As Mayor James J. Walker, Eddie posed for photographs and gave keys to the city to visiting sports figures, aviators, and crowned heads of state. As tickets to the *Follies* were often provided for important figures visiting the city, Eddie, as "The Mayor," had occasion to ad-lib greetings to visiting celebrities like Colonel Charles Lindbergh and long-distance swimmer Ruth Elder.

"You will go down in history," he said, presenting Elder with a key to the city, "as the only woman who was ever picked up on the ocean."

New York was the center of the world in the mid-'20s, and Broadway was the center of New York. There was a pride in being a New Yorker at this time, and the musical revue stage served, in part, to celebrate what seems, in retrospect, a modern Pax Romana. If a pseudo-Freudian narcissism (parodied in Cantor's song, "I Love Me") seemed at times to permeate the 1920s, the Broadway stage was in love with itself.

Ida had accepted the move back East with her customary pragmatism. The rented house in Great Neck was still running smoothly, and the girls had adapted to their new school with considerable ease. Their friends were children of such other top stars as the Marx Brothers, making for a total lack of jealousy or resentment.

The house, run as it was by servants, was not Ida's main concern. She was five months pregnant by the time the *Follies* opened. To Eddie, who wanted a large family, and Ida, raised in one, it was another blessing. But the pregnancy was difficult. Ida was now thirty-five and had not given birth in five years.

The eager baby was born two months premature on October 8, 1927. Ida had gone to see "a movie about airplanes [*Wings*]—I think it made me nervous" when she went into labor, calmly left the theatre, and had the Cantor chauffeur drive her to Brooklyn Jewish Hospital. A large tumor had pushed the baby out and then emerged itself, causing a hemorrhage that necessitated nineteen transfusions.

News photographs show Eddie standing over Ida's bed, looking properly astonished for the cameras. He is holding the new baby in his right arm, the fingers of his left raised to commemorate the birth of still another Cantor daughter. Ida is flat on her back, looking up at her husband and her daughter, smiling wearily. She had almost died.

Eddie, a good husband, spent every available moment at Ida's bedside until she returned to Great Neck. The Cantors soon decided to hire a permanent nurse to care for and raise the new baby, named Janet by her sisters.

"I had trained in pediatric nursing after arriving in New York from Ireland in 1925," recalled Winnie Brandley. "The Cantors hired me through a nurses' registry.

"Mr. Cantor was a very pleasant, very funny man. He was in the *Follies* when I first began, and so we saw him in the daytime, as he went to work at night. He always seemed to have time for the children."

Eddie, although not a perfect parent, truly loved his children. "He found it difficult to say good-bye to us when he was going out of town to work or we were going away to school or whatever," recalls Marilyn. "He would shake our hand and stoically say, 'It was nice meeting you. Hope to work on the bill with you again sometime.' The line came from his vaudeville days, when you would say good-bye to an act that had appeared on the same bill with you all week but whom you might not see again for years." Eddie spent as much time with his daughters as he could, given not just the demands of his career but the time he gave to a growing list of causes ranging from actors' unions to Surprise Lake Camp, a list that would only increase as the years rolled on.

Winnie Brandley said, "Mrs. Cantor had done a good job in raising the older girls. They fussed and fought a little over clothes and stuff like that but generally got along fine. When I got there, Margie was twelve. She was very bright. I used to help the other kids with homework after Janet, who was tiny, went to sleep. But Margie never needed any help. She was . . . unique."

Margie, now in puberty, was indeed unique, mature beyond her years and with a frequently baffling sense of obligation to the family. After Ida recovered and began to spend evenings in New York with Eddie, Margie would stay up for hours, checking on her sisters, bending over Janet's crib to see if she was breathing. Not until she heard her parents' car pull in would Margie sink into her bed and fall asleep.

With Ida out of danger and the *Ziegfeld Follies* "frozen," Eddie turned his seemingly inexhaustible energy to other fields. When Fanny Brice opened at the Palace on November 21, 1927, Cantor was on hand to take part in the Duncan Sisters' act on the same bill. On Saturday, December 3, at a luncheon of the Women's City Club at the Hotel Astor, he spoke about the need for playgrounds, pointing out that "playing without playgrounds" led to "yards like Sing Sing" far too often. The next night, he emceed the annual benefit performance for Surprise Lake Camp (now popularly identified as "the Eddie Cantor Camp") at the Ziegfeld Theatre. The all-star bill included Jackie Osterman, the first in a long line of Cantor protegés, a talented young singing comedian who would drink himself right out of a career and, finally, to death.

Cantor, as first vice president of the Jewish Theatrical Guild, addressed a joint meeting with the Catholic Actors' Guild at the Hotel Astor on Friday afternoon, December 16, by observing that those present would offer "a great opportunity for the Ku Klux Klan." Eddie predicted that all denominational guilds would one day unite as one, a thought endorsed by Father Martin Fahey, treasurer of the Catholic Guild.

Ziegfeld, while not frowning on charities, was nonetheless concerned about Cantor's innumerable benefit appearances—and his unreported performances at private parties for fees starting at five hundred dollars—which Ziegfeld feared would injure Eddie's health and place the show's run in jeopardy. Nor were all his fears unfounded. Performances from Thursday night, December 22, through Christmas eve were canceled when Cantor's personal physician, Dr. Alex L. Louria, ordered him to bed with a "mild case of the grippe." Cantor returned the following Monday, and the *Follies* played two more weeks on Broadway before opening a scheduled five-month tour in Boston on January 9, 1928.

The *Follies* grossed more than $70,000 in two weeks at the Colonial, followed by a week in Newark at similar figures. Thirty-five thousand dollars was great business at a top price of $3.30, but the *Follies* still lost money due to its high overhead. Even Ziegfeld, rarely one to value money highly, looked forward to the show's potentially profitable run at the spacious new Erlanger Theatre in Philadelphia.

Cantor's "grippe" of late December now returned with a vengeance. It was, he discovered, pleurisy, the illness that had floored him in Chicago two years earlier and of which he lived in fear. He still thought pleurisy had killed his father, Mechel; in fact, a variant of the disease had killed his mother, Meta.

On Friday, January 27, Eddie came to New York to play the Actors' Fund Benefit, his back strapped to lessen the debilitating pain of the pleurisy. Cantor finished out the *Follies* week in Newark, practically collapsing after the last show.

As the *Follies* cast and crew, complete with five seventy-foot baggage cars, went on to Philadelphia from Newark, Cantor returned to New York, where Dr. Louria described his ailment as "chronic pleurisy" and ordered a complete rest followed by a trip to either Florida or Texas. Cantor and the *Follies* were through for the season.

Eddie stayed in Great Neck for a week. By Saturday, February 4, he had recovered enough to attend a matinee of *The Five O'Clock Girl*, starring Mary Eaton, at the Forty-fourth Street Theatre.

The following Tuesday, as Cantor made plans for a trip to Miami, Ziegfeld filed a formal complaint against his star before the Council of Actors' Equity. Ziegfeld and Abe Erlanger, his backer, were incensed at the show's closing and were convinced Cantor was faking. Reports said Eddie had attended "several" Broadway shows and been seen driving his automobile down Broadway—an action scarcely possible, it was claimed, for someone with pleurisy. At the same time, Cantor had not visited the Ziegfeld office, nor had he communicated personally with the producer.

"Equity," ran Ziegfeld's statement, "called up Mr. Cantor on the phone and was told by a lady who claimed to be his nurse that he was asleep and could not be disturbed. At the same time, however, Mr. Cantor was sitting in the Hermitage Hotel."

Cantor, speaking from Great Neck that evening, denied that he had fabricated or exaggerated his illness. "Certainly I would not throw away $4,500 a week for at least six months just to aggravate Mr. Ziegfeld. The fact of the matter is that this pleuritic condition of mine must be cleared up before I will be able to do any more stage work. If Mr. Ziegfeld desires, I am quite willing to go to his doctor for examination, and if he says I am well enough to work I will return to the *Follies* the next day. As for my being in New York, for the past five days I have gone to town every day to take a treatment from Dr. William Bierman of 471 Park Avenue. Next Saturday, I am going away for a rest to Palm Springs, California, and shall not return till I am well."

Cantor offered further rebuttals to Ziegfeld's charges at a hearing in the Equity offices the following Thursday. After two hours, the meeting adjourned to the office of Dr. Jerome Wagner, Ziegfeld's own physician, who examined Cantor and said he was, indeed, suffering from pleurisy and in need of a protracted rest.

Eddie, vindicated, spent the next six weeks recuperating in Palm Springs with Ida. This was a complete rest, and Eddie passed the time by reading *Mendel Marantz*, a collection of stories about a listless East Side Jewish philosopher by David Freedman.

"What is love?" asked Mendel. "A cigar. The brighter it burns, the quicker it's ashes. What is marriage? The ash tray."

Eddie loved the book and made a mental note to contact Freedman when he returned to New York.

The Cantors arrived back East in April. Eddie was now well enough to accept a six-thousand-dollar filmhouse vaudeville engagement at Fox's Theatre in Philadelphia—until Ziegfeld, holding Eddie strictly to his contract, quashed the deal. Only after checking with his lawyers did Ziegfeld permit Cantor to play a special party for the Schlessinger family in Washington, booked by Billy Grady of the William Morris Agency.

It seemed like 1920 all over again: Ziegfeld versus Cantor. Eddie said that he would exercise a clause and cancel his contract with Ziegfeld if the producer did not secure a starring vehicle for him by the middle of May. Ziegfeld, seemingly unworried by the prospect, termed Cantor a "hypochondriac" who wanted to go back to motion pictures.

Meetings and negotiations followed. Eddie, always sensitive to what he saw as aspersions on his basic honesty, was now a millionaire, able to negotiate with Ziegfeld on a level of equality that he never would have dreamed of ten years earlier. There were, however, weaknesses in his position. He had made enemies of the Shuberts and had worn out his welcome in Hollywood, despite the recent birth of talking films. Cantor needed Ziegfeld almost as much as Zieggy needed him.

On May 2, 1928, the Ziegfeld office announced the "recent break" between Ziegfeld and Cantor had been "completely adjusted," the two men having drawn up a new contract for the two coming seasons. Cantor, the announcement said, had "given heavy bonds to cover the producer from any losses resulting from his dropping out of shows from sickness or any other reason." In turn, it was confirmed, Ziegfeld would star Cantor in a new musical comedy before the end of the year.

William Anthony McGuire's libretto for the new show, a musical version of Owen Davis's play *The Nervous Wreck*, cast Cantor as Henry Williams, a helpless hypochondriac sent out West for his health. Cantor knew that he could play the role after his recent illness. Ziegfeld thought so, too, calling it a case of "one hypochondriac playing another."

The show would be called *Whoopee*.

*Whoopee* started as a story called "The Wreck," written by Edith R. Rath in collaboration with Robert W. Davis, that began serializing in the *Argosy-All Story* Magazine of December 1921. Producers Albert Lewis and Max Gordon had the Pulitzer Prize–winning playwright Owen Davis adapt it for the stage under the title of *The Nervous Wreck* in 1923, and a 1926 film version had (the original) Harrison Ford, Phyllis Haver, and Chester Conklin in the leads.

Cantor was not yet involved in the show's preparations. He spent six weeks that summer in the famed Battle Creek Sanitarium, recuperating from the remnants of his pleurisy, doing what amounted to role research for *Whoopee*, and working on his autobiography, *My Life Is in Your Hands*, with the writer David Freedman.

After meeting him in person, Cantor was as impressed with the thirty-one-year-old Freedman as he had been with Freedman's book, *Mendel Marantz*. The son of Yankel Freedman, an editorialist for the *Jewish Daily Forward*, David had earned a Phi Beta Kappa key at Columbia, where he received both his B.S. and his M.A. degrees. He got a job with the New York *Evening Mail* after leaving college but was not successful as a reporter. He worked as a monitor in an orphan asylum before selling his first "Mendel" story to *Pictorial Review*. More successful "Mendel" stories followed, all of them reprinted in the book that Cantor read.

Freedman was a total extrovert, a Jewish Falstaff whose conversation was profane one moment, erudite the next. "Cantor complained of stomach trouble," Freedman said of their first meeting. "I recommended a tablet, and that sort of cemented our friendship. After that, we compared a lot of ailments we had in common."

*My Life Is in Your Hands*, written in the somewhat tiresome "tongue-in-cheek" style of the 1920s, was serialized by the *Saturday Evening Post* that fall, and brought out in book form by Harper and Brothers the following December. Extensive advertising resulted in huge sales.

Following a brief stay in Chicago, where he accepted agent Johnny Collins's offer of a September engagement at the Granada Theatre, Cantor returned to New York fully recovered—and in time to hear Ziegfeld veto his playing the lead in Paramount's sound movie of the play *Burlesque*. Ziegfeld, however, okayed Cantor's doing short films, and Eddie had Bobbe Arnst, a noted singer-dancer and the future wife of Johnny Weismuller, as his leading lady in "That Party in Person," a one-reeler shot at Paramount's Astoria Studio (where other Broadway stars, including the Four Marx Brothers, would make feature-length film versions of their stage shows in the months to follow).

Cantor returned to the recording studios for the first time in three years when he waxed "Sonny Boy" (from the yet unreleased Al Jolson film *The Singing Fool*) and the politically topical "It Goes Like This (That Funny Melody)" for Victor on September 6. Ten days later, he began his week at the Granada in Chicago.

Cantor used a "plant" (a person "planted" in the audience for a particular bit of business) for this engagement. Backstage before his first performance, Eddie instructed the "plant" to call out "She's Wonderful" when he asked the audience to request any popular song and wiped his face with his pocket handkerchief. At the first performance, Cantor became hot, pulled out his handkerchief and mopped his sweaty brow. The "plant" called out, "She's Wonderful," and Cantor, startled, quickly said, "Not now" and did another five minutes before pausing once again to wipe his forehead. Again, the plant called out, "She's Wonderful."

Eddie laughed this time and finally explained things to the audience. A short time later, Cantor walked off stage, returned to take an encore, asked the audience if there were any songs it wanted, pulled out his handkerchief, wiped his brow again, and waited.

Nothing happened. Cantor wiped his forehead once again; still nothing. Finally, he called out, "Now." Still nothing.

The plant found his way to Cantor's dressing room after the performance. "You're a fine one," Eddie told him. "Hollering at the wrong time, and then when I wanted you to holler, not a whisper."

"Don't holler at me," the plant replied. "The ushers threw me out after the second time."

Ziegfeld was now busy casting *Whoopee* in New York. He had already signed Ethel Shutta to play Eddie's nurse/love interest, Mary Custer; Frances Upton for the ingenue role of Sally Morgan; Ruby Keeler for the role of Harriet Underwood; and Ruth Etting for the singer Lesley Daw. William Anthony McGuire, Walter Donaldson, and Gus Kahn, in the meantime, had gone to a retreat in the Adirondacks to do further work on the score and libretto. Donaldson and Kahn then went to Chicago to complete the songs in company with Cantor. Chicago was Gus Kahn's home, and Eddie spent many happy hours in company with Donaldson (a bachelor at this point), Kahn, and his wife, Grace LeBoy.

"Walter Donaldson told my dad that he didn't like The Gimp," remembers Donald Kahn. "And that he wasn't going to write Ruth Etting a decent song. So he wrote her what he thought was this God-awful thing that went Dada-Da-Dada, Da-Dada, Da-Dada, and my dad wrote a lyric to it." The result, "Love Me or Leave Me," ironically became Ruth Etting's theme song.

Rehearsals started early in October. *Whoopee* was more than simply a vehicle for Eddie Cantor's talents. Based on a hit comedy, it boasted a fine score and was mounted with all the care and lavishness for which Ziegfeld was famous. Flo, in fact, spent hours going through hundreds of hats before he found the ten-gallon stetsons that the Ziegfeld Girls would wear. The sets were by Joseph Urban, whose great scenic work had transformed the *Follies* from a well-produced topical revue and girl show into a work of art in 1915. Seymour Felix did the dances, and George Olsen's band augmented the pit orchestra.

*Whoopee* epitomized what '20s audiences demanded from musical comedy. From the seminude showgirls parading as Indian maidens to the resplendent "Halloween Whoopee Ball," the show was breathtaking, tuneful, and, above all, funny, appeasing all the muses in a complete entertainment. Ziegfeld thought of all finales, then a most important part of any Broadway show, in terms of color. *Whoopee* had a pink and silver finale that even impressed the color-blind Cantor.

The show was still in need of work when it opened at the Nixon Theatre in Pittsburgh on Election Night. Added to the usual headaches was the sudden departure of Ruby Keeler, who left Pittsburgh to join Jolson, her new husband, in Los Angeles. Mary Jane Kittel, an attractive young blonde tapper, was put into Ruby's part, and *Whoopee* moved on to Newark, Washington, and finally, New York, opening at the New Amsterdam on Tuesday night, December 4, 1928.

That the show was a resounding hit is quite beyond dispute. Cantor, Ethel Shutta (a forgotten but truly delightful performer who returned to Broadway in the musical *Follies* in the 1970s), and Ruth Etting (whose three spoken lines drove The Gimp into ecstasies) came in for the critical raves, with Frances Upton and Paul Gregory almost wasted as romantic leads. Ziegfeld's breathtaking production, Urban's sets, and the score— "Makin' Whoopee," "Love Me or Leave Me," "I'm Bringing a Red, Red Rose," "Stetson"—all came together to create what would be the Roaring Twenties' last great show. The Broadway critics offered little except praise but were not oblivious to the production's faults. "It is not, of course, a perfect show," reported Richard Lockridge. "Even with such cutting as has no doubt already been done, it stretches out lengthily through the evening. Now and then its plot, based on Owen Davis' *The Nervous Wreck*, seems a little flat and we are left with the sad spectacle of Indians calling, solemnly and with much hitting of wrong notes, for justice. Now and then the funny lines are not so very funny; a little dismally fell the discovery that the tenor was not part Indian after all. With malice one searches for defects and brings up these. And *Whoopee* rolls over them."

The book of *Whoopee* did not at all times adhere to Davis's play, being studded, like most '20s musicals, with topical humor. "Look at a man like John Raskob," Cantor said in the first act. "There's a man for you who made eight millionaires. Think of it!" One of Eddie's pointed, eye-rolling pauses followed. Then he added sententiously, "That's two more than Peggy Joyce made!" The audience was naturally delighted. They were all New Yorkers, "in the know" about the often-married Peggy Hopkins Joyce. Cantor's line, though doubtless clever and sophisticated, was essentially comparable to a campus comic's "in" jokes about the drug scene, circa 1970.

Another scene had Cantor talking to a westerner who spoke of Pocahontas. "Pocahontas?" queried Eddie. "She saved John Smith's life?" The westerner nodded; Cantor leaned in further.

"Why didn't she do something for his brother Al?"

"Mr. Cantor," wrote Brooks Atkinson, reviewing for the *Times*, has never been so enjoyable a comedian. From the blackface singer of mammy songs, with a strong dash of Al Jolson in his style and an embarrassing devotion to soiled jesting, he has developed in *Whoopee* into a versatile and completely entertaining comic. At the close of the first act he bursts out of a gas stove oven as black as the proverbial ace of spades, and slips into that excited, breathless singing that used to be his stock in trade. It is as good as it ever was.

But Mr. Cantor in whiteface, palming himself off as a chef in a perilous situation or nervously holding up an automobile party with a jumpy revolver or playing Indian in a red union suit, is a comedian of deftness and appealing humor. He is sad; he is preoccupied; he is apprehensive or insinuating with those floating eyes. He opens eggs with a nutcracker and, in the excitement of a competition with another hypochondriac, he measures the lengths of their respective operation scars. Through it all he is better than ever before; and, like Beerbohn Tree's imposing "Hamlet" (if that was it) he is "funny without being vulgar."

*Whoopee* was an "integrated" book show only within limits; Cantor, once in blackface, sang two songs not in the score—"My Blackbirds Are Bluebirds Now" and the topical "Ever Since the Movies Learned to Talk" to smart accompaniment by Olsen. Unlike the smart bootlegger he had played in *Kid Boots*, his character in *Whoopee* stressed the weak side of the Cantor stage persona that would be exploited in the Goldwyn movies of the 1930s. But there was a difference. His films would feature Cantor as a nebishy and rather wishy-washy character. The character Henry Williams was adamant about his lack of health and seemed almost above the rest of the show's action, insulated by the thought of his own certain doom.

People in show business said that *Whoopee* would enjoy an even longer run than *Kid Boots*. Ziegfeld's only source of contention was George Olsen, who allegedly reserved his best song orchestrations for his wife, Ethel Shutta. Olsen and his orchestra left *Whoopee* at the end of January and were replaced by Paul Whiteman's Orchestra. The Rhythm Boys (Harry Barris, Al Rinker, and Bing Crosby) were then in Whiteman's contingent, making it the first and only time that Crosby did a Broadway show.

Ziegfeld's obvious attempt to show up Olsen was completely unsuccessful, however. Whiteman's accompaniment did not suit Cantor, and the larger orchestra cut into the show's profits. Whiteman left *Whoopee* in April, and Ethel Shutta, who had remained in the cast only at Cantor's insistence, left in May to have her second child.

Eddie Cantor had now reached the peak of his career on stage. His investments, under Lipsky's firm control, meant that he was a millionaire a few times over in the Great Bull Market of the late '20s, and a Cantor dream home in Great Neck was finished shortly after *Whoopee* opened.

The house was a true mansion. Having bought ten acres of land for $70,000, and having been told that it was worth $120,000, Eddie was $50,000 ahead on the house. Involved, as always, in a flock of other projects, Eddie left the planning up to others. With tens of thousands rolling in from Wall Street every week, he simply said to "get the best."

"The construction firm," he later claimed, "had never built a house before. They built banks. And like Fort Knox, the Great Neck place was made to last forever."

The house was of English Tudor design, two and one-half stories in height and constructed of brick, hollow tile, and stucco with exposed timbers. The entrance hall was trimmed in oak, paneled to the ceiling, with a dressing room, lavatory, and concealed phone booth. To the left, three steps led down to another small hall from which, through handcarved wooden grilled double doors, was the twenty-five-by-thirty-five-foot living room with an open fireplace. Across the hall from the living room was the twenty-by-sixteen wood-paneled library with another open fireplace. The dining room, twenty-four feet six inches long and nineteen and a half feet wide with walnut walls, had another open fireplace; a cheerful twelve-by-nineteen tiled breakfast room adjoined. The butler's pantry and large kitchen, three bedrooms for the servants, the servants' dining room, and bath made up the rest of the first floor.

The second floor contained two master bedrooms, each with its own bathroom, five guest bedrooms, two additional bathrooms, and a bedroom for the upstairs maid. The third floor was a large open attic with a spacious finished cedar room, while the basement had a large recreation or ball room, measuring twenty-three by twenty-four feet and complete with buffet bar with hot and cold water, a refrigerator, and a tiled lavatory. There were also a large room planned as a theatre, a completely equipped laundry, and several storerooms. The two-story garage had its own gasoline pump, held five to eight cars, and had two three-room apartments and a bathroom.

Thirty years later, Cantor recalled the "special doorknobs. . . . Our rugs were Aubusson—woven in France to fit our rooms. The main staircase was lit by stained-glass masks of comedy and tragedy. Handcrafted, of course, and as eerie—and expensive—as anything you've ever seen." It was, to say the least, baronial—a world removed from the basement Eddie had shared with his grandmother (and several young girls) a quarter of a century before.

That spring, on a Tuesday, Cantor and Ziegfeld were on adjoining tables in a health club, getting rubdowns. Ziegfeld told Cantor he had "everything"—a family, money, success, fame. . . . The list went on till Eddie interrupted, saying he did not have everything. He still did not have a Rolls-Royce like the ones he had seen the millionaires drive up in when they came to see the *Midnight Frolic* in 1916.

Ziegfeld dropped into Cantor's dressing room and suggested they have dinner at Dinty Moore's the following Saturday. On Forty-sixth Street sat a brand-new Rolls-Royce gray convertible with an orchid tied to the handle and a card from Ziegfeld.

"Dear Eddie. Now you have everything. Flo."

"Everything" included a valet named Eddie Frauchiger. Known as "Frenchy," he was actually Swiss, a diminutive, fun-loving player of practical jokes who kept Cantor feeling good in mind and body. Frenchy, scarcely more than five feet tall, would remain a fixture of Cantor's home and career for more than ten years, a friend to Eddie's children and, in time, his personal assistant.

Irving Cahn, a young reporter, sometimes spoke backstage with Cantor. "We chatted a number of times, and when he wasn't looking at one of the pretty girls passing by, he would concentrate on the conversation.

"He was a comedian onstage beyond delight. Offstage, he was a rather dreary fellow—quite serious, not the least bit funny."

Cahn was not the only one who felt that Cantor was not basically a happy man. Cantor's memories of his abject boyhood poverty were no doubt strong, but even they do not begin to explain Eddie's no-nonsense, often dour attitude toward stagework or his sometimes joyless backstage manner.

Clearly, Eddie felt something was missing in his life. He was now independently wealthy and had been one of the country's biggest stars for more than five years. At the age of thirty-seven, there seemed nothing more to prove, despite the advent of sound pictures. Eddie had, as yet, shown no great interest in the "talkers." Nor had Hollywood evinced strong interest in Cantor for the last two years, despite his obvious value for film musicals.

The season of 1927–28 was the most successful year in Broadway history, with scores of openings and new highs in receipts. With more than fifty theatres, activity along what was then called the "Main Stem" reached an all-time high.

The season of 1928–29 was another story. Many houses were dark on Labor Day, and panic spread through Broadway by Thanksgiving. More than twenty-five shows "laid off" the week prior to Christmas, and hit shows became rarities.

No one knew the reason for the panic, but hindsight points to the more general and widespread panic that would hit Wall Street the following October. Changing economic conditions become obvious in the theatre before anywhere else. From 1924 to 1928, Broadway grew too large for its comparatively limited audience, both in ticket prices and in the sheer volume of shows.

*Whoopee* was the great exception to the Broadway panic, grossing at or close to $50,000 a week from the time it opened on December 4. (Other exceptions were the Four Marx Brothers in *Animal Crackers* and Bert Lahr in *Hold Everything*.) No one knew that it would be Flo Ziegfeld's last big original hit production and one of Broadway's last big hit shows of the '20s.

If Wall Street was to crash within a year and destroy the world of Zieg-feld, no one knew it. On December 29, 1928, the New Amsterdam Roof Theatre, closed since the advent of Prohibition, reopened with a midnight club show featuring Eddie Cantor as master of ceremonies. The operation was short-lived, but it reflected the unchallenged position of not only Zieg-feld (whom a host of smash hit musicals had reestablished as the king of Broadway glamour in the preceding two years) but New York as the center of the world. To Eddie Cantor, hundreds of other Wall Street investors, thousands of well-to-do Americans, and millions of comparatively well-off people in the nation's middle class, prosperity had become "normal." There was no reason to suspect it would not always be so.

Cantor, his fortune guarded by Nathan S. Jonas, Dan Lipsky, and the briefcased army of Manufacturers Trust, was sitting so far on top of the world it seemed no harm could reach him. On Sunday night, March 10, 1929, the Jewish Theatrical Guild honored him with a testimonial dinner at New York's Hotel Commodore. Nearly twenty-five hundred people were reported to have attended, with the veteran actor William Collier serving as toastmaster and a dais that included Mayor James J. Walker, Police Commissioner Grover Whalen, the opera impresario Otto H. Kahn, Paul Whiteman, George Jessel, the former boxing champion James J. Corbett, Leon Errol, and William Fox. Walker was the keynote speaker.

"I see in Eddie Cantor something more than mere laughs," declared the mayor. "It is a long way from Market Street to the New Amsterdam Theatre and his name in lights, not in blocks or miles but in the struggle of life. As one who shares New York as a birthplace with him, and one to whom 'The Sidewalks of New York' is not a song but a hymn, I wish to state this is a joyous occasion, in honor of one of ours who has made the grade with glory to himself and all associated with him. Eddie Cantor is one who has brought a world of distinction to New York."

Eddie sang his response to the speeches with a special version of "Ma-kin' Whoopee," and the night concluded with entertainment courtesy of Errol, Jessel, and others.

Cantor had indeed come a long way—Horatio Alger with a Jewish coun-tenance set against a background of show business. The realization of his independent status—especially the fact that he made $140,000 on Wall Street in a single afternoon in early May—prompted an announcement in his dressing room on May 8, 1929.

Cantor, simply and sincerely, announced his retirement from the stage effective at the end of the 1929–30 season, when his Ziegfeld contract would expire. "I love the theatre," Eddie said, "and now that I am a mil-lionaire, why should I tie myself down to time schedules and be prevented from following my own inclinations? For instance, I haven't yet seen one of my daughters—I have five—graduate from school.

"I'm interested in philanthropic work and intend to devote much of my time to it. In the event that I should feel the urge to appear on the stage after my retirement, I can easily do so at benefits. Obligations to my manager have often prevented me from going away to take a much needed rest."

What Eddie did not mention was that Paramount now wanted him to remake *Kid Boots*—with sound, the original plot, and some of the songs from Ziegfeld's stage show.

Ziegfeld killed the *Kid Boots* deal a month later. He had soured on Paramount after two years of preparations for *Glorifying the American Girl*, the delays chiefly due to the advent of sound. The picture, which starred Mary Eaton, would go before the cameras at Paramount's Astoria, Long Island, studios that spring, with disappointing results. (One interpolated scene, supposedly a *Follies* sketch, showed Eddie and Lew Hearn in their sketch "Belt in the Back" from the Shubert *Midnight Rounders*.) Ziegfeld also had a deal pending with Sam Goldwyn for sound picture rights to *Whoopee*, with a possible option on *Kid Boots* as well.

Cantor, for his part, was also branching out, moving beyond the unwritten bounds for actors, not to mention testing Ziegfeld's patience and his contract.

The *Follies'* chief rival, since 1912, had been Jake Shubert's annual *Passing Show* at the Winter Garden, a revue strong on comedy (thanks to the comic Willie Howard) but weak on overall production values. Since the end of the war, two more major rivals had appeared: the former dancer George White's *Scandals* and Earl Carroll's *Vanities*, the latter with an emphasis on nudity.

On Friday, May 17, the Carroll office announced that Cantor would write the book for the next Carroll revue. David Freedman was available and eager for more money. Being Cantor's "ghost" on *Earl Carroll's Sketch Book*, as the new show would be called, would give him his first taste of writing successfully for performance.

It was, indeed, a new experience for Freedman—and an education. Under Cantor's tutelage, he wrote or rewrote scores of jokes and comic situations, some of them adopted from old burlesque scenes and other sources. The best scene in the *Sketch Book* involved Patsy Kelly, in a bathtub, Will Mahoney as her husband, and William Demarest as a plumber who walks right into the bathroom.

MAHONEY:   Hey, my wife's taking a bath.

DEMAREST:   I took my hat off.

The *Sketch Book* was a big hit when it opened on July 1, 1929, playing four hundred consecutive performances on Broadway—the longest run of any Carroll show.

Cantor, starring in *Whoopee* and still under contract to Ziegfeld, certainly could not appear in *Earl Carroll's Sketch Book*. In lieu of an appearance, a sound film was produced depicting Cantor and Carroll in the latter's office, Cantor showing Carroll the platinum watch he had received from Ziegfeld. Carroll thereupon proceeds to "top" Ziegfeld in the size of his offering by giving Cantor a grandfather clock.

*Earl Carroll's Sketch Book* began David Freedman's career as a comedy writer. Weeks after it opened, he received requests for vaudeville acts, jokes, and other special material from the top names in the business— Fanny Brice, Lou Holtz, the rising Jack Benny, and others.

Freedman's work increased until he had to hire others to help him meet the demand. The first job he gave to his staff was to expand the gag file begun under Cantor. In time, it would contain aproximately 150,000 cards from which old jokes could be taken and supplied with a new twist.

But it was with Cantor that his loyalty remained. If Eddie needed new gags to punch up a speech, Dave had ones for the occasion, or he wrote them. If the scripts in Paramount short subjects—Cantor did two more of them that season—needed editing, then David Freedman did it. In short, he became Cantor's right-hand man—the hand with the pen. It was common knowledge in show business, and the two men were sometimes called the Damon and Pythias of Broadway.

The day the *Sketch Book* opened, Eddie was elected president of the National Vaudeville Artists, succeeding Fred Stone, at the N.V.A. Clubhouse at 229 West Forty-Ninth Street. Others would have viewed the office simply as an honor. Cantor took it seriously and made a special trip to Saranac Lake for the opening of the new N.V.A. Sanitarium when *Whoopee* closed for three weeks during the heat of July. Eddie also agreed to serve as chairman of the theatrical panel of the American Arbitration Association.

Cantor's philanthropic work, his acceptance of high offices in various professional and philanthropic bodies, and his general involvement in both politics and "causes" was unprecedented among actors. Will Rogers, who poked gentle fun at politicians and seemingly represented the "common" man, raised no more money for good causes than did many other stars; he never was involved in actors' union politics and never campaigned, hard and openly, for any political candidate. Cantor did, and his activities along these lines would increase in the years to come.

Performances of *Whoopee* resumed on August 5. Six weeks later, on Sunday afternoon, September 15, Cantor unfurled the N.V.A. flag at Saranac, officially dedicating the new sanitarium to "members of our profession."

"I hope," he said, "the time will come when this place will be empty with an electric sign advertising chicken and hot waffles for one dollar. We have evolved a scheme whereby a day's receipts from all vaudeville and picture theatres will be donated to this institution.

"Our members will have on their membership cards addresses of physicians in New York, Chicago, and on the Coast so that they may avail themselves of expert medical advice. And in this way we hope to combat the inroads of tuberculosis. Nowadays, to go Shakespeare one better, it is not 'the play's the thing.' It is the player is the thing; and he is the backbone of the theatre.

"May God look down on these handicapped people and bring them a speedy recovery."

His various activities on behalf of the N.V.A., the Jewish Theatrical Guild, Surprise Lake Camp, and other bodies inevitably took their toll, and Eddie came down with a bad sore throat the last week in September. On Friday, September 27, accompanied by Benny Holtzman, the public relations man for *Whoopee*, he left for Fallsburgh, New York, to recuperate, leaving his understudy, Buddy Doyle, to play Henry Williams. Cantor, still a young man, could and did recover very quickly; he was back in *Whoopee* Monday night.

Events, ideas, and projects continued at the same hectic pace. (Cantor submitted an idea for a straight play to the producer Arthur Hopkins, a play he hoped to develop in collaboration with Arthur Richman until Hopkins said he was not interested.)

Margie was now fourteen and a half—smart, efficient, and devoted to her father. Increasingly, she acted as his secretary, typing letters to composers who wanted him to introduce their songs, actors who were looking for jobs, and the hosts of others who wrote to Eddie Cantor, the great star. He once took Margie to Atlantic City after a Saturday night performance of *Whoopee*. They spent all day Sunday there and lunched together in the hotel dining room before returning to New York in time for the Monday night performance. Margie wanted to have the chocolate cream pot for dessert but balked because it cost a dollar, and Eddie could not tempt her.

They left the dining room, walked down the boardwalk, and stopped at a brokerage house, where Eddie was able to inform his daughter that they had earned fifty thousand dollars in the market during lunch. Margie stopped, led her father back to the dining room, and ordered dessert.

The clouds had not yet darkened.

The six-month period from March 3 to September 3, 1929, was the "Great Bull Market." The aggregate value of stocks more than doubled in that period, and Eddie Cantor, star of *Whoopee*, father of five daughters, and one of the most most visible, best-loved stars in the nation, was worth more than five million dollars—the equivalent of almost one hundred million dollars in the 1990s—by Labor Day.

The economist Roger Babson launched the so-called Babson Break on Thursday, September 5. "Sooner or later," he told the National Business Conference, "a crash is coming, and it may be terrific." Seven weeks later, on October 24 (the infamous "Black Thursday"), the stock market crashed. Thirteen million shares were sold, as brokers frantically called clients to cover their margins to avoid losing their investments. The lucky ones were never contacted—meaning that they kept any money they did not have in the market. Others saw their fortunes disappear.

The market closed four hours late.

Cantor, who had lost hundreds of thousands in the market since early September, saw his losses go into the millions on October 24. Every night, as Ida met him at the stage door in their chauffeur-driven car, he had another grim report.

Eddie Cantor valued security more than perhaps any performer—Groucho Marx excepted—in the history of American show business. On the surface, he took the loss of his hard-earned fortune very well. Inside, he was devastated. More than fifteen years of work—his life—seemed suddenly wasted. He was back—on paper—to the poverty he had known as a child.

It was during these moments of crisis that Cantor proved his mettle. Emotionally tough, still a major star, with the support of his wife and their daughters, Eddie was able to use his new-found paper poverty as a source of material. On Friday night, he made a curtain speech at the New Amsterdam.

Well folks, they got me in the market just as they got everybody else. In fact, they're not calling it the stock market any longer. It's called the *stuck* market. Everyone is stuck. Well, except my uncle. He got a good break. He died in September. Poor fellow had diabetes at forty-five. That's nothing. I had Chrysler at a hundred and ten.

With the way the market has been running, many a man goes down to business in a Rolls-Royce and comes home in a Mack truck. If the market takes another slump, I know thousands and thousands of married men who will have to leave their sweethearts and go back to their wives. Everyone is singing the "Margin Song" from Wall Street: "Sucker come back to me."

Of course, if you can dig up the margin, you're all right. If not, brother, you're *gone*. Nowadays, when a man walks into a hotel and requests a room on the nineteenth floor, the clerk asks him: "For sleeping or jumping?"

I met one chap in the lobby of a hotel the other day, and he looked quite sleepy. And so I asked him. I said, "Why are your eyes half-shut?" He answered, "Eddie, I had to give up my room at 4:30 this morning. I had it on margin."

You know a lot of brokers down on Wall Street have devised a wonderful scheme. With each five shares of stock, they hand you a loaded gun. They don't tell you what to do with it, but you can use your own judgment.

Before I quit talking, I want to give you one sure tip on the market. Go out tomorrow and buy National Casket. You can't go wrong.

And by the way, have you noticed that the market is reflected even in the way women are dressing? Have you noticed how their skirts have dropped?

Personally, I shouldn't worry about my stocks. I know my broker is going to carry me. Yes, sir. He and three other pallbearers.

Eddie recorded this monologue for Victor the following Tuesday afternoon. As he spoke into the microphone, the market plummeted again. Near midnight, Eddie stepped into his waiting car and told his wife that they were, indeed, broke; not one cent remained of the five million dollars they had had eight weeks before.

Cantor pulled some sixty dollars from his pocket—all the money, at that moment, he had left. A minute later, Ida pressed something into his hand. It was a bracelet, a "trifle" Eddie had given her for her birthday five and a half months earlier.

"Poonelo, see what you can do with this," she said.

He and Ida talked for the remainder of the night. Two immediate courses of action were available: to sell the mansion, get rid of the help, and stop spending, or to go along as if nothing had happened. Eddie was still earning $4,500 a week in Whoopee.

"It'll do something to your personality to cut down. After all, you've only lost money. You still have your sense of humor. That's the one thing you didn't have on margin."

Eddie thought of ways to earn more money. Three nights later, as he lay awake in the small hours of the morning, he thought of a "gag" book about Wall Street and the market—really an expansion on the "curtain speech." Without hesitation, he woke Margie and began to dictate. Within a week, the book was finished. Eddie called it Caught Short: A Saga of Wailing Wall Street.

The book, like his monologue, was a tongue-in-cheek commentary on the Wall Street tragedy, allowing untold numbers of fellow sufferers, few of whom had Cantor's earning capacity, seemingly to commiserate with Eddie and to laugh at themselves. Simon and Schuster published it and sold one hundred thousand copies the first week. Sales soon reached half a million.

His grandmother had kept him from starvation as a boy. His wife, the "other woman" in his life, now kept Eddie from fear.

Both women, each in her own way, saved Eddie Cantor's life.

*Chapter 8*

# EYES ON THE MEDIUM

*"I hope you like* Palmy Days, *but it wasn't made for you.*
*It was made for the masses."*
—Eddie Cantor

ddie Cantor was not merely broke on October 31, 1929; he *owed* Manufacturers Hanover Trust $285,000—close to ten million dollars in the money of the mid-1990s. On paper, Cantor was in worse financial shape than he had been when living with his grandmother in the backyard house on Market Street.

The sudden loss of his wealth did not shake Cantor's faith in the American dream as it shook that of others in the theatre. He was still a young man, and the continued sight of his name in lights at the New Amsterdam served as nightly balm for the loss of his considerable fortune. Cantor's courage, born of his hard background on the Lower East Side sidewalks, always surfaced strongly in a crisis. It was "business as usual," and no one, save for Ida, saw him looking worried in the weeks after the crash.

He continued speaking out on actors' issues. The Broadway crisis of 1928–29 had caused managers and playwrights to explore the possibility of Sunday night performances. Cantor spoke at an Equity meeting called to vote on the proposal at the Hotel Astor on Monday afternoon, November 18.

"They say that there is a disease in the theatre; I claim it is a cancer. To cure cancer, the medical profession uses radium, and if Sunday night performances are permitted, it is comparable to alleviating the disease by treating it with dope. That won't cure it." The proposal was defeated by a ratio of three to one.

He soon went back to playing private parties. Even Ziegfeld offered no objections now, and Cantor earned five thousand dollars for singing all the

choruses of "Whoopee" at a cocktail party for guests of automobile magnate
Walter Chrysler. Eddie needed every cent.

*Whoopee* closed on Broadway on November 23, 1929, four weeks and two
days after "Black Thursday." Samuel Goldwyn had already bought the
movie rights from Ziegfeld, and plans now called for Cantor to tour in the
show through March 15. Goldwyn, and not Ziegfeld, was now firmly in
command.

Cantor, fearful and resentful, began bombarding Goldwyn with demands
in much the same way he had pestered J. J. Shubert nine years earlier.
BELIEVE IT BEST FOR SUCCESS OF PICTURE THAT I HAVE A HAND IN WRITING
OF SCRIPT, he wired from Chicago, where *Whoopee* had begun a six-week
run. Goldwyn calmly sent his writers, who had yet to put a word on paper,
out to visit Cantor. They listened to his numerous suggestions and answered every question with the key word "motivation." Every song or dance
or sequence, as they saw it—anticipating Rodgers and Hammerstein by
thirteen years—had to grow organically from the show's plot and characters. That, of course, was not how *Whoopee* was created.

Cantor also insisted that Goldwyn hire Busby Berkeley, choreographer
for *Earl Carroll's Vanities*, as the picture's dance director. Checking up on
Berkeley, Goldwyn learned he had a drinking problem. Nonetheless, he
soon gave in to Cantor's wishes. Berkeley was hired, beginning a career
that would revolutionize the American film musical.

Berkeley, William Counselman, the chief scenarist for Goldwyn, and
Thornton Freeland, who would direct the film *Whoopee*, met with Cantor when the show played Cleveland, the last stop on its tour. Cantor
and Berkeley went to Child's after the final performance, and "Bus"
sketched designs for the dance numbers on the backs of menus. The next
day, he entrained for Hollywood with Counselman and Freeland. Cantor
returned to New York and spent the next two weeks in conferences with
Ziegfeld.

Eddie still had one short left to make for Paramount, and he took care
of it on Friday, March 21. Arriving on the Astoria sound stage at 11:30
A.M., he did three takes of the short film (called *Insurance*) and sat down
for luncheon in the studio cafeteria at 1:30.

Cantor left for Hollywood the following Wednesday, a week ahead of
Ida, Winnie Brandley, and the girls. "We stayed at the Beverly Hills Hotel,"
remembered Winnie. "The older girls all loved it." Eight-and-a-half-year-
old Marilyn was a different story; she hated Hollywood from the start, despite the warmer climate's beneficent effect on her sinuses. Janet, who
would later dislike Hollywood intensely, was too young to care.

Eddie had little time to spend with his family on this trip. The film
version of *Whoopee* was scheduled to shoot and wrap in thirty-six days.
Indoor sequences were shot first, in Hollywood, with the outdoor scenes

filmed later, in Palm Springs. The principal Broadway cast of *Whoopee* was used for the movie version, with one notable exception: Frances Upton, who failed to pass Goldwyn's screen test.* Eleanor Hunt was jumped up from the chorus to play Sally Morgan.

The cast rose at 4:30 on the desert to start work at six. "This was June," remembered Cantor, "and by eleven A.M. you were falling down with the heat." Director Freeland had a crew "planting" poppies in the desert at five o'clock in the morning. As Eddie came onto the set, Eleanor came rushing up with a hundred poppies she had picked for him, her "leading man." Freeland almost died.

*Whoopee* is not so much a movie as a filmed stage show. Unlike similar such efforts, there is not even the pretense of an "adaptation" to the screen, only a judicious pruning of some dialogue and most of the Kahn-Donaldson stage score. There is the distinct feeling of being on a sound stage— *Whoopee* almost seems to be on tape rather than film—and the primitive two-color technicolor is so effective that one can practically see blue, a color that this process was unable to produce.

Busby Berkeley more than vindicated Cantor's choice of him as dance director. While his production numbers are not the isolated worlds within themselves that they would be in his coming days at Warners, Berkeley's imaginative use of the sound camera includes overheads (first seen in *The Cocoanuts*) and—a Berkeley original—the spotlighting of each individual beauty in his chorus (including Betty Grable) in a fast-paced series of charming head shots.

Cantor's performance is delightful, his timing perfect, and his rendition of a new song, "My Baby Just Cares for Me," provides some of the most inspiring, spontaneous moments in the history of film. Rivaling him is Ethel Shutta, whose comedy and singing of the rousing "Stetson" number make one wonder why she made no other pictures. Shutta would return to Broadway forty years later, introducing the song "Broadway Baby" in the Stephen Sondheim musical *Follies*.

Goldwyn, notwithstanding, was aghast at the dailies. The scenes and jokes that seemed so funny when he saw the show onstage now seemed corny and flat. His star remonstrated. "How can it be funny here with three of us sitting in a room? In a theatre, it plays to an audience of hundreds, and they *laugh*." Cantor's answer pacified Sam Goldwyn, but it only hints at the main problem. Like the material of standup comics, which is crafted toward small rooms, large rooms, television, or convention centers, the jokes and bits that made up '20s musicals were conceived in terms of a particular size audience. *Whoopee*, as Cantor predicted, would prove funny

---

*Upton played the Palace a year later. Following a featured role in *Hold Your Horses* at the Winter Garden (1933), she married future NFL commissioner Bert Bell and retired. Upton died in 1975.

and play well before large audiences in motion picture theatres. The same holds true for the film now. Audiences at the Museum of Modern Art howled at its comedy—both topical and otherwise—and cheered at the film's ending in the '70s. On small-screen television, played before an audience of ten or fewer people, the jokes and gags seem leaden and banal. (One becomes aware of pauses after lines and bits, as actors wait for laughs unlikely to come from audiences of two or three people watching TV in a living room.) All of Eddie Cantor's movies suffer on television; *Whoopee* simply dies.

The picture was completed by late June, only seven days behind schedule, and previewed in San Diego in July. Ziegfeld, virtually ignored during the filming, accompanied Cantor to the theatre, saying Hollywood was not the place for Eddie and urging him to return to Broadway. "Wait till we see the picture, Flo. If I squeeze your hand, we'll talk about another show." There was no squeeze; the film was good.

Cantor's personal contract with Goldwyn, calling for one more picture if the first one proved successful, was replaced on July 19 by a new three-film contract. Eddie had now cast his bread on the Pacific Ocean.

The Cantors left for New York three days later. Eddie fulfilled vaudeville engagements in Atlantic City (where burglars stole $20,000 worth of jewelry from Ida's bureau drawer) and Cleveland prior to the premiere of *Whoopee* at the Rivoli in New York on September 30—a major event for both the stage and the motion picture industries. *Whoopee* had been one of the biggest hit musicals in Broadway annals, and Eddie Cantor was one of the country's major stars. But the public, fed a steady diet of ineptly made film musicals, had tired of the genre. Were *Whoopee*—and Cantor—good enough to swim against the tide? "It's like standing trial," Cantor told the *New York Times*. "I've been good, the judge is nice—but how do I know what's going to happen?"

In point of fact, he was quite confident—a confidence borne out by the acclaims of colleagues and reviewers. *Whoopee*, trimmed of just three segments since the San Diego preview, was a greatly entertaining picture that echoed the exciting spirit of the Broadway show.

Mordaunt Hall in the *New York Times*:

So excellent is the fun furnished by Eddie Cantor in the Ziegfeld-Goldwyn technicolor screen adaptation of *Whoopee*, presented last night at the Rivoli before a smart audience, that those who had been compelled to fight their way through the throng on entering the theatre soon forgot their annoying experiences once the picture was under way. In this production, Mr. Cantor's clowning transcends even Mr. Ziegfeld's shining beauties, the clever direction and the tuneful melodies. And this is saying a great deal, for there is much for the eyes to feast on in the various scenes.

Eddie entertained for fifteen minutes at the premiere, following his cinematic self onstage with talk, gags, and a new song titled "Roll, Roll, Rolling Alone."

The Goldwyn contract, calling, as it did, for one picture a year, meant that Cantor could still star in Broadway shows. Two producers besides Ziegfeld made him offers, and one persistent rumor had him signed to star in *Mr. Cinders*, an English musical comedy, for Max Gordon.

Cantor was not interested. Living, as he was, on money from Sam Goldwyn, he realized he could make more in six weeks on a picture than in one year giving eight performances a week on Broadway—"important," he admitted, "to a guy who'd lost his shirt."

Broadway, though not dead, was in decline. The "Big Boom" years of the mid-'20s were over, and many Broadway actors were now trying to crash Hollywood. Cantor, though still paper poor, was in the most enviable position in the entertainment business—in demand as a star of the stage and of talking films.

His faith—in himself, in show business, in America, and God—had seemingly been vindicated. He had done everything "right." He also knew that many others had not fared as well.

Eddie and Ida left for Hollywood soon after the premiere of *Whoopee*. Their four older daughters were now attending school in Beverly Hills, and Cantor had no further business in New York just then. There were, moreover, meetings to attend regarding his next film for Goldwyn.

Eddie, still remembering the bullfight he had seen in Barcelona, wanted to play a matador; Goldwyn favored a less exotic setting. Producer and star were still discussing what to do when they, together with their wives, entrained for New York in November. Cantor had signed to do six weeks in RKO filmhouses at $7,500 a week.

Opening in Cleveland on December 6, he played two weeks at New York's Palace after Christmas, closing a strong bill that included, among others, Burns and Allen, dancer Joe Frisco, and the popular recording artist Marion Harris. Eddie was onstage for thirty-eight minutes, energetically singing "Ida, Sweet as Apple Cider" to his wife, in a box seat, in the finale.

It was the first time he'd sung "Ida" publicly since 1912. From this point on, the song would be identified with Eddie and his wife. References to Ida and their daughters now became, increasingly, a part of Cantor's act, just as the private Eddie, still crippled by the market crash and a return, on paper, to the poverty of his childhood, reached out to his wife and eldest daughter for support. Five daughters not only gave him great material; they made him seem more human—a family man. Not fathering a boy gave him the "common touch"—a seeming "failure" and frustration all of his success could neither help nor lessen.

Despite the reference to Janet's birth in the song "My Blue Heaven" four years earlier, this engagement at the Palace marked the start of the new Cantor image. Ida and the daughters would loom large as time wore on.

It was extremely cold that winter (1930–31), and Eddie was only too glad to accept a two-week engagement at the Floridian in Miami. Rudy Vallee, who was present at the opening, invited Cantor to appear on his radio show, *The Fleischmann Hour*, being broadcast from Miami via hookup.

*The Fleischmann Hour* was radio's first big musical-variety show hosted weekly by the same star—Vallee, a crooner who had never been on Broadway but whose famed opening line, "Hi-Ho, everybody," perfect "Yale" English, and singing (accompanied by his Connecticut Yankees) had made him a top star via the airwaves.

Cantor, on the Vallee program, was heard by more people than had seen him work onstage in twenty years. And Eddie, who had failed to impress on his last radio appearance two years earlier, came across quite well on Vallee's program. Mort Milman of the NBC Artists' Bureau made a mental note.

Eddie and Ida arrived back in Hollywood on Sunday night, February 15, 1931. *Palmy Days* was now the title of the Cantor vehicle Guy Bolton was preparing. The locale was a bakery, with the comedienne Charlotte Greenwood cast opposite Eddie as a physical culturist and the gorgeous "Goldwyn Girls" as bakers. Sam Goldwyn was now determined to become the Ziegfeld of Hollywood.

Cantor spent the next month attending story conferences, attempting to punch up the script with gags. The vogue for screen musicals had definitely passed, and *Palmy Days* was conceived as a comedy with songs—"Bend Down, Sister," sung by Greenwood, and "My Baby Said 'Yes,' " by Cantor. The romantic leads came in for scant attention.

Production dragged on to July. Previews of the film did not meet Goldwyn's expectations, and Mervyn LeRoy was called in to direct retakes and an added sequence in which Cantor sang "There's Nothing Too Good for My Baby" in blackface at a night club built into the bakery. The adding of another song scarcely made the film into a musical. Nor did the story build with the imagination necessary for a great screen comedy. And where Cantor as Henry Williams in *Whoopee* seemed strong and independent despite his hypochondria, the films for Goldwyn would now feature Eddie as a rather nebbishy character seeking to gain strength from the encouragements of ingenues, strong male romantic leads, and finally, in *Strike Me Pink*, a book.

With work on *Palmy Days* completed, Cantor turned his attention to other parts of show business. Mort Milman had recommended him to the J. Walter Thompson Agency, which wanted a big "name" star for the *Chase and Sanborn Hour*. Cantor signed to do seven weekly shows at two thousand dollars each. He was branching out, driven not only by his restless energy, his thirst for new ideas, and his boundless ego but by the ever-present fear of poverty. He had barely paid back all the money that he owed, and the show world he had known since his early adult years had now radically changed.

Vaudeville was waning, unable to compete with integrated musical comedy, talking films, radio, the Depression, and changing styles in popular entertainment. It looked tired and old-fashioned, and Edward Albee's insistence on putting performers in evening dress in an effort to escape the old "baggy pants" comedy stigma and bring "class" to vaudeville served only to make it look pretentious. Live engagements by top stars in movie houses were supplanting the old "two-a-day," and Eddie signed up to play dates for Paramount, United Artists, and RKO, including a return date at the Palace.

The Palace now let Cantor choose the "All-Star" acts on the bill with him, an arrangement no one would have dreamed of some years earlier, when no performer, no matter how successful, was accorded even featured billing at that fabled theatre. Jessel, then feuding with Cantor, nonetheless assumed that he would be on the bill—until Eddie offered the second comic spot to the dancer and dialectician Benny Rubin.

Cantor and Rubin wrote their material together. Once, when Eddie phoned to suggest that they rehearse that evening, Rubin said he was with friends in from New York—George Burns and Gracie Allen. Cantor, who had liked their work a year earlier, asked Rubin to bring them along.

"While we were rehearsing," Rubin recalled decades later, "George turned to Gracie and said, 'Googie, how would you like to be on a show like that?' She replied, 'Oh, my God—how could you wish for a thing like that!' Cantor, not knowing I had promised the spot to (Jesse) Block and (Eve) Sully, said, 'You want to be in the show? Easy,' picked up the phone, called Abe Lastfogel, and said, 'Benny and I want Burns and Allen for that bill we're going to do at the Palace.'" It would prove an important step for George and Gracie.

Cantor and Rubin traveled east by train, playing cards and going over bits of business. Eddie also spent time on the script for the first *Chase and Sanborn Hour*. The J. Walter Thompson Agency had lined up writers in New York, but Eddie wanted only tried and tested material he knew would get the laughs. To that end, he wanted the gag files and the brains of David Freedman.

Freedman had written most of Cantor's material for the past year, including books like *Between the Acts* (a small volume of amusing anecdotes and stories for which Eddie took sole credit), *Eddie Cantor's Song and Joke Book* (also "by Eddie Cantor"), and *Yoo-Hoo, Prosperity! The Eddie Cantor Five-Year Plan*, a fifty-six-page tongue-in-cheek solution to the Great De-

pression. Freedman had built his writing for comedians into a very lucrative business and had little interest in Eddie's offer to write his material on
the *Chase and Sanborn Hour* for $200 a week, 10 percent of Cantor's sal-
ary.

Eddie, chagrined, went to work on Freedman through his wife, the former Beatrice Goodman, during a cab ride in August. Cantor was escorting
Bea and the three Freedman sons to a ball game at Yankee Stadium.

"I don't know what it is with your husband. I'm getting two thousand a
week for this series, and I've offered him two hundred. If I stick with it,
and I mean to, I'll get more each time my contract is renewed, and he'll
be getting 10 percent of that."

Beatrice Goodman Freedman was a smart, aggressive woman with enormous influence on her husband. She got Dave to accept the Cantor offer.
The understanding, as she saw it, was that David would be Eddie's radio
writer and get 10 percent of whatever he made in that medium—forever.

But there are no "forevers" in the entertainment business. The Cantor-
Freedman "partnership" would end bitterly—and tragically—for David, Beatrice, and their children.

David Sarnoff, dictator of RCA for decades and founder of the National
Broadcasting Company, had first envisioned radio programming as a means
by which the public would be induced to buy radios. The programming, as
he saw it, would be educational, cultural, and sponsored by RCA at low
cost.

Westinghouse and AT&T, early competitors of RCA in the field of
broadcasting, introduced commercial messages, and Sarnoff soon saw the
futility of sticking to his plan. Much of early programming was nonetheless
devoted to "enlightening," "uplifting" discourses and "serious" music—including the half-hour *Chase and Sanborn* program on Sunday nights beginning in 1928.

*Chase and Sanborn* shifted its program emphasis to popular music late
in 1930, featuring musical theatre and film performers like Bernice Claire.
In January 1931, *Chase and Sanborn* took a major step and signed Maurice
Chevalier for twenty-six half-hour programs.

No other foreign performer until the Beatles captivated American audiences the way Maurice Chevalier did in the early 1930s. His magnetic
grin, romantic charm, and unique way of "putting over" many kinds of songs
made the Frenchman probably the world's top male star in those years, one
whose skill at comedy and music rivaled those of anyone in Hollywood or
on the New York stage. Chevalier was, at the same time, a perfectly acceptable romantic leading man. By the fall of 1929, he had displaced Al
Jolson as the screen's top star in musicals.

The *Chase and Sanborn* show was lengthened to an hour (8–9 P.M.)
following Chevalier's first four broadcasts. After seventeen full-hour
shows—at an unbelievable five thousand dollars a broadcast—Chevalier

left to spend the summer in his native France on board the liner *Paris* on July 1, 1931.

"Like it? Yes, very much" was how Maurice responded to a question about radio. But he liked the stage better because a performer could get a reaction to his work "immediately." The only way a radio star could tell if he was "going over," said the Frenchman, "was by whether his salary checks continued coming in"—and that, somehow, did not seem quite enough. Chevalier's days in American radio were over. Like most stage and film performers, he neither appreciated nor grasped the full significance of the new home "mass media."

Chase and Sanborn filled that summer with a series of female vocalists—Ruth Etting (five times), Bernice Claire, Marion Harris, Irene Bordoni, the contralto Elizabeth Lennox—and a "Male Trio" for one show in August. September 13 marked Cantor's debut.

Stage and film stars, like Chevalier, had appeared on weekly shows before. None, however, had lasted more than thirteen weeks (one "cycle") before frustration, boredom, and the constant need for new material forced them to quit or an indifferent sponsor let their option lapse. Cantor, from the onset, had determined to stick with it.

NBC supplied Cantor with an announcer, Jimmy Wallington, and a studio orchestra headed by David Rubinoff, a Russian-born violinist whom Rudy Vallee had "discovered" at the Paramount Theatre in New York the year before. A good violinist who regarded himself as one of the world's greatest artists, Rubinoff (who never used his first name) had become the conductor of the Chase and Sanborn Orchestra on January 11, four weeks before the first Chevalier broadcast.

The mustachioed Wallington had attracted attention as master of ceremonies for the short-wave programs broadcast by Station WGY, Schenectady, to Admiral Robert Byrd at the South Pole a year and a half earlier. He seemed older than his twenty-four years and had a natural, upbeat vocal quality that belied his slicked-down, formal physical appearance.

Before the broadcast started, he informed the studio audience that they were "guests of Chase and Sanborn," instructing them not to laugh or applaud except at signaled intervals. The 1931 audience did as it was told, disturbing Cantor with sphinx-like responses to his tried and tested gags.

Eddie, unlike other stars, had given considerable thought and preplanning to his stint on *Chase and Sanborn*. Remembering the thousands of letters that had followed his first commercial broadcast five years earlier, and mindful of Sam Goldwyn's dictum that films were for the "masses," Cantor had made up his mind to sound like a "man of the people." Not of Al Smith's East Side or the Jews, but as close to Will Rogers's America as Eddie Cantor could reasonably be.

Borrowing a page from Rogers's mock-presidential campaign (sponsored largely by *Life* magazine) in 1928, Cantor said he had come on radio to "run for president" and explained his platform in a song:

*I'm not a politician, so what I say is true.*
*If you send me to Washington, here's what I'll do for you:*
*Oh, when I'm the president, when I'm the president.*
*There won't be any landlords, when I'm the president.*

Eddie also introduced a song titled "(Potatoes Are Cheaper, Tomatoes Are Cheaper) Now's the Time to Fall in Love," philosophically finding a "plus" in the Depression. One of the few songs to attain popularity exclusively through live performances on radio, "Now's the Time to Fall in Love" became popular with everyone but farmers and second only to "Brother, Can You Spare a Dime?" as the national anthem of the Great Depression.

The script, concocted largely by Cantor, was clever, full of the irreverence for the new medium that he, as an established stage star, brought on with him. When Wallington, like other NBC announcers, sounded the three "chimes"—the signature of the National Broadcasting Company—Cantor exclaimed, "Lunch!"

However, Cantor's respect for the medium grew quickly. He soon realized that radio had implications far beyond not only the stage but also motion pictures. No longer were performers distant, almost abstract beings on a stage or movie screen. Being on weekly radio meant coming into America's living rooms and becoming, not merely a "guest" (as might have been the case with just one isolated broadcast), but an auxiliary member of the family. A radio performer touched the lives of every listener in a uniquely personal way, much like a doctor or a minister. It was an awesome power, unlike anything he had known as a stage or screen star.

Rudy Vallee had been on the air for more than two years at this point, but he never looked on radio as Cantor did. His *Fleischmann Hour* remained a musical "broadcast" just as Vallee remained a romantic singer, rather than a person. Eddie's references to his own wife and daughters and, increasingly, to his working life made him America's first "family" radio comedian, an icon of the airwaves who was also a "plain person" to the folks in the small towns throughout the country.

It was, moreover, all preplanned—not by Chase and Sanborn or the J. Walter Thompson Agency or by writers or psychiatrists but by Cantor. The urchin from the streets had sized up the whole situation and been smart enough to take advantage of it.

What makes this so amazing is that Cantor's shows initially were just a sideline venture. Five days after his first broadcast, Eddie opened a one-week engagement at the Brooklyn Paramount, playing five shows daily and providing the house with its largest gross in months despite a weak film (*Mad Parade*) as the "other" attraction. In the midst of all this, *Palmy Days* opened to one of the most epic exploitation campaigns in the history of New York City, including a gigantic parade of trucks that extended for two miles along Broadway, tremendous signs with life-size pictures of Cantor and the Goldwyn beauties, 250 lamp posts along Broadway from Forty-second to Fifty-ninth streets heralding the "Eddie Cantor *Palmy Days* 'Buy Now' Campaign," and huge flags with the names of the stars and the picture flowing from a score of office buildings.

Eddie attended the premiere at the Rialto on September 23. "Eddie Cantor's nimble and indefatigable shadow was very much in evidence at the Rialto last night," wrote Mordaunt Hall. "And when the picture came to an end, the owner of the shadow appeared on the stage and addressed the audience. In view of all that had happened during the unwinding of the film, it was surprising to observe that the performer was not perspiring and out of breath."

Reviews were pleasant, mostly identifying Eddie's female impersonation in the baking girls' bathing emporium as the funniest part of the movie. *Palmy Days*, while far from the best picture of the year, had enough diverse elements, including pretty girls, to satisfy the increasingly numerous people who thought Eddie Cantor was a funny, "nice enough fellow" on the radio.

"The wit," Hall observed, "may not be as nimble as Mr. Cantor's image, but it is good enough to make one laugh heartily several times and not really tedious during those moments when the crystal gazer is plotting." The picture, Eddie told the first-night audience before the film began, was made, not for them, "but for the masses." The "in" references to Cantor's Jewishness were absent, as were his East Side aggressiveness and the multiethnic layering of his comedy that reduced racism to absurdity. What remained was Cantor as "the little fellow," the great middle American Everyman who triumphed by his earnestness, aided by the love of a good woman (Charlotte Greenwood, in this instance). The formula, coupled with the Cantor timing, the spontaneous energy of his songs, and Goldwyn's beauties, made *Palmy Days* a success at the height of the Depression. Cantor's plugs for the film on the radio did not hurt grosses, either.

Cantor's "campaign" for the presidency, reiterated on his second *Chase and Sanborn* broadcast, rapidly became established in the public conscious. The New York *World-Telegram* radio editor Jack Foster, in his column for September 21, suggested that Cantor might "halt his mythic presidential campaign and boom himself for [Vice President Charles] Curtis' job."

The "campaign" trivialized national politics while promoting Eddie Cantor. Eddie's running was a gag, and everybody knew it. Still, there was the feeling that if any entertainer *could* be president, it probably was Cantor, not the smiling, "down-home," benign Will Rogers.

Despite his reputation as a bouncy Broadway musical comedy star, there was an element of earnestness in Cantor's phony campaign rhetoric, as if it seemed to presage some more serious involvement. Any listeners who got this feeling would be proven right within the next five years.

Cantor was still set to open at the Palace with Benny Rubin, and the two men spent their late nights socializing at Cantor's suite at the Pierre along with Block and Sully, Jack Benny and Mary Livingstone, Ed and Sylvia Sullivan, Benny Fields and Blossom Seeley, and Jack and Winnie Pearl. One night, Benny Fields announced that Gregory Ratoff was leaving the cast of *Girl Crazy*, then still in rehearsals, for another show and asked Rubin to take his place. Cantor was agreeable. "Why not," he said. "I'll make up with Jessel."

Jessel was certainly willing. Always working, when he wanted, as both an emcee and a monologuist, he knew he could make far more money— and come in for more attention—if he were to pair up with his "older brother" from the old "Kid Kabaret" days. Georgie would receive $3,500 a week for his work at the Palace, Eddie a record $8,800.

Cantor and Jessel spent three days and nights rehearsing in a suite at the Hotel Edison before Eddie had to leave for a week's engagement at United Artists' Grand Opera House in Philadelphia. Then it was back to New York for a week split between the Eighty-sixth Street Theatre and the Fordham in the Bronx. In between, Eddie continued with his Sunday evening broadcasts.

Cantor and Jessel opened at the Palace on Saturday, October 31, 1931, following the juggler Serge Flash and the Three Rhythm Boys (three black dancers programmed as "Tip, Tap, and Toe") onstage by way of an argument. Eddie scoffed at Georgie's sentimental songs, saying that he sang "My Mother's Eyes" in a way to make the heart bleed, while his mother lived only eight blocks away and Jessel had not been to see her in two months.

"Yeah, and you," retorted Jessel. "You're all over the stage, all hot and bothered with 'When I Get You in the Vestibule,' and at the same time your wife's the most discontented woman in Hollywood." The rest of the dialogue was in a similar vein, playing on the audience's familiarity with the stage personas of the performers and contrasting them with the performers' allegedly real private lives, of which the audience knew little or nothing.

Like other Palace bills in the last days of big-time vaudeville, the Cantor-Jessel program was not so much vaudeville as an integrated show that brought together all acts on the program. "Well, there's one thing Jessel can't do," Cantor remarked near the show's end, as he, onstage, applied his blackface. After singing "Dinah," he looked up and saw Jessel in blackface, followed by Burns and Allen and the other members of the cast in similar makeup.

*The Chase and Sanborn Hour* went on without interruption, Cantor using Sunday to rehearse, polish, and broadcast. His dialogue was quick and often complicated; yet, a true professional, he seldom blew a line. Cantor used every available minute to study the script, whenever he was not onstage with George Jessel, with his family, or attending to the thousand and one items that made up his average day.

He had found the audience's mandated silence maddening since the first broadcast, but Chase and Sanborn, despite his protests, did not want to change what they regarded as a basic concept of the medium. "If we were supposed to be at the north pole," he later recalled, "the advertising agency wanted those listening to think we *were* at the North Pole, not performing in a nice warm studio before nice warm people."

In October he and Jimmy did a sketch in which women took over men's jobs—Eddie as "Edwina" Cantor, Jimmy as "Jenny" Wallington. Ida and Jim's wife were seated in the first row, clad in furry caps and stoles. Eddie seized the moment to snatch away their outer garments. In a moment, he and the mustachioed Wallington were prancing around in the caps and stoles while the audience, despite the warning against laughing, howled.

Immediately following the broadcast, Cantor got a call from John Reber of the J. Walter Thompson Agency. "The show came alive," he said. "This is audience participation."

The results were dramatic. The audience was in, and warnings against laughing and applauding, except at certain intervals, were out. Within ten days, moreover, Chase and Sanborn re-signed Cantor for fourteen additional broadcasts, increasing his salary to $2,500 a show.

The *Chase and Sanborn Hour* used up material, ideas, and themes on a scale then unprecedented in show business history. Usually, the cast, as such, included Cantor, the NBC Orchestra under Rubinoff, and Wallington. Any other actors were paid out of Cantor's pocket, which explains why he, still battling his way back from insolvency, did not use guest stars. During that first season on the air for Chase and Sanborn, Eddie played brief "bits" as Rubinoff, Irish cops, and Jewish salesmen, answering his own lines in the manner of "voice-over" artists in TV cartoons. It nonetheless became apparent that the *Chase and Sanborn Hour* needed new voices. Shortly after opening at the Palace, Cantor approached George Burns about having Gracie appear on the show.

Burns, a showman just as shrewd as Cantor, was the "boss" of Burns and Allen; Gracie was the "star." George consented to his wife's appearance, figuring, quite rightly, that it would be good exposure. The team of Burns and Allen entered radio the following year, becoming and remaining stars for decades after vaudeville's demise.

Gracie Allen thus became Cantor's first radio guest star, playing a reporter sent to interview Eddie about his presidential candidacy. (Cantor himself had become the first radio star to guest-star on another program when he'd appeared on the Vallee show after his first three broadcasts for Chase and Sanborn.) As time wore on and budgets grew, he would use more guest stars on his own show and in time had a weekly cast of talent.

The Cantor-Jessel bill played nine weeks at the Palace, followed by engagements, without Burns and Allen, in Cleveland, Columbus, and the Balaban & Katz Chicago Theatre. The $44,000 gross in Cleveland broke all weekly records for that city, and *Variety* said they "almost literally broke the doors down at the Chicago," where Cantor did four shows a day.

The *Chase and Sanborn Hour* was broadcast from Chicago that week, with Jessel as guest star and Frankie Masters's Chicago Theatre Orchestra working in place of David Rubinoff's musicians. Cantor did the last two broadcasts on his contract from New York and left for Hollywood on February 9.

Cantor and Goldwyn had discussed the possibility of doing two pictures in 1932—*Ballyhoo* by Herbert Fields and *The Kid from Spain*. *Ballyhoo* was scrapped within two weeks of Cantor's arrival, and Goldwyn went ahead with the original plan for just one film a year—in this case, *The Kid from Spain*.

Nothing was ready, although Goldwyn was good to his word by involving Cantor in "every phase of production." Goldwyn acquiesced to having the songwriters Bert Kalmar and Harry Ruby write the screenplay, but he frowned on Cantor's idea of touring a preliminary version of *The Kid from Spain* to try out material and time the laughs. (The idea was later tried successfully by the Marx Brothers at M-G-M.)

To fill the time between story conferences and to make needed extra money, Cantor opened a week's engagement at Grauman's Chinese Theatre, fulfilling a promise he'd made to Sid Grauman in New York a decade earlier. Cantor sang and clowned all through the Grauman stage "prologue" to the Greta Garbo picture *Mata Hari* and immortalized his hand and foot prints (complemented by his hand-drawn "eye prints" and the words "Here's Looking at You, Sid") in the forecourt of that famous theatre on Wednesday, March 9. His daughters, being movie fans, were thrilled, but they never thought of "Daddy" as a movie star.

Neither could Flo Ziegfeld. Zieggy, ill since February and in worse financial shape than Cantor, wanted Eddie to return to the stage in a revival of *Whoopee* in tabloid (shortened) form for picture houses at a salary of $7,500 a week for two shows a day or $8,800 for three. The offers just made Eddie shake his head. Neither "tab" shows nor Broadway could offer him what he could make in pictures. And while Cantor wanted what he now termed "actor's music" (applause from a live audience), he was a Jewish father, a provider for his family—and not an idle dreamer like his father. Eddie would not commit economic suicide for Ziegfeld or any other producer.

The fact that Ziegfeld was ill made little difference. "Would like to do another show with you before I pass on," he wrote Cantor in June. Ziegfeld was not trading on sentimentality. He was dying. A severe case of the flu in early March, followed by a senseless round of orgies (as the aging Ziegfeld sought to regain his waning virility), had led to pleurisy—Cantor's own old foe.

Eddie was three thousand miles away and so busy with his career on the West Coast that there was little time to think of his old boss. The distance also served to make denial that much easier. The irony that Ziegfeld, his stage "father," was dying of the same disease that, he had been told, had killed his own father could not be have been lost on Cantor.

But his focus remained on *The Kid from Spain*. He wanted to go to Mexico for firsthand instruction on bullfighting until he found that the same training could be brought to Los Angeles. Technicolor, although hardly more advanced than it had been two years earlier, was favored by Cantor and Goldwyn until they learned it would cost $225,000 more than black and white. Scripting was still in preliminary stages in late April. To make matters even more unpleasant, Cantor underwent a tooth extraction that left part of the tooth's root in his gum; the resulting infection kept him in pain for a week.

Production, scheduled to begin on May 30, was postponed to mid-June and then into July. Cantor was now supervising all four writers, but work on the script continued slowly. Goldwyn still had not assembled a cast, although Lyda Roberti, then working on a film at Paramount, had been penciled in for the female lead. In early June, Cantor accepted a week's engagement at the Fox in San Francisco. William Perlberg of the William Morris Agency set the deal—a $10,000 guarantee with a split of the gross over $45,000. No one thought the gross would reach $45,000, and the $38,000 Eddie drew was enough for the house to clear a handsome profit. Other movie theatres, minus Eddie Cantor, broke into the black at less than half that figure.

The final script for *The Kid from Spain* was ready by the time Cantor got back to Los Angeles. One week later, it was cast, with rehearsals scheduled to start July 18. Goldwyn augmented his cast by getting the world-famous matador, the Brooklyn-born Sidney Franklin, who was in town for the Olympics, to play himself in the arena. When Franklin explained that truly ferocious bulls were needed, Goldwyn sent a scout to Mexico to buy five pedigreed Miuras.

The score included "In the Moonlight," "Look What You've Done," and "What a Perfect Combination," all performed by Cantor, the last augmented by a modest (by his later Warner standards) Berkeley production number. The amount of work done in the last two weeks of July was nothing short of tremendous.

In the midst of the rehearsals, Cantor received word that Ziegfeld was in Cedars of Lebanon Hospital in Los Angeles. Eddie went to see Ziegfeld on July 21, and was greeted by Ziegfeld's valet, Sidney. Told "the boss" was resting, Cantor left. Ziegfeld died the following day.

Will and Betty Rogers handled most of the funeral arrangements, Billie Burke insisting on a quiet, dignified ceremony with "only" a hundred personal friends in attendance. It was held at the Pierce Brothers Mortuary in Los Angeles, the service marred by a minister who repeatedly referred to Flo as "Zigfield," a common corruption of his name that Ziegfeld himself had detested.

That Cantor loved Ziegfeld is an overstatement. That Ziegfeld was a father figure to Cantor is undeniable. Flo was both producer—once again, the hated landlord—and a representative of the Anglo-Saxon establishment that Eddie longed to join. As Cantor's father figure, Ziegfeld also bore the brunt of Eddie's filial resentment. Cantor always demanded that his producers "be there," as his own father had not been. Ziegfeld usually was—unlike Jake Shubert—a negligent, "bad" father. But there were times when Flo had dragged his heels about getting vehicles for Eddie, and times when he insisted that Cantor work when he was really ill. Ziegfeld was not perfect, and Cantor was on those occasions—and some others—a rebellious child.

Eddie had nonetheless admired Florenz Ziegfeld. After Ziegfeld's death, that admiration turned to worship. Their fights, their mutual distrust and accusations, now seemed trivial. Ziegfeld would, in death, become the Broadway patriarch to Eddie, Fanny Brice, and hundreds of employees he had either featured, starred, or glorified.

Paramount invited Cantor to speak about Ziegfeld on a special newsreel in the days that followed. Eddie, who could generally find the time to do anything, refused. He said he was still too overcome with emotion about Ziegfeld, and this may very well have been true. Cantor was now forty, and his stage father was dead.

Cantor had daily discussions with Franklin and Charlie Chaplin, an admirer of Eddie's and another UA giant, about the bullfighting scenes in *The Kid from Spain*. Chaplin had an interest in the sport somewhat akin to Norman Mailer's fascination with professional boxing, and he was proud that the arena clowns in Spain were now called "charlots" in his honor. While still unhappy about sound films, Chaplin regarded music as one "of the most important emotional needs of mankind," and he viewed musicals as less destructive of "the great beauty of silence" than other talking pictures.

Cantor had no double for the comic bullfight scenes. "That was the original idea," he said, "but it didn't work because you needed such a long shot with a double that the scene had no kick, and I had to go in there myself. They put up buffers for me right in the ring so that in two steps to the right or left I could be out of the bull's path. I had a mental picture of where the buffers were, and I could duck in without thinking. The camera men were in a tower in the middle of the ring, something like the traffic towers they used to have on Fifth Avenue. Once, a big black devil charged the tower and plunked it right over. You never saw such frightened cameramen in your life.

"The stuff we got in the bullring was good, but it was mostly accidental, and don't let Goldwyn's press agents tell you anything else. You can't rehearse those bulls. They learn very quickly, and when they've been fooled by the cape once or twice they stop being fooled and charge for the man instead of the cape. For the practice scenes we used a steer. There were eleven cameras grinding from every angle all the time the real fighting bulls were in the arena."

*The Kid from Spain* has Cantor playing Eddie Williams, an innocent expelled from college with his friend, Ricardo (Robert Young; Cantor had rejected Cary Grant for the same role). After Eddie is forced to drive the car for an escaping gang of robbers, he fends off a detective by pretending to be a great bullfighter, Don Sebastian II.

When Eddie must inevitably fight a real bull, Ricardo gets one who will lie down at the sound of the word "popocatepetl." Eddie yells the word in the arena, unaware that the bulls have been switched. He ultimately chloroforms the bull in a slow-camera action sequence.

Cantor did his "bullfighting" by having two men hold a charged wire between him and the bull, a dangerous procedure that kept Eddie on edge until filming was completed. The scene got a fair share of laughs at a San Diego preview, but Goldwyn said the fight was "jumpy" and demanded retakes. Cantor and the director, Leo McCarey said the problem could be solved through editing, but Goldwyn was insistent, and the scene was reshot at a cost of more than sixty thousand dollars. It was, as Cantor would admit, improved.

Seen today, the camera tricks and the editing in the bullfight scene are obvious. Indeed, the best scenes in the film are those involving Cantor and Roberti, Eddie's "takes" to her advances holding up as minor masterpieces of comic acting. Roberti did well as Cantor's love interest, though one reviewer noted that she missed several opportunities for laughs.

Eddie and Ida had planned to sail back to New York through the Panama Canal. Retakes forced them to leave two weeks late, so they flew— much to their daughters' dismay—until Ida's stomach cramps made them switch to a train during the stopover in Chicago.

The Cantors arrived in New York on Wednesday morning, October 26, and settled into Delmonico's, the scene of New York nightlife in the storied 1890s. By three o'clock that afternoon, Eddie had finished breakfast, decided not to use a song about an old ladies' home, cut a huge number of gags from his radio script, tried out two new songs, and given a newspaper interview about *The Kid from Spain*.

Four nights later, Cantor opened his second season on the *Chase and Sanborn Hour*, falling back into his now-established image as a welcome guest in middle American living rooms. The "Cantor for President" theme was revived only long enough for him to seriously urge his listeners to "get out and vote" in the national election. Two days later, Roosevelt beat Hoover.

Suite 1602 at Delmonico's, Cantor's private office, now became a leading center of New York show business. Song pluggers might be found there any hour of the day, draped over chairs, resting on window sills, or simply standing, waiting for a chance to play their songs for Eddie Cantor.

Cantor usually wore a black silk robe on these occasions, going from one area of the room to another as he wolfed his lunch, ran over new material, tried out gags, and talked about everything from radio to politics.

Gags, he stressed, the lifeblood of comedians, were to be avoided in favor of material aimed at developing the performer's relationship to the listening audience. "At least 25 percent of the audience is made up of children. Comedy can be neither swift nor localized if it hopes to appeal to them. They respond best to sound gags—situations that end with a comic, repeated use of sound props—a bell, a whistle, or some other auditory gadget."

Cantor was now getting $2,500 a week on *Chase and Sanborn*, not including $750 for each "script," of which he pocketed two-thirds and gave Dave Freedman the remaining $250. Freedman thus got 10 percent of Cantor's weekly salary—according to Cantor.

Cantor's facility for creative financing meant that he had no need for an agent. But his various enterprises in films, radio, filmhouse vaudeville, not to mention endorsements, made him decide that a manager could take care of numerous details and enable him to spread his wings in even more directions.* Cantor's choice for this post was Benjamin F. Holzman.

Holzman, a year older than Cantor, had begun as cabaret editor of the New York *Press* in 1911; he switched to the *Evening Mail* five years later. Ziegfeld made him his director of publicity in 1924, and Holzman subsequently moved his newspaper activities to the New York *Journal*, where he remained until he founded his own publicity agency with Nat Dorfman three years later.

Ben had handled numerous affairs for Eddie during the run of *Kid Boots*, and Eddie liked his style. Affable and easy, good with details, Benny was a man of generally average abilities who laughed a lot and was neither stupid nor particularly brilliant. Holzman offset Cantor's offstage seriousness, just as his serenity seemed a counterpoint to Eddie's almost constant action. Holzman, who had come out to Hollywood to offer Cantor a new George White musical that summer, dissolved his partnership with Dorfman to become Eddie's new manager.

Benny, who functioned more as a stooge than a genuine manager, was a small-eyed man with thin hair and an angular face. A nondescript but pleasant man, he took care of various details for Eddie but never really handled his career or gave him valuable answers. Cantor had been in show business far longer than Holzman and had little need for anyone's advice on his career. He had done—and would do—very well using his own judgment.

*The Kid from Spain* opened at the Palace on November 17, 1932, inaugurating a straight picture policy at that fabled theatre that signaled the official end of vaudeville. Running 118 minutes, *The Kid from Spain* was a long feature for that era, although Cantor, ever mindful of the average

---

*Eddie accepted the presidency of the Jewish Theatrical Guild, vacant since the death of William Morris, at this time. He would be reelected every year until 1962.

man, had doubts about the wisdom of charging $2.20 a ticket in the midst of the Depression. Reviews were fair to excellent, the film being quite well paced, its cinematography a marked improvement over that in *Palmy Days*. Cantor, songs, comedy, the Goldwyn Girls, and Sam Goldwyn's publicity were all tremendous assets, but it was Cantor's plugging of the film on radio that made it a smash hit, one of only two hit movie musicals released in 1932. (The other was *Love Me Tonight*.) Cantor had been quick to realize how his exposure in one medium could greatly aid his success in another.

The spectacle of the film's opening did not prevent the astute Richard Watts Jr. from pointing out its defects in the New York *Herald Tribune*. *The Kid from Spain*, he wrote,

> is a spectacular and lavish screen musical comedy that suffers from such stage musical comedy defects as a routine book, much antique comedy and a score that is no better than it should be. There is an attempt to present the customary romance between a juvenile and an ingenue. The jokes are not being misrepresented by the news that one of them goes like this: "Are you a caveman at making love?" "Yes, one kiss and I cave in." The score permits Mr. Cantor to sing three times and Miss Lyda Roberti once, but save in a number called "In the Moonlight," there seems little about the music that is likely to keep the radio busy. A number of maedchen in uniform spring up as school girls in a boarding school chorus number, but they are soon forgotten.
>
> Mr. Cantor is probably as funny as his material permits. The engaging Miss Roberti is rather buried in the proceedings, which is quite a shame. The other members of the cast are, for one reason or another, negative.

*The Kid from Spain* was nonetheless a hit throughout the country. Cantor was now the number one star of radio and one of the nation's leading film stars. This conquest of the two leading media of the day, added to his reputation from the stage, made Eddie Cantor probably the top star in the world.

Material continued to be the chief problem of the *Chase and Sanborn Hour*. Cantor still had no set script team, outside David Freedman, and the fifth show of the season was set in the mythical kingdom of "Neurasthenia." *Variety* called it "vapid, awkwardly contrived stuff all the way through, with most of the cracks not only debilitated from age but over-strained by the effort to fit them into situations where they didn't belong." The following week's show, which burlesqued opera, did not fare much better, but the next program, a return to straight gags done with Wallington and insults aimed at Rubinoff, was deemed a big improvement.

Cantor returned to live stage work in December. Jessel was again his costar, and the two sang "Pals" as if they were in their seventies. They also burlesqued *Grand Hotel*, Cantor doing Garbo's part with Jessel as John Barrymore. The rest of Cantor's unit—which did four and five shows daily—included Jack Holland and June Knight in ballroom dances, the tall Colletta Ryan as Jessel's foil, the dancer Bobby Bixler, Rubinoff on violin, and an Alton-Bines chorus.

These Cantor "unit shows," natural successors to vaudeville, would be the mainstays of Eddie's stagework for much of the next twenty years. Offering "something for everyone," they proved the models for the USO shows of World War II and Bob Hope's TV specials of the 1960s.

Despite his dominance of the stage, film, and radio, Eddie had his detractors. Fred R. Pursel, manager of the Lyric Theatre in Simcoe, Ontario, said that Cantor, on the radio, was using old jokes that Pursel, as an old minstrel man, had heard and used "a hell of a long time ago. To make it worse, the jokes were even old when we used them. Then as a musician, I can't stand his sliding into notes." Cantor nonetheless came in first in one national poll after another as the nation's best-liked Air Act. The Cantor unit usually drew sellout crowds, and Chase and Sanborn, mindful of Cantor's $3,250 weekly salary—considerably lower than that of Jolson or Ed Wynn, neither of whom drew Eddie's ratings—agreed to let him broadcast from whatever city his tour brought him to on any Sunday night.

April 23 marked the final *Chase and Sanborn Hour* of the season, Cantor having already signed to do thirteen broadcasts the following season at five thousand dollars a broadcast. This, coupled with the money from his Goldwyn films and what he earned in stage tours, made Eddie the top money earner in show business.

He had not become complacent. Having come up in the theatre, Cantor was not used to the sycophancy demanded by newspaper radio columnists. He told the New York Council of the American Association of Advertising Agencies that critics favored those who paid homage to them—either verbally or otherwise—and could not therefore be trusted as barometers of quality, let alone of public taste. His charge grew out of his own experience. Cantor had been approached by several press agents who wanted him to play benefits or introduce songs in which they had an interest. If he did not "play ball" with them, they warned, he would not get to "first base" with certain radio columnists. Eddie never did, and found his radio show ignored in many papers in spite of its high ratings. Even *Variety*, despite the Cantors' friendship with its editor, Abel Green, and his wife, never formally reviewed the *Chase and Sanborn Hour* while Eddie was its star.

The New York radio editors and columnists responded with a vengeance. Ben Gross, Nick Kenny, and Mike Porter, among others, refuted Cantor's charges of "log-rolling," claiming that his efforts on behalf of George Jessel constituted the greatest form of log-rolling in show business.

The animosity between Cantor and the New York radio columnists would have intensified further had not Eddie left the air to make another film. Jimmy Durante, recently established as a star, was Eddie's summer replacement.

Goldwyn had toyed with the idea of having Eddie star in a musical version of *Androcles and the Lion*, complete with gags and Goldwyn Girls, but he soon abandoned the idea, having failed to reach terms with George Bernard Shaw. Goldwyn finally settled on *Roman Scandals*, the story of a young man transported, in a dream, to ancient Rome, where he finds the same corruption that exists in his own town.

Goldwyn wanted nothing but the best for this new Cantor vehicle. He liked the idea of an ancient Roman setting, and, in March, signed Robert Sherwood, author of *The Road to Rome*, and George S. Kaufmann, two of Broadway's leading playwrights, to write the story. The contract gave the writers escape clauses, allowing them to withdraw after writing either the original synopsis or the first draft of the screenplay.

Sherwood and, especially, Kaufmann had spurned Hollywood offers for years, preferring to reside and work near Broadway. Goldwyn, unlike the other major studio heads, agreed to have them work in New York and promised Kaufmann he would work without Cantor, the *buttinsky*.

The Cantors hung around New York for two weeks after Eddie's final *Chase and Sanborn Hour*. Cantor spent that time in meetings with Sam Goldwyn, recently returned from Europe, as well as the producer Arthur Hornblow Jr. and Frank Tuttle, who would direct *Roman Scandals*. The three men had planned a story conference with Kaufmann and Sherwood for Monday, May 8. Cantor, who was not invited, complained bitterly to Hornblow, who prevailed on Goldwyn to allow Eddie to sit in, over Kaufmann's objections, provided he sat quietly and just listened.

Cantor listened as Kaufmann read the story outline and some rough parts of a first draft of the screenplay. Eddie then asked if he could make a "single comment." Goldwyn nodded, and Cantor spoke—and spoke—for well over an hour, insisting on major revisions in what Kaufmann and Sherwood had written.

Kaufmann and Sherwood fired off a letter to Sam Goldwyn the next day, withdrawing from the project. A dispute over whether they would be paid for the first draft, rather than only the story, led to a law suit in 1934. It was settled three years later.

The Cantors, Goldwyn, Hornblow, and Tuttle left for California late in May. George Oppenheimer, who had turned out scripts for Groucho and Chico Marx's radio show, *Flywheel, Shyster, and Flywheel*, was hired to complete the screenplay, although Goldwyn, at Eddie's suggestion, would eventually hire William Anthony McGuire, Arthur Sheekman, and Nat Perrin as well. The more writers, the more gags, and Cantor was not comfortable without a lot of gags.

The finished script had Eddie as custodian of a small historical museum who befriends the homeless inhabitants of West Rome, whom Eddie persuades to live on the street in a sort of "Happy Hooverville," complete with smiling Goldwyn Girls in showers. Ordered to leave town, he finds himself in ancient Rome, where the political corruption rivals that found in West Rome—or, by inference, America. Waking up back in the present, Eddie finds he has the evidence to rid West Rome of its corrupt mayor.

The film's political overtones were, in the end, secondary to Cantor's all too limited physical comedy, his songs, and Busby Berkeley's production numbers, which were not as sharply defined as his work at Warners but did have the terrific Goldwyn Girls in opulent surroundings; in one magnificent "Slave Market" scene, completely, though discreetly nude under their long blonde wigs. Supporting Cantor were Edward Arnold, perfectly cast as the emperor, Verree Teasdale as the empress, David Manners and Gloria Stuart as the love interest, and Ruth Etting as a spurned courtesan who sings "No More Love," the picture's only love song.

Filming started in July and went on through mid-October. The gorgeous Gloria Stuart was impressed by Goldwyn's lavish production values, a far cry from the drabness often found at Universal, her home studio. Indeed, the slave market scene, together with the elaborate "Keep Young and Beautiful" production number, made *Roman Scandals* the most expensive musical in celluloid history. When a San Francisco preview made it clear that another song was needed, Cantor had the veteran songwriter L. Wolfe Gilbert dash off the topical, up-tempo "Put a Tax on Love," and the film went back into production.

The retakes finished, Cantor left for New York on November 9 with Gilbert and two other writers, Grant Garrett and Matt Brooks. All three were added to the *Chase and Sanborn* staff.

The trip east was a move for the entire family. Eddie and Ida had spent half of the previous two years in New York, and an epidemic of polio in southern California ("Daddy told us not to go in swimming"), coming after an earthquake in Long Beach, just outside Los Angeles ("The folks called from New York, and Mother wasn't satisfied till she had spoken to each of us individually"), led the Cantors to relocate once again.

The girls did not complain. Margie, a graduate of Beverly Hills High School, had recently dropped out of UCLA, refusing to see chemistry as a prerequisite to anything she considered worth doing with her life. Natalie left Santa Monica State College after six months because she hated cutting up dead frogs in zoology. Edna, at fourteen, had started high school. Marilyn was the happiest to move back to New York. At twelve, she thought that Broadway was more glamorous than Hollywood—an attitude that many shared in 1933.

The Cantors' new home in New York was the San Remo, a fashionable apartment complex at 145 Central Park West, near Seventy-fourth Street. For five hundred dollars a month, they had the top three floors—fourteen rooms comprising living room, kitchen, and servants' quarters on the first level, bedrooms on the second, and rehearsal space for Eddie on the roof.

Eddie's "staff," besides Frenchy and whatever pianists (including Harry Tobias) he used to rehearse numbers, now included Roy (Bunky) Arthur. Bunky, like thousands of other performers, had found life hard since the demise of vaudeville. "My father," recalls Janet, "ran into Bunky on the street and, sizing up the situation, told him he badly needed an assistant and offered him a job. We never knew what Bunky did, but he had his own little office." Bunky actually did little but run Eddie's errands. His wife, Mary, became one of Cantor's two secretaries, the other being Helen Kirke. Margie answered the voluminous fan mail, while Helen kept track of the innumerable phone calls and typed Eddie's writings, which included everything from gags to books. (Eddie contributed a section on his early days on Broadway to *Ziegfeld, the Great Glorifier*, a biography by David Freedman that was published as "by Eddie Cantor with David Freedman" by A. H. King the following year.)

Margie, now eighteen, attended Miss Semple's, a finishing school on Riverside Drive, before becoming Eddie's personal secretary at one hundred dollars a week. She was critical, attentive, perceptive, methodical, and so devoted to her father that she worried excessively about almost everything he did.

She attended nearly all of Eddie's broadcasts, standing in the back watching, listening to everything and cracking her knuckles. Extremely creative, Margie could have had a job as a director or writer on any one of a number of shows. Instead, she chose to stay close to her father.

Margie gradually usurped the duties of her mother, becoming major domo of the Cantor household as well as Eddie's confidante and primary adviser. Eddie greeted the entire family when he came home at night, but the one he *needed* to see was always Margie.

Ida was the mainstay of her husband's life, the successor to his grandmother in that respect and his life's companion. Their four younger daughters were love objects to Eddie, the family he'd wanted as a kid but never had. Margie, though, seemed different, not only to Eddie but to the family as well. The other family members never understood her devotion to their father, her unwillingness to permit anyone to "bother mother," or the obligation that she felt toward both her parents.

Margie had a boyfriend named Richard in high school, and she might have married him had her family not moved back to New York. Richard met another girl and married her. If Margie had regrets, she never voiced them.

And therein lies a tragedy, of sorts.

## Chapter 9

# THE PEAK

*"No one was bigger in film at the time. And no one was bigger in radio. He was just the biggest thing in show business at the time—in the U.S. or in Europe."*
—*Gerald Marks*

The Cantor girls found life at the San Remo interesting. Margie and Natalie shared one room, Edna and Marilyn another, and Al Jolson gave the family a new dog, named Jolie in his honor, who sadly was crushed to death by the heavy roof elevator door. Most of the family's adventures were not quite so tragic. Janet, not quite seven, gave Winnie the scare of her life by climbing up to the roof of the building on an outside ladder. Another time, a fire broke out on one of the lower floors, forcing an evacuation of the building. Margie, stark naked, looked down from her window and yelled, "Okay, boys, take me. Here I am."

The Cantors often entertained, their guests constituting a Who's Who of show biz in the early to mid-1930s: Block and Sully, Jolson, Jack Benny, Durante, Jessel, Burns and Allen, all of whom Eddie had either worked with in the recent past or known for years. The girls did not regard these people as celebrities; they were simply "Daddy's friends from show business."

Far more frequent guests were Ida's sisters and their husbands. Eddie and the girls found Ida's youngest sister, Nettie, by far the most amusing member of the Tobias family, especially when watching her take food. She ate quickly, without stopping, blissfully ignorant of her surroundings. "Ida, she's amazing," Eddie said on one occasion. "Listen." He proceeded to call Nettie one offensive name after the other as the woman went on shoveling food into her mouth, oblivious to what Eddie was saying.

The most traumatic times for the girls were their visits to Ida's parents. Janet remembers her maternal grandfather as "like a big teddybear—lovable and warm." By contrast, her grandmother was forbidding, miserable, "and a miser to boot." Rachel Slotzki Tobias had steadfastly refused to learn—

or, certainly, to speak—English for more than forty years. Her health declined rapidly during the Cantor family's first season at the San Remo. On May 5, shortly after the girls left for the West Coast, she died—unmourned by the Cantor girls, but not, it seems, by Eddie. "Mothers-in-law can be pretty nice people," he would one day write. "Take mine."

> As a cook, Ida's mother would have been tough competition for Oscar of the Waldorf, and she took great pains to pass on all her secrets to Ida, saying, "Eddie has a sensitive stomach. You must learn to cook fine food without spices."
> This sweet old lady had none of the traits supposedly typical of a mother-in-law, and it almost seemed libelous to label her this way. She was more like my own mother. Because I liked a certain kind of coffee cake, she would devote several hours every week to baking one, then travel two more hours on the subway to bring it to me. In family arguments, it was two against one—my mother-in-law and me against my wife. Poor Ida never had a chance.

Hardly a portrait of the strange and nasty miser Eddie's daughters so disliked. Rachel Slotzki Tobias doubtless had her good points. And she doubtless loved a son-in-law who made more money in a week than most men took home in a year.

Once again Cantor was active on behalf of actors. He had resigned as president of the National Vaudeville Artists when that body started passing baskets up and down the theatre aisles during intermissions—a desperate appeal for money that Cantor felt was beneath the dignity of what he saw as a profession. (Eddie thought the money could be raised through benefits.) Now, having been elected president of the Screen Actors' Guild during preparations for *Roman Scandals*, he wrote a personal letter to President Roosevelt, protesting details of the pending motion picture code, which sought to place a limit on the earnings of top film stars.

Roosevelt responded, and Cantor held a press luncheon at Sardi's on Monday, November 13, stating that he would meet with the president in Warm Springs, Georgia, nine days later. The president, said Cantor, had been "misinformed" regarding the situation in Hollywood. Eddie said he would bring to his attention "the unique personality and money-making power" of certain players who, being irreplaceable, were "worth what they can bring into the box office." The professional life of the average motion picture actor, Cantor maintained, was between four and five years, and salaries of five thousand dollars a week, since they lasted only part of the year, were seriously misleading to the public.

The Guild's chief objection to the code, said Cantor, was the clause that provided that actors who were under contract to one producer could not negotiate with other producers for six months before or after the time period covered by the existing contract. This, of course, was suicide for all but the wealthiest actors.

The meeting with Roosevelt, held three days after Cantor's return to the *Chase and Sanborn Hour*, turned into a rather harmless exchange of homey political outlooks. The president took note of Cantor's points, agreeing with him on the six-month clause but protesting Eddie's objection to the proposed $25,000 a year ceiling on film actors' salaries. "No one wants to take Ida's fur coat away from her, Eddie, or your car. But if the man around the corner is out of a job, his kids still have to eat. If we have to cut from the top to give them food, we'll cut."

Roosevelt thought enough of Cantor, his views, and his position as president of SAG—not to mention his potential public relations value as a star of films and radio— to appoint him to the Motion Picture Code Authority created by the National Recovery Administration. The president's motion picture code, with all of its now laughable restrictions, was held in abeyance for ninety days and finally tossed into the wastebasket. Stars were thus permitted to make more than twenty-five thousand dollars a year, opening the way to megamillion-dollar earnings in the last quarter of the century.

The new season on the *Chase and Sanborn Hour* saw the introduction of a new segment called "Night Court," in which Eddie, as the judge, first dismissed a small number of cases with absurd pronouncements, some of which contained sly comments on the nature of each offense, and then heard a serious case, generally one related to a public safety menace, poverty, or personal tragedy. On November 26, during the season's second show, the serious case involved a forty-six-year-old man who, depressed after having been out of work for two years and ashamed to face his wife and children, had attempted suicide. Eddie, as the judge, told him of men who, broke into their forties, had risen to be business leaders, produced great works of art, and left priceless legacies to future generations. Urging him to be a father to his children and not to give his family the burden of his suicide, Eddie gave the man a renewed sense of courage. It was a stirring scene and speech, made all the more so by the millions of similar people—out of work, despondent, looking for a figure to inspire them with hope.

Cantor's interest in poverty and failure was doubtless sparked by memories of his own boyhood and of his grandmother, who had found the strength to spend all but the final years of her life giving love and hope to him. Cantor did not want pity for the unemployed; he wanted them to have the caring that had sent him to Surprise Lake Camp in 1903. To poor people themselves, he sent out messages of optimism and courage. "Henry Ford was broke at forty. . . . Look at the deflation we're experiencing: 'Potatoes are cheaper, tomatoes are cheaper. Now's the time to fall in love.' "
Part of this, to be sure, was commercially inspired, the result of shrewd

appraisals of his audience's needs. Most of it, however, stemmed from Cantor's own beliefs.

Eddie truly loved performing, but he did not view it as his sole purpose in life. He had entered show business later than most entertainers of his era—as an intelligent young man of eighteen rather than as a stagestruck lad deep in the throes of puberty. As such, he had some sense of being a sojourner rather than a true "born-to-the-profession" entertainer. This helps explain his special vulnerability to the classic fear among successful entertainers that a "man will come up to the door and say, 'We've grown wise to you. You have to give it all back.' "

This sense of being a sojourner made him view the theatre as a facet of his life rather than his reason for existing. Cantor saw show business as, of course, a "way to make a living," but one that could be used to make the world a better place. The Educational Alliance, Will Rogers, Bert Williams, and, above them all, his grandmother, had made Eddie realize that there were things besides—and perhaps more important than—"mere" entertainment.

One who viewed himself as outside—or above—his chosen field in the 1930s had to have a very strong self-image; and from all indications, Cantor did. But did Eddie really see himself as the savior of show business, inaugurating a "new law"?

"I think Cantor was the kind of man who looked in the mirror and asked himself who he really was," said the long-time publicist Gary Stephens. "But I don't know if he could give himself an answer." Cantor, in short, was no saint, and he knew it. Being a "public entertainer" was a heavy burden for a mere mortal to carry, and Eddie surely had private doubts about his abilities and responsibilities. But there was little room in Cantor's fast-paced life for deep introspection. The only thing he felt he could do was keep working—for himself, his family, and the more-or-less "good world" that had been more than good to him.

There were other factors, to be sure, in Cantor's "public" role. The entertainment business, Cantor well knew, had no safety net. Public service made Eddie feel like a part of the "establishment," in terms of prestige (in an era when performers were still persona non grata in high social circles) and in gaining the illusion of security. Providing for his family and keeping the wolf from the door were still the top priorities for Cantor.

As a Jew, Cantor identified with the poor and downtrodden. And like many Jews, he felt vaguely uncomfortable with his wealth and his membership in the country's (largely non-Jewish) elite. Indeed, his sudden fall from wealth in 1929 may have convinced him that attempts at making big money were rooted in sin and therefore destined for disaster. God, thought Eddie Cantor, did not want him to be rich; He just wanted him to make a *very* good living. Cantor's actions in the future would serve to fulfill these beliefs.

Eddie's radio contract was renegotiated and extended after the first two broadcasts of the new season. The new agreement, set to run until December 1934, would raise his weekly salary to $7,500.

Cantor's insecurity about material—and his consequent reliance on gags to ensure laughs—led to a new career for Eddie Davis, a New York cab driver with a penchant for jokes. Davis's imaginative recollections, intended more for humor than for serious researchers, have him trying unsuccessfully for weeks to get to Cantor, gaining access only after renting a chauffeur's uniform and entering the stage door at NBC. "Once within, I took off the rented coat, pinned on my taxi badge, rounded a corner in the corridor and was astounded to find myself face to face with Eddie Cantor. Providence was with me.

" 'Mr. Cantor,' I announced, 'my cab is outside. I'll be waiting whenever you're ready.' Cantor, having no reason to say 'No,' replied with a detached 'Fine.' "

Davis's memoirs describe an impossibly frightening taxi ride, climaxed by the sale of five jokes to an understandably shaken Cantor at twenty dollars apiece. "After surviving several of my hair-raising chariot rides and buying a few more gags, Cantor concluded that his life would be safer if I could sell my taxi. To facilitate this, he gave me a permanent job on his writing staff." The absurdity, however, had its basis in reality: a new medium in constant need of fresh material with insufficient budgets for staffs of professional writers. It was every comedian for himself, and Cantor, facing increased competition from Ed Wynn, Burns and Allen, and Jack Pearl, was determined to remain the number one comic on radio. To him, that meant new gags.

While the new wave of radio comics built their interesting characters, Cantor stubbornly relied on corny, isolated jokes. Essentially a visual comedian with a strong talent for pantomime, Cantor was not naturally suited to radio. That he remained one of its top stars for many years was due to his pioneering efforts, his clever appeals to mass taste, and his prowess at selling his persona to various sponsors.

By the end of 1933, Cantor had totally recouped his losses from the 1929 crash and begun to stockpile what should have become a new fortune. *Roman Scandals* was greeted with overwhelming enthusiasm when it opened at the Rivoli, ensuring Cantor another quarter of a million dollars in personal income.

His yearly regimen was solidly established: make a picture in the summer, appear in filmhouse vaudeville in the fall and winter, and sandwich weekly radio broadcasts around every stage engagement. Cantor's now annual tour of picture houses began at the Brooklyn Paramount on January 5, 1934; Warner's Earle in Philadelphia and the New York Paramount followed.

He continued spouting his opinions, joining those comedians who thought live studio audiences were an unnecessary burden on radio comics

(Cantor may have been the biggest sinner when it came to playing to them instead of to the home listening audience), and expressing strenuous disapproval of any proposed changes in the chorus girl provisions of the Motion Picture Code Authority. Cantor said he would resign from the Authority if chorines' minimum salaries were reduced, though nothing had been said about this possibility; the producers' complaint concerned the proposed three-dollar-a-day layoff salary.

Following a Surprise Lake Camp benefit at the New Amsterdam Theatre on Sunday night, February 11, (the first since 1929), Eddie and Ida went to Hollywood, Florida, where they learned that the St. Louis businessman Maurice Weil had established an Eddie Cantor Fellowship at the Hebrew University in Jerusalem. Eddie quickly announced the establishment of an Ida Cantor Fellowship at the same university.

The *Chase and Sanborn Hour* continued unabated, broadcast from wherever Cantor was on any given Sunday evening, with or without Wallington or Rubinoff (played by Gregory Ratoff and Teddy Bergman, among others).

"Working with Eddie," recalled Bergman (later known as Alan Reed and best remembered as the voice of the cartoon character Fred Flintstone),

> was a great hunk of schooling for me, because I was able through the years that I was with him to grab off the hard won education that he had had all through the years from singing waiter on up. It was fascinating. I learned many things. I was really new at the time, and it led me to ask Eddie to help me with timing, because here I was getting laugh lines, joke things. I got a very interesting answer. I said, "Read it for me, and tell me how to time it." He said, "Nobody can tell you how to time it. You're gonna have to feel it. It'll come to you eventually. It's something that happens. It's different with every person, because you've got to adjust yourself to your audience. When you get it, you'll know it. I'll know it, too."
>
> The first couple of shows that I did, as Rubinoff, my timing was off, and I'd lose a few laughs that were written there. I didn't know how to do it. I was quite young when I joined Eddie. One day, about four months after I'd started the character, he said, "Now you've got it." It was one of the big days of my life. And I felt that I had it. I felt that I had learned from his suggestions, from observations, and from a feel inside, as he had said, of how to time. Timing is very important, and Eddie was a master of it.
>
> Another thing I learned from Eddie is that no two audiences are alike, and that you have to gear yourself to them. You'll have a few "test jokes," if you're working in comedy, and if you see they don't go, you must try the next one in a different way. Maybe they have to be a hit a little harder; maybe hit a little softer. I saw Eddie work differently from week to week, depending on the audience.

Cantor's increased salary allowed him to make use of other actors and guest stars. Georgie Price and Sophie Tucker guested on February 18, followed by Harry Richman on February 25 and Lillian Roth on March 4, giving the show added variety and spelling Eddie for brief periods of time. There was, however, no sustaining weekly talent until that spring, when Eddie heard Harry Einstein, an advertising copywriter for the Kane Furniture Company, give a hilarious "speech" in an impossible Greek dialect at a luncheon in Boston.

Cantor had Einstein (as "Parkyakarkus") on *Chase and Sanborn* the following Sunday, and he proved to be an overnight sensation. After three more broadcasts (at fifty dollars each), Einstein was signed to appear weekly at $250 a show.

"Parkyakarkus" tended to remain on the same vocal level for his whole three-minute segment, meaning that his language mixups verged on the annoying. Nonetheless, he was a welcome change of pace on *Chase and Sanborn*, and Einstein soon abandoned advertising copy to become the first great "second banana" in radio history.

Goldwyn, in the meantime, was selecting the new Goldwyn Girls for his next Cantor picture, tentatively titled *Treasure Hunt*. In April he persuaded Columbia to loan him the young Ann Sothern and, a short time later, George Murphy, an Irish song-and-dance man who, like Cantor, could speak Yiddish. The two men had little else in common.

The last *Chase and Sanborn Hour* of the season, on April 15, had Block and Sully, Georgie Price, and Frances Arms in addition to "Parkyakarkus"— all of them now under the personal management of Eddie Cantor. This meant Cantor could collect 10 percent of what he paid them for appearing on his show. The process, known as "double dipping," would become a part of entertainment on a larger scale in the 1950s, when MCA, a major talent agency, effectively became a producer; a government antitrust action subsequently forced MCA out of the agency business. Cantor, though, was not attempting to build an empire; he was simply trying to make a few dollars on the side in much the same way he had done, in other ways, on Henry Street some thirty years before.

Margie was now ensconced as her father's professional confidante, adviser, and "gal Friday." Eddie now spent more time with Margie than with anybody else, his youthful appearance, coupled with her serious demeanor, making them look more like brother and sister than father and daughter. This, no doubt, was just what Margie wanted. They took the train out to California three days after his last broadcast of the season, and Eddie did his usual kibitzing with Goldwyn's writers. Ida followed two weeks later with the younger girls.

Goldwyn soon had an unpaid consultant on the Cantor film. Marilyn, Eddie's twelve-year-old daughter, was one of Ethel Merman's biggest fans, having seen The Merm in several of her hit Broadway shows. Knowing Merman had completed work on *We're Not Dressing* at Paramount, Marilyn began badgering her father, practically demanding that Merman be hired for the Goldwyn picture. Eddie finally arranged for Marilyn to speak to Sam himself. Marilyn rose to the occasion and sold Goldwyn—something few adults in Hollywood could do—on using Merman in *Treasure Hunt*. "Marilyn would have made a great agent," says her sister Janet. "Aggressive and insistent. She could hammer down the doors."

Goldwyn, for the moment, was much more impressed with nineteen-year-old Margie. Having heard that "Night Court" had been her idea and seeing how she worked around her father, Goldwyn offered Margie a salaried position and an office of her own. Her only task would be to come up with ideas. "But Margie turned it down. She didn't want to take a job—or do anything, really—that was outside the family. That was just the way she was."

*Treasure Hunt* once more cast Cantor as a poor, boyish young man, heir to a considerable fortune. A crook and his moll try to muscle in on Eddie's money, with the woman (Merman) claiming to be Eddie's long-lost mother.

Cantor talked Goldwyn into reviving Irving Berlin's "Mandy" (introduced by Van and Schenck in the 1919 *Follies*) for a minstrel sequence in the second half of the film. The Nicholas Brothers (Fayard and Harold), signed out of the Cotton Club by Goldwyn, proved to be a highlight of the sequence.

The "Mandy" number also featured Merman, Murphy, and Ann Sothern. Eddie even made a joke of trying unsuccessfully to compete as a dancer with Fayard and Harold. "My brother Harold was only nine years old, and Goldwyn wanted him to be the interlocutor in that minstrel sequence," recalled Fayard. "But Cantor nixed it. He said, 'Children will steal any scene,' and that was that. But Harold got to do that song, 'I Want to Be a Minstrel Man,' that led into 'Mandy,' and it was Cantor's idea to have him reappear at the song's end and say the final line, 'and *me!*' " It provided a nice ending to the song and, coupled with their dancing—not yet quite as acrobatic as it would later become—propelled the Nicholas Brothers to national attention.

*Kid Millions*, as *Treasure Hunt* was retitled, was in production from July 16 to September 22, 1934, ten weeks of work that included a special color sequence showing Eddie's ice cream factory. The idea of making Eddie a poor orphan who provides free ice cream for poor kids was in keeping with Cantor's own background and his public image as a neighborhood boy who never forgot his roots.

Eddie's real-life associates included few "kids" from the neighborhood, Dan Lipsky having been persona non grata in the Cantor household since The Stock Market crash. (He had issued a press statement denying Cantor had been wiped out by the crash—an outright lie, lending credence to Ida's suspicions that Danny had used Eddie's money to his own advantage.) Most of Eddie's old boyhood friends had moved from the East Side, and the building at 47 Henry Street would shortly be demolished. Cantor made no attempt to save it, but later wept when he took one of his daughters on a walking tour and found the building razed.

Eddie, seconded by Margie, planned his final shows for Chase and Sanborn shortly after the Cantors' arrival back in New York on September 3. He had already signed with a new sponsor—Pebeco, the "Triple Action" toothpaste with milk of magnesia—for thirteen broadcasts beginning in February, leaving the two intervening months free for a trip to Europe.

As president of the Screen Actors' Guild, Cantor took a keen interest in Italy's Fascist government's refusal to allow American film studios to shoot or produce pictures in that country. His own films were popular with Italian audiences, and Eddie thought he could persuade Benito Mussolini to use American actors in Italian productions, thereby opening a new source of employment for SAG members.

Cantor was going to Europe ostensibly to publicize his own films—with a $25,000 "expense" contribution by Sam Goldwyn. This was, effectively, a tax dodge, although Cantor planned to do a little p.r. work in Paris and London.

In the meantime, he played filmhouse dates arranged by Abe Lastfogel, sandwiched carefully around his last eight Chase and Sanborn broadcasts. With Cliff Hall (Jack Pearl's "Sharlie") as straight man, the Nicholas Brothers, and the Twelve Aristocrats dance ensemble, Cantor opened at Poli's in Bridgeport, Connecticut, on October 22 and played other eastern cities through the middle of November, grossing $32,000 at the Earle in Philadelphia (as compared to Burns and Allen's $19,000 a week earlier). Kids sat through multiple performances at the Paradise Theatre in the Bronx until Cantor asked them to go home—a cue for them to rush the stage for autographs.

Cantor's last appearance on the *Chase and Sanborn Hour* came on November 25, 1934. Eddie had made plans to take Ida, Margie, and Natalie to Europe, feeling the trip would be ideal for his elder daughters. Fifteen-year-old Edna was to be left home with Marilyn and Janet.

Eddie later described Edna as "bawling all over the place. . . . 'Why are you leaving me here all alone if you really love me?' " Eddie finally capitulated and spent the next hour making frantic telephone calls to secure another ticket. Marilyn and Janet stayed behind with aunts and uncles, assorted friends, Winnie, and the Cantor staff of servants. Eddie, Ida, their three elder daughters, and Eddie's valet, Frenchy (who spent most of his time suffering from *mal de mer*) sailed on the *Rex* for Genoa, Italy, on Saturday, December 1, 1934.

Cantor almost did not get to see Benito Mussolini. "Daddy had left his card of admission at the hotel," Majorie told Radie Harris. "When he arrived at the palace, the guard at the gate refused to let him in." Cantor sent back to the hotel to get his admission card.

Mr. McBride of the American Embassy had prepped Cantor for his interview with Mussolini. "His office was probably the longest in the world," Cantor later recalled.

It took minutes to walk the length of it, and at the far end Mussolini would sit at a desk on a raised platform. The only furniture in the room was this desk and the chair he sat on and one other chair. Therefore, as one walked toward him down this long empty room, the dictator could size you up and under his gaze you were to feel smaller and smaller.

I go to the meeting. The door opens. It's all as McBride has told me: the endless room, Mussolini on the platform. But I have a trick of my own. The minute I come in I start to talk. Talk, talk, talk, whatever comes into my mind. Now he tries to hear what I'm saying, and it isn't easy at that distance. He even strains a little forward to listen, and he doesn't stare me down after all. He stands up and shakes hands. Then he pulls a handkerchief out of his pocket and starts waving it. "El Toro!" he says. "Cantor. El Toro!" He'd just seen *The Kid from Spain*.

Thinking Cantor's proposal would be good publicity for his regime, *Il Duce* turned Eddie over to his son-in-law, Count Ciano, who did not speak English. Cantor spent a long evening with him.

"What," he asked through an interpreter, "is this unholy alliance between Mussolini and Hitler?"

"When the time comes," Ciano replied. "Mussolini will take Hitler and. . . ." He zipped his finger across his throat.

*Roman Scandals* (dubbed in Italian, except for the songs) had made Cantor very popular in Italy. "The picture was playing in a fourth-run house when we arrived," reported Margie, "and since Daddy loves to get the reaction of that type of audience—they're far more honest than a preview or first-night audience—we slipped in, unannounced.

"The only reaction, however, that he got was from our own party, because as soon as word spread about that we were in the house, no one paid any attention to the picture but kept watching Daddy. He finally had to stand up and acknowledge the tremendous ovation."

The Cantors went to St. Moritz, Switzerland, from Rome, where Eddie found his daughters to be strictly indoor people. "I bought each of them a ski outfit—not to go skiing, just to get them outside the hotel into the crisp cold air. They never budged. Finally, I got angry. 'I bought the suits, you're going to wear 'em,' I said. So they put on the ski suits, and I had a sleigh waiting at the hotel door. It started to snow as we pulled away, just a light delicate little snow, and these dames all start to cry, especially Edna. As the bitter tears froze, she sobbed, 'We came here to have a good time, Daddy, not to get healthy.' "

They arrived in Paris on Saturday, December 29, Eddie augmenting United Artists French publicity chief Curtis Melnitz's efforts by sitting on the outside of the locomotive and crying, *"Vive la France."* He hosted a cocktail party at the Hôtel Crillon that evening, announcing to the press his scheme to make American pictures in Europe with American artists and American capital. Cantor claimed that Ambassador Straus as well as Mussolini were interested, although nothing more would be heard of the project.

When the Parisian songwriter Pascal Bastia said he wanted to sing Cantor a couple of songs, Eddie invited him to drop by his hotel suite the next morning, warning him that there was no piano. Bastia showed up with four moving men and a baby grand. The hotel employees were shocked, but Cantor scarcely blinked. Having worked for Ziegfeld and been a top star for years, he had long grown accustomed to pomp, circumstance, and efforts to impress.

London was next, and Margie came to disbelieve the popular conception of the English as restrained after they gave Eddie the most "rapturous" welcome he had received in all his years as a public figure: "At every theatre, nightclub, and restaurant, he was forced to take a bow. At the first soccer game he attended, sixty thousand people arose at his entrance. At Whitechapel, he was mobbed by five thousand fans. Huge placards at every newsstand heralded his every move. They were charming to Mother, Natalie, Edna, and me, too. The night we attended Leslie Henson's, the audience yelled, 'We want Ida! We want Ida!' until Mother, terribly embarrassed, responded with a bow."

The British Minister of Transport, Leslie Hore-Belisha, asked Eddie to repeat his "Drive Carefully . . . We Love Our Children" message on the BBC the evening after the Cantors' arrival. Just before the broadcast Margie spoke to a BBC official who said he thought the message was "too sentimental." Margie kept her silence, knowing it was too late for her father to switch topics. But she worried until several days later, when the BBC received thousands of letters from all over the United Kingdom. The broadcast, for which Eddie received five hundred dollars (promptly donated to charity), was a minor sensation.

The Cantors dined at the Savoy after the broadcast. Vic Oliver, an American comedian then married to Winston Churchill's daughter, Sarah, came over to their table, telling Eddie the "old gentleman" wanted to see him.

After the amenities, the sixty-year-old Churchill asked Cantor how many choruses of "Whoopee" he remembered. Eddie recalled five or six.

"I know *all* the choruses, my boy," said Churchill. Then and there, Great Britain's greatest statesman chanted half a dozen choruses Cantor had long since forgotten.

If Pascal Bastia's piano with four moving men had failed to impress Cantor in the slightest, Winston Churchill's "Makin' Whoopee" left the poor Jew from the Lower East Side speechless. This was it—total acceptance, on a common level, from an acknowledged leader of *the* leading Anglo-Saxon country. Eddie went back to his table and told Ida and the girls.

He had never been more touched.

Following more conferences with film producers, BBC officials, and reporters and a recording session for Rex-British Decca, sandwiched in among dinners, sightseeing, and other activities that thrilled the girls, the Cantors sailed back to New York on the *Ile de France* on January 9, 1935. Other passengers included the Russian bass Feodor Chaliapin and the violinist Mischa Elman, both of whom were praised by Eddie in the *New York Times*. Cantor, though, reserved his greatest praise for Mussolini.

"He's a great man. Everything in Italy is done for the people, and he never lies to them. If he tells them a new road will be opened at 3:30 P.M. on September 14, you can bet your last *lira* that it will be. Of course, we have had some great statesmen over here, but they would have been better if they had not kidded the people." Cantor would adopt a different tone toward Mussolini in years to come, after Fascist Italy invaded Ethiopia.

Following a meeting with Bill Hulburd over story and production on his next film for Sam Goldwyn, Eddie took Ida to Hollywood, Florida, to "rest" from their vacation, leaving Margie to run things at the San Remo. Eddie spent most of the time either reading in the sun or preparing radio scripts, mostly on the telephone to Phil Rapp in New York.

Rapp had replaced David Freedman as Eddie's principal writer prior to the Cantors' trip to Europe. There was no great public announcement; comedians acknowledged their writers as little as possible. But Cantor and Freedman—the Damon and Pythias of Broadway—were through.

Eddie had not dreamed, in the first weeks of his premier season on the air for Chase and Sanborn, that most of his yearly income would come from his radio work. As his number of shows per season increased, and his salary rose to seven thousand dollars a week, Eddie came to rue the quick and thoughtless deal he had pitched to Beatrice Freedman. In October, having signed with his new sponsor at ten thousand dollars a week, Cantor informed Freedman that their relationship had ended and stopped paying him his cut of the money. Freedman, urged on by his wife, Beatrice, raged, claiming their verbal agreement was binding for life. Eddie saw it differently.

In truth, though 10 percent had been agreed on, the verbal agreement—it was hardly a contract—had been rather vague as to the period it covered. Neither did it spell out whether either man could terminate it. "A verbal contract," as Sam Goldwyn once was quoted, "is not worth the paper it's written on." Cantor knew this long before he ever worked for Goldwyn.

Ben Bodec called Cantor's debut on Pebeco "a smackerino of a perfor-mance," noting that the half-hour format worked entirely to Eddie's advan-tage. The sports announcer Ted Husing proved a worthy temporary successor to James Wallington, and Cantor's crossfire with "Parkyakarkus," while "a little too fast for the average listener . . . was minimized by the deft dovetailing of the lines and the clearness with which they registered on the loudspeaker." The fact that Chase and Sanborn was no longer Cantor's sponsor was exploited in ways Bodec found both "adroit and diverting," and the gimmick was repeated on the following two shows.

The Crossley Reports, mass media's initial ratings system, showed that Cantor's first program for Pebeco had won the largest listening audience of any regular radio program in history—a triumph, not only for Cantor, his cast, and his crew, but also for William Paley's CBS, still a year away from threatening the dominance of NBC. The success of Cantor's Pebeco Show was an important milestone in the emergence of the so-called Tiffany Network.

The show was geared to the supposed mentality of the average radio listener in 1935, meaning that the humor was not too sophisticated: obvi-ous and leaden gags punched expertly across by Cantor with Ted Husing as the straight man, "Parkyakarkus's" mindless chatter, and some clever but eventually labored mixups between the old sponsor (Chase and Sanborn) and the new (Pebeco). Much more entertaining were the songs, especially two on the second broadcast.

Composer Gerald Marks wrote "Oh, Susannah, Dust Off the Old Pianna" with his lyricist-partners, Irving Caesar and Sammy Lerner. "Irving got a good response when he tried to sell it to Louis Bernstein [of Shapiro-Bernstein]," recalled Marks. "So he decided to publish it himself.

"Eddie Cantor was a natural for it. Eddie sometimes got up early, and he actually called me at six o'clock in the morning to come over and re-hearse the song. I got there by seven, and we worked. He was a very quick study. I remember his little daughter, Janet, coming into the room. Eddie laughed and gave her a quick pat on the backside."

"Oh, Susannah, Dust Off the Old Pianna" became one of Eddie's main-stays for the next few years. A more enduring hit was "Merrily We Roll Along," which Eddie wrote with Murray Mencher and Charlie Tobias. The strikingly upbeat song, first sung by Cantor on the second broadcast, be-came the instrumental theme song of the series, played between the pro-gram's different segments. Several months later, Warner Bros. bought it as the theme for its "Merry Melodies" cartoons, and the tune is now world-famous, known to millions unaware of the song's title or authorship or of the fact that Cantor introduced it.

Radio had become Cantor's mainstay, bringing his name and persona into millions of homes each week and ensuring his continued stardom. He was nonetheless still looking forward to his next Goldwyn film vehicle and seriously considering a return to the Broadway stage.

Vinton Freedley, the producer of *Anything Goes*, wanted to star Eddie in a Broadway show that would, in turn, be sold to Goldwyn as Cantor's next film vehicle. Having reached terms with Goldwyn in Hollywood, Freedley was amazed to find that Cantor would not take a salary—"just" 15 percent of gross receipts. Howard Lindsay and Russel (Buck) Crouse had agreed to do the book, with Cole Porter set to write the music and lyrics. Rehearsals would start in September, after Cantor finished his film work for 1935. No vehicle for that last film had been secured, but Goldwyn wanted the English detective novelist Joseph Fairlie to supply an original story and Frank Butler of the Hal Roach Studios to punch it up with gags.

Cantor had other ideas. He had loved *Three Men on a Horse*, the George Abbott play about a mild-mannered man with the uncanny knack of picking winners in horse races, and saw it—quite correctly—as a possible source for a great Cantor vehicle. The trouble was that Warner Bros. already owned 25 percent of *Three Men on a Horse*.

The owner could have been Sam Goldwyn. Cantor claimed that Fred Kohlmar, Sam's representative, had come across the unproduced play in New York the year before and had recommended that Goldwyn purchase a 25 percent interest for twenty-five thousand dollars. "The play was sent out," Cantor maintained. "Goldwyn never read it. He had someone else read it who turned it down." The Warners filled the breach.

While Goldwyn's people looked for other Cantor vehicles, Eddie focused mainly on his weekly show for Pebeco. Still president of the Screen Actors' Guild, he responded eagerly to the proposed unionization of actors in radio:

> There are many evils among present radio conditions, and many that can be corrected in orderly fashion through the right kind of actors' organization. It isn't the big fellows who are affected by abuses, but the little fellows who get it in the neck in radio as well as in any other business. Through sensible organization, the little fellows could obtain protection against prevailing evils.

Eddie lashed out at the exorbitant commissions being paid to actors' agents (30 to 45 percent), claiming that 10 to 15 percent, as in other fields, was sufficient remuneration. The then recently organized Associated Radio Artists eventually led to the formation of the American Federation of Radio Artists, with Cantor as its first president.

Cantor saw no contradiction between this and the small salaries he paid on radio, his double-deal signings of performers to managerial contracts, or his temper tantrums and demands for work from people who were sick or injured. (Ruth Marko still remembers the time Eddie insisted her husband, Robert, who was on his writing staff, meet him for a conference the day after he broke his arm.)

Cantor was no ogre. He simply thought that people in show business had, perforce, the same relentless drive and energy that had marked his career. Hence, he sometimes made the same impossible demands on them that he made on himself. The Eddie Cantor who demanded easier working conditions for chorus girls was Cantor the public figure; the other one was Cantor on the job. Neither was insincere.

Eddie Cantor was an emotional man who wept easily and unashamedly, laughed without restraint, and embraced old friends with genuine warmth. He had, however, a quick temper and did not shrink from confrontations regarding work performance.

Passion—for his family, his work, and the things he believed in—governed Eddie Cantor's day-to-day life every bit as much as careful reason guided his career. The result was a remarkably successful and rewarding life that Eddie, whatever little doubts he may have harbored, never failed to appreciate.

Eddie was now forming his own radio consultant business with Ben Holtzmann. Describing himself as a "program adviser" rather than a builder and producer, Cantor found his first customer in his own sponsor, Lehn & Fink, who wanted a new show to advertise their other product, Lysol. Eddie recommended a show utilizing exclusively feminine talent (including the announcer, orchestra, and singing star, with the young Jane Froman penciled in). Living with six women, not including Winnie, the cook, three maids, and two secretaries, had its influence on Cantor.

Warner Bros. turned down Goldwyn's offer of $90,000 for the film rights to *Three Men on a Horse*, and Sam looked into *Dreamland*, a series of stories about life in an amusement park that was set for publication in the *Saturday Evening Post*, as a source for Cantor's next film vehicle. Eddie was far from enthusiastic, and his mood was further clouded by a summons he received on Tuesday, April 2. David Freedman was suing him for a quarter of a million dollars.

The suit claimed that Cantor had promised Freedman 10 percent of his gross earnings as long as he "gave performances over the air." Freedman's services as writer, the complaint also alleged, were largely responsible for raising Cantor's weekly radio income from $2,500 to $10,000.

Cantor, true to form, did not avoid commenting on the suit, declaring that he had never had a verbal or any other contract with Freedman and that he had not told him his services were no longer required. Freedman, alleged Cantor, never wrote *for* him but rather wrote *with* him, serving at various times as one of anywhere from four to a dozen collaborators.

Eddie and Ida were certain that Freedman's wife had instigated the suit, but Cantor underscored his feelings about Freedman in an ad he took in the April 3, 1935, issue of *Variety*, expresssing his "deep appreciation" to

Philip Rapp, "my only collaborator." The break with David Freedman was now final.

Eddie, Margie, Rapp, and Harry Einstein sailed to Hollywood through the Panama Canal in May. Cantor made immediate plans for a Hollywood office for his radio consultant service but suffered "stomach pains" the following Sunday night and entered Good Samaritan Hospital on Monday.

Physicians, who first said Cantor needed treatment for a "minor stomach ailment," performed what was described as major surgery on Wednesday, May 22. "He had gallstones," Edna Cantor McHugh says. The extracted stones were facetiously mounted on black velvet, like a necklace, for home display.

Ida and the younger girls now came out from New York, and Eddie left the hospital to celebrate his twenty-first wedding anniversary on Sunday, June 9. The latest Cantor West Coast summer home was all prepared and rented—a luxurious house at 915 North Crescent Drive in Beverly Hills with a sloping driveway. "That's where I learned to rollerskate," remembers Janet Cantor. "Marilyn showed me how and then gave me a shove down the driveway. I crashed into the garage door, but I could skate!"

Samuel Goldwyn had several writers working on *Dreamland* by the time Eddie reached Hollywood, including Bayard Veiller, who walked out after four days. Eddie, getting daily shots delivered by a male nurse supplied by Good Samaritan, was angered when he found the script nowhere near completion. Three weeks of dissatisfaction culminated in a major blowup late that June, Cantor telling Goldwyn and his staff that he was having his local attorney and two lawyers in New York find ways to break his contract. Goldwyn and Abe Lehr quickly negotiated peace with Cantor through Ben Holzman, Sam agreeing to put two of Eddie's gags into the script of *Shoot the Chutes* (as the unfinished screenplay for *Dreamland* was titled) and to reimburse Eddie for the salaries paid to Rapp and Einstein since they had arrived in California.

Cantor also got Goldwyn's permission to try out material for *Shoot the Chutes* in a ten-day vaudeville booking at the Fox Theatre in San Francisco, Margie timing the laughs with a stopwatch. The "Cantor Unit," which now included Einstein, Rubinoff, and the Nicholas Brothers, moved on to the Los Angeles Paramount in early August, giving thirty-three performances in one week.

Goldwyn gave approval to a script for *Shoot the Chutes* by Frank Butler and George Haight several days later, just as Eddie was stunned by the news of Will Rogers's death in an airplane crash in Alaska. Will was fifty-five years old.

Eddie was in awe of Jolson, admired W. C. Fields, and loved Bert Williams. His high regard for Will, however, had little to do with Rogers's stage work. "Of first importance to [Will Rogers] always was his role as Mr.

Citizen," Cantor later claimed. The image was, it must be stressed, completely genuine.

Some have claimed that interest in politics and the "common man" was simply Rogers's gimmick—that he wooed politicians (the alleged targets of his humor) and built a career by painting himself as a downhome country boy in the manner of "Lonesome Rhodes" in Budd Schulberg's film, *A Face in the Crowd*. The evidence does not bear out this contention.

Rogers never claimed to be a revolutionary, and his oft-repeated trademark line, "I never met a man I didn't like," applied not just to cowboys, farmers, and factory workers but to businessmen and politicians. His daily newspaper columns often contained powerful accusations and insights disguised as harmless homilies, such as his observation, during the Depression, that the United States might become the first country to "go to the poor house in an automobile." Rogers, of course, lived well before the era of caustic political humorists like Mort Sahl, and it's doubtful if any comedian who essayed anti–political establishment material would have found a ready audiences before the middle 1950s.

Rogers's writings and speeches, however, did much to focus national attention on the devastating effects of the Great Depression on the lives of ordinary people. Perhaps his greatest contribution was as a good will ambassador, not just in representing the United States to Europe but in serving as conciliator between the big cities and the rest of the country before and during the Depression.

He did not trust the stock market and had something of the populist about him in his private life as well as on the radio and stage. But Rogers, because of his own beliefs and style, did not loudly champion truly controversial themes. Cantor, in the years that followed Will's death, surely did. Part of Cantor's activism was due to Hitler's rise. Much of it, however, grew out of Rogers's death, as if the passing of his friend and mentor had freed Eddie to assume the role of "Mr. Citizen" and push it one step further in a new public regime.

Eddie spent the weeks immediately following Will's death at work on the script for *Shoot the Chutes* with a team of five writers (Arthur Sheekman, Nat Perrin, Norman Taurog, Rapp, and Einstein). Walter DeLeon and Francis Martin were brought in for final polishing before rehearsals started on September 9. Filming began three weeks later, almost five months after Cantor's last broadcast for Pebeco. The delay had scuttled plans for Eddie's return to Broadway for Vinton Freedley, who eventually produced the show as *Red, Hot and Blue* starring Ethel Merman, Jimmy Durante, and Bob Hope.

Cantor, still smarting over *Three Men on a Horse* and angry over the time lost on *Shoot the Chutes*, had declared a private cold war against Goldwyn by the time that shooting started. "One day," he remembered, "he came on the set and I stopped working. I told the director I wouldn't do the scene until 'that man' left the set." Goldwyn's feelings gradually turned equally hostile.

The plot of *Shoot the Chutes* concerned Eddie Pink (Cantor), a meek man who gathers courage from a book on assertiveness and is hired to manage an amusement park. Gangsters, who have murdered the park's previous six managers, try, with the aid of Merman, a singer with whom Pink is hopelessly smitten, to force Pink to install their slot machines. Pink finally realizes she is in league with the gangsters, and the crooks are apprehended following a long chase on the Ferris wheel. Eddie winds up in the arms of his supportive secretary, played by the attractive Sally Eilers.

The high point of the comedy was Cantor's receipt of a shampoo treatment at the hands of a sideshow "grifter" salesman, his deadpan resignation to the indignity far funnier than any of the film's dialogue or its overlong chase sequence.

The Ferris wheel chase was one of the longest and most hazardous in motion picture history. When Eddie's first stunt double, Gordon Cravath, broke his leg in late October, Bobby Rose stepped in and broke his leg as well. The work was lengthy, dangerous, and, for Cantor, a wasted effort. Eddie Pink was the same insipid character he had been playing since *Palmy Days*, and *Shoot the Chutes* was a poor substitute for what he really craved.

The delayed start of shooting on *Shoot the Chutes* forced Cantor to start his radio season on the West Coast, sandwiching his broadcasts between filming. The season's first show featured a new character called Mr. Guffey, played by Sidney Fields, a comic signed by Cantor out of *Life Begins at Minsky's*. Fields's constant negativity as Mr. Guffey registered effectively against Cantor's gung-ho pace and set the stage for his Mr. Fields character on the Abbott and Costello syndicated television program of the '50s.

Cantor had a different orchestra conductor on every show for the first six months of the season—Gus Arnheim, Georgie Stoll, Jimmy Grier, Anson Weeks, Phil Ohman, Stoll again, and finally Lou Gress (who'd worked with Eddie on *Kid Boots*) beginning on November 10. The ratings, while not quite as high as those of six months earlier, still put the show among the top five programs despite mounting competition from a new wave of comics with vaudeville experience who were now coming into their own in radio: Jack Benny, Burns and Allen, and Fred Allen. These comedians, whose humor was verbal or, in Benny's case, deliberate, were suited to radio in a way that Cantor, for all his "theories" about radio audiences, never would or could be. Fred Allen, who featured classically droll material, called obvious, set jokes like those found on the Cantor program, "Eddie Cantor humor."

Nor had Cantor yet become the showman, as opposed to the performer. The seeds for this new role were planted at this time, however, by Sol Lesser, an early film exhibitor who had developed the child actors Jackie Coogan and Baby Peggy in the 1920s.

Lesser heard a seven-year-old boy soprano sing a difficult aria from *Rigoletto* at the home of Mario Marfioti, Grace Moore's vocal coach, and signed him to a contract. Lesser saw the youngster as a well-scrubbed Jackie Coogan who would sing his way to stardom with the right tear-jerking numbers. The boy, Bob Breen, was promptly redubbed "Bobby" Breen, and put into a film, *Let's Sing Again.*

Lesser, a star-maker with a genius for publicity, saw the possibilities of linking Bobby—the ultimate "boy" star and in Lesser's eyes a possible competitor with Shirley Temple—with Cantor, the man the world identified with having five daughters, but no son.

Would Cantor go for it? Sally Breen, Bobby's elder sister by ten years and the driving force behind the boy's budding career, had endeavored to have Bobby sing for Cantor months before, without success. Eddie was besieged by women carrying moppets of varying description and talent almost daily.

But Cantor listened to Sol Lesser. A new song had been written for Breen titled "Santa, Send My Mommie Back to Me," a tearjerker dreamed up for the approaching Christmas season. Cantor was sold on the idea of one broadcast after an audition.

Cantor welcomed Christmas rather early that year—on his broadcast of November 10, playing Santa Claus in a sketch segueing into Bobby's song. The response, from hundreds of middle-American listeners, was overwhelming. "I thought I was immune to all that sort of thing," Cantor was quoted as saying. "But that little kid singing that Christmas song made us all cry like babies."

Eddie resumed Christmas four weeks later, introducing "Santa Claus Is Coming to Town" on the December 8 show, but he did not have Breen back until December 29, when, surrendering to Lesser's constant urging, he and Bobby did a "Treasure Island" skit and Breen sang another ballad.

*Shoot the Chutes,* now titled *Strike Me Pink,* was finished by the middle of December, and Eddie stayed on the coast for the cutting and previews. He and Margie left for New York at the end of the month, rejoining Ida and the other girls at the San Remo after New Year's.

Ben Holzman had preceded Eddie back east by three weeks, wrapping up a number of details and making preparations for the New York broadcasts. Pebeco renewed Cantor's contract for nineteen additional weeks and moved his time slot up from 8–8:30 to 7–7:30, putting him opposite Jack Benny on NBC. This was rough competition, but Cantor had some ideas that he hoped would see him through.

Bobby Breen was signed for ten more broadcasts, and Cantor got an "exclusive" on his services in radio that amounted to a personal management contract with Eddie Cantor.* Publicity yarns planted with obliging

---

*Bobby would arrive in New York after finishing work on Sol Lesser's film, *The Show Goes On.*

magazine scribes touted Bobby as "the son that Eddie never had," hinting at a romance between Breen and Janet, Eddie's youngest daughter.

It was p.r. of the lowest sort in practice at the time, which meant the public loved it. Cantor and his writers played the Breen angle up big, portraying Eddie as the square, indulgent adult straight against Bobby's supposed smart lines in much the same way Danny Thomas would play straight for Rusty Haymer decades years later.

Strengthening his growing image as a humanitarian, Cantor kicked off his first New York broadcast of the season by announcing a five-thousand-dollar scholarship to be given to the writer of the best five-hundred-word essay on the topic "How Can America Stay Out of War?" The money, equivalent to well over $50,000 in the 1990s, would come out of Cantor's pocket, not that of his sponsor. Entries had to be postmarked no later than February 22 so that Cantor could announce the winner on the air for Pebeco on April 5.

"Every man, woman, and child in America is invited to enter," Cantor said. "There is only one condition: if the person who wins this scholarship does not wish to go to college, or cannot, he or she must designate another person to do so. Judging will be on the basis of the most constructive, sincere, and interesting letter, regardless of fancy writing or technical knowledge."

Cantor and, especially, his sponsor also thought the time had come to make peace with the New York radio columnists. At least thirteen of them attended a dinner Eddie sponsored the week after his return to New York broadcasts, burying the hatchet that had all but barred the Cantor name from radio columns since the early days of *Chase and Sanborn*.

Cantor's activity remained at the same ceaseless, breakneck pace. Later in January, he emceed the President's Birthday Ball in Brooklyn. (Similar balls were held in all parts of the country under the auspices of the President's Birthday Committee.) Eddie was also preparing a new unit show for picture house appearances.

"Parkyakarkus" seemed better on the stage of Philadelphia's Earle Theatre than on the radio. His first routine with Cantor wound up with his singing a "Greek version" of "The Music Goes Round and Round." Cantor did his Shirley Temple takeoff, introduced a song, "You Hit the Spot," made a plug for his "Peace" essay contest, and sang "Let Them Keep It over There," a philosophy that, while in keeping with the contest, would prove untenable in the near future. Wallington, the Frazee Sisters, and the Three Gobs (black tap dancers in sailor outfits), rounded out the program.

The next three broadcasts were done from Miami, Eddie's now-established winter rest home. He returned to New York in March, and an Eddie Cantor testimonial dinner at the Hotel Astor on Saturday night, April 4, netted $25,000 for the American Jewish Congress. Cantor's speech on this occasion stood in marked contrast to what might have been expected from someone who was sponsoring a peace essay contest in 1936.

Eddie said he intended to go "from one end of the country to the other" in an effort to raise funds to take as many Jewish children out of Germany as possible. Cantor said that eighty million dollars had been poured into the United States for propaganda, much of it anti-Semitic.

"If you don't think this propaganda is taking effect, you don't know what is happening," he said. "Formerly, when you went into a moving picture house and Hitler appeared on the screen, you heard nothing but hisses. Now when you see him you only hear two hisses to a hundred cheers— Hitler, the man who just won such an overwhelming victory over nobody."

Cantor first became aware of Hitler's villainy through his voracious reading and through his contacts with both Jews and non-Jews in politics on both sides of the Atlantic. But how he guessed—correctly—the true extent of the threat in the mid-1930s can be explained only in light of his intelligence, awareness, and acute sensitivity to anything that touched Jews. At a time when Joseph P. Kennedy was urging American film studios to "go easy" on Nazi Germany, and before most Jews sensed the extent of Nazism's menace, Eddie Cantor, the eye-rolling, prancing, and hand-clapping musical comedy star of the 1920s, the purveyor of corn humor on the radio, sounded the alarm on Adolf Hitler. And Cantor, in his way, would make a difference.

Eddie announced the winner of the peace essay contest over the air for Pebeco the following evening. He was Lloyd Lewis, an eighteen-year-old farm youth and high school student from Plattsburg, Clinton County, Missouri, who had spent "only thirty minutes" outside Missouri. Lewis's essay was selected as the best of the approximately 212,000 received from all parts of the United States.

> Peace is an expensive luxury. The supreme good in the mind of the average man is not the building of peace among nations but the securing of the advantages of his own nation before that of any or all other nations. As long as this is true, every man is the raw material of an army; and popular psychology supports our own economic nationalism in a tendency toward international strife. It will not be until we are ready to put international good above national advantage that we shall be prepared for peace.

The editorial page of the *New York Times* reprinted this excerpt on Tuesday, April 7. "Eddie Cantor," said the *Times*, "may feel that he has made a substantial and inspiring international contribution . . . the award was deserved, for no one of this multitude of youth could have written a better paragraph than that which was embodied in his essay."

The *Times* was more correct than it imagined. Lewis, who had never before ridden on a train, was a guest at a farewell party at the Kansas City airport prior to his flight to New York on Thursday, April 9. As he flew in, forces were at work to discredit him.

A woman member of the New Jersey Joint Council of International Relations noticed that the published excerpts from the winning essay matched part of an article written by Dr. Frank Kingdon, president of the University of Newark, for the December 1935 issue of *Peace Digest*. She notified Dr. Kingdon, who tried, in vain, to reach Cantor by telephone on Saturday, April 11.

Lewis, in the meantime, had been warmly greeted by Cantor and put up as his guest at the San Remo. Lewis, described as a "long-faced, grinning strippling," was certainly a revelation to the Cantor girls. A real-life embodiment of the character played on film by Slim Sommerville, he was a junior at Plattsburgh High School "down on Smith's Fork of the River Platte" in Missouri whose best subjects were manual training and mechanical drawing.

The *Newark News*, Dr. Kingdon's hometown paper, ran a story about Lewis's deception on Monday, April 13. A *News* reporter reached Cantor that morning.

A shocked Cantor spoke to Lloyd. "He said that no one had told him the essay had to be original," Eddie recalled years later. While Cantor went to see his lawyers, Lewis, in a press conference in Benny Holzman's office, unperturbedly told newsmen he did not see what the fuss was all about.

> Mr. Gillian—that's my history teacher—gave us this subject, "How to Keep America Out of War," as part of our class work. My brother Harry and me have been boarding at Hetty Robertson's place in Plattsburg all winter, on account of it's right cold out on our farm and the roads get bad.
>
> I see where I have to get me some material to write that essay and I asked Mrs. Robertson did she have anything and she had this magazine. She gets it all the time. I looked it over and I reckoned I might get some stuff out of it—and I did.
>
> It was filled with lots of words that was a bit too big, and I took some of them out and put in words I thought of. I didn't think, at the time, that I'd get anywheres with it. Thought it was a good-enough piece, but I was sure they'd be better ones than that. I didn't think it was so hot.

Cantor, far more shaken and, for once, at a loss for words, said, "I feel badly. It's a terrible thing."

Lloyd Lewis was sent home by plane that evening, Eddie coming out of shock to ask reporters not to "ride this boy to the point where he'll jump out a window. . . . He's just a kid. He's had a big disappointment already." The reporters of the day complied.

Cantor announced a new winner, the runner-up, Owen W. Matthews III of Portland, Oregon, the following Sunday evening. Matthews, an honor student who had been graduated from Jefferson High School the previous

June, was an Eagle Scout who used his experiences at the 1933 World Boy Scout Jamboree in Godollo, Hungary, as an example of how international youth conferences "would do more for world peace than any meeting of diplomats." Matthews, who had hoped to work his way through Oregon State College as an engineering major, went instead to M.I.T. Cantor attended his graduation.

Cantor had been among those Broadway stars who did their own business and contract negotiations, guarding their independence, proudly jealous of their knowledge of the show world, and reluctant to "give away" 10 percent of their earnings. Now, upon his return from Miami, Eddie signed with the William Morris Agency. He had decided that "a good agent will get you much more salary than the commission amounts to."

The Morris agents, under Abe Lastfogel, operational head of the agency since the death of William Morris in 1932, set to work on Cantor's behalf, not just lining up more filmhouse dates (the number of which depended on how soon Samuel Goldwyn would want Eddie to start work on his next picture) but improving his lot in radio as well. Pebeco paid Cantor handsomely, but the Morris Agency put together a new contract with the Texas Company, producers of Texaco gasoline. Eddie would become the "Mayor of Texaco Town" on CBS on Sunday nights from 8:30 to 9:00 beginning in September. The new contract would allow Cantor to do most or all of his broadcasting from the West Coast, with the company absorbing any line costs. This would make a major change in the lives of his family.

Cantor's last broadcast for Pebeco was on May 10, 1936. The following day, he, Ida, the girls, Frenchy, Winnie, and the rest of the retainers took the superchief out to California. The family would never live on the East Coast again.

The reason was simple. Eddie's film work was in southern California. Broadcasting from there would mean that he would never have to sacrifice months of lucrative radio work while waiting for Sam Goldwyn's writers to finish a script. It was economically sensible and far less hectic; and the weather was much better.

To Marilyn and Janet, the move was like a prison sentence. Marilyn had long since become a dyed-in-the-wool Broadway buff, but Janet, now eight and a half, simply loved the San Remo, her friends from school, and the Ethical Culture School that she attended. A sweet and simple little girl who took things at face value—qualities her status as the baby of the family did nothing to undercut—she had found Ethical Culture's lessons on humanity entirely consistent with the secular and happy world around her. Her parents were publicly and nominally Jewish—Eddie still shunned pork and shellfish—but they paid no attention to religion except on Yom Kippur, when they went to synagogue without the younger children.

Sidney Skolsky once wrote that Eddie wanted to "start his own religion"—a ridiculous and untrue statement, on the surface. But Cantor's brand of broad-based ecumenism was as close to a "world" religion as a Jew was likely to believe in—especially one who still observed the dietary laws. ("You can eat pork if you wish," said Ida to the servants. "But please don't let Mr. Cantor see or smell it.") Ritual observance being just a safety ring around the core of a religion, it was only a small step from nonobservance to nonbelief for Eddie's daughters.

Winnie's home-grown Irish devotion to the Catholic religion puzzled Janet. The Cantors' maids, also Irish Catholics, tried, without success, to answer Janet's queries about why they went to mass or felt that God existed. Winnie's answer was "It's my faith, child. I just try to accept it."

Janet respected Winnie, but she could never see a reason for religion. If her sisters' faith was "secular agnosticism," hers was a sure atheism. Future events, like the slaughter of six million Jews in Europe, served only to reinforce her views.

Cantor traveled with his family as far as Cleveland, the Morris office having booked Eddie and his unit show into the RKO Palace. The following week, they were at Chicago's Palace Music Hall, breaking all attendance marks for Windy City theatres.

The Chicago Palace went to six shows on Saturday for the first time in its history. The only problem seemed to be the young people who stayed in their unreserved seats for show after show, while others waited on line, unable to get in. Eddie asked the kids to leave as "a personal favor" and promised to sing songs for them on their way out.

Cantor took personal ads in the Chicago newspapers apologizing to those who had tried to see his shows but failed—a great, transparent piece of self-promotion. The final gross was $35,200, better than the mathematical gross possibiities of the theatre at that scale. Eddie came away with $17,600 for his unit, personally netting about ten thousand dollars. "Breaking records is something that my father did so often that it wasn't news to us," remembers Janet. "It was just something he did."

The trade was not quite so blasé. Leo Spitz, the future president of Universal-International, wired Cantor from New York: TO BREAK A RECORD NOW AND THEN IS NOT UNUSUAL, BUT TO DO IT AS CONSISTENTLY AS YOU HAVE OVER A PERIOD OF YEARS STAMPS YOU AS THE OUTSTANDING BOX OFFICE ATTRACTION IN SHOW BUSINESS.

Cantor nonetheless felt stymied and betrayed in Hollywood. Goldwyn had reportedly bid $200,000 for Billy Rose's *Jumbo* as a vehicle for Cantor but allowed the deal to fall through. Eddie really fumed when Goldwyn, with no other script prepared, refused to loan him out to Warners to make *Three Men on a Horse*.

Eddie and Ida went to Honolulu for a brief vacation. Goldwyn was still bidding for the composer Vincent Youmans to write the score for a still plotless, untitled Cantor vehicle, with the writer Arthur Kober having flown in from New York to work on the nonexistent script. Returning to L.A.,

Eddie spoke with representatives of the J. Walter Thompson Agency about doing *Three Men on a Horse* on the Lux Radio Theatre, until Warners dragged their contract out and said that they forbade it.

Eddie took another vacation in Santa Barbara, more to get away from the frustrations than to get a real rest. He was eager to return to work—on radio, in films, or on the stage.

On Monday, July 27, Cantor reported to his office on the UA lot and learned that Goldwyn still had nothing planned. Angry and disgusted, he again offered to buy his way out of his contract. When that was refused, he walked off the lot and asked his lawyers to seek ways that he could sue Sam for his release.

Goldwyn found out quickly about Eddie's plans and became, for once, as angry as his star. Negotiations quickly followed between the lawyers, Cantor agreeing to reimburse Goldwyn for expenses incurred in preparing his latest—unnamed and unscripted—picture.

A statement went out to the press on Saturday, August 1:

"Upon Mr. Eddie Cantor's request for a release from his contract, I have today terminated our contractual agreement."

Cantor, Bobby Breen, and Harry Einstein left to play a week in San Francisco three days later, breaking all house records at the Golden Gate Theatre. Eddie, who spent his offstage moments showing the essay contest winner Owen Matthews around town, turned most of his attention to a pending deal with Twentieth Century-Fox when he returned to Hollywood. He conferred with Joseph M. Schenck, Darryl F. Zanuck, and William Goetz on the preliminaries before bringing in Abe Lastfogel, Benny Holtzman, and Abe Berman, his personal attorney, for final negotiations.

The terms called for three films in two years, with a guarantee of $200,000 a picture—$50,000 more per picture than he had been getting from Sam Goldwyn. Cantor was delighted with Lastfogel's contribution and made the Morris Agency his representative for films as well as radio and stage work.

Tentative plans called for the first film to start early in February. Cantor, in the meantime, prepared for his first season as "the Mayor of Texaco Town."

# Chapter 10

# ``BEFORE I'M A PERFORMER . . .''

*"The Jews of this country have only three things to fear: Bernard*
*Baruch, the motion picture industry, and Eddie Cantor."*
—Father Charles Coughlin

The career of Eddie Cantor, distinguished by its shrewd, adaption to new mediums, switched gears after Cantor left Goldwyn. The change was hardly noticed at the time, although it was well marked, sudden, and, in its own way, profound. Cantor had decided that his youth was over. He would now become the first in a long line of superstars to "reinvent" himself.

His first show for Texaco signaled a new era for broadcasting as well. *Texaco Town* was a well-rehearsed, well-mounted program featuring a singing chorus, special-material numbers, and musical introductions (generally "Pony Boy") for all individual performers. A special song, whose lyrics included a sly reference to Eddie's sexual prowess as the father of five daughters, heralded Cantor as "the Mayor of Texaco Town."

The major highlight of the first show was the debut of a new, anonymous young singer introduced as Bobby Breen's friend, the daughter of the fire chief. The girl devastated listeners with one of the most unforgettable renditions of Arditi's *"Il Bacio"* in the annals of music. The applause from the studio audience was overwhelming, but Cantor still did not identify the singer.

The obvious ploy worked, as thousands of listeners wrote in asking about the unnamed sensation. The girl, as it turned out, had just completed her first movie, *Three Smart Girls*. Her name was Deanna Durbin.

Deanna, thirteen years of age, had been brought to sing for Cantor by Rufus LeMaire, now the casting director for Universal Pictures. The audition, held in the conductor Alfred Newman's bungalow on Chaplin's UA lot shortly before Cantor's split with Goldwyn, proved a revelation. At thirteen, Deanna's voice was fully developed, a high soprano that would have been welcomed in the world of opera with very little additional training.

Cantor was even more amazed at the girl's poise as she auditioned. She was totally calm, sure of her material, and as fully professional as any top star in the business. She was also cheerful, well mannered, and bright—qualities she would project on screen and which would make her Universal's top box-office star until Abbott and Costello's film smash in *Buck Privates*.

Eddie Cantor's influence on the career of Durbin has been overstated many times and dismissed, unfairly, as inconsequential at others. She was under contract to Universal at the time of her "discovery" by Cantor. Eddie, however, made her into an easily recognizable commodity on *Texaco Town*, promoting her to stardom months before the release of her full-length film debut. The trailer for *Three Smart Girls* included the following message:

> Deanna Durbin has as much poise as any star in Hollywood. Her voice is magnificent, and she is loaded with the type of talent and personality rarely seen in persons of her age.
>
> *Eddie Cantor*

Cantor and his writers soon concocted a fictional radio "romance" between Deanna and the nine-year-old Bobby Breen, played largely for laughs. When they had a "quarrel," Bobby cried on Eddie's shoulder, "I gave that girl the best years of my life."

Cantor was now firmly established in the public mind as the "discoverer of talent," eclipsing Gus Edwards by the immediacy and magnitude of the stars he created. And whereas Edwards was remembered chiefly by those in show business, Cantor was considered the premier star maker by the masses of radio listeners.

In a sense, he was giving back to others the same chance he had gotten as a kid. That Cantor had entered show business as a young adult, and not as a child, was obscured by his repeated references to his role in Edwards's "Kid Kabaret," and the fact that Breen and Durbin had been "screened" by pros like Lesser and LeMaire was seldom mentioned. Cantor was the great "Columbus of Show Business," the humanitarian-showman who gave stardom to deserving, talented young people in much the same way Santa Claus dispensed his gifts at Christmas.

When Deanna Durbin appeared for the second time on *Texaco Town*, she was introduced by name for the first time and sang "A Heart That's Free" from the M-G-M film *San Francisco*. "Everytime I hear this little girl sing," said Eddie, "I want to go home and stab my five daughters. Not that they haven't any talent. My girls are all right. Of course, they don't sing, they don't dance, they don't play musical instruments. But gosh, do they tear stockings. Ohh!"

It was on *Texaco Town* that Cantor's daughter became regular props for their father. "Take my daughters—please" was the unofficial theme of Cantor's show, which included seemingly innocuous jokes like this:

My daughter Janet pouted at the small strawberries on our break-fast table. I said, "When I was your age, I never had *any* strawber-ries—or any waffles or orange juice or corn flakes, either." She said, "Gee, Daddy, aren't you glad you're living with us now!"

"It made me cringe," remembered Janet. "I didn't gloat because my fa-ther starved as a kid. That joke made me out to be a brat."

The jokes about Eddie's older girls usually concerned their spending money on new clothes or other vanities. What hurt the girls was Eddie's increasingly used tag line, "Oh, I've got to marry them off."

Many listeners soon came to believe that the Cantor girls were "square" and unattractive. They were neither, but hearing themselves referred to as "Eddie Cantor's homely daughters" on one program was enough to shake their still emerging self-confidence.

If Margie was the only daughter involved with her father's day-to-day life and career, the ringleader of the Cantor girls, her special status was not evident on the radio. Janet, because of her youth, was the only one among them who had a clearcut identity for Cantor's radio listeners. (Mar-gie was perhaps best known by name thanks to the song "Margie" and to her place as Eddie's eldest daughter. What distinguished Cantor's daughters as a group, however, was their albatross status 'round their famous father's neck.

The Dionne quintuplets are today remembered as the five most famous sisters of the century. Cantor's daughters, in their day, were every bit as famous. And, except for Margie (who thought in terms of what was good for Daddy), the girls hated their "celebrity."

Edna, the most independent of the Cantor girls, was also the most crit-ical of Eddie. If Edna did not like his jokes or songs, she told him so in a matter-of-fact manner. Eddie did not always take her criticism—or that of her sisters—very well.

When they told him not to risk doing a Christmas sketch, he argued long and loudly over dinner. Finally, only partly pretending to be impatient, Eddie rose and headed upstairs, muttering, "Afraid. Afraid of everything. They're probably afraid to go to the bathroom 'cause a rat'll bite 'em. . . ."

"He was wonderful when we were kids—playing with us and springing lots of harmless practical jokes," said Janet. "But he couldn't seem to deal with us when we reached our teen years. We were children to him, not women."

Eddie's only comments about his girls' looks were negative. Recalling Ida's bulk after the births of their first two children, Eddie rode his daugh-ters hard about their weight.

"He still loved chocolate," said Janet, "so he would often bring home milkshakes and candy. But then he'd nag us about our weight. None of us were ever really heavy, but between the lack of compliments, the gags about having to marry us off, and the nagging, we felt really unattractive."

The November 8 *Texaco Town* ran about a half minute short, and Eddie filled the time by speaking of his four upcoming broadcasts in New York. The CBS switchboard in New York was immediately flooded with requests for tickets.

The Texas Oil Company, mindful of New York's premiere status in entertainment and thinking it advisable to use the talent then available on Broadway, had readily agreed to let its star do part of his first season's broadcasts from Manhattan. Cantor had his own reasons for moving the show east. The William Morris Agency had booked him and his radio cast into the RKO Boston for Thanksgiving Week.

Playing with the film *The Smartest Girl in Town*, the Cantor show grossed $48,800. More remarkable than the gross was the money earned by Cantor. The Morris Agency had gotten him a $15,000 guarantee against 50 percent of the gross, by which terms Cantor got a whopping $24,400, less the money he paid his unit. Eddie walked away with close to twenty thousand dollars.

Deanna Durbin made her commercial stage debut in this RKO program, singing *"Il Bacio"* and "Make Believe" from *Show Boat*. The applause was overwhelming; Cantor finally stepped in to move the show along. "Parkyakarkus," Wallington, Betty Jane Cooper (the tap-dancing Mrs. Wallington), and the conductor-violinist Jacques Renard (whose waistline made him a predictable target for Eddie's "insult" jokes) made up the balance of the unit.

Another reason for the trip to New York was the lawsuit launched by David Freedman, Eddie's former coauthor, chief radio writer, and friend.

Freedman had continued his career on Broadway since leaving Cantor's fold, providing the librettos for the *Ziegfeld Follies* of 1936, *White Horse Inn*, and *The Show Is On*. He was still the top writer in radio, and his clients now included Fanny Brice, Jack Benny, and Fred Allen.

The trial opened before Justice Ferdinand Pecora in New York State Supreme Court on Monday, December 8, 1936. Samuel Leibowitz, the plaintiff's counsel, in his opening remarks, identified Freedman as "the all-important man in the background of much of the defendant's success." Freedman, he alleged, had built up Cantor's career on the air until Cantor had gone from earning $2,000 a week to $10,000. It was then, said Leibowitz, that Cantor began to ease him out: "He even went so far as to steal one of Mr. Freedman's assistants so he could have cheaper labor. Finally, after much stalling, Cantor broke the contract without legal or just cause."

"We know of no law that binds one man to another for the rest of his life," Cantor's attorney, David L. Podell, countered. "We contend we never made any such crazy agreement anyway.

"Freedman, all will agree, is a very capable writer, but he never wrote a script for any living stage performer until 1931, when Mr. Cantor engaged him. Remember, Mr. Cantor was even then an established comedian, and he had written many, many of his own sketches."

Podell told the jury that "association" with Cantor had resulted in Freedman's getting as much as $1,500 for articles that would otherwise have brought him not more than $150. Cantor and Freedman, Podell claimed, made new working agreements from year to year, as documentary evidence would prove; no contract was made as described by the plaintiff.

Testimony was to begin the next morning. When that time came, however, Samuel Leibowitz rose and said: "I am sorry to inform the court that Mr. Freedman, the plaintiff, is dead." The overweight Freedman had died of a heart attack early that morning.

Cantor's sense of guilt was only slightly less apparent than his shock and obvious discomfort. He had privately blamed the suit on Dave's wife, Beatrice, whom he had used to get Freedman to write for *Chase and Sanborn* in the first place. His remarks to the press were coated with denial and attempts at rationalization.

"It is the most distressing thing that could have happened. Dave Freedman had great talent, and he died in the very prime of his life. I feel that, in his heart, Dave Freedman knew I was his friend and it would not have been long before we were back working together again.

"Life is a cockeyed business. We're fighting each other today; we're working together tomorrow. I cannot sufficiently emphasize the admiration I had for Dave's talents. I am deeply sympathetic toward the family."

*Freedman versus Cantor* was declared a mistrial. Beatrice Freedman did not file a new suit.

Cantor stopped off on his way back to the West Coast to open the Chicago branch of his drive to get five hundred Jewish children out of Germany. Starting his activities on Wednesday morning, December 16, Eddie raised $18,000 at a private lunch at the Standard Club, enough to rescue fifty children. That afternoon, at a tea party, he raised $3,600 more. Dinner brought another $3,600. On Thursday morning he got $1,500 in pledges from the local Jewish Council, and Hadassah pledged a total of $7,200 that afternoon. A dinner given by L. L. Cohen in Glencoe for ten major Jewish philanthropists in Chicago brought another $7,500.

Cantor also hosted Mayor Ed Kelly's two-hour annual Christmas frolic before twenty-three thousand people in Chicago Stadium. He even took time out to put over an advertising stunt with a local agency for $10,000, to be divided among four charities. Eddie stayed in Chicago past the time intended, lost his reservation on the train to the West Coast, and wound up sleeping in an upper berth—an odd situation for one of the world's biggest stars.

No performer had pursued a cause like this before. No one, until Cantor, had asserted himself publicly in behalf of a specific group of people. And no actor until Cantor had taken up the cudgel against political phi-

losophies or governments, except during a war. It was one thing to sell
Liberty Bonds or appear at a benefit for charitable causes. It was quite
another for a star to stick his neck out on a controversial topic. For Cantor,
representative of major sponsors' products, it meant risking major income
and, quite possibly, his entire career.

Harry Einstein now served notice, wanting either his release or a substantial
raise. Sid Silvers had bombed as Al Jolson's second banana on *Cafe Trocadero*, and Jolson was willing to pay Einstein plenty to replace him. Cantor,
who never felt that anyone was irreplaceable, immediately let Harry go and
temporarily replaced him with vaudeville comedian Harry Savoy, whose
trademark expression, "I'll give you a hit on the head," has outlived his own
fame. Savoy was neither billed nor introduced in his first show—a Cantor
ploy to excite listener's curiosity and avoid giving new supporting talent too
much recognition.

Cantor, as the quintessential professional, seemed more sympathetic to
people who worked in fields other than show business. Sam Kurtzman
worked his way through the University of Pennsylvania's dental school as
one of Eddie's collaborators on radio and magazine material. "I've been
associated with Eddie Cantor for three and a half years," he wrote *Variety*
on June 3, "and all the time I was on his staff I received weekly checks
with the stipulation that if school should get tough, I was to forget Eddie
and concentrate on dentistry; the checks would come in just the same. He
followed out this promise to the letter. It was swell of him." Kurtzman
graduated on June 9 and went on to a career in dentistry.

Cantor did not confine his philanthropy to major causes that might provide favorable publicity and hone his public image as a great humanitarian.
The story of Sheila Rogers, née Sylvia Solomon, best exemplifies the private
philanthropy that represents, perhaps, the best in Eddie Cantor.

Sylvia was nine years old and living in Brooklyn when her parents separated for the third and final time. Her mother was a practical nurse who
earned barely enough to cover their expenses, yet she bought Sylvia a radio
for her tenth birthday. The year was 1935.

"Suddenly," Sylvia recalled, "I had many new friends—all on the radio.
One man sounded so warm and friendly. He talked about his wife and
daughters and made you feel that you were involved."

What followed was a true-life *Purple Rose of Cairo*. Sylvia wrote a poem
about Cantor and sent it to him care of NBC. In about a week, there came
a thank you note, and Sylvia, in need of a new father, adopted Eddie Cantor. She wrote to him from that point on and always got a warm note in
reply.

In November 1938, having read that Cantor would be staying at the
Sherry Netherland Hotel while in New York, Sylvia began a vigil outside
the hotel. When Eddie finally appeared, she introduced herself and referred

to their "correspondence"—and to the scrapbooks she had filled with Cantor pictures.

Cantor asked her to see him in his suite the following day. When she got there, Eddie introduced her to his guest star for the week, the romantic, sophisticated actor Leslie Howard. Eddie also gave Sylvia two V.I.P. tickets to the broadcast.

From that time on, Sylvia Solomon had reserved seats to every Cantor broadcast in New York. Sometimes, Eddie took the teenager to Lindy's following the show.

The grateful girl began an Eddie Cantor Fan Club, whose sign-carrying members greeted Eddie when he arrived at Grand Central Station, saw his broadcasts at Radio City, and saw him off when he returned to Hollywood. "We became good friends," remembers Sylvia. "I remember once he called me on the phone. We really didn't have a phone, but Mr. Parrish, who owned the local candy store, sent kids to people's homes to let them know they had a call. I threw a coat over my pajamas, ran down the three flights of stairs, and rushed across the street to Parrish's. I knew Eddie Cantor had just visited President Roosevelt in Washington and wondered if someone might be playing a joke on me. Nonetheless, I picked up the phone and said, 'Hello.'

" 'Sylvia?' The voice on the other end of the line was unmistakably that of Eddie Cantor. 'Do you know it's harder to get to you than to the president of the United States?' "

Roosevelt was not too big, or Sylvia Solomon too small, to be involved with Eddie Cantor. Eddie, like his political idol, Al Smith, could walk with both the great and the humble and seem to be "all things to all people."

Eddie was the keynote speaker at Sylvia's graduation from Thomas Jefferson High School in June 1941, and when the principal insisted on introducing him, Eddie made a special point of thanking Sylvia Solomon, "without whom I would not be here today."

On March 29, 1947, Eddie gave Sylvia away at her wedding. To this day, she regards Cantor as the father of *six* daughters.

Sylvia says "there was something very *chamish* [Jewish-folksy] about Eddie." There is no doubt that Cantor's bond was especially strong with his Jewish listeners. They felt not only pride in him but a total identification with him as a Jew, a father, a public figure, and a humanitarian who practiced the time-honored Jewish values of community service, *stuccoh* (charity), and concern about all aspects of society. Millions of Americans welcomed Cantor into their homes as a guest via radio, but Jews regarded him as a beloved leader of the Jewish-American community—good humored and benign, but courageous when it came to doing good for worthy causes and performing *mitzvahs* (good deeds) for children, the unfortunate, and the poor.

Eddie's use of his family, his personal life, background, and experiences and his public consciousness made him the first star to transcend stardom and become a total person to his audiences. To Jews, it's safe to say, he was much more. Cantor seemed to many the epitome of *Yiddishkeite*—a blend of model citizen and personal humanitarian, with a folksy, self-deprecating humor that belied his total faith in himself, his people, and his God. He made one feel good to be a Jew.

Cantor, in a sense, made "stardom" an embodiment of Jewish virtue—concern for the community and for individuals, good works, and charity. He was the "total citizen" (and total Jew) who knows no sharp division between public good and private.

The Cantors had been living in a home rented from Charlie Chaplin since arriving from New York the previous May. In March, they made a major move: the purchase of an eighteen-room dwelling at 1012 North Roxbury Drive in Beverly Hills for $133,000. This would be known as the "big house" to the family—the quintessential "Cantor Home for Girls."

Six-thirty was dinnertime, and woe betide the Cantor girl who missed it. It was the one time of the day for the entire family, and guests, to dine together, exchange news and ideas, and, above all, learn from Eddie. "And we learned plenty," points out Janet. "He made us aware of politics and social issues, encouraging us to have a point of view. He'd state his own, but he always wanted us to think, even if we disagreed. And I have to say that he was usually right concerning what was doing in the world. I'll always be grateful for the solid sense of values he gave us."

Frenchy was still Cantor's valet, and others who had worked for Eddie at the San Remo were likewise now ensconced at North Roxbury. Mary Arthur worked as the house secretary, and a room was set aside as Roy Arthur's office, although it still was difficult to tell what Bunky did there except for "odds and ends." If someone needed airline tickets, Bunky made the reservations. If props were needed for the radio show, he knew where to get them. Arthur also took care of unusual assignments. Once, Eddie needed a large sum of cash brought from the house to the Warner Bros. studio to pay his radio cast. Bunky got the money, stuck it in two shopping bags, and brought it on the bus. "Bunky, don't tell me you brought all that money down by bus in shopping bags," said Cantor, as if setting up a punch line. "Who's gonna bother an old man with shopping bags?" responded Arthur in his old, established manner, sounding like Lon Chaney Jr. in *Of Mice and Men*.

The house had everything except a pool—a requirement for Hollywood—and Margie bought one from her savings. The Cantor home soon became one of the busiest houses in Hollywood, playing host to the friends of all five daughters, old friends of the Cantors, and, occasionally, neighbors; Ira Gershwin lived across the street.

These first years at the "big house" were the peak of Margie's life. The backyard became a movie set, and Margie directed her four sisters and their friends in amateur movies so professionally done that M-G-M once tried to buy one as a short subject.

Margie had a wonderful and wild sense of humor that belied her somber look. Fanny Brice and her two children, Fran and Bill, were frequent visitors at North Roxbury Drive, with Bill sometimes pressed into service as "announcer" for Margie's radio "broadcasts." He could seldom make it through the first page of the script without laughing.

Her high school sweetheart, Richard, was now married. Margie, though, soon had a new companion, a man ten years older, several inches shorter, and, over all, less worthy than herself. He was, moreover, married, although estranged from his wife.

His name was Sidney Skolsky.

Born in New York City on May 2, 1905, Skolsky attended New York University before becoming a press agent for producers, notably Earl Carroll and George White. The city then had about a dozen daily papers, and Skolsky sold an idea called "Tin-types" to the New York *Sun*. Vignette biographies of Broadway greats, his pieces were cornucopias of half-truths, lies, old hearsay, and anecdotes—exactly what the public wanted. At the age of twenty-four, Skolsky took over Mark Hellinger's Broadway column for the New York *Daily News*. Four years later, he moved to Hollywood and wrote a column on the doings of its citizens with the trademark slogan "Don't Get Me Wrong—I Love Hollywood."

Love it he did. Skolsky was the first New York columnist to migrate to Hollywood. When his paper asked him to return to New York, he said, "Broadway is passé. Broadway has gone to Hollywood. If they can bring back the Broadway I left, I'll go back."

Skolsky's main hangout was Schwab's, the famous Hollywood drugstore where Lana Turner was allegedly "discovered." He had some trouble getting there each day because he did not drive—a rarity, if not a sin, in Hollywood. Sidney, his wife, Estelle, and their two daughters, Nina and Steffi, lived, not particularly happily, but well in Hancock Park.

Skolsky was, at this time, not unhandsome, with a thick head of curly hair and an intellectual yet strangely forceful manner unlike that of many of the far less educated columnists the Cantors had played host to over the past decade. Extremely lithe and standing only five foot four in height, he carried himself like a man much taller. There was, if one looked hard enough, a lot of Eddie Cantor in the still young Sidney Skolsky.

His relationship with Margie, which her father either refused or pretended not to notice, would last more than twenty years.

Roxbury Drive was primarily a matriarchy. Most of its inhabitants were women, and the benevolent male breadwinner was away most of the time.

Clothes and how to wear them were important. Ida had the same flat derrière as all her daughters except Natalie, an attractive young woman with a well-shaped, feminine bottom that her father made the target for his well-intentioned but insensitive humor.

"What a *zet*," Eddie would roar and double up with laughter, sounding more like Natalie's teasing brother than her father. The girl soon became morbidly self-conscious because of what seemed like Daddy's criticism. The attentions of her high school boyfriend, the handsome Joseph Metzger, helped her to develop some self-confidence.

Joe Metzger had trained for the 1936 U.S. Olympic swimming team until his heavy smoking habit cut down on his wind. Radiating self-confidence, he found it easier to rely on his looks and charm and, it is alleged, chicanery than work. Joe never held a job for very long.

Joe and Natalie announced their engagement shortly after the Cantors moved into their new home on Roxbury Drive, and Joe soon launched a string of new business ventures, aided by both Natalie and Eddie. Most notable among these was the Eddie Cantor Gift Shop on Vine Street in Hollywood, a modest store in which the Metzgers and two hirelings sold porcelain and silver bric-a-brac. Tourists loved the Eddie Cantor Gift Shop stickers that were put on every package, but the store folded within a year, the victim of, some say, Joe Metzgeritis.

As Ida and the girls prepared for the big wedding, Eddie readied himself for *Ali Baba Goes to Town*, the script that had replaced *Saratoga Chips* as his first vehicle at Twentieth Century-Fox. Eddie Stanley, a comedian half-jokingly promoted as "Eddie Cantor's nephew," took over as Cantor's summer radio replacement as the director David Butler readied *Ali Baba*.

*Ali Baba Goes to Town* combined the fantasy elements of Cantor's Goldwyn pictures with topical political satire. Eddie's character, a movie fan, finds himself in ancient Baghdad and solves all the country's problems by implementing his own version of Roosevelt's New Deal. The score included just three songs—"Swing Is Here to Sway," "Laugh Your Way Through Life," "Vote for Honest Abe," the latter two with the same music.

A chase scene in which Eddie rode a flying carpet proved as hazardous as the Ferris wheel sequence in *Strike Me Pink*. Several stuntmen were injured in a sequence where the carpet caught on fire, and Eddie, whose foot was seriously burned during one take, was elected an honorary member of the "Hollywood Stunt Men" (founded "Friday the 13th, 1313") by "Chief Executioner" Harold Perry.

As work preceded on *Ali Baba Goes to Town*, Ida was summoned east by the illness of her father. David Tobias had married a younger, generous, and gracious woman a year after Rachel's death and had enjoyed two years of great happiness until his final illness.

His granddaughters remember David as a sweet man who abhorred violence of any kind. (David was amazed that things like boxing were allowed when Eddie took him to the fights in California.) He was seventy when he died in New York.

Eddie's recollections of his father-in-law would seldom go beyond the picture of a rather naive, bourgeois businessman who managed to feel smugly and myopically superior in the face of Eddie's own phenomenal accomplishments. While it is true that David was not humbled by his son-in-law's success, there is no indication that he failed to appreciate Eddie's position in the entertainment world. David Tobias, like most older immigrants from Europe, simply had no interest in show business.

On Monday, August 16, 1937, in the midst of preparations for the new season on *Texaco*, Cantor was named president of the new American Federation of Radio Artists at the first meeting of the AFRA board of directors in the offices of the Actors' Equity Association, 45 West Forty-seventh Street in New York City. Lawrence Tibbett, Helen Hayes, Jascha Heifetz, James Wallington, and Norman Field were elected vice presidents, with Lucille Wall as recording secretary and George Heller as treasurer. A formal application for a charter from the Associated Actors and Artistes of America, the AFL affiliate that had Actors' Equity and SAG under its umbrella, was made by the AFRA directors.

Cantor had completed two years in office as president of SAG in 1935. He had long served as a self-appointed spokesman for the broadcasting field, calling his own New York press conferences to air his latest feelings, condemnations, and accusations against the ratings agencies (as soon as his own ratings slipped in the mid-'30s) and various industry practices. And, of course, he was the spokesman for "the actors." The presidency of the new union seemed not only natural for Cantor, but almost his by right.

Eddie's second season as Mayor of *Texaco Town* began on Wednesday evening, September 29, 1937. The switch from Sundays to Wednesdays forced no change in closing signatures; "I Love to Spend Each Sunday with You" became "I Love to Spend Each Wednesday with You" with no complaints from anyone, including the song's authors. Pinky Tomlin and Helen Troy (as the babbling Saymore Saymore), who had been featured performers on the summer replacement show, were Cantor's guests on this first broadcast. Bert wrote in *Variety*:

> Seven years consecutive as a big-league comic is a career in radio. And, in starting his seventh term, Cantor is still strong. Always a smart showman, he realizes he cannot carry a program on his own shoulders alone these days. His aggregation of supporters not only is strong, but they complement his personality adroitly. This is a switch from the Sunday night spot with which he's been identified.
>
> Just one item might be criticized. Cantor is still treating Deanna

Durbin as his young, eyelid fluttering protegé. True, he brought her
up the ladder via his program, but today she's full-fledged in her own
right and deserves that recognition. Miss Durbin had only one number, the *Madame Butterfly* aria, "One Fine Day." She might rate more
attention.

Darryl F. Zanuck's determination to launch Eddie Cantor's first film for
Twentieth Century-Fox with the utmost fanfare led the studio publicity
department to concoct "Eddie Cantor's 25th Anniversary Week" for October 24–30, 1937, as *Ali Baba* opened in New York and the Cantors returned
to Hollywood from a few days in Palm Springs.

The high point of this "Anniversary Week"—really the silver anniversary
of Cantor's first season with "Kid Kabaret"—was a special banquet at the
Ambassador Hotel in Los Angeles. At the banquet, a benign and laudatory
Friar's Roast, sans profanity and emceed, nonetheless, by Jessel, Jack
Benny, Irvin S. Cobb, Darryl Zanuck, Dr. A. H. Giannini, California Government Frank F. Merriam, and Louis B. Mayer preceded Cantor on the
speaker's dais. Eddie, for probably the first time in his life, groped for words
in public. Never had a studio welcomed a new star into its precincts with
such overblown, pretentious adulation. Never would the returns be so meager.

*Ali Baba Goes to Town*, previewed at Grauman's Chinese Theatre in
Hollywood on October 15, received a fine review from *Flint in Variety*, who
shrewdly observed that it would do terrific business, assuming "that the
mass population of America which patronizes the picture theatres is ready
to laugh at recent and current nipups in Washington."

They were not. The film premiered in New York to only fair reviews,
but grosses during the first week were nonetheless impressive. What
shocked Zanuck and Cantor were the second week's grosses. The Cantor
fans—and they were legion—had been enough to buoy the first week's
grosses in every major city, but the bulk of moviegoers stayed away on
reading the reviews and hearing word of mouth.

The days of star comedians who shouldered major films were over. This
was the age of "screwball comedy," with stars like Cary Grant and Irene
Dunne—easier on the eyes and frequently more pleasant over the course
of a long picture. The antic comics who had built their stardom on the
stage were now reduced to second leads, their dominance confined to radio
and stage work.

*Ali Baba* was, essentially, the plot of *Roman Scandals* in the setting of
*Kid Millions*, but without the Goldwyn Girls and substituting a lame send-
up of the New Deal for the comedy and glamour that had marked the
Goldwyn pictures. Obvious satire and the lack of biting wit—improbable
to begin with, given Cantor's friendship and respect for F.D.R.—doomed
*Ali Baba* from the outset.

Even the film's topical humor was dated. Roosevelt was in his second

(*Above*) Eddie Cantor, Jean Bedini, and Roy Arthur.
(*Below*) Eddie Cantor and Al Lee.

(*Above*) *Ziegfeld Follies* of 1919. *Left to right*: Johnny Dooley, Eddie Cantor, Gus Van, Bert Williams, Joe Schenck, Eddie Dowling, Rae Dooley. (*Below, left*) Eddie Cantor and Dan Lipsky. (*Below, right*) Jobyna Howland and Cantor in *Kid Boots* (1924).

*(Above, left)* Roy Arthur, Eddie, and Roy's wife, Mary. *(Above, right)* Mainstays of *The Chase & Sanborn Hour*, 1931-34: David Rubinoff, Eddie Cantor, Jimmy Wallington. *(Below)* Eddie in *The Kid From Spain* (1932).

(*Above*) Cantor and the Goldwyn Girls in the "Keep Young and Beautiful" production number from *Roman Scandals* (1933); Lucille Ball to Eddie's right, Barbara Pepper second from his left. (*Below*) The Brood, 1930s: Eddie, Ida, Margie, and Natalie; Marilyn and Janet in the foreground.

(*Above*) Sally Eilers, Eddie, Gordon Jones, and Helen Lowell in *Strike Me Pink* (1936). (*Below*) June Lang, Eddie Cantor, and Louise (Gypsy Rose Lee) Hovick in *Ali Baba Goes To Town* (1937).

(*Above*) Cary Grant, Jeanette MacDonald, Eddie Cantor. (*Below*) Cantor in
*Banjo Eyes* (1941), his final Broadway show.

EDDIE CANTOR

(*Above*) How many different "Eddie Cantors" were there? (*Below, left*) Eddie and Bob Hope. (*Below, right*) Eddie and Joan Davis in *If You Knew Susie* (1948).

(*Above*) Cantor and Al Jolson. (***Below, left***) Eddie and Ida, 1948.
(*Below, right*) Eddie at home. "The Apostle of Pep" spent the last twelve years of his life in physical decline.

term when *Ali Baba Goes to Town* was written. A satire on the New Deal might not have won commercial favor three or four years earlier. It would, however, have been topical, making the film either a huge hit or a colossal bomb. By 1937, a gentle satire on the Roosevelt revolution was good for only a few knowing chuckles. Nor did "Swing Is Here to Sway" provide a bridge to an emerging audience of young people. If anything, it served to underscore the fact that Cantor seemed increasingly old-fashioned.

*Ali Baba Goes to Town* lost money. A subsequent $1,025,000 suit for plagiarism, filed by Andreas Michael, was settled out of court.

Cantor's relationship with Franklin D. Roosevelt is easily exaggerated but too often dismissed. He was certainly closer to F.D.R. than any entertainer had ever been to a president, and if most of their conversations were by telephone instead of face to face, the results were scarcely less significant.

The president, through White House aide Marvin McIntyre and others, planned to launch a national campaign in 1938 to combat polio. Impressed with Cantor's record as a power in mass media (often in support of the New Deal), and having long received Eddie's telegrams, the president asked Cantor what he thought about persuading a million people to contribute a dollar each.

Cantor knew his audience. Observing that the million might dwindle down to two or three hundred thousand if the president was not reelected, he suggested something more permanent, more amenable to mass mobilization, and more effective in identifying the bulk of Americans with Franklin D. Roosevelt: asking ten million people to contribute a dime each to the White House.

So was born the March of Dimes, its name, Cantor's own creation, prompted by *The March of Time*, a popular newsreel series (and the inspiration for "News on the March," Orson Welles's opening newsreel in *Citizen Kane*). The March of Dimes was officially launched one week before the president's annual ball on Saturday, January 29.

"The March of Dimes will enable all persons, even the children, to show our president that they are with him in this battle against this disease," Cantor stated in a special wire. "Nearly everyone can send in a dime, or several dimes. It is a small amount and the plan might seem insignificant. However, it takes only ten dimes to make a dollar and if a million people send only one dime each, the total will be $100,000."

Cantor said that a number of star names had promised to support and implement the appeal, including Jack Benny, Jack Haley, Bing Crosby, Rudy Vallee, Deanna Durbin, Jascha Heifetz, Lily Pons, Lawrence Tibbett, Edgar Bergen, and Kate Smith. Eddie waxed a special introduction to the Crosby-Connee Boswell recording of "Alexander's Ragtime Band" for Decca on January 26, with receipts going to the March of Dimes. The three artists autographed the first copy off the press; Cantor sold the second copy for five hundred dollars.

Eddie made the appeal on broadcast after broadcast. "Always," he remembered, "the minute we'd go off the air, the phone would ring. Not a secretary, but the president himself to say, 'Bless everybody and thank you.' "

Eddie's daughter Edna, eighteen, now planned to wed the twenty-one-year-old James McHugh Jr., son of the composer of such popular song hits as "I Can't Give You Anything But Love," "I Feel a Song Coming On," and "On the Sunny Side of the Street." Eddie announced their engagement in January, with the wedding set for May.

There almost was no wedding, or any other thing, for Edna, however. She sustained what were described as "minor injuries" in newspaper accounts of an automobile collision in Beverly Hills. The injuries, in fact, were anything but minor. The force of the impact had sent Edna through the windshield, severely cutting her around the face, especially the mouth, and necessitating plastic surgery.

Morris Levine, the driver of the other car, who was entirely at fault, nonetheless sued Cantor for $21,342. Celebrity status, in the thirties, was becoming costly.

Not that Cantor needed things to spur him on in his pursuit of "making a good living" in show business. It was soon announced that Eddie would again switch over to a new sponsor—this time to the R. J. Reynolds Tobacco Company, as star of the half-hour *Camel Caravan* on NBC. (The closing song would now be "Each *Monday* with You.")

Nor had Cantor given up on stage work. He and Deanna Durbin left Los Angeles for New York late in February, staying at the Sherry Netherland while Eddie finalized plans for a two-hour show combining his own "Radio Revue" with Ted Lewis's "Rhythm Rhapsody."

Booked by the increasingly powerful Music Corp. of America, the Cantor and Lewis units played the Civic Auditorium in Cleveland for the Shriners and Convention Hall in Philadelphia as the first attraction of a huge entertainment project sponsored by the Artisans Extension Committee. Eddie came on five times at each show, bantering with Lewis, acting as straight man for Bert (Mad Russian) Gordon, imitating Mae West ("which gets the howls"), and singing his old hits in blackface for a finish. Cantor's deal had been arranged by his new son-in-law, Jimmy McHugh Jr.

Eddie Cantor's *Camel Caravan* debuted to lukewarm reception on March 28, 1938. Bob Landry called it "mixed up" and "spotty." Intellectually aware of the demands of radio, Cantor the performer nonetheless directed much of his performing to the studio audience, his interpolated bits of spontaneous physical comedy leading Landry to complain that what "was going on in CBS' hall wasn't correlated with the vibrations coming out of the loudspeaker."

Deanna Durbin sang "Loch Lomond" on this, her last broadcast for

Cantor. Durbin's manager, Jack Sherrill, had been talking to a couple of possible sponsors in an effort to get Deanna her own show for the fall. In the meantime, she returned to Hollywood and Universal Pictures.

Cantor the activist, Cantor the expresser of opinions, was supremely active in the months that followed. He had urged newspaper radio editors to attack the Cooperative Analysis of Broadcasting (Crossley ratings) in a talk at Cavanaugh's restaurant in New York prior to his first broadcast for Camels, saying that the sampling was too small, that homes without telephones were not canvassed, and that the C.A.B. figures were becoming too influential. William Esty sidestepped making comment.

Cantor's comments were put forward, at least partially, to "explain" why "the Mayor of *Texaco Town*" had been trounced by Jack Benny in the ratings. "It wasn't fair to ask the radio audience to choose between two favorites," he said later. Eddie would have made a great politician.

Other ideas centered around vaudeville units. Cantor now envisioned a permanent variety circuit consisting of himself, half a dozen other top-name radio comics, and a number of pop dance bands. Eddie said they owed it to themselves and to the hundreds of show people, including individual acts, choruses, and musicians, as well as to the stagehands, managers, and other background people who would find employment. He labeled "stupid" the exhibitors who had described his recent shows with Ted Lewis as "unfair" competition and expressed keen interest in current negotiations involving AFRA, the networks, and their advertising agencies.

"My father read voraciously," says Janet Cantor Gari. "Mother read novels—sometimes two or three at once; we used to tease her about it, but she thought it was the most natural thing in the world. Daddy read nonfiction—history, politics, civics, contemporary philosophy—books, newspapers, and magazines.

Reading and listening had caused Cantor to become increasingly alarmed at the sitation in Germany. While in Philadelphia with Lewis on March 17, he had told the Associated Press that it had gotten so "that people [in Europe] will laugh at a fellow on the stage, then stop to find out his nationality before they clap."

Cantor's Jewishness, tempered by his longing for acceptance by the mainstream Anglo-Saxon culture, was nonetheless definite and uncompromising under pressure. The Cantors may have had a Christmas tree, but Eddie still insisted on not eating ham or shellfish. Once, to appease Natalie, he'd let her take him to a new "in" restaurant in New York. In an unintentional repetition of the scene at Jack (Twin) Sullivan's twenty years earlier, Eddie ordered a slice of melon, which arrived nearly covered with a strip of ham.

This time, Cantor was indignant. "Take it back," he told the waiter. "I didn't ask for it with ham. And don't just take the ham off. Give me a different piece. I suppose if I ordered chocolate pudding, it would come with a piece of ham sticking out of the middle." Eddie turned to Natalie. "Next time," he said, "back to Lindy's!"

Jews across America were painfully aware of the rabid, vicious anti-Semitism common in central and eastern Europe, but few Americans—Jews or Christians—were willing to believe that Adolf Hitler wanted to kill every Jew in Europe or the world. Eddie Cantor, a driven man in his own right, and nurtured by the stories of pogroms in Russia, seemed to grasp, instinctively, the demon that drove Hitler.

Speaking before one thousand guests at a Hadassah Society fund-raising dinner in Washington, D.C., on Thursday night, March 31, 1938, Cantor said that Hitler had "made it his business to exterminate Jewry. . . . Even in Hollywood, where the motion picture industry is run by Jews, I have a bodyguard."

Eddie said that his radio sponsors had "been told I was using the radio for Jewish propaganda and have been threatened with boycott of their products."

Less than two weeks later, on Tuesday afternoon, April 12, Cantor called Hitler "murderer, kidnapper, and number one gangster of the world" before a gathering of eleven hundred listeners at the annual donor luncheon of the New York chapter of Hadassah at the Waldorf-Astoria. Speaking of the persecution of Jews in Germany and Austria and of Hitler's efforts "to justify" his anti-Semitic program to the rest of the world, Cantor said, "We do not combat him as a business but as a sideline. We fight Hitler five minutes a day, and Hitler is fighting twenty-four hours. We are too smug. We say here in America that 'It can't happen here,' but I say, 'It can happen here.' " Cantor condemned the Nazi camps in the United States and said the Nazis were "pouring millions of dollars into this country for propaganda."

The $15,000 raised at the luncheon would relocate forty-two children from central Europe to Palestine. Cantor knew that there were many children more.

Colonel Josiah C. Wedgwood, a Labor member of the British Parliament, commended the work of Hadassah in Palestine, for Arabs as well as Jews, and expressed the wish that Hitler might observe the organization's activities. Far more prophetic was Phelps Adams, head of the Washington bureau of the New York *Sun*, who said "the Jews in Palestine will never be at home there until they have overcome the Arab hatred that is spreading today more rapidly and more extensively than I care even to think about." Adams had returned from an assignment in Palestine four months earlier.

Cantor's speech and other exertions, most of them in behalf of Jewish causes, weakened him in the days that followed. He was running a temperature on Monday, April 18, and was accompanied to the studio by his physician for the Camel show that evening. Eddie played a benefit for a

Jewish philanthropic institution on Wednesday evening, April 20 against his doctor's orders and came down with a bad case of the flu.

The Sunday night rehearsal for that week's *Camel Caravan* was canceled, and Rudy Vallee subbed for Eddie on the next night's program, doing what *Variety* reported as a "straight, dignified m.c. and solo song routine. It was a straight musical revue. There wasn't a laugh in the half-hour from tune-in to tune-out. . . . [This] demonstrated radio's helplessness in substituting a comedy program at the last moment."

A recovered Cantor returned to *Camel Caravan* the following Monday. Eddie could not attend a dinner in his honor at the Ninety-second Street YMHA on Wednesday evening, May 4 (Ida, who had joined him in New York, accepted an award on his behalf), but he and former governor Al Smith were guests of honor at the fiftieth anniversary of the founding of the Reiss home the following Saturday evening. After one more Camel show, Eddie, his wife, and radio cast left for Hollywood and the seven final broadcasts of the season.

Following the last show, on June 27, Eddie, Ida, Natalie, her husband, Joe, and the ten-year-old Janet left for the East Coast. Eddie had vowed to raise one hundred thousand dollars for the evacuation of Jewish children from Central and Eastern Europe to Palestine. England, he had now determined, was the place to get the money.

They sailed from New York on July 6, docking in Plymouth and proceeding on to London. It was Janet's first trip without Winnie, who, on her own for the first time in more than a decade, soon met a young man named Leonard Hanson. The couple were soon engaged.

Eddie and Ida dined with Ambassador and Mrs. Joseph P. Kennedy in London, an odd pairing, since Kennedy had urged filmmakers to "go easy on the Nazis." The conversation was, unfortunately, not recorded.

Sheffield, Leeds, Glasgow, Manchester, and Newcastle made up Cantor's intinerary for July 17–22. "Daddy sang song after song in Glasgow," Janet says, "but didn't get one pledge. Finally, he said he would not sing another song till someone pledged some money, and the pounds poured in."

Cantor received an ovation from the BBC studio audience before he opened his mouth for a twenty-minute appearance on the *Sing-Song* program of Saturday, July 23. He told stories, gently ribbing the London traffic, and sang several songs, including "Making the Best of Each Day" and "Lambeth Walk" from the English show *Me and My Girl*. Eddie later appeared at a midnight benefit show at the Hyams Bros. State Cinema in Kilburn, netting $25,000.

Cantor raised $85,000 in four days and wound up with closer to $250,000 than the $150,000 he had set as his goal.

The Cantor party sailed for home aboard the *Normandie* on Wednesday,

July 27, along with Darryl Zanuck. He and Eddie used the time on board to talk about the second Cantor vehicle for Twentieth Century-Fox. Zanuck had offered Harry Warner $100,000 for the rights to *White Horse Inn*, but Eddie favored buying *Pins and Needles*, a pro-union, somewhat left-wing revue, from the Labor Stage and pinning on the story of a stagestruck dress-firm foreman. *The People's Choice*, built around the theme of "Mr. Average Man" and the products he chose on the basis of radio commercials, was the final selection.

On Wednesday, August 3, two days after his arrival in New York, Cantor was honored with a testimonial luncheon at the Hotel Astor by the national boards of Hadassah and the Committee of One Thousand for Youth Aliyah. Mrs. Herbert H. Lehman, the wife of New York's governor, was on hand to extend official greetings.

Cantor did not let the luncheon pass without excitement. Warning of the spread of anti-Semitism in the United States, he bitterly denounced Henry Ford for having accepted a decoration from the German government the previous Saturday. Ford had received the Grand Cross of the German Eagle, a decoration for distinguished foreigners, on the occasion of his seventy-fifth birthday, the first time the award had been made in America.

Ford's well-known anti-Semitism was doubtless a major factor in his getting the award. Cantor, though, chose to ignore it. "I question the Americanism of Henry Ford for accepting a citation from the biggest gangster in the world. Mr. Henry Ford, in my opinion, is a damned fool for permitting the world's greatest gangster to give him this citation. Doesn't he realize that the German papers, reporting the citation, said all Americans were behind Nazism?

"Whose side is Mr. Ford on? I question Mr. Ford's Americanism and his Christianity. I don't think he is a real American or a good Christian. The more men like Ford we have, the more we must organize and fight.

"We can smell the smoke in this country, and we've got to start now to save ourselves. Don't think we are safe here, because we are not."

Asserting that the Nazi government had "reached people in the highest places in this country," Cantor claimed he had been barred at certain places, which he did not care to name, because he was Jewish.

Cantor received a small scroll sent from the Jewish refugee children of Kvutzat Aryeh, near Hedera in Palestine, a settlement founded with money he had raised and that was named in his honor, the word "Aryeh" being a Hebrew translation of "Edward" and meaning "lion." A message was read from James G. McDonald, former High Commissioner for German Refugees at the League of Nations, to "my friend, Eddie Cantor, distinguished artist, great American, and magnificent humanitarian."

Eddie took part in *Alexander's Ragtime Band*, the CBS radio tribute to Irving Berlin, that evening, singing "My Wife's Gone to the Country" and performing with Al Jolson. He, Ida, Janet, and the Metzgers entrained for California the next day.

Cantor and Zanuck had come to a new agreement: Eddie would not make any more pictures for Twentieth Century-Fox.

Cantor gave his reasons in a letter to *Variety*.

September 4, 1938
Beverly Hills, Calif.

Editor, *Variety*:

Darryl Zanuck and I disagreed over my next story. I felt, and still feel, that it is time to get away from the formula pictures I have been making. It is important at this time to make a big musical, where I can play "Eddie Cantor" for a change.

Despite the fact that *Ali Baba Goes to Town* will gross $2,000,000, it is my contention that one who has been successful in the theatre, as in my particular case, will be successful on the screen. I want to sing and I want to play something else besides an insipid character which the audience does not believe.

The disagreement with Zanuck was, believe me, a friendly one. At the present time, negotiations have been opened up between two studios and myself, so that maybe, before you go to press, I will know my future plans for the screen.

Eddie Cantor

Metro-Goldwyn-Mayer and RKO were the studios in question. Abe Last-fogel handled the negotiations, Cantor agreeing to make one picture for RKO "within five months" for a guarantee and a percentage and another for Metro within twelve months for a flat sum only. Izzy Ellison and Joe Quillen, two of Eddie's radio writers, were put to work on a screen-play.

Eddie attended a recovered Edna's wedding on September 17. McHugh Jr., long neglected by his father, was a young man bursting with ambition. Employed by MCA, he looked forward to a professional alliance with his new father-in-law that would elevate him to the ranks of the top agents in the show world.

The newlyweds' frequent dinners with the Cantors always ended up with Ida and Edna getting together in one room while Jimmy talked to Eddie about business in another.

Eddie and his son-in-law had similar ideas about show business. The public taste—what would later be termed the "lowest common denominator"—was what mattered. "You should see the grosses of his latest picture," was Eddie's response when Edna or his other daughters panned a certain star. "I don't care," Edna would say, "he's still a lousy actor."

Edna, who had never liked her status as "one of the five Cantor daughters," grew to resent not only these nights but the other evenings Jimmy spent away from home with clients, real and potential, of both sexes.

Fanny Brice was Cantor's guest star on the new season's first Camel show on Monday night, October 3, playing "Baby Snooks" and saying she had come to play with Eddie's "little boy." The script had Eddie saying that he did not have one, to which Baby Snooks asked her inevitable "Why?" It was a good broadcast, one of the best opening shows of Cantor's recent seasons, but the question of "a son for Cantor" remained a major part of Eddie's public stock of gags. "We never minded that part," Margie said, "because we always knew that such a nonexistent person would have had a very tough time." The girls felt that a boy would have been under tremendous pressure to excel but that, at the same time, he would have been chastised by their father if he excelled too much in the "wrong" field—especially one too close to show business. The purely hypothetical "son of Cantor" might have pleased his father if he had become a top-notch medical researcher—a nonthreatening, humanitarian profession unconnected to the world of entertainment.

There is, however, little to suggest that Cantor craved a son. Eddie seemed quite comfortable with the "Cantor Home for Girls," which was actually a prosperous version of the home he had grown up in on the East Side of New York. Ida had succeeded Esther, the Cantor daughters had replaced the Polish servant girls, the food was better, and there were more rooms. Little else separated 47 Henry Street and 1012 North Roxbury Drive.

Cantor loved his daughters, but he related to them best when they were small. When Janet was three or four, she looked forward with delight to her nightly ritual with Daddy.

> He would come upstairs when I was tucked in bed and lie down next to me. I can still smell his cologne and his hair tonic [Vitalis], which stayed comfortingly on my pillow after he left. "Okay," he said solemnly, "I'll stay a little while, but remember, the first one who laughs goes to Mexico." Then he'd make up nonsense stories or ask impossible riddles with answers that would send me into terminal giggles. He'd then give me one more chance to miss the train to Mexico, and I'd try my hardest to keep a straight face, but if his words didn't do it, his rolling eyes or comical expressions would send me into spasms of laughter.
>
>   "Well, that certainly does it," he'd announce, sliding off my bed. "I guess I have to go down and make your reservation." After a dozen kisses and maybe a tickle or two, he'd quietly leave my room, and I'd snuggle down warm and happy, wondering where and what Mexico was.

Winnie, not Ida, had raised Janet. "Mother was to me a presence rather than a person," she has confessed. "She looked nice, she smelled nice, and she felt nice; she had gorgeous skin. But she had absolutely no patience.

She used to ask me why I spoke so fast. It was because I had to get the words out while I still held her attention."

Janet's little world cracked on October 7, 1938, the day that Winnie married Leonard Hanson and moved out. (The wedding had been held on Janet's birthday, at her own request.) Hanson was, however, an indulgent man who did not mind having the child Winnie loved so much spend a night at his home once a week during the first year of their marriage.

From this point, however, it was Margie, not Ida, and, increasingly, not Winnie, who raised Janet. The twelve-and-a-half-year age difference between them seemed, in fact, like twenty-five, given Margie's mature outlook and appearance.

"She made learning fun for me. She'd say, 'I think I have a book you might enjoy.' And it would be one of the classic novels. She was a very fine teacher. But she was great at almost everything she did," Janet recalled.

Little Janet's alleged "boyfriend," Bobby Breen, was dropped from Cantor's cast later that season. Eddie had been paying Bobby, now eleven, five hundred dollars a broadcast when he used him, sometimes when he didn't. If the show ran too long at rehearsals, or if Breen seemed tired or not in good voice, Cantor often sent him home but paid him all the same.

Bobby's elder brother, Mickey, eager to usurp his sister Sally's role as Bobby's "manager," met with Cantor in Sol Lesser's office to "negotiate" a new contract. Mickey Breen spent five minutes delivering a long list of demands, walking up and down "like a big impresario, like a Sol Hurok," as Cantor would remember. The phrase "We want" preceded each demand: He, Mickey Breen, as Bobby's agent, would approve his material, select his songs, and so on. "We want a thousand dollars. . . ."

Eddie finally asked Mickey if he was through."

"Yes, Uncle Eddie, I'm through."

"Good," Cantor responded. "So is Bobby."

Eddie later maintained that Mickey's attitude had ended his desire to use Bobby. But Breen was also getting older. At eleven, he was no longer the adorable child he had been at eight. And Bobby's boy tenor, though impressive, was not really thrilling, except when coming from the mouth of a small child.

Breen's career from that point on was not very successful; Cantor had him on his show again a couple of years later and invited him to appear with him on television in the early '50s. An attempt at a Breen comeback in the '60s proved abortive. "If a child can spell at six," Cantor observed, "it's great. At twenty—who cares?"

Eddie's attitude toward Breen was, though decent, ultimately cynical, due in large part, it must be said, to the family's own attitude. Breen was a commodity, a product of Sol Lesser that Cantor used to the advantage of his radio show and the Cantor public image. Other "bright young talents" would appear on Cantor's program in the years that followed—with less effective results than those enjoyed by Breen and Durbin.

Cantor and his cast, which now included Vick Knight as producer, the conductor Edgar (Cookie) Fairchild, the announcer Walter Wolf King, Bert Gordon, Sid Fields, the writers Quillen, Ellison, Rapp, and Joe Donahue (the contact man for William Esty), entrained for New York on Tuesday, November 1. It was still thought wise to broadcast part of every season from New York, and Eddie was scheduled to emcee the "Night of Stars" Benefit for Jewish Refugees in Palestine at Madison Square Garden.

Cantor's compulsive need for gags led him to augment his regular writing staff with outside contributors. "Ernie Lehman had an aunt named Bea Landau who was a friend of the Cantors," recalled David Brown.

So Ernie and I interviewed the family and wrote a magazine piece called "The Cantor Home for Girls." Cantor liked it so much that he invited us up to his apartment at the Sherry Netherland and said, "Boys, I'd like to give you the opportunity to write some stuff for me." And he assigned us to write material for "Mr. Guffy," the contrarian, played by Sidney Fields.

We also wrote for the guest spots, like one for Helen Mencken, and for the "Mad Russian." We worked on special material. We were not on the regular payroll because I think Eddie may have used this as his own idea. He paid us by personal check from a Hollywood branch of the Bank of America, and we were paid according to the number of jokes he used. We would attend a dry-run rehearsal at what is now the Ed Sullivan Theatre, and we'd clock the number of laughs. We knew the jokes that survived were the ones that got the biggest laughs. Two shows were given—one for the east and another for the Mountain and Pacific times. We'd celebrate according to the number of jokes that remained in.

In the midst of this, he became enamored of our work enough to ask us to write a screenplay for him. He had bought a novel called *The Flying Yorkshireman* by an Englishman named Alec Knight. It was about a man who could fly, a wonderful book. The author of that book was killed in World War II, and Cantor, for some reason, couldn't sell the idea of the picture.

Lehman, who would write several top screenplays (*The Sweet Smell of Success* and *Somebody Up There Likes Me*, among others), wrote a short piece called "The Life of Sammy Hogarth" in 1948. Published in *Liberty*, it is a bitter satire, written in the style of a minor-league Ring Lardner, about a fictitious radio comedian who postures as a public humanitarian while exploiting everyone on his staff, from his writers to his chauffeur. Hogarth's daughter, Clarabelle, has been driven into a sanitarium by "funny" jokes "about poor Sammy Hogarth bein' stuck with a homely daughter and how dumb she was and how was he ever goin' to get rid of her." Hogarth winds up hiring and firing male talent without mercy in a vain attempt to get his daughter married.

"The Life of Sammy Hogarth," which the author admittedly based on Eddie Cantor, is a deadly assault with not so much a rapier as a gigantic broadsword. Lehman had no quarrel with his subject, but he was cynical about him and the "Cantor Home for Girls" and was influenced by stories he had heard from Cantor's other writers. "The Life of Sammy Hogarth" is fiction, but it throws a glaring spotlight on an unpleasant side of Cantor's life. Eddie *was* often pushy and manipulative when he dealt with people in show business. And, despite the fact that he believed in all the causes he championed, he certainly did posture.

"I'll never forget the day I introduced him to my future husband, Dr. Monroe Engelbert, a dentist," recalled Sheila Rogers. Eddie spoke in general about the future of the world or something like that, pointing toward the sky. He never looked at Monroe, who was sort of disappointed. I guess the world was Eddie's audience."

President Franklin D. Roosevelt again played a small but highly publicized role in Cantor's life. In a message to the nation that Thanksgiving (November 24), Roosevelt referred to a telegram he had received from his good friend, "Eddie Cantor, the comedian," who said:

> MAY YOU AND YOURS HAVE A HAPPY THANKSGIVING. I AM GRATEFUL THAT I LIVE IN A COUNTRY WHERE OUR LEADERS CAN SIT DOWN ON THANKSGIVING AND CARVE UP A TURKEY INSTEAD OF A MAP.

Cantor later said he wept when he heard the president call him his "friend" and quote his telegram to the entire nation. However, research in the archives of Hyde Park, repository of Roosevelt's presidential correspondence, including copies of every telegram sent or received during F.D.R.'s three and one-quarter terms in office, has not turned up the telegram in question. Chances are that the telegram, as such, never existed.

Lending support to this theory is the fact that Cantor had been stopped from giving the same message on his own show by the William Esty Agency just three nights earlier. (The agencies were by then the all-powerful representatives of the sponsor, and they disliked controversial material that might offend people with differing political viewpoints.) It is probable that Cantor spoke to someone at the White House, who relayed the censored message to the president. Roosevelt, a consummate politician, found it not just flattering but useful.

Cantor continued his nonstop activities in New York in the weeks that followed, hosting a luncheon in honor of Ben Bernie's fifteenth anniversay on Monday, December 19, and starting the new March of Dimes campaign with a major appeal on the *Camel Caravan* of January 9, 1939, the same broadcast in which Bert Parks succeded Walter Wolf King as Cantor's announcer.

Eddie had heard the twenty-four-year-old Parks, a CBS announcer for the previous few years, on a midnight radio show emanating from the great Cotton Club in Harlem. The voice was young and warm, with what Cantor heard as a slight southern accent. (Parks was from Atlanta.)

Parks became the singing partner of Kay St. Germain and the target of the well-worn Cantor campaign to find husbands for his daughters. The following dialogue was typical:

CANTOR:  Bert, haven't I been treating you well on this program.

PARKS:   Yes, sir, Mr. Bossman. You've been like a father to me.

CANTOR:  That's it. I want to be more like a father-in-*law*. You've got to eat. Come on home and have dinner at our house.

        (*Pause*)

CANTOR:  You like good food, don't you, Bert?

PARKS:   Yes, it's just . . . I'm afraid that dinner might turn out to be a wedding feast. I'm not quite ready, Mr. C.

Natalie and Edna, both married now, could almost laugh along with their father's radio audience. Marilyn, at seventeen, could not. Overweight and still beset by asthma, she had nonetheless decided on a show business career. She so informed her father after he returned from New York late that month.

Eddie later said he "saw no signs of talent" in Marilyn. His words at the time, however, were little short of brutal: Marilyn had not yet blossomed as a beauty, and she could neither sing nor dance. The only thing she had to recommend her for a career in show business, as Eddie saw it, was her name—Marilyn Cantor. ("And how far do you think that will eventually take you?" he asked.) Marilyn, however, had at least one quality in common with her father—sheer determination. Eddie reluctantly allowed her to attend the American Academy of Dramatic Arts in New York.

Marilyn, despite her teen-aged handicaps, had gone where angels—and her sisters—feared to tread. Margie's admonition not to "make a scene" in public, be obtrusive, or in any way detract from "Daddy" had at last been trashed. Entering show business was the ultimate infringement.

Five minutes seldom passed before Eddie and Marilyn were locked in battle. "My father loved to argue," Janet recalls, "but Marilyn would *really* get him upset."

Cantor's activity in filmhouse variety had decreased markedly since 1936, as RKO and other chains gradually eliminated vaudeville. One of Eddie's last unit shows, the "*Camel Caravan* Revue," opened San Francisco's new California Auditorium on March 3, 1939. This was part of that city's Golden Gate Exposition, and Eddie brought in a chorus line of sixteen dancers to complement Ann Miller, Bert Parks, Bert Gordon, Kay St. Germain, Sid Fields, and Cookie Fairchild and Adam Carroll in piano duets. The remainder of the program was typical post-Ziegfeld Eddie Cantor: a line of comic chatter about Rudy Vallee (some of which seemed in poor taste, according to reviewers), a couple of Hitler jokes, several up-tempo songs, the Shirley Temple takeoff, and a heartfelt patriotic message warning of the dangers overseas.

The Cantors returned east in May and spent a weekend up at Grossinger's, the premier resort of the Catskills. Eddie spoke at the first observance of "New Citizens Day" at the Central Park Mall on Friday night, June 2, and the *New York Times* said that his "arrival on the platform was the signal for cries of glee. He reminded the group of the heterogeneous racial character of the American nation, and closed with a declaration that everyone who enjoys its privileges should 'thank God on your knees every night' for citizenship in this country"—almost the same closing speech he'd made in San Francisco.

Eddie and Ida celebrated their twenty-fifth wedding anniversary with a dinner in the Perroquet Suite of the Waldorf-Astoria. About a hundred of their friends were present, including many who had attended their wedding in Brooklyn on June 9, 1914, but not including President Roosevelt, whom Cantor had invited, "along with two of your friends from England"—a cryptic reference to the visiting King George and Queen Elizabeth.

Eddie seemed to think there was a chance that they would come—unlikely as that might have been in those days before actors became international role models. It might not have occurred to him that reigning British monarchs would not socialize with Jews. Then again, that might have been his very point. Cantor, the old street kid, sometimes stuck his face out very subtly, as if daring the non-Jewish world to punch him in the nose.

Every ten years, it seemed, Cantor faced a crisis. In 1909 he had been stranded on the road with Frank B. Carr's *Indian Maidens*. In 1919 his position in the Actors' Strike had cut his income and threatened his career. In 1929 the Wall Street crash had wiped out his five-million-dollar fortune and left him $280,000 in debt.

Now, in 1939, would come another challenge. On Tuesday afternoon, June 13, the Cantors were guests at a luncheon in the Cafe Tel Aviv of the Jewish Palestine Pavilion at the New York World's Fair. Their hosts were the eighteen thousand members of the New York chapter of Hadassah. Following the luncheon, Eddie gave a speech titled "Human Values Today and Tomorrow" at the Temple of Religion.

Cantor used his speech to go on the attack against, not Hitler, Nazism, or the various real and potential enemies faced by Judaism in Europe, but a target closer to home—Father Charles E. Coughlin.

Father Coughlin was ordained a priest in 1916 and became pastor of the Shrine of the Little Flower in Royal Oak, Michigan. Ten years later he made his first broadcast, speaking on morality and Christian virtue. Father Coughlin continued his broadcasts on an increasingly regular basis to an ever-widening audience over the next four years, now and again touching on politics.

Coughlin's broadcasts took a much more controversial tone as the United States plunged into the Great Depression. In 1931 the Columbia Broadcasting System tried to censor an attack by Coughlin on the Treaty of Versailles and received 1,250,000 letters of protest.

Father Coughlin had become a listening habit for more than thirty million Americans, a political force, and a demagogue. Eighty-five members of Congress petitioned President Roosevelt to send the radio priest as an official adviser to the London Conference on economics in 1933. A national poll the following year named Coughlin the most powerful and popular man in the United States after Franklin D. Roosevelt—the priest's archfoe.

Coughlin attacked the New Deal in broadcast after broadcast, calling it a mask that would put the country in the hands of communists and other groups not well liked by the great majority of Americans. "The New Deal is not the New Deal," Coughlin once asserted. "It's the Jew Deal." The sentence struck responsive chords among Americans pauperized by the Depression and ready to find groups on which to focus their resentment, hate, and fear. Rumor, mostly current among Nazi Bund members, Coughlinites, and other Jew-baiters unfamiliar with the president's Dutch ancestry, said Roosevelt's real name was Rosenfeld.

In 1935, twenty thousand Coughlinites packed Madison Square Garden to hear the priest deliver a particularly bitter attack on the New Deal. In one speech, Coughlin called the president "the great liar and betrayer," and his bishop, who had up until then backed him fully, made Coughlin apologize to the chief executive. That same year, Coughlin called Roosevelt the "scab president."

Coughlin joined forces with Gerald L. K. Smith, the well known race-baiter from Louisiana, and Dr. Francis Townsend (originator of the Townsend Plan) to form the Union Party in 1936. Their candidate, Congressman William Lempke, received nine hundred thousand votes in that year's presidential election. During this campaign, the priest began to couple his denunciations of President Roosevelt with attacks on "Jewish bankers," and the Catholic Layman's League condemned him for "cowardly Jew-baiting and shameless use of the cloth to insult the president."

Coughlin's broadcasts were carried over forty-seven radio stations, and his National Union for Social Justice had eight and a half million members. He received as much as one million letters and cards a week and retained four secretaries and a reported 106 clerks.

Cantor had been seething about Father Coughlin privately for years. Not before his speech at the Hall of Religion, however, did he find an opportunity to vent his rage in public.

"Father Coughlin is not only anti-Christian," Cantor proclaimed, "he is anti-American as well. He should be considered not only as an enemy of Jews, but of all America." Proceeding to detail and damn the priest's phobic anti-Semitism, Eddie left the platform feeling he had gotten something off his chest, unmindful and uncaring of any potential consequences.

Cantor's days, in truth, were far too filled for worry. On Friday, June 16, he joined the Theatre Arts Committee in petitioning Congress not to drop the WPA fine arts projects, including, most important from the Committee's standpoint, the Federal Theatre Project. Unable to reach President Roosevelt's secretary on the phone, Eddie sent the following telegram to Marvin McIntyre at the White House:

> One of the finest things this administration has done has been the Federal Arts Project. At a time when America sorely needed a spiritual uplift, the Federal Theatre Project came along. It is my belief that not only would the curtailment of this project work havoc on thousands of actors, writers and producers, but it would be greatly resented by the masses who, because of its small admission scale, have had their only source of flesh and blood entertainment. I am sending this telegram as a protest to those in Congress who can't see beyond the budget.

Despite all protests, the presentation of a special show in its support by the Screen Actors' Guild, and Cantor's seemingly close ties with Roosevelt, the project was indeed scrapped. Gone was the first and last attempt by the United States to provide major funding of the arts.

The next day—Saturday, June 17—Cantor resigned from the Council of the American Federation of Actors, the union representing performers in nightclubs and other variety fields. The American Federation of Actors had been organized by Ralph Whitehead in 1932 with Cantor himself as president. The first union for variety performers since the White Rats lost their charter in 1916, the AFA was formed chiefly to combat abuses by nightclub owners who forced performers to work outside jobs for nothing. Fred Keating, Rudy Vallee, and Sophie Tucker succeded Cantor, in turn, as its president.

When an article in *The Hollywood Reporter* in the spring of 1939 accused Whitehead of misusing AFA funds, Tucker had the American Association of Actors and Artists' auditors (parent union of Equity, SAG, and the A.F.A.) go over his books. The report said the books were balanced but allowed that there might have been misuse of funds.

At that point, Eddie called both Sophie and Harry Richman, urging both to resign. Neither did, and Tucker called a 2:00 A.M. meeting of the AFA at the Hotel Edison for Tuesday, June 20, 1939. She wanted a vote of confidence from the members.

The Sunday prior to the meeting, Cantor, still president of AFRA, and Vallee urged the members not to give that vote of confidence and to wait until the trial on July 10 of charges preferred against the AFA by the parent union.

Tucker's meeting was a shambles. She was heckled by "The Ferrets," the announced opposition, as she tried to read the auditors' report. She made references to Cantor, pointing out his absence from the meeting and accusing him of "deserting his brothers and sisters" and "making things tough for his old friend, Sophie Tucker." The meeting ended in a riot.

Cantor sent a telegram to Tucker: YOU HAVE BEEN MISLED IN THIS PRESENT CONTROVERSY AND AS A FRIEND I PLEAD WITH YOU TO RESIGN AS QUICKLY AS POSSIBLE OR YOU TOO WILL INNOCENTLY INVOLVE YOURSELF.

Tucker read the telegram to the press on Wednesday, June 21. "Eddie, my boy," she said, "even a murderer is entitled to a trial. Eddie, you have found us guilty without hearing our evidence. I suggest that you withdraw your resignation until this investigation is completed."

The Associated Actors and Artistes of America (also known as the Four A's) pulled the AFA charter, and Tucker responded by getting a new one from IATSE, the powerful stagehands' union whose president was soon under investigation.

Eddie's life continued to be volatile. He had anticipated being picked up for another season on the *Camel Caravan*. When, however, the R. J. Reynolds Tobacco Company did not advise its representative, the William Esty Agency, that it would renew Cantor by June 20, industry tongues wagged. The rumors were confirmed by Monday night, June 26, Cantor's final broadcast. He would not be renewed.

It was too late to secure another sponsor. Eddie Cantor would be without his own radio show for the first time in eight years.

Cantor was not shocked. He knew that letters had poured in to R. J. Reynolds and the Esty Agency from Coughlin fans around the country who had read about his speech in local newspapers.

> When the time arrives that one Jew can speak for all Jews and Americans—then—but not until then, I'll say Hitler is right.
> —Edna Boyle Andersen, Brooklyn, N.Y.

> We, the undersigned, take this opportunity to advise you that, to a man, we are boycotting your products until such time that Mr. Cantor will publicly retract and apologize for the remarks made against Father Coughlin, etc.—or until such time as Mr. Cantor is replaced on your programs.

Other letters referred to the " 'Smear Father Coughlin' campaign being carried on by the Jews and the Communists in this country," including one letter addressed, not to Camels, but to Cantor by Raymond J. Winslow of Bellaire, Long Island, New York. "Is it anti-American and anti-Jewish to request the Jews of this country to join with all religious creeds in a concerted attack against all foreignisms? That's all Father Coughlin did." The William Esty Agency had approached Cantor about apologizing or retracting or modifying his remarks. He had refused. "Before I'm a performer, I'm an American," he told them. "Before I'm an American, I'm a Jew. And before I'm a Jew, I'm a man."

Eddie did not try to call upon his status as a long-established favorite— "a guest in millions of American homes"—to force Esty or Reynolds to renew his contract. It was not simply a case of stacking his popularity against that of Father Coughlin. Stars' self-righteous cries for "justice" in their own behalfs were dismissed as childish temper tantrums in 1939. The only way to keep one's self-respect, look graceful, and retain one's public image was to maintain silence. Cantor made no public statements. He had simply lost his sponsor and had no plans for next season. Privately, however, he would not back down.

There was something very genuine in Cantor when push came to the inevitable shove. Despite his ego and his frequently manipulative, street kid's cynicism, Eddie believed in his causes. It was Cantor's faith and courage, pure and almost knightly, that made him seem so noble in a crisis.

## Chapter 11

# ``WE'RE HAVING A BABY''

*"The stage was his medium."*
—Natalie Cantor Clary

Cantor appeared unconcerned about his sudden and forced exit from the airwaves. Deep inside, he fought to keep his fears in check, to keep the demons from "doing something to him" that would destroy what remained of his still viable career. For the most part, he succeeded.

Eddie's unflappable demeanor was born, in part, of the old actor's belief that the time to put one's best foot forward and deny life's problems is when things are at their worst. Also, he believed that he was in the right—a political show biz martyr in the fight against right-wing religious bigots such as Father Coughlin and the Nazi hordes who were their (welcome or not) allies. He had been careful not to worry his four younger daughters when the market crashed ten years before. Now his confident manner was displayed, not just for them, but for the public. Commiserating with a country that had been through the worst market plunge in history was one thing. A major star's having what amounted to "sponsor trouble" was another. Eddie's answer was to totally ignore not having his own radio show—in public and at home.

In contrast, Margie worried, seeming to carry the burden of every negative thought so that her father could remain the same seemingly optimistic "Apostle of Pep" he had been as far back as she could remember.

If her sisters complained about the food at any meal, Margie would explain that they had to cut down on expenses. She—they—the entire household had to pitch in during what she saw as a true crisis. In fact, the family finances were in good shape thanks to Eddie's mammoth (by the standards of the '30s) earnings since the 1929 crash. But Margie's fierce devotion to her father would not let her find peace. She seemed, in fact, to bear the weight of every problem that came near the Cantor family, as if that was her duty.

Cantor was scarcely any less active without a weekly show. Three days after his last Camels broadcast, Eddie opened a week's engagement at Loews State in New York, supported by his former radio contingent, the socialite Cobina Wright Jr., Harrison and Fisher, and the teen-age Ann Miller. It was a typical Cantor unit stage show, Eddie getting a phenomenal 50 percent of the gross and "gearing himself for maximum possible revenue," in the words of Ben Bodec.

> During the supper show of the opening day (Thursday) he told a capacity audience that he had just been informed by the manager that up to 6 p.m. he had broken all house records. That 50-50 angle reflected itself in his next statement. He pleaded with the audience that they be good sports, if they had already seen the complete bill, and leave so that 1,000 people waiting outside could get in. The existing flock must have been puzzled by the appeal because, while there were standees and a hefty line at the box office, the lobby was clear.

The Cantors spent the remainder of the summer at their home in California, Eddie getting a long overdue rest except for the time he devoted to the various actors' unions.

The American Federation of Actors lost its AFL charter on Friday, July 14, 1939, following four days of investigation by the Four A's into charges of misuse of funds and mismanagement. Cantor immediately became temporary president of the American Guild of Variety Artists (AGVA), a new union created to absorb the AFA membership. A constitution for AGVA had already been drawn.

Sophie Tucker fumed. "Now I can understand why Eddie Cantor was very desirous of having me resign from the Federation on the ground I was being misled. It is all very funny."

Cantor telegraphed his New York press agent, Irving Mansfield, the following Wednesday, saying that Miss Tucker was "slamming me around only because she is disappointed that Ralph Whitehead was found guilty on all charges and that the charter was taken from the American Federation of Actors." Eddie claimed he had conferred with Laurence Beilenson, Los Angeles attorney for the Screen Actors' Guild, and James Cagney on the feasibility of having Sophie named first president of AGVA.

The situation dragged on into August, Tucker and Harry Richman, chairman of the AFA Council, having been suspended from membership in all Four A's bodies. Cantor, in another telegram, condemned the "silence" of the American Federation of Labor's executive council in settling the jurisdictional issue between the Four A's and IATSE. He described the silence as "ominous" because "back of the wall of silence we know there is the figure of Ralph Whitehead."

Cantor accused Whitehead of "attempting to hide behind the skirts of Miss Tucker, whose life has been devoted to the entertainment of the public."

The AFA council voted to disband the union, giving AGVA a clear field in variety. Although it has never been a strong union, AGVA still exists, a living testament to the near impossibility of organizing variety performers into a viable organization.

Cantor was reelected president of the American Federation of Radio Artists at its national meeting in Chicago on August 26. Eddie was still in Beverly Hills, going over plans for filmhouse vaudeville, preparing radio guest shots, and reading scripts for films at RKO and M-G-M.

He now had a new valet-masseur. Edmund Frauchiger having returned to Switzerland to pursue a career in osteopathy, Eddie hired a Norwegian, Maurice Nielson, at Frenchy's recommendation.

The differences between Frenchy and Maurice were marked. Maurice was tall, quite dignified, a Seventh-Day Adventist, and very religious. Like Frenchy, he was kind, totally devoted to Cantor, and a conscientious valet who laid out his color-blind boss's clothes, checked to see his tie was straight, and massaged his aging muscles daily.

The William Morris Agency had lined up a series of film house engagements for the Cantor unit, starting with the Stanley Theatre in Pittsburgh on September 29. They were at the RKO Boston on October 18, 1939, when Natalie gave birth to a son, Michael Jay, in Los Angeles.

Cantor announced the event onstage for the remainder of the week. The audience applauded, but there might have been some gasps. Cantor, more perhaps than any other performer, personified high energy and youth. All his movies cast him as a young man, presumably in his mid-twenties, and Cantor's slight appearance, energy, and youthful-looking face, helped along by careful makeup and photography, allowed him to play the roles with reasonable conviction. Cantor's blend of shy/sly innocence augmented the impression.

Viewing him onstage, as master of his unit, one could see that Cantor was a man into his forties. But a grandfather? Eddie's proud admission seemed to shatter all illusion.

Cantor had been reshaping his image for the past two years, assuming the role of a show business elder statesman, gradually becoming less performer and more showman. This included being the "Columbus of Show Business." In November, the Cantor unit played the Balaban & Katz Chicago Theatre, where Eddie did what Gold (*Variety*) said was an "out-and-out selling job on a little tap dancer, Ruth Daye." Leni Lynn, another thirteen-year-old soprano Cantor thought might be a second Deanna Durbin, had been with the show since Pittsburgh. Like most Cantor discoveries, neither Ruth nor Leni remained in the spotlight long.

Eddie went to Palm Springs for a brief vacation, played a week in Cincinnati with his unit show, and returned to California. The script of his new picture was now ready.

Cantor claimed that *Forty Little Mothers* was based on the plot of a French movie he and Ida had seen in New York. "I asked Metro to get the story for me to do in Hollywood. The head men looked at the film and agreed. So here I am a school teacher, and I think we've got something. I know that everybody says the world wants to laugh. But mere laughter is not sufficient. The world wants a good cry, too. It wants to think a little bit; it wants to be stirred."

The plot concerned an out-of-work teacher (Eddie) who talks a young woman out of committing suicide and then finds a baby boy whom he thinks has been abandoned. Arrested on a minor charge, he gets a job at a girls' school through the intervention of the judge, an old classmate, and brings the baby (whom he now calls "Chum") with him. The students, resentful of the fact that Eddie is replacing an extremely handsome teacher fired for inciting their affections, discover the baby and rejoice at getting the goods on their new, unwanted teacher. When he reproaches them, they turn around and become "Forty Little Mothers" to the baby. The baby's mother (the same woman he had saved from suicide) eventually reappears, and the head of the school (Judith Anderson), who had wanted to fire Eddie after discovering the baby's presence, relents and lets him stay. Presumably, he marries the baby's mother, who has been deserted by her husband.

Among the picture's "Forty Little Mothers" was the beautiful Diana Lewis, wife of William Powell. Another was Bonita Granville, daughter of Bernard Granville, a well known musical comedy performer of the 1910s. "Bonita is the finest little actress I know. She's only sixteen now, and in a few years I predict she'll be the Bette Davis of Hollywood." It was Eddie, the Columbus of Show Business, once again "discovering" young talent.

Cantor's acting in *Forty Little Mothers*, somewhat labored in a scene where he confronts the girls, is generally subdued, and his scenes with "Chum" ("Baby Quintella" in the credits) are wonderful depictions of paternal love. The scenes, in fact, were shot shortly after Eddie passed out cigars at the studio on January 19, the day his daughter Edna presented him with his first granddaughter. Judith McHugh came into the world at Cedars of Lebanon Hospital weighing eight pounds, two and one-half ounces, with Dr. Irving LeRoy Ress attending. Eddie saw the baby two days later, during a brief break from filming.

Production ended Friday, February 23, having taken seven weeks. Cantor was now talking to Sam Goldwyn about a nonmusical remake of *Whoopee*— if M-G-M would consent to postpone a second picture.

Another Cantor project was an all-black Broadway stage show written by himself and John B. Hymer. Eddie returned to New York in March to cast it, publicize *Forty Little Mothers*, and see about a new radio sponsor through agent Jimmy Saphier.

Publicity for *Forty Little Mothers* consisted of a luncheon in Cantor's honor given by the Grand Street Boys Association on the Lower East Side on April 17, prior to the picture's world premiere at Loews Canal, near Eddie's birthplace. Cantor and George Jessel entertained, having broken in their material at the State Theatre in Hartford, and a parade was held from Madison and Pearl streets to the Canal Theatre. A more ambitious stage show accompanied the picture's official premiere at the Capitol Theatre the following evening.

Cantor and Jessel's new material included a takeoff on *Gone With the Wind*, with Cantor as Scarlett and Jessel as Rhett Butler. Jokes about George Jessel's marriage to the sixteen-year-old Lois Andrews, the supporting acts, and songs by Cantor and Jessel made up the balance of the program, climaxed by a scene about Gus Edwards. Cantor now seemed dated in the days of Benny Goodman, his still obvious popularity increasingly nostalgic.

The Cantor of eight years before was a young forty who had met the challenge of commercial radio with enthusiasm and ideas that reflected, at the least, a showman's appreciation of the new medium. Now he seemed to be resting on his laurels. He was close to fifty, with two married daughters, another daughter of twenty-five, and two grandchildren.

He did not identify with the "new" show biz. The new sound known as "swing" seemed more than just a new development in popular music. It was, much more than jazz, a break with the old, pre-Depression culture that could not be wedded comfortably with musical comedy or, indeed, the "presentation" style of show business. Swing was not theatrical, and it featured, not performers, but musicians. Performers, such as Cantor, who relied on their stage presence, inborn sense of showmanship, audience rapport, and humor now looked corny and old-fashioned. The '20s and art deco were now history. So, too, it seemed, was Eddie Cantor.

Nor was *Forty Little Mothers* a success. Walt, in *Variety*, scored its "dated scripting and erratic direction. . . . Story is not too well constructed, and bends in many spots in trying to get over plausibility. Cantor provides a broad interpretation of the prof., straining unsuccessfully to achieve spontaneous comedy in lines and situations that are absent from the script." Neither did the first week's gross at the Capitol—$35,000—merit another week for Cantor's unit, with or without *Forty Little Mothers*.

Recent viewings of the film do not bear out Walt's pronouncements. Busby Berkeley's direction is amazingly taut. Indeed, the picture's major flaw is its simplicity. The plot, fairly tight at the beginning, meanders after Eddie is established in his teaching job, and the titular motif of forty little mothers takes up a brief moment near the film's end that makes no contribution to the picture. The picture's only song, a ballad titled "Little Curly Hair in a High Chair," worked well within the context of the film but failed to become a hit in its own right. (Cantor's commercial recording pales beside his rendition of the song to "Chum" in the movie.)

Cantor's self-confidence, however, was unshaken by the film's lukewarm reception. A reshuffling of radio comics' sponsors meant that Fred Allen would be going from Bristol-Myers to Texaco. And Jack Benny's contract was up for renewal.

Benny's success on radio was not only consistent; he actually improved each season. The increased sureness of his impeccable timing, his overall confidence, his top writers, and his expanding cast of characters—including Eddie (Rochester) Anderson, the announcer Don Wilson, and a series of tenors that would culminate in Dennis Day—were the ingredients, along with Benny's charm and willingness to be identified as both the stingiest man in the world and a vain egomaniac. Young & Rubicam, his account agency, had guaranteed to get him a new sponsor at more money.

Benny, a proud Jew in his own right, urged the agency to get Cantor a new show as well. As a result, Young & Rubicam gave Cantor the first half of the hour slot vacated by Allen at a base salary of $10,000 a week, plus an added bonus predicated, for the first time in radio history, on his Crossley rating. His sponsor would be Bristol-Myers.

Cantor's rating had to exceed twenty points. If the rating averaged twenty-five points over the thirty-nine-week cycle, he would get a bonus of $39,000. If the average was not achieved, he would get $200 per point for the rating that his program hit between twenty and twenty-five points—a strange contract for a man who had attacked the Crossleys for the past three years. Cantor, nonetheless, was back in radio. He hired Joe Quillan and Izzy Ellison as writers and exercised his personal contract with producer Vick Knight, forcing him to leave the Rudy Vallee *Sealtest Show*.

Eddie spent the next two months working for good causes—emceeing a Red Cross rally in New York on Sunday afternoon, May 28—and against Adolf Hitler, whom he seemed to consider his own personal enemy. On July 11, he was the principal guest speaker at the District Convention of Grand Lodge No. 6, B'nai B'rith, at the Municipal Auditorium in Omaha, drawing cheers and laughter with lines like:

> From now on, every man's business must become his sideline, and his chief business that of helping in the government's defense program.

> I'd rather live under an unbalanced budget than an unbalanced dictator.

Too many Americans take liberty for granted—like many men take their wives.

At Boys' Town, he embraced the famous Father Flanagan for newspaper photographers. "Hurry up," he yelped, "much as I like Father Flanagan, he's no Myrna Loy."

In Atlantic City on Saturday, July 13, Cantor urged the people of the United States to "get serious," declaring that it was time to "think seriously about hates, and their threat to America."

We've got to start now—this moment—to see things clearly. We have had it too soft, but unless we wake up it won't be that way long. . . . Every man, woman and child you see on the Boardwalk today will be called upon to make some sacrifice.

We've got to forget talking about five-day weeks, and no work on Saturdays, because the dictators are working seven days a week— and nights, too, figuring out what they can do to us. Anti-Semitism is only one of their schemes—it says "you hate me because I hate you." And then what happens—a country is broken, easily conquered. It's too bad the anti-Semitists can't see it works both ways.

He was back in New York on July 22, telling one and all about a play by two collegians and a youth in civil service. Cantor said he planned to coproduce and star in this new play, into which four songs would be inserted. *Sweet Land of Liberty*, the all-black show he had been planning to produce, had since been shelved. The script, said Cantor, poked fun at the White House, which, he claimed, would be sacrilegious "in this hour of danger."

Cantor flew back to Los Angeles the following Sunday, having agreed to retain Harry Von Zell from Fred Allen's program as his announcer. The remainder of the cast was finalized on the west coast: the female vaudeville team of (Nan) Rae & (Maude) Davis and Tommy Mack for comedy support, Bobby Sherwood as conductor, and Dinah Shore as vocalist.

Dinah, a Jewish girl from the deep South, was, at this time, an extraordinary singer—musical, expressive, with what seemed like a coating of honey on the inside of her throat. She would soon become the top female vocalist in the nation.

Cantor sailed back east through the Panama Canal, arriving in New York aboard the U.S. liner *Manhattan* on September 10. In an interview, he said he hoped to organize a radio show in behalf of refugee British children and announced that he was going to open his own home in Great Neck—still unsold—for one hundred British youngsters.

"Aside from humanitarian reasons, I want to pay back England for her help in aiding my fund to assist refugees from German territories. English people gave the fund $560,000. It is ironic that many who gave money to my fund now need aid for their own children."

Eddie agreed to appear on *America's Famous Fathers* over WJZ and several dozen other stations. This was a sustaining (noncommercial) show at the time Cantor taped it. Hours later, it was sold to Julius Grossman Shoes, which Eddie learned only when he saw ads in New York papers. He then announced he would sue Grossman, NBC, and Ray Green of the Kermit-Raymond Corporation, producers of the series.

"I didn't want to appear on the show, anyway," said Cantor, "but the Young & Rubicam publicity department persuaded me to do it. They said it would help publicize my series for Sal Hepatica, so I finally agreed to do it. However, it was strictly with the understanding that the series was a sustainer. I look like a dope, and I make Bristol-Myers look like dopes to have it announced that I'm being sponsored by Julius Grossman shoes the very night before my own series goes on the air." The show was yanked an hour before air time.

*Time to Smile*, Cantor's new show for Bristol-Myers, premiered the following evening with superlative results. The script was far superior to those for *Camel Caravan*, with Von Zell put to good use as the target of Maude Davis's man-chasing humor. Eddie scored with a burlesque of quiz shows, and Dinah Shore's success was nothing short of phenomenal—one of the best introductions of a talent in radio history. "Cantor not only glutted the air with laughs," Ben Bodec wrote, "he so projected Dinah Shore that listeners got an entirely new vista of this girl's singing talents. Judging from her performance on that broadcast, Miss Shore stacks up as radio's new vocal sensation."

Ben Holtzmann, Cantor's personal manager for almost a decade, now told Eddie that he wanted to go into radio production on his own. Eddie wished him well but warned him of the pitfalls. Within six weeks, Holtzmann had decided to join the William Morris Agency on the West Coast as a general talent agent, representing, chiefly, Eddie Cantor.

Holtzmann's position as Cantor's "personal manager" was soon filled by Jack Crandall, a customer's man in a New York brokerage house who had done various "gopher" work for Cantor and George Olsen in the '20s. Crandall's wife, a former Broadway showgirl named Alice Monroe, was found dead in the bathroom of their New York home on June 10, 1939, officially the victim "of a heart attack brought on by acute indigestion" but reportedly a suicide at thirty-five years old.

Crandall himself was uncouth and unattractive, and he had little sensitivity or tact, making him a strange candidate for the job of Eddie Cantor's personal manager. "He was strange, period," remembers Janet Cantor. "He used to sleep on top of the bed fully dressed because he said if he got into bed he'd die. He eventually had shock treatment, which left him with trouble with his memory—meaning he'd call Margie at all hours because he couldn't remember things like the name of the fourth chorus girl from the end in *Whoopee*."

Crandall rendered personal, rather than professional, service, making sure of Eddie's hotel accommodations, train tickets, and other sundries; he never did—or could—function as an agent. Eddie's daughters advised him to replace Crandall every time he made a major mistake—which was often. "If I let him go, he'll kill himself" was all Eddie would say. Even relegating Jack to a "make-believe job," like Bunky's, seemed to be out of the question.

Crandall did, however, know insurance. He made sure Cantor had plenty of life insurance (medical coverage was a rarity in the early 1940s), which kept Eddie's daughters supplied with annuities years after their father's death.

Crandall's son Edward was likewise, a strange person—entirely nonsocial, often found standing in corners of the Cantor home during his not infrequent visits. When certain items turned up missing, the girls—privately—blamed him. Their suspicions were lent credence when the younger Crandall was arrested on a minor charge. Cantor provided young Crandall's bail.

Cantor, although not a patient man at work, was nevertheless loyal to a fault with his employees. Crandall's greatest liability was not, at the time, readily apparent. One of his supposed jobs was taking care of the Cantor investments, and the family lost out on many millions of dollars due to opportunities he failed to advise Eddie to grab. Chief among these was the purchase, at a low price, of the entire block of Hollywood and Vine through Sunset and Vine. Ida urged Eddie to buy the buildings; Crandall advised against it.

"Ida, I'm an actor," Eddie told his wife, "What do I know about real estate?" Ida merely sighed and returned to her knitting, painting, and card playing. She had accepted her lot—a life as the most famous "nonshow business person in show business," living in retirement with virtually no worries, cares, or power.

The Cantors returned to the West Coast in December, and Eddie did *Time to Smile*, with weekly guest stars ranging from Margaret Hamilton to Rita Hayworth. He guest-starred on the Burns and Allen Show in January, running afoul of NBC, then in the midst of a giant war with ASCAP, when he wanted to sing a new song they considered too similar to "Birth of the Blues." (Cantor substituted "Lazy Mary, Won't You Get Up?")

While Cantor was on the West Coast, plans were under way for his return to Broadway. Georgie Hale, the nominal producer of the Jolson show *Hold onto Your Hats*, wanted to star Cantor in a show about the new Selective Service System. Max Gordon had a vehicle for Cantor titled *Glam-*

*our Boy.* Al Lewis planned to star Cantor in *Christopher Columbus, Jr.*—if Eddie would supply most of the money.

Cantor was mentioned as a possible replacement for Jolson when Al quit the cast of *Hold onto Your Hats* early in February. One month later, it was said Jules Levey would produce *Hold onto Your Hats* for Universal, with Cantor in the role Jolson had played on Broadway.

Cantor moved his radio show to New York in mid-March. More film-house engagements began with three performances in Lowell, Massachusetts, where he broke the house record with a gross of $5,500. A long weekend in Hartford had the usual lines around the block for the five shows on Sunday; business on Saturday had been surprisingly weak.

Cantor, always sensitive to changing tastes—whatever his personal reaction to them—now stocked his troupe with more purely musical performers and fewer comedians. He and Fields (Mr. Guffy) were the only comics on the bill in Hartford, with Dinah Shore, the ballet dancer Gloria Gilbert, the Clyde McCoy Band with vocalist Dick Lee, the pianist Bob Nelson, the three Bennett Sisters, and Olive Major, another Deanna Durbin type of vocalist—but without Durbin's charm or beauty—making up the remainder of the program.

Olive, a sad-eyed thirteen-year-old only child, was born in Santa Barbara. Edna's husband, Jimmy McHugh Jr., heard her sing in Hollywood in early 1940 and insisted Eddie give her an audition.

"I was so nervous I don't think I could describe it," Olive said. "But Mr. Cantor was wonderful. He listened, and I kept looking at him out of the corner of my eye, trying to find out what he was thinking. And then when I was all through, he said he liked it."

Cantor had her study voice for six months. Finally, deciding she was ready for limited activity, Eddie put her on his Christmas *Time to Smile* broadcast. Olive remained a Cantor "regular" on radio and in his unit stage show for the balance of the season.

She was a serious girl who liked to read and collect records. She was also writing a book about a young man looking for a job in London about 1825. Olive said the book was very "psychological."

Her ambition was to sing at the Met. Unlike Deanna, who reportedly had asked for an ice cream soda and a trip to the top of the Empire State Building, Olive's first request in New York was to see the Met's stage entrance. Like most Cantor "discoveries," she vanished in a year.

Plans for *Hold onto Your Hats* were scuttled after United Artists vice president Arthur Kelly offered Cantor a three-year contract as actor and producer. The agreement called for Eddie to star in a minimum of one picture a year with options on two additional films every twelve months, with or without Cantor on screen. Production on the first film would begin that summer.

Cantor's attorney, Joe Ross, came in from the coast for the negotiations. United Artists was reputedly willing to aid in the financing, but Cantor said he was prepared to provide all the necessary money from personal friends eager to invest.

Among those "friends" was the multimillionaire Jock Whitney. To tie his first UA film in with Whitney's "Pan American Conference," Cantor envisioned a Latin American theme, with music ranging from the Cuban congarlumba to the Argentine samba and tango.

Eddie took lessons in Spanish and Portuguese for eight weeks. "As and when I go to South America, I want to be able to stand up on a platform or dais and answer questions that will help the cause of democracy in the native language of the country. And I want to have a good enough understanding of words so that I can put some humor into my answers. That's always the most effective way of creating good will."

But the unsettled monetary state of United Artists forced Cantor to let the deal simmer. He had no interest in buying the block of UA stock held by the estate of Douglas Fairbanks but hoped, in vain, that the company's future would be settled by July.

In the meantime, there were radio and more public events. Cantor was there when New York celebrated "I Am an American Day" on Sunday, May 18, 1941. Bill Robinson personally guaranteed that Hitler would "never get past Yankee Stadium" if he ever started for Harlem.

As Bristol-Myers picked up its option for another Cantor season on radio, Eddie picked up his option on Dinah Shore, whose Columbia recording of "Yes, My Darling Daughter" had been one of the best sellers of the season. Dinah had outgrown her status as "Eddie Cantor's vocalist"— but not Eddie Cantor's contract.*

Cantor did his final broadcast of the season on June 25 and spent a fairly quiet summer at North Roxbury, broken only by an occasional weekend in Palm Springs. Eddie got the surprise of his life when he found that the house down there belonged to him—a gift from Ida.

He truly loved the house. Not till after Ida's death would it be sold, and then because it served to remind Eddie of her absence.

Plans for Cantor's return to the Broadway theatre under the Al Lewis banner were now closer to fruition. Cantor wanted a show based on his own life, which could then be turned into a movie. The show would be called *Banjo Eyes*.

This play was changed completely in July, when Cantor decided to make *Banjo Eyes* into a musical version of his cherished *Three Men on a Horse*.

---

*Miss Shore, however, was not with the Cantor unit when it played a two day weekend (June 21–22) at the Steel Pier, Atlantic City. "Cantor works at top speed," wrote Carter in *Variety*, "his songs, yarns and patter never failing to please his responsive listeners. His song from former years, 'Making the Best of Each Day,' with interspersed references to his personal life and family, went over big." There were the usual lines.

Partly through necessity, as it still owned the rights, he managed to get Warners to finance the project as a source for a film vehicle.

On Tuesday, August 12, three days after emceeing a free show for the San Francisco *Examiner*, Cantor left for New York to start work on *Banjo Eyes*. He wanted everything to be first class. When Rodgers and Hart declined to do the score, Cantor and Lewis secured Vernon Duke and John LaTouche, who had written *Cabin in the Sky*. Their work on *Banjo Eyes* would prove less memorable.

June Clyde, a player in several Hollywood musicals of the early 1930s and the wife of Thornton Freeland, director of the film version of *Whoopee*, was chosen to play Sally Trowbridge, Eddie's wife in *Banjo Eyes*. Audrey Christie left the Chicago company of *My Sister Eileen* to play Mabel, a striptease artist who disrobed at every opportunity. Added to the principals was an attractive chorus line including Betty Boyce (a former Jolson paramour), Shirl Thomas, and Florence Foster. Wishing to make *Banjo Eyes* a "show" in the best Broadway tradition, Cantor did not use a single member of his radio cast.

*Banjo Eyes* stuck closely to the script of *Three Men on a Horse*, with a few variations. In his dreams, a greeting card salesman, Erwin Trowbridge (Cantor), talks to a horse ("Banjo Eyes") who gives him tips on real races. The tips invariably pan out, but the horse insists that Trowbridge never bet on races. When a gang hears of his pickings and forces Trowbridge to put money on a race, "Banjo Eyes," true to his word, stops talking.

Cantor still saw *Three Men on a Horse* as the ideal vehicle for him. The major catch was Eddie's age. The boyishness and innocence that had been such a staple of his early shows and character were gone. In its place was a sure-footed, obviously mature star—likable but obviously no boy, either in appearance or in the minds of a public that knew he was returning to the Broadway stage after an absence of twelve years.

*Banjo Eyes* barely infringed on Cantor's weekly show for Bristol-Myers. Eddie's second season as the star of *Time to Smile* opened with a guest appearance by the Shakespearean actor Maurice Evans on September 3, 1941. The script was original and clever, with topical humor and fine, logical transitions between one part of the program and the next. Evans proved himself adept at comedy, singing a parody of "Daddy," bantering with Cantor, and telling the Mad Russian he did not believe that he had ever been in Moscow—or could get in. Gordon's next line—"You're not the only one that can't get into Moscow"— a reference to the stalled Nazi drive, drew loud and sustained applause from the studio audience. Ben Bodec called the show "a consistently explosive half-hour. The only regretful thing about this program was the spotting and stingy use made of Dinah Shore. She was in for a briefie at the opening of the proceedings and back again at the fadeout to join Cantor in a reprise of the same number." Cantor, having long recognized the value of using his stardom in one medium to publicize his efforts in another, had been careful to include a brief reference to *Banjo Eyes* in the program's opening crossfire.

The show's book was completed by the middle of September, and rehearsals started on October 7. The madness implicit in rehearsing for a Broadway show and preparing, rehearsing, and performing a weekly network radio show at the same time did not daunt Eddie Cantor. Not since the early '30s had the star of a radio show attempted to carry a Broadway show at the same time. Cantor had the energy, the discipline, the ego, and the drive to do what seemed impossible, without so much as rolling his big eyes at what seemed like a Herculean labor.

*Banjo Eyes* opened to a sold-out audience at the Shubert Theatre in New Haven on Friday night, November 7, 1941. The consensus, voiced by Bone. (*Variety*) was that the show's major drawback was its score, that the book stuck too closely to the original stage play (with the exception of an army camp scene in which Cantor drew "consistent laughs"), and that the show's major strengths were Cantor, the DeMarcos, and the lavishness of its production values. Even the finale, in which Cantor did a few of his old hits in blackface, did not go well at the opening, due largely to an ill-advised "buildup" that had Eddie blacking up onstage—described as "a dead spot" by Bone. Drastic work was clearly needed.

An improved *Banjo Eyes* opened at the Colonial Theatre in Boston the following Tuesday evening. By now, the book had been trimmed back so much that Elinor Hughes, reviewing the show in the Boston *Herald*, thought it "had a way of getting lost in the shuffle" of production values, dancing, "lively songs," and beautiful girls. The capacity house, "sold out to the rafters and with standees three deep," allowed *Banjo Eyes* to gross more than $18,000 in six performances that week—not spectacular compared to the $30,000 for eight performances racked up by *Sons o' Fun*, Olsen and Johnson's sequel to *Hellzapoppin'*. *Banjo Eyes* still needed work.

Cantor's weekly broadcasts meant there were no Wednesday night performances of *Banjo Eyes*—the first time in history a Broadway show gave a reduced number of weekly performances in order to accommodate a star's obligations in a different medium. Seven shows a week instead of eight made it that much harder for the show to make a profit. *Banjo Eyes* grossed only $60,000 over three weeks at the Colonial, having given only twenty performances.

Three new songs were added by the time the show opened a three-week engagement at the Forrest Theatre in Philadelphia. Since Vernon Duke and John Latouche had started work on *A Lady Comes Across*, a new musical for England's Jessie Matthews, Cantor got Harold Adamson to write "Make with the Feet," "It Could Only Happen in the Movies," and "I Gotta Keep Rollin'," the "tuneful tale of a taxi driver," sung by Romo Vincent.

The following Sunday morning, a day that Cantor planned to spend preparing for his next broadcast, the Japanese bombed the U.S. naval base at Pearl Harbor, Hawaii.

Eddie spent most of that afternoon on the telephone. *Banjo Eyes* already had an army scene, interpolated without too much rhyme or reason aside from its undoubted topicality and its relevance to the year-old Selective Service Act. Young men had been subject to a draft into the "peace"-time army for more than a year.

When Congress approved President Roosevelt's request for a declaration of war against Japan and Germany declared war on the United States, Cantor knew he wanted a new song. He got it, not from Adamson, but from Charlie Tobias. "We Did It Before (And We Can Do It Again)" was a rousing, jubilant martial call designed to allay Americans' fears about the long, hard years of war ahead. *Banjo Eyes* was getting further and further from the strict adherence to the story line it had observed in New Haven, without becoming a much better show. If anything, it was now close to a revue.

Eddie's daughter Janet, who flew in as the show moved in to New York, saw her parents looking drawn and haggard after a rehearsal that went into the early hours of the morning. "I Gotta Keep Rollin' " was cut, and a new song, written to fill in a stage wait, was provided called "We're Having a Baby," its double-entendre lyrics given added meaning by Eddie's pointed phrasing and his rolling eyes.

When opening night came, less than twelve hours later, Cantor looked well rested and excited—the picture of a man about to tackle a big moment with self-confidence and relish. All the constant work, he knew instinctively, had not been wasted. *Banjo Eyes* was ready for the toughest Broadway critics, including John Mason Brown, who perhaps summed it up best:

> Eddie Cantor remains a remarkable performer. The all-too-many years which separate his personal reappearance on Broadway last night from the Ziegfeldian days when he was cavorting in *Whoopee* have not diminished his vitality. Although he may now and then become a bit winded as he rushes through a song, his prancings up and down the proscenium have lost nothing of their bounce.
>
> Even so, it is hard to become enthusiastic about *Banjo Eyes*. It is meant for those who not only like Mr. Cantor (which is easy enough to do) but who also do not mind musical comedies when they are being just like all other indifferent musical comedies, with some vaudeville and night club talent thrown in. Judging from the reactions of last night's audience, however, I am happy to report that there seems to be plenty of theatregoers who dote on both.

*Three Men on a Horse* was one of those delicious comedies of characters (e.g., "tough guys," "mousy greeting card writer") that have long since passed from vogue. It was likewise thought to be the type of comedy best suited to adaption as a musical. Assembled as a quick and easy vehicle for its star, Eddie Cantor, and doctored into better shape during seven weeks of tryouts, *Banjo Eyes* failed to make use of the great elemental forces that made *Three Men on a Horse* the great play it had been in the hands of a true theatre genius like George Abbott. *Guys and Dolls* would be the show that *Banjo Eyes* might well, and should, have been. Cantor likewise would have fared much better had his songs been tailored to the character of Trowbridge; what he got were mediocre Eddie Cantor numbers. The non-musical scene in which Cantor, as Trowbridge, thought up rhymes for greeting cards, was one of the high points of the production.

Another asset was Virginia Mayo, whom Gertrude Lawrence, in the crowd of first-nighters that included Ida, all of Eddie's daughters, and the usual Broadway habitués, described as "something you expect to see dancing on the lawn when you're a child." Others in the show included the beautiful blonde showgirl Adele Jergens, who would star in second features at Columbia within the next few years. Adele reminded Eddie of the Ziegfeld show girls, who were courted by millionaires. "I had this doctor," Adele recalled, "who admired me and bought me a fur coat. He dropped me off at the theatre one night, and when Eddie saw me wearing the mink coat, he brought me into his dressing room to show Ida."

There was another girl who spent a lot of time in Eddie's dressing room when Ida was not there. She was Jacqueline Susann, the twenty-three-year-old wife of Cantor's New York press agent, Irving Mansfield.

"I've never seen such ambition" was the way that Eddie, one of the most ambitious men in the history of American show business, described Jackie to his daughter, Marilyn. Jacqueline Susann was dark, quite attractive (not at all the hard-looking woman she would become) and, by her own admission, "sick for Jewish comedians." Eddie was Jewish, a comedian, and twenty-six years older than Jackie. Doubtless, he reminded her of Bob Susann, her father, a good-looking artist and a playboy.

Jacqueline had been in a Broadway play titled *My Fair Ladies* that ran thirty-two performances beginning March 23, 1941. She could neither sing nor dance, and she was not really a showgirl. Her presence in the cast of *Banjo Eyes* was due less to her husband's influence with Cantor than to her own dogged persistence.

Many thought she and Eddie were lovers, and the rumors were encouraged by the ruthlessly ambitious Susann. Kate Witkin, a dancer in the show, remembered Jackie as behaving "so unprofessionally" during rehearsals. "She was in the opening scene, and in rehearsal when her scene came everybody had to wait; someone would have to go looking for Jackie. She may have been off with Cantor." Jackie made sure she was seen leaving the Essex House late at night when Ida made a brief trip out of town.

*Banjo Eyes* was not a great show, and Mansfield had his work cut out for him as its p.r. man. A special party celebrating Cantor's twenty-fifth anniversary on Broadway was held on the Hollywood Theatre stage on Tuesday afternoon, March 24, with Ziegfeld alumni Peggy Hopkins Joyce, Margaret St. Clair, Gladys Feldman, Gertrude Vanderbilt, Irene Delroy, Tot Qualters, Annette Herbert, and Ethel Shutta in attendance. Gene Buck, in a short speech, commended Cantor's theatrical accomplishments. An award, commemorating "twenty-five years of Page One performances," was presented to Cantor at the seventh annual ball of the Newspaper Guild at the Hotel Astor on Friday, April 10.

Cantor had been suffering from hemorrhoids for days when he visited Dr. Joseph S. Diamond's office at 16 East 83rd Street for what the *New York Times* described as "a slight operation" on Monday morning, April 13, 1942. No operation was performed, however, and Eddie returned to the Essex House later that day. The papers did not specify his malady, and Cantor was expected to rejoin the cast of *Banjo Eyes* on Thursday evening.

Dr. Diamond had decided that Cantor would need, in fact, an operation. Eddie entered Sydenham Hospital on Tuesday afternoon, April 14; the rest of that week's performances were canceled. By Wednesday morning, Dr. Diamond reportedly told Cantor that he would have to stay off his feet for "several weeks," and Cantor called Warner representative Bernard Klawans. *Banjo Eyes* would have to close.

Bell Telephone Company workmen spent Wednesday installing a special line to Cantor's bedside, so that *Time to Smile* could go on *almost* as usual. Eddie, from his bed, "cut in" on his own show, as an obviously altered *Time to Smile* relied mainly on its guest host, Phil Baker.

Klawans told the press that *Banjo Eyes* might be reopened at a later date. Several comedians, including Jack Haley, were offered Cantor's part, but all declined to follow Eddie in a vehicle that had been named for him. More than thirty-five thousand dollars in advance sales was refunded, and the final balance sheet showed *Banjo Eyes* $100,000 in the red.

The cast felt Eddie had deserted them—that he, like many stars of radio and screen, had tired of doing the same show, night after night, and wanted to return to California. Cantor seems to have been willing to do the show until the end of his radio season. His ailment might have incapacitated Eddie for a brief time, yet it is hard to think that a case of hemorrhoids, all by itself, would have forced him to leave *Banjo Eyes* for good.

Cantor "set the record straight" on April 22. "For ten days prior to Sunday, April 12, I played while suffering intense pain. The following day, upon advice of my physician, an emergency operation was performed. Complications set in which necessitated a second operation and while I am permitted casual activity my doctors inform me that it would be at least a month before I could undertake eight performances a week in *Banjo Eyes*. It is my hope to keep in touch with all members of the cast so that if all goes well we might reopen in the fall."

The show did not reopen. Eddie was now fifty and no longer capable of sustaining the rigors of a tough and fast-paced musical comedy seven or eight times weekly. Giving one's all, as Eddie felt obliged to do, on Broadway was a young man's game.

*Banjo Eyes* would be Cantor's final Broadway show.

*Chapter 12*

# THE OTHER MADONNA

*"A strange female curtain-climber, with a trick of punching herself in
the jaw and a curious resemblance to Olive Oyl in the cartoons."*

Variety described 1941–42 as Cantor's "most successful radio work since
1933." That assessment considered only the ratings, however. Artisti-
cally, *Time to Smile* had but one major asset—Dinah Shore.

His writers now had Eddie playing the straight man throughout most of
the program. Gone were most of the boyishly effeminate inflections, the
infectious Cantor enthusiasms, and the delightful "Ohs" of fear. The "modern" Cantor simply walked (or talked) through the motions; the energy, the
character, the classic *shtik* were missing.

The Cantor of the '40s read through sketches in a detached, vaguely
condescending manner, and his "stooging" for Bert Gordon and numerous
guest stars sounded like a stage manager reading the script for an actor's
audition—repeating the gag lines, not to the "comic" but to the audience,
as if trying to explain the joke.

Cantor did the final nine broadcasts of the season from the West Coast,
six of them from military installations, with Bristol-Myers's full cooperation.
"It was great for Dinah," recalls Janet. "She had always been insecure about
her appearance, and the soldiers going wild about her made her feel good
about herself." Dinah's healthy appetite for men would later become well
known among Hollywood insiders. (Her lovers in the 1950s would include
another Cantor discovery, Eddie Fisher.)

Cantor's writers had all heard the rumors of his adventures with women
ranging from Lillian Lorraine to comedienne Collette Lyons, and they
tended to be cynical about his public image as the nation's "family comedian." It had become Eddie's habit to hold court in bed on weekday mornings, his writers sitting alongside as he critiqued their efforts, told them

what was "really needed" for the next week's show, and read the mail. On one occasion, they concocted a poison pen letter: "Dear Eddie Cantor: You no good S.O.B. You pretend to be this great family man, but you screw every young girl you can get your hands on. I hope your stinking show goes off the air and you wind up in hell. A fan."

They mailed the letter in a green envelope and then waited, poker-faced, for its arrival. Cantor opened it, read it through without changing expression, folded it up carefully, and put it back in the envelope.

"What was that one?" one of the men queried.

"Someone wants me to sing 'Margie,' " replied Cantor, unperturbed.

Cantor offered little argument when Jack Warner told him *Banjo Eyes* would not work as a film. The comedy, the dances, even the idea of a horse with Cantor's trademarked "banjo eyes," belonged completely to the theatre. A new deal was soon struck that would enable Eddie and Dinah Shore to appear together in a new film, *Thank Your Lucky Stars*.

Production for the film was scheduled to begin in September, but by the middle of July no songwriters had been hired. Nor had the screenplay, by Herman J. Mankiewicz, been completed. Cantor filled in the long wait with other business. He left Los Angeles on August 14, stopping off in Rochester to host a show at which a government citation was presented to the Eastman Kodak Company. In New York, he appeared on *Star-Spangled Rhythm* and played himself on a Philip Morris Playhouse Presentation of his own life story.

He spoke out about the war work being done by show business stars. "After all, Donald Nelson, as the best purchasing agent in the country, is more important heading the War Production Board than handling a gun. Well, the same analogy holds true for Bob Hope, Abbott & Costello, Kay Kyser, or anybody of that calibre—all of whom are more important selling war bonds and maintaining morale than they would be as doughboys." Eddie hoped President Roosevelt would speak out in behalf of these and other stars and "spare the top names the many snide remarks now coming their way because the public doesn't realize they are as much a part of the war effort as the industrial or mercantile exec parked behind a desk in Washington as a dollar-a-year man." Cantor had a date with Roosevelt's press secretary, Stephen Early, on August 26, but canceled it to appear at the Harvest Moon finals at Madison Square Garden that evening. Ed Sullivan, who had needled Cantor about walking out on *Banjo Eyes* in April, was one of the most powerful columnists in the country after Winchell. Eddie had long learned that fighting the big writers did no good.

Cantor returned to the West Coast right after Labor Day, and *Time to Smile* started its third season in Camp Callan, California. Eddie, ever conscious of his audience, had geared the script entirely to servicemen. Craps and the pursuit of sex were favorite topics, and any joke that had a sergeant as its butt was good for "seven" on the belly laugh scale. It was humor aimed at the "boys in uniform," which Cantor knew would be okay with the millions of grateful listeners at home.

This unblushing, calculated tailoring of material to the lowest common demoninators of Eddie's studio and radio audiences is why these *Time to Smile* shows are not enjoyed today. Fred Allen and his writers wrote largely to please themselves, and their work retains an often biting point of view that remains timeless to most true lovers of humor. Cantor's jokes are obvious and betray him as a comedian straining for the cheap laughs. This was the Eddie Cantor of the '40s, whose unit shows and camp broadcasts were the ancestors of Bob Hope's vapid TV specials of the 1960s.

Cantor, who received more requests to do broadcasts from camps and bases than any other highly rated star, did his next two shows from Camp Haan and March Field.

Nothing seemed important but the war. The Treasury Department asked Cantor for a recording of "Pass the Ammunition," in which several government messages were blended on *Time to Smile*. Eddie did the October 23 broadcast from the Hollywood Canteen, with Ida in the kitchen making sandwiches for servicemen. Bert Gordon got a call from his draft board despite having the remnants of a wound from World War I, and the Cantors opened up their home on North Roxbury Drive to furloughed servicemen on weekends.

With two units in front of the camera (Eddie and Joan Leslie on one stage, Dinah Shore on another), four in rehearsal, and two more preparing for rehearsals, *Thank Your Lucky Stars* was the busiest production on the Warner lot in several years. Personnel on all production phases ran to six hundred people.

*Thank Your Lucky Stars* integrated an essentially studio revue with a weak story line that allowed for an interesting concept—Cantor, in a double role, as Eddie Cantor, an obnoxious star who refuses to let the producers of a benefit show use Dinah Shore unless he can appear himself and take complete control, and as a celebrity bus driver and tour guide, "cursed" to see his own career destroyed because he looks like Cantor. In the end, he saves the benefit by impersonating the egomanical star.

That Cantor, as producer, had agreed to spoof himself so mercilessly speaks volumes about his own self-image. Shrewd enough to know the public would in no way identify the "Eddie Cantor" in *Thank Your Lucky Stars* with the lovable family man, humanitarian, and discoverer of talent they heard every week on radio, Cantor allowed his screenwriter, Mankiewicz, to have carte blanche. The result is a devastating caricature of the Cantor many in show business knew.

His daughters were appalled, not only because "Eddie Cantor" was obnoxious but because their father's other character, "Joe Sampson," was himself a somewhat nasty little man only slightly less objectionable than the big star. In a day when most stars were identified with the characters they played, *Thank Your Lucky Stars* was unprecedented self-deprecation, especially for Cantor, who had for years obscured the line between his private self and his public image. If Cantor, as he claimed, feared the day would come when a man would knock on the door and say, "Cantor, we've found you out," then *Thank Your Lucky Stars* was a confession before the fact, a turning state's evidence to get a lighter sentence.

*Thank Your Lucky Stars* includes a now prized clip of Bette Davis singing "They're Either Too Young or Too Old," Jack Carson and Alan Hale performing "Way Up North" with all the energy and camp now associated with vaudeville, and a long production number titled "Ice Cold Katie (Won't You Marry the Soldier?)" with an all-black cast that included Hattie McDaniel. Miss McDaniel was also a regular on *Time to Smile* that season, talking about her "boy friend, Cecil," an Army recruit, a great one with the "galloping ivories."

Bert Gordon, Dinah Shore, and the teen-aged Shirley Dinsdale were the other Cantor regulars that season. Dinsdale, one of the few great female ventriloquists before Shari Lewis, had a rather saucy pigtailed dummy named Judy Splinters. They were often seen on TV in the late 1940s and '50s.

There were, as always, those unbilled actors and actresses, hired as needed, who played whatever bit parts were in each week's script. One of them was a young Irish-Catholic woman named Billie Belleport. Cantor's need to dominate attractive non-Jewish women would have a profound effect on her.

"Cantor liked the girls," remembers Jean Vanderpyle (later the voice of Wilma in *The Flintstones*). "And he liked to goose them. He would wait until they were on the air, so that they couldn't protest and no one would know. On one occasion, he goosed Billie, who was a sweet, naive thing. She was so unprepared that she went, 'Oh, Mr. Cantor!' and he had to quickly cover. The studio audience knew exactly what had happened; it was so obvious, and Cantor was fuming; he came storming off the set: 'Don't ever use that girl again.' Billie was so upset that she finally said, 'I'm through with show business,' and became a nun."

The need for retakes kept *Thank Your Lucky Stars* in production into March 1943. Cantor, in the meantime, was negotiating with the agent Bill Miller to have the comic Joe Besser on *Time to Smile* when he arrived in Hollywood for film work at Columbia.

Besser had established himself as America's leading "swish" comedian in *Sons o' Fun*, Olsen and Johnson's successor to *Hellzapoppin'* at the New York Winter Garden. Cantor had made use of Besser's catchphrase, "not so fa-a-st," in repartee with Janet Blair in February, prompting Joe to wire him on Tuesday, March 2, requesting he refrain from using that line and "You crazy, you" on future broadcasts. Besser claimed that Cantor had used both lines on his last two shows, giving them to Lionel Stander on February 24.

Cantor's reply was the epitome of condescension.

> As time goes on and you become more successful in radio, you will find not only Eddie Cantor and Lionel Stander and Phil Baker, but all the comedians using your catch phrase. It happened with the late Joe Penner's "Wanna buy a duck?" It happened with Jack Pearl's "Vas you dere, Sharlie?" It happened with my own "Mad Russian" and his "Shall I tell him?" You should be heartened by the compliment rather than taking it too hard. To stop the use of a popular catch phrase would be like stopping our American boys at Guadalcanal, or any other place where they start going. Don't be silly, little boy. If it was my desire to hurt you, I wouldn't have spent an hour with your agent last Friday trying to arrange a deal where I could have you exclusively for radio.

Besser listened to his agent, swallowed his pride, and appeared on Cantor's show.

Bristol-Myers renewed Cantor for the 1943–44 season, despite his disappointing Hooper ratings.

The ratings for the week ending March 31, 1943, were typical:

1. Bob Hope
2. *Fibber McGee and Molly*
3. Edgar Bergen
4. *Aldrich Family*
5. Walter Winchell
6. *Lux Radio Theatre*
7. *Maxwell House Coffee Time* (Frank Morgan/Fanny Brice)
8. *Mr. District Attorney*
9. *Sealtest Village Store* (Rudy Vallee/Joan Davis)
10. *Screen Guild Players*
11. Abbott and Costello subs
12. Jack Benny subs
13. Fred Allen
14. *Take It or Leave It*
15. Kay Kyser

Cantor was nowhere. As usual, he assailed the ratings as inaccurate barometers of public taste, not indicative of product sales and generally useless. That his sponsors bought his points says volumes about Cantor as a salesman.

In terms of explaining away ratings, placing blame on things like time frames, passing fads, and matters best described as "acts of God," Eddie Cantor, in the '40s, had no equal. His reasons seemed compelling and logical and, given his track record, sounded like they came from an experienced pro at the peak of his powers with little to prove.

One aspect of the Cantor *shtik* that had remained unchanged since the mid-'30s was Eddie's desperate desire to marry off his daughters to some nice handsome young man with a bright future. "Two down, three to go" was Cantor's response when Von Zell, on the April 7 show, asked him how many of his daughters were married. That show featured the tenor Dennis Day, a Benny sidekick, as guest.

Much of the show was built around Eddie's not-so-subtle efforts to steal Dennis from Benny so he could marry one of Cantor's daughters. (Janet was still fifteen.) Toward the end of the program, just before announcing yet another "telegram request" for servicemen's morale, Cantor thanked his guest. "Dennis, remember I'm not trying to take you away from Jack. Call me at CRestview 6-1394." It was an ad-lib, and the number was real—Cantor's home telephone number.

Within a minute, Eddie's house was barraged by phone calls from men wanting to get to know "any of the daughters," "the oldest daughter," "the youngest daughter," any combination of them, or all three. "Have you lost all sense?" Ida asked her husband when he got home later. The line between the Cantor private life and the life of Eddie Cantor, entertainer, had long since been nonexistent to the public. Now it seemed blurred to Eddie.

Cantor's action was essentially that of a premedia performer from a more benign time when actors were regarded as mere tradesmen, rather than the kind of celebrities that Hollywood—and Cantor's career on the radio—had made them. Whatever Eddie's influence had been in that regard, he himself remained something of an old-time stage performer, one born and nurtured in the days before the Lindbergh baby kidnapping made stars hire bodyguards and distance themselves from an increasingly celebrity-conscious public.

The incident, which never made the papers, was quickly forgotten, except perhaps by those who tested the phone number—and the Cantor household. Whether by coincidence or not, the twenty-eight-year-old Margie now decided to leave the Cantor "big house" and try it on her own in Manhattan.

Margie moved to New York ostensibly to embark on a career as a free-lance writer. It was, predictably, short-lived. As Eddie Cantor's daughter, working in the shadow of her father, she had never experienced failure. Now she was amazed to find her work rejected, not once but, it seemed to her, unceasingly. Margie soon abandoned all her writing aspirations and took a job as a secretary in a New York theatrical agency.

The June 23 show, with the man-chasing comedienne Vera Vague gushing over leathernecks at the El Toro, California, marine base, was Cantor's last of the season. Eddie, Ida, their daughter Edna and her husband, Jimmy—now his father-in-law's agent at MCA—left for New York later that same week. Margie had lined up almost a hundred actors to audition for Eddie's next film, *Show Business*.

Eddie, hard at work for the war effort, spoke at the official launching of the Liberty ship *George M. Cohan* at the Bethlehem-Fairfield shipyards in Baltimore on Sunday, July 4. After singing "Harrigan," "Give My Regards to Broadway," "You're a Grand Old Flag," and "Over There," Cantor paid his respects to the memory of Cohan, his adversary in the Equity Strike of 1919, who had died that past November.

"If there ever was one man who was a symbol of our great nation, that man was George M. Cohan. He always tried to project the spirit of America. His songs came from the pen and the heart. He waved the flag because he loved it. He gave it a 'permanent wave,' " said Cantor, coining yet another of his play-on-word slogans. Sincere or not, the tribute was most fitting. Georgette Cohan, daughter of George M., was not available to christen the new ship, so the ritual bottle-breaking was done by Margie in her first public appearance.

The war, even more than the Depression, had given Americans a sense of unity and purpose. While Cantor did not go overseas to entertain the troops during the war, he served as the entertainment industry's unofficial spokesman on the home front.

> When a visiting star wants to emphasize the evil of absenteeism [of workers from Defense Plants], he must not preach. It's one thing for me to say, "Of course, if you stay away it doesn't help Mr. Whiskers, but it does help the Man with the Moustache," That's all right, I think because I then go into my song-and-dance, then back again when I might observe, "Well, if my coming here saves you the bother of going out for your entertainment and theatrical diversion, that means so much time and labor saved for the building of another ship." I know it works because I've seen it work.
>
> Nobody wants to be preached at. What's more, and justifiably, that kind of wrong libretto invariably fetches a crack. "Yeah, then why aren't you at the front; at least we're here on the home front," and all is lost.

Cantor was decidedly on "the home front." On Wednesday afternoon, he took charge of the War Bond and Stamp booth in the lobby of the Palace. The next day, he was at a rally at the Polo Grounds. That night, he addressed the final preliminary meeting of the National Entertainment Industry Council at the Hotel Astor on entertainment and its relation to the national morale.

Eddie spoke at the RKO Radio Pictures Convention at the Waldorf-Astoria the following Monday. This appearance was tied in, not to the war effort, but to *Show Business*, a semiautobiographical film that became less and less autobiographical as the final script took form. The talent that Margie had assembled provided a few minor players for the picture, but Eddie had a much harder time finding a suitable replacement for Dinah Shore on his radio program. He had auditioned almost forty singers.

Bert Gordon, "The Mad Russian," who intended to leave *Time to Smile* for a part in a Broadway show, soon changed his mind and stuck with Cantor. Dinah had received lucrative offers for radio shows, not to mention further roles on screen. Warners wanted her for the role of Nora Bayes in *Shine On Harvest Moon*, but Dinah chose to sign with Samuel Goldwyn, who cast her opposite Danny Kaye in *Up in Arms*, an updated *Whoopee* with an army background. Dinah played Ethel Shutta's old role as the nurse, Mary Custer.

Eddie, Ida, and the McHughs left New York on Tuesday morning, July 13, stopping off en route to the West Coast to attend fund-raising events in several midwestern cities. Margie went back with them, having quit her job. Within the month, she had resumed, not just her role as major domo of 1012 North Roxbury, but her old relationship with Skolsky. Margie never tried to leave the nest again.

A souvenir of Margie's New York escapade went back west with the Cantors, according to Janet.

Margie, when she came to New York, dated Milton Pickman—a nice man, And we all got to know Milton's brother, Jerry. When everyone went back to California, Jerry came down to supposedly see them off and got on the train. They said, "all aboard," and he didn't get off. And so, it was "Ah, ha ha. Jerry's coming out to California." Everyone assumed he was gonna turn around and go back. But he didn't. He came to stay with us, and would not go away.

He wore all my father's suits until he grew too fat from all the food that he was eating. Then my father decided to give him some busy work. They were trying to find the "typical G.I.," so he put him in charge of that and set up an office in the playroom.

Jerry would butt into absolutely everything. If two of us were having an argument, he'd put in his two cents. There was an extra car around the house; no one knew how we'd acquired it, but it was there. As soon as I was old enough to drive I was tickled it was there, because it meant *freedom*. In southern California, you *must* drive. But I was still stuck because Jerry would often be out in the car.

There was Jerry at all times, and he was getting on all our

nerves—a lot. And my folks, being the kind of people they were, did not know how to say just, "Bye, Jerry."

So they decided to close the house and tell him they had found termites and were going to exterminate. That's how we got rid of Jerry Pickman.

P.S.: Jerry ended up getting a great big job at Columbia Pictures, saying he had been Eddie Cantor's righthand man. And I'm sure he bluffed his way through that job, too.

*Time to Smile* began its fourth season on September 29, 1943, with the twenty-two-year-old Nora Lou Martin as Cantor's new vocalist. "While no Dinah Shore," wrote Ben Bodec, "Miss Martin is endowed with plenty of vocal appeal. Listeners are certain to take to her soft, insinuating style and penchant for embroidering her final few bars with a flourish of flute-like coloratura. She's a little different from the general run of name pop singers, and that difference, plus a natural feel for melody, should gain for Miss Martin a snug little niche in radio."

Eddie had signed Nora, a native of Portland, Oregon, after hearing her sing on station KFWB in Hollywood. As he'd done with Olive Major and other singers he felt had potential, Cantor sent her to a well-respected vocal coach. The man reportedly told Eddie that he was not needed: "She can sell a song as well as I could ever teach her." Nora would spend two seasons as Eddie Cantor's vocalist and then vanish completely.

*Show Business* was now set to roll October 25, with Edwin Marin as director, George Murphy and Constance Moore as the principal love interest, Nancy Kelly, and Joan Davis.

Madonna Josephine Davis was born in St. Paul, Minnesota, on June 29, 1907, the daughter of a train dispatcher, LeRoy Davis, and his wife, Nina. A natural "ham," Joan played the Pantages Circuit, billed as the "Toy Comedienne," at the age of six, worked as a salesgirl following graduation from Mechanic Arts High School, and reentered vaudeville at twenty. Vaudeville was then failing, and the eight years that Davis spent on the circuits, while providing her with a living and invaluable experience, were not uniformly pleasant. She married her straight man, Serenus (Si) Willis, in Chicago on August 31, 1931, and gave birth to a daughter, Beverly, two years later.

Darryl F. Zanuck signed Davis to a five-year contract in 1936, and Joan's popularity rose in a succession of Twentieth Century-Fox efforts like *Thin Ice, Sally, Irene and Mary, My Lucky Star, Hold That Co-ed,* and *Sun Valley Serenade.* She scored a major hit as the "scream specialist" Camille Brester in *Hold That Ghost* (Universal, 1941) with Abbott and Costello and became a regular on Rudy Vallee's NBC show, *Sealtest Village Store,* the same year. Jack Haley had replaced Vallee (who had gone into the Coast Guard) by the time *Show Business* started filming, making Joan, to listeners, the mainstay of the program.

"I've known Joan for years," Cantor would tell reporters. Their meetings had been few and incidental—on the lot of Twentieth Century-Fox during the filming of *Ali Baba Goes to Town*. Fifteen years his junior, Joan liked and idolized Eddie Cantor. He admired her talent as well: a mugging, physically angular comedienne on the lines of Fanny Brice who played upon her supposed lack of grace. Joan, both verbally and physically, "spoke Eddie Cantor's language."

Joan's forte was physical comedy—not the pantomime that Eddie did but the kind dependent on athletic skill and control of one's body. She was also acrobatic and could dance, which made Eddie just a tad self-conscious. A few "bells" and half a dozen basic time steps from his *Follies* days was the extent of Cantor's dancing, not counting the agile prancing and stylized "stage walks" he did in his songs.

As producer of the film, he "ordered" himself to take lessons. It was like bailing water on an ocean liner. Cantor had great difficulty following choreography and drove dance director Nick Castle to distraction with his slip-ups. When, at one point, someone else made a mistake, Eddie comically reacted by exclaiming, like a schoolboy, "It wasn't me." A close examination of the final film of *Show Business* finds him moving his lips in a dance sequence with Davis, Moore, and Murphy—counting in an almost vain attempt to keep in step.

Constance Moore says she loved doing that picture.

In fact, I loved everything about it, especially the long lunch hours. Lunch would be called at twelve, and instead of being back at one, as everyone else was, Eddie and Joan would come sauntering in sometime between two and four. But since he was the producer of the picture, not a word was said.

Eddie and Joan were mad for each other. It's hard to say exactly when their relationship began, but it soon became obvious. The rest of the company never discussed it. We tried to pretend that they were studying the script, but there was very little doubt they were having a physical relationship. They spent so much time in his trailer. They would try to find Eddie, who was both the star and the producer, but Maurice, his valet, would have orders he and Joan were not to be disturbed. Once, somebody knocked on the trailer door and said, "Mr. Cantor, you're wanted on the set," and Joan yelled, "He's not done yet."

I think the reason we tried to ignore their affair was that it contrasted so sharply with the image we all seemed to have of Cantor. I know I had pictured him as the ideal family man. He seemed to constantly talk about his wife, Ida, on the radio. The reality was something different, but we all thought the Cantor we heard on the air was real.

Eddie and Joan seemed to enjoy each other tremendously. Neither one was sixteen anymore, and I think they were glad to have found each other.

Rumors of the Cantor-Davis "romance" (if such it truly was) spread quickly through the entertainment business but were kept from the public by a press that observed a strict "hands-off" policy regarding the affairs of married stars. Several "blind items" in Dorothy Kilgallen's column proved the lone exception.

Margie's reaction to the columns was "blind fury" at Kilgallen, whose thinly disguised anti-Semitism was further fueled by Cantor's firing of her husband years earlier. The Cantor sisters frequently discussed "the rumor" but never dared to mention it to Ida.

"Ida Cantor and my mother were close friends, and Ida was what then was called 'long suffering,'" recalled Budd Schulberg. "Everybody knew about the affair with Joan Davis—everybody in the business. The public always thought Eddie Cantor was the same man they heard on the radio."

Production on *Show Business* was finished before New Year's. Several weeks later, on Thursday morning, January 27, Eddie, Ida, Nora Martin, and Cookie Fairchild boarded the *Lark* for San Francisco, where Cantor would begin a twenty-four hour marathon broadcast to sell war bonds at 5 A.M. Saturday.

This vigil was preceded by several laughable publicity stunts and stories, including Eddie's being drilled, massaged, and sparred with by the world wrestling champion Steve (Crusher) Casey. Dr. J. C. Geiger, head of San Francisco's Public Health Department, was at Radio City to "stand by to swab Cantor's throat or give him a hypo," while George Mardikian, proprietor of the Omar Khayyam Restaurant, was there to furnish pots of steaming coffee (which Cantor did not drink) and platters of Armenian food.

Eddie was on station KPO for what turned out to be more than thirty-three hours beginning at six o'clock Saturday morning, January 29. Nora Martin was there as "supporting talent," Cookie Fairchild conducted the orchestra, and the producer Don Thompson's staff prepared more than one hundred thousand words of copy, but the vigil was essentially a one-man show. Cantor sang more than one hundred songs, told every joke he knew, danced around for the benefit of the studio audience, kissed babies, and auctioned off captured articles of war (including a sniper's rifle for $350,000).

More than seventeen thousand persons crowded into the studio at various stages of the marathon broadcast. (Admittance was by purchasing a bond.) Cantor's only extended break was his appearance as a guest at a $500,000 luncheon given by a San Francisco businessman, Louis Lurie, in the KPO studios.

At ten minutes to six, John W. Elwood, the general manager of KPO, took over to commend Eddie for his show and to applaud Ida, who had stood by during the long vigil. "In those closing moments," said *Variety*, "Cantor reached new heights as a radio figure. Speaking for himself and Elwood, his pledge to the men at the fighting front will be long remembered:

> Every night, before I go to sleep, I have a question I ask myself—a question I'd like to have our listeners engrave upon their hearts as it is upon mine: "What have I done today that is worthy of the boy who lost his life in some far-off place, fighting for me and the things for which I stand?"
> And let's remember not only the boys who gave their lives, but let's remember the boys who want to live . . . and bring them safely home."

The Cantors remained in San Francisco for ten hours more, Eddie thanking those who'd made the broadcast possible. They then flew back to Los Angeles to celebrate Eddie's birthday in the Roxbury house that evening.

The final total raised by this direct ancestor of telethons exceeded forty million dollars—an astronomical sum for 1944, the equivalent of almost half a billion 1997 dollars. There had never been a benefit or broadcast like it, and Eddie spent the day of his "official" fifty-second birthday catching up on needed sleep.

"The Trial of Adolf Hitler," a minicomedy-drama written by L. Wolfe Gilbert, made up the final minutes of *Time to Smile* on February 16. The skit, like almost all of Cantor's radio material, was neither real drama nor insightful humor. Hitler was, predictably, depicted as a simple buffoon and, in "attempting to solve the what-to-do-with-Hitler problem, which has the economists and political seers working overtime, Cantor, through his comedy medium, only managed to make it appear ridiculous. This is one question," said *Variety*, "that's just a bit too important to be treated with levity."

Cantor started a "Search for G.I. Joe" contest on the following week's broadcast, having placed five thousand dollars in a trust fund to be given to the most "representative soldier" after the war. The five thousand dollars may have been symbolic; it was the same amount Cantor was demanding as a weekly pay raise to remain with Bristol-Myers.

Eddie had been dissatisfied with his $10,000 weekly salary for some time, as well as with the show and its writing staff. (His lack of affection for the writing staff was returned by them in kind.) He had already talked Eddie Beloin, Jack Benny's former writer, into joining the staff of *Time to Smile* at a whopping $2,000 a week. Cantor, of course, did not want to foot the bill.

Eddie's contract called for one more season, but he was already threatening to sign with Colgate-Palmolive, a direct product competitor of Bristol-Myers, which had offered him a lucrative three-year pact.

Cantor got his way; Hubbell Robinson Jr., radio director of Young & Rubicam, got him a new two-year contract with Bristol-Myers. The new pact gave Eddie full control of the show, made sure Bristol-Myers paid for all expenses incidental to camp broadcasts, and guaranteed mention of *Time to Smile* in practically all ads for Bristol-Myers products.

One week later, Cantor breezed through the Brown Derby, collecting bets. Several ad agencies executives had felt "sorry" that he was on opposite the red-hot Frank Sinatra. Eddie had bet them that he would double Sinatra's Crossley rating before the end of the season. At the season's end, the latest Crossley listings won Cantor the bet with points to spare.

The reason for this startling development was Cantor's shrewd assessment of the radio audience. Transistor radios had not made their appearance in 1944, and radio dials, still housed in the nation's living rooms, remained under the control of adults—the audience for Cantor's jokes and homilies since 1931.

With *Show Business* scheduled to open at the Palace on May 11, Cantor took his radio troupe east after the April 12 broadcast of *Time to Smile*. Cantor and Company played military hospitals along the way, beginning with one in Topeka, Kansas.

Yet another Cantor "anniversary"—allegedly his thirty-five years in show business—was used as publicity for *Show Business*. A banquet, with George Jessel and Jimmy Walker as toastmasters, was planned for the Hotel Astor on Sunday, May 7, with nine actors' guilds and unions as sponsors: Equity, AFRA, ASCAP, Catholic Actors' Guild, Episcopal Actors' Guild, Negro Actors' Guild, Jewish Theatrical Guild, and AGVA. Proceeds would go to Surprise Lake Camp.

Cantor and Company arrived in New York from Utica on Sunday morning, April 23. Eddie was greeted with a cheerful "thank you" from Sammy Weiss, a drummer with Paul Whiteman's Orchestra at a rehearsal for the Philco *Radio Hall of Fame* that afternoon.

"It's thanks for twenty-five years ago," Weiss told the bewildered Cantor, "when the Eddie Cantor Boys' Camp took me from an East Side tenement district and gave me a couple of swell vacation weeks."

"Well, if you're that grateful," Cantor said, "how about kicking in and making some other kid happy today?" Weiss donated twenty-five dollars.

The banquet at the Astor drew a capacity audience of fifteen hundred, a turn-out speaker Fannie Hurst said was as much a tribute to show business as to Cantor. That cued Eddie into talking of his campaign on the "Purple Heart Circuit," saying it should be the proud duty of all showmen to entertain and divert the nation's wounded heroes during their convalescence.

On Thursday, May 18, Cantor joined the Ed Sullivan entourage visiting

Halloran Hospital on Staten Island. Similar engagements were sandwiched around rehearsals and broadcasts of *Time to Smile* and two appearances on television from Philadelphia, the first one a gesture to J. H. Carmine, vice president of Philco and a pioneer in television. Carmine would be speaking at the Poor Richard Club, where the telecast would be shown as a special feature. It marked the first practical intercity chain telecasting; New York and Philadelphia were linked by Philco's new television transmitter at Mount Rose, New Jersey.

The song "We're Having a Baby" had been submitted in advance to NBC, and Cantor's representatives were told that certain parts of the lyrics were "objectionable." When Cantor raced into the studio from a hospital engagement in St. Albans, New York, and learned of the deletions, he protested and threatened to cancel the program. "Our program director was faced with the alternative of cancelling the whole show or permitting the song to go and cutting the part deemed objectionable to NBC," said C. L. Menser, the network's vice president in charge of programs. "He chose the latter course, and this had and has our complete approval."

The special press turnout for the occasion in New York and for the Poor Richard Club guests in Philadelphia were completely unaware of the situation until the camera was distorted and the sound turned off in the middle of the song's second chorus. "It was history-making, all right," said Carmine. "We usually get sound without sight over the air, but here was sight without sound."

Cantor was incensed, castigating what he termed the "pettiness and poor judgment of minor NBC officials." That he was not being paid for the "experiment" and tribute to Carmine was, to him, a minor point. The action, Eddie felt, was a reflection on him, a man who had recently been honored by show business and the world at large on his thirty-fifth anniversary as an entertainer. "No risqué performer could last thirty-five days, much less thirty-five years." Cantor saw himself as a conscientious public entertainer, a father, a "clean-living American." Eddie pointed out that he had recently, on May 8, signed to do the song (with Nora Martin) in the forthcoming Warner Brothers picture *Hollywood Canteen*.

As if to prove his point, Eddie said that he and Nora would reprise the song on the Philco *Radio Hall of Fame* in Philadelphia on Sunday night. This "simulcast" (broadcast and televised) was the final week of the *Hall of Fame* radio series and featured an all-star bill made up of Cantor, Jolson, Paul Whiteman, and Benny Goodman in addition to the arranger-music critic Deems Taylor and the announcer Ben Grauer.

NBC did not censor Cantor this time, but the government-owned Canadian Broadcasting Corporation, forewarned of Cantor's reprise, blanked out the offending lyrics for its twenty-two affiliated stations.

*The Evangelist*, the weekly publication of the Albany Catholic Diocese, upheld the censor's actions. Commenting on reports that Cantor was "blazing mad" at the interruption, the diocesan publication wondered if he realized how "mad" thousands of responsible persons in respectable American family circles must get when they are forced to dial out his frequent sorties into the realm of the vulgar and double-meaning sex references for his gags on the radio. The broadcasting censors have been more than lenient with him; and with a few others of similar mentality.

N.B.C. officials rightly attached importance to the Cantor case. When, as and if television comes into general use, it is only proper to get it off on the right foot, for the sake of the people's welfare and the industry's profits as well as for the progress of the art.

While the editorial criticized Cantor, the paper on another page headlined a National Catholic Welfare Council News Service report, "Eddie Cantor Honored by Catholic Veterans."

Eddie and Ida celebrated their thirtieth wedding anniversary with eighteen friends, including Margie, Edna, Marilyn, Nettie, and her husband, Henry Bernstein, at a private dinner party in the Perroquet Suite of the Waldorf on June 9. But Cantor's troubles with the NBC censor Clarence L. Menser were not over, and the two men had it out prior to the *Time to Smile* broadcast of Wednesday, June 14. Cantor, true to his word, had signed Joe Besser as guest.

Menser, sitting in the control booth at rehearsals, called Cantor in after Besser had gone through his lines and said that the material could not be aired.

Cantor pointed out that Besser's "swish" humor had been accepted on the Fred Allen show on CBS and accused Menser of trying to persecute him, a charge Menser denied. As for CBS, said Menser, "that's up to CBS."

Half an hour later, Besser went through a blue-penciled routine with Harry Von Zell while Cantor and Menser sat in the control room. The new lines didn't work, but Menser said Besser would go on with those new lines or not at all. Besser quit the show, with Cantor's consent.

Eddie filled the spot with an extra song. The season ended one week later, Cantor saying he would not mind leaving NBC for good.

More entertaining of wounded servicemen in hospitals, more bond rallies, and other work, both for the war and for more commercial causes, filled the weeks that followed. Cantor entertained wounded veterans at Walter Reed Hospital in Washington, D.C., on Saturday, June 24, and was at a war bond rally on the Monument grounds that night. Returning to the West Coast in July, he signed "The Mad Russian" for the following season and to a three-year personal management contract. Eddie also signed Leonard Suess as musical director for *Time to Smile*, replacing Cookie Fairchild, as well as Bea Walker, a pianist he had met in New York.

Cantor, Constance Moore, and George Murphy recorded tunes and skits from the film *Show Business* for the Armed Forces Radio Services "Mail Call" series. On other days, Eddie was at Warners, filming his scene for the picture *Hollywood Canteen*, with Nora Martin. Prior to their duet of "We're Having a Baby," Cantor made his entrance carrying a tray for servicemen at the Canteen, reprising, a capella, a line from the song, "We're Staying Home Tonight (My Baby and Me)" from *Thank Your Lucky Stars*, his only prior film for Warners.

One of the soldiers says the drinks Eddie has been serving really go quickly. "Yes," Cantor replies, "I wish I could get rid of my daughters this fast."

"I still get comments from people on that one," says Janet.

People really thought that we were ugly. Marilyn once waited for him in the front of the lobby after a show. A couple of young guys were out there who made some comments about her being quite an eyeful, which she was. Marilyn was a very attractive young woman; she looked a little like Linda Darnell.

Then one of them wondered whether "Eddie Cantor's ugly daughters" were there. Neither of them knew who Marilyn was, so she waited for Daddy to come out and then called across the lobby, so that those two guys couldn't miss it, "Daddy, I'm over here!"

Marilyn had graduated from the American Academy of Dramatic Arts in March 1942, with "Daddy" himself as principal speaker. Eddie, still in *Banjo Eyes*, had warned the graduates that they were about to enter a "hard profession" and urged them never to give up trying and praying for success.

Marilyn never did. A good comedienne, she tried to be a singer, billing herself as "Marilyn Curtis" for a gig at Leon and Eddie's in midtown New York in order to convince Daddy she was not trading on his name. Cantor sent an opening night telegram to her dressing room signed "Eddie Curtis," but even the kindest critics could only advise Marilyn to stay away from ballads.

She thought Broadway was her home, but Broadway had no place for Marilyn Cantor. As the years went by, she taught acting, produced an off-Broadway show called *Curtain Going Up*, and spent a lot of time in all-night delis.

Following a tour of six California service hospitals with his latest unit show, Eddie opened his fifth season on *Time to Smile* with Joan Davis as guest star. Well scripted, in the Cantor fashion, the show contained a running gag in which two stooges intermittently broke in with jingles advertising different fictitious products. Cantor closed the show with his new "Give a Gift to a Yank Who Gave" campaign, an appeal for the benefit of hospitalized GIs.

Two days later, an exhausted Eddie Cantor was in Cedars of Lebanon

Hospital, suffering from strep throat and what Dr. Elmer Belt called a "run-down condition." He was out of the hospital within three days.

Fewer guest stars were in evidence that season. The child actor Billy Gray joined the cast in October and became the only Cantor protégé to achieve greater fame years after his discovery by Eddie when he played Bud on *Father Knows Best*

There were also the now standard Cantor projects. Eddie was appointed chairman of the March of Dimes of the Air for the eighth consecutive year, and another essay contest, with the theme "Juvenile Delinquency, Its Cause and Solution," was won by Charles Byrne, a seventeen-year-old student at Minneapolis Senior Vocational High School. ("If parents would discipline children at as early an age as possible and instill in them, through kindness and understanding, respect for the rights and property of others, they would save themselves and their children much misery later on.")

The Cantors certainly knew where all their children were. Around this time, Natalie and her son, Michael, together with Edna and her daughter, Judy, moved back into the big house. The girls' marriages were in big trouble, with divorces inevitable in both cases. Janet was moved downstairs only weeks before her graduation from Beverly Hills High School in February 1945.

"My graduation present was a trip to New York," she recalled. "I saw all the shows, and it was the most thrilling experience I'd had since the folks moved us to L.A. nine years earlier."

The trip to New York merely whetted young Janet's appetite. Shortly after her return to California, she left for New York on her own without her parents' knowledge, showing up at the apartment of Toby Garson, Harry Ruby's married daughter. The outraged Toby, ten years Janet's senior, demanded that she call home at once.

Eddie and Ida both insisted that Janet return home until she was eighteen. This was not a spontaneous declaration but the result of a "conference" with Margie, one of many held in Ida's room when matters of importance required discussion.

To Eddie, Ida's room was the Supreme Court of the family. "A child runs away . . . a child wants to leave college . . . or wants to get married . . . or is having a baby . . . or there's trouble in paradise and talk of a divorce. All in Ida's room." But never in Eddie's. A concession to the old adage that "mothers raise daughters," it was also a reflection on how Eddie viewed his home life. The house was the domain of Ida and the girls. He was Eddie Cantor, the orphan boy, an outsider who ate with them at half past six, had a room there, loved them all, and paid the bills—more of a Dutch uncle than a father, except when they gained weight or tried to go into show business. The "Little Janet" joke that ended with "Gee, Daddy, aren't you glad you're living with us now" said far more about Eddie's viewpoint than about his youngest daughter's.

Jimmy McHugh Sr. and Harold Adamson were working on the songs

for *It Happened in Mexico*, Cantor's second film for RKO, which was scheduled to film that summer with Joan Davis in the female lead. Joan's popularity was at an all-time high; the Hooper ratings for the first eight days
of April put her show in third place (behind Bob Hope and *Fibber McGee*)
with a rating of 26.0; Cantor, at 17.2, was twelfth.

Eddie and Ida headed east after the broadcast of May 30, stopping off
in Salt Lake City for a war bond show. After the regular show, for which
the audience purchased $206,000 in war bonds, Cantor bid $25,000 for a
pair of nylon hose. In supporting the war effort, Cantor practiced what he
preached.

The season's three remaining shows were done from the NBC studios
in New York. Eddie took the opportunity of being in New York to sound
off, through *Variety*, about radio's shortcomings in developing new talent.
"I say that radio, with all its wealth, should do what DuPont does when it
experiments with plastics, nylons, cellophane . . . and all by products. Standard Oil probably spent millions before anything like ethyl gasoline came
out. . . . What would it cost to subsidize new writers for thirteen or twenty-
six weeks? They're bound to come up with at least one good idea which
will pay off everything."

The Cantors celebrated their thirty-first wedding anniversary at the Per-
sian Room of the Plaza Hotel. The next week, they were down on Henry
Street, together with two carloads full of well-wishers, touring East Side
restaurants like the Old Roumanian and the Cafe Royale. Residents of
Henry Street came out of their apartments, some by way of fire escapes,
and the Cantor contingent soon numbered in the hundreds as Eddie, unconcerned, refreshed his own and Ida's memories regarding the old land-
marks.

They visited the local settlement house, and Eddie, forced to make a
speech, said his days on the East Side, in this same Riis House, were the
happiest of his life.

He was being politic, of course, pouring out the same nostalgia that had
now become a staple of the public Eddie Cantor. Perhaps his words were
also an admission that his life had not, in some strange way, been totally
fulfilling—that, despite the happy image he projected to his family and
public, he felt somehow cheated.

Filmhouse vaudeville, successor to the grand old "two-a-day," disappeared
rapidly after 1936, and Cantor's "unit shows" became a rarity. Eddie's public life—his work for charities, the honors and the awards—took their
place. Cantor appeared at Philadelphia's Convention Hall on Monday, June
18, selling 3,500 people $1,500,000 worth of E bonds. Cantor and his radio
troupe arrived in Boston the following Saturday and entertained seven thousand convalescing American servicemen (twenty-five hundred of whom had
been rescued from Nazi POW camps) at Camp Myles Standish, fifty miles
outside the city. The next night, Eddie was at the "Back to Bataan" show

at Boston Garden, where Governor Maurice Tobin made him an honorary
citizen of the Commonwealth of Massachusetts, to resounding cheers and
applause.

Eddie and Ida left for California two days later. Nora Martin, having,
like so many, worn out Eddie Cantor's welcome, would not be returning
for a third season on *Time to Smile* in September. Monica Lewis, a beautiful, petite young blonde who had appeared with Eddie in Boston, had
already been suggested as Nora's replacement.

Cantor also considered Adele Clark, a former WAC, as his new female
vocalist. He soon decided, however, on Thelma Carpenter, a former vocalist
for Count Basie who had recently appeared in *Memphis Bound*, a black
American adaptation of Gilbert and Sullivan's *H.M.S. Pinafore* starring Bill
(Bojangles) Robinson that ran for less than five weeks at the Broadway
Theatre.

"Basie was great, but I figured two years with him was enough," Carpenter recalled.

> I was singing at Le Ruban Bleu, and this girl came in looking like
> something dug out of a bag of rags. She looked so bad, they didn't
> want to let her in, but she said she needed to speak to Thelma Car-
> penter. I met her in the back, and she told me they were looking for
> a singer to succeed Nora Martin on the Eddie Cantor show, and that
> I was up for it.
>
> I spoke to Imogene Coca, and she said, "You don't believe her,
> do you?" I just said, "That's what she said." Sure enough, a week
> later, Cantor's publicity man came in and sat in the front with some
> people from the radio show. He saw me after the performance and
> told me I was being considered for the job as vocalist.
>
> They came again a few nights later, along with Margie, Cantor's
> oldest daughter. Cantor himself came after that. About this time,
> Paul Kapp, whose brother Jack was head of Decca Records, said he'd
> represent me, and he closed the deal.

Thelma was signed for three initial broadcasts with the usual options.

> They signed me but said not to tell anybody. Even when the time
> came to leave for the West Coast, I only told my mother I was going
> out to work in California. I phoned her on the day of the broadcast,
> and she asked me where I was working. I said, "Turn the radio on
> to NBC at nine o'clock and you'll find out."

The NBC publicity had already begun, and Thelma Carpenter's picture
appeared in major newspapers from coast to coast: the first black female
vocalist on a major mainstream program in network radio history. "The
Kansas City *Star* was the only paper that refused to run my picture,"
Thelma recalled. "All the other ones did—even those in the deep south."

Young & Rubicam, Bristol-Myers's ad agency, while not opposed to Thelma, tended to think of her in a stereotyped role and actually suggested she be cast as Cantor's maid.

Cantor had the courage to ask why. "I didn't cast Dinah Shore or Nora Martin as maids. They were my vocalists, like Thelma. That's how Thelma will be introduced—as my vocalist."

Thelma went on, as his vocalist, scoring effectively with "Happiness Is a Thing Called Joe." Following the second program, Cantor signed her for the next six months.

Thelma's role on Cantor's show was remarkably free from stereotyping, and the writers struck a doubtless unintended blow for black pride when the former world light heavyweight boxing champion Billy Conn was a guest on the program in November. Conn, a Caucasian, had been knocked out in a bid for Joe Louis's world heavyweight title in 1941 and, with the war over, was looking toward a return bout in June.

CANTOR:      Thelma, really, don't think that you're under pressure, but which man are you rooting for in June?

CARPENTER: Well, I can only say: May the better man win—again.

The audience roared, knowingly.

"I was late for one performance," she remembered. "They actually told me to say 'I'm late' as I came to the microphone, but I stuck in 'I cried' on top of that, and Cantor ad-libbed back, 'What were they, tears of ink?' He actually repeated the line at the Waldorf-Astoria that evening while I was at their table, and I saw his wife give him one of those looks, you know?" The remark may seem hopelessly at odds with Cantor's otherwise crusading liberalism, unless one recalls Cantor's non-aversion to racial humor, his remarkable innocence in many areas, and the fact that blacks were still unusual in main-stream circles. Given those conditions, one may understand this side of Eddie Cantor. In the 1990s, we can only express shock.

That fall, Eddie began a number of new projects. He opened a second "Give a Gift to a Yank Who Gave" campaign, made his dramatic radio debut as Mr. Miller in Arch Oboler's play of the same name on KHJ on October 4, guested on Danny Kaye's *Pabst Blue Ribbon Show* of November 9, and huddled with his writers on *Come On Along*, the new title of his pending second film for RKO.

*Come On Along* called for nineteen days of on-location shooting, and the coming rainy season, coupled with the RKO studio strike, caused production to be postponed until May. Eddie accordingly made plans to spend six to eight weeks in New York starting in November in order to comply with a request by Bristol-Myers, head up Victory Bond rallies through the east, and produce *Nellie Bly*, a Broadway show about the female reporter assigned to beat Phileas Fogg's fictitious eighty-day circumnavigation of the globe in the Jules Verne novel *Around the World in Eighty Days*.

As always, Cantor's radio contingent made the trip across the country.

"I was walking ahead of him," remembered Thelma Carpenter. "All of a sudden, he gave me this sort of playful smack on my bottom. I turned around and gave him a look that could have killed; I didn't care if he was my boss.

"I saw Mrs. Cantor give him a look, too."

Janet, now eighteen and free to move to New York, went east with her parents. Neither Eddie nor Ida was happy with "losing" their youngest daughter, who moved into the Belmont Plaza with her good friend, Sunny Sauber, in Manhattan.

If the Cantors had lost one daughter, they had regained two.

Natalie and Joe had divorced in the spring. Joe was then calling himself a "toy manufacturer." "What he was," says someone close to Natalie, "was a crook. He was involved with many things at many different times, all of them of an unstable nature. He overreacted to everything. His highs were too high, his lows were too low, his anger was too great, and everything was too much. There was nothing in moderation with Joe. And I think he was extremely self-centered."

Metzger claimed it was none of her business when Natalie inquired where he had been late at night. "He told me I was interfering with his life," said Natalie, adding he was "not very sociable."

"He could charm the pants off anyone he wanted to, which is why he got away with things as long as he did. I'm sure that he was seeing other women, too." The latter was the straw that broke Nat's back. The Metzgers and the McHughs moved into North Roxbury Drive in January 1945, ostensibly to "work things out" under the Cantor "big house" roof.

Jimmy McHugh Jr.'s functional alcoholism and unexplained absences, not to mention his twenty-five-hour-a-day obsession with being a Hollywood agent, had been driving Edna to distraction. The end came when Edna heard rumors that Jimmy was seeing another woman. On April 20, he returned to North Roxbury Drive to find his bags all packed and outside the door.

The divorces of both married Cantor daughters came up within five weeks of each other late that spring. Both were uncontested and were decided with brief, if painful, appearances in court. Edna testified before Superior Judge Ruben S. Schmidt on May 7, saying that her husband would stay away from home all night about once every two weeks. "I would have no idea where he was. He kept me nervous and tense and I had to have medical attention." The court approved an agreement through which McHugh promised to pay 20 percent of his net income, with a minimum of $3,600 a year guaranteed, for support of Edna and six-year-old Judy. Edna also received $10,818 in cash, $1,200 in bonds, and other property.

Natalie's case against Joe Metzger came up before Superior Judge Jess E. Stephens on June 11. Her official complaint was similar to Edna's: that her husband stayed away from home late at night without explanation, em-

barrassed her in front of friends, and upset her so much that she had to
have medical attention.

Metzger, who was in no position to pay alimony, agreed to pay seventy-
five dollars a month for the support of their son, Michael. The court granted
a request for a nominal award of one dollar per month alimony in order to
preserve the judge's jurisdiction to grant a larger amount later, if application
was made. Metzger never saw the boy again.

*Nellie Bly*, the Broadway show that Eddie was producing, opened its first
tryout at the Forrest Theatre in Philadelphia on Saturday night, December
1, 1945. The Debonairs' precision dancing was extremely well received,
unlike the show.

"It will take a great deal more than routine doctoring to put *Nellie Bly*
in the upper brackets," wrote Waters in *Variety*. "A major surgical is, in
fact, indicated. It might even find greater favor in Hollywood than on
Broadway if a too-premature opening in New York doesn't ruin its film
chances."

Cantor left for the West Coast on Thursday, January 17, 1946, four
days before *Nellie Bly* opened at the Adelphi Theatre on Broadway to two
favorable notices and half a dozen bad ones. The show grossed nearly
$32,000 in its first eight performances, but most of that was due to advance
sales. Box office business declined markedly after the opening, and a closing
notice was put up on Monday, January 28, following two long-distance
telephone calls between Cantor and his lawyer and representative, Abe Berman. *Nellie Bly* closed on February 9, having cost Cantor personally more
than $100,000, not to mention time and work.

At the same time, Bill Dozier, executive assistant to RKO studio chief
N. Peter Rathvon, bluntly told Eddie that the studio did not want *Show
Business Out West*, the script that had replaced *Come On Along*. RKO was
then producing several big westerns, all in color, and thought a burlesque
on the order of the Cantor picture—in plain black and white, no less—
would be bad business that same season. Cantor shook his head and told
his writers to come up with a new theme.

To make matters worse, the Canadian Broadcasting Company had
banned *Time to Smile* "for a number of reasons, but mainly because it did
not meet CBC standards of program acceptance." The CBC did not elaborate, but the theatre page of the February 15 *Montreal Gazette* had a
photograph of Cantor dusting off a microphone with the caption, "Keep It
Clean, Cantor."

The CBC ban, the result of a decision by its Program Acceptance Committee in Toronto, was the result of Eddie's repeated gags about his sexual
prowess in fathering five daughters. Innocuous by today's standards, and
by those of Broadway, they were nonetheless risqué for commercial radio
in the 1940s.

Cantor considered Thelma Carpenter another problem. "He thought the company she kept was not that good," remembers one close to the scene, "that she hung around with a wild crowd, and that it was not good for herself or for the show." Carpenter was let go after a total of twenty-five broadcasts.

Thelma had her own ideas concerning her dismissal. "A few of Cantor's people were members of the Communist Party," she later claimed. "A lot of writers belonged to it at the time. Some of Cantor's men tried to get me to come to a meeting, but I'm a Catholic, and we were told to stay away from communism. Well, Manning Ostroff was Cantor's producer, and he was 'in there,' and before I knew it, I was fired—gone." Fourteen-year-old Patsy Bolton became female vocalist for the balance of the season.

The only good news seemed to be in the recording studio. Late in February, Eddie waxed a new song, "One-Zy, Two-Zy," for Pan-American Records in Hollywood, followed by "Josephine, Please No Lean on the Bell" and the old standby, "Makin' Whoopee."

Cantor often introduced "Josephine," an Italian dialect song with an extensive patter, by claiming it was "given" him by his old friend Durante. In fact, the writers—one of whom, the veteran Harry Pease, had written "I Don't Want to Get Well" in 1917—had simply brought the song to Cantor. The Pan-American recording has a verve, an energy, not found in Cantor's later (1957) version and showed that Eddie could do special material comparable to that done by Danny Kaye in the same period.

Danny Kaye was a smash hit in every entertainment medium except radio. Some blamed his problem there on poor material; others said he simply was "not right" for radio. Whatever the true reason (Fred Allen said he sounded like a cross between Eddie Cantor and Milton Berle), the failure of his 1945–46 series for the Pabst Breweries of Milwaukee was one of the major points of conversation in the entertainment world. Determined to wipe the egg off their corporate faces—and to show everyone in advertising that the *Pabst Blue Ribbon Show* could be the top program in radio— Pabst approached Eddie Cantor with one of the most lucrative offers in the history of radio: $20,000 per broadcast.

The contract, slated to begin in September 1947—leaving Cantor one more season for Bristol-Myers and Kaye one more for Pabst—was revised six days after Eddie's final broadcast of the season (from Denver, which had tied with Des Moines as the safest city in the country in connection with the Safety First Campaign Cantor had initiated on April 10). In the new deal, Bristol-Myers released Cantor from his contract, Pabst switched from CBS to NBC, and Eddie replaced a quickly ousted Kaye on the *Pabst Blue Ribbon Show* a year before the surprised Danny thought that it would happen. (Groucho Marx referred to Cantor as the "double-crosser.")

Several days later, it was announced that Joe Quillen and Bobby O'Brien would leave Cantor—with the latter's assumed blessings—to join Nat Linden on Joan Davis's writing staff for Swan Soap on CBS. Joan herself was still set as costar of Eddie's second film for RKO—if and when a script could win approval.

Eddie had decided to get rid of "The Mad Russian" and did so with a letter to Bert Gordon saying that "The Russian" was ready for his own show and it wasn't "quite fair holding" him to his contract. Gordon did not know whether Cantor was being kind or sarcastic—pretty much exactly as intended.

The summer passed in rest, relaxation, and conferences and included a week at the Milwaukee Centurama in Juneau Park on the shores of Lake Michigan. Cantor arrived in Milwaukee on Saturday, July 27, to prepare for the show in the Central Amphitheatre and to confer with his new sponsor, Pabst. "Marilyn and I flew out for that one," recalled Janet. "Marilyn had a part in the show as a young woman who came up to get Daddy's autograph. For one show, we decided to surprise him, and I came up to play the part instead of Marilyn. Daddy grabbed me by the wrist and held me so tight for the entire sketch I almost screamed. He was trying to keep me steady and make sure I wasn't nervous. I wasn't nervous; I was just in pain."

Following his work in the Milwaukee Centurama, Eddie and the press were guests of Pabst president Harris Pearlstein in the Pump Room of the Ambassador Hotel in Chicago on Thursday, August 8.

The three-year pact with Pabst was iron-tight and called for the most extensive ad campaign to publicize a star in radio history. Pabst and Cantor offered three thousand dollars in cash for the NBC station promotion manager who came up with the best ad campaign. It was announced that Eddie would be Pabst's "calendar boy" for 1947, with copies sent to some 150,000 inns and taverns.

*The Eddie Cantor Pabst Blue Ribbon Show* premiered at 10:30 P.M. on Thursday, September 26, 1946, with the lively prattle of Burns and Allen as guests and Margaret Whiting as female vocalist. Cantor had again relied on smarts, rather than talent, in assembling a first-rate program.

Harry Von Zell was retained as announcer. Best remembered for his work on the Burns & Allen TV show, he would spend a total of nine years with Eddie Cantor. "Some people who worked with Eddie will say he was sometimes a difficult man," said Von Zell several years before dying of cancer in 1981, "that he sometimes tended to be aggressive, stubborn, and rather cantankerous. And in all honesty, I have to say he could be difficult. He was what you call a fighter. When he felt that what he wanted to do was right, he was a hard man to whip. And sometimes he fought when it wasn't really necessary; it wasn't all that important. But that came from his background, in the ghetto, where he *had* to fight . . . in order to exist."

Eddie remained dissatisfied with the script of *Rich Man, Poor Man*, his latest stab at a film vehicle, after about half a dozen rewrites. The plot concerned a vaudeville couple who retire to a country inn in New England but find the locals snobbishly resentful until they find a letter from George Washington that proves one of their ancestors was a hero—and makes them heirs to a fabulous fortune from the United States government. The major defect was the lack of opportunity for comedy. It was too much plot and far too much Joan Davis—with Cantor's acquiescence—an accommodation to another performer that Eddie had never allowed before (much less endorsed) in his entire professional life.

Part of this "new outlook," to be sure, involved his evolution from performer to showman. For the ten years past, he had become less a comedian than an ambassador of good will, less an entertainer than a lecturer, wise moralist, and, at times, friendly conscience.

Another part involved Joan Davis. She and Eddie had a kind of symbiotic outlook he had never and could never have shared with Ida. For all her undeniably wise counsel, Ida had never become "part of show business," in speech, dress, looks, or outlook. As much as they still loved each other, there was much that Eddie and Ida Cantor did not have in common.

To her granddaughter, Judy, Ida was "like Auntie Mame—without the taking off and traveling and being a single woman."

> She was always beautifully dressed, beautifully jeweled. She was not particularly domestic in the sense of keeping house and cooking. She was forced by his career to find her own life, which she did. My grandmother spent a good deal of her time playing cards. She had a gang of women who came over every day, and a deli truck would pull up and all this marvelous food would come out.
>
> She loved to gamble, and would fly off to Vegas at the drop of a hat. Ida was very generous and would give everybody all these wonderful silver dollars after she got back. She was a great lady, great sense of humor, lots of fun, and led a really charmed life.

Ida Tobias Cantor was a practical woman who could catch a rat down in Palm Springs and drown it in the toilet. She was, at the same time, a rather proper post-Victorian Jewish lady who never uttered a four-letter word—knowingly, that is.

Ida was given to malapropisms that Norman Lear could never have gotten past the network censors for *All in the Family*. On one occasion, she discussed the coming rental of a summer home—a duty Ida always handled—with her daughters. "That agent thinks he's smart," she said. "But if he wants to be like that, I won't worry. *I* have an ace up my hole!"

She wanted to have her dog mated, and a vet gave her the name of a society woman in Beverly Hills who owned a similar breed. Ida called her up and said, "Yes. This is Mrs. Cantor. Dr. Huff gave me your name because I want to get my dog laid."

She had heard the word and simply thought it was correct. On one occasion, her daughters tried to get her to say some word that she knew was off-color. "Oh," she gasped, "I couldn't do that." And she never did.

Her Victorian innocence made the strongest and coarsest of men watch their language. Ida's card games took in not only her woman friends but various Hollywood characters, like the stand-up comic B. S. Pulley. A heavy-set and vulgar man later best known for his performance as Big Julie in *Guys and Dolls*, he tiptoed around daintily and was the perfect gentleman when entering the Cantor home, generally through the kitchen, to play cards with Ida and the others. (The only one not allowed in the game was Eddie, a notorious sore loser.)

Eddie took the writing staff to Palm Springs to polish *Rich Man, Poor Man* while Jimmy McHugh Sr. and Harold Adamson finished work on the songs in LaQuinta. Cantor always hollered about "tried and tested" material whenever he felt uneasy about any show business project. This time was no exception, and RKO paid the publisher Shapiro-Bernstein $20,000 for unlimited use of the song "If You Knew Susie," which became the film's new title. Joan, predictably, played Susie, the first and only time she played the title role in any motion picture—a fortieth birthday present from her costar, Eddie Cantor.

*The Eddie Cantor Pabst Blue Ribbon Show* was not among the top fifteen shows in the Hooper ratings (which outstripped the Crossleys in the eyes of postwar sponsors) at the end of 1946. Fighting frantically to regain the position he had occupied with *Time to Smile*, Eddie brought Bert Gordon back on a semiregular basis and booked the hottest guest stars he could get over the next four months: Jack Benny, Cary Grant, Charles Boyer, Van Johnson, Al Jolson (at the height of *The Jolson Story* craze), Bob Hope, and Dennis Day. A late surge in the ratings convinced Pabst to exercise its option. Cantor's five-figure weekly radio salary was secure for another year.

Cantor was now fifty-five, graying rapidly and feeling a little run-down on occasion. He rested that summer, except for one spontaneous, exhausting trip to San Francisco with George Jessel, where Eddie appeared on two radio shows and wound up doing five shows at the Fox with Jessel, Martha Stewart, and June Haver. Cantor also went to New York in late August, narrating a special WNBC radio program on the life of Elizabeth Blackwell, America's first woman doctor, who founded the New York Infirmary, the first hospital ever to open its doors to the sick and poor, regardless of race or creed. The Infirmary, then seeking contributions for a modern twelve-story medical center, was located on New York's East Side, making it a natural project for Cantor.

One week later, Eddie received the United Jewish Appeal's 1947 Humanitarian Award at a dinner in his honor at the Bellevue-Stratford Hotel in Philadelphia. Barney Balaban of the Chicago theatre-owning family made the presentation as chairman of the UJA's film division. Cantor and Balaban entrained for Chicago several days later.

Early in November, with *If You Knew Susie* in production, Joan Davis filed suit for divorce against her husband, Si Wills, charging mental cruelty. The suit was uncontested, and the divorce was granted four weeks later. Joan's marriage, never a great love fest, had become a casualty of her friendship with Eddie.

Two weeks after that, *If You Knew Susie* was completed. Cantor and Davis, who had seemed like soulmates for four years, were never close again.

## Chapter 13

# COLGATE COMEDY HOUR

*"Apparently, there's nothing wrong with television*
*that a real showman can't cure."*
—*Jack Gould, the* New York Times

[E]ddie Cantor's professional life stagnated in the late 1940s. His radio show continued to have its old audience, and he still made occasional appearances with hastily improvised "unit" shows culled largely from his radio ensemble. But the hostile critical reaction to *If You Knew Susie* meant that Cantor's film career was over. He was now an institution, no longer one of the world's biggest stars.

This left Eddie free to play the doting grandfather to Michael and Judy, both of whom had lived—with their respective mothers, Natalie and Edna—in the house at North Roxbury Drive for the last three years.

"I grew up in that house," remembers Judy.

And I have absolutely glorious memories of that house and my grandparents, especially my grandfather. My cousin Michael and I were the "kings of the house," and anything we did was just considered cute.

I was the apple of my grandfather's eye. Nobody, especially my mother, liked to go down to the house in Palm Springs, but my grandfather adored it, and sometimes he would throw me in the car and we'd drive down together. Those are some of my most beautiful memories, he and I in that big blue Cadillac convertible, driving to Palm Springs.

He was extraordinarily energetic, the same at home as when he was performing. In fact, I think he was the original "streaker." We'd be in the middle of dinner, and he'd get up and drop his pants and exit. He was always clowning, very fun to be with. I adored him. Being the second generation, I think my cousin Michael and I enjoyed him more than the daughters did.

Cantor still continued his enormous work for charity, and received innumerable honors. The Beverly Hills B'nai B'rith women's organization acclaimed him "Man of the Year" before an audience of more than one
thousand religious, civic, and entertainment leaders in Los Angeles's Biltmore Bowl on Wednesday, April 14. George Jessel served as emcee, and
the evening wound up with a two-hour show that included Dinah Shore,
Al Jolson ("What did we need him for?" Eddie whispered to Dinah), Danny
Thomas, Gertrude Niesen, Abe Burrows, and Dennis Day. Eddie officiated
at the opening of the United Jewish Appeal drive in San Diego later that
month.

NBC wanted Cantor for a sixty-minute *Ziegfeld Follies*, but Eddie was
much more concerned about his late-night (10:30–11:00) regular Thursday
time slot, telling NBC he would "look elsewhere" if it was not changed.
Cantor's last two broadcasts of the season aired at nine as a result.

Eddie, still disgruntled with his ratings, tried to make sure 1948–49
would be his best season since before the war by signing new talents like
Toni Harper, a nine-year-old black singer whose recording of "Candy Store
Blues" had been number fifteen on *Billboard*'s rhythm-and-blues jukebox
chart. Dinah Shore returned as Cantor's regular vocalist, accepting $1,250
a week to fit one song and a small portion of a Pabst Blue Ribbon broadcast
into her other professional commitments.

Eddie sold Pabst another summer show similar to the annual fill-in
shows he had been selling sponsors in the past, using his regular winter
cast with frequent mentions of himself in each week's script.

Maurice Neilson had not been in his native Norway for ten years when
he, Eddie, and Ida sailed on the S.S. *Stockholm* on Saturday, April 3,
1948. Eight days later, they arrived in Stockholm, where Eddie received
a cable from the Lord Mayor, asking him to broadcast for the United
Nations Children's Relief Fund on Tuesday, July 20. "They know I am
working with such programs in the U.S.," Cantor said. He lost no time
accepting.

Eddie lauded the Swedish tourist service and received an offer to visit
a camp for displaced persons in Germany during his visit to Denmark. In
truth, Cantor found the Scandinavian countries uncomfortable, not due to
the people—he thought it fascinating when a young woman cut his hair in
Stockholm and another ("much older") woman gave messages—but to the
food. Whether it was simple lack of food at Stockholm's Grand Hotel and
other places or the Scandinavian cuisine, Cantor found very little to eat in
Sweden. (Ida did a painting titled "Eddie Waiting for Breakfast" when they
got back home.) Cantor also found the Norse countries duller than popularly believed, except for the man who started speaking Yiddish to him in
a Turkish bath.

The Cantors passed from Germany to France, where Eddie ate his fill,
saw the DP rehabilitation camps, and heard Richard Josef Inger, the "Pa-

lestinian Chaliapin," sing in Paris. Cantor was determined to present Inger in concert in America and spoke about it to Jack Kapp, the head of Decca Records, after he and Ida got back to New York.

When he returned, Cantor stepped into a whirl of conferences, lunches, and professional engagements. The William Morris office quickly booked him at fairs in Erie and Reading, Pennsylvania. Eddie then began a series of personal appearances in twelve key cities in behalf of the United Jewish Appeal for Overseas Children's Relief.

His third season on the air for Pabst Blue Ribbon did not have an encouraging beginning. "Not even a master craftsman like Eddie Cantor, with eighteen years of radio and forty years of show business behind, can surmount the impost of a script that lacks the incandescence so vital to his type of jesting," Helm wrote in *Variety*. "Try as he would, and no one tries harder to make every line count, NBC's new 'man Friday' couldn't give his season opener the high comedic content which has so consistently been his measure."

William Powell's timing was off in his guest cross-fire with Cantor. Billie Burke was back for another "giggly" bit, and Dinah Shore delivered one song for her $1,250. All in all, it was an inauspicious start to what would prove to be Eddie's last season at the helm of a prime-time network radio variety program.

In fact, it scarcely mattered. Radio, as it had been for twenty years, was dying, and forty-year-old Milton Berle had singlehandedly sold millions of TV sets in the past twelve months alone.

Pabst and its agency, Warwick and Legler, wanted Eddie to jump straight into a weekly "live" television show in the fall of 1949. Cantor hedged, wanting to do no more than one program a month, and Paul Warwick made a special, although fruitless, trip to Hollywood that winter, attempting to sign Eddie to a contract.

Cantor was still cooperating on Pabst Beer promotions, broadcasting from Peoria and Milwaukee that spring as part of Pabst "Blue Ribbon Week." Negotiations for TV with Pabst looked quite encouraging at this point, Eddie saying that his first NBC-TV show would be kinescoped from the West Coast on the fourth of October.

While Cantor was negotiating with Paul Warwick and Erv Staudinger of Warwick and Legler, Ida was in New York, planning to show the town to one of her friends from Hollywood. The plan was ruined when a viral infection laid Ida up for two weeks in her suite at the Savoy-Plaza. She and her friend then returned to Los Angeles, where Ida checked in for a brief stay at Cedars of Lebanon Hospital.

Eddie, in the interval, had spent most of his nonworking time in Palm Springs, accompanied by Vivienne Bowes, an all-purpose secretary, p.r. copywriter, and "Gal Friday" who had gradually attached herself to Cantor.

Eddie had already canceled a planned vaudeville tour of the Midwest, conserving, for a change, his vaunted energy and looking, with no little trepidation, to the fall.

Like most contemporary radio stars, Cantor was in no hurry to do television. "Sure, TV is coming, and the so-called big names will be at the station when it arrives—but I don't think it will be for several years. The following is a helluva thing for me to say, but it will give you something to think about. The big comics are a little bit too old and tired to memorize and rehearse a full half hour of entertainment each week. This means that people in control of TV will be forced to get some new faces whether they like it or not. When television gets around to me, I promise you that I shall not do more than twenty shows in a year. I'd like time to prepare, rehearse thoroughly, and feel perfectly at ease. I look upon a television show as an engagement at the Palace or the New Amsterdam Theatre or Loews State. You've got to be good—and the only way you can be good is to be sure."

Cantor left rehearsals for his final broadcast of the season to fly to New York for conferences with NBC president Niles Trammel and CBS board chairman William S. Paley. Paley was then starting the final "talent raid" on NBC that would make CBS the top TV network for the following two decades. Crosby, Burns and Allen, Jolson, and Jack Benny were among the biggest stars to fall into his fold. Trammel, anxious to hold on to any top name that he could, agreed to find Cantor a radio sponsor for the coming season and a television contract for twelve shows a year, beginning in the fall of 1950.

*The Eddie Cantor Pabst Blue Ribbon Show* went on the air for the last time on June 24, 1949. Bobby Breen, then twenty-one, was the guest star, providing an additional nostalgic tinge to what had long since become a show for "old folks" over forty.

Trammell did not get Cantor another variety show for the coming season. All the major money was now headed for TV, and sponsors would no longer shoulder Cantor's twenty-thousand-dollar-a-week radio budget. Trammell's answer was for Cantor to host *Take It or Leave It*, a popular game program whose origins went back to April 21, 1940, when it debuted over CBS with Bob Hawk as its host.

Each contestant on the show had to select a category from a list (e.g., "First Names of People," "Cards and Card Games," "Titles in Literature," "Detectives") and then answer progressively more difficult questions for prizes starting at a dollar. The amount was doubled with each question, stopping at sixty-four dollars, with the contestant having the option of stopping at each level and taking whatever money he had won. If, however, he missed any question, all the money won was forfeit. It was truly "Take It or Leave It."

As with Groucho Marx's ratings smash, *You Bet Your Life*, the success of the show was due more to the host's interviewing skills than to the questions or the modest sums involved. Phil Baker, who succeded Hawk, enjoyed six years as host and was noted for his shameless hinting at the answers to contestants. Garry Moore, fresh from four years on the air with Jimmy Durante, followed Baker in 1947, when the program switched to NBC. Cantor followed Moore after two seasons.

The show might have seemed a comedown, had Cantor been less aware of the economic realities of radio in 1949. He had already forgone Pabst's offer of a television series in favor of one from Colgate-Palmolive, which would not begin until the fall of 1950. In the meantime, there was *Take It or Leave It*, a show with little overhead aside from Eddie's salary and whose very title mirrored Cantor's situation.

Cantor, in the east, killed time attending baseball games and spent the Fourth of July weekend at Grossinger's, then celebrating its forty-fifth anniversary. Ida joined him in New York a few days later, and the Cantors sailed for France aboard the *America* on Saturday, July 9, 1949.

Cantor visited war veterans in Paris before he and Ida left to spend ten days in Cannes, where Eddie tentatively accepted an offer from Val Parnell and Harry Foster to perform at the world-famous London Palladium the following summer. A strong supporter of the Marshall Plan, Cantor transcribed a broadcast for the European Cooperation Administration the evening before he sailed for home on the *Queen Mary*.

Ida left for California shortly after their arrival in New York. Eddie assembled yet another "unit" company, including Cookie Fairchild and Vivienne Bowes, who came in from the West Coast, and did shows for the UJA in Buffalo and for the Knights of Columbus in Detroit. He continued to drop in and out of New York on fair dates and other personal appearances over the next few weeks. Sandwiched in were tapings of *Take It or Leave It*. Four had been completed by the time the first one aired.

Jose of *Variety* said *Take It or Leave It* was "a natural" for Cantor, citing his "ability to ad lib . . . dress up the occasion with song, and handle contestants in a manner that can provide entertainment for listeners." The show might well indeed have been a TV vehicle for Eddie, had NBC not eagerly looked forward to a Cantor prime-time variety show. *You Bet Your Life* had made Groucho Marx a radio favorite. A Cantor show along the same lines seemed a waste of an invaluable and versatile performer at the time.

Cantor continued taping two or more *Take It or Leave It* shows whenever he could slot them in between other commitments. He was back at Grossinger's for Labor Day weekend, where the agent Milton Blackstone persuaded him to hear a client of his sing at a rehearsal for the evening show. Eddie "didn't seem particularly impressed" but agreed to let the young man do two songs that night.

Performing for an audience that understood interpolated Yiddishisms, Cantor did some of the best stand-up work of his long career, far more spontaneous and real than he had ever been on radio, to judge from a surviving tape of that night's program. Playing off his audience as well as any seasoned nightclub comic, he spun easily among insult humor, knowing insights into household annoyances, and left-handed compliments aimed at life in the Catskills. His singing, by contrast, was embarrassing—barely in time with the orchestra. His voice was hoarse and creaky, miles below the still light, youthful tenor he had shown on several recordings for Decca five years earlier.

Then he introduced the singer Blackstone had forced on him. The response was overwhelming, as the younger man's clear, strong, vibrant voice rang out in three songs. Some said Blackstone stocked the room with claques (paid applauders). The tape, however, tells a different story.

"I think you'll make a living," Cantor told him onstage, flavoring his compliments with the major concern of the typical Jewish father-in-law. "You'll do all right. Ladies and gentlemen, this boy isn't just a crooner; he's a singer. He'll join my unit—yes, he'll join my unit—for fair dates in Lancaster and Reading and then for longer dates in Chicago and Omaha. Then, I'll take him home to meet my daughters."

Cantor's young discovery was Eddie Fisher.

Fisher had been bouncing in and about show business since the age of thirteen, when he'd won a radio talent contest on the Horn and Hardart *Children's Hour*. Managed for the past three years by Milton Blackstone, he had been a "production singer" at the Copacabana, an "intermission singer" at the New York Paramount, and a favorite on *Teen Time*, a local Philadelphia radio show that featured the latest in pop music. Cantor, though, would spell the difference. Never before had one big-name performer "made" another in the sense that Cantor would "make" Eddie Fisher.

The Cantor unit played Atlantic City the weekend after Labor Day, followed by returns at Reading and Lancaster. Then it was back to New York, where Cantor's friend Francis Cardinal Spellman asked him to set up a radio show to raise money for his pet charity, the New York Foundling Hospital. Within forty-eight hours, Cantor had secured time from NBC and lined up Bob Hope, Bing Crosby, Jack Benny, Jimmy Durante, Dinah Shore, Hank Russell's Orchestra, Manny Ostroff as producer, and himself as the emcee. A UJA luncheon drive at the Hotel Commodore was next, Cantor establishing a record for one-shot fund-raising with $1,253,800 in cash.

Cardinal Spellman's car drove Eddie to the airport when he left for Omaha, where the Cantor unit was scheduled to play three days at the Ak-Sar-Ben Shrine Auditorium. A ten-day stint at the Electrical Exposition at the Coliseum in Chicago followed. It was the typical Cantor unit show, with an opening balancing act (The Glenns), "the Mad Russian," a new female vocalist (Vickee Richards), a novelty tap clacker, David Powell, the young Fisher, and Cantor; Vivienne Bowes served as a walk-on "stooge."

The show grossed over $80,000 over the ten days, including several extra matinees and a midnight show on Saturday, October 8. Thirty thousand dollars of it went to Cantor and his unit, which meant that Eddie walked away with twenty thousand before taxes—good money for ten days of work in 1949.

Cantor left for the West Coast by plane, leaving the troupe to drive to Hollywood in its Cadillac convertible. Fisher had a learner's permit and enjoyed doing some of the driving till they got to Kearney, Nebraska, where he hit a soft shoulder on the road, jammed his foot down on the brake, and turned the car over in a ditch. "Everyone was shaken up, but nobody was hurt," Fisher remembered. "We scrambled out, and I just walked away, laughing."

It was nervous laughter. Fisher had seen Cantor bawl out other people for "the most trivial offenses." He was sure Cantor would fire him. "I called him on the phone, told him what had happened, and waited for the explosion. There was a pause. 'Well,' he said finally, 'it's a good thing nobody was hurt. Why don't you all stay overnight where you are and take the train in the morning. Don't worry about a thing.' I hung up the phone with one more reason to be grateful to Eddie Cantor."

Following a four-day trip to San Francisco—where Cantor was greeted by Mayor Elmer Robinson, did a Community Chest show, taped two *Take It or Leave It* shows, and introduced Fisher, his "new protege," to an audience at the Golden Gate Theatre—Cantor "rested" at home for ten days. He showed Fisher around Hollywood and, true to his word, had him to his house for dinner. Margie, Natalie, and Edna, not to mention Mike and Judy, were all present, but the beauty of the Cantor girls was lost on Eddie Fisher. "They were *below average*," he has chortled. In truth, he did not care for Jewish women, and, despite Cantor's obvious Jewishness, expected his host's daughters to be Hollywood starlets with classic American beauty features. At twenty-one, Fisher was also thirteen years Margie's junior, twelve years younger than Natalie, and nine years younger than Edna. It is extremely doubtful that Cantor thought Fisher would marry one of his daughters. He did not, however, think that he would find them totally sexless.

Cantor's grueling schedule continued. On December 2, he emceed a show at Purdue University, Lafayette, Indiana, accompanied by Fisher and Sid Fields. Ida, during this time, was in New York seeing Janet.

Janet had become involved with Roberto Gari, a young dancer-artist who had been in the chorus of *Nellie Bly* and did superb imitations of Bette Davis and Judy Holliday. "My parents did not want me to marry him," Janet now confesses. "Why? I guess they knew it wouldn't work before I did."

It was Ida's job to dissuade Janet and, predictably, she failed. Janet married "Gari," as she called him, in a civil ceremony on Saturday, December 3. Ida made a lame, transparent excuse and stayed in bed. Anything seemed better than attending.

Eddie flew into New York as soon as Ida called him.

We planned a small reception in our apartment for a few friends after the wedding. That's where we were when mother called, saying she was at the Waldorf and asking us to come on over, with our friends, to meet some friends of hers.

We went. I remember the Waldorf elevator doors opening and seeing wing-tipped shoes. I knew who they belonged to, so I followed them up and saw my father's face.

I was startled when we reached their suite. They had a hundred people there, with lavish spreads of food and drinks. Gari and I stayed for a brief time because we didn't feel comfortable among my parents' friends.

The two oldest Cantor daughters were the most loyal to the family and to their father's wishes. Edna was the wildly artistic one, Marilyn the streetwise, born-to-show-business hellion. Janet was the intelligent baby, a little like the ingenue in *Guess Who's Coming to Dinner*.

The absence of his long-familiar radio variety show had caused Cantor to fill the last few months of 1949 with a string of live performances and personal appearances, with and without Fisher and the "Eddie Cantor Unit." But repeated tapings of *Take It or Leave It* had made Eddie feel restless. He needed something different, a new challenge. The answer, largely Cantor's own, was a one-man show—Eddie with two pianists in a one- to two-hour program.

Ida did not want Eddie to try it, fearful he would be hurt, disappointed, and disillusioned with his own abilities in his late fifties. Logically, it was a risk with little point of gain; Cantor had enjoyed several brilliant careers with another seemingly assured in television. Eddie, however, was determined. Opening at the University of Maine, before an audience who'd never seen him in their lives but knew his voice from radio and his face from the movies, Eddie was not sure if he could "get across to the younger generation who hadn't been born when I was on Broadway."

Cantor, although no teen idol, was still a major, although slightly passé, star. Advance sales were so good that two performances were given. Eddie did not mind; it gave him a chance to further hone the act for more prestigious dates to follow. He opened with "There's No Business Like Show Business," not yet the banal, shopworn phrase it later would become, and told stories (of varying veracity). He also sang his famous songs.

Cantor later said it "was one of the great nights of my life." Certainly, it was successful, and the idea that college kids were applauding someone from the East Side with a sixth grade education made the night more important to Eddie than the larger triumphs he had enjoyed in the past.

The tryout having proved successful, Eddie returned west for a vacation in Palm Springs with Ida. Cantor was already scheduled to do his one-man show, officially titled *My Forty Years in Show Business*, at the University of Arizona in February. Now he accepted a much more ambitious booking from Sol Shapiro of the William Morris Agency: Carnegie Hall in New York, under the auspices of the One World Committee, on Tuesday night, March 21.

George Tibboth, composer of "The Woody Woodpecker Song," and Arthur Siegel, who would later write songs for the great 1952 edition of Leonard Sillman's *New Faces*, were Cantor's two accompanists at Carnegie. He opened with a well-delivered, predictably warm-humored wisecrack when the thunderous three-minute ovation that greeted his appearance finally died down: "I don't think I should do this to Jascha Heifetz." A subsequent remark, however, defied all convention.

We're gonna talk about show business, a show business that many of you knew, that I know—and still know. And it should be a very nostalgic evening—things that you've heard time and time again. And it may recall memories of a much more pleasant day, a day without the H-bomb or Senator McCarthy or other evil things that want to destroy mankind.

Several months earlier, Cantor had instructed Eddie Fisher to keep his "mouth shut" about attending a left-wing affair in Chicago—wise advice to a vulnerable youngster on his way up the show biz ladder at the time. Cantor saw himself in an entirely different light, going in where others dared not tread and challenging the potent—and, if anything, still growing—power of Joseph McCarthy and the communist witch hunts of the early 1950s in the same way he had challenged Father Coughlin more than ten years earlier. The next day's papers, reluctant to cause trouble for a much-beloved performer—or to spread comments harmful to McCarthy— carefully omitted any mention of Cantor's open statements against the powerful United States senator from Wisconsin, disappointing Eddie, who was anxious for the fight.

Carnegie Hall was sold out for *My Forty Years in Show Business*, and three hundred special chairs were put up on the stage for those willing to pay the regular admission price just to watch Cantor's back. Eddie told them they'd been cheated, drawing a huge chuckle from the audience out front, and proceeded to give each of them a single dollar refund from his pocket.

Cantor then felt more at ease; in ten more minutes he was, in his own words, "feeling fine. The nervousness of an entertainer melts once the audience starts to laugh and applaud. And the greatest tribute is when you want them to be silent and they are—when the silence is thunderous."

This tension, the subtle yet dynamic interplay between audience and performer, was the foundation on which such greats as Jolson, Brice, Cantor, Harry Lauder, Albert Chevalier, Josephine Baker, and others of the live stage rested their careers. Eddie was no longer the young, energetic, singing comedian whose depiction of the lamb being led to the slaughter, with his rolling eyes and clapping hands, whose wisenheimer, rather pushy Jewish ways had endeared him to Broadway audiences of the 1920s. Long gone was the bashful, almost impish joy of Cantor the young sex fiend, blushing at the charms of a seductress, somewhat fearful and yet joyful at the prospects of the bedroom. His "character," as such, was now the wise, quietly strong, and highly creditable elder statesman of a show business he gratefully acknowledged had given him a life beyond the dreams of poor boys growing up on New York's Lower East Side in the early 1900s. He spoke honestly, sincerely, without too much false modesty or undue pride, of his relationships with Ziegfeld, Will Rogers, W. C. Fields, Bert Williams, Fanny Brice, Al Jolson, and the other great names of the Broadway years before the Great Depression, of Al Smith and Franklin D. Roosevelt, and, at the beginning of the program, his grandmother, Esther. The high, brilliant singing voice of the late '20s was long gone. In its place was a love, good will, and genuine enthusiasm for his songs, like "Charley My Boy," "My Best Girl," "Dinah," and "Makin' Whoopee," Eddie closing the show with a medley of "Margie," "Ida, Sweet as Apple Cider," and "If You Knew Susie." Cantor reappeared onstage to receive the One World Award Citation in recognition of his efforts for world peace and the LaGuardia Citation from the Non-Sectarian Anti-Nazi League for his humanitarian work. The modest, orchestraless program was acclaimed a triumph by the audience and critics.

"Cantor spent from 8:50 to 10:25 uninterruptedly—as solid a one-man show as could be desired," Abel Green wrote in *Variety*.

> He was gay, serious and quasi-tragic in the cavalcade of emotions. . . . A sentimental crack about hoping his "grandmother could only be here; when I was a kid in Henry Street she always said 'go and play in the hall' and I'd have liked her to see me play in the hall—Carnegie Hall" was a natural. None of the nostalgia or sentimental thereafter was sticky. With the innate showmanship of veteran trouping, Cantor's routine thereafter was as objective as a reporter's. His closeups on the greats with whom he became associated, and vice versa, were projected in matter of fact manner. His career, by now more or less public information, requires no gilding, hence his raconteuring has greater authority by underplaying.

The New York daily newspapers were equally enthusiastic, granted that Cantor was a long-accepted favorite and could expect good reviews in the early 1950s, a decade that would reverence the '20s with the same thirty-year-anniversary nostalgia that the 1980s would hold for the '50s. Ward Morehouse of the *World Telegram & Sun* said he might be inclined to vote for *My Forty Years in Show Business* as the "best play of the season"—a tribute to a veteran entertainer not meant to be taken literally, but indicative of the respect both Cantor and his program had inspired.

Cantor spent the next two weeks alternating performances of *My Forty Years in Show Business* in Cleveland and Rochester and at William and Mary College in Virginia with speaking engagements for the UJA in Cincinnati and Norfolk and tapings of *Take It or Leave It* in New York. One-man shows at Congregation Beth Yeshurun, Houston, and Oklahoma A&M followed in mid-April before he returned to L.A. with Ida.

Eddie was now set as one of four rotating stars on the weekly TV show *Colgate Comedy Hour*, which meant script conferences with the writers, Charles Isaacs and Artie Stander. Cantor was out by the pool, getting a massage from Maurice, when they first arrived.

Isaacs later recalled Cantor's referring to himself in the third person, leaping off the table, and pacing up and down the patio in the nude as he discussed ideas, one of which was used for the first show. The writers worked two days and were invited back for lunch. "As before," Isaacs remembered, "we were told to go out into the backyard. Eddie had finished having his rubdown and was now lying stretched out naked in the sun. When he heard us coming along the patio he jumped up and greeted us.

" 'We'll go inside and have a bite of lunch. We're very informal here.'

"Artie and I looked at each other and shrugged. Neither of us had ever eaten lunch with our clothes off."

Eddie wound up reading most of their material while seated on the toilet bowl, the writers "nervously" awaiting his decision in the living room. "There, in the porcelain sterility of that little room, a $50,000 television show was being born.

"Eddie came into the living room. 'Boys, these could be very funny . . . yes, very funny.'

" 'They're smart,' I said, 'but very solid.'

" 'Let's eat,' Eddie said and started for the dining room. As we sat down, Cantor said, 'Boys, don't be too clever. From me they expect hilarity.' "

Cantor was in Chicago for the Jefferson Jubilee Celebration of the SuperMarkets Institutes's Convention at the Stevens Hotel and at Chicago Stadium with Jessel on May 18. He and Ida were en route to Israel, the state that Cantor, more than any other American celebrity, had done so much to foster.

Grossinger's threw them a bon voyage party on Sunday, May 21, Eddie raising $220,000 to give to the Israeli government in June. After giving a talk for the UJA in New Haven on the twenty-fourth and attending an interfaith meeting in Boston with Eleanor Roosevelt and Notre Dame football coach Frank Leahy the following day, Cantor spoke before the convention of the International Ladies Garment Workers in Atlantic City on Saturday, May 27. Instead of asking for donations to the state of Israel, Cantor urged Americans to invest in the country.

Eddie, Ida, the New York restauranteur Mac Kriendler, and Mr. and Mrs. Yoland Markson, who had been instrumental in raising millions for the UJA, were met by a welcoming committee that included U.S. Ambassador James G. McDonald, government officials, and representatives of the UJA when they arrived in Tel Aviv on Monday, June 12. It was the first time a great American star had come to Israel, and Cantor, described as having "raised more money for Israel than any other individual," finished his first tour of immigrant camps by having lunch at Youth Aliyah's transit camp in Nathanya the following day. Impressed by the spirit of the people in the camps but appalled by the conditions under which they lived, Cantor thought the solutions were to raise as much money as possible in the shortest period and to urge businessmen to "get in on the ground floor" of Israel. He was already doing both.

Youth Aliyah, then caring for sixteen thousand children, mostly orphans, dedicated a building at the newest Israeli settlement, Maaleh Ha-Hamishma, near Jerusalem, in Cantor's name on June 26. Eddie himself spoke to everyone in Israel, from bricklayers to government officials, including President Chaim Weizmann at the latter's home in Rehovoth. He and Ida then went on to France, where Cantor finalized plans for his NBC-TV premiere, organized a U.S. personal appearance tour under the sponsorship of B'nai B'rith, and played a special benefit accompanied by Paul Baron's Orchestra. He also took a signed ad in the New York *Herald Tribune* continental edition to promote the recently formed "Hullo, America," an organization set up for the benefit of U.S. students in Paris.

The Cantors arrived back in New York aboard the United States liner *America* on Wednesday, July 12. Eddie had agreed to speak at the Hadassah convention at the Waldorf-Astoria on August 21 if the organization gave him a check for one million dollars made out to Youth Aliyah. Hadassah readily complied.

As one of the national chairmen of the UJA's nationwide campaign, Cantor received a check for $1,500,000 at a luncheon held in his honor by the United Jewish Appeal of Greater New York at the Hotel Commodore on July 19. "The people of Israel," he stressed, "are ready to welcome every Jew who needs a home there, but they will not be able to maintain the present flow of immigration unless we here in the United States realize that there are many thousands of Jewish lives still to be saved and that only our maximum effort and highest devotion can achieve this all-important objective."

Ida left for the West Coast the following day. After thirteen years, the Cantors had made plans to sell their North Roxbury home because of the high taxes, the large staff required to maintain the house, and the fact that all their daughters were now grown. Natalie and Edna were buying their own houses, and it seemed the time had come to sell the "Cantor Home for Girls."

The work of moving was done gradually. Eddie gave fourteen crates of priceless radio transcriptions dating back to 1931 to Jerry Lewis. The Cantors would be spending most of the new season in New York, and the pain of leaving their old house was eased by the knowledge that Eddie, at fifty-eight, would be one of the top stars in what promised to be the ultimate medium: television.

Top radio stars had dreaded the advent of television. It seemed like the Norse Ragnarok, the foretold "Twilight of the Gods"—an end, a doom they knew was inevitable but tried to pretend was in the distant, unimaginable future.

Radio, in truth, had been the Promised Land for the handful of vaudeville comics, Broadway musical comedy stars, and other performers who had managed to make the transition to the ether. They were getting paid thousands a week to do, as it eventually developed, one half-hour show a week—a show in which they read lines off a script while standing before a camera wearing street clothes. Television would require them to memorize a script each week, rehearse the blocking, and worry about every aspect of performance, with the chances good to excellent that a major mishap would occur before ten million people over live television. And live TV was largely all there would be until *I Love Lucy*.

Charles Friedman and Manning Ostroff were overseeing preparations for the first Colgate show by the time Cantor spoke at a UJA luncheon in New York. "We are in a war in Korea and we don't know where we'll be fighting next," said Eddie, his words more prophetic than he realized.

Cantor then left for the annual WCCO aquatennial radio show before a live audience of ten thousand in the Minneapolis Auditorium on July 22. Eddie crowded in several UJA fund-raising affairs on this trip and took time out, in Chicago, to expound on his views on television.

Cantor said he hoped that television did not fall into "the same groove" as radio had concerning the role of the studio audience: "Why should you jeopardize the show for twenty million viewers for the benefit of one thousand or so in the studio, as too many are doing today?" Cantor would live to see the day when shows were shot on film, without the benefit of studio audiences, but not long enough to see the return of the studio audience in the early 1970s. He vowed that he would play the *Colgate Comedy Hour* "for one guy—the camera man." Cantor had long voiced the same attitudes about having studio audiences in radio, only to relentlessly play to them when he went before the microphone. He would commit much the same sin on national TV.

The *Colgate Comedy Hour* would rotate four big comic stars (originally Cantor, Martin and Lewis, Fred Allen, and Bobby Clark) in the all-important 8–9 P.M. slot on NBC on Sunday nights, opposite Ed Sullivan's two-season-old *Toast of the Town* variety show on CBS. Cantor, true to his word, shouldered most of the fast-paced program himself. But he was smart enough, as always, to surround himself with solid pros, most of the young talent picked from current Broadway shows.

The program had the gimmick of a novel "story line," Cantor addressing the executives at a Colgate-Palmolive banquet, telling of his plans for the first show. The scene then segued into a big production chorus number, "This Is Broadway," featuring Tommy Wonder of *Tickets Please*, Danny Daniels of *Kiss Me, Kate*, Helen Wood and Janet Gaylord of *Gentlemen Prefer Blondes*, Charlotte Fayne, Lou Wills Jr., Rudy Tone, and the ballet team of Joy Williams and Val Buttignal. Subsequent numbers were introduced by Cantor's off-camera voice: "We're Having a Baby," a skit about inspection at an army training camp, and "Belt in the Back" with Eddie, Joseph Buloff, and Lew Hearn.

Peruvian coloratura Yma Sumac did an Inca "Hymn to the Sun" before Cantor did a "next-to-closing" park bench scene with Frank Albertson as a backstage doorman who "knew Cantor" in the *Follies* days. This in turn segued into Eddie in blackface, straw hat, and big glasses for a medley of "How Ya Gonna Keep 'Em Down on the Farm?," "Now's the Time to Fall in Love," "Ain't She Sweet?," "Charlie My Boy," "Ma," and "Waiting for the Robert E. Lee," Lou Wills Jr. "doubling" the dancing.

The ratings showed that Cantor's long-anticipated network television debut had outdrawn *Toast of the Town*. The Audience Research Bureau's survey, based on one thousand five hundred telephone calls in New York, Washington, Cleveland, and Chicago, gave the *Colgate Comedy Hour* a 32.1 rating, compared to 27.4 for Sullivan. The same survey gave Cantor an incredible 49.9 percent share of the audience against 24.6 percent for *Toast of the Town*.

The critical response was much more overwhelming. George Rosen of *Variety* said the premiere Colgate show "established Cantor, a veteran of forty years as a luminary in all phases of the entertainment industry, as a TV natural. And, like Bob Hope before him, he effected the transition into the 'glamor' medium with a finesse and sureness that automatically sparked the medium and paved the way for a whole new career for the comic."

Jack Gould of the *New York Times* said the "ageless Eddie was the exuberant trouper of tradition, singing, wise-cracking, dancing and thoroughly enjoying himself. This morning he is TV's undisputed new hit. . . . Eddie acted as if he had been brought up in video. Relaxed and self-assured, he imbued the whole sixty-minute proceedings with a pep and zest characteristic of the best that can be seen on Broadway."

There was hardly a dissenting voice across the nation. Norman Clark of the Baltimore *News-Post* said that "Eddie was born to make people laugh, tap their feet, and applaud." Andy Wilson of the Detroit *Times* said he "proved that the knack of delighting audiences in other media is with him in television." Larry Wolters of the Chicago *Tribune* said Cantor had "always been a visual comedian, so he is back in his element on TV." Mitchell Swartz of the Philadelphia *Daily News* said, "With the ease of the veteran showman he is, Eddie Cantor scored a success in his TV debut last night on the new *Colgate Hour* program."

The truth was that Cantor, for all his years of popularity on radio, was much more suited to TV. Ben Gross of the New York *Daily News* said, "Cantor came into his own, for the first time in the many years he has been on the air. . . . He is the dynamic comedian that he was in the days of the *Ziegfeld Follies*. He sings, he dances, he acts with cyclonic energy. One must see him to appreciate what he puts into his work."

Eddie reveled in the kudos for two days before leaving for Dallas, where he kicked off a thirty-three-stand tour of *Forty Years in Show Business*, including a return at Carnegie.

Wrote Herm Schoenfeld in *Variety*:

> This performance by Cantor was in many ways a tougher assignment than his earlier stand in the Hall. Not only was Cantor going over the same route in reprising his forty-one-year-old career in show business, but there was the factor of his regular monthly appearance on TV which might have been expected to take the edge off his in-the-flesh show. But Cantor, who has been a standout in every facet of show business from his childhood vaude start with Gus Edwards through legit, silent films, talkers, radio and now TV, once again gave double-ply proof that talent and basic entertainment values can sell in any and every medium.

Cantor's second Colgate show proved that the success of the first one was not accidental. Eddie introduced "Maxie the Taxi," a talkative, not altogether sweet cab driver, on this broadcast, took part in two other skits, and sang "Dinah" in a big production number at the finish. "The veteran comic demonstrated that he not only can hold his own with the best of the new crop of TV talent, without resorting to oldie material," *Variety* reported, "but in fact sparked a production that was as fresh, scintillating and beautifully coordinated as video has seen this season."

More one-man concerts followed in Toronto, Buffalo, New Orleans, Houston, Oklahoma City, Birmingham, and other cities. At 4 A.M. in Mobile on October 24, Cantor was awakened by a call from NBC in New York. Al Jolson had died in San Francisco two and a half hours earlier. NBC was paying tribute to him on a special broadcast and wanted Cantor at their studio in Mobile by 6 A.M. Eddie, his heart racing, quickly got up and got dressed.

That night, he did his one-man show on schedule at the Fort Whiting Auditorium in Mobile. There was a portion of the show in which he sang a parody of "Ol' Man River" titled "Ol' Man Jolson," kidding Al:

> Ol' man Jolson, that ol' man Jolson.
> He's older than Johnson, together with Olsen.
> But ol' man Jolson, he just keeps goin' along.

"The music started," Eddie recalled, "but I couldn't sing it. Instead, I talked to the audience of the Jolson I knew. I was crying, and so were they. The king was gone, the greatest minstrel of them all."

Cantor, like many in show business, knew Al Jolson as an egocentric, often overbearing person who had little or no real private life—a strange man at home only on the stage. Jolson's ego, although monumental, encompassed a view of himself only as a performer, in contrast to Cantor's more horizontal self image as a "citizen of the world." Jolson's passing nonetheless seemed to touch Cantor deeply. Jolson, to Cantor's generation, personified not only the entertainment world but the best—"the magic"—all performers *wished* they had. There was, it had been said, "a little of Al Jolson in all of us." There was certainly a bit of him in Cantor.

Perhaps the passing of his somewhat older musical comedy contemporary—his "rival"—made Cantor more cognizant of his own mortality. Eddie was now fifty-eight; his daughters were all grown, and he and Ida were giving up their "permanent" residence after more than thirteen years. Everything seemed transient.

Cantor did another *Forty Years in Show Business* at Philadelphia's Academy of Music the following evening and returned to New York for more Colgate show rehearsals. He scrapped the original finale in favor of a "Salute to Al Jolson." The salute, he knew, had to be meaningful while skirting what the industry might term dubious sentimentality.

He succeeded admirably. *Variety* called the third Cantor Colgate show

> by far, the best to date, even exceeding his preem, which set a top standard. The Cantor segment comprised knowing entertainment with a showmanly savvy that was marked by smooth production and excellent components.
>
> Cantor's growth in this medium is becoming increasingly evident. He isn't relying exclusively on the wealth of material that he's accumulated through his forty-one years in show business. Rather, he's come up with a characterization that promises to become a warm bit of Americana. His second "Maxie the Taxi" sequence in the series had a glowing type of homey humor. These conversations of a hack driver with his fares radiate a cordial feeling that promises to make this character one of his better tele developments.

This being his first display since the death of his lifelong friend, Al Jolson, Cantor devoted the finale to reminiscences of Jolie. It had reverence and nostalgia without becoming maudlin. Bit was excellently staged with one of Jolie's diskings to the pantomime of Bob Gari. Tribute also served to introduce Mrs. Cantor (Ida), which had as its by-product one of the better ad-libs. Mrs. Cantor fluffed her one speech, which led the comic to observe: "For one line you don't divorce a woman."

Five more one-man concerts followed, including one at St. Louis's Kiel Auditorium, where Cantor drew a paying audience of three thousand for the benefit of the St. Louis Heart Association. His fourth Colgate show, on December 3, paired Eddie with Connie Sawyer in a sketch about a nearsighted couple. Pianist Joe Bushkin, rather than the orchestra, accompanied Cantor on "Oh, Susannah! Dust Off the Old Pianna" and "Ballin' the Jack," while *Babes in Toyland*, the finale, fit in with the Christmas season.

The Sherman & Marquette Agency had a new animated commercial (drawn by Robert Gari, Janet's husband) showing Eddie, Ida, and their five daughters shampooing with Colgate-Palmolive's Halo. That the girls were grown and on their own with two divorces in their wake did not matter at all. The Cantor girls had long since taken on lives of their own that had nothing to do with Margie, Natalie, Edna, Marilyn, or Janet.

Eddie and Ida went to Palm Springs for two weeks at this point, returning to New York in time for Eddie to begin a series of shows in Veterans Administration and Army hospitals at Kingsbridge Hospital, the Bronx, on Christmas Day, and do his fourth *Colgate Comedy Hour* on New Year's Eve with his guests, Ed Wynn, Danny Thomas, and the composer Sigmund Romberg. Manning Ostroff, an old Cantor hand, replaced Charles Friedman as producer-director the next day. (Friedman became the producer for Abbott and Costello, replacements for Fred Allen in the Colgate lineup. The pace and the reshuffling were frantic; Allen himself wound up a panelist on *What's My Line*, his humor—not to mention his decidedly "unshow biz" looks—unappealing to comedy-variety show viewers of the early 1950s. Cantor, his professional enemy, said Allen's lack of success occurred because "Allen doesn't like the audience, and on TV, they get a chance to see it.")

Cantor's sixth show for Colgate was called "uninspired . . . mainly because of weak scripting. Comic himself, appearing in almost every skit, ran through the show with his usual uninhibited antics, displaying plenty of energy and effort. But, with the exception of the final production number, a reprise of Cantor's Ziegfeld days which paid off nostalgically, the program was seldom lifted off the ground."

A scheduled two-night concert stand at the RKO Theatre in White

Plains was canceled on the advice of Cantor's doctors. Eddie's schedule in the last six months had been truly horrific. Nonetheless, his cancellations were remarkable. Cantor had missed dates before, but not as a precaution. Something was terribly wrong.

Eddie and Ida flew down to Miami Beach for a vacation, ran into a storm, and headed back within a week. Eddie's seventh *Colgate Comedy Hour* rested on a "then and now" routine about how people danced in the old days compared to the then present era. Eddie sang "(Potatoes Are Cheaper—Tomatoes Are Cheaper) Now's the Time to Fall in Love" with the chorus bringing the song up to date by singing, rather drearily, "Potatoes Are Dearer." Lena Horne guested with sensational renditions of "Where or When" and " 'Deed I Do," while Eddie, as "Maxie the Taxi," tried to convince an eight-year-old boy to run away from home. In another bit, Eddie and Charlie Cantor were in drag as two gossipy housewives in a supermarket. *Variety* called it one of Cantor's "best shows yet," but Eddie's dicing and slicing of the same nostalgia formulas was growing a bit tiresome. Cantor's ratings nonetheless continued high, and Colgate soon persuaded him to star for two weeks in a row. Cantor, almost instinctively, accepted and resumed his killing pace. He returned to Miami for three concerts at the Municipal Auditorium, sponsored by the local American Legion post; emceed the Al Jolson Memorial, dedicated to interracial amity, at the Lord Tarleton Hotel on Sunday night, March 5, stayed at the Roney Plaza for a week of "rest"; and did his one-man show at the George Washington Hotel in Jacksonville on March 9 before returning to New York.

The March 25 *Colgate Comedy Hour* was essentially "My Forty Years in Show Business," intercut with a filmed guest appearance by Jimmy Durante. Cantor used his own life story as a peg for a "salute to show business," "for without show business, this could never happen." The program climaxed with a pitch for the United Services Organization, with Secretary of Defense George C. Marshall appearing in a film clip from Washington.

On the following week's program, Cantor presented "bright new talent"—six young professional acts he said would one day rate star billing: the soprano Evelyn Gould, Joel Grey, the baritone William Warfield, Tony & Eddy, the violinist Michelle Auclair, and Marilyn Colby, who performed a duet with Cantor of "How Could You Believe Me . . . When You Know I've Been a Liar All My Life." Cantor brought out Eddie Fisher, who had emerged as a major recording artist, at the finish of the program for a sendoff prior to his army induction.

The new Colgate show—Cantor's third within five weeks—was somewhat below par, although *Variety* called Bob Gari's Judy Holliday impression a "good bit." Eddie felt increasingly run down and shifted more and more of the performing burdens on the *Colgate* show to younger players. The live one-man shows nevertheless continued. Cantor was at Grossinger's for the benefit of the Damon Runyon Cancer Fund on April 25, and the

Knights of Pythias brought him to Pittsburgh for two nights at the Syria Mosque in behalf of the National Foundation for Infantile Paralysis.

The awards also continued. On Thursday, May 3, Eddie was honored "for his efforts to foster mutual understanding among all peoples" at a one hundred dollar-a-plate dinner for the benefit of the New York University Chair of Hebrew Culture and Education at the Waldorf-Astoria Two nights later, the Jewish Theatrical Guild tendered a dinner to Cantor and George Jessel, also at the Waldorf. Eddie received the Williamsburg Settlement's gold medal for "humanitarianism and Americanism" the following evening and the Michael Award "for deep devotion to causes of humanity in stimulating public interest and support of American institutions" the night after that.

After a surprise birthday party for Ida at the Cantors' Sutton Place South apartment and a guest-starring assignment on Jimmy Durante's *Four-Star Revue* on NBC, Eddie turned his full attention to his eleventh show for Colgate. The skits were overlong and not well written; Cantor teamed in two more sketches with Charlie Cantor, one as schoolboys and the other, once again, as women. Eddie's guests included Joel Grey and PFC Eddie Fisher. "Maxie the Taxi" was back for the eighth time.

Cantor could barely speak when he woke up the next morning. By midday, he was in Doctors Hospital with a ruptured blood vessel in his vocal chords. Danny Thomas substituted for him on Milton Berle's *Texaco Star Theatre* the following evening.

Cantor's daughter Janet was then working for Henry Dunn at AGVA.

Somehow, a rumor got out that Eddie Cantor had died. Henry Dunn came over to me in the afternoon, the day after Daddy went in the hospital, and told me that my father was dead. I burst into tears, but I didn't want to believe him. I called my father's room at the hospital and said, "Daddy, I know you can't talk now, but if you're there, please tap three times on the phone." Three taps followed from his end, and so I ran out, got a cab, and ran into his room. I threw my arms around him and told him someone had told me he was dead. He shut his eyes and shook his head and hugged me. All because Henry Dunn wanted to be the big shot who broke the "news."

Eddie was discharged on Tuesday morning, June 5. Not yet entirely recovered, he nonetheless began rehearsals for the next Colgate show and received the degree of doctor of humane letters from Philadelphia's Temple University on June 14.

Eddie Cantor's twelfth and final *Colgate Comedy Hour* of the 1950–51 season had Milton Berle, Jack E. Leonard, and Dagmar (of *Broadway Open House*, forerunner of the *Tonight Show*) as the principal guests, Phil Foster as Maxie the Taxi's passenger, songs by the young Junie Keegan, and appearances by Cantor's daughter Marilyn and Ida. *Variety* called it "an hour of varied entertainment, some good, some bad, that literally threw the book at the viewer, spanning such diversified items as a gratuitous deadpan plug by Cantor on behalf of doctors ('Pay your doctor bills, they've got to eat, too') to a ten-minute tribute to Irving Berlin."

Eddie left for the West Coast a few days later, checking into Cedars of Lebanon Hospital in time for minor surgery on July 3. "Just spent miserable week of surgery," he wired a friend in New York two weeks later. "Returned from hospital feeling much better. Took a bigger cut than anyone at (blank) studio. Hope to be east next month."

Before he left the hospital, extensive tests revealed both the source of Cantor's four-month-old exhaustion and the results of his mad, punishing schedule: he had suffered a "silent" heart attack. "The doctors warned him to slow down at that point," Janet recalls. "But of course, he didn't."

Eddie spent that summer resting at the new Cantor home, a pleasant one-and-a-half-story dwelling at 9360 Monte Leon Lane, adequate but modest when compared to the large house on North Roxbury Drive. The Cantors now had only a cook, a housekeeper, and Maurice on retainer. Gone forever was the wonderful, half-mad atmosphere of the old "Cantor Home for Girls."

Cantor returned to New York looking well rested, and the season's first *Colgate Comedy Hour* opened with a smash production number built around his singing of a new song titled "This Is My New York," by Jerry Seelen and Sy Miller. Ironically, the show marked Eddie's farewell to New York as a performer. The *Colgate Comedy Hour* was going west.

Despite his energy, his comparatively youthful appearance for a man close to sixty, and the work demands he made on himself, Cantor was more conscious of the passing years than perhaps any of his contemporaries, including Ed Wynn, who was roughly five years older. Mindful of the warning he had received from his doctors, Eddie wanted to do TV in a more relaxed atmosphere, and he looked forward to doing the *Colgate Comedy Hour* from the West Coast even more than he had welcomed his move west in radio in 1936.

"It will be particularly beneficial to the not-so-young talent, like myself, Durante, Wynn, and others, who can enjoy the comforts of home and family and free themselves of the unnecessary involvements and confusions attending a New York origination. I can assure you we'll be better as a result."

The first *Colgate Comedy Hour* from the West Coast, on September 30, 1951, was only the second live coast-to-coast telecast in history, the first being the signing of the peace treaty with Japan in San Francisco several weeks earlier. The reception was lauded for its clarity, a vast improvement over the kinescopes West Coast production had necessitated in the past. National TV had arrived.

Instead of traveling to various cities with his one-man show, Cantor now went down to Palm Springs to relax after the program. He had already signed to do a weekly radio show for Philip Morris, a combination of his one-man concert show and an amplified d.j. program in which Eddie used old records as a springboard to tell anecdotes about the greats he'd known through forty years.

The program proved successful in what was left of commercial radio in that uncomfortable period between the desertion of the network shows and the birth of rock 'n' roll. NBC wanted Eddie to expand the show to an hour, hoping to attract more lucrative sponsors if Philip Morris decided to drop out. The program was relatively easy for Cantor to do, assisted, as he was, by Margie, his secretaries, and various TV writers. Cantor, the nation's premiere nostalgist after Jessel, had wanted to do this sort of show for almost three years, and he saw it as great fun, not to mention easy money, after decades of breakneck performing.

Cantor's activity was now confined to his monthly show for Colgate, the weekly half-hour radio program, and occasional outside appearances like the "Bonds For Israel" rally at which he and Lucille Norman entertained. He also did his one-man show at a B'nai B'rith benefit in San Francisco on Saturday night, November 17, grossing $13,800 at the three thousand five hundred-seat Opera House.

Much of the December 9 *Colgate Comedy Hour* was aimed at the audience at the El Toro, California, marine base. Wolf calls greeted the show girls stepping out of sheet music covers as Cantor sang "Dinah," "Ida," "Margie," and "If You Knew Susie." Also on this show was Robert Clary, the Jewish French refugee from a German concentration camp who later became famous as Corporal LeBeau on TV's *Hogan's Heroes*.

Only two weeks later, Eddie was back with a Christmas show. "Cantor," said *Variety*, "who's always been associated with daughters, got entangled with an adopted son, and it didn't come off as anticipated. The novelty of the situation was lost in a mess of over-sentimentality. . . . Stuffy Singer did nicely, though, as the youngster." Bobby Breen, Cantor's original "son," now twenty-five, made an appearance, dueting with his old recording of "Ave Maria," made when he was eight. *Variety* identified the "major adult guest" as "Farley Granger, who maintained the juvenile character of the show by the calibre of the lines allotted to him."

After one more Colgate show, on January 20, with singer-dancer Sharon Baird, Robert Clary, and the Herman McCoy Swing Choir, the Cantors left for New York City. The occasion was Eddie's sixtieth birthday party, held in the grand ballroom of the Hotel Commodore.

Admission to the dinner, which was sponsored by the Greater New York Committee of the State of Israel Bonds, was by purchase of a thousand-dollar Israeli bond. Rudolf G. Sonneborn, president of the American Financial and Development Corporation, which was directing the $500,000 American Israeli bond issue, announced that the event resulted in the sale of $2,616,000 in bonds. Speakers included Vice President Alben W. Barkley, Mayor Vincent Impellitteri, and Walter White, executive secretary of the National Association for the Advancement of Colored People. Eddie was presented with an engraved cable from Prime Minister David Ben-Gurion, who said he hoped Mr. Cantor would continue "to dispense both humor and humanity as generously as before and thus witness the growth of a productive Israel to which you have devoted such efforts." Former American Ambassador to Israel James G. McDonald presented Ida with a silver tray, and Basil O'Connor, president of the National Foundation for Infantile Paralysis, lauded Cantor on behalf of the March of Dimes campaign. Eddie also received a leather-bound volume with hundreds of personal tributes from stars of the entertainment world.

Vice President Barkley, acting on behalf of the Israel bond drive, gave Cantor a gold relief plaque of a map of Israel with the inscription "His life has been a noble testament of devotion and self-sacrifice for the Jewish people and all mankind; his towering achievements for Israel have been an inspiration and a beacon to all American Jews."

In Eddie's honor, the name of lower Henry Street had been temporarily changed to Cantor Street by Manhattan Borough President (later New York Mayor) Robert F. Wagner.

That was Eddie Cantor's sixtieth birthday. His life, from this point on, would run downhill.

Cantor spoke at the thirteenth annual conference of the Council of Organizations of the United Jewish Appeal of Greater New York at the Hotel Astor on Sunday, February 3, 1952. He and Ida then returned to California, where Eddie joined rehearsals for the Colgate show of February 17. It would be an especially noteworthy show, from the standpoints of entertainment, history, and race relations.

The guests included Sharon Baird (her third straight Cantor Colgate program), Doris Singleton, and the Will Mastin Trio, composed of Mastin (a veteran showman, fourteen years older than Cantor), Sammy Davis, and the twenty-six-year-old Sammy Davis Jr.

Davis, brought up in show business, could do "everything" and do it with panache—sing, dance, do impressions, and play several instruments. He was, in short, a phenomenal performer, destined for quick stardom. Davis gave an all-out performance on the Colgate show and stood there, smiling and perspiring as a more than impressed Cantor came on, joining the applause.

Cantor, ever the showman, took the handkerchief from his breast pocket, the handkerchief that had become a symbol of his own performance, waved behind him as he made his exit at the close of countless upbeat songs, and mopped young Sammy's forehead.

The next day, Janet presented Eddie with his second grandson, Brian

Milo, in New York. Eddie was again ecstatic. He was not prepared for what would follow in the next few days in the wake of Davis's appearance.

Vicious, racist mail poured in to NBC. ("Eddie Cantor: How dare you mop that coon's face with your handkerchief on national TV?") Cantor still remembered Bert Williams's words at New Year's, but he had never seen the ugly feelings that were exposed in these letters. Even the mail received by R. J. Reynolds after Eddie's speech on Father Coughlin did not have the naked viciousness that these contained.

Cantor was a rather naive man in many respects. Things—and people— seemed, to him, divided sharply into "good" (his grandmother, benefits, chocolate) and "bad" (anti-Semites like Hitler, Coughlin, and people who opposed Israel). He had grown up with a Jewish Russian immigrant woman who spoke virtually no English, in a largely Jewish neighborhood, and gone into a business that was practically a world unto itself. The show world, to be sure, was often harsh. But Cantor himself had lived a very blessed, almost fairytale life in which he had experienced few serious wrongs; those he had committed had been seemingly forgiven by his grandmother or Ida.

The choice was easy now. The bigots had thrown down the gauntlet, and Cantor, the crusader, could not possibly back down. He had said the Mastin Trio would be back on his next program. Now he told the same to NBC, to Colgate, and to his writers. Let the racists do their worst.

In the meantime, Eddie and Ida went to Miami Beach, where Cantor raised $11,340,000 for the UJA in a single luncheon at the Saxony Hotel. The Cantors then went to New York to see their newest grandchild, leaving the following Tuesday for another UJA luncheon in Houston. It was then back to Los Angeles for the *Colgate Comedy Hour* of March 16 before a studio audience made up almost entirely of U.S. Air Force personnel.

It was one of Cantor's best shows of the season, emphasizing straight variety rather than production and skits. "Guest lineup," said *Variety*,

> was topped by Dorothy Kirsten, who scored solidly in both her vocal chores and the comedy skits, in which she displayed a neat and per- sonable ability to gag it up. But it was Sammy Davis, Jr., fronting the Will Mastin Trio, who walked away with the guesting honors, repeating the socko work he did on Cantor's last previous show. Spot- ted in two places on the bill, he wowed with his versatility in terping, singing, impersonations and the like. Latter bit, incidentally, also gave Cantor a chance to make with the miming, and he handled his impressions okay.

Eddie even mopped Sammy's face with his handkerchief again.

Cantor's next *Colgate Comedy Hour*, done before the armored tank corps of Camp Irwin, California, at El Capitan Theatre four weeks later, featured Joe E. Brown as the principal guest star, but his "brief stints were accompanied by off-timing and fluffs that failed to salvage the portions in which he worked. Otherwise, this was a show that was pretty notable for the energy exhibited by the veteran star, Cantor, who never lets up for a moment."

Those words became especially appropriate on April 29, when Cantor opened a new concert tour in behalf of the American Red Cross at the Naval Recreation Auditorium in Boston. Admission was a pint of blood, and Eddie played to an overflow crowd of nearly five thousand, with hundreds more kept out because of the fire laws. The trip had come about when Natalie complained she was the only one on line to give blood at the Red Cross Bank. Eddie made a few phone calls and found there was, indeed, a blood shortage that year.

Doctors had warned him not to undertake this tour, but Eddie did not listen. Lung ailments—tuberculosis, pleurisy, pneumonia—were still the health threats Cantor feared. Margie was the only one who ever feared Eddie would die of a heart attack. And Margie, Eddie well knew, *always* worried. He did the tour, following the Boston date with appearances in Baltimore, Pittsburgh, Cincinnati, Cleveland, Buffalo, and Chicago.

Eddie made an appearance at the American Heart Association rally in St. Louis on May 6 and then took the train back to California. In Buffalo he had revealed plans for a blood donor circuit with at least a hundred entertainers.

The tour had brought in sixty-three thousand pints of blood. Cantor had paid his own expenses. He would pay much more within the next six months.

After more radio shows and a *Colgate Comedy Hour* on which Cantor appeared as himself, Maxie the Taxi, a boxer, and an old man in the park, Eddie did more one-man shows for the blood banks in San Jose and Oakland. His twelfth and final Colgate show of the season, coming on the eve of his thirty-eighth wedding anniversary, turned out to be one of his best shows of the season. He and Ida stepped out of a wedding cake to renew their wedding vows at the start of the program, and Eddie serenaded her with "Ida, Sweet as Apple Cider" on a traveling piano at the program's end.

So ended Cantor's second season for Colgate-Palmolive. Not as consistently successful as his first, it nonetheless satisfied the sponsors and most long-time Cantor fans who did not mind his increased reliance on nostalgia, lack of comic focus, and increasingly tired singing voice.

Eddie took part in a Friars testimonial dinner tribute to Judy Garland at the Biltmore Bowl on Sunday, June 29, and rested for the balance of the summer. He had another Red Cross tour planned for the fall and had worked out a new deal for *Then and Now*. Cantor had become a huge stockholder in the new Welch Wine and, not wanting it to seem that he was trying to get rich by hawking his own product under the guise of sponsorship, refused to have Welch replace Philip Morris. The show would now be done as a sustainer.

Cantor, still thinking that no job was either too big or too small, began the season with a three-day stint as guest star of the Fifth Annual Package Store Dealers Convention in San Antonio, August 24–26, 1952. His first *Colgate Comedy Hour* was scheduled for September 28, with Dorothy Lamour, long a Cantor favorite, Eddie Fisher, and the Will Mastin Trio as guests. Cantor rehearsed long and hard, determined to begin the season with a great show that would rival the first programs of his first season for Colgate.

As work proceeded, an event in the life of one of Eddie's daughters took place that would affect not just the Colgate show, but Cantor's life as well. An operation to remove a scar on Edna's chin that had been left by a mastoid operation was performed two days before the Colgate show was taped. Eddie was at Cedars as his daughter, bandaged at the chin but semiconscious, her face a ghastly white, was wheeled past him to recovery.

It was a new experience for Eddie. He had been shielded from having to cope with others' injuries, from scraped knees to Edna's serious automobile accident in 1937, by either Margie or career demands. This time, the reality hit home. His daughters were not little girls who never grew up. They were real, mortal people.

Later, home on Monte Leon Lane, Eddie collapsed into tears.

He experienced chest pains shortly before airtime on Sunday. Cantor went on with the program, which Helm of *Variety* said "sped through the Sabbath hour with sparks of wit flying in all directions." Lamour worked well in two skits and Sammy Davis Jr. further established himself as "one of the great talents in show biz." Cantor was rushed to the office-home of his physician, Dr. Julius Kahn, when the program was finished. Kahn took an electrocardiograph that showed no alarming symptoms, and the Cantors, both relieved, went to Yom Kippur services.

Arriving home, they went to their respective bedrooms, Eddie's earliest bedtime in years. At 4 A.M., he was awakened by severe chest pains. Attempting to arise, Eddie found that he had trouble breathing.

He half-crawled to Ida's room, got the door open, and awakened her with gasps and moans. Panic-stricken, Ida reached for the phone and called, not Eddie's doctor or an ambulance, but Margie.

At this, the moment Margie had been dreading since the age of nine, she stayed calm and worked quickly, calling for an ambulance, alerting Dr. Kahn, throwing on her clothes, and rushing to her parents' home.

She got there before the ambulance and had Eddie lie down. When the ambulance arrived, about five minutes later, the stunned medics made him sit up; lying down, they said, was bad for the victims of heart attacks. It was one of the few big mistakes regarding her father that Margie ever made.

Kahn was joined by his associate, Dr. Edward Shapiro, at Cedars of Lebanon Hospital. The two physicians then brought in Dr. Eliot Corday as consultant.

Another electrocardiogram showed definite damage to the heart. Kahn told newsmen that Cantor had "collapsed" due to "complete exhaustion" and been brought to the hospital "for observation" and a "complete rest." There was no sense in wrecking Cantor's image by saying that the ageless "Apostle of Pep" had suffered a major heart attack.

A six-week stay at Cedars was essential. No phone calls were permitted, and no visitors allowed. One week into his stay, Corday told Cantor some good news: he now could sit up and dangle his legs over the side of the bed.

Eddie did so. The "Apostle of Pep" had come full cycle.

## Chapter 14

# `` . . . AND YOU HAVE TO GIVE IT ALL BACK''

*"I don't want to die a rich man."*

Cantor was depressed, "first because I thought I was dying, then because I realized I wasn't. How could I ever entertain again? How could I raise money or sell bonds if I couldn't get around to make people laugh?"

Although he had increasingly become more of a humanitarian and show-man than a performer, Cantor nonetheless had been an entertainer for more than forty years and had been identified with energy and youth. Many of his older contemporaries had died in the past half dozen years—W. C. Fields, Al Jolson, Fanny Brice. Will Rogers had been dead for seventeen years and Bert Williams for thirty. Cantor found himself asking why Jolson, victim of a heart attack, and Brice, who had died of a burst embolism, had died while he had lived. He asked it in the same way he had asked why he had been sent to Surprise Lake Camp and why he had become a rich, famous entertainer while another boy from the East Side had wound up in the electric chair. The answer, as he saw it, was the act of an essentially benign universe. God was good, the world was good (with a few villains), and God had spared his life in the same way that "somebody" (the good people who founded and ran the Educational Alliance) had sent him to Surprise Lake Camp in 1903.

Cantor never *stopped*, and if his body could not function, his mind worked all the harder. His incapacitation forced him to reflect on his life, past and present. There were, presumably, regrets. But surely his involve-ment with performers' unions and humanitarian efforts had more than made up for whatever sins he had committed.

Cantor doubtless saw himself as one of those slightly wayward young-sters played by Mickey Rooney at Metro-Goldwyn-Mayer—someone who proved himself to be on the side of the angels by some noble deed before the film's conclusion. Life, to Eddie Cantor, was like an M-G-M movie—with a few aspects that could not be shown in films. Ida, as he saw it, lived a great life, enjoyed her fame and privileged position, and was mother to five girls, each of whom was happy. No, Eddie could tell himself, he had done very well.

Even the depression that had gripped him when the thought occurred that he would never entertain again now faded as the letters came—from governors and mayors, from General Dwight D. Eisenhower aboard his presidential campaign train, hundreds of letters from servicemen, ex-servicemen, and civilians, many of them fans since the days of the *Follies*.

> There were letters from people telling me that they'd just con-
> tributed to the blood bank because they knew I wanted that work to
> go on. There were letters advising me to take it easy, not to jump up
> and down when I came back. They were praying for me, they said.
> Ida heard from one church where a hundred people had that day
> lighted candles—for me. Can you imagine what this does for a guy
> flat on his back? Every letter was like a blood transfusion. I'd heard
> laughter and applause, sure, for forty-five years; but I hadn't realized
> that there was love behind the laughter.

Nor, indeed, had any entertainer's illness brought forth this kind of a response from the public. Cantor was now reaping—on his back, as he would emphasize—the rewards of the persona he had put forth on the radio.

Ida, Marjorie, Natalie, and Edna were at the hospital daily. Marilyn and Janet flew in from New York. Jimmy Durante made a number of trips, sitting in the corridor outside Eddie's room at first, when there were no visitors allowed, then coming in to bring Eddie his warm and truly genuine good cheer. Predictably, Abe Lastfogel came, too.

Lastfogel cared about his clients, and his trip to Cantor's bedside was more than cynical professionalism. It was Cantor who asked him to assure Colgate that he would be back on the air for them in January.

In November, Eddie left the hospital and gradually returned to work. Fortunately, he had taped a number of *Show Business—Then and Now* radio shows before the near-fatal heart attack. By December 1, he had taped half a dozen more shows and discussed material for his next *Colgate Comedy Hour*.

There was other work as well. Shortly before his heart attack, Cantor had made preliminary recordings, accompanied only by a piano, for *The Eddie Cantor Story*, a picture that, at long last, was to go into production.

The phenomenal success of Columbia's *The Jolson Story*, released in the fall of 1946, led Jack Warner, who had lost out on the Jolson picture, to secure the rights to Cantor's story. The actual deal with Warner Bros., by which Eddie would receive one-third of all profits on *The Eddie Cantor*

*Story*, was set by Abe Lastfogel in June 1947, with Cantor receiving a fifty-thousand-dollar advance for working with the writers. Then titled *All My Life*, the movie was to star a young unknown as Cantor, with Eddie supplying his offscreen voice for the songs.

Gordon MacRae, then a Warner contract player, was set for the role of Cantor six months later as part of a new deal that guaranteed Cantor one million dollars, spread out over ten years. These plans were scuttled when Warners' script department could not come up with a suitable story line.

A renewed effort in the fall of 1948 brought Cantor to the Warner lot in Burbank almost every day to talk with writers. Eddie said he wanted to make the story as accurate as possible—"taking the halo off my noggin."

Musical "biopics" of those days did not—could not—tell the truth about their subjects. Movies were about ideals, and no one thought to deal with Cantor's rumored marital infidelity, frequent hypocrisy, or haranguing of subordinates. "Taking the halo off my noggin" did not mean self-flagellation.

Jack Warner dropped the project in November 1948, convinced that a two-million-dollar project was too risky for the times. Two months later, Sidney Skolsky, who had sold Columbia's Harry Cohn on doing *The Jolson Story*, teamed with Eddie to produce the picture independently, but no progress was made until late 1951, when Warner picked up the project and made Skolsky the associate producer. Margie, from the day that Sidney first became involved, thought of *The Eddie Cantor Story* as "her" picture. The film would be a monument to Daddy, with her and her sisters dealt with fleetingly, at best.

Within four months, it was announced that Keefe Brasselle would play the title role in *The Eddie Cantor Story*, with production due to start on June 1, 1952. Inevitable delays postponed the project to the following season.

In December, Cantor made the final tracks that would be used in the production. He recorded twenty songs, his standards from the twenties, including "If You Knew Susie," "Makin' Whoopee," "Margie," "Bye, Bye, Blackbird," "Ma," and "Yes Sir, That's My Baby," plus the inevitable "Ida," "Josephine, Please No Lean on the Bell," and others. (Missing were "You'd Be Surprised" and "Dinah.") The musical arrangements were first rate, and the vocals were better than might be expected, considering that Cantor had suffered a major heart attack less than three months earlier and that his voice had lost its former brilliance after World War II. Production was now set for January, with Brasselle as Cantor and Marilyn Erskine as Ida.

Cantor's return to the Colgate show was made almost anticlimactic by the fact that his three major segments—a "Maxie the Taxi" sketch with Arnold Stang, a well-enacted wedding pantomime with Dinah Shore, and a re-creation of him and Dinah performing for the GIs at San Francisco's Presidio in 1943—were done on film. Cantor did not move much, looked tired in his few live segments, and relied, more than ever, on nostalgic reminiscing.

Ida had insisted on filming. "I want a 'live' husband," she had said, not dreaming—or caring—that film would come to dominate TV within the next ten years. After the show, the Cantors went down to Palm Springs, arriving back in Hollywood for Eddie's sixty-first birthday on January 31.

Cantor's next *Colgate Comedy Hour*, on February 15, relied less on his own performing talents and more on those of his guests. There was another "Maxie the Taxi," a child impressionist named Danny Richards, a GI skit with Hal March and Tom D'Andrea, and a segment with Frank Loesser in which he and Eddie dueted on "Baby, It's Cold Outside"—all of it on film.

Another vacation in Palm Springs was followed by negotiations with Charles Barry of NBC. The network, knowing Cantor might retire, tempted him to sign for one more season at a huge increase in pay. Cantor's ratings remained high, and the *Colgate Comedy Hour* was still opposite *The Talk of the Town*. Eddie signed, hoping that he would return to normal after a rest in the summer.

George Jessel and Harry Ruby were Cantor's *Colgate* guests on March 15, and the singers Connie Russell and Billy Daniels made their second appearances. One week later, Eddie returned for a special all-star 100th edition of the *Colgate Comedy Hour*, with Bob Hope, Donald O'Connor, Abbott and Costello, and Martin and Lewis. Three weeks later, he was back in his regular slot with Gloria Grahame, the Will Mastin Trio (in their fourth appearance), and Russell, whom Eddie optimistically signed to a seven-year personal management contract.

Cantor spent the summer resting. Marilyn and Janet came in from New York to see him, and the usual arguments ensued regarding politics, the latest styles, marriage, children, and the changing tastes in entertainment. "I was always being told not to upset him, but I said I'd tell him if he was wrong, and that was it," remembers Janet. Eddie, though, had reason to be in good spirits. *The Eddie Cantor Story*, Warners told him, was a certain winner, and Cantor felt that his career, and his life, would be rejuvenated once the picture was released.

Cantor's fourth season for Colgate started on October 18, 1953, with Jack Benny as the guest. The show was good enough, but nothing like the *Colgate Comedy Hours* of 1950–52. Nor was Eddie the same Cantor.

Eddie Fisher was on the next show, with Frank Sinatra as a surprise guest. A sequence on a surviving kinescope shows Cantor seated on the edge of the stage, talking with the audience. Eddie holds his left arm as he rises, as if suffering a stroke. He looks impatient, angry with himself and with the world for his obvious discomfort and inability to perform.

Two weeks later, Cantor announced that he was not resigning with NBC and was through with hour shows on television. "It's become increasingly difficult to get good material, especially when writers take time off between shows. They get out of the mood. The hour show is too fatiguing on the performer, and takes too much out of him. By filming one half-hour show weekly, I can deliver a better show, one not so wearing on physical effort."

*The Eddie Cantor Story*, in the meantime, was set to premiere in New York on December 23, the same night Eddie would be the subject of Ralph Edwards's *This Is Your Life*.

As Cantor's heart attack made him a risky candidate for any surprise show, he became the only subject in the history of *This Is Your Life* to be told well in advance about the program—a fact Edwards revealed before Cantor walked onstage.

Danny Lipsky was the first "voice from the past." He was certainly not a voice of the Cantor present, having been unwelcome in the Cantor home for years. Ida, his arch-enemy, was next, followed by George Jessel and Jimmy Durante. A live segment from New York, where crowds were lined up for the premiere of *The Eddie Cantor Story*, introduced Margie, Marilyn, and Janet.

Margie, looking uncomfortable in one of her few public appearances, recited a tribute to "Daddy," followed by an ad-libbed crack by Marilyn: "She remembered her lines!" Margie, far from happy, turned away as Edwards introduced her younger sister. Marilyn was the performer among the daughters, and she had made sure no one could deny it.

After Natalie, Michael, Edna, and Judy came out to embrace Eddie in Hollywood, the scene shot back to New York City. Eddie Fisher was there, paying tribute to his benefactor, as was Keefe Brasselle.

"Keefe," said Cantor, via hookup, "if this film does not make you a major star, I don't know what. Congratulations and best wishes."

*The Eddie Cantor Story* rolled, and the results were devastating—an embarrassing indictment of Warner Bros., if not the entire studio system.

Brasselle looked and acted like a caricature of Eddie Cantor—pop eyes produced by spirit gum and ears that made him look like a cross between Eddie and Dick York of *Bewitched* fame. Adding to the ludicrousness was the way Brasselle played his subject in the picture's off-stage scenes: bugging his eyes and speaking in a voice that sounded more like Henry Aldrich than Eddie Cantor. Cast in what had been hyped as a triumph, Brasselle seemed like a third-rate entertainer giving a bad Cantor imitation on the Gus Sun time in Steubenville, Ohio.

Almost as bad was the script. After describing young Cantor's rise in early-twentieth-century show business—the film had Eddie with Gus Edwards's troupe as a preadolescent—and the death of "Grandma Esther" (there is a total absence of ethnic flavoring), the film degenerates into a bad imitation of *The Jolson Story*, with Cantor focused totally on his career, "neglecting" his wife and five daughters. The film asserts that after Cantor's heart attack, which brings him to his "senses," he finds new purpose in performing for charity (this despite the fact that Cantor had done an enormous amount of benefit and charity work since World War I and was forced to dramatically *decrease* this activity following his heart attack).

Reviewers of the 1950s rarely trashed the films of major studios with the incisive vehemence they would deploy in later years. *The Eddie Cantor Story*, nonetheless, did not receive the raves that Cantor, Skolsky, Warners, or Brasselle had eagerly anticipated. There were, in fact, a fair number of pans.

Margie, who took every setback to her father as a personal loss, was frankly devastated. Skolsky was her lover, and she felt that she, as well as he, had let her father down. The picture depressed Eddie, too. Before it opened, he had thought Brasselle was "marvelous." Gradually, after having seen the picture two or three times, the novelty of being the subject wore off, and he viewed Brasselle's performance as a totally absurd impression and the script as a labored remake of *The Jolson Story*. When he realized the flaws in the production, he could only comment on how the project had gotten totally away from both himself and Sidney Skolsky.

Cantor walked through the next Colgate show in New York with his guests, Dennis Day, George Gobel, Donald O'Connor, and Durante, and attended the opening of the Greater New York March of Dimes campaign at Gracie Mansion on Tuesday night, January 5, 1954. Talks with NBC, the major purpose of the trip for Eddie, were less fruitful. Eddie needed a less taxing work load, but he also wanted money he could not get from the network for a weekly thirty-minute filmed show. He returned to the West Coast, disgusted and in doubt about his future in show business.

Eddie pushed himself through three more shows for Colgate over the next fifteen weeks. Many of his segments were now filmed, but the scheduling pressures of live TV were still too much for Cantor's damaged heart. His contract was expiring, and Eddie did not want any renewals. Neither, at this point, did Colgate; the show's ratings had slipped badly.

In July, it was announced that Cantor had been signed to produce and host thirty-nine half-hour filmed TV shows for Ziv Television Programs. He himself would star in one-third of the programs, and Ziv held a yearly option to renew. It marked the first time a major star had deserted the major networks for a syndicated program. The contract, calling for a similar number of radio variety programs, was easily the largest of its kind in TV history, involving, as it did, a total investment of more than nine million dollars over the seven-year life of the contract.

The radio shows made sense, as transcribed programs had been enjoying good local sales, in contrast to the remaining network product. Cantor's old radio scripts were polished up, rewritten, and recycled, with Ziv providing a full orchestra, Eddie's former announcer, Jimmy Wallington, and supporting talent—four unknowns named Patti, Dorothy, Roy, and Ronnie. The radio shows were transcribed at the rate of three a week.

Thirteen TV shows were filmed that summer, and the syndicated *Eddie Cantor Comedy Theatre* made its first appearance on home TV screens early in February 1955. The first episode, titled "Now in Rehearsal," had a variety-show format. It was basically *The Colgate Comedy Hour* on film, complete with Eddie playing his own passenger in "Maxie the Taxi."

It all looked tired. The idea of Eddie "having his own theatre" seemed hopelessly contrived, and the cleverness and energy that had made "The Mayor of Texaco Town" viable in 1937 were absent in the writing and performing. Eddie did his best, rolling his eyes and seeming to be very interested in his new "theatre," but everything he did, especially the old songs, only underscored the fact he was an old man going through the motions. Moreover, scripts of the succeding shows—those that Cantor starred in and those he merely hosted—were lame and uninspired. *The Eddie Cantor Comedy Theatre* looked like fake, low-budget show biz—a big deal over nothing. Eddie personally rewrote script after script but made little change in the results.

As if to get his mind off of the Ziv shows, Cantor turned his attention to writing a book. The failure of *The Eddie Cantor Story* had led him to consider a new autobiography. Late that January, around the time of his "official" sixty-third birthday, he saw "The Story I've Never Told," a piece on the film star Joan Crawford in *The Women's Home Companion*, and contacted the author, Jane Kesner Ardmore.

Jane, the author of two novels (*Women, Inc.*, and a Civil War story called *Julia*) in addition to her magazine work, lunched with Cantor in late February. "Eddie has also read my stories on Fred Allen and Jack Benny," Jane wrote her family on March 10, "and wants me to do a story on him. It may be a book possibility. He's a fascinating man, talks a mile a minute, and has anecdotes every second. He would be easy to work with."

"The first time I went to see him," Jane recalls, "we had lunch."

Then he took me into the den and we had a long talk. When I asked if I could use a remark of his to the effect that Fred Allen was a bust on television because he hates people and they know it, whereas Durante loves people and they know it, he said, "Janie, one thing about me—nothing I ever say is off the record."

I was ill for a week. Then I went back, had lunch with Eddie again, told him I thought that he had book material, and gave him what I thought should be the title—*Take My Life*. My idea was to organize the chapters into groupings like "The Women in My Life," "The Men in My Life," "The Rest of My Life," which would be about politics and fund-raising, and "The Best of My Life," which would be about the development of his personal philosophy following his heart attack.

I usually saw Eddie twice or three times weekly. He would always open the front door himself and then ask, "What are we gonna talk about today?" If he knew we were going to discuss W. C. Fields, for example, he would open the door and do an imitation of Fields. He really got into whatever we were doing.

He was a very vital guy, and the words just poured out of him. He talked very, very rapidly, and I quickly realized I'd need a stenographer to take down what he said. When I told him that, he said, "Why not use mine?"

Olive Kelsie thus took down, in shorthand, everything that Cantor said and gave her typewritten transcriptions to Jane Kesner Ardmore. The interviews proceeded for six months, Eddie talking about topics ranging from his work for charities to Ida and their daughters.

His heart attack had softened Eddie, made him more reflective. He still, however, believed what he wanted to believe. All the girls were happy with their lives. Natalie was "the kindest person I know and a born mother." Janet had "a beautifully successful marriage."

Jane Kesner Ardmore did not ask questions about Eddie's rumored affairs with women, from Ziegfeld chorines to Joan Davis. It was Eddie's story, told in his own words, and not a public confession. Nor did publishers, much less the public, want anything more damning or revealing. It was the 1950s, a decade of "normalcy," of quiet reassurance in the face of an uncertain world of H-bombs and an undercurrent of youth culture and rebellion set to erupt in the sixties. Even the tongue-in-cheek raciness of the 1920s that had permitted Eddie to recall honestly his youthful affair with Fania had been replaced by a gentle haziness that allowed only a brief, cryptic reference to his being "involved" with a girl of nineteen when he first met Ida. This time, Eddie said he left the girl for Bubba's meatballs after only "a few days."

He tried to tell Jane, and the readers, that there were "just as many divorces in Newark" as there were in Beverly Hills and pointed out the number of stars, like himself, who had been married to the same person for twenty-five years or more. Show business had nothing to do with having a happy marriage.

It was all so reassuring, so nostalgic. Even the chapters that dealt with what now would be termed Cantor's "activism" were sanitized, the threats the Cantor family had received in the '30s long forgotten.

In retrospect, not all the shows of *The Eddie Cantor Comedy Theatre* were wholly without merit. "The Play Pen," starring Edward Arnold as a baby furniture kingpin who gets even with the partner who had framed him by turning the prison workplace into a rival factory, was a solid blending of good concept, solid writing, and fine acting. There was also "Commercially Ever After," starring Eddie as himself (the role he played in all his starring

Ziv shows), the star of a weekly network variety show who makes up a fictitious sponsor when he finds none are available for the new season.

Most, however, were embarrassing affairs, a waste of film and airtime. Far fewer local stations bought the show than Ziv had anticipated, and the company made little protest when Cantor offered to buy out their options.

So ended the Ziv shows—Cantor's most excruciating professional failure.

Eddie went to New York in September 1955 and appeared at a "miniature" USO Camp Shows fund-raiser on a stand at the northeast corner of West Thirty-sixth Street and Seventh Avenue at noon on Wednesday, the fourteenth. The major purpose of the trip, however, was to be with Janet, whose second child was born three days later. It was a daughter, named Amanda.

"We named her that so we could call her 'Mandy,' like the song," Janet recalls. "But we never did; the nurse at the hospital said her name, 'Amanda Gari,' was musical; I guess she thought it sounded like a Spanish guitar." Amanda, who would be only nine when her grandfather died, would have a special bond with him. Slight and dark, with large eyes, she was the only member of the family who looked like Eddie. He doted on her as much as his failing health permitted in his nine remaining years.

Back in L.A., Eddie suffered troubles with his prostate two months later (the press reported he had kidney stones) and was forced to cancel what would have been his first live TV appearance in two years—a guest shot on Milton Berle's *Texaco Star Theatre* the following Tuesday, November 29. His doctors wanted Cantor to enter Cedars of Lebanon, but Eddie, who said he'd had enough of hospitals, persuaded them to let him remain at home under his wife's care. A few hours later, he was rushed to Cedars for observation and treatment. An operation was finally begun on Tuesday, December 6, and quickly aborted when Eddie went into shock on the operating table.

Cantor, under heavy bundles to protect him from the cold, was taken from the operating room on a stretcher. At one end were two nurses, monitoring the I.V. bottles. At the other were two doctors, monitoring Eddie, who looked tiny and pathetic in the middle of it all.

Eddie saw his daughter Margie, terror-stricken, as they went into the hall. Quickly putting aside his own panic, he beckoned Margie.

She rushed over and leaned down to hear what she thought might be her father's last words. "Guess what?" he said. "We won first prize. Best float in the Rose Bowl Parade."

Eddie's deteriorating heart, coupled with his gall bladder condition, made him a prisoner of diet. The list of prohibitions now included fried foods, fish, eggs, liquor (no great loss to Eddie), almost all delicatessen food (a big loss), and most sweets (a still bigger one). Eddie moaned.

"He's just doing beautifully," Ida told the press. "The doctors are pleased, and he is singing and talking and acting gay. I'd love to keep him in the hospital for a week, but he's too frisky, I'm afraid. He'll probably be out in four or five days."

It was the same line she had used since Eddie's heart attack three years earlier. No one wanted an entertainer who could no longer perform. A strong front was essential. If Eddie wanted to be candid when the crisis passed, as he had been after his heart attack, then that was up to him.

Cantor stayed in Cedars until the day before Christmas.

Margie left for New York as soon as Eddie was out of danger. After New Year's party at Gari and Janet's, she passed out on the bed by 3 A.M.

"Margie seemed about the same as always," recalled Janet "but she talked about some trouble she'd had on the coast that fall. One morning, she'd had trouble putting on one of her stockings because her knee was swollen. Her doctor said she had phlebitis and had recommended treatment. That was all we knew at the beginning of 1956."

That year, Jane Kesner Ardmore took the notes Olive Kelsie had kept and wrote the book *Take My Life*. The "Women in My Life" section had chapters on "Grandma Esther," "Ida," "Fanny Brice," and "The Girls from Show Business." "The Girls" (meaning his daughters) were relegated to "The Rest of My Life," as, indeed, they always had been. Margie, in accordance with the public "Cantor's daughters" image (and her parents' sense of family democracy), shared equal space with her four sisters.

It was a classic case of a ghost writer's setting down exactly what the star would have written. But unlike David Freedman, Jane had made the book sound as if it truly had been written by Eddie Cantor. Thanks to Olive Kelsie's excellence at shorthand, in large measure it had been.

In March, a few weeks after Margie's return to the West Coast, Eddie made his first professional appearance since his prostate trouble, appearing in an episode of *The Louella Parsons Show* titled "Climax." The effort was a modest one, but Cantor liked the possibilities it raised.

He'd hated the Ziv shows, been completely disappointed by *The Eddie Cantor Story*, and realized that his days as a full-force musical comedy performer in any medium were over. The solution seemed to be to go back to the route he had explored in *Forty Little Mothers* and become a "dramatic" actor.

To that end, he signed a one-year contract with the William Morris Agency on April 10, 1956. The six-page form contract listed Abe Lastfogel, Bert Allenberg, Sam Weisbord, and Morris Stoller as Cantor's agents under the Morris umbrella.

Within a week, the Morris office had him signed to star in a film version of *The Fifth Season*, a comedy Menasha Skulnik had starred in on Broadway. It would be an independent venture, produced by Gregory Ratoff but distributed by Twentieth Century-Fox.

Eddie arrived in New York on Thursday, April 25, but left for a speaking engagement at Brandeis University the following day. He was also guest speaker at the Greater Boston Defend Israel Dinner at the Hotel Statler on Saturday night.

"You don't tell a kid after its born, 'You're out on your own,' " he said. "Our good President Eisenhower and our secretary of state, Mr. [John Foster] Dulles, believe a mighty arsenal is a deterrent to war. If that's good enough for the U.S., then it's good enough for Israel, too." Eddie also spoke at Israeli bond rallies in Paterson, New Jersey, and Baltimore.

Cantor spent the next two weeks in talks regarding *The Fifth Season*, the publication of *Take My Life* by Doubleday, and other business matters. He had at least one conference with Hubbell Robinson Jr. about doing a drama titled "Sizeman and Son" on CBS's *Playhouse 90* in the fall. Cantor was already studying the script for "George Has a Birthday," an upcoming comedy on NBC's half-hour *Matinee Theatre*.

While Eddie went from one conference to another, Ida was stricken with what was first reported as "a mild coronary thrombosis" at the Essex House apartment. Taken to Mount Sinai Hospital for treatment, she was found to have an insufficient heartbeat. Margie promptly flew in from the coast, while Eddie made plans to return to California. "George Has a Birthday" would be done live from Hollywood on Monday, June 11.

"George Has a Birthday," which featured Lillian Bronson, Madeline Holmes, and Mae Clarke, was an innocuous playlet about a mild elevator operator who comes into an inheritance on his fifty-fifth birthday. The script, more suited to a thirty-minute episode of *Alfred Hitchcock Presents* than to a full hour presentation, required little acting effort on Eddie's part. Its nominal acceptance by the public nonetheless encouraged him, and he plunged into the script for "Sizeman and Son" with, perhaps, more confidence than might have been deserved.

Ida, having flown in from New York, was checked into Cedars of Lebanon Hospital. Pacemakers were not yet available; the prescription then was a costly month-long stay for "observation." Released in August, Ida resumed her painting, undisturbed, while Margie entered the same hospital for an operation on the lump behind her knee. It had failed to respond to treatment, but neither Margie nor her doctors were prepared for what was found.

The lump was cancerous. Margie had a sarcoma, a type of cancer physicians of the time were powerless to cure. The removal of the lump, they now told Margie, would give her a period of remission—three months, six months, or perhaps a year. It was almost certain to return.

Margie kept the news to herself and, with doctors' assurances that the news would be kept private, left Cedars of Lebanon. Her sister Natalie knew the truth, but Margie did not tell her friends, her other sisters, or—especially—her parents.

On October 5, with work on "Sizeman" in its final stages, Edward R. Murrow invaded Monte Leon Lane for his CBS-TV program, *Person to Person*, a weekly show on which Murrow interviewed, by remote hookup, a star in his or her own home. Eddie was shown on his patio, chatting amiably and proceeding in to where Ida—"The Duchess," as he called her—was knitting on the sofa. References to Cantor's upcoming performance in "Sizeman and Son" on *Playhouse 90* were carefully included.

"Sizeman," which also featured Nan Boardman, Mona Freeman, and Peter Lorre, showed Eddie "acting" (too obviously, one feels) his part as the owner of a garment house whose son (played by Farley Granger), returned from Army duty overseas, harbors both writing ambitions and left-wing ideals.

The kind critical reaction led Eddie to make plans for more such acting roles. Plans for *The Fifth Season* were scuttled by top-level brass at Twentieth Century-Fox, but Jackie Gleason, a long-time admirer of Cantor's, devoted his January 12 variety show to a Cantor birthday tribute called "At Sixty-Five."

Gleason did not appear on the program, broadcast live from L.A. starring Cantor. Eddie's opening song, "Waiting for the Robert E. Lee," segued into a production number. At one point, Cantor seemed to lose the orchestra and "talk" the song for a few lines. Visibly disgruntled at the song's conclusion, he said he usually complained that the orchestra was too loud. "This time," he said, "I couldn't hear it."

It was true, but no musicians were at fault. It took a few scenes, including a good number called "That's My Daughter—That's My Dad," performed with Marilyn, before Eddie realized he was having another heart attack.

He did one scene late in the show from a chair, apologizing to the audience but giving no indication he was experiencing an attack. Following the program, an ambulance took Eddie to the hospital, with Marilyn beside him.

Cantor, in the words of his physician, Dr. Elliot Corday, "sat up and enjoyed a good breakfast" at Cedars of Lebanon the following morning. Press releases said that Eddie had collapsed from "exhaustion." Those close to the scene knew better.

Cantor was released a few days later, with increased warnings against "getting upset" and the usual admonitions to "take it easy." Four weeks later, the Cantors left Beverly Hills for Miami Beach, where Eddie's birthday was celebrated, fifteen days late, at a special dinner session of the Israel Bond Organization at the Fontainbleau Hotel.

Former President Harry Truman, the keynote speaker, sharply criticized the Eisenhower Doctrine as "too little and too late" in seeking to counteract the Soviet Union's arming of Middle East nations. The text of Truman's speech was printed in the nation's major dailies:

> I am very happy to join with you this evening in honoring this great American comedian, Eddie Cantor. For about four decades now he has helped us to laugh—in bad times as well as good—and that is a real public service and one for which we ought to be very thankful.
>
> However, you do not honor him tonight so much for his accomplishments as a comedian as for his warm heart and his constant efforts in behalf of youth and the unfortunate and the oppressed of the earth.
>
> Eddie Cantor has always worked to bring happiness into the lives of others. It is only natural that one of his abiding interests should be the State of Israel—which was founded, and exists today, to provide a refuge and a new life for the most bitterly persecuted minority history has ever known.

Truman's speech and Cantor's birthday celebration were telecast, via closed circuit, to fifteen cities, including New York. Marilyn and Janet came down for the big event, sharing both their parents' joy—a joy that was brought down to earth on at least two occasions.

The first time was the night before the dinner, when their father began looking pale. Ida immediately reached into her purse and broke a vial of amyl nitrate under his nose. Then she calmly led Eddie upstairs, assuring Marilyn and Janet that their father was "all right" but adding that he had to get to bed. Eddie had recovered by the morning.

The other time was the day following the party, when Ida entered the Miami Heart Institute with apparent heart trouble. Eddie told the Associated Press she was "having no particular trouble—no heart attack or anything like that. She was just emotionally upset . . . that thing the other night was just too much for her."

Ida was discharged the following Tuesday. The attack was a recurrence of the trouble she had had the year before—an insufficient heart beat.

On Thursday, March 21—four weeks after the Cantors returned to California—the Academy of Motion Picture Arts and Sciences announced that it was giving a special honorary Oscar to Eddie Cantor for his work in behalf of the motion picture industry as an entertainer and as a humanitarian.

Eddie became short of breath while waiting in the wings at that year's nationally televised ceremony, held at the Pantages Theatre six nights later. He took a pill as an aide helped him remove his dinner jacket and was led to the stage door for some fresh air.

A few moments later, he walked onstage to receive his award. After he walked off to the applause of hundreds gathered in the theatre, not to mention millions watching on TV, a policeman and a doctor helped him to his waiting car.

Cantor later denied reports that he had suffered a heart attack, claiming merely to have "tired" from the evening's great excitement. He had known, after the Gleason telecast, that his days as an entertainer were over. Now he realized that his life as a public figure would be increasingly limited as well.

He was sixty-five, practically still in middle age by the standards of the 1990s. His mental faculties were as sharp as ever, and the realization that his life would be increasingly one of confinement caused him considerable sadness. He had enjoyed one of the finest show business careers in history, dozens of awards, and the knowledge that he had raised untold millions of dollars for good causes. He and Ida had been married more than forty years, and Eddie was the father of five daughters with four grandchildren. He could, and did, increasingly look back.

Eddie and Ida picked up their first Social Security checks April 21, driving up in their 1957 Cadillac to collect checks for February and March in the amount of $323.40.

"The government complicates everything," Eddie told W. Robert Thompson of the *Hollywood Citizen-News*. "If I can simplify it by showing that owning a Cadillac, which Mrs. Cantor gave me, does not prevent a person from collecting his insurance premiums, then I have helped a great many people.

"You see, Social Security is not charity. It is an insurance policy that everyone pays on during their productive years. Edmund Gwenn, for instance, is past seventy, and we had to call him to come down and get his check when he wasn't working in a movie. Jack Benny should have been here years ago."

The Cantors were giving all their checks to Surprise Lake Camp—a very generous gesture, considering that Eddie, whose income had been slashed over the past two years, was not nearly as rich as most people believed.

Eddie had one last performing chore—a months-old commitment to record his old songs for RCA with special spoken introductions. The songs would be released on a twelve-inch LP.

The recordings were done over three days in June, with backing by a vocal group at the last session. The orchestrations were imaginative, if somewhat camp at times, but Eddie's voice had thickened considerably in the last four years, due in no small measure to the medication necessitated by his steadily worsening heart condition. June 26, 1957, the last recording date, marked the real end of the career of Eddie Cantor.

Margie exhibited more energy and verve in the thirteen months following her operation than she had since her teens. "Gari, the two kids, and I would spend our summers with the folks in California," Janet recalls. "I remember Margie swimming in the ocean down at Edna's place in Malibu for the first time in years that summer [1957]. For awhile there, I guess she hoped she'd beaten it. We all did."

Early in the morning of October 18, a car driven by Jack Young of 335 Cloverdale Avenue, Los Angeles, failed to stop for a red light at the intersection of Wilshire Boulevard and Doheny Drive and headed straight for Margie's Volkswagen. She swerved quickly, thus avoiding a head-on collision. The larger auto slammed into her car's rear, and both autos were severely damaged. Neither Young nor Shirley Silverman, his passenger, were injured. Skolsky, who was seated next to Margie, was treated for a sprained wrist at the Beverly Hills Emergency First Aid Station. Margie went to Cedars, suffering from a brain concussion and a broken collarbone.

"Three days later," she reported, "the doctors were asking me who the president was and other stupid questions. I later found out I hadn't been able to give answers to them for the first two days."

Margie later said she wished she had died then. Her cancer returned with a vengeance a short while later.

New areas of pain appeared throughout her body, and her sisters "just kept inventing excuses for her to go back to the hospital. Margie was given cobalt treatments; they didn't have any other therapy except nitrogen mustard.

Doctors drew outlines on her body with magic marker before giving her the treatments and asked her to monitor any new pains she felt. She did so, and wrote "detour" on herself each time she started a new line.

"I sometimes couldn't believe the conversations I was having with her; they were so macabre," recalled Janet.

> But that was how Margie lived with it. She was so funny about it that you found yourself kidding with her. She once said to me, "I went to the dentist today. He wants to do some work on my gums. What am I gonna tell him—I don't care if I have the best mouth in the cemetery." That was the way she taught us to deal with it.

Eddie spent 1958 writing magazine stories, making sporadic walk-on guest appearances—on *The Eddie Fisher Show* on NBC, the Tenth Annual Awards Ceremony of the American Television Arts and Sciences [the Emmies] on April 15, George Jessel's syndicated *Show Business* (twice)—and beginning a new book, *The Way I See It*, with Phyllis Rosenteur.

That fall, Eddie also played on his image as a successful husband and family man to host a fifteen-minute NBC radio talk show called *Family Living*. Topics included "Can There Be Happiness Without Money?," "Child Adoption," and "Oddball or Conformist." Each show had a topic with two guests: a clergyman or lay authority and a celebrity, who gave his views upon the subject and swapped harmless banter with Eddie. The program (which featured such absurdities as the multimillionaire Bob Hope pontificating on happiness without money) ended after thirteen weeks.

If some of Eddie's philosophy may seem banal—even downright naive— by post–1965 standards, his blunt and forthright comments on political and labor union matters went on unabated. On Saturday, November 1, 1958, the National Council for Industrial Peace distributed a statement he had issued calling right-to-work laws a "threat to majority rule." Cantor compared the acts with others that had destroyed freedom in Nazi Germany, Fascist Italy, and the Soviet Union.

"The union shop," he declared, "is democratic, the most democratic method the workers have to deal with their employers. There can be no union shop unless a majority of the employees of any business or industry vote for a union shop."

He had now accepted his retirement from show business. When a cousin, Celia Margolin, asked for help in getting a magazine article made into a television spectacular, Eddie wrote that he had been "relatively inactive professionally for some time now and am frankly not in a position to be of help to you in seeing that the idea gets to the right people. My own little activity is confined to 'guest shots' here and there, and, believe it or not, I am not even acquainted with most of the VIPs now in command at the networks." It was all sadly true.

Margie's cancer was now beyond all control, and an operation was performed to relieve a growth that had developed in her bile duct. Eddie and Ida knew something was serious, but no one mentioned cancer. Margie went to Cedars every second week for cobalt treatments but continued with her brave, wisecracking front for her sisters and, above all, for her parents.

On the night of March 25, 1959, as her father was involved with final details on *The Way I See It*, Margie, in great pain, went into the hospital. This time, Ida went to Cedars with her eldest daughter.

When Margie undressed, Ida gasped. She was little except skin and bones. No one could deny the nature of the illness any longer, but it took Eddie a while to come to grips with what was happening. Margie had remained a constant—his adviser, his personal manager, and, to some extent, his confidante—through the last twenty-five years. Ida had accepted this in the same way her sisters had; it was *right*—the natural order of things. Margie was just Margie, the born leader.

Margie, mindful of the shock her emaciated body had given her mother, refused to have "the folks" visit at Cedars. She even refused painkillers in the late afternoons and early evenings until after she had called them at seven o'clock—always very chatty, letting them hear no reminder of the cancer that was killing her. A nurse—the same one who had taken care of Ida and her new baby when Janet had been born in Brooklyn Jewish Hospital more than thirty years earlier—said she did not know, on numerous occasions, where Margie got the strength to make the phone calls. She was wasting away daily, still alert but always getting weaker.

Elizabeth Taylor, in the hospital at the same time for a minor ailment, made herself a nuisance, and the nurses loathed her. Those same nurses adored Margie. She was polite, kind, sweet, often funny, and courageous.

Only once—towards the end, as she began to lose her grip on the world—did Margie falter. On that occasion, she mistakenly accepted medication prior to her 7 P.M. call to her parents. The effect was quite profound. "Daddy, mother," she cried into the telephone that evening. "Why haven't you been here to see me?"

"I know it's a weird thing to say," says Janet, "but, in a way, I'm glad she lingered after she was no longer conscious because I could see she was hallucinating; she was imagining she was directing a show. I came in one time, and she was singing 'Summertime' in her beautiful voice at the top of her lungs. She was enjoying herself. The Margie I knew was gone, but the Margie who should have been was finally there."

There came a time, in early May, when Janet asked the nurse if Margie could be saved if a cure for cancer were available right then and there. The answer was that she could not. She was literally a physical shell of herself, not conscious but with a heart still strongly beating. "What is keeping her alive?" asked Janet. "Her heart just keeps on beating," said the nurse. "I don't know why."

Ida's birthday was on May 15, and the girls felt that Margie was somehow waiting for the day to pass. They knew she would not die on such a day. Nor did she.

On Sunday, May 17, Janet asked the nurse if she thought Margie could somehow still hear her. "I don't know," replied the nurse, "but I talk to her every day. I'll let you try." And so Janet began.

"Margie, it's okay. Everything is taken care of. The folks are all right, and all of us are all right, and you can go to sleep. It's okay, Margie."

Margie died later that day.

The Cantors were told separately. Ida was at home, and Eddie was out for the daily constitutional his doctors had prescribed. Maurice found him, and Eddie solemnly, instinctively, rolled up his sleeve for the sedative he knew was coming.

"Is she gone?" he asked, almost rhetorically. Maurice simply administered the injection and drove Eddie back to Monte Leon Lane. Ida was not told until the doctor had arrived. She cried, "No, no!" and accepted her own sedative.

Eddie and Ida were brought together in a room a short time later. They hugged and then fell into each other's arms, sobbing hopelessly, "Our baby. Our little girl."

Their other daughters stood by helplessly, yet somehow lost in wonder.

Even to Natalie, Margie had seemed always an adult. Now they realized that she, like them, had been a daughter of their parents.

Margie had not consciously sought death, and yet the onslaught of her cancer followed closely, and then mirrored, her father's physical and professional decline. Margie worried about who would take care of "the folks" until the time she finally lost consciousness. And yet the thought of burying her parents—especially her father—had always been her greatest dread, her nightmare. That awful task had now been spared her. But the family would never be the same.

Margie's personal checking account, still unbalanced and long since forgotten, contained six thousand dollars at her death. The money was divided among her sisters. Janet used her share to take her family to Europe. "We felt Margie would have enjoyed that," said Janet. "She would have loved giving it to us."

Once the summer passed and the initial shock and grief at Margie's death had slowly worn away to emptiness, Eddie once again appeared in public. On September 23, he received the Al Jolson Memorial Medal at the Hollywood Bowl from the Veterans of Foreign Wars for his work in entertaining servicemen. One week later, he appeared on the *Today Show* to publicize *The Way I See It*, recently released to stores by Prentice-Hall.

In November, Eddie gave an interview to Liz McGuinness of the Los Angeles *Mirror-News*, sipping tea and munching on cake as he spoke. "I've tried very hard in this book to have people avoid the mistakes I've made in my life; to write the book took sixty-seven years of living and learning. . . . I think the book can prevent many heart attacks if people will read what I have to say."

"An interview with Cantor," wrote McGuinness, "is like almost none other. It is liable to wander from his new book to his pride in the new State of Israel, advice to husbands and wives, juvenile delinquency, and more general Cantor philosophy." An example of the philosophizing: "My grandmother once warned me, 'Don't go so fast or you'll miss the scenery.' It took me so many years to catch up with her meaning. For instance, I was at the birth of only two of my five daughters, was at none of their graduations. Then I realized what she meant."

Most of the philosophy revolved around the things Eddie had thought about, apparently for the first time, while recuperating from his first heart attack, when he could not entertain or write or listen to new songs or talk with writers.

"I think the greatest kick I've gotten out of life," he now maintained, "more than from appearing with Ziegfeld, in *Whoopee* or other shows, was when Jonas Salk mentioned that I helped start the March of Dimes from whence came the polio vaccine . . . that I might have helped save the life of a kid some place."

The book was the counsel of a famous man who hoped he'd found the

real secret of life after his heart attack and wished to share it with the
world—the final testament of a man who was more than an entertainer.
Some parts of *The Way I See It* are amazingly perceptive; much is balm for
a performer who, in his mid-sixties, could no longer perform.

Ida suffered another attack on Wednesday evening, December 30, 1959,
and was listed in satisfactory condition at Cedars of Lebanon the following
Sunday. She was released before the middle of January, although neither
she nor Eddie could attend Marilyn's wedding to announcer-actor Mike
Baker in New York on February 28.

Marilyn had met Mike through Henry Morgan, a great radio humorist
who is now remembered chiefly as a panelist on TV's *I've Got a Secret*. As
the romance blossomed, Mike went out to meet Eddie and Ida. Baker
passed muster as a man who would make "a good living." Eddie joked that
the only hard part would be living with Marilyn.

The marriage ceremony was performed at the home of the officiating
rabbi, Dr. Samuel M. Segal of Mount Nebo Congregation, with Janet attending her sister. Baker eventually served four terms as president of the
New York local of the American Federation of Television and Radio Artists—following in Eddie's footsteps, to be sure.

Baker's self-assurance, authoritativeness, and extremely logical mind
served as perfect complements to Marilyn's volatile personality, and the two
have enjoyed a long marriage.

Her last attack had greatly weakened Ida. Often, she was too weak to come
into the dining room for dinner. Eddie visited her bedroom at these times
to chat and joke with her and try to keep her going. Eddie's efforts in this
line kept him going as well.

Margie's death, in truth, had sapped her parents' will to live. Eddie
suffered yet another heart attack late that summer and remained in Cedars
till the beginning of October. This time, there was little pretense; doctors
frankly described the heart condition as "chronic" and said it was "better
to keep him here where he will remain quiet. When we release him, he
will become more active, and we don't want that now."

Eddie was quite stoic. He had come to grips with death through Margie
and offered no complaints. "Nobody lives forever," he joked with his nurses.
Nor did Eddie seem to want to.

He took it easy now. Cantor's only work in early '61 was a monthly
reminiscence column for the *Diners Club Magazine* called "In One Era and
Out the Other." It was nostalgic, pleasant, and not too taxing to write.
Eddie had become the nation's number one nostalgist, no longer for commercial purposes but simply because losing himself in the past was far less
painful than living in the present.

In March, his health somewhat improved, Eddie began a series of 260
five-minute taped radio programs for Lika Productions of New York. Called

*Ask Eddie Cantor,* each segment featured Eddie answering a question with a reminiscence, homespun wisdom, and, at times, a spin of an old record.

As with many, if not most, such series, almost all the "letters" were fictitious, Eddie's real "fan mail" consisting mostly of reminiscences from people who had seen his old films in the 1930s. Few, if any, contained questions suitable for a five-minute radio show. The "question-letters" were provided by Joe Franklin.

That same month, Louella Parsons announced that Edna's daughter, Judy McHugh, would wed Eddie Kafafian on June 30. Kafafian, who'd been writing the "Clef Dwellers" column and other musical articles for *Variety*, was about to join the MacFadden-Eddy public relations firm. Judy, who had worked for her paternal grandfather, Jimmy McHugh Sr., in the music business, was a copywriter for the publicity firm of Lewin, Kaufman and Schwartz.

Cantor's life was now routine and slow. He rose at about nine and answered mail until noon. (Eddie still got around two hundred letters a week.) He took an hour's walk each day and an afternoon nap, worked on his column or the taped radio show on days when he felt up to it, and went to the movies. "It's nice to know," he told Bob Thomas of the L.A. *Mirror-News*, "that you can go to bed at 10:30, about the time you would be starting the second act of a show."

He and Ida went to Palm Springs in the winter. Eddie had, at all costs, to avoid excitement, and he usually did. A viral infection confined him to Monte Leon Lane when Eddie Fisher and "a committee of industrialists and show business figures including Jack Benny and George Jessel" sponsored an Eddie Cantor Golden Jubilee Salute at the Ambassador Hotel's Cocoanut Grove on Tuesday evening, July 25, 1961. Beverly Hills financier Barry Mirkin, chairman of the committee, headed a delegation of celebrities who later presented a ten-thousand-dollar check to Ida, representing Eddie, for Surprise Lake Camp.

Ill health also prevented Cantor from receiving the Medallion of Valor from Eleanor Roosevelt on behalf of State of Israel Bonds at the Beverly Hilton on November 28, 1961. Jack Benny presented it to him at his home in Beverly Hills on February 5, 1962, with Victor M. Carter, general chairman of the local drive, and Louis H. Boyar, national chairman of the trustees, in attendance.

Boyar was chairman at the 1962 Inaugural Conference for Israel Bonds celebration of Eddie's seventieth birthday at the Fontainebleau Hotel, Miami Beach, on February 24. Jack Benny accepted a silver Torah breastplate symbolizing the Twelve Tribes of Israel from the Israel Bond Organization on Eddie's behalf. That night, Cantor was the subject of tributes by Israeli Premier David Ben-Gurion (via cable), Edward G. Robinson, Sophie Tucker, and Ed Sullivan. Eddie himself remained in California, which he had not left since 1957.

The Arab League also took note of Cantor's work for Israel, blacklisting him, along with six American companies, in a statement issued in Damascus, Syria, on Sunday, October 22, 1961. Cantor was accused of "Zionist affiliations and material support of Israel."

Cantor, when apprised of this, reacted the same way he had toward Father Coughlin. "I have no wish," he said, "to make those people laugh who have made my people cry."

Eddie, who finished more than two hundred five-minute radio shows by the end of February, taped the remaining sixty in the following three months. He now did no work beyond his column for *The Diners Club*, answering his daily mail, and continuing the fight to watch his health and keep alive.

He seldom lacked for visitors. In July, Janet, Gari, and their children came to visit for two months. Amanda, then approaching seven, still remembers the night she turned on the TV and saw the opening credits of an ABC situation comedy titled *Margie*.

*Margie*, then on the last legs of its lone season on the air, starred Cynthia Pepper as Margie Clayton, an attractive teen-age high school student in a small New England town during the 1920s. The opening consisted of a doo-wacka-doo introduction and a boisterous rendition of the song "Margie."

Gari burst into the room and cut the sound off. "Are you crazy?" he asked his small daughter. Gari may have overreacted, but his concern was quite real. The song would have reduced his famous father-in-law to tears and might, he feared, have brought on another heart attack.

Eddie still felt Margie's loss. One time, Janet watched him as he napped, a smile on his face. Then he woke and blinked, uncomprehendingly. Tears welled in his eyes as the reality set in.

"In your dreams, nobody's missing," Eddie told his youngest daughter. Margie was still in his dreams.

He was not prepared for what would follow.

The nurse who cared for Ida was a good one. In early 1962, as Ida grew weaker, the nurse kept a close watch, not only taking care of her daily needs but acting as a medic.

Ida suffered what was described as a "seizure" in February and was confined to bed thereafter, with her nurse in 'round-the-clock attendance. On Monday night, August 6, her heart stopped beating, but the nurse's immediate therapy restarted it within half an hour. Two nights later, shortly after 6:30, Janet, still in L.A., got a call from the nurse, asking that she come at once.

Natalie was staying with Eddie and Ida; Marilyn was in New York, while Edna, Janet learned, was on her way from Malibu. "I did all I could, honey," the nurse said. "I just couldn't save her."

Ida had been dead less than an hour. "Her cheeks were still rosy when

I saw her," Janet recalled. "She looked as if she was sleeping, and I spoke to her, waiting for her to wake up. She never did."

Eddie was left sleeping in his room, as no one dared tell him the news until he was sedated. In the meantime, Ida's body was picked up and moved to the Groman Mortuary at 830 West Washington Boulevard in Los Angeles.

The furniture from Ida's room was moved to a storage center, and the girls went through their mother's personal belongings. There was no petty selfishness, only rational consideration for each other's needs, those of Ida's sisters, and their father. The closeness of the Cantor sisters was never more apparent. All the work was done within two hours.

In the morning, a doctor came, gave Eddie a sedative, and told him that his wife had died. Cantor went into a state of shock.

"My father is all right," said Edna, reached by newsmen. "I can't say any more."

Eddie, still in shock and weaker than before, could not attend the funeral on Friday. Rabbi Edgar F. Magnin officiated, reading selections from the Book of Psalms and a brief eulogy. "People who are worthwhile do not need a eulogy," he said. "Their works is their life written in the hearts of their family and friends." The Cantors, said the rabbi, were "outstanding for their wholesomeness in show business."

The girls had not revealed when the service would be held. Only twelve people were there as a result, with no celebrities among them.

Ida Tobias Cantor, age seventy, was laid to rest in the same Hillside crypt that held the body of her eldest daughter, Margie.

Ida's will, dated October 26, 1960, and filed for probate in Los Angeles Superior Court three weeks after her death, placed all of her estate in trust for Eddie's benefit. The probate petition gave no estimate of value other than that the estate would exceed $25,000. The will directed that the proceeds go to their four daughters after Eddie's death.

Janet spent as much time with her father as she could before returning to New York. At one point, Eddie turned his back to her and sobbed into his pillow about Ida. "I wrote her from camp," he cried, remembering the year they had first met.

He, who had not slept in the same room with Ida in almost two decades, now could find no sleep without her. His suffering continued until he slept with Ida's dog at the foot of his bed.

The Palm Springs house was sold. Bought by Ida, it made Eddie think only of her and was too painful to reside in. His health was another factor; even traveling to Palm Springs was too much for Cantor now.

Eddie only gradually recovered from the shock of losing his wife of forty-eight years. Early in October, still confined to Monte Leon Lane, he and the television-radio executive Harry Maizlish sought two hours of donated network time to raise $15,000 for the projected Salk Foundation Program. The program, "conceived and developed" by the two men and titled "Something to Remember," never got beyond the talking-planning stages.

On November 13, Cantor received the first annual Screen Actors' Guild Award "for outstanding achievement in fostering the finest ideals of the acting profession and advancing the principles of good citizenship." Jack Benny accepted the award for Eddie at that evening's annual meeting of the Guild at the Beverly Hilton, with a private presentation to Eddie that same evening at his home by SAG president George Chandler.

On February 20, 1963, Los Angeles Superior Court was informed that Eddie Cantor needed expense money from his late wife's estate for medical care. Ida's total estate had come to more than $300,000, with a probable annual income of $10,000. Eddie, whose earnings had been meager since the middle 1950s, now needed $1,706 a month for 'round-the-clock nurses and $400 monthly for doctors' bills and other medical expenses. Judge Clarke E. Stephens granted Eddie $5,000 a month for six months or until an inventory of Mrs. Cantor's estate was filed with the court.

The column for *Diners' Club* Magazine continued, and *As I Remember Them*, Eddie's first book since *The Way I See It*, was on the fall list of the publisher Duell, Sloan & Pearce.

*As I Remember Them* was a weak collection of anecdotes, some true, some outright fabrications, about Will Rogers, Jolson, W. C. Fields, Fanny Brice, and other Cantor colleagues and contemporaries, with short chapters on more current stars like Danny Kaye and Danny Thomas. A thin volume, it served only to keep Cantor's name alive during the 1963–64 season as, weakened more and more by both his diet and his heart, he continued both to write and to explore ideas.

One of these ideas, announced in a full-page ad in the August 14, 1963, issue of *Variety* and titled *The Three Brothers*, was about Harry, Charley, and Henry Tobias. "I'm writing four hours a day," Cantor told Hal Humphrey one week later, "which includes doing my regular column for *Diners' Club* magazine. I like it, and anyway the doc insists I do it to keep my mind off myself."

The awards continued. AFTRA, acting on a suggestion made by Charlie Cantor, gave Eddie a scroll in recognition of his dedicated service to his fellow performers and his pioneering work in radio and television. Jack Benny made the presentation to Eddie at Monte Leon Lane at noon on Tuesday, September 10, 1963, the thirteenth anniversary of his smash debut on TV's *Colgate Comedy Hour*.

In January, Jessel flew to Washington to confer with President Lyndon B. Johnson on a proposed medal for Cantor, honoring him for his humanitarianism, with special emphasis on his work for the March of Dimes. The

medal, approved and presented to Cantor at his home by California Governor Pat Brown, with Jessel in attendance, on January 31, 1964, Eddie's
seventy-second birthday, read as follows:

> President of the United States of America awards this commen-
> dation to Eddie Cantor for the distinguished services to his nation
> during his illustrious career. Mr. Cantor has given unstintingly of his
> time, talent and energy to humanitarian causes of every description.
> Lighting the personal burdens of the peoples of the nation, his efforts
> have made possible major achievements in the constant struggle
> against disease and poverty. He has exemplified a spirit of selfless-
> ness, courage and service that reflects the highest credit to himself
> and his country. He has earned the esteem and admiration of his
> countrymen and the enduring gratitude of this republic.

A photograph of Eddie, taken on that day, shows him looking frail. He
was not the vulnerable but energetic Cantor of the 1920s but an old man,
looking somewhat like a turtle, with a sadly lined, drawn face, seemingly
amazed at the proceedings. Eddie was still alert mentally, however, and as
forthright in his opinions as he had been thirty years earlier.

February 4, 1964

Gov. Pat Brown
Executive Mansion
Sacramento, Calif.

> In spite of my illness, this January 31st was the most thrilling
> birthday of my life. The citation from the president was over-
> whelming, but equally overwhelming was the honor of having the
> best governor California ever had right here in my home to present
> it to me. I cannot thank you enough for taking time from all your
> other pressing duties for this. Since then, I feel better than I have
> in a year. Now if you can just arrange such an occasion every other
> day or so, I'll be back in shape in no time. Seriously, I am convinced
> that should we meet again after November, I shall be addressing you
> as "Mr. Vice Pres." and that's as it should be. Nowhere in this coun-
> try is there a more dedicated servant of the people than California's
> beloved Governor Pat Brown. Best wishes for continued success in
> your excellent work and my warm personal regards.

Eddie Cantor

He continued writing as much as possible, though now he was so weak
that he could scarcely hold a pen. "His hands had been so strong," remembers Janet. "It was really sad to see him now; he couldn't hold a brush to
comb his hair." Edna visited as often as she could, lying next to Eddie on
his bed, watching boxing on TV with him, and betting on the fights.

The writer Bob Thomas came to visit at this point, but the Eddie Cantor he saw "was far from the vital, kinetic figure who had danced across the Ziegfeld stage and the screens of movie houses. His speech had grown slow and heavy-tongued, evidence of the heart attacks that had withdrawn him from the entertainment scene. He moved with the deliberateness of a man who knew he was existing on borrowed time. But his mind was sharp as ever; his memory seemed unimpaired as he reached back to those days he liked to recall."

Janet brought the kids out to the coast again that summer. One day, she tried to take him for a ride in the car to break his monotony and get him out of the house, which had become almost a prison. Eddie got out of bed and made it to the door when he stopped suddenly and shook his head. He simply could not make it.

Janet returned to New York before Labor Day, but the West Coast branches of the Cantor family made sure Eddie had plenty of company for dinner. Tuesday nights were Michael Metzger's turn and Eddie's favorite "laugh" night of the week on television since the demise of *Your Show of Shows*—*The Red Skelton Hour*.

Cantor had effectively retired from show business at the dawn of rock 'n' roll. "Swing," the first pop music aimed at younger people, had left adults bemused in the mid '30s. Rock 'n' roll, however, seemed both foreign and bewildering to anyone past forty. Eddie shook his head in disapproval and disinterest when rock groups like the Rolling Stones appeared on Skelton's show. He did not understand why groups like this were popular with anyone. Presley had been a joke to the established show crowd, but at least the man was some kind of performer. The Stones' music to Cantor was nothing—loud, musically discordant, utterly without charm, and obnoxious. Skelton more than made up for it, however. That was show biz—funny, bright, and warm at the same time. He loved it.

"Even before Red's sign-off," Mike Metzger recalls, "Gramps was up in front of the used-brick fireplace doing the Old Soft Slipper and belting out 'Harrigan' for me and the night nurse, Margaret Collins.

"Please do not do that, Mr. Cantor."

"Gramps, enough. Margaret's having a stroke."

"That's better than a heart attack." He rolled his eyes.

More than ever now, he cherished memories of the show world he'd known. Jessel visited and made jokes about Michael's beatnik clothes. Harry Ruby also dropped by frequently. Eddie's other guests included younger stars like Jerry Lewis and Eddie Fisher.

Don Carle Gillette, editor of *Hollywood Reporter*, asked Cantor what he thought of the reaction against blackface, which he'd used almost exclusively from 1911 to 1918 and reprised in many shows and films. Cantor was crestfallen. "He did not think blackface comedy teams such as Amos 'n' Andy created an unfavorable image of the Negro race," Gillette reported.

Audiences knew that these shows were designed strictly for entertainment, he said, and were not to be taken seriously.

"The most colorful and enjoyable days of the vaudeville era, according to Cantor, was when the public—black and white—was allowed to laugh at the innocent humor of Dutch comedians such as Weber & Fields, the blackface comedy of McIntyre & Heath, and the laughs created by Italian, Hebrew, Irish, and other comics who could make fun without being hamstrung by ethnicity and ideology. 'When this kind of harmless humor was banned,' said Cantor, 'it took half the fun out of show business.' "

In September, he prepared a tape-recorded message for a banquet celebrating Jimmy Durante's fiftieth year in show business. Much of the tape, including a song, was assembled from older recordings. He sounded sadly weak and feeble in the new parts.

Three weeks later, Eddie wrote his last piece, a short obituary tribute to Harpo Marx for *Variety*.

In the early evening of October 10, he suddenly felt pain. Natalie had just finished preparing dinner, and Margaret asked her to keep the food warm while she took Eddie to his room for oxygen. Natalie looked in several times to find her saying, "Take a deep breath, Mr. Cantor. Take a deep breath." The last time, Margaret paused and said to call the doctor. Natalie called him, as well as Edna, who was up from Malibu and at a nearby friend's house.

Edna hurried over. The doctor arrived a short while later, at 7:25 P.M. He was five minutes too late.

Eddie Cantor, the first performer to go beyond performing and become a welcome "member of the family" to millions upon millions of Americans, was dead.

*Epilogue*

# "OLD PERFORMERS NEVER DIE . . ."

t was news when Eddie Cantor died, but not big news. He had been retired for too long in an era before TV interviews were common, and at least five years before the "nostalgia" craze of 1969–72. News of Cantor's death was lost in the barrage of publicity surrounding the Beatles.

The *New York Times* reported his death on its front page, but the tributes were indeed few; Jackie Gleason announced that "a great man died the other day" and asked for a moment of silence. Most of the news items mentioned Cantor's efforts on behalf of humanitarian causes and noted that his passing marked the third recent death of a celebrated comedian from the "Golden Age of Show Business"—first Gracie Allen, then Harpo Marx, now Eddie Cantor.

The family was informed of his passing in quick order. Natalie telephoned Edna and then Marilyn and Janet in New York. When Janet told her nine-year-old, Amanda, that grandpa had died, she screamed and cried hysterically. Amanda, like her brother, Brian, and their cousins, Mike and Judy, had truly and wholeheartedly loved Grandpa.

Cantor was laid out at the funeral home. "The funeral director asked us if we wanted to view the body," recalled Janet. "None of us did; we didn't want to remember him that way. But Maurice did the kindest thing. He looked in to make sure that Daddy's tie was on straight."

It marked his final task for Eddie.

George Jessel, still the "Toastmaster General of the United States," had naturally wanted to deliver Eddie's eulogy. But Cantor had expressly said that he wanted a private funeral—something Natalie and Edna were only too willing to have—and all four daughters knew that Jessel, "though he loved our father," would have relished and enjoyed his task a bit too much for comfort. Knowing that reporters and photographers would descend nonetheless, they asked the funeral home not to make public either the time or the place of the service. Jessel, quite predictably, was outraged and arranged for a special Eddie Cantor memorial service at Grossinger's Catskills Resort Hotel for May 28.

Michael and Judy, Eddie's two oldest grandchildren, also had misgivings about the private funeral. "He was a public figure," insists Judy. "You really can't deny that. Why have him go quietly away?"

There were, and still are, plenty of misgivings about Natalie's decision to give Eddie's personal belongings—scrapbooks, plaques, citations, papers, the remains of fifty years in entertainment—to UCLA, which promised to create a special Cantor Archive and Collection, a promise never realized.

"They gave all that material away without any consideration for us, the grandchildren, and future generations," said Judy. "They just shut the book on everything so fast."

The liquidation of Cantor's estate began on February 4, 1965, when Dr. Thomas J. Cline and his wife, Ruth, bought Eddie's home on Monte Leon Lane after a bid of $112,000. Selected items from the Cantor estate brought two thousand dollars at the Ames Art Galleries ("Beverly Hills' only Auction Rooms") at 8725 Wilshire Boulevard later that month.

On March 15, 1965, five months after Eddie's passing, a preliminary inventory and appraisal of Cantor's personal and real estate property was filed in Los Angeles Superior Court by a court-appointed appraiser, N. Jeffries Weiner. Weiner's figures showed $23,858 in stock, $13,015 in Israeli bonds, $19,668 from a commercial account in the City National Bank of Beverly Hills, $5,075 from the Security Mutual Life Insurance Company, twelve life insurance policies valued at $208,029, $27,000 (a one-half interest) from the sale of Beverly Hills real estate, and a check from the Screen Actors' Guild death benefit fund for $117. A California state inheritance tax of $6,175 was shown.

The official total was $319,814, a respectable sum for an upper-middle-class businessman before the steep inflation of the 1970s but not the figure many had expected from a man who'd been the biggest earner in show business in the 1930s.

Not much was said about it in the press, but there are explanations for the modest figure. There were the trust funds Eddie had established for his daughters, the increasingly huge sums he'd spent on medical care over the final decade of his life, his own generosity toward charities, and the fact that Cantor, although a sharp bargainer for his own services in show business, had little understanding of investments.

It is safe to say that Cantor's daughters would be fabulously wealthy had Eddie followed not Jack Crandall's advice, and certainly not Lipsky's, but that of his wife, Ida. Business—outside the show world—was the one area in which Cantor was conscious of his lack of education and blindly accepted bad professional advice. The 1929 stock market crash had made Eddie more conservative but hardly any wiser.

Cantor had once said he did not want to die a rich man. Fate, and his bad judgment, made sure he did not.

On May 15, 1965, a little over seven months after her father's passing, Natalie Cantor Metzger married Robert Clary, the Jewish-French performer Eddie had promoted on the *Colgate Comedy Hour*, in Las Vegas. Natalie was forty-nine, Robert almost ten years younger.

Eddie, who never understood his daughters' needs with any great profundity, was nonetheless perceptive about Nat's and Robert's romance. "She loves that boy," he'd said to other members of the family, years before Natalie realized it herself.

Edna, increasingly reclusive, has never remarried, living by herself in the beach house in Malibu she purchased back in 1956. A gourmet cook specializing in desserts, she is the author of four cookbooks, has written a weekly column for a Malibu newspaper, and, in keeping with her father's sense of social responsibility, is a veteran of the Selma civil rights march of 1965.

Marilyn wrote the original story for *Sidney Shorr*, a television movie starring Tony Randall that became the TV series *Love, Sidney*. Her never-boring marriage to Mike Baker produced a son, Jed, now a child psychologist, and a daughter, Lynne, an attorney married to another lawyer, Andrew Eichner, by whom she has twin sons, Sam and Joe. Marilyn is still a firebrand in her mid-seventies but is a doting grandmother as well.

Janet divorced Roberto Gari in 1969 and is now pursuing a career as a composer-lyricist, having written words and music for a musical titled *Such a Pretty Face*.

The Cantor grandchildren have done well with their own lives. Michael Metzger is a Hollywood writer and producer, while Judy's marriage to Eddie Kafafian produced a son, now active as a musical performer in Los Angeles under the name Lee Newman.

Brian Gari had a brief marriage to the dancer-actress Darla Hill in the 1980s. Amanda Gari is married to Bert Abel, and they have a daughter, Allison.

Winnie Brandley Hanson died, age eighty-eight, in 1994, a year that also brought the death of Arthur Siegel, the young composer who had accompanied Eddie in his Carnegie Hall concert and became the "brother" Cantor's daughters never had.

Eddie's grandchildren and great-grandchildren, notably Brian Gari and Lee Newman, are actively engaged in trying to promote the Cantor legacy. Brian, a devotee of Jimmy Webb, has rescued priceless radio transcriptions, produced a number of Cantor CDs, and written notes to a laser-disc collection of his grandfather's UA films. Lee incorporates a few of Eddie's songs into his nightclub act.

There is today a small audience for Cantor's work. Repeated screenings of the Cantor-Goldwyn films in the early 1990s led to the formation of the Eddie Cantor Appreciation Society. The membership, although several hundred, hardly signals a mass Cantor revival. Eddie, like other stage performers once considered gods of entertainment, has not stood the test of time with a generation reared on rock 'n' roll. Cantor's look at the Rolling Stones on *The Red Skelton Hour* was as far as he would ever get to the age of Vietnam, hippies, and yippies. He simply did not relate to it; nor do we, by and large, relate to him.

It goes beyond the differences in music. Cantor belonged to "presentation" show biz, as opposed to the "tribal" show business of rock, which has made not only Cantor and the other former greats of entertainment seem helplessly old-fashioned, but has likewise made all "acts," from magic acts (sans grand illusions) to novelties like "The Banana Man" and animal acts, seem trivial, bizarre, and hopelessly absurd.

It would have been interesting to get Cantor's reaction to the world of 1966–71. He remained an independent-thinking liberal who, unlike Jessel and Winchell, had not swung over to the political right at the time of his death. Cantor probably would not have supported U.S. involvement in Vietnam, although he would have deplored the riots and burnings of the flag and would certainly have condemned the shootings of four students at Kent State. He would probably not have blamed the yippies, hippies, rioters, or looters for anything. But he would have stared, sadly and uncomprehendingly, at society, at the "mistakes" people were making, and tried to reason why the gentle times he'd known in his youth—and, increasingly, the Broadway he had known from 1917–29—had changed, had disappeared, had passed him by.

Cantor gradually retreated from memory in the years following his death. The Jews in major cities seemed to remember him the longest. To their children, he was just a Jewish name, a vague show business amalgam of Harry Golden and Al Jolson.

The March of Dimes is now taken for granted. It is less important in this age of government support for research, and few indeed know Cantor was its founder. Many of the charities he championed have either disappeared or have become a part of the "establishment." Even Eddie's great work for the State of Israel is no longer seen as totally benign.

The joyous, vaguely ethnic, willing but virginal Eddie Cantor that Broadway audiences knew throughout the 1920s is little more than a dim memory to the rapidly diminishing numbers of people who saw him. What remains, outside of a few films, some kinescopes, and radio transcriptions, is the public show world of today.

Cantor transformed show business from a self-contained profession into a public trust and took its membership from an insular and largely ignored "race" of "show folk" to a worshipped aristocracy with feudal obligations to the public and society. The idea of actors as role models with public responsibilities, and as people whose perceived private lives are public property, began with Eddie Cantor on the *Chase and Sanborn Hour*.

In making actors into public figures, Cantor made "actor" synonymous with "star" in the mind of the public and obscured the line between actors and other public figures. Ronald Reagan might not have gotten Eddie's vote, but his career in politics owed much to Cantor's influence.

If Cantor actually created modern stardom, was he himself a suitable role model? Eddie lived at a time when men compartmentalized their lives, when the home and the outside world were not readily confused. Cantor certainly never confused them. And if, as he maintained, he never placed career before his family, he often used that family to further his career. In doing so, however, he created modern stardom—a pantheon of blessed gods and goddesses as far removed from the itinerant actors of the early 1900s as Esther's basement apartment was from the famed "Cantor Home for Girls" of the 1930s, when Eddie Cantor touched the lives of millions.

# NOTES

## Chapter One

Sources for this chapter include United States and New York census records for 1910, extensive interviews with Janet Cantor Gari, Cantor's two autobiographies (*My Life Is in Your Hands* and *Take My Life*), an brief interview with Theodore Levy, Esq., a notice Cantor placed in the New York Times (1947) mentioning the names of four of his grade school teachers (other than Catherine Luddy), *The History of Surprise Lake Camp*, and theatrical trade papers (re: *Billy the Kid*).

## Chapter Two

*Take My Life*, the 1910 census, the Earl Wilson interview with J. C. Weir, and theatrical trade weeklies were the principal sources for this chapter. Jessel's book *So Help Me* was also helpful.

## Chapter Three

*So Help Me* provided some of the information on Gus Edwards. The trades helped trace both the act's route and what acts appeared on the same bills. Cantor and Jessel both remembered meeting Jolson when *Kid Kabaret* played Oakland/San Francisco. The Cantor-Tobias wedding certificate gave a few details, and *The Era*, a British theatrical trade weekly, provided information on Cantor and Lee at the Oxford. The material on *Canary Cottage* is from the show's program, Cantor's reminiscences, and contemporary reviews. Miles Kreuger's interview with Anna Held's daughter, numerous writings on Flo Ziegfeld, and a visit to Esther Kantrowitz's grave yielded the remaining information.

## Chapter Four

An interview with Doris Eaton, detailed combings of trade papers, Cantor's writings, and an interview with Natalie Cantor Clary provided most of the material.

## Chapter Five

The Shubert Archives, housed in New York's Lyceum Theatre Building, was the chief source of material. Trade and daily newspapers and the interview with Natalie filled out the balance of the chapter.

## Chapter Six

Natalie, *Variety*, numerous reviews in daily papers, Eddie's memoirs, interviews with Harry Fender, Doris Eaton, and Arthur Tracy, plus viewings of the films *Kid Boots* and *Special Delivery* provided most of the material.

## Chapter Seven

Sources included *My Life Is in Your Hands*, interviews with Winnie Brandley and Janet Cantor, publicity material for *Whoopee*, an interview with Irving Kahan, weekly issues of *Variety*, and various writings on the Wall Street crash.

## Chapter Eight

The interviews with Janet, Winnie, and Natalie, screenings of the short *Insurance*, *Whoopee, Palmy Days, The Kid from Spain*, and *Roman Scandals*, several biographies of Samuel Goldwyn, trade and daily papers, and transcriptions of the *Chase and Sanborn Hour* were the sources for this chapter.

## Chapter Nine

Janet's reminiscences of life at the San Remo, an article by Margie on the trip to Europe, screenings of *Kid Millions* and *Strike Me Pink*, transcriptions of the *Chase and Sanborn Hour* and the Eddie Cantor *Pebeco Show*, coverage of Cantor's doings in *Variety*, and several pieces in The *New York Times* were the chief sources of material.

## Chapter Ten

Transcriptions of *Texaco Town*, a screening of *Ali Baba Goes to Town*, interviews with Janet, Ruth Marko, Sheila Rogers, David Brown, and Ernest Lehman, articles on Father Coughlin, letters in the Eddie Cantor Collection at the Magic Castle in Los Angeles, various daily papers, and weekly reports in *Variety* made up the sources.

## Chapter Eleven

Janet Cantor is the source for much of the material on Margie, *Variety* for Ben Bodec's review of the Cantor Unit at Loews State and Eddie's doings re: the start of AGVA. Michael Metzger's birth announcement by his grandfather in Boston was published in the L.A. press. Cantor's comments on the origin of *Forty Little Mothers* appeared in *Variety*, and his passing out cigars at Judy McHugh's birth was likewise carried in the L.A. papers. The film was viewed (as were, indeed, all Cantor features). The Jack Crandall information is from Janet; that on Olive Major is from contemporary p.r. pieces. The *Banjo Eyes* material is based on interviews with Virginia Mayo, Adele Jurgens, and contemporary trade and daily newspapers, while the information on Jacqueline Susann is from *Lovely Me*, Kate Witkin, and Irving Cahn.

## Chapter Twelve

*Variety*, an interviews with Cantor auxiliary staff writer Mort Lockman (later a top gagman for Bob Hope and others), Bob Feldman, Janet Cantor, and Jean Vanderpyle were extremely helpful re the first part of this chapter. The dialogue from the *Time to Smile* broadcast of April 7, 1943, was taken from an audio transcription of the broadcast. Interviews with Thelma Carpenter, Budd Schulberg, Judy McHugh, Irving Cahen, and Joe Franklin made up the information for the balance of the chapter, along with certain quoted portions of *Take My Life*.

## Chapter Thirteen

Judy McHugh, *Variety*, Janet Cantor, Eddie Fisher, an audio copy of the Carnegie Hall concert, an article by Charles Isaacs ("Through Every Medium with Burnt Cork and Five Daughters") in the January 5, 1955, issue of *Variety*, and several pieces in the *New York Times* provided most of the material. *Variety, Yes I Can* (the autobiography of Sammy Davis Jr.), and Arthur Penn, plus viewings of several *Colgate Comedy Hour* kinescopes, were also very helpful.

## Chapter Fourteen

*Take My Life*, the Warner Archives, viewings of the Cantor episode of *This Is Your Life*, several Ziv shows, kinescopes of *George Has a Birthday*, *Sizeman and Son*, and "At Sixty-Five" (the special Cantor birthday celebration on *The Jackie Gleason Show* sans Gleason), David Brown, Jane Kesner Ardmore, Janet Cantor, and several daily papers were of great value. Janet was the primary source for Margie's final years. An interview with Phyllis Rosenteur, readings of Cantor's writings for the *Diners' Club* Magazine, transcriptions of *Ask Eddie Cantor*, interviews with Brian and Amanda Gari, *As I Remember Them*, Michael Metzger's writings in The Eddie Cantor Appreciation Society's monthly organ, a Bob Thomas interview with Cantor published in the L.A. *Mirror-News*, and several pieces in the *New York Times* were helpful. A copy of Eddie's letter to then Governor Pat Brown is in the Cantor collection at the Magic Castle in Los Angeles. Natalie Cantor proved an excellent source for information on her father's death.

## Epilogue

The *Hollywood Reporter*, the *New York Times*, Janet Cantor, Judy McHugh, Cantor's will (filed for probate), and numerous clippings in the Academy of Motion Picture Arts & Sciences Library were the sources here.

# BIBLIOGRAPHY

## Books by Eddie Cantor
### (chronologically arranged)

*My Life Is in Your Hands*, as told to David Freedman. New York: Harper & Brothers, 1928. (New edition, with additional chapter, published by Blue Ribbon Books, New York, 1932.)

*Caught Short: A Saga of Wailing Wall Street*. New York: Simon & Schuster, 1929.

*Between the Acts*. New York: Simon & Schuster, 1930.

*Eddie Cantor's Song and Joke Book*. Chicago: Pryor Press, 1930.

*Yoo-Hoo, Prosperity! The Eddie Cantor Five-Year Plan*. New York: Simon & Schuster, 1931.

*A Book Full of Laughs*, with David Freedman. New York: Simon & Schuster, 1932.

*Your Next President*, with David Freedman. New York: R. Long & R. R. Smith, Inc., 1932.

*Eddie Cantor Song and Joke Book for 1934*. New York: M. Witmark & Sons, 1934.

*Ziegfeld, The Great Glorifier*, with David Freedman. New York: A. H. King, 1934.

*World's Book of Best Jokes*. Cleveland: World Publishing Co., 1943.

*Take My Life*, with Jane Kesner Ardmore. New York: Doubleday & Company, 1957.

*The Way I See It*, with Phyllis Rosenteur. Englewood, N.J.: Prentice-Hall, 1959.

*As I Remember Them*. New York: Duell, Sloan & Pearce, 1963.

# STAGEOGRAPHY

## FRANK B. CARR'S INDIAN MAIDENS

| 1908 Dec. | 25–26 | Shenandoah | Shenandoah, Pa. |
|---|---|---|---|
| | 28 | | |
| | 29 | Opera House | Carbondale, Pa. |
| | 30 | Broad Street | Pittstown, Pa. |
| | 31 | Grand Opera House | E. Stroudsburg, Pa. |
| 1909 Jan. | 1 | | |
| | 2 | | |
| | 4 | | |
| | 5 | Fulton Opera House | Lancaster, Pa. |
| | 6 | | |
| | 7 | Opera House | Columbia, Pa. |
| | 19 | Rosedale Opera House | Chambersburg, Pa. |
| | 20 | | |
| | 21 | | |
| | 22 | | |
| | 23 | Cambria | Johnstown, Pa. |
| | 25 | | |
| | 26 | Mishler | Altoona, Pa. |
| | 27 | | Piedmont, W. Va. |
| | 28 | | Keyser, W. Va. |
| | 29 | | Hendricks, W. Va. |
| | 30 | | Davis, W. Va. |
| Feb. | 1 | | |
| | 2 | | |

3
4   Masonic Opera House    Hinton, W. Va.

June–Sept.     Carey Walsh's      Coney Island, N.Y.
Oct. 1909–June, 1910—Runner, J. C. Weir & Co., New York, N.Y.
Aug. 1910–Jan., 1911—Stock Clerk, National Cloak and Suit Co.

## Vaudeville

| 1911 | Feb. | Manhattan | New York, N.Y. |
|------|------|-----------|----------------|
| | March 6–8 | Hippodrome | Utica, N.Y. |
| | March | | Troy, N.Y. |
| | March | | Schenectady, N.Y. |
| | March | | Mechanicville, N.Y. |
| | April | West Side | New York, N.Y. |

## People's Vaudeville Co.

| 1911 | May 15–17 | Lyric | Hoboken, N.J. |
|------|-----------|-------|---------------|
| | 18–20 | New Lyceum | Elizabeth, N.J. |
| | 22–24 | Royal | Brooklyn, N.Y. |
| | 25–27 | Lyric | Brooklyn, N.Y. |
| | 28 | Amphion | New York, N.Y. |
| | 29–31 | Lyric | Hoboken, N.J. |
| | June 1–3 | New Lycem | Elizabeth, N.J. |
| | 5–7 | Royal | Brooklyn, N.Y. |
| | 8–10 | Lyric | Brooklyn, N.Y. |
| | 12–14 | Lyric | Hoboken, N.J. |
| | 15–17 | New Lyceum | Elizabeth, N.J. |
| | 19–21 | Royal | Brooklyn, N.Y. |
| | 22–24 | Lyric | Brooklyn, N.Y. |
| | 26–28 | Lyric | Hoboken, N.J. |
| | June 29–July 1 | New Lyceum | Elizabeth, N.J. |
| | July 3–5 | Royal | Brooklyn, N.Y. |
| | 6–8 | Lyric | Brooklyn, N.Y. |

## BEDINI & ARTHUR

| 1911 | Aug. 21–26 | Hammerstein's Victoria | New York, N.Y. |
|------|------------|------------------------|----------------|
| | Oct. 9–14 | Orpheum | Des Moines, Iowa |
| | 16–21 | Orpheum | Omaha, Neb. |
| | 23–28 | | |
| | Oct. 30–Nov. 4 | | |
| | Nov. 6–11 | Columbia | St. Louis, Mo. |
| | 13–18 | Majestic | Chicago, Ill. |
| | 20–25 | Lyric | Dayton, Ohio |
| | Nov. 27–Dec. 2 | Keith's | Indianapolis, Ind. |
| | Dec. 4–9 | Hopkins' | Louisville, Ky. |

| 11–16 | Keith's | Cincinnati, Ohio |
| 18–23 | Orpheum | Memphis, Tenn. |
| 25–30 | Orpheum | New Orleans, La. |
| | | |
| Jan. 22–27 | Hippodrome | Cleveland, Ohio |
| Jan. 29–Feb. 3 | Grand Opera House | Pittsburgh, Pa. |
| 5–10 | Hammerstein's Victoria | New York, N.Y. |
| 12–17 | Proctor's | Newark, N.J. |
| 19–24 | Alhambra | New York, N.Y. |
| Feb. 26–March 2 | Fifth Avenue | New York, N.Y. |
| March 4–9 | Bushwick | Brooklyn, N.Y. |
| 11–16 | Grand Opera House | Syracuse, N.Y. |
| 18–23 | Greenpoint | Brooklyn, N.Y. |
| 25–30 | Keith's | Boston, Mass. |
| April 1–6 | | |
| 8–13 | Shea's | Buffalo, N.Y. |
| 15–20 | Shea's | Toronto, Ont. |
| 22–27 | | |
| April 29–May 4 | National | Boston, Mass. |
| May 6–11 | Bronx | Bronx, N.Y. |
| 13–18 | Colonial | New York, N.Y. |
| 20–25 | Orpheum | Brooklyn, N.Y. |
| May 27–June 1 | New Brighton | Brooklyn, N.Y. |
| June 3–8 | Hammerstein's Victoria | New York, N.Y. |
| 10–15 | | |
| 17–22 | | |
| 24–29 | Keith's Union Square | New York, N.Y. |
| July 1–6 | Henderson's | Coney Island, N.Y. |
| 8–13 | | |
| 15–20 | Savoy | Atlantic City, N.J. |
| 22–27 | Keith's | Philadelphia, Pa. |
| July 29–Aug. 3 | Fifth Avenue | New York, N.Y. |

## KID KABARET

Dialogue by Thomas J. Gray. Lyrics by Will D. Cobb and Thomas J. Gray. Book and Music by Gus Edwards. Staged by Gus Edwards. Scenic Effects by Dodge & Castle. Costumes by Madame Freisenger and Browning, King & Co.

### Cast

| | |
|---|---|
| Jefferson, Butler in Chief | EDDIE CANTOR |
| Roly-Poly | WILL RIALTO |
| B. Fuller Melody | B. FULLER |

| | |
|---|---|
| Carlton Terrace Jr. | EDDIE BUZZELL |
| Annette, Carlton's Sweetheart | ENID MOREL |
| Annabella O'Hara, Kid-Kut-Up | EVELYN MCVEY |
| Mutky, Little Bit Yiddish | GEORGIE JESSEL |
| Millie Bon Bon, from Paris, Ky. | LILLIAN LIPMAN |
| Chauncey Pickadilly | AL HINSTON |
| Rosie, Flower Girl | RUTHIE FRANCIS |
| Tutti, Spearmint Salesman | JACK BARTON |
| Bud Weiser, in wrong | LOU EDWARDS |
| The Little Violinist | BETTY WASHINGTON |
| Lillie | ALICE HARTY |
| Tillie | MARIE SMITH |

Scene—Dining Room of Mr. and Mrs. Carlton Terrace.
Time—Five Minutes after Ma and Pa leave the house.

## Musical Review

| | |
|---|---|
| "Start Something" | Jeff and Co. |
| "Gee, It Must Be Tough" | Tutti |
| "That English Rag" | Chauncey |
| "You've Got to Stop a Pickin' " | Annette |
| "I'll Get You" | Annabella, Mutky |
| Violin Specialty | Betty Washington |
| "What Ja Ma Call 'Im" | Annette, Jeff, Bud & Co. |
| Dance Specialty | Bud Weiser |
| "Mimic Land" | |
| David Warfield | Mutky |
| Raymond Hitchcock | Rosie |
| Al Jolson | Jeff |
| Finale—"Favors" | Entire Company |
| Ballet Dance on Table | Alice Harty |

| | | |
|---|---|---|
| 1912 Sept. 2–7 | Hammerstein's Victoria | New York, N.Y. |
| 9–14 | | |
| 16–21 | Chase's | Washington, D.C. |
| 23–28 | Maryland | Baltimore, Md. |
| Sept. 30–Oct. 5 | Palace Music Hall | Chicago, Ill. |
| Oct. 7–12 | Majestic | Milwaukee, Wisc. |
| Nov. 18–23 | Shea's | Buffalo, N.Y. |
| 25–30 | Shea's | Toronto, Ont. |
| Dec. 2–7 | | |
| 9–14 | Orpheum | Brooklyn, N.Y. |
| 16–21 | Colonial | New York, N.Y. |
| 23–28 | Poli's | New Haven, Conn. |
| 1913 Jan. 20–25 | Bronx | Bronx, N.Y. |

| | | |
|---|---|---|
| Jan. 27–Feb. 1 | Poli's | Hartford, Conn. |
| Feb. 8–13 | | |
| 10–15 | Alhambra | New York, N.Y. |
| 17–22 | | |
| Feb. 24–March 1 | Fifth Avenue | New York, N.Y. |
| March 3–8 | Keith's | Boston, Mass. |
| 10–15 | | |
| 17–22 | | |
| 24–29 | Keith's | Philadelphia, Pa. |
| March 31–April 5 | Grand | Pittsburgh, Pa. |
| 7–12 | Majestic | Chicago, Ill. |
| 14–19 | | |
| 21–26 | | |
| April 28–May 3 | Keith's | Cincinnati, Ohio |
| May 5–10 | | |
| 12–14 | | |
| 15–17 | Grand | Macon, Ga. |
| 19–24 | | |
| 26–31 | Temple | Detroit, Mich. |
| June 2–7 | | |
| 9–14 | | |
| 16–21 | Orpheum | Winnipeg, Man. |
| 23–28 | (Travel) | |
| June 30–July 5 | Orpheum | Spokane, Wash. |
| July 7–12 | Orpheum | Seattle, Wash. |
| 14–19 | Orpheum | Portland, Ore. |
| 21–26 | (Travel) | |
| July 27–Aug. 9 | Orpheum | San Francisco, Calif. |
| Aug. 11–16 | Orpheum | Oakland, Calif. |
| 18–20 | Orpheum | Sacramento, Calif. |
| 21–23 | Orpheum | Stockton, Calif. |
| Aug. 25–Sept. 6 | Orpheum | Los Angeles, Calif. |
| 8–13 | (Travel) | |
| 15–20 | Orpheum | Salt Lake City, Utah |
| 22–27 | Orpheum | Denver, Colo. |
| Sept. 29–Oct. 4 | Orpheum | Lincoln, Neb. |
| Oct. 6–11 | Orpheum | Sioux City, Iowa |
| 13–18 | Orpheum | Des Moines, Iowa |
| 20–25 | Orpheum | Kansas City, Mo. |
| Oct. 27–Nov. 1 | Orpheum | Omaha, Neb. |
| Nov. 3–8 | Orpheum | Minneapolis, Minn. |
| 10–15 | Orpheum | St. Paul, Minn. |
| 17–22 | Orpheum | Duluth, Minn. |
| 24–29 | (Travel) | |
| Dec. 1–6 | Columbia | St. Louis, Mo. |
| 8–13 | Orpheum | Memphis, Tenn. |
| 15–20 | Orpheum | New Orleans, La. |
| 22–27 | | |

Dec. 29–Jan. 3
1914 Jan. 4–10    Majestic            Dallas, Texas
      11–17       Majestic            Houston, Texas
      18–24       Majestic            San Antonio, Texas
      26–31
   Feb. 2–7       Keith's             Knoxville, Tenn.
      9–14        Lyric               Birmingham, Ala.
      16–21       Lyric               Richmond, Va.
      23–28
   March 2–7
      9–14
      16–21       Palace              New York, N.Y.
      23–28
March 30–April 4  Alhambra            New York, N.Y.
   April 6–11     Orpheum             Brooklyn, N.Y.
      13–18       Shea's              Buffalo, N.Y.
      20–25       Shea's              Toronto, Ont.
April 27–May 2    Grand               Pittsburgh, Pa.
   May 4–9        Temple              Detroit, Mich.
      11–16       Temple              Rochester, N.Y.
      18–23
      25–30       Keith's             Atlantic City, N.J.

## CANTOR & KESSLER

1914 June 22–27   Oxford              London, Eng.

## NOT LIKELY

1914 July 6–18    Alhambra            London, Eng.

## CANTOR & LEE

1914 Oct. 12–17   Bushwick            Brooklyn, N.Y.
      19–24       Maryland            Baltimore, Md.
      26–31
   Nov. 2–7       Keith's             Columbus, Ohio
      9–14        Keith's             Indianapolis, Ind.
      16–21       Palace Music Hall   Chicago, Ill.
      23–28       Columbia            Grand Rapids, Mich.
Nov. 30–Dec. 5    Majestic            Milwaukee, Wisc.
      7–12        Columbia            St. Louis, Mo.
      14–19       Orpheum             Memphis, Tenn.
      20–26       Orpheum             New Orleans, La.

1915 Feb. 8–13    Keith's             Louisville, Ky.
      15–20       Vaudeville          Fort Wayne, Ind.
      22–27       Keith's             Cincinnati, Ohio
   March 1–6      Temple              Detroit, Mich.

|  |  |  |
|---|---|---|
| 8–13 | Temple | Rochester, N.Y. |
| 15–20 | Orpheum | Harrisburg, Pa. |
| 22–27 | Grand | Syracuse, N.Y. |
| March 29–April 3 | Orpheum | Brooklyn, N.Y. |
| April 5–10 | Colonial | New York, N.Y. |
| 12–17 | Alhambra | New York, N.Y. |
| 19–24 | Keith's | Philadelphia, Pa. |
| April 26–May 1 | Orpheum | Montreal, Que. |
| May 3–8 | Prospect | Brooklyn, N.Y. |
| 10–15 | Keith's | Boston, Mass. |
| 17–22 | | |
| 24–29 | | |
| May 31–June 5 | | |
| June 7–12 | | |
| 14–19 | Keith's | Washington, D.C. |
| 21–23 | Harlem Opera House | New York, N.Y. |
| 24–26 | | |
| June 28–July 3 | Shea's | Buffalo, N.Y. |
| 5–10 | | |
| 12–17 | | |
| 19–24 | | |
| 26–31 | Morrison's | Rockaway, N.Y. |
| Aug. 2–7 | Henderson's | Coney Island, N.Y. |
| | | |
| Sept. 20–25 | Maryland | Baltimore, Md. |
| Sept. 27–Oct. 2 | Keith's | Providence, R.I. |
| Oct. 4–9 | Alhambra | New York, N.Y. |
| 11–16 | Bushwick | Brooklyn, N.Y. |
| 18–23 | Prospect | Brooklyn, N.Y. |
| 25–30 | Colonial | New York, N.Y. |
| Nov. 1–6 | Orpheum | Brooklyn, N.Y. |
| 8–13 | Keith's | Philadelphia, Pa. |
| 15–20 | Hippodrome | Youngstown, Ohio |
| 22–27 | Keith's | Toledo, Ohio |
| Nov. 29–Dec. 4 | Keith's | Columbus, Ohio |
| Dec. 6–11 | Palace Music Hall | Chicago, Ill. |
| 13–18 | Orpheum | St. Paul, Minn. |
| 20–25 | Orpheum | Minneapolis, Minn. |
| Dec. 27–Jan. 1 | Orpheum | Winnipeg, Man. |
| 1916 Jan. 3–5 | Grand | Calgary, Alb. |
| 6–8 | (Travel) | |
| 10–15 | Orpheum | Seattle, Wash. |
| 17–22 | Orpheum | Portland, Ore. |
| 24–29 | (Travel) | |
| Jan. 31–Feb. 5 | Orpheum | Oakland, Calif. |
| Feb. 7–19 | Orpheum | San Francisco, Calif. |
| 21–22 | Clunie | Sacramento, Calif. |
| 23–24 | T.& D. | Stockton, Calif. |

|  |  |  |
|---|---|---|
| 25–26 | White | Fresno, Calif. |
| Feb. 28–March 11 | Orpheum | Los Angeles, Calif. |
| March 13–18 | (Travel) | |
| 20–25 | Orpheum | Salt Lake City, Utah |
| March 27–April 1 | Orpheum | Denver, Colo. |
| April 3–5 | (Travel) | |
| 6–8 | Orpheum | Des Moines, Iowa |
| 10–15 | Orpheum | Kansas City, Mo. |
| 17–22 | Orpheum | Omaha, Neb. |
| 24–29 | Orpheum | St. Paul, Minn. |

## CANARY COTTAGE

A Farce with Music. Produced by Oliver Morosco. Book by Oliver Morosco and Elmer Harris. Lyrics and Music by Earl Carroll. Staged by Frank Stammers. Scenery by Robert McQuinn.

### Cast

| | |
|---|---|
| Michael O'Finnegan | LAURENCE WHEAT |
| "Sam" Beverly Moon | EDDIE CANTOR |
| Mrs. Hugg | GRACE ELLSWORTH |
| Pauline Hugg | EUNICE BURNHAM |
| Billy Moss | HERBERT CORTHELL |
| Nip | O. W. EDWARDS |
| Tuck | M. EDWARDS |
| Jerry Summerfield | CHARLES RUGGLES |
| Trixie Fair | LOUISE ORTH |
| Blanche Moss | TRIXIE FRIGANZA |
| Mitzie | BESSIE BAKER |
| Mabel | VIRGINIA TAVARES |
| Hal | LOUIS STRANGARD |

Orchestra under direction of Louis Gottschalk

#### ACT I

| | |
|---|---|
| Opening Ensemble | Chorus and O'Finnegan |
| Dance Intermezzo | Morin Sisters |
| "Such a Chauffeur" | Mrs. Hugg and Pauline |
| Quartette | Mrs. Hugg, Pauline, O'Finnegan, Sam |
| "But in the Morning" | Billy, Nick and Tuck |
| Grotesque | Edwards Bros. |
| "Old Man Methuselah" | Jerry and Boys |
| "I Never Knew" | Trixie and Jerry |
| "It Ruined Marc Antony" | Sam |
| "Canary Cottage" | Jerry, Trixie and Chorus |
| Fire Ensemble | Principals and Chorus |
| "The Syncopated Harp" | O'Finnegan and Chorus |
| Nouvelle Danse Acrobatique | Morin Sisters |

| "Follow the Cook" | Blanche and Chorus |
| Finale with Quartette | Blanche, Jerry, Pauline, Trixie |

ACT II

| Opening Ensemble | Jerry, Sam, Mrs. Hugg, Chorus |
| Canary Waltz | Morin Sisters |
| "The More I Love My Dog" | Blanche and Chorus |
| Fantasie L'Ostriche | Bessie Morin |
| "It's Always Orange Day in California" | Pauline, O'Finnegan, Chorus |
| "I'll Marry No Explorer" | Sam |
| Canary Gallop | Morin Sisters |
| Finale | Company |

| 1916 May 18–20 | Empress | San Diego, Calif. |
| May 21–July 15 | Mason Opera House | Los Angeles, Calif. |
| July 16–Sept. 9 | Cort | San Francisco, Calif. |

## ZIEGFELD MIDNIGHT FROLIC (FOURTH EDITION)

A Musical Revue in Two Parts by Gene Buck and Dave Stamper. Staged by Ned Wayburn. Sets by Joseph Urban. Produced by Florenz Ziegfeld Jr.
Orchestra under direction of Ford Dabney

PART I

| 1. "When He Comes Back to Me" | L. Haynes, O. Thomas, Chorus |
| 2. "The Hesitation Blues" | William Rock, Frances White |
| 3. Milo | |
| 4. "The Baloonatics" | Sybil Carmen and Chorus |
| 5. Lucy Gillette | |
| 6. "My Puerto Rican Maid" | Peggy Brooks and Chorus |
| 7. A New Nut | Eddie Cantor |
| 8. "Every Girl Is Fishing" | Frances White and Chorus |

PART II

| 9. "My Dancing Girl" | William Rock, Frances White |
| 10. Song | Peggy Brooks |
| 11. "High Life" | Bird Millman |
| 12. "Don't You Wish You Were a Kid Again?" | Sybil Carmen, Brady's Collies |
| 13. "Mavis" | Lawrence Haynes |
| 14. "Oh, You Gray-Haired Kid" | William Rock, Frances White |
| 15. Dance | Adelaide Bell |
| 16. "My Midnight Belle" | Mabel Ferry and Chorus |
| 17. "The Musical Dromeos" | Arnaut Bros. |
| 18. "The Melting Pot" | Lawrence Haynes |
| 19. Finale | Entire Company |

| 1916 Oct. 3–April 7 | New Amsterdam Roof | New York, N.Y. |

# ZIEGFELD FOLLIES OF 1917

A Musical Revue in Two Acts and Nineteen Scenes. Book and Lyrics by Gene Buck and George V. Hobart. Music by Dave Stamper and Raymond Hubbell. Patriotic Finale by Victor Herbert. Scenery by Joseph Urban. Staged by Ned Wayburn. Produced under the Personal Direction of Florenz Ziegfeld Jr.

PRINCIPALS: Will Rogers, Bert Williams, W. C. Fields
　　　Fanny Brice, Eddie Cantor, Walter Catlett
　　　Irving Fisher, Tom Richards, Allyn King
　　　Russell Vokes, Peggy Hopkins, Fred Heider
　　　Marion and Madeline Fairbanks, May Carmen
　　　Helen Barnes, Lilyan Tashman, Bruce McKay
　　　Clay Hill, Malcolm Hicks, Gus Minton, Dolores
　　　Peter Ostrander, Edith Hallor, Don Barclay
　　　Kathryn Perry, Charles Scribner, Joseph Kilgour
　　　Carl Hyson, Hans Wilson, Dorothy Dickson
　　　Emily Drange, Doris Lloyd, Gladys Loftus
　　　Ethel Delmar, Marie Wallace, Dorothy Leeds
　　　Betty Browne, Marcelle Earle, Margaret St. Clair
　　　Florence Kern, Mary Arthur, Edythe Whitney
　　　Claremont Carroll, Eleanor Lang, Cecile Markle

ACT I
　　　Scene 1—"The Episode of an Arabian Night in New York"
　　　Scene 2—"The Episode of the Purse"
　　　Scene 3—"The Episode of the Garden of Girls"
　　　Scene 4—"The Episode of the Dog"
　　　Scene 5—"The Episode of the Tennis Match"
　　　Scene 6—"The Episode of the *Ziegfeld Follies* Rag"
　　　Scene 7—"The Episode of the Information Bureau"
　　　Scene 8—"The Episode of the Telephone Wires"
　　　Scene 9—"The Episode of the Eddiecantor"
　　　Scene 10—"The Episode of the Patriotism"
　　　Scene 11—"The Episode of the American Eagle"

ACT II
　　　Scene 1—"The Episode of the Wedding Morning"
　　　Scene 2—"The Episode of the Williamswarbles"
　　　Scene 3—"The Episode of the Mississippi Levee"
　　　Scene 4—"The Episode of New York Streets and Subway"
　　　Scene 5—"The Episode of the Fannybriceisms"
　　　Scene 6—"The Episode of the Chinese Lacquer"
　　　Scene 7—"The Episode of the Willrogersayings"
　　　Scene 8—"The Episode of an Arabian Night (three hours later)"
　　　　　Orchestra under direction of Frank Darling

ACT I

"My Arabian Maid"　　　　　　　　　Irving Fisher, Allyn King, chorus
(Raymond Hubbell-Gene Buck)

| | |
|---|---|
| "The Arabian Fox Trot" | Doris Lloyd, Arabian Dancers |
| "Beautiful Garden of Girls" | Edith Hallor |
| (Raymond Hubbell-Gene Buck) | |
| "*Ziegfeld Follies* Rag" | Fanny Brice, Follies Dancers |
| (Dave Stamper-Gene Buck) | |
| "The Potato Bug" | Fred Heider |
| "Hello, My Dearie!" | Edith Hallor |
| (Dave Stamper-Gene Buck) | |
| "The Modern Maiden's Prayer" | Eddie Cantor |
| (James F. Hanley-Ballard MacDonald) | |
| "That's the Kind of a Baby for Me" | Eddie Cantor |
| (J. C. Egan-Alfred Harriman) | |
| "Can't You Hear Your Country Calling?" | Tom Richards |
| (Victor Herbert) | |

ACT II

| | |
|---|---|
| "Because You Are Just You" | Irving Fisher |
| "Because You Are Just You" | Irving Fisher |
| "Same Old Moon" | Edith Hallor |
| (Dave Stamper-Gene Buck) | |
| "Home, Sweet Home" | Bert Williams |
| (Ring W. Lardner) | |
| "Unhappy" | Bert Williams |
| (Henry Creamer-J. Turner Layton) | |
| "Just You and Me" | Fanny Brice, Eddie Cantor |
| (Dave Stamper-Gene Buck) | |
| "Egyptian" | Fanny Brice |
| (Leo Edwards-Blanche Merrill) | |
| "Chu-Chin-Chow" | Allyn King |
| (Dave Stamper-Gene Buck) | |

| | | |
|---|---|---|
| 1917 June 4–9 | Nixon's Apollo | Atlantic City, N.J. |
| June 12–Sept. 15 | New Amsterdam | New York, N.Y. |
| Sept. 17–Oct. 27 | Colonial | Boston, Mass. |
| Oct. 29–Nov. 10 | Forrest | Philadelphia, Pa. |
| Nov. 12–17 | Academy of Music | Baltimore, Md. |
| 19–24 | National | Washington, D.C. |
| Nov. 26–Dec. 1 | Nixon | Pittsburgh, Pa. |
| Dec. 3–8 | Euclid Ave. Opera House | Cleveland, Ohio |
| 10–22 | Detroit Opera House | Detroit, Mich. |
| Dec. 23–March 2 | Illinois | Chicago, Ill. |
| 1918 March 3–9 | American | St. Louis, Mo. |
| 11–16 | Grand Opera House | Cincinnati, Ohio |
| 18–23 | English's Opera House | Indianapolis, Ind. |
| 25–30 | Hartman | Columbus, Ohio |
| April 1–6 | Majestic | Buffalo, N.Y. |
| 8–13 | Princess | Toronto, Ont. |
| 15–20 | His Majesty's | Montreal, Que. |

## ZIEGFELD MIDNIGHT FROLIC (SEVENTH EDITION)

A Musical Revue in Two Parts by Gene Buck and Dave Stamper. Staged by Ned Wayburn. Sets by Joseph Urban. Produced by Florenz Ziegfeld, Jr.
Orchestra under direction of Ford Dabney

PART I

| | | |
|---|---|---|
| 1. | "We Are the Bright Lights of Broadway" | Yvonne Shelton and Eight Ziegfeld Girls |
| 2. | "The Motor Girls" | Frank Carter and Six Ziegfeld Girls |
| 3. | "Swinging Along" | Lillian Lorraine |
| 4. | "A Syncopated Frolic" | Ann Pennington |
| 5. | Mr. Rogers and Mr. Cantor | Will Rogers, Eddie Cantor |
| 6. | "The Spring Drive" | Lillian Lorraine |
| 7. | PATRIOTIC PICTURES | Arranged by Ben Ali Haggin |

PART II

| | | |
|---|---|---|
| 8. | "Queen of the Wire" | Bird Millman |
| 9. | "Fresh from the Bronx" | Eddie Cantor |
| 10. | "The Broadway Blues" | Lillian Lorraine and Girls |
| 11. | "Timely Topics" | Will Rogers |
| 12. | The Creator of "Jazz" Dancing | Frisco |
| 13. | "I Ain't Married No More" | Bert Williams |
| 14. | "Oriental Jazz" | Ann Pennington |
| 15. | "Victory" | Lillian Lorraine and Nine Ziegfeld Girls |
| 16. | TABLEAUX: "The Road To Victory" | Arranged by Ben Ali Haggin |

April 25–May 12    New Amsterdam Roof    New York, N.Y.

## ZIEGFELD FOLLIES OF 1918

A Musical Revue in Two Acts and Twenty-Six Scenes. Book and Lyrics by Rennold Wolf and Gene Buck. Music by Louis A. Hirsch and Dave Stamper. Scenery by Joseph Urban. Staged by Ned Wayburn. Produced under the Personal Direction of Florenz Ziegfeld Jr.

PRINCIPALS: Will Rogers, W. C. Fields, Eddie Cantor,
Marilyn Miller, Frank Carter, Ann Pennington,
Lillian Lorraine, Allyn King, Harry Kelly,
Gus Minton, Kay Laurel, Bee Palmer, Frisco,
Bert Savoy, Jay Brennan, Charlotte LeGrande,
John Blue, Dolores, Billie Ritchie, Clay Hill,
Kathryn Perry, Dorothy Leeds, Gladys Feldman,
Martha Mansfield, Dorothy Miller, Olive Osborne,
Julie Ross, Florence Atkinson, Gladys Ziellan,

Sylvia Ellias, Rose Dolores, Diana Allen,
Marie Wallace, Fairbanks Twins, Edith Hawes,
Ruth Taylor, Pauline Hall, Simon D'Herleys,
Carol Young, Mildred Richardson, Muriel Miles,
Annette Herbert, Helen Lloyd, Martha Wood,
Hazel Washburn, Nan Larned, Irene Wilson,
Theresa Rubins, Virginia Young, Leonard Baron

ACT I

Scene 1—"The Warring World"
Scene 2—"The Follies"
Scene 3—"The Peaches of 1918"
Scene 4—"A Patent Attorney's Office"
Scene 5—Specialty (W. C. Fields)
Scene 6—"Starlight"
Scene 7—"In Old Versailles"
Scene 8—Indian Dance (Ann Pennington)
Scene 9—"A Miniature"
Scene 10—"Timely Topics" (Will Rogers)
Scene 11—Finale
Scene 12—"Forward, Allies" (Ben Ali Haggin Tableau)

ACT II

Scene 13—"The Lower Regions"
Scene 14—Marilyn Miller as "Billie Burke"
Scene 15—"Blue Devils"
Scene 16—"A Game of Golf" (W. C. Fields)
Scene 17—"Poor Little Me"
Scene 18—"The Aviator's Test"
Scene 19—"Since The Men Have Gone to War"
Scene 20—"Any Old Time At All"
Scene 21—"A Dream"
Scene 22—"Fresh From The Bronx" (E. Cantor)
Scene 23—"Garden of Your Dreams"
Scene 24—"Getting Acquainted"
Scene 25—"Jazz Dance"
Scene 26—Finale

ACT I

"Starlight"
(Dave Stamper-Gene Buck)
"In Old Versailles"
(Louis A. Hirsch-Gene Buck)
"When I Hear A Syncopated Tune"                    Marilyn Miller
(Louis A. Hirsch-Gene Buck)
"When I'm Looking At You"
(Dave Stamper-Gene Buck)

| "I'm Gonna Pin A Medal On | Frank Carter |
| The Girl I Left Behind" | |
| (Irving Berlin) | |
| "Ship Song" | Addison Young |
| (Louis A. Birsch-Gene Buck) | |

ACT II

| "Marriage of Convenience" | Marilyn Miller |
| (Louis A. Hirsch-Gene Buck) | |
| "The Blue Devils" | Lillian Lorraine |
| "Poor Little Me" | Marilyn Miller |
| "Since The Men Have Gone To War" | Allyn King |
| "Any Old Time At All" | Lillian Lorraine |
| (Louis A. Hirsch-Gene Buck) | |
| "But After The Ball Was Over" | Eddie Cantor |
| (Arthur J. Jackson-Bud DeSylva) | |
| "Garden of My Dreams" | Lillian Lorraine, |
| (Dave Stamper-Louis A. Hirsch- | Frank Carter |
| Gene Buck) | |
| "I Want To Learn To Jazz Dance" | Bee Palmer |
| (Dave Stamper-Gene Buck) | |

| 1918 June 15 | Nixon's Apollo | Atlantic City, N.J. |
| June 18–Sept. 14 | New Amsterdam | New York, N.Y. |
| Sept. 16–Oct. 5 | Colonial | Boston, Mass. |
| Oct. 7–26 | Globe | New York, N.Y. |
| Oct. 28–Nov. 9 | Forrest | Philadelphia, Pa. |
| Nov. 11–16 | Academy of Music | Baltimore, Md. |
| 17–23 | National | Washington, D.C. |
| 25–30 | Nixon | Pittsburgh, Pa. |
| Dec. 2–7 | Euclid Ave. Opera House | Cleveland, Ohio |
| 9–21 | New Detroit | Detroit, Mich. |
| Dec. 22–March 1 | Colonial | Chicago, Ill. |
| 1919 March 2–8 | American | St. Louis, Mo. |
| 9–15 | | Kansas City, Mo. |
| 16–23 | Grand Opera House | Cincinnati, Ohio |
| 24–29 | English's Opera House | Indianapolis, Ind. |
| March 31–April 5 | Hartman | Columbus, Ohio |
| April 7–12 | Majestic | Buffalo, N.Y. |
| 14–19 | Princess | Toronto, Ont. |
| 21–26 | His Majesty's | Montreal, Que. |
| April 28–May 10 | Colonial | Boston, Mass. |

˅˅˅Cantor also appeared in the Eighth Edition of the Ziegfeld *Midnight Frolic* at the New Amsterdam at two intervals when the influenza epidemic forced the closing of all theatres in Boston and Philadelphia and the *Follies* cast was called into New York.

## ZIEGFELD FOLLIES OF 1919

A Musical Revue in Two Acts and Twenty-Three Scenes. Book and Lyrics by Rennold Wolf and Gene Buck. Music by Dave Stamper. Additional Songs by Irving Berlin. Ballet Composed by Victor Herbert. Scenery by Joseph Urban. Staged by Ned Wayburn. Produced under the Personal Direction of Florenz Ziegfeld Jr.

PRINCIPALS: Bert Williams, Eddie Cantor, Marilyn Miller
  John Steele, Eddie Dowling, George LeMaire
  Gus Van, Joe Schenck, Rae Dooley, Johnny Dooley
  George LeMaire, Mary Hay, Fairbanks Twins
  Jessie Reed, Phil Dwyer, Mildred Sinclair
  Martha Pierce, Margaret Irving, Alta King
  Addison Young, Simone D'Herlys, Lucille Levant
  Hazel Washburn, Kathryn Perry, Delyle Alda
  Betty Francesco, Ethel Hallor, Mauresette
  Florence Ware, Marcelle Earle, Jack Lynch
  Wesley Pierce, Willie Newsome, Ziegfeld Girls

### ACT I
Scene 1—"The *Follies* Salad"
Scene 2—"Hail to the Thirteenth Folly"
Scene 3—"A Pet"
Scene 4—"A Spanish Frolic"
Scene 5—"My Baby's Arms"
Scene 6—"Sweet Sixteen"
Scene 7—"The Popular Pests"
Scene 8—"Tulip Time"
Scene 9—"The Seldom Misses"
Scene 10—"Shimmy Town"
Scene 11—"The Epostle of Pep"
Scene 12—"I Love a Minstrel Show"
Scene 13—"The *Follies* Minstrels"

### ACT II
Scene 1—"Harem Life"
Scene 2—"The Guy Who Guards the Harem"
Scene 3—Songs (Bert Williams)
Scene 4—"The Circus Ballet"
Scene 5—"Melody Fantasy and Folly"
Scene 6—"At the Osteopath's"
Scene 7—"Prohibition"
Scene 8—Song (Van and Schenck)
Scene 9—"Tambourine Girl"
Scene 10—"Victory Arch" (Finale)

### ACT I
"The *Follies* Salad"                    Eddie Dowling

| | |
|---|---|
| "My Baby's Arms" | Delyle Alda |
| (Harry Tierney-Joseph McCarthy) | |
| "Sweet Sixteen" | Marilyn Miller |
| (Dave Stamper-Gene Buck) | |
| "Tulip Time" | John Steele, Delyle Alda |
| (Dave Stamper-Gene Buck) | |
| "Shimmee Town" | Johnny and Rae Dooley |
| (Dave Stamper-Gene Buck) | |
| "You'd Be Surprised" | Eddie Cantor |
| (Irving Berlin) | |
| "I'd Rather See a Minstrel Show" | |
| (Irving Berlin) | |
| "Mandy" | Van and Schenck |
| (Irving Berlin) | |
| "Harem Life" | Hazel Washburn |
| (Irving Berlin) | |
| "I'm the Guy That Guards The | Johnny Dooley |
| Harem" | |
| (Irving Berlin) | |
| "A Pretty Girl Is Like a Melody" | John Steele |
| (Irving Berlin) | |
| "You Cannot Make Your Shimmy | Bert Williams |
| Shake on Tea" | |
| (Irving Berlin) | |
| "A Syncopated Cocktail" | Marilyn Miller |
| (Irving Berlin) | |
| "My Tambourine Girl" | Jessie Reed |
| (Irving Berlin) | |
| "We Made the Doughnuts Over There" | Follies Girls |

| | | |
|---|---|---|
| 1919 June 10–14 | Nixon's Apollo | Atlantic City, N.J. |
| June 16–Aug. 23 | New Amsterdam | New York, N.Y. |
| Aug. 25–Sept. 13 | A.E.A. Strike | |
| Sept. 15–Dec. 6 | New Amsterdam | New York, N.Y.*** |
| Dec. 8–20 | New Detroit | Detroit, Mich. |
| Dec. 21–March 6 | Colonial | Chicago, Ill. |
| March 7–13 | | |
| March 15–20 | English's Opera House | Indianapolis, Ind. |
| March 22–27 | Euclid Ave. Opera House | Cleveland, Ohio |
| March 29–April 3 | | |
| April 5–10 | Grand Opera House | Cincinnati, Ohio |
| April 12–17 | Nixon | Pittsburgh, Pa. |
| April 19–24 | Academy of Music | Baltimore, Md. |
| April 25–May 1 | National | Washington, D.C. |
| May 3–15 | Forrest | Philadelphia, Pa. |
| May 17–29 | Colonial | Boston, Mass. |

***Cantor also appeared in the Ninth Edition of the Ziegfeld *Midnight Frolic* October 3–December 6, 1919.

## ZIEGFELD FOLLIES OF 1920

A Musical Revue in Two Act and Twenty-Five Scenes. Book and Lyrics by Gene Buck. Music by Dave Stamper. Additional Lyrics and Music by Irving Berlin. Special Music by Victor Herbert. Scenery by Joseph Urban. Staged by Edward Royce. Produced Under the Personal Direction of Florenz Ziegfeld Jr.

(Eddie Cantor's "specialty" comprised Scene 12 of Act II during the first week of this show's Broadway run.)

1920 June 22–26   New Amsterdam   New York, N.Y.

## GEORGE LEMAIRE'S BROADWAY BREVITIES

An Entertainment in Two Acts and Nineteen Scenes. Lyrics by Blair Treynor. Music by Archie Gottler. Dances and Ensembles Staged by Jack Mason. Art Direction by Herbert Ward. Presented by Rufus LeMaire.

ACT I

Scene 1—Prologue
Scene 2—Times Square
Scene 3—"A Will and a Way"
Scene 4—The Birch Forest
Scene 5—Ninety Days from Broadway
Scene 6—"Spanish Love"
Scene 7—"Stage Door Blues"
Scene 8—That Inimitable Comedian—Bert Williams
Scene 9—"At The Dentist's Office"
   A patient          EDDIE CANTOR
   Dr. Payne          GEORGE LEMAIRE
Scene 10—Mt. Blanc, Switzerland

ACT II

Scene 1—"The Kiss"
Scene 2—"Lu Lu"
Scene 3—The Smart Bootery
Scene 4—A Fifth Avenue Shop Window
Scene 5—"The Usual Thing"
Scene 6—A Roof Garden of a Modern Apartment
   Mr. Moe Goldfarb        EDDIE CANTOR
   Mr. Ponzi Dough         GEORGE LeMAIRE
   The Ladies              Peggy Parker, Genevieve
                           Houghton
Scene 6—A Roof Garden of a Modern Apartment
            Typical Restaurant Revue Scene
   EDDIE CANTOR, GEORGE LeMAIRE, Genevieve Houghton,
         Peggy Parker, Marcelle Barnes, Florence Kern
Scene 7—Eddie Cantor
Scene 8—"A Picture of You"
Scene 9—Finale: The Marble Steps

EDDIE CANTOR, GEORGE LeMAIRE,
EDITH HALLOR, BERT WILLIAMS,
Entire Ensemble
Orchestra under direction of Louis Gress

### ACT I

| | |
|---|---|
| "The Usual Opening Chorus" | Entire Ensemble |
| "I Love To Dance" | Teck Murdock, Virginia Roche, Peggy Mitchell, Alvah Fenton, Ona Hamilton |
| "Love, Honor and Oh, Baby!" | Eddie Buzzell, Peggy Parker |
| "Spring Dance" | Natalie Kingston and Girls |
| "The Dance of Nymphs" | Ula Sharon |
| "The Lady Beautiful" | Edith Hallor |
| "Stage Door Blues" | Misses Kerns, Berg, Hughes, Callahan, Levon, Westcott, Worth and Barnes |
| (Harry Ruby-Bert Kalmar) | |
| "Snow Flakes" | E. Hallor, Hal Van Rensellear |
| (George Gershwin-Arthur Jackson) | |

### ACT II

| | |
|---|---|
| "Lu Lu" | Edith Hallor and Girls |
| (George Gershwin-Arthur Jackson) | |
| "Beautiful Faces Need Beautiful Clothes" | Edith Hallor and Girls |
| (Irving Berlin) | |
| "I'm a Dancing Fool" | William Sully and Girls |
| "Drigo's Polka" | Ula Sharon |
| "Won't You Let Me Take a Picture of You?" | Vera Grosset and Kodak Girls |

1920 Sept. 16–25    Lyric          Philadelphia, Pa.
Sept. 29–Nov. 27   Winter Garden   New York, N.Y.

## THE MIDNIGHT ROUNDERS

A Musical Revue in Two Acts and Twenty-Eight Scenes. Book by Harold Atteridge. Lyrics by Alfred Bryan. Music by Jean Schwartz. Staged by Lew Morton. Musical Numbers Staged by Jack Mason. Entire Production Staged under the Personal Direction of J. J. Shubert.

### ACT I

Scene 1—Prologue: "Make Believe Land"
Scene 2—"The Land of Blues"
Scene 3—"The Heart Burglars"
Scene 4—"Children Not Wanted"
Scene 5—"Oriental"

Scene 6—"A Comedian Wanted"
| | |
|---|---|
| A Man About Town | JOHN BYAM |
| Another Man About Town | EDDIE CANTOR |

Scene 7—"Joyland"
Scene 8—"Just Clothes"
Scene 9—At The Stage Door of the Winter Garden
Scene 10—"Toyland"
Scene 11—"Insurance"
| | |
|---|---|
| The Doctor | JOE OPP |
| The Stenographer | MABEL OLSON |
| The Patient | EDDIE CANTOR |
| Applicants | BETTY PECAN, ALICE FORREST |

Scene 12—"Just Dancing"
Scene 13—A Few Songs (Green and Blyler)
Scene 14—Cafe de La Paix
| | |
|---|---|
| The Deacon | HARRY KELLY |
| Crabapple | LEW HEARN |
| The Manager | JOE OPP |
| A Waiter | EDDIE CANTOR |
| A Man About Town | JOHN BYAM |
| A Man From Home | JOHN DOUGHERTY |
| A Quiet Man | C. E. WHEELER |

Scene 15—More Dance
Scene 16—"The Wedding of the Sun and the Moon"

ACT II

Scene 1—"Playland"
Scene 2—"A Jazz Vampire" (Jane Green)
Scene 3—Cameo
Scene 4—"The Story of the Waltz"
Scene 5—"The Storytellers"
"A Jazz Vampire" (Jane Green)
Scene 6—"Joe's Blue Front"
| | |
|---|---|
| The Proprietor | JOE OPP |
| The Salesman | EDDIE CANTOR |
| The Prospective Victim | LEW HEARN |

Scene 7—"Nonsense"
Scene 8—"Heavenly Body"
Scene 9—Just Songs (Eddie Cantor)
Scene 10—"Looking Backwards"
Scene 11—Dancing
Scene 12—Century Promenade
Orchestra under direction of Louis Gress

ACT I
| | |
|---|---|
| "Romantic Blues" | Jane Green, Girls, Penn Quartette |

"Heartbreakers" John Byam, Ten Heart Burglars
"A Mouthful of Kisses" Muriel Deforrest

ACT II

"My Lady of the Cameo" Nan Halperin, John Byam, Girls
"Whisper in My Ear" Francine Dunlap, Chorus
"Beautiful Shoulders" Helen Bolton, Girls

| | | |
|---|---|---|
| 1920 Nov. 29–Dec. 18 | Sam S. Shubert | Philadelphia, Pa. |
| Dec. 20–25 | Auditorium | Baltimore, Md. |
| Dec. 27–Feb. 19 | Majestic | Boston, Mass. |
| 1921 Feb. 21–26 | Shubert-Majestic | Providence, R.I. |
| Feb. 28–March 5 | Court Square | Springfield, Mass. |
| March 7–12 | Sam S. Shubert | New Haven, Conn. |
| 14–19 | Parsons' | Hartford, Conn. |
| 21–26 | Broad Street | Newark, N.J. |
| March 28–April 2 | Crescent | Brooklyn, N.Y. |
| April 3–9 | Poli's | Washington, D.C. |
| 11–23 | Alvin | Pittsburgh, Pa. |
| April 25–May 7 | Shubert-Detroit | Detroit, Mich. |
| May 9–21 | Hanna | Cleveland, Ohio |
| 23–28 | Teck | Buffalo, N.Y. |
| May 30–June 4 | Globe | Atlantic City, N.J. |

## FRIARS' FROLIC

June 12, 1921 Manhattan Opera House New York, N.Y.

## MIDNIGHT ROUNDERS

| | | |
|---|---|---|
| Aug. 28–Sept. 3 | Garrick | Detroit, Mich. |
| Sept. 4–Oct. 1 | Apollo | Chicago, Ill. |
| Oct. 2–29 | Garrick | Chicago, Ill. |
| Oct. 30–Nov. 26 | Great Northern | Chicago, Ill. |
| Nov. 27–Dec. 3 | Sam S. Shubert | Kansas City, Mo. |
| Dec. 4–10 | Jefferson | St. Louis, Mo. |
| 11–17 | Davidson | Milwaukee, Wisc. |
| 19–24 | | |
| 26–31 | Murat | Indianapolis, Ind. |
| 1922 Jan. 1–7 | Sam S. Shubert | Cincinnati, Ohio |
| 9–14 | Garrick | Detroit, Mich. |

## MAKE IT SNAPPY

A Revue in Two Acts and Twenty-Seven Scenes. Produced by the Winter Garden Company. Book and Lyrics by Harold Atteridge. Eddie Cantor's Scenes by Harold Atteridge and Eddie Cantor. Music by Jean Schwartz. Staged by J. C. Huffman. Numbers Staged by Allan K. Foster. Stage Settings by Watson Barratt. Entire Production Staged Under the Personal Supervision of J. J. Shubert.

ACT I

Scene 1—Prologue: Mr. and Mrs. Playgoer.
Scene 2—Main Street.
Scene 3—Dance Town.
Scene 4—The Broadway Modiste Shop.
Scene 5—The Stage Door.
Scene 6—A Bouquet of Girls.
Scene 7—A Bit of Kipling.
Scene 8—In Front of the Police Station.
Scene 9—The Police Station.
Scene 10—Esquimoland.
Scene 11—Broadway Impressions.
Scene 12—Joe's Blue Front.
Scene 13—In Old Madrid.
Scene 14—Cafe DeGrande.

ACT II

Scene 1—The Princess Beautiful.
Scene 2—Step in My Taxi.
Scene 3—A Fragonard Picture.
Scene 4—The Price.
Scene 5—Only Man I Ever Loved.
Scene 6—The Sheik.
Scene 7—Stepville.
Scene 8—Butterflies.
Scene 9—Eddie Cantor.
Scene 10—In Lampland.
Scene 11—Finale.

Orchestra under direction of Louis Gress

ACT I

| | |
|---|---|
| "Blossom Time" | John Byam and Blossom Girls |
| "Good-Bye, Main Street" | Tot Qualters, Lew Hearn, Marie Burke, John Byam, and Main Street Steppers |
| "When the Wedding Chimes Are Ringing" | J. Harold Murray, Dolly Hackett and Bridesmaids |
| "Cheeky Kiki" | Nan Halperin and Kiki Girls |
| "To Make Them Beautiful Ladies" | Margaret Wilson and Some Winter Garden Beauties |
| "Bouquet of Girls" (Jean Schwartz-Harold Atteridge) | John Byam and Nosegays |
| "I Learned About Women from Her" (Adapted from Kipling's poem) | J. Harold Murray |
| Humoresquimos | Tot Qualters, Carlos and Inez |
| "The Flapper" | Nan Halperin |
| "My Castillian Girl" | Marie Burke and Beauties |

| | |
|---|---|
| "Won't You Buy a Flower?" | Conchita Piquer |
| "Hootch Rhythm" | Tot Qualters, Inez and Carlos |
| (Jean Schwartz-Alfred Bryan) | |
| *Some Songs | Eddie Cantor |
| "Tell Me What's The Matter. Lovable Eyes" | J. Harold Murray, Dolly Hackett, Hackett, Lew Hearn, Conchita Piquer and Lovable Girls |
| (Jean Schwartz-Harold Attridge) | |

ACT II

| | |
|---|---|
| "My Fragonard Girl" | Margaret Wilson and Girls |
| (Jean Schwartz-Alfred Bryan) | |
| "He Was the Only Man I Ever Loved" | Nan Halperin |
| "Desert Rose" | J. Harold Murray and Roses |
| (Jean Schwartz-Harold Atteridge) | |
| "The Sheik" | Eddie Cantor |
| "Gay Butterfly on the Wheel" | Marie Burke and Butterflies |
| (Jean Schwartz-Alfred Bryan) | |
| *Some Songs | Eddie Cantor |
| "Lamplight Land" | Margaret Wilson, J. H. Murray |

*Songs sung by Cantor during the run of this show:
   "The Sheik of Araby"
   (Ted Snyder-Harry B. Smith-Francis Wheeler)
   "Waikiki, I Hear You Calling Me"
   (Harry Ruby-Bert Kalmar)
   "The Wedding Ring Don't Mean a Thing When You're Married"
   (Fred Fisher-Eddie Cantor)
   "My Yiddisha Mammy"
   (Jean Schwartz-Eddie Cantor-Alex Gerber)
   "Don't (Don't Stop Loving Me Now)"
   (James F. Hanley-Joe Godwin-Murray Roth)
   "I Love Her—She Loves Me"
   (Eddie Cantor-Irving Caesar)
   "Where the Bamboo Babies Grow"
   (Walter Donaldson-Lew Brown)
   "Lovin' Sam, the Sheik of Alabam' "
   (Milton Ager-Jack Yellen)
   "I Go So Far with Sophie"
   (Abner Silver)
   "I'll Be in My Dixie Home Again Tomorrow"
   (Roy Turk-J. Russel Robinson)
   "Little Rover (Don't Forget to Come Back Home)"
   (Walter Donaldson-Gus Kahn)

| | | | |
|---|---|---|---|
| 1922 | Feb. 14–18 | Auditorium | Baltimore, Md. |
| | Feb. 20–March 18 | Sam S. Shubert | Philadelphia, Pa. |

| | | |
|---|---|---|
| March 20–25 | Teck | Buffalo, N.Y. |
| March 27–April 1 | Hanna | Cleveland, Ohio |
| April 3–8 | Alvin | Pittsburgh, Pa. |
| April 13–July 1 | Winter Garden | New York, N.Y. |

## Vaudeville

| | | |
|---|---|---|
| 1922 Aug. 13–19 | Garden Pier | Atlantic City, N.J. |
| Aug. 20–26 | | Astoria, N.Y. (?) |

## MAKE IT SNAPPY

| | | |
|---|---|---|
| Sept. 18–23 | Majestic | Brooklyn, N.Y. |
| 25–27 | | |
| 28–30 | Lyceum | Rochester, N.Y. |
| Oct. 2–7 | Royal Alexandra | Toronto, Ont. |
| Oct. 9–14 | Hanna | Cleveland, Ohio |
| 16–21 | Alvin | Pittsburgh, Pa. |
| 23–28 | Auditorium | Baltimore, Md. |
| Oct. 30–Nov. 4 | Shubert-Majestic | Providence, R.I. |
| Nov. 6–Dec. 2 | Sam S. Shubert | Boston, Mass. |
| Dec. 4–9 | Broad Street | Newark, N.J. |
| 17–23 | Poli's | Washington, D.C. |
| 25–30 | | |
| Dec. 31–Jan. 6 | Garrick | Detroit, Mich. |
| 1923 Jan. 7–March 10 | Apollo | Chicago, Ill. |
| March 12–17 | Hartman | Columbus, Ohio |
| 18–24 | Sam S. Shubert | Cincinnati, Ohio |
| 25–31 | Jefferson | St. Louis, Mo. |
| April 1–7 | Sam S. Shubert | Kansas City, Mo. |
| 8–14 | Davidson | Milwaukee, Wisc. |
| 15–21 | Garrick | Detroit, Mich. |
| 23–28 | | |
| April 30–May 26 | Chestnut St. Opera House | Philadelphia, Pa. |

## Keith Vaudeville*

| | | |
|---|---|---|
| 1923 June 4–9 | Orpheum | Brooklyn, N.Y. |
| June 11–23 | Palace | New York, N.Y. |

*Cantor "doubled" into the *Ziegfeld Follies* of 1922, New Amsterdam Theatre, New York, N.Y., replacing Will Rogers, during this three-week (June 4–23, 1923) period.

## ZIEGFELD FOLLIES OF 1922 (NEW EDITION)

| | | |
|---|---|---|
| 1923 June 25–Aug. 4 | New Amsterdam | New York, N.Y. |

## Keith Vaudeville

| | | |
|---|---|---|
| 1923 Aug. 6–11 | Globe | Atlantic City, N.J. |
| Aug. 13–Sept. 15 | Lay-off; vacation. | |
| Sept. 17–22 | Riverside | New York, N.Y. |
| 24–29 | Alhambra | New York, N.Y. |
| Oct. 1–6 | Bushwick | Brooklyn, N.Y. |

## KID BOOTS

A Musical Comedy of "Palm Beach and Golf." Produced by Florenz Ziegfeld Jr.
Book by William Anthony McGuire and Otto Harbach. Music by Harry Tierney.
Lyrics by Joseph McCarthy. Staged by Edward Royce.

| | | |
|---|---|---|
| Herbert Pendleton | | PAUL EVERTON |
| Peter Pillsbury | | HARRY SHORT |
| Herbert Pendleton | | PAUL EVERTON |
| Harold Regan | | JOHN RUTHERFORD |
| Menlo Manville | | HARLAND DIXON |
| Miss Stymie | | AVONNE TAYLOR |
| Miss Brassey | | MADELYN MORRISEY |
| Miss Putter | | JOAN GARDNER |
| Miss Cleek | | KATHARINE STUART |
| Miss Driver | | DIANA STEGMAN |
| Miss Mashie | Society Buds | SONIA IVANOFF |
| Miss Fairway | | SYLVIA KINGSLEY |
| Miss Foursome | | BETTY GREY |
| Miss Hazard | | PERLE GERMOND |
| Miss Green | | EUNICE HALL |
| Miss Pinn | | MURIEL MANNERS |
| Miss Stroke | | VELMA ZIEGLER |
| Tom Sterling | | HARRY FENDER |
| Polly Pendleton | | MARY EATON |
| First Golfer | | MORTON MCCONNACHIE |
| Second Golfer | | JACK ANDREWS |
| First Caddie | | DICK WARE |
| Second Caddie | | WILLIAM BLETT |
| Third Caddie | | FRANK ZOLT |
| Fourth Caddie | | WALDO ROBERTS |
| Fifth Caddie | | LLOYD KEYES |
| Kid Boots | | EDDIE CANTOR |
| Beth | | BETH BERI |
| Carmen Mendoza | | ETHELIND TERRY |
| Jane Martin | | MARIE CALLAHAN |
| Dr. Josephine Fitch | | JOBYNA HOWLAND |
| Randolph Valentine | | ROBERT BARRAT |
| Federal Officer | | VICTOR MUNROE |

Ensemble
GEORGE OLSEN AND HIS ORCHESTRA

ACT I

Scene 1—Exterior of Everglades Golf Club, Palm Beach, Fla.
Scene 2—The Ladies' Locker Room.
Scene 3—The Caddie Shop
Scene 4—Patio of the Everglades Club.

ACT II

Scene 1—The Trophy Room.
Scene 2—The Eighteenth Hole.
Scene 3—Exterior of Caddie House—"The Nineteenth Hole."
Scene 4—The Cocoanut Ball.

Orchestra under direction of Louis Gress
Orchestrations by Frank Barry

ACT I—"GOING OUT"

| | |
|---|---|
| "A Day at the Club" | Ensemble |
| "The Social Observer" | Menlo Manville and Ensemble |
| "If Your Heart's in the Game" | Polly and Tom Sterling |
| "Keep Your Eye on the Ball" | Boots and Caddies |
| "The Same Old Way" | Carmen Mendoza and Tom Sterling |
| "Someone Loves You After All" | Boots, Polly, and Ensemble |
| "The Intruder Dance" | Jane Martin, Menlo Manville |
| "We've Got to Have More" | Horton Spurr and Caddies |
| "Polly Put the Kettle On" | Tom Sterling and Ensemble |
| "Let's Do and Say We Didn't" | Boots and Jane Martin |
| "In the Swim at Miami" | Carmen, Beth, and Ensemble |
| "Along the Old Lake Trail" | Polly and Gentlemen |
| "On with the Game" | All Members of the Club |

ACT II—"COMING IN"

| | |
|---|---|
| "Mah Jong" | Ensemble |
| "Bet on the One You Fancy" | Ladies and Gentlemen |
| "I'm in My Glory" | Menlo Manville, Beth |
| "A Play Fair Man" | Polly, Carmen, Tom, Harold |
| "Win for Me" | Boots, Polly, Carmen, and Ensemble |
| "The Cake Eaters' Ball" | Jane Martin, Menlo Manville |
| "Down 'Round the 19th Hole" | Boots, Howland, Pillsbury, Pendleton and Caddies |
| "The Cocoanut Ball" | George Olsen Orchestra |
| "When the Cocoanuts Call" | Carmen, Beth, Ensemble |
| "In the Rough" | Eddie Cantor of *ZIEGFELD FOLLIES* |
| Presentation of the Cup | Polly |
| "That's All There Is" | Company |

| | | |
|---|---|---|
| 1923 Dec. 3–8 | New Detroit | Detroit, Mich. |
| 10–15 | Grand Opera House | Cincinnati, Ohio |

| 17–22 | National | Washington, D.C. |
|---|---|---|
| 24–29 | Nixon | Pittsburgh, Pa. |
| Dec. 31–Aug. 30 | Earl Carroll | New York, N.Y. |
| 1924 Sept. 1–Feb. 21 | Selwyn | New York, N.Y. |
| 1925 Feb. 23–April 11 | Colonial | Boston, Mass. |
| April 13–18 | Sam S. Shubert | Newark, N.J. |
| 20–25 | Werba's Brooklyn | Brooklyn, N.Y. |
| April 27–May 23 | Forrest | Philadelphia, Pa. |
| Sept. 14–26 | Ohio | Cleveland, Ohio |
| Sept. 27–Jan. 24 | Woods | Chicago, Ill. |
| 1926 Jan. 25–Feb. 6 | Lay-off; Cantor illness. | |
| Feb. 8–13 | English's Opera House | Indianapolis, Ind. |
| 14–20 | American | St. Louis, Mo. |
| 21–27 | Sam S. Shubert | Kansas City, Mo. |
| Feb. 28–March 6 | Davidson | Milwaukee, Wisc. |
| March 8–13 | New Detroit | Detroit, Mich. |
| 15–20 | Nixon | Pittsburgh, Pa. |
| 22–27 | National | Washington, D.C. |
| March 29–April 3 | Sam S. Shubert | Newark, N.J. |
| April 5–10 | Lyceum | Rochester, N.Y. |
| 12–17 | Ford's | Baltimore, Md. |
| 19–21 | Court Square | Springfield, Mass. |
| 22–24 | Worcester | Worcester, Mass. |
| April 26–May 1 | Sam S. Shubert | New Haven, Conn. |
| May 3–5 | Shubert-Majestic | Providence, R.I. |
| 6–8 | Parsons' | Hartford, Conn. |

## Paramount Vaudeville

Oct. 9–22　Rialto　New York, N.Y.

## All-Star Benefit/Surprise Lake Camp

March 20　Casino　New York, N.Y.

## Orpheum Vaudeville

1927 May 8–14　Orpheum　San Francisco, Calif.
15–21　Orpheum　Los Angeles, Calif.

## ZIEGFELD FOLLIES OF 1927

A Musical Revue in Two Acts and Twenty-Four Scenes. Sketches by Harold R. Atteridge and Eddie Cantor. Lyrics and Music by Irving Berlin. Ballets by Albertina Rasch. Dialogue Staged by Zeke Colvan. Dances Staged by Sammy Lee. Scenes by Joseph Urban. Costumes Designed by John W. Harkrider. Presented by Abraham L. Erlanger and Florenz Ziegfeld Jr. Produced by Florenz Ziegfeld Jr.

PRINCIPALS: Eddie Cantor, Ruth Etting, Frances Upton
Cliff Edwards, Irene Delroy, Franklyn Baur

Brox Sisters, Helen Brown, William H. Power
Dan Healy, Harry McNaughton, Andrew Tombes
Claudia Dell, Lee Russell, Paul Chezzi
Phil Ryley, Frank Phillips, Jack Stevens
Evelyn Grove, Jean Ackerman, Bonnie Murray
Gladys Renneck, Muriel Finley, Claire Luce
Gertrude Williams, Lora Foster, Edith Hayward
Catherine Moylan, Jean Ackerman, Pirkko Ahlquist
Gladys Rennick, Gertrude Williams, Bonnie Murray
Mignon Dallett, Catherine Moylan, Jean Audree
Margaret Mayer, Ross Hines, Peggy Chamberlin
Frank Sherlock, Kae Carroll, Bob Ingersoll
Myrna Darby, Eileen Cullen, Al Siegal
Albertina Rasch Dancers, Ziegfeld Girls

### ACT I

Scene 1—The Office of Florenz Ziegfeld
Scene 2—"The Star's Double"
Scene 3—"Ribbons and Bows"
Scene 4—The Trans-Atlantic Flight
Scene 5—"Shaking the Blues Away"
Scene 6—"The Doll Toto"
Scene 7—"Innovation"—At Palm Beach
Scene 8—"Maybe It's You"
Scene 9—"It Won't Be Long Now"—A Taxi Ride
Scene 10—"Rainbow of Girls"
Scene 11—Eddie Cantor Himself
Scene 12—"It's Up to the Band"
Scene 13—Finale

### ACT II

Scene 1—"At the City Hall Steps"
Scene 2—"Getting a New Dress"
Scene 3—"Near the Bridge"
Scene 4—"Learn to Sing a Love Song"
Scene 5—"A Ballet Master's Idea of the Spoken Drama"
Scene 6—"Tickling the Ivories"
Scene 7—"The Jungle-Jingle"
Scene 8—"Now We Are Glorified"
Scene 9—"The New York Dog Shop"
Scene 10—Cliff Edwards (Ukelele Ike)
Scene 11—Finale

### ACT I

| | |
|---|---|
| "Ribbons and Bows" | Irene Delroy |
| "Shaking the Blues Away" | Ruth Etting, Jazzbow Girls |
| "Ooh, Maybe It's You" | Irene Delroy, Franklyn Baur |
| "Rainbow of Girls" | Franklyn Baur |
| "You've Got to Have 'It' " | Eddie Cantor |

| "It All Belongs to Me" | Lora Foster |
| "It's Up to the Band" | Brox Sisters, Male Ensemble |

ACT II

| "Jimmy" | Ruth Etting, Ingenues |
| "Learn to Sing a Love Song" | Franklyn Baur |
| "Tickling the Ivories" | Ruth Etting |
| "Jungle Jingle" | Brox Sisters |

| 1927 Aug. 2–13 | Colonial | Boston, Mass. |
| Aug. 16–Jan. 7 | New Amsterdam | New York, N.Y. |
| 1928 Jan. 9–21 | Colonial | Boston, Mass. |
| Jan. 23–28 | Sam S. Shubert | Newark, N.J. |

Vaudeville

| Sept. 16–22 | Granada | Chicago, Ill. |
| Sept. | Marlboro | Chicago, Ill. |

## WHOOPEE

A Musical Comedy in Two Acts and Twelve Scenes. Produced by Florenz Ziegfeld Jr. Book by William Anthony McGuire, based upon the comedy, *The Nervous Wreck*, by Owen Davis. Music by Walter Donaldson. Lyrics by Gus Kahn. Sets by Josef Urban. Dialogue Staged by William Anthony McGuire. Ensembles Staged by Seymour Felix. Costumes by John W. Hark-rider.

ACT I

Scene 1—Mission Rest, California.
Scene 2—Black Top Canyon, a mountain road.
Scene 3—The Gas Station.
Scene 4—Kitchen of Bar M Ranch.
Scene 5—The Corral.
Scene 6—Bar M Ranch.

ACT II

Scene 1—The Reservation of the Mohave Tribe.
Scene 2—A Poppy Field.
Scene 3—Interior of Ranch House, Bar M Ranch.
Scene 4—Indian Retreat.
Scene 5—"Halloween."

| Leslie Daw | RUTH ETTING |
| Pearl | OLIVE BRADY |
| Betty | GLADYS GLAD |
| Mable | JOSEPHINE ADAIR |
| Estelle | JEAN ACKERMAN |

| | |
|---|---|
| Alice | ADELE SMITH |
| Irene | KATHERINE BURKE |
| Virginia | MYRNA DARBY |
| Lucille | MURIEL FINLEY |
| Vivian | FREDA MIERSE |
| Judson Morgan | LOUIS MORRELL |
| The Padre | FRANK COLLETI |
| Jim Carson | JACK SHAW |
| Pete | FRANK FREY |
| Joe | BOB RICE |
| Jack | JACK GIFFORD |
| Mary Custer | ETHEL SHUTTA |
| Sheriff Bob Wells | JOHN RUTHERFORD |
| Sally Morgan | FRANCES UPTON |
| Brand Iron Edwards | JAMES P. HOUSTON |
| Henry Williams | EDDIE CANTOR |
| Wanenis | PAUL GREGORY |
| Black Eagle | CHIEF CAUPOLICAN |
| Jerome Underwood | SPENCER CHARTERS |
| Chester Underwood | ALBERT HACKETT |
| Timothy Sloane | JACK SHAW |
| Harriet Underwood | RUBY KEELER |
| Andy Nab | WILL H. PHILBRICK |
| Morton | BOB RICE |
| Yvonne | BERNICE MANNERS |
| Ma-Ta-Pe | SYLVIA ADAM |
| Comulo | JAMES P. HOUSTON |
| An Indian | EDOUARD GROBE |
| Tejou | JACK SHAW |
| Yolandi | TAMARA GEVA |
| Eleanor | OLIVE BRADY |

Ensemble
GEORGE OLSEN AND HIS ORCHESTRA
Pit Orchestra Under Direction of Gus Salzer

Mary Jane Kittel replaced Ruby Keeler on Monday, November 12, 1928, during out-of-town try-outs in Pittsburgh.

ACT I

| | |
|---|---|
| "It's a Beautiful Day Today" | Ensemble |
| "Here's To the Girl of My Heart" | Wanenis, Cow Boys |
| "I'm Bringing a Red, Red Rose" | Sally Morgan, Wanenis |
| "Gypsy Joe" | Leslie Daw, Dancers |
| "Makin' Whoopee" | Henry Williams |
| "Go Get 'em" | John Rutherford, Ensemble |
| "Until You Get Somebody Else" | Henry, Sally |

| | |
|---|---|
| "Taps" | Harriet Underwood |
| "Come West, Little Girl, Come West" | Mary Custer, Cow Boys |
| "Where Sunset Meets the Sea" | Leslie Daw, Ensemble |
| Gypsy Dance | Tamara Geva, Ensemble |
| "Stetson" | Mary Custer, Cow Boys |
| The Singing Waiter | Henry Williams |
| Finale | Entire Company |

ACT II

| | |
|---|---|
| "The Song of the Setting Sun" | Black Eagle and Tribe |
| "Love is The Mountain" | Black Eagle, Wanenis, Ma-Ta-Pe |
| "Red Mama" | Harriet Underwood |
| "We'll Keep On Caring" | Sally Morgan, Wanenis |
| Mohave War Dance | |
| Invocation to the Mountain God | |
|     (a) The Parade, (b) The Dance, (c) The offering of Beauty | |
| "Halloween Tonight" | George Olsen Orchestra |
| "Love Me or Leave Me" | Leslie Daw |
| Modernistic Ballet in Black | Tamara Geva |
| "Halloween Whoopee Ball" | Mary Custer, Ensemble |

| | | |
|---|---|---|
| 1928 Nov. 6–17 | Nixon | Pittsburgh, Pa. |
| 19–24 | Sam S. Shubert | Newark, N.J. |
| Nov. 26–Dec.1 | National | Washington, D.C. |
| Dec. 4–July 13 | New Amsterdam | New York, N.Y. |
| 1929 July 15–Aug. 3 | Lay-off; vacation. | |
| Aug. 5–Nov. 23 | New Amsterdam | New York, N.Y. |
| Nov. 25–Dec. 21 | Colonial | Boston, Mass. |
| Dec. 23–28 | Ford's | Baltimore, Md. |
| Dec. 30–Jan. 11 | Garrick | Philadelphia, Pa. |
| 1930 Jan. 13–18 | Wilson | Detroit, Mich. |
| Jan. 19–March 1 | Illinois | Chicago, Ill. |
| March 2–8 | American | St. Louis, Mo. |
| 10–15 | Ohio | Cleveland, Ohio |

## Eddie Cantor

| | | |
|---|---|---|
| 1930 Aug. 31–Sept. 6 | Steel Pier | Atlantic City, N.J. |
| Sept. | | Cleveland, Ohio |
| Oct. 13–18 | George Olsen's | Culver City, Calif. |
| Dec. 6 | Palace | Cleveland, Ohio |
| Dec. 27–Jan. 9 | Palace | New York, N.Y. |
| 1931 Jan. 17–23 | Albee | Brooklyn, N.Y. |
| Feb. | Floridian | Miami, Fla. |
| Sept. 18–24 | Paramount | Brooklyn, N.Y. |

## Eddie Cantor Unit *

*Cantor, George Jessel, George Burns & Gracie Allen, Janet Reade, Rhythm Boys (3), Serge Flash, Miacahua (Cleveland), Noble Sissle's Orchestra (Cleveland), Benny Meroff Band (Chicago).

| | | | |
|---|---|---|---|
| 1931 | Oct. 17–23 | Grand Opera House | Philadelphia, Pa. |
| | 24–27 | 86th Street | New York, N.Y. |
| | 28–30 | Fordham | Bronx, N.Y. |
| | Oct. 31–Jan. 1 | Palace | New York, N.Y. |
| 1932 | Jan. 4–10 | Civic Auditorium | Cleveland, Ohio |
| | 11 | Memorial Auditorium | Columbus, Ohio |
| | 15–21 | Chicago | Chicago, Ill. |

## Eddie Cantor Unit*

*Cantor, George Jessel, David Rubinoff, Jack Holland & June Knight, Bobby Bixler, Coletta Ryan.

| | | |
|---|---|---|
| Dec. 23–29 | Paramount | Brooklyn, N.Y. |
| Dec. 30–Jan. 5 | Earle | Philadelphia, Pa. |
| 1933 Jan. 6–12 | Paramount | New York, N.Y. |
| 13–19 | | |
| 20–26 | Paradise | Bronx, N.Y. |
| 28 | | Springfield, Mass. |
| 29 | | Albany, N.Y. |
| 30 | Palace | Rochester, N.Y. |
| 31 | Century | Buffalo, N.Y. |
| Feb. 1 | Mosque | Pittsburgh, Pa. |
| 2 | | Reading, Pa. |
| 3 | | Richmond, Va. |
| 6 | | Roanoke, Va. |
| 7 | | Raleigh, N.C. |
| 8 | | Atlanta, Ga. |
| 9 | | Macon, Ga. |
| 10 | | Jacksonville, Fla. |
| 15–16 | | Miami, Fla. |
| 20 | | Palm Beach, Fla. |

## Eddie Cantor

March 11–16    Fox    Washington, D.C.

## Eddie Cantor-George Jessel

| | |
|---|---|
| March 17–18 | Newark, N.J. |
| 26 | New Orleans, La. |
| 27 | Houston, Texas |
| 28 | San Antonio, Texas |

| | | |
|---|---|---|
| 29 | | Fort Worth, Texas |
| 30 | | Dallas, Texas |
| 31 | | Tulsa, Oklahoma |
| April 1 | | Kansas City, Mo. |
| 2 | | Des Moines, Iowa |
| 3 | Orpheum | Minneapolis, Minn. |
| 4 | | |
| 5 | | |
| 6 | | |
| 7 | | |
| 8 | Sam S. Shubert | Cincinnati, Ohio |

## Eddie Cantor Unit*

*Cantor, David Rubinoff, Florence Desmond, Bob Ripa, George Prentiss, Norman Gast, Chilton & Thomas, Chaney & Fox, chorus line, house orchestras. Films: *Fog* (Columbia), Brooklyn; *Miss Fane's Baby Is Stolen* (Paramount), New York.

| | | |
|---|---|---|
| 1934 Jan. 5–11 | Paramount | Brooklyn, N.Y. |
| 12–18 | Earle | Philadelphia, Pa. |
| 19–25 | Paramount | New York, N.Y. |

## All-Star Benefit/Surprise Lake Camp

1934 Feb. 11    New Amsterdam    New York, N.Y.

## Eddie Cantor Unit*

*Cantor, Cliff ("Sharlie") Hall, David Rubinoff, Nicholas Brothers, The 12 Aristocrats; house orchestras.

| | | |
|---|---|---|
| 1934 Oct. 24–26 | Poli's | Bridgeport, Conn. |
| Nov. 2–8 | Earle | Philadelphia, Pa. |
| 9–15 | Paradise | Bronx, New York |
| 16–22 | Metropolitan | Brooklyn, N.Y. |

## Eddie Cantor Unit*

*Cantor, David Rubinoff, Harry Einstein ("Parkyakarkus"), The Orientals, The Dicksons, Jay Seiler, Penn Theatre Orchestra.

1935 March 15–21    Penn    Pittsburgh, Pa.

## Eddie Cantor Unit*

*Cantor, David Rubinoff, Harry Einstein, Nicholas Brothers, house orchestras.

| | | |
|---|---|---|
| July 23–Aug. 1 | Fox | San Francisco, Calif. |
| Aug. 2–8 | Paramount | Los Angeles, Calif. |

## Eddie Cantor Unit*

*Cantor, James Wallington, Harry Einstein, Stone and Vernon (5), Frazee Sisters (2), Three Gobs, Earle Theatre Orchestra/dir. Louis Gress.

1936 Feb. 14–20   Earle        Philadelphia, Pa.

## Eddie Cantor Unit*

*Cantor, James Wallington, Harry Einstein, Bobby Breen; film: *The Bridle Path* (RKO).

1936 May 15–21   Palace        Cleveland, Ohio
         22–29   Palace        Chicago, Ill.

## Eddie Cantor Unit*

*Cantor, Harry Einstein, Bobby Breen, film: *The Last Outlaw* (RKO).

1936 Aug. 7–13   Golden Gate   San Francisco, Calif.

## Eddie Cantor Unit*

*Cantor, Harry Einstein ("Parkyakarkus"), Deanna Durbin, James Wallington, Betty Jane Cooper, Jacques Renard and violin, RKO Keith's Orchestra; film: *Smartest Girl in Town* (RKO).

1936 Nov. 28–Dec. 4   Keith's   Boston, Mass.

## Eddie Cantor and Ted Lewis*

*Cantor, Lewis, Snowball Whittier, Bert Gordon ("The Mad Russian"), Vyola Vonn, Harris & Shore, Gaye Dixon, Betty Dickerson, Loretta Lane, Sylvia Manon & Co., Four Kraddocks, Ben Yost's Varsity Eight.

1938 March 13–14   Civic Auditorium   Cleveland, Ohio
          16–18   Convention Hall    Philadelphia, Pa.

## Eddie Cantor's *Camel Caravan Revue**

*Cantor, Ann Miller, Bert Gordon, Sidney Fields ("Mr. Guffey"), Bert Parks, Kay St. Germain, Edgar (Cookie) Fairchild & Adam Carroll, Fanchon and Marco Girls, Walter Roesner's California Auditorium Orchestra.

March 3–9   California Auditorium   San Francisco, Calif.

## Eddie Cantor Unit*

*Cantor, Ann Miller, Bert Gordon, Sidney Fields, Bert Parks, Kay St. Germain, Fairchild & Carroll, Cobina Wright Jr., Harrison & Fisher (dance team), Ruby Zwerling's State Theatre Orchestra; film: *It's a Wonderful Life* (M-G-M).

1939 June 29–July 5   Loew's State   New York, N.Y.

## Eddie Cantor Unit*

*Cantor, Bert Gordon, S. Fields, Leni Lynn, Fairchild & Carroll, Joyce Hunter, Stuart Morgan Dancers (4), Norma Shea, Stanley Theatre Orchestra (16); film: *These Glamour Girls* (M-G-M).

1939 Sept. 29–Oct. 5   Stanley   Pittsburgh, Pa.

## Eddie Cantor Unit*

*Cantor, Bert Gordon, Sidney Fields, Fairchild & Carroll, Jean Mona, Joyce Hunter, Leni Lynn, Stuart Morgan Dancers, house orchestras; films: *Two Bright Boys* (Universal), Boston; *Fast and Furious* (M-G-M), Brooklyn.

1939 Oct. 12–18   Keith's              Boston, Mass.
          19–25   Loews Metropolitan   Brooklyn, N.Y.

## Eddie Cantor Unit*

*Cantor, Bert Gordon, Sidney Fields, Fairchild & Carroll, Ruth Daye, Joyce Hunter, Leni Lynn, Stuart Morgan Dancers, Chicago Theatre Orchestra; film: *The Cat and the Canary* (Paramount).

1939 Nov. 3–9   B. & K. Chicago   Chicago, Ill.

## Eddie Cantor Unit

1939 Dec. 1–6   Albee   Cincinnati, Ohio

## Eddie Cantor Unit*

*Cantor, George Jessel, Gracie Barrie, Buster Shaver w/Olive and George Brasnow, Stuart Morgan Dancers (4), Don Albert's WHN Orchestra (18); film (N.Y. engagements): *Forty Little Mothers* (M-G-M).

1940 April 16   State           Hartford, Conn.
           17   Loews Canal     New York, N.Y.
        18–24   Loews Capitol   New York, N.Y.

Eddie Cantor Unit

1941 March 23    Auditorium    Lowell, Mass.

Eddie Cantor Unit*

*Cantor, Dinah Shore, Sidney Fields, Olive Major, Gloria Gilbert, Clyde McCoy Orchestra w/Bennett Sisters (3), Dick Lee, Bob Nelson, Sam Kaplan's State Theatre Orchestra; film: *Mr. District Attorney* (Republic).

1941 April 12–14    State    Hartford, Conn.

Eddie Cantor Unit*

*Cantor, Sidney Fields, Olive Major, Gloria Gilbert, Edgar (Cookie) Fairchild, Walter Dare Wahl, Eddie McKnight's Steel Pier Orchestra (9); film: *Road Show* (UA).

1941 June 20–21    Steel Pier    Atlantic City, N.J.

## BANJO EYES

A Musical Comedy in Two Acts and Twelve Scenes. Book by Quillan and Elinson, based on the play, *Three Men On A Horse*, by John Cecil Holm and George Abbott. Lyrics by John LaTouche. Music by Vernon Duke. Staged by Hassard Short. Dances by Charles Walters. Settings by Harry Horner. Gowns and Costumes by Irene Sharaff. Presented by Albert Lewis.

### Cast

| | |
|---|---|
| Miss Clark | JACQUELINE SUSANN |
| Mr. Carver | E. J. BLUNKALL |
| Erwin Trowbridge | EDDIE CANTOR |
| Sally Trowbridge | JUNE CLYDE |
| Harry, the Bartender | RICHARD ROBER |
| Charlie | BILL JOHNSON |
| Ginger | VIRGINIA MAYO |
| The DeMarcos | SALLY AND TONY DE MARCO |
| Patsy | LIONEL STANDER |
| Frankie | RAY MAYER |
| Mabel | COLLETTE LYONS |
| The General | JOHN ERVIN |
| The Captain | JAMES FARRELL |
| The Filly | RONNIE CUNNINGHAM |
| "Banjo Eyes" | MAYO AND MORTON |
| The Quartette | GEORGE RICHMOND, HARRY BOERSMA, DOUG HAWKINS, GEO. LOVESEE |

ACT I
Scene 1—The Display Salon of the Carver Greeting Card Co.

Scene 2—The Bar in a Midtown Hotel.
Scene 3—Mabel's room, in the same hotel.
Scene 4—The Dream Pastures.
Scene 5—Mabel's Room.


### ACT II

Scene 1—The Bar.
Scene 2—Erwin's Home, Jackson Heights.
Scene 3—The Dream Pastures.
Scene 4—Mabel's room.
Scene 5—Camp Dixon.
Scene 6—The Clubhouse, Belmont Park.
Scene 7—The Grandstand, Belmont Park.


### ACT I

| | |
|---|---|
| "The Greeting Cards" | Carver, Girls and Boys |
| "I'll Take the City" | Erwin, Boys and Girls |
| "The Toast of the Boys At the Post" | Mabel and Quartette |
| "I've Got to Hand It to You" | Bill Bailey and Dancers |
| "A Nickel to My Name" | Charlie, Quartette, Girls |
| "Who Started the Rhumba?" | Erwin, Banjo Eyes, Ensemble |
| "It Could Only Happen in the Movies" | Erwin and Mabel |
| (Lyrics by Harold Adamson) | |


### ACT II

| | |
|---|---|
| "Make with the Feet" | Mabel and the DeMarcos |
| (Lyrics by Harold Adamson) | |
| "We're Having a Baby" | Erwin and Sally |
| (Lyrics by Harold Adamson) | |
| "Banjo Eyes" | Erwin, Bill Bailey, Banjo Eyes, Ensemble |
| "We Did It Before" | Captain and Boys |
| (Cliff Friend-Charles Tobias) | |
| "Not a Care in the World" | Charlie and Ensemble |
| Eddie Cantor Medley | Erwin |
| Finale | Entire Company |

| | | | |
|---|---|---|---|
| 1941 | Nov. 7–8 | Sam S. Shubert | New Haven, Conn. |
| | Nov. 11–29 | Colonial | Boston, Mass. |
| | Dec. 2–20 | Forrest | Philadelphia, Pa. |
| | Dec. 25–April 12 | Hollywood | New York, N.Y. |


## Military Hospitals

| | | | |
|---|---|---|---|
| 1944 | April | | Topeka, Kansas |
| | April | | Utica, New York |
| | May 18 | Halloran Hospital | Staten Island, N.Y. |
| | June 24 | Walter Reed Hospital | Washington, D.C. |
| | Aug. 17 | | Mare Island, Calif. |

## Eddie Cantor Unit

1945 June 18 Conventional Hall    Philadelphia, Pa.
      23   Camp Myles Standish   Boston, Mass.
      24   Boston Garden        Boston, Mass.

## Vancouver Diamond Jubilee

1946 July 1–13   Timber Bowl   Vancouver, B.C.

## Centurama

1946 Aug. 2–8   Juneau Park   Milwaukee, Wisc.

## Eddie Cantor
### Film: *If You Knew Susie* (RKO).

1948 Feb. 22   Golden Gate   San Francisco, Calif.

## Eddie Cantor/Fair Dates

1948 Aug. 26–27   Erie, Pa.
     Aug. 28–29       Reading, Pa.

## Eddie Cantor-Dinah Shore/Service Shows

Nov. 1948   San Francisco, Calif.

## Eddie Cantor Unit*

*Cantor, Bert Gordon, Sidney Fields, Eddie Fisher, Vickee Richards, The Glenns (3), David Powell, Vivian M. Bowes, Lou Breese Orchestra (8).

1949 Sept. 3   Grossinger's                 Catskill, N.Y.
         13   Warner                        Atlantic City, N.J.
    22–24   Ak-Sar-Ben Shrine Temple   Omaha, Neb.
Sept. 30–Oct. 9   Coliseum                  Chicago, Ill.
    Dec. 2   Purdue University        Lafayette, Ind.
         5   Forum                         Montreal, Que.
         7   Convention Hall         Philadelphia, Pa.

## MY FORTY YEARS IN SHOW BUSINESS

1950 Jan. 24   University of Maine     Orono, Maine
   Feb. 27   University of Arizona   Tucson, Ariz.
March 21   Carnegie Hall           New York, N.Y.
      26   Public Hall             Cleveland, Ohio
      28   Masonic Auditorium    Rochester, N.Y.

| April 3 | William and Mary College | Norfolk, Va. |
|---|---|---|
| 16 | Cong. Beth Yesurun | Houston, Texas |
| 18 | A. & M. | Stillwater, Ok. |
| Sept. 15 | Palace | Dallas, Texas |
| 17 | City Auditorium | Denver, Colo. |
| 19 | Memorial Hall | Pueblo, Colo. |
| 21 | Auditorium | Milwaukee, Wisc. |
| 23 | Murat | Indianapolis, Ind. |
| 26 | Arena | Niagara Falls, N.Y. |
| 27 | Memorial Auditorium | Providence, R.I. |
| 28 | Symphony Hall | Boston, Mass. |
| 30 | Carnegie Hall | New York, N.Y. |
| Oct. 1 | Memorial Auditorium | Stamford, Conn. |
| 9 | Massey Hall | Toronto, Ont. |
| 10 | City Auditorium | London, Ont. |
| 11 | Kleinhan's Music Hall | Buffalo, N.Y. |
| 12 | Massey Hall | Toronto, Ont. |
| 17 | Municipal Auditorium | New Orleans, La. |
| 18 | Municipal Auditorium | San Antonio, Texas |
| 19 | Music Hall | Houston, Texas |
| 21 | Auditorium | Oklahoma City, Ok. |
| 22 | Convention Hall | Tulsa, Oklahoma |
| 24 | Fort Whiting Auditorium | Mobile, Alabama |
| 25 | Municipal Auditorium | Birmingham, Ala. |
| 30 | Academy of Music | Baltimore, Md. |
| Nov. 9 | Medina Shrine Temple | Chicago, Ill. |
| 10 | Kiel Auditorium | St. Louis, Mo. |
| 12 | Memorial Auditorium | Louisville, Ky. |
| 14 | Masonic Temple | Chicago, Ill. |
| 17 | Convention Hall | Camden, N.J. |
| 20 | Bushnell Auditorium | Hartford, Conn. |
| Dec. | Norton Air Force Base | San Bernardino, Calif. |
| 25 | Kingsbridge Hospital | Bronx, N.Y. |
| 1951 Jan. 4 | Mitchell Field | Garden City, N.Y. |
| 5 | Veterans Hospital | Castle Point, N.Y. |
| 10 | Hotel Astor | New York, N.Y. |
| 11 | Fort Monmouth | Asbury Park, N.J. |
| 12 | Fort Dix | Wrightstown, N.J. |
| 14 | Valley Forge Hospital | Phoenixville, Pa. |
| 16 | Fort Jay | Governor's Is., N.Y. |
| Feb. 12 | Massey Hall | Toronto, Ont. |
| 16 | Temple University | Philadelphia, Pa. |
| Feb. 27–March 1 | Auditorium | Miami Beach, Fla. |
| March 9 | George Washington Hotel | Jacksonville, Fla. |
| April 25 | Grossinger's | Catskill, N.Y. |
| 29–30 | Syria Mosque | Pittsburgh, Pa. |
| Sept. 3 | Veterans Hospital | Albany, N.Y. |
| 11 | Catholic Youth Center | Scranton, Pa. |

| Nov. 16 | U.S. Naval Hospital | Mare Island, Calif. |
|---|---|---|
| 17 | Opera House | San Francisco, Calif. |
| 27 | Russ Auditorium | San Diego, Calif. |
| 29 | U.S. Naval Hospital | Oceanside, Calif. |
| 1952 April 29 | Navy Recreation Aud. | Boston, Mass. |
| 30 | Lyric | Baltimore, Md. |
| May 1 | Syria Mosque | Pittsburgh, Pa. |
| 2 | Music Hall | Cincinnati, Ohio |
| 3 | Severance Hall | Cleveland, Ohio |
| 4 | Kleinhan's Music Hall | Buffalo, N.Y. |
| 5 | Board of Trade Aud. | Chicago, Ill. |
| 27 | | San Jose, Calif. |
| 28 | | Oakland, Calif. |

# FILMOGRAPHY

### WIDOW AT THE RACES
*(Edison, 1913)*

**Cast**

Truly Shattuck, Eddie Cantor, George Jessel

### KID BOOTS
*(Paramount, 1926)*

| | |
|---|---|
| Production: | June–July, 1926 |
| Premiere: | October 9, 1926, Rialto Theatre, New York, N.Y. |
| Length: | 8,565 ft. |

| | |
|---|---|
| Director: | Frank Tuttle |
| Scenario: | Luther Reed, Tom Gibson |
| Source: | Based on the musical comedy by Wm. Anthony McGuire and Otto Harbach |
| Photography: | Victor Milner |

**Cast**

| | |
|---|---|
| Kid Boots | EDDIE CANTOR |
| Jane Martin | CLARA BOW |
| Polly Pendleton | BILLIE DOVE |
| Tom Sterling | LAWRENCE GRAY |
| Carmen Mendoza | NATALIE KINGSTON |
| George Fitch | MALCOLM WAITE |
| Herbert Pendleton | WILLIAM WORTHINGTON |
| Carmen's lawyer | HARRY VON METER |
| Tom's lawyer | FRED ESMELTON |

## SPECIAL DELIVERY
*(Paramount, 1927)*

Production: January, 1927
Premiere: April 25, 1927, Paramount theatre, New York, N.Y.
Length: 5,524 ft.

Director: William Goodrich (Roscoe Arbuckle)
Scenario: John Goodrich
Titles: George Marion, Jr.
Source: Story idea by Eddie Cantor
Photography: Henry Hallenberger

### Cast

| | |
|---|---|
| Eddie | EDDIE CANTOR |
| Madge | JOBYNA RALSTON |
| Harold Jones | WILLIAM POWELL |
| Harrigan, a fireman | DONALD KEITH |
| Flannigan, a cop | JACK DOUGHERTY |
| Nip | VICTOR POTEL |
| Tuck | PAUL KELLY |
| The Mother | MARY CARR |

## THAT PARTY IN PERSON
*(Paramount, 1928)*

Length:   9 minutes

### Cast
Eddie Cantor, Bobbe Arnst

### Score
"Hungry Women"   EDDIE

## ZIEGFELD MIDNIGHT FROLIC
*(Paramount, 1929)*

Length:   19 minutes

### Score
"Eddie Cantor's 'Automobile Horn' Song"

## THE COCK-EYED NEWS
*(Paramount, 1929)*

Length:   8 minutes

### Score
"If you Knew Susie"   EDDIE

## GETTING A TICKET
*(Paramount, 1929)*

Length:   11 minutes

**Cast**

Eddie        EDDIE CANTOR
Policeman    CHARLES WILSON

**Score**

"My Wife Is on a Diet"    EDDIE

GLORIFYING THE AMERICAN GIRL
*(Paramount, 1929)*

Producer:    Florenz Ziegfeld, Jr.
Director:    Millard Webb
Screenplay:  J. P. McAvoy, Millard Webb

Premiere:    Dec. 7, 1929, Paramount Theatre, New York, N.Y.
Length:      8,071 ft. (96 minutes)

Eddie Cantor did his famous sketch, "Joe's Blue Front" (also known as "Belt in the Back") in one scene of this backstage musical, chronicling the rise of Gloria Hughes (Mary Eaton) to stardom in the *Ziegfeld Follies*.

INSURANCE
*(Paramount, 1930)*

Length:    9 minutes

Doctor    CHARLES WILSON
Eddie     EDDIE CANTOR

**Score**

"Now That the Girls Are Wearing Long Dresses"    EDDIE

WHOOPEE
*(Samuel Goldwyn/United Artists, 1930)*

Production:    May-June 1930
Premiere:      September 30, 1930. Rivoli Theatre, New York,
               N.Y.
Length:        8,393 ft.

Producers:     Samuel Goldwyn, Florenz Ziegfeld Jr.
Director:      Thornton Freeland
Scenario:      William Conselman
Source:        The musical comedy by William Anthony Mc-
               Guire
Music:         Walter Donaldson
Lyrics:        Gus Kahn
Photography:   Lee Garmes, Ray Rennahan, Gregg Toland
Film Editor:   Stuart Heisler
Sound:         Oscar Lagerstrom

## Cast

| | |
|---|---|
| Henry Williams | EDDIE CANTOR |
| Mary Custer | ETHEL SHUTTA |
| Wanenis | PAUL GREGORY |
| Sally Morgan | ELEANOR HUNT |
| Sheriff Bob Wells | JOHN RUTHERFORD |
| Judd Morgan | WALTER LAW |
| Black Eagle | CHIEF CAUPOLICAN |
| Ma-Ta-Pe | LOU-SCHA-ENYA |
| Jerome Underwood | SPENCER CHARTERS |
| Chester Underwood | ALBERT HACKETT |
| Harriet Underwood | MARIAN MARSH |
| Timothy Sloane | JACK SHAW |
| Andy McNabb | WILL H. PHILBRICK |

### Ensemble

Joyzelle Cartier, Betty Grable, Virginia Bruce
Muriel Finley, Dorothy Knapp, Claire Dodd
Dean Jagger, Theodore Larch, Budd Fine
Gene Alsace, Frank Rice, Edmund Cobb
Martin Faust, Arthur Dewey, William J. Begg
John Ray, Frank Lanning, Paul Panzer

## GEORGE OLSEN AND HIS MUSIC

### Score

| | |
|---|---|
| Cowboy Number | CHORUS |
| "I'll Still Belong to You" | WANENIS |
| (Nacio Herb Brown-Edward Eliscu) | |
| "Makin' Whoopee" | HENRY |
| Mission Number | CHORUS |
| "A Girl Friend of a Boy Friend of Mine" | HENRY |
| "My Baby Just Cares for Me" | HENRY |
| "Stetson" | MARY |
| "The Song of the Setting Sun" | BLACK EAGLE |
| "My Baby Just Cares for Me" (reprise) | HENRY |

## PALMY DAYS
### (*Samuel Goldwyn/United Artists, 1931*)

| | |
|---|---|
| Production: | June–July 1931; Aug. 1931 (retakes/add. scenes) |
| Premiere: | September 23, 1931, Rialto Theatre, New York, N.Y. |
| Length: | Nine reels; 7,081 ft. (80 minutes) |

| | |
|---|---|
| Producer: | Samuel Goldwyn |
| Director: | Edward Sutherland |
| Ensembles: | Busby Berkeley |
| Screenplay: | Eddie Cantor, Morrie Ryskind, David Freedman |
| Continuity: | Keene Thompson |
| Film Editor: | Sherman Todd, Stuart Heisler |

Photography: Gregg Toland
Sound: Vinton Vernon
Conductor: Alfred Newman
Sets: Richard Day, Willy Pogany
Costumes: Alice O'Neill
Gowns: Gabrielle Chanel

## Cast

| | |
|---|---|
| Eddie Simpson | EDDIE CANTOR |
| Helen Martin | CHARLOTTE GREENWOOD |
| Joan Clark | BARBARA WEEKS |
| A. B. Clark | SPENCER CHARTERS |
| Steve Clayton | PAUL PAGE |
| Yolando | CHARLES MIDDLETON |
| Joe the Frog | GEORGE RAFT |
| Plug Moynihan | HARRY WOOD |
| Man at Seance | ARTHUR HOYT |

## Ensemble

Loretta Andrews, Virginia Bruce, Edna Callahan
Georgia Coleman, Nadine Dore, Ruth Eddings, Betty
Grable, Virginia Grey, Olive Hatch, Amo Ingraham
Jean Lenivick, Betty Lorraine, Neva Lynn, Nancy
Nash, Fay Pierre, Nita Pike, Dorothy Poynton
Hylah Slocum, Betty Stockton, Hazel Witter

## Score

"Bend Down, Sister"                                    HELEN AND GIRLS
(Con Conrad-Dave Silverstein-Ballard MacDonald)
"Yes, Yes!"                                            EDDIE AND ENSEMBLE
(Con Conrad-Cliff Friend)
"There's Nothing Too Good for my Baby"                 EDDIE
(Harry Akst-Eddie Cantor-Benny Davis)


## THE KID FROM SPAIN
### *(Samuel Goldwyn/United Artists, 1932)*

Production: July–October 1932
Premiere: November 17, 1932, Palace Theatre, New York, N.Y.
Length: Eleven reels; 9,176 ft. (104 minutes)

Director: Leo McCarey
Screenplay: William Anthony McGuire
Photography: Gregg Toland
Ensembles: Busby Berkeley
Conductor: Alfred Newman
Art Director: Richard Day
Costumes: Milo Anderson

## Cast

| | |
|---|---|
| Eddie | EDDIE CANTOR |
| Rosalie | LYDA ROBERTI |
| Ricardo | ROBERT YOUNG |
| Anita | RUTH HALL |
| Pancho | JOHN MILJAN |
| Alonzo Gomez | NOAH BEERY |
| Pedro | J. CARROL NAISH |
| Crawford | ROBERT EMMET O'CONNOR |
| Jose | STANLEY FIELDS |
| Gonzalez | PAUL PORCASI |
| Dalmores | JULIAN RIVERO |
| Martha Oliver | THERESA MAXWELL CONOVER |
| Dean | WALTER WALKER |
| Red | BEN HENDRICKS, JR. |

## Ensemble

## Score

| | |
|---|---|
| "In The Moonlight" | EDDIE |
| "Look What You've Done" | EDDIE, ROSALIE |
| "What A Perfect Combination" | EDDIE, CHORUS |

## ROMAN SCANDALS
*(Samuel Goldwyn/United Artists, 1933)*

| | |
|---|---|
| Production: | July–October 17, 1933 |
| Premiere: | November 27, 1933, Los Angeles |
| Length: | 10 reels (92 minutes) |

| | |
|---|---|
| Director: | Frank Tuttle |
| Original Story: | George S. Kaufman, Robert E. Sherwood |
| Screenplay: | William Anthony McGuire (Additional material by George Oppenheimer, Arthur Sheekman, and Nat Perrin) |
| Photography: | Gregg Toland and Ray June |
| Film Editing: | Stuart Heisler, Sherman Todd |
| Sets: | Richard Day |
| Costumes: | John W. Harkrider |
| Conductor: | Alfred Newman |

## Cast

| | |
|---|---|
| Eddie (Oedipus) | EDDIE CANTOR |
| Princess Sylvia | GLORIA STUART |
| Josephus | DAVID MANNERS |
| Emperor Valerius | EDWARD ARNOLD |
| Empress Agrippa | VERREE TEASDALE |
| Olga | RUTH ETTING |

### The Goldwyn Girls
Lucille Ball, Bonnie Bannon, Dolores Casey, Rosalie Fromson
Jane Hamilton, Vivian Keefer, Mary Lange, Katharine Mauk
Gigi Parish, Barbara Pepper, Theo Phane, Iris Shunn

### Score

| | |
|---|---|
| "Build a Little Home" | EDDIE |
| "No More Love" | OLGA |
| "Keep Young and Beautiful" | EDDIE, CHORUS |
| "Put a Tax on Love" | EDDIE |
| "Build a Little Home" (reprise) | EDDIE, ENSEMBLE |

## KID MILLIONS
### *(Samuel Goldwyn/United Artists, 1934)*

| | |
|---|---|
| Production: | July 16–September 4, 1934 |
| Premiere: | November 11, 1934, Rivoli Theatre, New York, N.Y. |
| Length: | Ten reels (90 minutes) |

| | |
|---|---|
| Director: | Roy Del Ruth |
| Screenplay: | Arthur Sheekman, Nat Perrin, Nunnally Johnson |
| Source: | Original story |
| Photography: | Ray June |
| Ensembles: | Seymour Felix |
| Conductor: | Alfred Newman |
| Lyrics: | Gus Kahn, Harold Adamson |
| Music: | Walter Donaldson, Burton Lane |

### Cast

| | |
|---|---|
| Eddie Wilson | EDDIE CANTOR |
| Jane Larrabee | ANN SOTHERN |
| Dot | ETHEL MERMAN |
| Jerry Lane | GEORGE MURPHY |
| Ben Ali | JESSE BLOCK |
| Fanya | EVE SULLY |
| Colonel Larrabee | BURTON CHURCHILL |
| Louie the Lug | WARREN HYMER |
| Sheik Mulhulla | PAUL HARVEY |
| Khoot | OTTO HOFFMAN |
| Nora ("Toots") | DORIS DAVENPORT |
| Herman | ED KENNEDY |
| Oscar | BRADLEY FIELDS |
| Adolph | JOHN KELLY |
| Pop | JACK KENNEDY |
| Stymie | STYMIE BEARD |
| Leonard | LEONARD KILBRICK |
| Slade | GUY USHER |

THE NICHOLAS BROTHERS

### The Goldwyn Girls

## Score

| | |
|---|---|
| "When My Ship Comes In" | EDDIE |
| "An Earful of Music" | DOT |
| "Your Head on My Shoulder" | JERRY, JOAN |
| "I Want to Be a Minstrel Man" | HAROLD NICHOLAS, CHORUS |
| "Mandy" | EDDIE AND ENSEMBLE |
| "Okay, Toots" | EDDIE |
| "Ice Cream Fantasy" | EDDIE |

## STRIKE ME PINK
### *(Samuel Goldwyn/United Artists, 1936)*

| | |
|---|---|
| Production: | September 30–December 1935 |
| Premiere: | January 16, 1936, Radio City Music Hall, New York, N.Y. |
| Length: | 11 reels; 8,997 ft. (100 minutes) |

| | |
|---|---|
| Producer: | Samuel Goldwyn |
| Director: | Norman Taurog |
| Screenplay: | Walter DeLeon, Francis Martin, Frank Butler |
| | (Additional Dialogue: Phil Rapp) |
| Source: | The novel *Dreamland* by Clarence Budington Kelland |
| Photography: | Merritt Gerstad |
| Film Editor: | Sherman Todd |
| Conductor: | Alfred Newman |

## Cast

| | |
|---|---|
| Eddie Pink | EDDIE CANTOR |
| Joyce Lennox | ETHEL MERMAN |
| Claribel Higg | SALLY EILERS |
| Parkyakarkus | HARRY EINSTEIN |
| Hattie Carson | HELEN LOWELL |
| Butch Carson | GORDON JONES |
| Vance | BRIAN DONLEVY |
| Copple | WILLIAM FRAWLEY |
| Marsh | DON BRODIE |
| Selby | CHARLES MCAVOY |
| Thrust | JACK LaRUE |
| Killer | EDWARD BROPHY |
| Rita | RITA RIO |
| Pitchman | CLYDE HAGER |

## Score

| | |
|---|---|
| "First You've Got Me High" | JOYCE |
| "Shake It Off with Rhythm" | JOYCE |
| "The Lady Dances" | EDDIE, CHORUS |
| "Calabash Pipe" | EDDIE, JOYCE |

## ALI BABA GOES TO TOWN
*(Twentieth Century-Fox, 1937)*

Production: July–September 1937
Preview: October 22, 1937, Roxy Theatre, New York, N.Y.
Length: 10 reels, 7,402 ft. (81 minutes)

Producer: Darryl F. Zanuck
Director: David Butler
Ensembles: Sammy Lee
Screenplay: Harry Tugend, Jack Yellen
Story: Gene Towne, Graham Baker, Gene Fowler
Photography: Ernest Palmer
Film Editor: Irene Morra
Costumes: Gwen Wakeling
Conductor: Louis Silvers

### Cast

| | |
|---|---|
| Aloysius Babson (Ali Baba) | EDDIE CANTOR |
| Yusuf | TONY MARTIN |
| Sultan Abdullah | ROLAND YOUNG |
| Sultana | LOUISE HOVICK (GYPSY ROSE LEE) |
| Princess Miriam | JUNE LANG |
| Prince Musah | DOUGLAS DUMBRILLE |
| Broderick (Ishak) | JOHN CARRADINE |
| Dinah (Deenah) | VIRGINIA FIELD |
| Boland | ALAN DINEHART |
| Omar the Rug Maker | MAURICE CASS |
| Tramps | WARREN HYMER |
| | STANLEY FIELDS |
| Captain | PAUL HURST |
| Radio Announcer | SAM HAYES |
| Selim | DOUGLAS WOOD |
| Assistant Director | SIDNEY FIELDS |
| Chief Councilor | FERDINAND GOTTSCHALK |
| Doctor | CHARLES LANE |
| Captain of Guards | JIM PIERCE |

### Score

| | |
|---|---|
| "Laugh Your Way Through Life" | ALOYSIUS |
| "Swing Is Here to Sway" | ALI BABA AND ENSEMBLE |
| "Vote for Honest Abe" | ALI BABA, SULTAN, YUSUF |

## FORTY LITTLE MOTHERS
*(M-G-M, 1940)*

Production: December 26, 1939–February 23, 1940
Previewed: April 13, 1940, Grauman's Chinese, Hollywood
Premiere: April 17, 1940, Loews Canal, New York, N.Y.
Length: 88 minutes

Producer: Harry Rapf
Director: Busby Berkeley
Screenplay: Dorothy Yost, Ernest Pagano
Source: The play *Monsieur Petiot*, by Jean Guitton
Photography: Charles Lawton
Film Editor: Ben Lewis

### Cast

| | |
|---|---|
| Gilbert J. Thompson | EDDIE CANTOR |
| Madame Granville | JUDITH ANDERSON |
| Mlle. Cliche | NYDIA WESTMAN |
| Marian Edwards | RITA JOHNSON |
| Doris | BONITA GRANVILLE |
| Marcia | DIANA LEWIS |
| Eleanor | MARGARET EARLY |
| Judge Joseph M. Williams | RALPH MORGAN |
| Janette | MARTHA O'DRISCOLL |
| Lois | CHARLOTTE MUNIER |
| Betty | LOUISE SEIDEL |
| Chum | BABY QUINTANILLA |
| Mama Lupini | EVA PUIG |
| Professor Lange | ALDEN CHASE |

### Score
"Little Curly Hair in a High Chair"  GILBERT


## THANK YOUR LUCKY STARS
*(Warner Bros., 1943)*

Production: November 1942–March 1943
Premiere: October 1, 1943, Strand Theatre, New York, N.Y.
Length: 127 minutes

Producer: Mark Hellinger
Director: David Butler
Screenplay: Norman Panama, Melvin Frank, James V. Kern
Orig. Story: Everett Freeman, Arthur Schwartz

### Cast

| | |
|---|---|
| Joe Sampson/Eddie Cantor | EDDIE CANTOR |
| Pat Dixon | JOAN LESLIE |
| Tommy Randolph | DENNIS MORGAN |
| Dinah Shore | DINAH SHORE |
| Dr. Schlenna | S. Z. SAKALL |
| Farnsworth | EDWARD EVERETT HORTON |
| Nurse Hamilton | RUTH DONNELLY |
| Girl with book | JOYCE REYNOLDS |
| Barney Jackson | RICHARD LANE |
| Don Wilson | DON WILSON |
| Angelo | HENRY ARMETTA |

### Score

| | |
|---|---|
| "Now's the Time to Fall in Love" | EDDIE CANTOR |
| "The Dreamer" | DINAH SHORE |
| "We're Staying Home Tonight" | EDDIE CANTOR |
| "I'm Riding for a Fall" | TOMMY AND PAT |
| "Thank Your Lucky Stars" | DINAH SHORE |
| "No, You—No, Me" | TOMMY AND PAT |
| " 'Way Up North" | JACK CARSON, ALAN HALE |
| "Love Isn't Born, It's Made" | ANN SHERIDAN |
| "Ice Cold Katie" | ENSEMBLE |
|   Soldier | WILLIE BEST |
|   Ice Cold Katie | RITA CHRISTIANI |
|   Gossip | HATTIE MCDANIEL |
|   Justice | JESS LEE BROOKS |
|   Trio | FORD, HARRIS, AND JONES |
|   Gambler | MATTHEW JONES |
| "That's What You Jolly Well Get" | ERROL FLYNN, ENSEMBLE |
| "They're Either Too Young or Too Old" | BETTE DAVIS |
| "How Sweet You Are" | DINAH SHORE |
| "Good Night, Good Neighbor" | TOMMY, ALEXIS SMITH, CHORUS |

## SHOW BUSINESS
### (RKO, 1944)

Production: October 25–December 1943
Premiere: May 10, 1944, Palace Theatre, New York, N.Y.
Length: 92 minutes

### Cast

| | |
|---|---|
| Eddie Martin | EDDIE CANTOR |
| George Doane | GEORGE MURPHY |
| Joan Mason | JOAN DAVIS |
| Constance Ford | CONSTANCE MOORE |
| Nancy Gaye | NANCY KELLY |
| Charles Lucas | DON DOUGLAS |
| Director | FORBES MURRAY |
| Desk Clerk | BERT MOORHOUSE |
| Nurse | CLAIRE CARLTON |
| Army Doctor | RUSS CLARK |
| Head Waiter | CHEF MILANI |
| Taxi Driver | RALPH DUNN |
| Harold | STYMIE BEARD |
| Page | HARRY HARVEY JR. |
| Call Boy | BILLY BESTER |

### Score

| | |
|---|---|
| "They're Wearing 'Em Higher in Hawaii" | GEORGE |
| "The Curse of an Aching Heart" | EDDIE |
| "I Want a Girl" | GEORGE, CONNIE, EDDIE, JOAN |
| "It Had to Be You" | GEORGE, CONNIE |

| | |
|---|---|
| "Makin' Whoopee" | EDDIE |
| "Why Am I Blue?" | CONNIE |
| "While Strolling in the Park One Day" | GEORGE, EDDIE |
| "Dinah" | EDDIE, GEORGE, JOAN, CONNIE |
| "The Daughter of Rosie O'Grady" | EDDIE, GEORGE |
| "Alabamy Bound" | EDDIE |
| "I Don't Want to Get Well" | EDDIE |
| "You May Not Remember" | GEORGE |

## HOLLYWOOD CANTEEN
### *(Warner Bros., 1945)*

Eddie Cantor appeared as himself in this all-star extravaganza, interwoven with a fictional plot involving Joan Leslie (as herself) and a sailor played by Robert Hutton.

| | |
|---|---|
| Premiere: | December 15, 1944, Hollywood Theatre, New York, N.Y. |
| Length: | 124 minutes |

| | |
|---|---|
| Producer: | Alex Gottieb |
| Director: | Delmer Daves |
| Screenplay: | Delmer Daves |

"We're Having A Baby"   EDDIE CANTOR AND NORA MARTIN

## IF YOU KNEW SUSIE
### *(RKO, 1948)*

| | |
|---|---|
| Production: | October–November 1947 |
| Premiere: | February 22, 1948, Palace Theatre, New York, N.Y. |
| Length: | 90 minutes |

| | |
|---|---|
| Producer: | Eddie Cantor |
| Director: | Gordon M. Douglas |
| Screenplay: | Warren Wilson, Oscar Brodney |
| Music: | Jimmy McHugh |
| Lyrics: | Harold Adamson |

### Cast

| | |
|---|---|
| Sam Parker | EDDIE CANTOR |
| Susie Parker | JOAN DAVIS |
| Junior | BOBBY DRISCOLL |
| Marjorie Parker | MARGARET KERRY |
| Mike Garrett | ALLYN JOSLYN |
| Mr. Whitley | CHARLES DINGLE |
| Steve Garland | SHELDON LEONARD |
| Zero Zantini | JOE SAWYER |
| Grandma | MABEL PAIGE |
| Marty | DOUGLAS FOWLEY |
| Handy Clinton | DICK HUMPHREYS |
| Mr. Clinton | HOWARD FREEMAN |
| Joe Collins | PHIL BROWN |

| | |
|---|---|
| Mrs. Clinton | ISABEL RANDOLPH |
| Count Alexis | SIG RUMAN |
| Chez Henri | FRITZ FELD |

### Score

| | |
|---|---|
| "My, How the Time Goes By" | SAM |
| "If You Knew Susie" | SAM |
| (Joseph Meyer-B. G. DeSylva) | |
| "My Brooklyn Love Song" | MARTY, MARJORIE |
| (Ramez Idriss-George Tibbles) | |
| "What Do I Want with Money?" | SAM |
| "We're Living the Life We Love" | SAM, SUSIE |

## THE STORY OF WILL ROGERS
### *(Warner Bros., 1952)*

| | |
|---|---|
| Length: | 109 minutes |
| Producer: | Robert Arthur |
| Director: | Michael Curtiz |
| Screenplay: | Frank Davis, Stanley Roberts, John C. Moffitt |
| Source: | "Uncle Clem's Boy," a story by Betty Blake Rogers |

### Cast

| | |
|---|---|
| Will Rogers | WILL ROGERS JR. |
| Betty Rogers | JANE WYMAN |
| Clem Rogers | CARL BENTON REID |
| Cora Marshall | EVE MILLER |
| Bert Lynn | JAMES GLEASON |
| Dusty Donovan | SLIM PICKENS |
| Wiley Post | NOAH BEERY, JR. |
| Mrs. Foster | MARY WICKES |
| Dave Marshall | STEVE BRODIE |
| Orville James | PINKY TOMLIN |
| Sally Rogers | MARGARET FIELD |
| Art Frazer | VIRGIL S. TAYLOR |
| Mr. Cavendish | RICHARD KEAN |
| Joe Arrow | JAY SILVERHEELS |
| Florenz Ziegfeld, Jr. | WILLIAM FORREST |
| Pres. Woodrow Wilson | EARL LEE |
| Tom McSpadden | BRIAN DALY |
| Eddie Cantor | EDDIE CANTOR |

### Score
"Ma (He's Making Eyes at Me)"    EDDIE CANTOR

## THE EDDIE CANTOR STORY
### *(Warner Bros., 1953)*

| | |
|---|---|
| Premiere: | December 25, 1953, Paramount Theatre, New York, N.Y. |
| Length: | 115 minutes |

Producer: Sidney Skolsky
Director: Alfred E. Green
Screenplay: Jerome Weidman, Ted Sherdeman, Sidney Skolsky
Orig. Story: Sidney Skolsky

## Cast

| | |
|---|---|
| Eddie Cantor | KEEFE BRASSELLE |
| Ida Tobias Cantor | MARILYN ERSKINE |
| Grandma Esther | AILEEN MACMAHON |
| Harry Harris | ARTHUR FRANZ |
| Eddie (as a boy) | RICHARD MONDA |
| Ida (as a girl) | SUSAN ODIN |
| Harry (as a boy) | OWEN PRITCHARD |
| David Tobias | ALEX JERRY |
| Rachel Tobias | GRETA GRANDSTEDT |
| Leo Raymond | DOUGLAS EVANS |
| Jimmy Durante | JACKIE BARNETT |
| Gus Edwards | HAL MARCH |
| Lillian Edwards | ANN DORAN |
| Florenz Ziegfeld Jr. | WILLIAM FORREST |
| Diamond Jim Brady | CHARLES MORTON |
| Will Rogers | WILL ROGERS JR. |

## Score

| | |
|---|---|
| "Meet Me Tonight in Dreamland" | EDDIE (AS A BOY) |
| "Bedelia" | EDDIE (AS A BOY) |
| "Will You Love Me in December As You Do in May?" | EDDIE (AS A BOY) |
| "Be My Little Baby Bumble Bee" | "KID KABARET" ENSEMBLE |
| "If I Was a Millionaire" | "KID KABARET" ENSEMBLE |
| "Love Me and the World Is Mine" | EDDIE AND QUARTET |
| "Row, Row, Row" | EDDIE |
| "How Ya Gonna Keep 'Em Down on the Farm?" | EDDIE |
| "Oh, You Beautiful Doll" | EDDIE |
| "If You Knew Susie" | EDDIE |
| "Pretty Baby" | EDDIE |
| "Yes Sir, That's My Baby" | EDDIE |
| "Bye, Bye, Blackbird" | EDDIE |
| "Josephine, Please No Lean on the Bell" | EDDIE |
| "Makin' Whoopee" | EDDIE |
| "Ida, Sweet as Apple Cider" | EDDIE |
| "Now's the Time to Fall in Love" | EDDIE |
| "When I'm the President" | EDDIE AND CHORUS |
| "One Hour with You" | EDDIE |
| "Yes, We Have No Bananas" | EDDIE |
| "You Must Have Been a Beautiful Baby" | EDDIE |
| "Ida, Sweet as Apple Cider" | EDDIE |
| "Margie" | EDDIE |
| "Ma (He's Making Eyes at Me)" | EDDIE |

# RADIOGRAPHY

## STARRING RADIO SERIES

### *The Chase & Sanborn Hour* (NBC)

Time Slot:   Sun., 8:00–9:00 P.M. (EST)
Sponsor:   Chase and Sanborn Coffee Co.
Announcer:   James Wallington
Conductor:   David Rubinoff

| | | | | |
|---|---|---|---|---|
| Broadcast from New York, N.Y.: | Sept. | 13, 1931–Dec. | 27, 1931 | (16) |
| Broadcast from Cleveland, Ohio: | Jan. | 3, 1932–Jan. | 10, 1932 | ( 2) |
| Broadcast from Chicago, Ill.: | Jan. | 17, 1932 | | ( 1) |
| Broadcast from New York, N.Y.: | Jan. | 24, 1932–Jan. | 31, 1932 | ( 2) |
| Broadcast from New York, N.Y.: | Oct. | 30, 1932–Jan. | 22, 1933 | (13) |
| Broadcast from Albany, N.Y.: | Jan. | 29, 1933 | | ( 1) |
| Broadcast from New York, N.Y.: | Feb. | 5, 1933–Feb. | 12, 1933 | ( 2) |
| Broadcast from Jacksonville, Fla.: | Feb. | 19, 1933 | | ( 1) |
| Broadcast from New York, N.Y.: | Feb. | 26, 1933–March | 5, 1933 | ( 2) |
| Broadcast from Washington, D.C.: | March | 12, 1933 | | ( 1) |
| Broadcast from New York, N.Y.: | March | 19, 1933 | | ( 1) |
| Broadcast from New Orleans, La.: | March | 26, 1933 | | ( 1) |
| Broadcast from Des Moines, Iowa: | April | 2, 1933 | | ( 1) |
| Broadcast from New York, N.Y.: | April | 9, 1933–April | 23, 1933 | ( 3) |
| Broadcast from New York, N.Y.: | Nov. | 19, 1933–Feb. | 18, 1934 | (14) |
| Broadcast from Hollywood, Fla.: | Feb. | 25, 1934–March | 11, 1934 | ( 3) |
| Broadcast from New York, N.Y.: | March | 18, 1934–April | 15, 1934 | ( 5) |
| Broadcast from New York, N.Y.: | Oct. | 7, 1934–Nov. | 25, 1934 | ( 8) |

Total Broadcasts: 77

### The Eddie Cantor Pebeco Show (CBS)

| | | | |
|---|---|---|---|
| Time Slot: | Sun., 8:00–8:30 P.M. (EST) | (Feb. | 3, 1935–April 28, 1935) |
| | | (Sept. | 29, 1935–Dec. 29, 1935) |
| | Sun., 7:00–7:30 P.M. (EST) | (Jan. | 5, 1936–May 10, 1936) |
| Sponsor: | Pebeco Toothpaste | | |
| Announcer: | James Wallington | | |
| Conductor: | David Rubinoff | (Feb. | 3, 1935–April 28, 1935) |
| | Gus Arnheim | (Sept. | 29, 1935) |
| | George Stoll | (Oct. | 6, 1935, Nov. 3, 1935) |
| | Jimmy Grier | (Oct. | 13, 1935) |
| | Anson Weeks | (Oct. | 20, 1935) |
| | Phil Ohman | (Oct. | 27, 1935) |
| | Lou Gress | (Nov. | 10, 1935–May 10, 1936) |

| | | |
|---|---|---|
| Broadcast from New York, N.Y.: | Feb. 3, 1935–April 28, 1935 | (13) |
| Broadcast from Los Angeles, Calif.: | Sept. 29, 1935–Dec. 29, 1935 | (14) |
| Broadcast from New York, N.Y.: | Jan. 5, 1936–Feb. 16, 1936 | ( 7) |
| Broadcast from Hollywood, Fla.: | Feb. 23, 1936–March 15, 1936 | ( 4) |
| Broadcast from New York, N.Y.: | March 22, 1936–May 10, 1936 | ( 8) |

Total Broadcasts: 46

### Texaco Town (CBS)

| | | |
|---|---|---|
| Time Slot: | Sun., 8:30–9:00 P.M. (EST) | (Sept. 20, 1936–May 30, 1937) |
| | Wed., 8:30–9:00 P.M. (EST) | (Sept. 29, 1937–March 23, 1938) |
| Sponsor: | Texaco Gasoline | |
| Writers: | Sam Kurtzman, John Rapp, Bob Ross (1937–1938) | |
| Announcer: | James Wallington | |
| Conductor: | Jacques Renard | |
| Cast: | Sid Fields as "Mr. Guffy" | |
| | Deanna Durbin, Bobby Breen, Pinky Tomlin | |
| | Vyola Vonn | (Nov. 10, 1937–Feb. 9, 1938) |
| | Bert Gordon | (Dec. 1, 1937–March 23, 1938) |

| | | |
|---|---|---|
| Broadcast from Los Angeles, Calif.: | Sept. 20, 1936–May 30, 1937 | (37) |
| Broadcast from Los Angeles, Calif.: | Sept. 29, 1937–March 23, 1938 | (26) |

Total Broadcasts: 63

### Camel Caravan (NBC)

| | | |
|---|---|---|
| Time Slot: | Mon., 7:30–8:00 P.M. (EST) | |
| Sponsor: | R.J. Reynolds Tobacco Co. | |
| Announcer: | Walter Wolf King | (March 28, 1938–June 27, 1938) |
| | | (Oct. 3, 1938–Jan. 2, 1939) |
| | Bert Parks | (Jan. 9, 1939–June 26, 1939) |

Conductor: Edgar (Cookie) Fairchild
    Cast: Bert Gordon             (March 28, 1938–Jan.   23, 1939)
          Bobby Breen
          Kay St. Germaine       (Feb.      6, 1939–April   24, 1939)

| | | |
|---|---|---|
| Broadcast from Los Angeles, Calif.: | March 28, 1938–June 27, 1938 | (14) |
| Broadcast from Los Angeles, Calif.: | Oct. 3, 1938–Oct. 31, 1938 | ( 5) |
| Broadcast from New York, N.Y.: | Nov. 7, 1938–Jan. 9, 1939 | (10) |
| Broadcast from Los Angeles, Calif.: | Jan. 16, 1939–Feb. 27, 1939 | ( 7) |
| Broadcast from San Francisco, Cal.: | March 6, 1939 | ( 1) |
| Broadcast from Los Angeles, Calif.: | March 13, 1939–May 1, 1939 | ( 8) |
| Broadcast from New York, N.Y.: | May 8, 1939–June 26, 1939 | ( 8 |

Total Broadcasts: 53

*Time To Smile* (NBC)

Time Slot: Wed., 9:00–9:30 P.M. (EST)
  Sponsor: Bristol Myers
Announcer: Harry Von Zell
Conductor: Bobby Sherwood        (Oct.    2, 1940–June   25, 1941)
          Cookie Fairchild        (Sept.   3, 1941–April   19, 1944)
          Vincent Tranco       (April 26, 1944–June   21, 1944)
          Leonard Sues         (Sept. 27, 1944–June   19, 1946)
  Vocalist: Dinah Shore          (Oct.    2, 1940–June   23, 1943)
          Nora Martin          (Sept. 29, 1943–June   20, 1945)
          Thelma Carpenter    (Sept. 26, 1945–March 13, 1946)
          Patsy Bolton         (March 20, 1946–June   19, 1946)
  Writers: Joe Quillen, Irving Ellinson, Johnny Rapp

| | | |
|---|---|---|
| Broadcast from Los Angeles, Calif.: | Oct. 2, 1940–March 12, 1941 | (24) |
| Broadcast from New York, N.Y.: | March 19, 1941–June 25, 1941 | (15) |
| Broadcast from New York, N.Y.: | Sept. 3, 1941–Nov. 5, 1941 | (10) |
| Broadcast from Boston, Mass.: | Nov. 12, 1941–Nov. 26, 1941 | ( 3) |
| Broadcast from Philadelphia, Pa.: | Dec. 3, 1941–Dec. 17, 1941 | ( 3) |
| Broadcast from New York, N.Y.: | Dec. 24, 1941–April 15, 1942 | (17) |
| Broadcast from Fort Monmouth, N.J.: | April 22, 1942 | ( 1) |
| Broadcast from Los Angeles, Calif.: | April 29, 1942–May 6, 1942 | ( 2) |
| Broadcast from Santa Ana, Calif.: | May 13, 1942 | ( 1) |
| Broadcast from San Francisco, Cal.: | May 20, 1942 | ( 1) |
| Broadcast from Los Angeles, Calif.: | May 27, 1942 | ( 1) |
| Broadcast from Camp Haan, Calif.: | June 3, 1942 | ( 1) |
| Broadcast from Long Beach, Calif.: | June 10, 1942 | ( 1) |
| Broadcast from March Field, Calif.: | June 17, 1942 | ( 1) |
| Broadcast from Los Angeles, Calif.: | June 24, 1942 | ( 1) |
| Broadcast from Camp Callan, Calif.: | Sept. 30, 1942 | ( 1) |
| Broadcast from Santa Ana, Calif.: | Oct. 7, 1942 | ( 1) |
| Broadcast from Camp Elliot, Calif.: | Oct. 14, 1942 | ( 1) |
| Broadcast from Camp Haan, Calif.: | Oct. 21, 1942 | ( 1) |

| | | | |
|---|---|---|---|
| Broadcast from March Field, Calif.: | Oct. | 28, 1942 | ( 1) |
| Broadcast from Los Angeles, Calif.: | Nov. | 4, 1942–Feb. 24, 1943 | (17) |
| Broadcast from Camp Elliot, Calif.: | March | 3, 1943 | ( 1) |
| Broadcast from Palm Springs, Calif.: | March | 10, 1943 | ( 1) |
| Broadcast from March Field, Calif. | March | 17, 1943 | ( 1) |
| Broadcast from Pasadena, Calif.: | March | 24, 1943 | ( 1) |
| Broadcast from Los Angeles, Calif.: | March | 31, 1943–June 16, 1943 | (12) |
| Broadcast from El Toro Base, Calif.: | June | 23, 1943 | ( 1) |
| Broadcast from Los Amedos, Calif.: | Sept. | 29, 1943 | ( 1) |
| Broadcast from Los Angeles, Calif.: | Oct. | 6, 1943–April 19, 1944 | (29) |
| Broadcast from New York, N.Y.: | April | 26, 1944–June 21, 1944 | ( 9) |
| Broadcast from Los Angeles, Calif.: | Sept. | 27, 1944–May 23, 1945 | (35) |
| Broadcast from New York, N.Y.: | May | 30, 1945–June 20, 1945 | ( 4) |
| Broadcast from Los Angeles, Calif.: | Sept. | 26, 1945–Oct. 31, 1945 | ( 6) |
| Broadcast from New York, N.Y.: | Nov. | 7, 1945–Dec. 26, 1945 | ( 8) |
| Broadcast from Staten Island, N.Y.: | Jan. | 2, 1946–Jan. 9, 1946 | ( 2) |
| Broadcast from New York, N.Y.: | Jan. | 16, 1946 | ( 1) |
| Broadcast from Los Angeles, Calif.: | Jan. | 23, 1946–June 12, 1946 | (21) |
| Broadcast from Denver, Colo.: | June | 19, 1946 | ( 1) |

Total Broadcasts: 238

### The Eddie Cantor Pabst Blue Ribbon Show (NBC)

| | | |
|---|---|---|
| Time Slot: | Thurs., 9:00–9:30 P.M. EST | |
| Sponsor: | Pabst Beer Co. | |
| Announcer: | Harry Von Zell | |
| Conductor: | Edgar (Cookie) Fairchild | |
| Vocalists: | Margaret Whiting | (Sept. 26, 1946–June 19, 1947) |
| | CeCe Blake | (Sept. 25, 1947–Oct. 23, 1947) |
| | | (Nov. 6, 1947) |
| | | (Dec. 4, 1947) |
| | Dinah Shore | (Oct. 1, 1948–June 24, 1949) |
| Writers: | Jay Sommers, Jess Goldstein | |
| Producer: | Vick Knight | |

| | | | |
|---|---|---|---|
| Broadcast from Los Angeles, Calif.: | Sept. | 26, 1946–June 19, 1947 | (39) |
| Broadcast from Los Angeles, Calif.: | Sept. | 25, 1947–Dec. 18, 1947 | (13) |
| Broadcast from Van Nuys, Calif.: | Dec. | 25, 1947 | ( 1) |
| Broadcast from Los Angeles, Calif.: | Jan. | 1, 1948–Feb. 12, 1948 | ( 7) |
| Broadcast from San Francisco, Calif.: | Feb. | 19, 1948 | ( 1) |
| Broadcast from Los Angeles, Calif.: | Feb. | 26, 1948–June 15, 1948 | (17) |
| Broadcast from Los Angeles, Calif.: | Oct. | 1, 1948–March 18, 1949 | (24) |
| Broadcast from Peoria, Ill.: | March | 25, 1949 | ( 1) |
| Broadcast from Milwaukee, Wisc.: | April | 1, 1949 | ( 1) |
| Broadcast from Los Angeles, Calif.: | April | 8, 1949–June 24, 1949 | (12) |

Total Broadcasts: 116

## *Take It Or Leave It* (NBC)

Time Slot:   Sun., 10:00–10:30 P.M., Sept. 11, 1949–June 4, 1950
  Sponsor:   Eversharp

Total Shows: 39 (pre-recorded)

## *Show Business Old and New* (NBC)

Time Slot:   Sun.,   9:30–10:00 P.M., Oct. 14, 1951–Jan.  6, 1952
             Tues., 10:00–10:30 P.M., Jan. 15, 1952–May 13, 1952
  Sponsor:   Philip Morris

Total Shows: 31 (pre-recorded)

Time Slot:   Thur., 9:30–10:00 P.M., Oct. 2, 1952–July 1, 1954
             (not on October 30, 1952, March 5, May 14, May 21, June 11,
             and Aug. 5, 1953; March 4 and May 6, 1954)
  Sponsor:   Sustaining

Total Shows: 84 (pre-recorded)

## *The Eddie Cantor Show* (Ziv)

Time Slot:   30 minutes; syndicated
Announcer:   James Wallington
Vocalists:   Roy Edwards, Patti Lewis
Cast:   Dorothy Carless, Ronnie Harris
Opening Theme:   "We Want Cantor"/"When You're Smiling"

Total Shows: 258 (pre-recorded)

## *Family Living* (NBC)

Time Slot:   30 minutes
Announcer:   Guy Wallace

Total Shows: 13

## *Ask Eddie Cantor* (Lika)

Time Slot:   5 minutes

Total Shows: 260 (pre-recorded)

## GUEST RADIO APPEARANCES
### (Principal Network Broadcasts)

*Warner Bros. Vitaphone Jubilee* (CBS), Oct. 1, 1928, New York
*Majestic Theatre of the Air* (CBS), Jan. 6, 1929, New York

*Old Gold Cigarette Program* (CBS), Feb. 5, 1929, New York
*Old Gold Cigarette Program* (CBS), Dec. 12, 1929, New York
*Radio Follies* (CBS), Feb. 4, 1931, Miami, Fla.
*Rudy Vallee Fleischmann Hour* (NBC), Feb. 5, 1931, Miami
*Sunkist Musical Cocktail* (CBS), May 6, 1931, Los Angeles
*Rudy Vallee Fleischmann Hour* (CBS), Oct. 1, 1931, New York
*Jack Benny Chevrolet Show* (NBC), April 1, 1934, New York
*Rudy Vallee Fleischmann Hour* (NBC), April 23, 1936, New York
*Al Jolson's Cafe Trocadero* (CBS), Jan. 19, 1937, Los Angeles
*Burns & Allen Grape Nuts Show* (NBC), Oct. 25, 1937, Los Angeles
*25 Years in Show Business* (CBS), Oct. 28, 1937, Los Angeles
*Council of Stars* (CBS), Jan. 22, 1939, Los Angeles
*Good News of 1939* (NBC), April 27, 1939, Los Angeles
*Red Cross War Fund Program* NBC), May 26, 1940, New York
*Burns & Allen Spam Show* (NBC), Jan. 6, 1941, Los Angeles
*Star Spangled Vaudeville* (NBC), Aug. 23, 1942, New York
*Philip Morris Playhouse* (CBS), Aug. 28, 1942, New York
*Packard Bell Christmas Show* (CBS), Dec. 25, 1942
*Take It Or Leave It* (CBS), Jan. 3, 1943, Los Angeles
*March of Dimes* (NBC), Jan. 23, 1943, Los Angeles
*Joan Davis Show* (NBC), Dec. 17, 1943, Los Angeles
*Frank Sinatra Program* (CBS), Jan. 5, 1944, Los Angeles
*March of Dimes* (NBC), Jan. 23, 1944, Los Angeles
*Joan Davis Show* (NBC), Feb. 25, 1944, Los Angeles
*Jack Benny Grape Nuts Show* (NBC), Feb. 27, 1944,
    Los Angeles
*Radio Hall of Fame* (NBC), April 23, 1944, New York
*Radio Hall of Fame* (NBC), May 28, 1944, Philadelphia
*Danny Kaye Pabst Blue Ribbon Show* (CBS), Jan. 6, 1945, L.A.
*The Baby Snooks Show* (CBS), Sept. 16, 1945, Los Angeles
*The Jack Benny Program* (NBC), Feb. 10, 1946, Los Angeles
*Maxwell House Coffee Time* (NBC), Oct. 3, 1946, Los Angeles
*Maxwell House Coffee time* (NBC), Dec. 26, 1946, Los Angeles
*Bob Hope Pepsodent Show* (NBC), April 1, 1947, Los Angeles
*The Jimmy Durante Show* (NBC), Oct. 8, 1947, Los Angeles
*Bob Hope Pepsodent Show* (NBC), Nov. 18, 1947, Los Angeles
*Maxwell House Coffee Time* (NBC), March 4, 1948, Los Angeles
*Carnival of Stars* (CBS), May 10, 1948, Los Angeles
*The Jack Benny Program* (NBC), Dec. 12, 1948, Los Angeles
*The Railroad Hour* (ABC), Jan. 3, 1949, Los Angeles
*Maxwell House Coffee Time* (NBC), April 21, 1949, Los Angeles
*The Jack Benny Program* (NBC), May 8, 1949, Los Angeles
*Suspense* (CBS), December 22, 1949, Los Angeles
*Chesterfield Supper Club* (NBC), Feb. 23, 1950, Los Angeles
*The Big Show* (NBC), Nov. 19, 1950, New York
*The Jack Benny Program* (NBC), Dec. 10, 1950, New York
*The Big Show* (NBC), Jan. 21, 1951, New York
*The Big Show* (NBC), March 18, 1951, New York

## GUEST RADIO APPEARANCES
(Principal Non-Network Broadcasts)

Untitled (WDY), Feb. 10, 1922, Roselle Park, N.J.
Vaughn de Leath (WDT), 1924, New York [several broadcasts]
*Eveready Hour* (WEAF), Nov. 2, 1926, New York
N.A.G. Test. to Bill Robinson (WINS), Dec. 8, 1940, New York
*Arch Oboler Plays* (KHJ), Oct. 4, 1945, Los Angeles
*So This Is Paris* (NNF), June 25, 1949, Paris, France

# TELEVISIONOGRAPHY

## STARRING TELEVISION SERIES

*Colgate Comedy Hour* (NBC)

Time Slot:  Sun., 8:00–9:00 P.M.
Sponsor:  Colgate-Palmolive-Peet
Director:  Charles Friedman  (1950–51)
             Manning Ostroff  (1951–52)
             Sid Kuller       (1952–53)
                            (1953–54)
Producer:  Sam Fuller
Writer:  Manning Ostroff
Ensembles:  Dick Barstow
Conductor:  Al Goodman
Announcer:

Telecast from New York:    Sept. 10, 1950–Sept.  9, 1951
Telecast from Los Angeles:    Sept. 30, 1951–May  16, 1954

### Guests

| | | | |
|---|---|---|---|
| 1950 | Sept. | 10 | Ima Sumac, Tommy Wonder, Danny Daniels, Joseph Buloff |
| | Oct. | 8 | (no guest) |
| | Nov. | 5 | (no guest) |
| | Dec. | 3 | Joe Bushkin, Mrs. Franklin D. Roosevelt |
| | Dec. | 31 | Ed Wynn, Danny Thomas, Sigmund Romberg |
| 1951 | Jan. | 28 | Basil O'Connor, Estelle Sloan, Dave Powell, Lee Fairfax |
| | Feb. | 25 | Lena Horne, Jack Albertson, Chris Barbery |
| | March | 25 | Jimmy Durante and Eddie Jackson |

|  |  |  |  |
|---|---|---|---|
| | April | 1 | Johnny Weissmuller |
| | April | 22 | Anne Jeffreys, Johnny Weismuller, Hal Loman |
| | May | 27 | Connie Haines, Joel Grey, Charlie Cantor, Herbert Colman |
| | June | 17 | Milton Berle, Jack Leonard, Phil Foster, Dagmar |
| | Sept. | 9 | Cesar Romero |
| | Sept. | 30 | (no guest) |
| | Oct. | 28 | Cesar Romero, Sheilah Graham, Arthur Blake |
| | Nov. | 25 | Cesar Romero, Eddie Fisher |
| | Dec. | 9 | Nillson Twins, Tom D'Andrea, Larry Blake, Robert Clary |
| | Dec. | 23 | Bobby Breen, Farley Granger, Sharon Baird |
| 1952 | Jan | 20 | Herman McCoy Swing Choir, Robert Clary, Sharon Baird |
| | Feb. | 17 | Will Mastin Trio, Doris Singleton, Sharon Baird |
| | March | 16 | Dorothy Kirsten, Will Mastin Trio, Sharon Baird |
| | April | 13 | Joe E. Brown, Constance Moore, Dave Barry, Sharon Baird |
| | May | 18 | Cesar Romero, Rusty Draper, The Szonys |
| | June | 8 | Ida Cantor, Pat O'brien, Kay Starr, Harry Von Zell |
| | Sept. | 28 | Dorothy Lamour, Eddie Fisher, Will Mastin Trio |
| 1953 | Jan | 18 | Dinah Shore, Joel Grey, Arnold Stang, The Tokayers |
| | Feb. | 15 | Frank Loesser, Connie Russell, Billy Daniels |
| | March | 15 | George Jessel, Harry Ruby, Connie Russell, Billy Daniels |
| | March | 22 | 100th Anniversary Program |
| | April | 12 | Gloria Grahame, Will Mastin Trio |
| | May | 3 | Connie Russell |
| | May | 10 | Jan Pearce, Connie Russell, Billy Daniels |
| | June | 7 | Jack Benny, George Jessel, Dinah Shore, Jimmy Wallington |
| | Oct. | 18 | Jack Benny, Connie Russell, Billy Daniels |
| | Nov. | 29 | Brian Donlevy, Eddie Fisher, Connie Russell |
| | Dec. | 27 | Jimmy Durante, Donald O'Connor, Dennis Day, George Gobel |
| 1954 | Jan. | 31 | Groucho Marx, Wally Cox, Marilyn Cantor, Connie Russell |
| | March | 7 | Audrey Hepburn, William Holden, Grace Kelly |
| | April | 4 | Daryl F. Zanuck, Connie Russell, Billy Daniels |
| | May | 16 | Milton Berle, Eddie Fisher, Connie Russell |

*Eddie Cantor Comedy Theatre* (Frederic W. Ziv Co., 1954–55)
Syndicated, 30 minutes
Host: Eddie Cantor

| | |
|---|---|
| "Now in Rehearsal" | Eddie Cantor, Brian Aherne |
| "Nearly Normal" | Don Defore, Pat Crowley |
| "The Big Bargain" | James Gleason, Billie Burke |
| "The Hypochondriac" | E. Cantor, Reg. Denny, E. Fisher |
| "A Hunting We Will Go" | Lizabeth Scott, Craig Stevens |
| "The Suspicious Husband" | Buddy Ebsen, Bonita Granville |
| "Garage" | Eddie Cantor, Connie Russell |
| "The Romance Wrecker" | Charles Coburn, Cathy Downs |
| "The Atomic Brain" | Allyn Joslyn, Marie Windsor |
| "The Mink Coat" | Eddie Cantor, Jean Parker |
| "The Finer Points" | Robert Strauss, Jack LaRue |
| "The Helper" | Eddie Cantor, Marjorie Reynolds |

| | |
|---|---|
| "Commercially Ever After" | Eddie Cantor, John Gallaudet |
| "The Practical Joker" | Joe E. Brown, Dorothy Grainger |
| "The Sure Cure" | Peter Lorre, Veda Ann Borg |
| "The Critics" | Eddie Cantor, Honey Brothers |
| "This Marine Went to Town" | Victor McLaglan, Stan Freberg |
| "Always the Butler" | Basil Rathbone |
| "A Night at the *Follies*" | Eddie Cantor, Joe Besser |
| "V for Victoria" | Mona Freeman, Peter Leeds |
| "How Much for Van Such" | Vincent Price |
| "Dying to Love" | Eddie Cantor, Jane Frazee |
| "Bombshell Goes to College" | Joan Blondell, Michael Fox |
| "Call Me Irving" | Johnny Johnson, Mary Beth Hughes |
| "Ten Thousand Years from Now" | Eddie Cantor, Reginald Denny |
| "What Do You Want in a Show" | Three Stooges, Ida Cantor |
| "The Playboy" | Rudy Vallee |
| "Man Who Liked Little People" | Edmund Gwenn |
| "Lieutenant Was No Gentleman" | Ann Sheridan |
| "The Song Plugger" | Eddie Cantor, David Rose |
| "Four Strikes" | Pat O'Brien, Vera Marshe |
| "Square World of Pennyworth" | Buster Keaton |
| "The Hollywood Story" | Johnny Johnson |
| "The Tester" | Alan Young |
| "Strange Little Stranger" | Tommy Noonan, Joyce Holden |
| "And Now from the Audience" | William Frawley |

## NETWORK GUEST APPEARANCES

*Philco Relay Program* (NBC), May 25, 1944, Philadelphia
*Radio Hall of Fame* (ABC), May 28, 1944, Philadelphia
*United Jewish Appeal* (NBC), Oct. 28, 1950, New York
*The Comedy Hour* (NBC), Oct. 29, 1950, New York
*Four-Star Revue* (NBC), Jan. 3, 1951, New York
*Four-Star Revue* (NBC), Jan. 10, 1951, New York
*The Comedy Hour* (NBC), April 8, 1951, New York
*Four-Star Revue* (NBC), May 16, 1951, New York
*Damon Runyon Memorial Fund* (NBC), June 10, 1951, New York
*Broadway Open House* (NBC), June 14, 1951, New York
*Colgate Comedy Hour* (NBC), September 2, 1951, New York
*Texaco Star Theatre* (NBC), September 18, 1951, New York
*What's My Line?* (CBS), January 27, 1952, New York
*Horn & Hardart Children's Hour* (NBC), Feb. 3, 1952, New York
*Hope-Crosby Olympic Telethon* (NBC), June 21, 1952, Los Angeles
*Dinah Shore Chevrolet Show* (NBC), Jan. 29, 1953, Los Angeles
*Coke Time* (NBC), January 6, 1954, Los Angeles
*All-Star Revue* (NBC), April 4, 1953, Los Angeles
*RCA Victor Show* (NBC), November 9, 1953, Los Angeles
*Dinah Shore Chevrolet Show* (NBC), Dec. 15, 1953, Los Angeles
*This Is Your Life* (NBC), December 23, 1953, Los Angeles
*Buick-Berle Show* (NBC), January 5, 1954, Los Angeles

*Coke Time* (NBC), January 6, 1954, Los Angeles
*RCA Victor Show* (NBC), February 22, 1954, Los Angeles
*Coke Time* (NBC), March 5, 1954, Los Angeles
*Colgate Comedy Hour* (NBC), March 14, 1954, Los Angeles
*Coke Time* (NBC), June 18, 1954, Los Angeles
*Betty White Show* (NBC), Sept. 9, 1954, Los Angeles
*Coke Time* (NBC), December 22, 1954, Los Angeles
*This Is Your Life* (NBC), (J. Grossinger), Dec. 29, 1954, Los Angeles
*This Is Your Life* (NBC), (Belle Baker), June 1, 1955, Los Angeles
*This Is Your Life* (NBC), (Bela Herskovitz), Feb. 8, 1956, Los Angeles
*Milton Berle Show* (NBC), Feb. 21, 1956, Las Vegas (Color)
*Matinee Theatre* (NBC), (*George Has A Birthday*), June 11, 1956
*Playhouse 90* (CBS) (*Sizeman and Son*), October 18, 1956
*Coke Time* (NBC), December 21, 1956, Los Angeles
*Academy Awards Show*, March 27, 1957, Hollywood
*Masquerade Party* (NBC), May 29, 1957, Los Angeles
*What's My Line* (CBS), June 2, 1957, New York
*Tonight: America After Dark* (NBC), June 17, 1957, Los Angeles
*Arlene Francis Show* (NBC), September 20, 1957, Los Angeles
*Eddie Fisher Show* (NBC), February 4, 1958, Los Angeles
*Eddie Fisher Show* (NBC), May 27, 1958, Los Angeles
*Eddie Fisher Show* (NBC), October 28, 1958, Los Angeles
*George Jessel's Show Business*, 1958, Los Angeles
*George Jessel's Show Business*, 1958, Los Angeles
*You Asked For It* (ABC), March 1, 1959, Los Angeles
*The Big Time*, November 17, 1959 (Color), Los Angeles
*The Future Lies Ahead* (NBC), January 22, 1960 (Color), Los Angeles

# DISCOGRAPHY

June 28, 1917. New York, N.Y.
Unaccompanied.

61723     To Max Hart [Private Recording]     Columbia

July 12, 1917. Camden, N.J.
With Victor Orchestra under direction of Rosario Bourdon.

B-20216     "The Modern Maiden's Prayer"     Victor 18342 (1)
    (James F. Hanley–Ballard MacDonald)

B-20217     "That's the Kind of a Baby for Me"     Victor 18342 (2)
    (J. C. Egan–Alfred Harriman)

November 1917. New York, N.Y.
With Studio Orchestra.

"The Modern Maiden's Prayer."     Aeolian Vocalion 1220
(James F. Hanley–Ballard MacDonald)
"That's the Kind of a Baby for Me"     Aeolian Vocalion 1220
(J. C. Egan–Alfred Harriman)
"Down in Borneo Isle"     Aeolian Vocalion 1228
(Henry Creamer–J. Turner Layton)
"Hello, Wisconsin"     Aeolian Vocalion 1228
(Harry Ruby–Bert Kalmar–Edgar Leslie)
"The Dixie Volunteers"     Aeolian Vocalion 1233
(Harry Ruby–Edgar Leslie)
"I Don't Want to Get Well"     Aeolian Vocalion 1233
(Harry Jentes–Howard Johnson–
Harry Pease)

June 1919. New York, N.Y.<br>With Pathe Orchestra

| | | |
|---|---|---|
| 67833 | "Oh! The Last Rose of Summer"<br>(Harry Ruby–Eddie Cantor–Phil Ponce) | Pathe 22163 (1) |
| 67834 | "You Don't Need the Wine"<br>(Harry Akst–Howard E. Rogers) | Pathe 22163 (1) |

July 1919. New York, N.Y.<br>With Emerson Orchestra.

| | | |
|---|---|---|
| 4467 | "You Don't Need the Wine"<br>(Harry Akst–Howard E. Rogers) | Emerson 1071 (2, 3) |

July 1919. New York, N.Y.<br>With Emerson Orchestra.

| | | |
|---|---|---|
| 4508 | "Don't Put a Tax on the Beautiful<br>Girls"<br>(Milton Ager–Jack Yellen) | Emerson 1071 (2, 3) |
| 4509 | "When They're Old Enough to Know<br>Better"<br>(Harry Ruby–Sam M. Lewis–Joe Young) | Emerson 1094 (1, 2) |

August 1919. New York, N.Y.<br>With Pathe Orchestra

| | | |
|---|---|---|
| 67952 | "I've Got My Captain Working for Me<br>Now"<br>(Irving Berlin) | Pathe 22201 (1) |
| 67953 | "When They're Old Enough to Know<br>Better"<br>(Harry Ruby–Sam M. Lewis–Joe Young) | Pathe 22201 (1) |

August 1919. New York, N.Y.<br>With Pathe Orchestra.

| | | |
|---|---|---|
| 67977 | "I've Got My Captain Working for Me<br>Now"<br>(Irving Berlin | Pathe 22201 (1) |
| 67979 | "Don't Put a Tax on the Beautiful<br>Girls"<br>(Milton Ager–Jack Yellen) | Pathe 22260 (1) |

September 1919. New York, N.Y.<br>With Emerson Orchestra

| | | |
|---|---|---|
| 4629 | "I Used to Call Her Baby"<br>(Cliff Hess–Howard Johnson–<br>Murray Roth) | Emerson 10102 (3, 4) |
| 4630 | "Give Me the Sultan's Harem"<br>Abner Silver–Alex Gerber) | Emerson 10105 (1,2,3) |

September 1919. New York, N.Y.
With Emerson Orchestra.

| | | |
|---|---|---|
| 4670 | "You'd Be Surprised" (Irving Berlin) | Emerson 10102 (1, 2, 3) |

September 1919. New York, N.Y.
With Pathe Orchestra.

| | | |
|---|---|---|
| 68091 | "At the High Brown Babies' Ball" (Ernie Erdman–Sid Erdman– Benny Davis) | Pathe 22260 (1) |

October 1919. New York, N.Y.
With Emerson Orchestra.

| | | |
|---|---|---|
| 4734 | "Oh! The Last Rose of Summer" (Harry Ruby–Eddie Cantor–Phil Ponce) | Emerson 10134 (4, 6) |

October 1919. New York, N.Y.
With Emerson Orchestra.

| | | |
|---|---|---|
| 4759 | "When It Comes to Loving the Girls" (Jack Glogau–Joe Burns– Murray Kissen) | Emerson 10105 (2, 3) |
| 4760 | "Come On and Play Wiz Me" (Harry Ruby–Bert Kalmar–Edgar Leslie) | Emerson 10119 (1, 3) |

October 1919. New York, N.Y.
With Emerson Orchestra.

| | | |
|---|---|---|
| 4779 | "All the Boys Love Mary" (Gus Van–Joe Schenck– Andrew B. Sterling) | Emerson 10119 (1, 2) |
| 4780 | "You Ain't Heard Nothing Yet" (Al Jolson–Gus Kahn–Bud DeSylva) | Emerson 10134 (2) |

November 1919. New York, N.Y.
With Pathe Orchestra.

| | | |
|---|---|---|
| 68188 | "When it Comes to Loving the Girls" (Jack Glogau–Joe Burns– Murray Kissen) | Pathe 22318 (1) |
| 68189 | "I Never Knew I Had a Wonderful Wife" (Albert von Tilzer–Lew Brown) | Pathe 22318 (1) |

June 1920. New York, N.Y.
With Emerson Orchestra.

| | | |
|---|---|---|
| 41171 | "The Argentines and the Greeks" (Arthur M. Swanstrom-Carey Morgan) | Emerson 10200 (3) |
| 41172 | "Noah's Wife Lived a Wonderful Life" (Ernie Erdman–Abe Olman–Jack Yellen– Roger Lewis) | Emerson 10200 (1) |

July 1920. New York, N.Y.
With Emerson Orchestra.

41207    "The Older They Get, the Younger They   Emerson 10212 (2, 3)
Want 'Em."
(Clarence Gaskill–Al Dubin)

41208    "Snoops, the Lawyer"                Emerson 10212 (2)
(Harry Ruby–Bert Kalmar)

August, 1920. New York, N.Y.
With Emerson Orchestra.

41239    "She Gives Them All the Ha! Ha! Ha!"    Emerson 10292 (2, 3, 4)
(Albert von Tilzer–Lew Brown)

September 1920. New York, N.Y.
With Emerson Orchestra.

41375    "Dixie Made Us Jazz Band Mad"      Emerson 10263 (1, 2, 3)
(Irwin Dash–Howard Johnson–William
K. Wells)

41376    "When I See All the Loving They      Emerson 10263 (1, 2, 3)
Waste"
(Art Johnston–Sam Ward–Hopwood
De Rob)

October 1920. New York, N.Y.
With Emerson Orchestra.

41453    "I Wish That I'd Been Born in Borneo"   Emerson 10301 (5, 6, 7)
(Walter Donaldson-Grant Clarke)

November 1920. New York, N.Y.
With Emerson Orchestra.

41494    "Palesteena"                     Emerson 10292 (1, 2)
(Con Conrad-J. Russell Robinson)

December 1920. New York, N.Y.
With Emerson Orchestra.

41534    "Margie"                        Emerson 10301 (1, 2, 3)
(Con Conrad–Benny Davis–J. Russell
Robinson)

December 1920. New York, N.Y.
With Emerson Orchestra.

41551    "You Oughta See My Baby"       Emerson 10327 (1, 2)
(Fred E. Ahlert–Roy Turk)

January 1921. New York, N.Y.
With Emerson Orchestra.

41631    "Timbuctoo"                    Emerson 10352 (1, 2, 3)
(Harry Ruby–Bert Kalmar)

41632    "I Never Knew I Could Love Anybody"    Emerson 10349 (2, 3)
         (Tom Pitts–Raymond Egan–
         Roy K. Marsh)

                      June 1921. New York, N.Y.
                      With Emerson Orchestra.
41852    "Anna in Indiana"                      Emerson 10397 (2)
         (Harry Rose–Billy Gorman–
         Eddie Gorman)

                  April 28, 1922. New York, N.Y.
                      With Columbia Orchestra.
80328    "I Love Her, She Loves Me"             Columbia A3624 (3)
         (Irving Caesar–Eddie Cantor)

                   May 10, 1922. New York, N.Y.
                      With Columbia Orchestra.
80342    "I'm Hungry for Beautiful Girls"       Columbia A3624 (2)
         (Fred Fisher–Billy Rose–Wilbur Held)

                   July 5, 1922. New York, N.Y.
                      With Columbia Orchestra.
80439    "Oh, Is She Dumb!"                     1-2-3 Rejected
         (Archie Gottler–Grant Clarke–
         Edgar Leslie)
80440    "Susie"                                Columbia A3682 (2)
         (Harry Ruby–Bert Kalmar)

                  July 28, 1922. New York, N.Y.
                      With Columbia Orchestra.
80439    "Oh, Is She Dumb!"                     Columbia A3682 (6)
         (Archie Gottler–Grant Clarke–
         Edgar Leslie)

                October 30, 1922. New York, N.Y.
                      With Columbia Orchestra.
80636    "(I Go So Far with) Sophie"            Columbia A3754 (2)
         (Abner Silver)
80637    "He Loves It"                          Columbia A3754 (3)
         (Pete Wendling–Grant Clarke–
         Edgar Leslie)

                December 13, 1922. New York, N.Y.
                      With Columbia Orchestra.
80715    "Joe Is Here"                          Columbia A3784 (2, 3)
         (Harry Ruby–Bert Kalmar)
80716    "How Ya Gonna Keep Your Mind on        Columbia A3784 (2)
         Dancing?"
         (James F. Hanley–Lew Brown)

May 4, 1923. New York, N.Y.
With Columbia Orchestra.

| | | |
|---|---|---|
| 81004 | "I Love Me (I'm Wild About Myself)" (Edwin J. Weber–Will Mahoney– Jack Hoins) | Columbia A3906 (1) |
| 81005 | "Ritzi Mitzi" (Con Conrad–Irving M. Bibo– Howard Johnson) | Columbia A3906 (2) |

June 12, 1923. New York, N.Y.
With Columbia Orchestra.

| | | |
|---|---|---|
| 81073 | "Oh! Gee, Oh! Gosh, Oh! Golly, I'm in Love" (Ernest Breuer–Ole Olsen– Chic Johnson) | Columbia A3934 (2) |

June 14, 1923. New York, N.Y.
With Columbia Orchestra.

| | | |
|---|---|---|
| 81076 | "Eddie (Steady)" (Charles Tobias–Eddie Cantor) | Columbia A3934 (2, 6) |

July 26, 1923. New York, N.Y.
With Columbia Orchestra.

| | | |
|---|---|---|
| 81148 | "No, No, Nora" (Gus Kahn–Ernie Erdman–Ted Fiorito) | Columbia A3964 (1, 2) |
| 81149 | "Yes! We Have No Bananas Blues" (James F. Hanley–Robert A. King– Lew Brown) | Columbia A3964 (2, 3) |

January 4, 1924. New York, N.Y.
With the Georgians/directed by Frank Guarente.

| | | |
|---|---|---|
| 81459 | "O, Gee, Georgie" (Al Sherman–Jack Meskill–Willie Raskin) | Columbia 56-D (3) |
| 81460 | "If You Do What You Do" (Roy Turk–Lou Handman– Eddie Cantor) | Columbia 56-D (2) |

April 4, 1924. New York, N.Y.
With Columbia Orchestra.

| | | |
|---|---|---|
| 81666 | "I'll Have Vanilla" (Arthur Terker–Redmond Farrar– Eddie Cantor) | Columbia 120-D (2) |
| 81667 | "On a Windy Day 'Way Down in Waikiki" (Harry DeCosta–Eddie Cantor) | Columbia 120-D (4) |

May 14, 1924. New York, N.Y.
With Columbia Orchestra.

| | | |
|---|---|---|
| 81779 | "Oh, Papa" | Columbia 140-D (2) |
| | (David Elman) | |
| 81780 | "Monkey Doodle" | Columbia 140-D (3) |
| | (Ted Morse–Dorothy Terriss–Leo Wood) | |

July 18, 1924. New York, N.Y.
With Columbia Orchestra.

| | | |
|---|---|---|
| 81878 | "Charley, My Boy" | Columbia 182-D (2) |
| | (Gus Kahn–Ted Fiorito) | |

August 8, 1924. New York, N.Y.
With Columbia Orchestra.

| | | |
|---|---|---|
| 81904 | "No One Knows What It's All About" | Columbia 196-D (3) |
| | (Harry Woods–Billy Rose) | |

September 12, 1924. New York, N.Y.
With Columbia Orchestra.

| | | |
|---|---|---|
| 140037 | "Doodle-Doo-Doo | Columbia 213-D (3) |
| | (Art Kassel–Mel Stitzel) | |

October 14, 1924. New York, N.Y.
With Columbia Orchestra.

| | | |
|---|---|---|
| 140106 | "How I Love That Girl" | Columbia 234-D (1) |
| | (Ted Fiorito–Gus Kahn) | |

November 17, 1924. New York, N.Y.
With Columbia Orchestra.

| | | |
|---|---|---|
| 140145 | "Those Panama Mamas" | Columbia 256-D (1) |
| | (Irving M. Bibo–Howard Johnson) | |

December 29, 1924. New York, N.Y.
With Columbia Orchestra.

| | | |
|---|---|---|
| 140213 | "Goo-Goo-Goodnight, Dear" | Columbia 277-D (3) |
| | (Cliff Friend) | |

January 6, 1925. New York, N.Y.
With Columbia Orchestra.

| | | |
|---|---|---|
| 140223 | "Laff It Off!" | Columbia 283-D (3) |
| | (Harry Ruby–Bert Kalmar) | |

April 6, 1925. New York, N.Y.
With Columbia Orchestra.

| | | |
|---|---|---|
| 140499 | "If You Knew Susie" | Columbia 364-D (3) |
| | (Joseph Meyer–B.G. DeSylva) | |

April 27, 1925. New York, N.Y.
With Columbia Orchestra.

140558     "We're Back Together Again"                1-2-3-4 Rejected
           (James V. Monaco–Sidney Clare)

June 1, 1925. New York, N.Y.
With Columbia Orchestra.

140558     "We're Back Together Again"                Columbia 397-D (7)
           (James V. Monaco–Sidney Clare)
140641     "Row, Row, Rosie"                          Columbia 415-D (1)
           (George W. Meyer–Alfred Bryan)

September 10, 1925. New York, N.Y.
With Columbia Orchestra.
Matrices 140926 and 140928 are monologues.

140925     "Oh! Boy, What a Girl"                     Columbia 457-D (3)
           (Frank A. Wright–Bud Green–
           Frank Bessinger)
140926     "Jake, the Plumber"                        1-2 Unissued
           (Lew Brown)
140928     "Eddie's Trip Abroad"                      1-2 Unissued
           (Eddie Cantor)

September 6, 1928. New York, N.Y.
With George Olsen and His Music.

BVE-46989  "Sonny Boy"                                1-2-3-4 Unissued
           (Jolson–DeSylva–Brown–Henderson)
BVE-46990  "That Funny Melody"                        1-2 Unissued
           (Cliff Friend–Irving Caesar)

December 18, 1928. New York, N.Y.
With Victor Orchestra under direction of Nat Shilkret.

BVE-49001  "Makin' Whoopee"                           Victor 21831 (2)
           (Walter Donaldson–Gus Kahn)
BVE-49002  "Hungry Women"                             Victor 21831 (4)
           (Milton Ager–Jack Yellen)

January 28, 1929. New York, N.Y.
With Victor Orchestra under direction of Nat Shilkret.

BVE-49688  " 'Automobile Horn' Song"                  Victor 21862 (2)
           (Gaskill–Tobias–Bennett–Carlton)
BVE-49689  "I Faw Down and Go 'Boom' "                Victor 21862 (2)
           (James Brockman–Leonard Stevens–
           B.B.B.)

April 5, 1929. New York, N.Y.
With Victor Orchestra under direction of Leonard Joy.

BVE-51610  "Hello, Sunshine, Hello"                   Victor 21982 (3)
           (Henry Tobias-Jack Murray-
           Charles Tobias)

BVE-51611    "If I Give Up the Saxophone"      Victor 21982 (3)
           (Sammy Fain–Irving Kahal–
           Willie Raskin)

October 29, 1929. New York, N.Y.<br>With Victor Orchestra under direction of Leonard Joy.<br>Matrix BVE-57130 is a monologue.

BVE–57128    "Does an Elephant Love Peanuts?"    1-2-3-4 Unissued
           (James F. Hanley)
BVE-57129    "My Wife Is on a Diet"        Victor 22189 (3, 4)
           (Charles Tobias–George J. Bennett)
BVE-57130    "Eddie Cantor's Tips on the Stock    Victor 22189 (4)
           Market"
           (Eddie Cantor)

August 23, 1931. Hollywood, Calif.<br>With Gus Arnheim and his Cocoanut Grove Orchestra.

PBVE-68306    "There's Nothing Too Good for My    Victor 22851 (2)
           Baby"
           (Harry Akst–Eddie Cantor–
           Benny Davis)

September 1931. New York, N.Y.<br>With Orchestra.

K-623    "Cheer Up" [*Ballyhoo* Theme Song]    Durium De Luxe K-6
           (Misha Portnoff–Wesley Portnoff–
           Norman Anthony)

November 2, 1932. New York, N.Y.<br>With Columbia Orchestra under direction of Ben Selvin.

152316    "What a Perfect Combination"    Columbia 2723-D (3)
           (Harry Ruby–Harry Akst–Bert Kalmar–
           Irving Caesar)
152317    "Look What You've Done"        Columbia 2723-D (3)
           (Harry Ruby–Bert Kalmar)

April 16, 1934. New York, N.Y.<br>With Studio Orchestra.

15075    "Over Somebody Else's Shoulder"    Melotone 13001 (1)
           (Al Sherman–Al Lewis)
15076    "The Man on the Flying Trapeze"    Melotone 13001 (1)
           (Hugo Frey–Walter O'Keefe)

September 12, 1934. Los Angeles, Calif.<br>with Studio Orchestra.

LA-204    "Mandy"                  Melotone 13183 (A)
           (Irving Berlin)
LA-205    "An Earful of Music"          Melotone 13183 (A)
           (Walter Donaldson–Gus Kahn)

| LA 206 | "When My Ship Comes In" | Unissued |
| | (Walter Donaldson–Gus Kahn) | |
| LA-207 | "Okay, Toots" | Melotone 13184 (A) |
| | (Walter Donaldson–Gus Kahn) | |

October 1, 1934. Los Angeles, Calif.
With Studio Orchestra

| LA-206 | "When My Ship Comes in" | Melotone 13184 (C) |
| | (Walter Donaldson–Gus Kahn) | |

January 1935. London, England.
With Orchestra under direction of Jay Wilbur.

| F-1117 | "That's the Kind of a Baby for Me" | Decca F-6748 (3) |
| | (J.C. Egan–Alfred Harriman) | |
| F-1118 | "Making the Best of Each Day" | Decca F-6748 (1) |
| | (Murray Mencher–Charles Tobias– | |
| | Sidney Clare) | |

January 26, 1938. Los Angeles, Calif.
With Connie Boswell and Bing Crosby.
With Orchestra under Direction of Victor Young.

| DLA-1152 | "Alexander's Ragtime Band" | Decca 1887 (A) |
| | (Irving Berlin) | |

July 23, 1938. London, England.
with Ambrose and his Orchestra.

| F-2822 | "Says My Heart" | Decca F-6741 (1) |
| | (Frank Loesser–Burton Lane) | |
| | "Little Lady Make Believe" | |
| | (Nat Simon–Charles Tobias) | |
| F-2823 | "Lambeth Walk" | Decca F-6741 (2) |
| | (Noel Gay–Douglas Furber– | |
| | L. Arthur Rose) | |

November 26, 1939. Los Angeles, Calif.
With Orchestra under Direction of Jerry Joyce.
Matrix LA-2049 with Mitchell Boychoir

| LA-2049 | "The Only Thing I Want for Christmas" | Columbia 35325 |
| | (Vic Knight–Johnny Lange–Lew Porter) | |
| LA-2050 | "If You Knew Susie" | Columbia 35325 |
| | (Joseph Meyer–B.G. DeSylva) | |

February 29, 1940. Los Angeles, Calif.
With Orchestra under direction of Jerry Joyce.

| LA-2171 | "Little Curly Hair in a High Chair" | Columbia 35428 |
| | (Nat Simon–Charles Tobias) | |
| LA-2172 | "Margie" | Columbia 35428 |
| | (Con Conrad–Benny Davis– | |
| | J. Russell Robinson) | |

May 6, 1941. New York, N.Y.
With Studio Orchestra.

| | | |
|---|---|---|
| 69143 | "Makin' Whoopee" <br> (Walter Donaldson–Gus Kahn) | Decca 3798 |
| 69144 | "Yes Sir, That's My Baby" <br> (Walter Donaldson–Gus Kahn) | Decca 3798 |
| 69145 | "Oh! Gee, Oh! Gosh, Oh! Golly, I'm in Love" <br> (Ernest Breuer–Ole Olsen– Chic Johnson) | Decca 3873 |
| 69146 | "They Go Wild, Simply Wild, Over Me" <br> (Fred Fisher–Joseph McCarthy) | Decca 3873 |

March 19, 1942. New York, N.Y.
With Orchestra under direction of Harry Sosnik.

| | | |
|---|---|---|
| 70539 | "We're Having a Baby" <br> (Vernon Duke–Harold Adamson) | Decca 4314 |
| 70540 | "Now's the Time to Fall in Love" <br> (Al Sherman–Al Lewis) | Decca 4314 |

October 17, 1944. Los Angeles, Calif.
With Nora Martin.
With Orchestra under direction of Victor Young.

| | | |
|---|---|---|
| L-3648 | "Around and Around and Around" <br> (Dave Franklin) | Decca 23592 |
| L-3649 | "You Kissed Me Once" <br> (Sol Marcus–Edward Seiler) | Decca 23592 |

October 31, 1944. Los Angeles, Calif.
With Orchestra under direction of Victor Young.

| | | |
|---|---|---|
| L-3668 | "If You Knew Susie" <br> (Joseph Meyer–B.G. DeSylva) | Decca 23986 |
| L-3669 | "You'd Be Surprised" <br> (Irving Berlin) | Decca 23987 |
| L-3670 | "Dinah" <br> (Harry Akst–Sam M. Lewis–Joe Young) | Decca 23988 |
| L-3671 | "Ma (He's Making Eyes at Me)" <br> (Con Conrad–Sidney Clare) | Decca 23723 |

November 1, 1944. Los Angeles, Calif.
With Orchestra under direction of Victor Young.

| | | |
|---|---|---|
| L-3673 | "Alabamy Bound" <br> (B.G. DeSylva–Bud Green– Ray Henderson) | Decca 24597 |
| L-3674 | "Margie" <br> (Con Conrad–Benny Davis– J. Russell Robinson) | Decca 23723 |
| L-3675 | "Ida, Sweet as Apple Cider" <br> (Eddie Munson–Eddie Leonard) | Decca 23987 |

L-3676        "How Ya Gonna Keep 'Em Down on        Decca 23988
              the Farm?"
              (Walter Donaldson–Sam M. Lewis–
              Joe Young)


              February 1946. Hollywood, Calif.
              With Cliff Lange's All-Star Orchestra.
ST-71         "One-Zy, Two-Zy"                      Pan American 036
              (Dave Franklin–Irving Taylor)


              March 1946. Hollywood, Calif.
              With Rafael Mendez and his Orchestra.
ST-83         "Josephine, Please No Lean on the     Pan American 044
              Bell"
              (Duke Leonard–Ed G. Nelson–
              Harry Pease)
ST-84         "Makin' Whoopee"                      Pan American 044
              (Walter Donaldson–Gus Kahn)


              August 28, 1946. Los Angeles, Calif.
              Narration.
              With Orchestra under direction of Carmen Dragon.
5656          "Tweedle De Dee and Tweedle De        Royale 18145
              Dum" (Part 1)
5657          "Tweedle De Dee and Tweedle De        Royale 18145
              Dum" (Part 2)
5658          "Tweedle De Dee and Tweedle De        Royale 18145
              Dum" (Part 3)
5659          "Tweedle De Dee and Tweedle De        Royale 18145
              Dum" (Part 4)


              September 29, 1949. Chicago, Ill.
              With Orchestra.
VB-1935       "I Never See Maggie Alone"            Victor 54-0005
              (Everett Lynton–Harry Tilsley)
VB-1946       "Oh! Gee, Oh! Gosh, Oh! Golly,        Victor 30-0010
              I'm in Love"
              (Ernest Breuer–Ole Olsen–
              Chic Johnson)
VB-1947       "The Old Piano Roll Blues"            Victor 30-0010
              (Cy Coben)


              January 30, 1950. New York, N.Y.
              With Orchestra under direction of Henri Rene.
              With Three Beaus and A Peep.
VB-3171       "Enjoy Yourself"                      Victor 20-3705
              (Carl Sigman–Herb Magidson)

| | | |
|---|---|---|
| VB-3172 | "I Love Her Oh! Oh! Oh!" (James V. Monaco–Ed P. Moran–Joseph McCarthy) | Victor 20-3705 |
| VB-3173 | "Now I Always Have Maggie Alone" (Everett Lynton–Harry Tilsley) | Unissued |

March 23, 1950. New York, N.Y.
With Lisa Kirk.
With Sammy Kaye and His Orchestra.

| | | |
|---|---|---|
| VB-3922 | "The Old Piano Roll Blues" (Cy Coben) | Victor 20-3751 |

April 2, 1954. Los Angeles, Calif.
With Studio Orchestra.

| | | |
|---|---|---|
| 12416 | "Maxie the Taxi"—Part 1 (Warren Foster–Tedd Pierce) | Capitol 32159 |
| 12417 | "Maxie the Taxi—Part 2 (Warren Foster–Tedd Pierce) | Capitol 32159 |

June 24, 1957. Hollywood, Calif.
With Orchestra under direction of Henri Rene.

| | | |
|---|---|---|
| H4PB-3096 | "Waiting for the Robert E. Lee" (Lewis F. Muir–L. Wolfe Gilbert) | Victor LX 1119 |
| H4PB-3097 | "Ballin' the Jack" (Chris Smith–Jim Burris) | Victor LX 1119 |
| H4PB-3098 | "If You Knew Susie" (Joseph Meyer–B.G. DeSylva) | Victor LX 1119 |
| H4PB-3099 | "Josephine, Please No Lean on the Bell" (Duke Leonard–Ed G. Nelson–Harry Pease) | Victor LX 1119 |

June 25, 1957. Hollywood, Calif.
With Orchestra under direction of Henri Rene.

| | | |
|---|---|---|
| H4PB-3100 | "Ain't She Sweet?" (Milton Ager–Jack Yellen) | Victor LX 1119 |
| H4PB-3101 | "Makin' Whoopee" (Walter Donaldson–Gus Kahn) | Victor LX 1119 |
| H4PB-3102 | "Margie" (Con Conrad–Benny Davis–J. Russell Robinson) | Victor LX 1119 |
| H4PB-3103 | "How Ya Gonna Keep 'Em Down on the Farm?" (Walter Donaldson–Sam M. Lewis–Joe Young) | Victor LX 1119 |

June 26, 1957. Hollywood, Calif.
With Orchestra under direction of Henri Rene.
With Bill Thompson Singers.

| | | |
|---|---|---|
| H4PB-3104 | "Baby Face" | Victor LX 1119 |
| | (Harry Akst–Benny Davis) | |
| H4PB-3105 | "Ma (He's Making Eyes at Me)" | Victor LX 1119 |
| | (Con Conrad–Sidney Clare) | |
| H4PB-3106 | "Yes Sir, That's My Baby" | Victor LX 1119 |
| | (Walter Donaldson–Gus Kahn) | |
| H4PB-3107 | "Ida, Sweet as Apple Cider" | Victor LX 1119 |
| | (Eddie Munson–Eddie Leonard) | |

1960. Hollywood, Calif.

| | |
|---|---|
| "Carnegie Hall Concert" (Re-creation) | AFLP 702 |

# INDEX

Abbott, George, 171, 226
Abbott and Costello, 184, 230, 233, 237, 272, 285
*Abbott and Costello Show, The*, 175
Abel, Allison, 310
Abel, Bert, 310
Abramowitz (Lazarowitz), Mindel, 3
Academy of Motion Picture Arts and Sciences, 294
Academy of Music (Baltimore), 72
Academy of Music (Philadelphia), 271
Actors' Equity Association (AEA), 71, 75–77, 121, 135, 193, 209, 235, 241
Actors' Fund Benefit, 121
Adams, Phelps, 198
Adamson, Harold, 224, 225, 245, 254
Adelphi Theatre (New York), 250
Aeolian-Vocalian Co., 64
"Ain't She Sweet?," 117, 269
Akst, Harry, 109
Albany Catholic Diocese, 242
Albee, Edward, 99, 116, 141
Albee Theatre (Brooklyn), 116
Albertson, Frank, 269
*Aldrich Family*, 233
"Alexander's Ragtime Band," 195
*Alexander's Ragtime Band*, 200
Alger, Horatio, 129
Algonquin Hotel (New York), 104
Alhambra Theatre (London, Eng.), 42
Alhambra Theatre (New York), 38
*Ali Baba Goes to Town*, 192, 194–195, 201, 238
*All in the Family*, 253

*All My Life. See* Eddie Cantor Story, The
Allen, Fred, 175, 186, 217, 218, 231, 233, 243, 251, 269, 272, 288
Allen, Gracie, 141, 147, 308
Allen, Maud, 32
Allen, Woody, 57
Allenberg, Bert, 291
Alliance Camp (Cold Spring, N.Y.), 11–15, 66, 79, 101, 104, 112, 114, 119, 120, 132, 160, 163, 241, 282, 295, 301
Alton-Bines, 154
Ambassador Hotel (Chicago), 252
Ambassador Hotel (Los Angeles), 194, 301
*American*, 260, 267
American Academy of Dramatic Arts (New York), 206, 244
American Arbitration Association, 131
American Association of Advertising Agencies, 154
American Broadcasting Co. (ABC), 302
American Embassy (Italy), 167
American Federation of Actors (AFA), 209–210, 213–14
American Federation of Labor (AFL), 76, 193, 213–14
American Federation of Radio Artists (AFRA), 171, 193, 197, 214
American Federation of Television and Radio Artists (AFTRA), 300, 304
American Financial and Development Corp, 276
American Guild of Variety Artists (AGVA), 213–14, 241, 274
American Heart Association, 279

American Jewish Congress, 177
American Legion, 273
*American* Magazine, 102
American Red Cross, 279
American Society of Composers, Authors, and
    Publishers (ASCAP), 103, 220, 241
American Telephone and Telegraph (A.T.& T.),
    142
American Television Arts and Sciences, 296
American Theatre (St. Louis), 78
*America's Famous Fathers*, 219
Ames Art Galleries (Beverly Hills), 309
*Amos 'n' Andy*, 306
Amphion Theatre (New York), 28
Anderson, Eddie (Rochester), 217
Anderson, Judith, 215
Anderson, Maxwell, 103
Andrews, Lois, 216
*Androcles and the Lion*, 155
*Animal Crackers*, 128
*Anything Goes*, 171
Apollo Theatre (Chicago), 86, 91, 108
Apollo Theatre, Nixon's (Atlantic City), 61
Applebaum's Bicycle Shop (New York), 14
*Aquitania*, 42
Arab League, 302
*Arabian Nights*, 61
Arbuckle, Roscoe, 113
Arden, Edwin, 71
Arditi, Luigi, 183
Ardmore, Jane Kesner, 29
*Argosy-All Story* Magazine, 122
Aristocrats, Twelve, 166
Armed Forces Radio Services, 244
Arms, Frances, 164
Arnheim, Gus, 175
Arnold, Benedict, 9
Arnold, Edward, 156, 289
Arnst, Bobbe, 123
Arnstein, Jules W. (Nick), 66
*Around the World in Eighty Days*, 248
Arthur, Mary, 157, 190
Arthur, Roy (Bunky), 30–33, 42, 54, 157, 190,
    220
Artisans Extension Committee, 196
*As I Remember Them*, 304
*Ask Eddie Cantor*, 300–302
Associated Actors and Artistes of America
    (AAAA), 193, 209, 210, 213, 214
Associated Press, 113, 197, 294
Associated Radio Artists, 171
Astaire, Fred and Adele, 103
Astor, Hotel, 120, 135, 177, 200, 227, 236,
    241, 277
Astoria (Queens Co., N.Y.) Studio, 123, 130,
    136
Astors, 52
"At Sixty-Five," 293
"At the City Hall Steps," 116, 118

"At the Osteopath's," 72, 73, 81
Atkins, Ira, 9
Atkinson, Brooks, 117, 125
Atteridge, Harold, 86, 88, 117
Auclair, Michelle, 273
Audience Research Bureau, 269
Auditorium (Baltimore), 88
Auditorium (Minneapolis), 268
"Ave Maria," 276
"Aviator's Test, The," 68, 73
Avon Hotel (New Haven), 84
*Awful Truth, The*, 105

*Babes in Toyland*, 272
Babson, Roger, 132
"Baby, It's Cold Outside," 285
"Back to Bataan" Show, 246
*"Bacio, Il,"* 183, 186
Bacon, Frank, 75
Bacon, Lloyd, 75
Baird, Sharon, 276, 277
Baker, Jed, 310
Baker, Josephine, 265
Baker, Lynne, 310
Baker, Mike, 300, 310
Baker, Phil, 227, 233, 260
Balaban, Barney, 254–255
Balaban & Katz, 147, 214
"Ballet Master's Idea, A," 116
*Ballyhoo*, 148
"Ballin' The Jack," 40, 272
Baltimore *News-Post*, 270
Banana Man, The, 311
*Banjo Eyes*, 222–28, 230, 244
Bank of America, 204
Barkley, Alben W., 277
Baron's Orchestra, 267
Barris, Harry, 126
Barry, Charles, 285
Barrymore, John, 154
Basie, Count, 247
Bastia, Pascal, 168, 169
Battle Creek Sanitarium, 123
Bayes, Nora, 44, 58, 236
Beatles, The, 142, 308
Bedini, Jean, 31–35, 42, 53, 54
Bedini & Arthur, 30–35, 37, 57, 58, 115
Beilenson, Laurence, 213
Bell Telephone Co., 227
Belleport, Billie, 232
Bellevue-Stratford Hotel (Philadelphia), 254
Belmont Plaza (New York), 249
Beloin, Eddie, 240
Belt, Dr. Elmer, 245
"Belt in the Back." *See* "Joe's Blue Front"
Ben-Ami, Jacob, 89
"Benches in the Park," 30
"Bend Down, Sister," 140
Bennett Sisters, 221

Benny, Jack, 131, 146, 158, 175, 176, 186, 194, 195, 197, 217, 233, 234, 240, 254, 259, 261, 285, 288, 295, 301, 304
Ben-Gurion, David, 277, 301
Bergen, Edgar, 195, 233
Bergman, Teddy, 163
Berkeley, Busby, 136–137, 149, 156, 216
Berle, Milton, 251, 258, 274, 290
Berlin, Irving, 23, 28, 33, 72, 73, 74, 109, 115, 117, 165, 200, 275
Berman, Abe, 182, 250
Bernie, Ben, 205
Bernstein, Henry, 243
Bernstein, Louis, 170
Besser, Joe, 232–233, 243
Beth Yeshurun, Congregation (Houston), 266
Bethlehem-Fairfield Shipyards (Baltimore), 235
*Between the Acts*, 141
Beverly Hills Emergency First Aid Station, 296
Beverly Hills High School, 156, 245
Beverly Hills Hotel, 136
Beverly Hilton Hotel, 301, 304
*Bewitched*, 286
Bierman, Dr. William, 121
*Big Boy*, 106, 108, 109
*Billboard, The*, 41, 71, 257
*Billy the Kid*, 16
Biltmore Bowl (Los Angeles), 257, 279
"Birth of the Blues," 220
Bixler, Bobby, 154
Blackstone, Milton, 260–261
Blackwell, Elizabeth, 254
Blair, Janet, 233
Blanche, Wm. (Shorty), 64, 66
Block, Paul, 98
Block & Sully, 141, 146, 158, 164
Bloomer, Leonard, 12
Bloomer, Mrs., 12
Blyler, Jimmy, 86–87
B'nai B'rith, 217, 256, 267, 276
Boardman, Nan, 293
Bodec, Ben, 170, 213, 219, 223, 237
Bolger, Ray, 34
Bolton, Guy, 140
Bolton, Helen, 83
Bolton, Patsy, 251
*Bombo*, 91
Booth, Edwin, 85
Bordoni, Irene, 143
Boston Garden, 247
Boston *Herald*, 105, 224
Boswell, Connee, 195
Bow, Clara, 111
Bowery Amphitheatre (New York), 29
Bowes, Vivienne, 258, 260, 261
Boyar, Louis H., 301
Boyce, Betty, 223
Boyer, Charles, 254
Boyle Anderson, Edna, 210

Boy's Town, 217
Brady, Diamond Jim, 21, 52, 53, 104
Brandeis University, 292
Brandley, Winnie, 119, 136, 166, 172, 180, 181, 199, 202, 203, 310
Brasselle, Keefe, 284, 286, 287
Breakers, The, 90
Breen, Bobby, 176–177, 182, 183, 184, 203, 259, 276
Breen, Mickey, 203
Breen, Sally, 176
Brice, Fanny, 39, 41, 59–63, 66, 69, 70, 98, 120, 131, 150, 186, 191, 202, 233, 238, 265, 282, 291, 304
Brice, Frances, 191
Brice, Lew, 41
Brice, William, 191
Bristol-Myers, 217, 219, 222, 223, 229, 233, 240–41, 248, 251
British Broadcasting Co. (BBC), 168–169, 199
"Broadway Baby," 137
*Broadway Brevities*, 81–83
*Broadway Open House*, 274
Broadway Theatre (New York), 247
Bronson, Lillian, 292
Brooklyn *Eagle*, 90
Brooklyn Jewish Hospital, 119, 298–99
Brooks, Matt, 156
Brooks, Peggy, 54
"Brother, Can You Spare a Dime?," 144
Brown, David, 204
Brown, Joe E., 278
Brown, John Mason, 225
Brown, Louise, 109
Brown, Gov. Pat, 305
Brown Derby (Hollywood), 241
Buck, Gene, 51–52, 59, 67, 227
*Buck Privates*, 184
Buloff, Joseph, 269
Burke, Billie, 53, 70, 149, 258
*Burlesque*, 123
Burns, George, 141, 147
Burns and Allen, 139, 141, 146, 147, 158, 162, 166, 175, 252, 259
*Burns and Allen Show*, 220
Burrows, Abe, 257
Bushkin, Joe, 272
Bushwick Theatre (Brooklyn, N.Y.), 44
"But After the Ball Is Over," 69
Butler, Frank, 171, 173, 192
Butler, Sheppard, 91
Buzzell, Eddie, 34, 36
"By the Light of the Silvery Moon," 34
"Bye, Bye, Blackbird," 284
Byrd, Robert, 98, 143
Byrne, Charles, 245

*Cabin in the Sky*, 223
Caesar, Irving, 170

Cafe Tel Aviv, 207
Cafe Royale (New York), 246
*Cafe Trocadero*, 188
Cagney, James, 213
Cahn, Irving, 128
California Auditorium (San Francisco), 206
"Call of the '60s, The," 55
Callahan, Marie, 95, 96, 111
Callan, Camp (Calif.), 231
*Camel Caravan*, 196, 198–99, 206, 210, 213, 219
*Camel Caravan Revue*, 206–7
Canadian Broadcasting Corporation, 242, 250
*Canary Cottage*, 47–51, 55, 58
"Candy Store Blues," 257
Cantor, Charlie, 273, 274, 304
Cantor, Edna June, 73, 77, 79, 82, 86, 101, 110, 111–12, 114, 136, 148, 156–58, 166–69, 173, 180, 185, 196, 201, 206, 215, 221, 226, 235, 236, 243, 245, 249, 262, 263, 268, 272, 280, 283, 286, 291, 296, 301–3, 305, 307, 308, 310
Cantor, Esther. *See* Lazarowitz (Kantrowitz), Esther
Cantor, Ida. *See* Tobias (Cantor), Ida
Cantor, Janet Hope, 119–20, 136, 139, 148, 156–58, 165, 166, 170, 173, 177, 180, 181, 185, 190, 197, 199, 200, 202–3, 206, 219, 225, 226, 229, 234, 244, 245, 249, 252, 262–63, 272, 274, 275, 277, 283, 285, 286, 289, 290, 291, 294, 295–300, 302–3, 305, 306, 308, 310
Cantor, Marilyn, 86, 110–12, 114, 119, 136, 148, 156–58, 164–66, 173, 180, 206, 226, 243, 244, 252, 263, 272, 275, 283, 285, 286, 291, 293, 294, 300, 302–3, 308, 310
Cantor, Marjorie, 46–47, 51, 63, 64, 77, 79, 82, 86, 101–2, 110, 111–14, 119–20, 132, 134, 136, 148, 156–58, 164, 166–69, 173, 176, 180, 185, 190–91, 202, 203, 206, 212, 220, 226, 234–36, 243, 245, 247, 262, 263, 272, 276, 279, 280–81, 283, 284, 286, 287, 290–93, 295–300, 302, 303
Cantor, Meta. *See* Kantrowitz (Iskowitz), Meta
Cantor, Natalie, 48, 51, 63, 77, 79, 82, 86, 101–2, 110, 111–12, 114, 136, 148, 156–58, 166–69, 180, 192, 197–200, 206, 214, 226, 245, 249–50, 262, 263, 268, 272, 279, 283, 286, 289, 291, 292, 299, 302–3, 307–310
*El Capitan* Theatre (Hollywood), 278
Capitol Theatre (New York), 216
Carey Walsh's (Coney Island, N.Y.), 22–24
Carless, Dorothy, 288
Carlos & Inez, 89
Carmine, J.H., 242
Carnegie Hall (New York), 264–65, 310
"Carolina," 43
Carpenter, Thelma, 247–51
Carr, Frank B., 21–22, 27, 207

Carr, Lily. *See* Carrera, Liane
Carrera, Liane, 49–50
Carroll, Adam, 207
Carroll, Earl, 47–49, 130–31, 136, 191
*Carr's Thunderbolts*, 21
Carson, Jack, 232
Carter, Frank, 68, 69–70, 76, 78
Carter, Victor M., 301
Casey, Steve (Crusher), 239
Casino Theatre (New York), 114
Caruso, Enrico, 47
Case, Theodore, 98
Castle, Nick, 238
Catholic Actors' Guild, 120, 241
Catholic Layman's League, 208
Catlett, Walter, 61, 63
*Caught Short*, 134
Cavanaugh's (New York), 197
Cedars of Lebanon Hospital (Los Angeles), 149, 215, 244–45, 258, 275, 280, 281, 290–93, 296, 297, 300
Central Amphitheatre (Milwaukee), 252
Central Park Mall (New York), 207
Century Theatre (New York), 67, 81, 83, 84, 88
Chain & Archer, 115
Chaliapin, Feodor, 169
Chandler, George, 304
Chanel No. 5, 99–100
Chaney, Lon, Jr., 190
Chaplin, Charlie, 39, 111, 150, 183, 190
"Charley, My Boy," 265, 269
Charlot, Andre, 42
Chase and Sanborn, 170
*Chase and Sanborn Hour*, 140–48, 151–56, 160–64, 166, 169, 177, 187, 312
Chase and Sanborn Orchestra, 143, 160
Chelsea Yacht Club (Atlantic City), 34, 41, 46
Chestnut Street Opera House (Philadelphia), 91
Chevalier, Albert, 265
Chevalier, Maurice, 142–43
Chicago Stadium (Chicago), 187, 266
Chicago Theatre (Chicago), 147, 214
Chicago Theatre Orchestra, 148
Chicago *Tribune*, 91, 270
*Children's Hour*, Horn and Hardart, 261
Child's (Cleveland), 136
Chinese Theatre, Grauman's (Hollywood), 148, 194
Chonklin, Chester, 123
Christie, Audrey, 223
*Christopher Columbus, Jr.*, 221
Chrysler, Walter, 135
Churchill, Sarah, 168
Churchill, Winston, 168–169
Ciano, Count, 167
*Citizen Kane*, 195
"City Hall." *See* "At The City Hall Steps"
City National Bank (Beverly Hills), 309

Civic Auditorium (Cleveland), 196
Claire, Bernice, 142–143
Claridge, Hotel (New York), 79
Clark, Adele, 247
Clark, Bobby, 269
Clark, Norman, 269
Clark, Thomas W., 13–14
Clarke, Mae, 292
Clary, Robert, 276, 310
Claudius, Dane, 55
Claudius & Scarlet, 55
"Climax," 291
Cline, Ruth, 309
Cline, Dr. Thomas J., 309
Clinton Music Hall (New York), 18
Clyde, June, 223
Cobb, Irvin S., 194
Coca, Imogene, 247
"Cocoanut Ball, The," 97–98
*Cocoanuts, The* (film), 95, 137
Cohan, George M., 76, 85, 104, 235
Cohan, Georgette, 235
Cohen, L. L., 187
Cohn, Harry, 284
Colby, Marilyn, 273
*Colgate Comedy Hour*, 89, 266, 268–80, 283–
    85, 287, 288, 304, 310
Colgate-Palmolive, 241, 260, 269, 272, 278,
    279, 283, 285, 287
Coliseum (Chicago), 261
Collier, William, 129
Collins, Margaret, 306, 307
Collins, Johnny, 123
Colonial Theatre (Boston), 63, 70, 105, 120,
    224
Colonial Theatre (Chicago), 77
Colonial Theatre (New York), 54–55
Columbia Amusement Co., 22
Columbia Broadcasting System (CBS), 170,
    180, 186, 196, 200, 206, 208, 243, 251,
    259, 269, 292
Columbia Graphophone Co., 90
Columbia Pictures, 164, 226, 232, 237, 283,
    284
Columbia Theatre (St. Louis), 45–46
Columbia University, 123
*Come On Along*, 248, 250
"Commercially Ever After," 289–290
Commodore, Hotel (New York), 104, 129, 261,
    267, 276
Concourse Plaza (New York), 101
Conn, Billy, 248
Connecticut Yankees, 140
Conrad, Con, 82
Convention Hall (Philadelphia), 196, 246
Coogan, Jackie, 175, 176
Cooper, Betty Jane, 186
Cooper, Lew, 51
Cooperative Analysis of Broadcasting (CAB),
    197

Copacabana (New York), 261
Corbett, James J., 129
Corday, Dr. Eliot, 281, 293
Cort Theatre (San Francisco), 50
Cosmopolitan Pictures, 98
Cotton Club (New York), 165, 206
Coughlin, Charles E., 207–12, 264, 278, 302
Counselman, William, 136
Couthoui, Mrs., 88
Craig, Miss, 13
Crandall, Edward, 220
Crandall, Jack, 219–20, 309
Cravath, Gordon, 175
Crawford, Joan, 288
Crillon, Hotel, 168
Crosby, Bing, 126, 195, 259, 261
Crossley Reports, 170, 197, 217, 241, 254
Crouse, Russel (Buck), 171
*Curtain Going Up*, 244
Curtis, Charles, 145

Dabney, Ford, 51–52
"Daddy," 223
Dagmar, 274
Damon Runyon Cancer Fund, 273
"Dance of the Seven Veils, The," 32
D'Andrea, Tom, 285
Daniels, Billy, 285
Daniels, Danny, 269
Darnell, Linda, 244
Davies, Marion, 98
Davis, Benny, 82
Davis, Bette, 215, 232, 262
Davis, Eddie, 162
Davis, Joan, 233, 237–39, 244, 246, 251–55,
    289
Davis, LeRoy, 237
Davis, Margie, 82
Davis, Maude, 219
Davis, Nina, 237
Davis, Owen, 122, 125
Davis, Robert W., 122
Davis, Sammy, 277
Davis, Sammy, Jr., 277–78, 280
Davis & Bryan Theatrical League, 101
Day, Clarence, 4
Day, Dennis, 217, 234, 254, 257, 287
Daye, Ruth, 214–215
Dazie, Mlle., 32
de Croux, Etienne, 111
Debonairs, The, 250
Decca Records, 195, 247, 261
" 'Deed I Do," 273
DeForrest, Dr. Lee, 98
DeForrest, Muriel, 83
DeLeon, Walter, 174
Delmonico's (New York), 151
Delroy, Irene, 116, 227
DeMarcos, The, 224
Demarest, William, 130

DeMilt, Joseph, 113
"Dentist's Office, The," 81
*Desire Under The Elms*, 103
Detroit Theatre, New (Detroit), 96
Detroit *Times*, 270
Diamond, Dr. Joseph S., 227
Diamond Tony's (Coney Island, N.Y.), 22, 23
Dickens, Charles, 64
Dillingham, Charles B., 53, 65, 67, 91
"Dinah," 109–10, 146, 265, 270, 276, 284
*Diners Club Magazine*, 300, 302, 304
Dinsdale, Shirley, 232
Dinty Moore's, 127
Dionne Quintuplets, 185
"Dixie Volunteers, The," 63
Dockstader's Minstrels, Lew, 29
Doctors Hospital (New York), 274
"Dog Shop, The," 116
"Doin' the Eddie Cantor," 88
Dolce Sisters, 38
Dolly Sisters, 38
Donahue, Joe, 204
Donaldson, Walter, 124, 137
Dooley, Johnny, 72, 73, 75, 76
Dooley, Rae, 73, 75, 76
Dorfman, Nat, 152
Doubleday & Co., Inc., 292
Dowling, Eddie, 75
Doyle, Buddy, 132
Dozier, Bill, 250
*Dreamland. See* Strike Me Pink
"Dreams of Long Ago," 47
*Dresser, The*, 86
Dudley, Gertrude & Co., 28
Duell, Sloan & Pearce, 304
Duke, Vernon, 223, 224
Dulles, John Foster, 292
Dumas, Alexandre, 64
"Dumber They Come, The Better I Like 'Em, The," 102
Duncan Sisters, 34, 120
Dunn, Caesar, 102
Dunn, Henry, 274
Dunne, Irene, 105, 194
DuPont, 246
DuPonts, 52
Durante, Jimmy, 23–24, 155, 158, 174, 251, 260, 261, 273–75, 283, 286–88, 307
Durbin, Deanna, 183–84, 186, 193–97, 203, 214–15, 221

Earl Carroll Theatre (New York), 97–98, 100, 101
Earle Theatre (Philadelphia), 162, 166, 177
Early, Stephen, 230
Eastman Kodak Co., 230
Eaton, Doris, 69
Eaton, Mary, 95, 97, 100, 109, 121, 130
Ed Sullivan Theatre (New York), 204
Eddie Cantor Appreciation Society, 311

*Eddie Cantor Comedy Theatre, The*, 287–91
Eddie Cantor Fan Club, 189
*Eddie Cantor Five-Year Plan*, 141
Eddie Cantor Night (1925), 106
Eddie Cantor Theatrical Enterprises, 90
Eddie Cantor Fellowship, 163
Eddie Cantor Gift Shop, 192
Eddie Cantor Golden Jubilee Salute, 301
*Eddie Cantor Show, The* (Ziv), 287–88
*Eddie Cantor Story, The*, 283–88, 291
*Eddie Cantor's Song and Joke Book*, 141
"Eddie Cantor's 25th Anniversary Week," 194
Eddie Fisher Show, The, 296
"Eddie (Steady)," 107
Edison, Hotel (New York), 146, 209
Educational Alliance, 11, 161, 282
Educational Alliance Community House, 11, 15
Educational Alliance Camp. *See* Alliance Camp
Edwards, Gus, 30, 34–35, 37–39, 41, 109, 117, 184, 216, 270, 286
Edwards, Ralph, 286
Edwards, Roy, 288
Eichner, Andrew, 310
Eichner, Joe, 310
Eichner, Sam, 310
"Eight Blue Devils, The," 89
Eighty-sixth Street Theatre (New York), 146
Eilers, Sally, 175
Einstein, Harry, 164, 170, 173, 174, 177, 182, 186, 188
Eisenhower, Dwight D., 283, 292
Elizabeth, Queen (Consort), 207
Elder, Ruth, 118
Electrical Exposition (Chicago), 261
Elks (B.P.O.E.), 21
Eliot, George, 64
Ellison, Izzy, 201, 204, 217
Elman, Mischa, 169
Elwood, John W., 239–40
Emerson, 74, 78, 80, 85, 87, 90
Empire State Building (New York), 221
Empress Theatre (San Diego), 49
*Engaged To Be Married*, 102
Engelbert, Dr. Monroe, 205
Episcopal Actors' Guild, 241
Erlanger, Abraham L., 62, 68, 76, 116, 121
Erlanger Theatre (Philadelphia), 120
Errol, Leon, 86, 87, 96, 129
Erskine, Marilyn, 284
Essex House (New York), 226, 227, 292
Esty, William, 197
Esty Agency, William, 204, 205, 210, 211
Ethical Culture School (New York), 180
Etting, Ruth, 117–18, 124, 125, 143, 156
European Cooperation Administration, 260
*Evangelist, The*, 242–43
Evans, Maurice, 223
"Ever Since the Movies Learned to Talk," 126
*Eveready Hour*, 112–13

*Face in the Crowd, A,* 174
Fahey, Father Martin, 120
Fairbanks, Douglas, 222
Fairchild, Edgar (Cookie), 204, 207, 239, 243, 260
Fairlie, Joseph, 171
*Family Living,* 296–97
Famous-Barr Co. (St. Louis), 78
Fania, 18–19, 62, 118, 289
*Father Knows Best,* 245
Fay, Frank, 58
Fayne, Charlotte, 269
Federal Theatre Project, 209
Feldman, Gladys, 227
Felix, Seymour, 124
Fender, Harry, 95, 100
Ferber, Edna, 103
Ferrets, The, 210
*Fibber McGee and Molly,* 233, 246
Field, Norman, 193
Fields, Benny, 146
Fields, Herbert, 148
Fields, Sidney, 175, 204, 207, 221, 262
Fields, W.C., 52, 59–64, 66, 68–69, 77, 86, 99, 173, 265, 282, 289, 304
Fifth Avenue Theatre (New York), 35
*Fifth Season, The,* 292, 293
Fisher, Eddie, 229, 261–64, 273, 274, 280, 285, 286, 301, 306
Fisher, Irving, 61
Fitzgerald, F. Scott, 104
Fitzgerald, Lillian, 89
Fitzgerald, Zelda, 104
*Five O'Clock Girl, The,* 95, 121
Flanagan, Father, 218
Flash, Serge, 146
*Fleischmann Hour, The,* 140, 144, 147
*Flintstones, The,* 163, 232
Flippen, Jay C., 106
Floridian, The (Miami), 140
*Flying Yorkshireman, The,* 204
*Flywheel, Shyster, and Flywheel,* 155
Fogg, Phileas, 248
*Follies,* 125, 137, 238
*Follies* (Ziegfeld) (generic), 80, 86, 87, 95, 97, 103, 116, 130, 269, 270, 283
*Follies* of 1907, 59
*Follies* of 1910, 59, 60
*Follies* of 1911, 60
*Follies* of 1915, 50, 59, 124
*Follies* of 1916, 50, 60
*Follies* of 1917, 59–64, 66, 69, 73
*Follies* of 1918, 66–72, 73, 95
*Follies* of 1919, 72–79, 89, 95, 165
*Follies* of 1920, 77, 79, 81, 85
*Follies* of 1922, 91–93
*Follies* of 1924, 106
*Follies* of 1925, 108
*Follies* of 1926, 116
*Follies* of 1927, 116–21

Fontainbleau Hotel (Miami Beach), 293, 301
Ford, Harrison, 123
Ford, Henry, 81, 160, 200
Fordham Theatre (Bronx, N.Y.), 146
Forrest Theatre (Philadelphia), 64, 71, 224, 250
Fort Whiting Auditorium (Mobile), 270
*Forty Little Mothers,* 215–17, 291
Foster, Florence, 223
Foster, Harry, 260
Foster, Jack, 145
Foster, Phil, 274
*Four-Star Theatre,* 274
Fox, Harry, 38
Fox, Madge, 99
Fox, William, 129
Fox Theatre (San Francisco), 149, 173, 254
Fox's Theatre (Philadelphia), 122
Foy, Eddie, Sr., 65
Francis, Ruthie, 37, 38
Franklin, Joe, 229, 301
Franklin, Sidney, 149, 150
Frauchiger, Eddie (Frenchy), 128, 157, 166, 180, 190, 214
Frazee Sisters, 177
Freedley, Vinton, 171, 174
Freedman, Beatrice. *See* Goodman (Freedman), Beatrice
Freedman, David, 122–23, 130–31, 141–42, 152, 153, 157, 169, 172–73, 186–87, 291
Freedman, Yankel, 123
Freeland, Thornton, 136–37, 223
Freeman, Mona, 293
Friars' *Frolic,* 85
Friedman, Charles, 268, 272
Friganza, Trixie, 49–50, 58, 59
Friml, Rudolf, 103
Frisco, Joe, 52, 139
Froman, Jane, 172
Fuller, Miss, 13
"Fun in Hi Skul," 34

Gain, William, 27–28
"Gang's All Here, The," 107
Garbo, Greta, 112, 148, 154
Garden Pier (Atlantic City), 90
Gari, Amanda, 290, 295, 302, 308, 310
Gari, Brian, 277–78, 295, 308, 310–11
Gari, Roberto, 5, 262, 272, 273, 291, 295, 302, 310
Garland, Judy, 279
Garon, Tubby, 115
Garrett, Grant, 156
Garrick, David, 85
Garrick Theatre (Chicago), 88
Garrity, Mr., 88
Gaylord, Janet, 269
Geiger, Dr. J. C., 239
Gellis, Isaac. *See* Isaac Gellis Meats
*Gentlemen Prefer Blondes,* 269

George VI, King, 207
"George Has a Birthday," 292
*George M. Cohan*, 235
George Washington Hotel (Jacksonville, Fla.), 273
Gerry Society, 39
Gershwin, George, 36, 96, 103
Gershwin, Ira, 190
Gerson, Mr., 88
"Getting a Ticket," 92
Giannini, Dr. A. H., 194
Gilbert, Gloria, 221
Gilbert, L. Wolfe, 156, 240
Gilbert and Sullivan, 247
Gillette, Don Carle, 306–7
*Girl Crazy*, 146
*Girl Friend, The*, 114–15
"Give a Gift to a Yank Who Gave," 244, 248
*Give My Regards to Broadway*, 235
*Glamour Boy*, 220–221
Gleason, Jackie, 293, 295, 308
Glenns, The, 261
Globe Theatre (Atlantic City), 85, 93
Globe Theatre (New York), 71, 116
Glogau, Jack, 72
*Glorifying the American Girl*, 130
Gobel, George, 287
Gobs, Three, 177
Goetz, Coleman, 71
Goetz, William, 182
*Gold Diggers, The*, 105
Golden, Harry, 311
Golden Gate Exposition (San Francisco), 206
Golden Gate Theatre (San Francisco), 182, 262
Goldstein, Jonah, 9
Goldwyn, Samuel, 126, 130, 136–40, 143, 148–51, 153–56, 164–66, 169, 171–75, 180–83, 192, 194, 215, 236, 311
Goldwyn Girls, The, 140, 144–45, 153, 155, 156, 164, 194
*Gone With the Wind*, 216
Good Samaritan Dispensary (New York), 10
Good Samaritan Hospital (Los Angeles), 173
Goodman, Al, 47–49
Goodman, Benny, 216, 242
Goodman (Freedman), Beatrice, 142, 169, 172, 187
Gordon, Bert, 196, 204, 223, 229, 232, 233, 236, 243, 252, 254, 261
Gordon, Cliff, 21
Gordon, Max, 122, 139, 220
Gordon, Ruth, 104
Gould, Evelyn, 273
Gould, Jack, 269
Grable, Betty, 137
Gracie Mansion (New York), 287
Grady, Billy, 122
Grahame, Gloria, 285
Granada Theatre (Chicago), 123

Grand Central Station (New York), 109, 110, 189
*Grand Hotel*, 154
Grand Hotel (Stockholm), 257
Grand Opera House (New York), 19
Grand Opera House (Philadelphia), 146
Grand Street Boys Association (New York), 216
Granger, Farley, 276, 293
Granlund, Nils T., 100
Grant, Cary, 151, 194, 254
Granville, Bernard, 215
Granville, Bonita, 215
Grauer, Ben, 242
Grauman, Sid, 148
Gray, Billy, 245
Gray, Lawrence, 111
Great Northern Theatre (Chicago), 88
Greater Boston Defend Israel Dinner, 292
Green, Abel, 154, 265
Green, Jane, 86–87
Green, Ray, 219
Greenwood, Charlotte, 47, 140, 145
Gregory, Paul, 125
Gresheimer, Fred, 70
Gress, Lou, 175
Grey, Joel, 273, 274
Grier, Jimmy, 175
Griffith, Raymond, 49–50
Groman Mortuary, 303
Gross, Ben, 154, 270
Grossinger's (Catskills, N.Y.), 207, 260–61, 273, 309
Grossman Shoes, Julius, 219
*Guess Who's Coming to Dinner*, 263
"Gus Edwards' Song Revue," 37, 40, 45
Gus Sun Circuit, 286
*Guys and Dolls*, 226, 254
Gwenn, Edmund, 295

Haan, Camp (Calif.), 231
Hadassah, 187, 198, 200, 207, 267
Haight, George, 173
Hale, Alan, 232
Hale, Georgie, 89, 220
Hale, Philip, 105
Haley, Jack, 195, 227, 237
Hall, Cliff, 166
Hall, Mordaunt, 112, 114, 138, 145
Hall of Religion, 207, 208
Halloran Hospital (Staten Island, N.Y.), 242
"Halloween Whoopee Ball," 125
Halperin, Nan, 89
Hamilton, Margaret, 220
*Hamlet*, 126
Hammerstein, Oscar I, 30
Hammerstein, Oscar II, 30, 96, 136
Hammerstein, William, 30, 54
Hammerstein's Theatre (New York). *See* Victoria Theatre (New York)

Hanson, Leonard, 199, 203
"Happiness Is a Thing Called Joe," 248
"Happy Hooligan," 12
Harbach, Otto, 93, 97
Harding, Warren G., 75
Harper, Toni, 257
Harper and Brothers, 123
"Harrigan," 235, 306
Harrimans, 52, 57, 62
Harris, Elmer, 49
Harris, Marion, 139, 143
Harris, Radie, 167
Harris, Ronnie, 288
Harrison & Fisher, 213
Hart, Lorenz, 114, 223
Hart, Max, 39, 41–44, 51, 55, 59, 60, 68, 80, 81, 84, 85, 87, 91, 99
Hartford *Union*, 84
Hartman Theatre (Columbus), 91
Harvard Union, 105–6
Harvest Moon Finals, 230
Hasty Pudding Club, 106
Haver, June, 254
Haver, Phyllis, 123
Haverly's Minstrels, 29
"Hawaii, America Loves You," 53
Hawk, Bob, 259–60
Hayes, Helen, 193
Haymer, Rusty, 177
Haynes, Lawrence, 54
Hayworth, Rita, 220
"He Seldom Misses," 73
Hearn, Lew, 83, 87, 90, 130, 269
Hearst, William Randolph, 10, 53
"Heart That's Free, A," 184
Hebrew Free Burial Society, 5
Hebrew University (Jerusalem), 163
Heifetz, Jascha, 193, 195, 264
Held, Anna, 25, 49, 51, 70, 80
Heller, George, 193
Hellinger, Mark, 191
*Hellzapoppin'*, 224, 232
Henry Hall (New York), 6, 17
Henson, Leslie, 168
Herbert, Annette, 227
Herman McCoy Swing Choir, 276
Hermitage Hotel (New York), 121
Hershfield, Harry, 110
Higler, James, 45–46
Hildegarde, 34
Hill, Darla, 310
Hill, Walt, 41
Hillside Theatre, Loews (Jamaica, N.Y.), 116
Hinston, Al, 37
Hitchcock, Raymond, 39
Hitler, Adolf, 167, 174, 178, 198, 207, 217, 222, 235, 240, 278
Hoffman, Aaron, 80
Hoffman, Gertrude, 32
*Hogan's Heroes*, 276

*Hold That Co-ed*, 237
*Hold Everything*, 128
*Hold On to Your Hats*, 220, 221
*Hold That Ghost*, 237
Holland, Jack, 154
Holliday, Judy, 262, 273
Hollywood Bowl, 299
Hollywood Canteen, 231
*Hollywood Canteen*, 242, 244
Hollywood *Citizen-News*, 295
*Hollywood Reporter, The*, 209, 306–307
Hollywood Theatre (New York), 227
Holman, Jack, 13, 98
Holmes, Madeline, 292
Holtz, Lou, 74, 131
Holtzmann, Benny, 132, 152, 172, 173, 176, 179, 182, 219
Hooper Ratings, 233, 246, 254
Hoover, Herbert C., 151
Hope, Bob, 154, 174, 230, 231, 233, 246, 254, 261, 269, 285, 297
Hopkins, Arthur, 132
Hopwood, Avery, 105
Hore-Belisha, Leslie, 168
Hornblow, Arthur, Jr., 155
Horne, Lena, 273
"Hot Footin'," 109
"How Can America Stay Out of War?," 177–80
"How Could You Believe Me When I Said I Loved You?," 273
"How Ya Gonna Keep 'em Down on the Farm?," 269
"How Ya Gonna Keep Your Mind on Dancing?," 91
Howard, Leslie, 189
Howard, Sidney, 103
Howard, Willie, 106, 130
Howland, Jobyna, 95, 105
Hudson *Dispatch*, 29
Huff, Dr., 253
Hughes, Elinor, 224
Hugo, Victor, 64
Hulburd, Bill, 169
Hullo, America, 267
Humphrey, Hal, 304
Hunt, Eleanor, 137
Hurok, Sol, 203
Hurst, Fannie, 241
Husing, Ted, 170
Huston, Walter, 110
Hyams Bros. State Cinema (Kilburn, Eng.), 199
Hyde Park (New York), 205
Hymer, John B., 216
"Hymn to the Sun," Inca, 269

I Am an American Day, 222
"I Can't Give You Anything But Love," 196
"I Can't Make My Eyes Behave," 25, 49

"I Don't Want to Get Well," 251
"I Feel a Song Coming On," 196
"I Gotta Keep Rollin'," 224, 225
"I Love a Minstrel Show," 72
"I Love Her—She Loves Me," 89
*I Love Lucy*, 268
"I Love to Spend Each Sunday With You," 193, 196
"I Never Knew I Could Love Anybody," 87
"I Want to Be a Minstrel Man," 165
"I Wish That I'd Been Born in Borneo," 82
"Ice Cold Katie," 232
Ida Cantor Fellowship, 163
"Ida, Sweet as Apple Cider," 139, 265, 276, 279, 284
"If I Was a Millionaire," 34
"If You Do What You Do," 102
"If You Knew Susie," 106, 254, 265, 276, 284
*If You Knew Susie*, 252–56
*Ile de France*, 169
"I'll Marry No Explorer," 49
Illinois Theatre (Chicago), 108
"I'm Bringing a Red, Red Rose," 125
"I'm Hungry for Beautiful Girls," 89
"I'm Making a Study of Beautiful Girls," 72
Impellitteri, Vincent, 277
Imperial Theatre (New York), 29
"In My Merry Oldsmobile," 34
"In One Era and Out the Other," 300
"In the Moonlight," 149, 153
*Indian Maidens*, 21–22, 72, 207
Inger, Richard Josef, 257–58
*Insurance*, 136
International Association/Theatre Stagehands and Employees (IATSE), 76, 210, 214
International Ladies Garment Workers Union, 267
Interstate Circuit, 40
*Irene*, 94
Irving, Sir Henry, 85
Isaac Gellis Meats, 13
Isaacs, Charles, 266
Iskowitz, Meta. *See* Kantrowitz (Iskowitz), Meta
Iskowitz, Mechel, 4–6, 9, 121, 148
Israel Bond Organization, 293
"It All Belongs to Me," 117
"It Could Only Happen in the Movies," 224
"It Goes Like This," 123
*It Happened in Mexico*, 246
"It Ruined Marc Antony," 49
"It Won't Be Long Now—A Taxi Ride," 116, 118
*I've Got a Secret*, 300
"I've Got My Captain Working for Me Now," 74

*Janice Meredith*, 98–99
Janis, Elsie, 44
Jaycox, Catherine, 12

Jaycox, William O., 12
Jefferson High School, Thomas (New York), 189
Jefferson High School (Portland, Ore.), 179
Jergens, Adele, 226
Jessel, George, 30, 34, 37–43, 98, 102, 110, 129, 141, 146–48, 153–54, 158, 194, 216, 241, 254, 257, 266, 276, 285, 286, 296, 301, 304–6, 308–9, 311
Jewish Council (Chicago), 187
*Jewish Daily Forward*, 123
Jewish Palestine Pavilion, 207
Jewish Theatrical Guild, 120, 129, 132, 152, 241
"Joe's Blue Front," 87, 88, 89, 130, 269
Johns, Brooke, 92
Johnson, Lyndon B., 304
Johnson, Van, 254
Jolson, Al, 38–40, 58, 68, 73, 85, 90, 91, 103, 104, 106, 108, 109, 123, 125, 142, 154, 158, 173, 188, 200, 220, 221, 223, 242, 254, 257, 259, 265, 270–72, 282, 284, 304, 311
*Jolson Story, The*, 283, 286, 287
Jonas, Nathan S., 67, 79, 97, 114, 129
"Josephine, Please No Lean on the Bell," 251, 284
Joyce, Peggy Hopkins, 125, 227
*Judge*, 43
*Julia*, 288
*Jumbo*, 181
"Jump Jim Crow," 29
"Juvenile Delinquency: Its Cause and Solution," 245

Kafafian, Eddie, 301, 310
Kafafian, Lee. *See* Newman, Lee
Kahn, Donald, 124
Kahn, Gus, 124, 137
Kahn, Dr. Julius, 280–81
Kahn, Otto H., 129
Kalmar, Bert, 148
Kane Furniture Co., 164
*Kansas City Star*, 247
Kantrowitz, Abraham, 3
Kantrowitz, Annie, 6, 67
Kantrowitz, Esther. *See* Lazarowitz (Cantor), Esther
Kantrowitz, Irwin, 6
Kantrowitz, Jack, 13
Kantrowitz (Iskowitz), Meta, 3–6, 46, 121
Kantrowitz, Murray, 13
Kantrowitz, Minnie, 6
Kapp, Jack, 247, 258
Kapp, Paul, 247
Kathryn Perry & Co., 73
Kaufman, George S., 103, 155
Kaye, Danny, 236, 248, 251, 304
Kean, Edmund, 85
Keating, Fred, 209

Keegan, Junie, 274
Keeler, Ruby, 124, 125
"Keep Young and Beautiful," 156
Keith, B. F., 36
Keith Vaudeville Exchange, 54–55, 81, 83, 92, 99, 117
Keith's Theatre (Atlantic City, N.J.), 42
Keith's Theatre (Boston, Mass.), 46, 186
Keith's Theatre (Indianapolis), 32
Keith's Theatre (Knoxville, Tenn.), 40
Keller, Henrietta, 39
Kelly, Arthur, 221
Kelly, Ed, 187
Kelly, Harry, 83
Kelly, Nancy, 237
Kelly, Patsy, 130
Kelly, Paul, 114
Kelly, Walter C., 30
Kelsie, Olive, 289, 291
Kennedy, Joseph P., 178, 199
Kennedy, Rose, 199
Kenny, Nick, 154
Kent State University, 311
Kermit-Raymond Corp., 219
Kesner Ardmore, Jane, 288–89, 291
Kessler, Sammy, 41–42
KHJ, Television Station (Los Angeles), 248
*Kid Boots*, 93–103, 105–11, 113, 126, 130, 152, 175
*Kid Boots* (film), 110–12
*Kid from Spain, The*, 148–53, 167
"Kid Kabaret," 35, 37–41, 146, 184, 194
*Kid Millions*, 164–165, 194
Kiel Auditorium (St. Louis), 272
Kilgallen, Dorothy, 239
King, A. H. (Publishers), 157
King, Walter Wolf, 204, 206
*King Lear*, 65
Kingdon, Dr. Frank, 179
Kingsbridge Hospital (Bronx, N.Y.), 272
Kingsley, Walter J., 100, 110
Kingsley, Sidney, 9
Kiraly, Stage Manager, 52
Kirke, Helen, 157
Kirsten, Dorothy, 278
*Kismet*, 42
*Kiss Me. See Make It Snappy*
*Kiss Me, Kate*, 269
Kittel, Mary Jane, 125
Klaw, Marc, 116
Klawans, Bernard, 227
Knight, Alec, 204
Knight, June, 154
Knight, Vick, 204, 217
Knights of Columbus, 260
Knights of Pythias, 274
Kober, Arthur, 181
Kohlmar, Fred, 171
KPO, Television Station (San Francisco), 239
Kriendler, Mac, 267

Ku Klux Klan, 104, 120
Kurtzman, Sam, 188
*Kvutzat Aryeh* (Palestine), 200
Kyser, Kay, 230, 233

Labor Stage, 200
*Lady Be Good!*, 96, 103
*Lady Comes Across, A*, 224
Lahr, Bert, 128
Lake Surprise Camp. *See* Alliance Camp
"Lambeth Walk," 199
Lambs Club (New York), 72
Lamour, Dorothy, 280
Landau, Bea, 204
Landry, Robert, 196
Lardner, Ring, 62, 204
*Lark*, 239
Lasky, Jesse, 98, 112, 114, 115
Lastfogel, Abe, 141, 166, 180, 182, 201, 283, 284, 291
LaTouche, John, 223, 224
Lauder, Harry, 265
"Laugh Your Way Through Life," 192
Laurie, Joe, Jr., 113
Lawrence, Gertrude, 103, 226
Lazarowitz (Kantrowitz), Esther, 3–22, 24–26, 29, 31, 33, 35, 37, 42, 47, 54–56, 73, 134, 161, 202, 265, 278, 286, 289, 291, 299
Lazarowitz, Javel, 3
Lazarowitz, Mindel. *See* Abramowitz (Lazarowitz), Mindel
"Lazy Mary, Won't You Get Up?," 220
League of Nations, 200
Leahy, Frank, 267
Lear, Norman, 253
LeBoy, Grace, 124
Lee, Al, 43–48, 58
Lee, Dick, 221
Lee, Lila (Cuddles), 34
"Lefty Louie," 9
Lehman, Ernie, 204
Lehman, Mrs. Herbert H., 200
Lehn & Fink, 172
Lehr, Abe, 173
Leibowitz, Samuel, 186–87
LeMaire, George, 72–73, 81–82, 88
LeMaire, Rufus, 73, 183, 184
Lempke, William, 208
Lennox, Elizabeth, 143
Leon and Eddie's (New York), 244
Leonard, Jack E., 274
LeRoy, Mervyn, 140
Lerner, Sammy, 170
Leslie, Joan, 231
Lesser, Sol, 175–76, 184, 203
"Let Them Keep It Over There," 177
"Let's Do and Say We Didn't," 96
*Let's Sing Again*, 176
Levey, Jules, 221
Levi Simpson's (New York), 31

Levine, Morris, 196
Levy, Sammy, 8, 9
Levy, Theodore, 8
Lewin, Kaufman & Schwartz, 301
Lewis, Albert, 122, 221–23
Lewis, Diana, 215
Lewis, Jerry, 268, 306
Lewis, Lloyd, 178–179
Lewis, Monica, 247
Lewis, Patti, 288
Lewis, Sam M., 109
Lewis, Shari, 232
Lewis, Ted, 196–97
*Liberty* Magazine, 204
*Life* Magazine, 143
*Life Begins at Minsky's*, 175
"Life of Sammy Hogarth, The," 204
*Life With Father*, 4
*Lightnin'*, 75
Lika Productions (New York), 300
Lillie, Beatrice, 103
*Limelight*, 39
Lincoln, Abraham, 85
Lincoln School (New York), 112
Lindbergh, Charles, 118, 234
Linden, Nat, 251
Lindsay, Howard, 171
Lindy's (New York), 189, 198
Lipman, Lillian, 37
Lipsky, Daniel, 11, 13, 17–18, 67–68, 73, 74,
    79, 84–85, 90–92, 98, 126, 129, 165–66,
    286, 309
Little, Harry, 37
"Little Curly Hair in a High Chair," 217
Livingstone, Mary, 146
Lloyd, Harold, 98
"Loch Lomond," 196
Lockridge, Richard, 125
Loesser, Frank, 285
Loew, Marcus, 28, 80, 98
Loews Canal Theatre (New York), 216
Loews State Theatre (New York), 213, 259
Loews Theatres, 115
London Conference on Economics, 208
London Theatre (New York), 21
"Look What You've Done," 149
Lord Tarleton Hotel (Miami), 273
Lorraine, Lillian, 52, 69, 70, 71, 229
Lorre, Peter, 293
Los Angeles *Mirror-News*, 299, 301
Los Angeles Superior Court, 303, 304, 309
*Louella Parsons Show, The*, 291
Louis, Joe, 248
Louria, Dr. Alex L., 120–21
*Love Letters*, 113
"Love Me or Leave Me," 124, 125
*Love Me Tonight*, 153
*Love, Sidney*, 310
Lowe, Joshua, 37
Loy, Myrna, 218

Luddy, Catherine, 13
Lurie, Louis, 239
*Lux Radio Theatre*, 182, 233
Lyceum Theatre, New (Elizabeth, N.J.), 28
Lynn, Leni, 214
Lyons, Collette, 230
Lyons' Corner House (London, Eng.), 42–43
Lyric Theatre (Brooklyn, N.Y.), 28
Lyric Theatre (Dayton, Ohio), 32
Lyric Theatre (Hoboken, N.J.), 28, 29
Lyric Theatre (Philadelphia), 81
Lyric Theatre (Simcoe, Ont.), 154

McBride, Mr., 167
McCarey, Leo, 151
McCarthy, Joseph, 93
McCarthy, Sen. Joseph, 264
McCoy Band, Clyde, 221
McCree, Junie, 21, 30
McDaniel, Hattie, 232
McDonald, James G., 200, 267, 277
MacFadden-Eddy, 301
MacGowan, Kenneth, 89
McGuinness, Liz, 299
McGuire, Wm. Anthony, 93, 97, 111, 122,
    124, 155
McHugh, James, 196, 201, 245, 254, 301
McHugh, James, Jr., 196, 201, 221, 235, 236,
    249
McHugh, Judith, 215, 245, 249, 253, 256,
    262, 286, 301, 308–10
McIntyre, Marvin, 195, 209
McIntyre & Heath, 307
MacRae, Gordon, 284
McVey, Evelyn, 37
"Ma, He's Making Eyes At Me," 269, 284
Mack, Tommy, 218
Mackaye, Dorothy, 114
*Mad Parade*, 144
Mad Russian, The. *See* Gordon, Bert
*Madame Butterfly*, 194
*Madame X*, 31
Madison Square Garden (New York), 104–5,
    204, 208, 230
Magnin, Rabbi Edgar F., 303
Mahoney, Will, 130
Mailer, Norman, 150
Maizlish, Harry, 303–4
Majestic Theatre (Brooklyn), 90
Majestic Theatre (Chicago), 32
Majestic Theatre (Houston), 40
Majestic Theatre (Milwaukee), 45
Major, Olive, 221, 237
*Make It Snappy*, 88–91, 117
"Make Believe," 186
"Make with the Feet," 224
"Making the Best of Each Day," 199, 222
"Makin' Whoopee," 125, 129, 136, 168–69,
    251, 265, 284
Malitz, Joe, 22, 23

"Mandy," 72, 165, 290
*Manhattan*, 218
Manhattan Opera House (New York), 85
Manhattan Theatre (New York), 27–28
Mankiewicz, Herman J., 230, 231
Manners, David, 156
Mansfield, Irving, 213, 226
Manson Sisters, 28
Manufacturers Hanover Trust Co., 67, 79, 97, 129, 135
Marceau, Marcel, 111
March, Hal, 285
March Field (Calif.), 231
March of Dimes, 195–96, 205, 245, 277, 287, 299, 304, 311
*March of Time, The*, 195
Mardikian, George, 239
Marfioti, Mario, 176
"Margie," 82, 185, 230, 265, 276, 284, 302
*Margie*, 302
Margolin, Celia, 297
Marin, Edwin, 237
*Mark (Variety)*, 41
Marko, Robert, 171
Marko, Ruth, 171
Marks, Gerald, 170
Markson, Mr. and Mrs. Yoland, 267
Marshall, George C., 273
Martin, Francis, 174
Martin, Nora Lou, 237, 239, 242, 244, 247, 248
Martin & Lewis, 269, 285
Marx, Adolph (Harpo), 34, 104, 307, 308
Marx, Julius (Groucho), 34, 133, 155, 251, 259
Marx, Leonard (Chico), 104, 155
Marx, Milton (Gummo), 34
Marx Brothers, 34, 89, 95, 119, 123, 128, 148
Marshall Plan, 260
Mason Opera House (Los Angeles), 49
Masonic Hall (New York), 85
Masonic Opera House (Hinton, W. Va.), 22
Masons (F. & A.M.), 85–86
Massachusetts Institute of Technology (M.I.T.), 180
"Master and Man," 43–45, 48–49
Masters, Frankie, 148
Mastin, Will, 277
*Mata Hari*, 148
Matthews, Jessie, 224
Matthews, Owen W., 179–80, 182
*Matinee Theatre*, 292
"Maxie the Taxi," 89, 270, 271, 273, 274, 279, 284, 285, 288
*Maxwell House Coffee Time*, 233
Mayer, Louis B., 194
Mayflower Hotel (New York), 64
Mayo, Virginia, 226
Mayor of Broadway "Election," 100–101
"Mayor of Texaco Town, The," 183, 288

*Me and My Girl*, 199
"Me and My Shadow," 117
"Me, Too," 112
Mechanic Arts H.S. (St. Paul), 237
Melnitz, Curtis, 168
*Memphis Bound*, 247
Mencher, Murray, 170
*Mendel Marantz*, 122, 123
Mencken, Helen, 204
Mendelssohn, Felix, 32
Menser, C. L., 242–43
Merchants Trust Co., 112
Merman, Ethel, 164–65, 174–75
Merriam, Frank F., 194
"Merrily We Roll Along," 170
*Merry Melodies*, 170
Metro-Goldwyn-Mayer (M-G-M), 148, 184, 191, 201, 214, 215, 282–83
Metropolitan Opera House (New York), 221
Metzger, Joseph, 192, 199, 200, 249–50
Metzger, Michael, 214, 245, 250, 256, 262, 286, 306, 308–10
Miami Heart Institute, 294
Michael, Andreas, 195
*Midnight Frolic* (Fourth Edition), 50–55, 57–59, 74, 127
*Midnight Frolic* (Seventh Edition), 67, 70
*Midnight Frolic* (Eighth Edition), 70, 71, 87
*Midnight Rounders*, 81, 83–88, 130
Miller, Ann, 206, 213
Miller, Bill, 232–33
Miller, Marilyn, 68, 69, 70, 73, 76, 78–81, 86, 95, 98
Miller, Mrs. 69–70
Miller, Sy, 275
Milman, Mort, 140
Milwaukee Centurama, 252
"Mimic Land," 39
Miner's Bowery Theatre (New York), 20–21, 24
*Minick*, 103
Minneapolis Senior Vocational H.S., 245
Minton, Gus, 61
Mirkin, Barry, 301
*Miss Springtime*, 52
*Mr. Cinders*, 139
*Mr. District Attorney*, 233
"Mr. Gallagher and Mr. Shean," 92
"Modern Maiden's Prayer, The," 61, 63
Molasso, 32
Monroe (Crandall), Alice, 219
Montreal *Gazette*, 250
Moore, Constance, 237, 238, 243–44
Moore, Gary, 260
Moore, Grace, 176
Moore, Owen, 73
Moore, Victor, 19
Morehouse, Ward, 266
Morgan, Henry, 300
Mount Nebo Congregation (New York), 300

Mount Sinai Hospital (New York), 292
Mt. Zion Cemetery (Maspeth, N.Y.), 56
Morel, Enid, 37, 40
Morgan, Frank, 233
Morosco, Oliver, 47–48, 50–51, 55
Morris, William, 110, 180
Morrison's Music Hall (Rockaway, N.Y.), 35
Moses, Mr., 12
Motion Picture Code Authority (MPCA), 160, 163
Mullett, Mary B., 102
Municipal Auditorium (Miami), 273
Municipal Auditorium (Omaha), 217
Munn Lodge No. 203, F. & A.M., 85
Murphy, George, 164, 165, 237, 238, 243–44
Murrow, Edward R., 293
Museum of Modern Art (New York), 138
Music Corporation of America (MCA), 164, 196, 235
"Music Goes 'Round and 'Round, The," 177
*Music Master, The*, 39
Mussolini, Benito, 166–169
"My Baby Just Cares For Me," 137
"My Baby Said 'Yes'," 140
"My Best Girl," 265
"My Blackbirds Are Bluebirds Now," 126
"My Blue Heaven," 139
*My Fair Ladies*, 226
*My Forty Years in Show Business*, 263–66, 270, 271
"My Landlady," 59
*My Life Is in Your Hands*, 123
*My Lucky Star*, 237
"My Mariucca Take A Steamboat," 15
"My Mother's Eyes," 146
*My Sister Eileen*, 223
"My Wife's Gone to the Country," 200
Myles Standish, Camp, 246

NAACP, 277
National Broadcasting Co. (NBC), 89, 113, 142–44, 162, 170, 176, 188, 219, 220, 237, 242–43, 246, 247, 251, 252, 257–61, 267, 270, 276, 278, 285, 287, 292, 296
NBC Artists Bureau, 140
NBC Orchestra, 143, 147, 148
National Business Conference, 132
National Catholic Welfare Council News Service, 243
National Cloak & Suit Co., 25
National Council for Industrial Peace, 297
National Entertainment Industry Council, 236
National Foundation for Infantile Paralysis, 274, 277
National Recovery Administration (NRA), 160
National Theatre (San Francisco), 39
National Union for Social Justice, 208
National Vaudeville Artists (NVA), 131–132, 159
NVA Clubhouse (New York), 131

NVA Sanitarium (Saranac Lake, N.Y.) 131
Naval Recreation Auditorium (Boston), 279
Negro Actors' Guild, 241
Neilson, Maurice, 214, 238, 257, 266, 275, 298, 308
*Nellie Bly*, 248, 250, 262
Nelson, Bob, 221
Nelson, Donald, 230
Nelson, Eddie, 113
*Nervous Wreck, The*, 122–123, 125
*Nervous Wreck, The* (film), 123
New Amsterdam Roof Theatre (N.Y.), 50–51, 54, 70, 129
New Amsterdam Theatre (New York), 50, 52, 61, 63, 69, 76, 77, 79, 125, 129, 133, 135, 163, 259
New Citizens Day, 207
*New Faces* (1952), 264
New Jersey Joint Council of International Relations, 179
New Plantations Club (New York), 109
"New Teacher, The," 34
New York *American*, 54
New York Bureau of Licenses, 67
New York Central Railroad, 11
New York *Commercial*, 97
New York *Daily News*, 191, 270
New York *Evening Journal*, 10, 152
New York *Evening Mail*, 123, 152
New York *Evening Sun*, 73
New York *Evening Telegram*, 54, 62
New York Eye and Ear Infirmary, 114
New York Foundling Hospital, 261
New York *Globe*, 67, 68, 73, 89
New York *Herald*, 54, 62, 92
New York *Herald Tribune*, 153, 267
New York Infirmary, 254
New York *Press*, 152
New York State Supreme Court, 186
New York *Sun*, 191, 198
New York *Telegram-Mail*, 100
New York *Times, The*, 64, 71, 98, 109, 112, 114, 125, 138, 169, 178, 207, 227, 269, 308
New York *Tribune*, 62
New York University, 191, 274
New York *World*, 62
New York *World-Telegram*, 145, 266
Newark *News*, 179
Newman, Alfred, 183
Newman, Lee, 310, 311
Newspaper Guild, 227
Nicholas I, Czar, 31
Nicholas II, Czar, 3
Nicholas, Fayard, 165
Nicholas, Harold, 165
Nicholas Brothers, 165, 166, 173
Nicolai, George, 113
Niesen, Gertrude, 257
"Night Court," 160, 165
Night of Stars, 204

Nixon Theatre (Pittsburgh), 125
*No Foolin'. See* Follies *(1926)*
"No More Love," 156
Non-Sectarian Anti-Nazi League, 265
*Normandie*, 199
Norman, Lucille, 276
*Not Likely*, 42–43
Notre Dame, University of, 266
"Now in Rehearsal," 288
"Now's The Time to Fall in Love," 144, 160, 269, 273
Nugent, J. C., 102

Oboler, Arch, 248
O'Brien, Ray, 108, 251
O'Connor, Basil, 277
O'Connor, Donald, 285, 287
*Of Mice and Men*, 190
"Oh, Gee! Georgie," 102
"Oh, Gee! Oh, Gosh! Oh, Golly! I'm in Love," 91
"Oh, How She Could Yacki Hacki Wicki Wacki Woo," 52, 53
"Oh, Susannah, Dust Off the Old Pianna," 170, 272
Ohio Theatre (Cleveland), 107
Ohman, Phil, 175
*Oklahoma*, 96
Oklahoma A&M University, 266
"Ol' Man River," 271
Old Roumanian (New York), 246
Oliver, Vic, 168
Olsen, George, 98, 104, 107, 112, 124, 126, 219
Olsen & Johnson, 224, 271
Olympic Games (1932), 149
Omar Khayyam Restaurant (San Francisco), 239
"On the Sunny Side of the Street," 196
"One Fine Day," 194
One World Committee, 264, 265
O'Neill, Eugene, 103
"One-Zy, Two-Zy," 251
Opp, Joe, 83, 87
Oppenheimer, George, 155
Oregon State College, 180
Orpheum Circuit, 38–39, 47–48
Orpheum Theatre (Brooklyn, N.Y.), 46, 91
Orpheum Theatre (Des Moines, Iowa), 32
Orpheum Theatre (Los Angeles), 47, 49, 115
Orpheum Theatre (San Francisco), 39, 115
Oscar of the Waldorf, 159
Osterman, Jack, 120
Ostroff, Manning, 251, 261, 268, 272
Ouimet, Francis, 94
"Over There," 235
Oxford Theatre (London, Eng.), 42

*Pabst Blue Ribbon Show*, 248, 251, 252, 254, 256–59

Pabst Breweries, 251, 252, 254, 257, 258, 260
Package Store Dealers Convention, Fifth Annual (San Antonio), 280
Palace Music Hall (Chicago), 45, 181
Palace Theatre, RKO (Cleveland), 181
Palace Theatre (New York), 41, 91, 92, 120, 139, 141, 145–47, 152, 235, 241, 259
Palace Theatre Building (New York), 43
"Palesteena," 82
Paley, William, 170, 259
Palladium (London), 260
Palmer, Bee, 70, 71
*Palmy Days*, 140, 144–45, 153, 175
"Pals," 154
Pan-American Conference, 222
Pan-American Records, 251
Pantages, Alexander, 237
Pantages Theatre (Los Angeles), 294
Paradise Theatre (Bronx, N.Y.), 166
Paramount, 110–12, 114–15, 123, 130, 136, 141, 149, 150
Paramount Theatre (Brooklyn), 144, 162
Paramount Theatre (Los Angeles), 173
Paramount Theatre (New York), 114, 143, 162, 261
*Paris*, 143
"Paris By Night," 32
Parks, Bert, 206
Parkyakarkus. *See* Einstein, Harry, 164
Parnell, Val, 260
Parrish's Candy Store (New York), 189
Parsons, Louella, 301
"Pass the Ammunition," 231
*Passing Show, The* (Shubert) (generic), 80, 130
Pastor, Tony, 36
Pastor's Theatre (New York), 16
Pathe (Recording Co.), 74, 78, 87
*Peace Digest*, 179
Pearl, Jack, 146, 162, 166, 233
Pearl, Winnie, 146
Pearlstein, Harris, 252
Pease, Harry, 251
*Pebeco Show, Eddie Cantor*, 166, 170, 171, 174, 176, 177, 180
Pecora, Ferdinand, 186
Pefsner, Leon, 31
Peggy, Baby, 175
Penner, Joe, 233
Pennington, Ann, 69, 70, 71, 73, 92
*People's Choice, The*, 200
People's Vaudeville Co., 28–29
Pepper, Cynthia, 302
*Perils of Pauline*, 43
Perlberg, William, 149
Perrin, Nat, 155, 174
Perry, Harold, 192
Perry, Kathryn, 73
*Person to Person*, 293
Phi Beta Kappa, 123
Philadelphia *Daily News*, 270

Philadelphia *Inquirer*, 82
Philco, 242
Philip Morris, 276, 280
*Philip Morris Playhouse*, 230
Phonofilm, 98
Piantadosi, Al, 72
Pickford, Mary, 73
Pickman, Jerry, 236–37
Pickman, Milton, 236
*Pictorial Review*, 123
Pierce Brothers Mortuary (Los Angeles), 149
Pierre Hotel (New York), 145
Pig 'n' Whistle Coffee Shop (L.A.), 50
Pike Street Synagogue (New York), 14
*Pinafore, H.M.S.*, 247
*Pins and Needles*, 200
Plattsburgh High School (Mo.), 179
"Play Pen, The," 289
*Playhouse 90*, 292–93
Plaza Hotel (New York), 246
Podell, David L., 186–87
Poli's Theatre (Bridgeport), 166
Polo Grounds (New York), 235
Pons, Lily, 195
"Pony Boy," 183
Poole, Bessie, 63, 66
Poonelo, 44
"Poor Pauline," 43
Poor Richard Club (Philadelphia), 242
"Popular Pests, The," 72
Porter, Cole, 171
Porter, Mike, 154
"Potatoes Are Cheaper." *See* "Now's the Time to Fall in Love"
Powell, David, 261
Powell, William, 113, 215, 258
Prentice-Hall, Inc., 299
President's Birthday Committee, 177
Presidio (San Francisco), 284–85
"Pretty Girl Is Like a Melody, A," 72
*Pretty Mrs. Smith*, 47
Price, Georgie, 164
Price, Guy, 50
*Private Izzy Murphy*, 110
Proctor, F.F., 36
Proctor's 58th Street Theatre (New York), 25–26
Producing Managers' Association, 75–76
Public Health Dept. (San Francisco), 239
Purdue University (Lafayette, Ind.), 262
P.S. 1 (New York), 8
P.S. 2 (New York), 8
P.S. 126 (New York), 7–8
P.S. 177 (New York), 14–15, 107
Pulitzer Prize, 122
Pulley, B. S., 254
Purple Heart Circuit, 241, 243
*Purple Rose of Cairo*, 188
Pursel, Fred R., 154
"Put a Tax on Love," 156
"Put Both Hands Up," 23

Qualters, Tot, 227
*Queen Mary*, 260
Quillen, Joe, 201, 204, 217, 251
Quintella, Baby, 215

Radio City (New York), 189, 246
Radio City (San Francisco), 239
Radio Corporation of America (RCA), 142
RCA Camden, 295
*Radio Hall of Fame, Philco*, 241, 242
Radio-Keith-Orpheum (RKO), 139, 141, 186, 201, 206, 214, 246, 248, 250, 252, 254
RKO Boston Theatre. *See* Keith's Theatre (Boston)
RKO Theatre (White Plains, N.Y.), 272–73
*Radio Revue*, Eddie Cantor, 196
Rae, Nina, 218
Rae & Davis, 218
"Ragtime Violin," 33, 58
Ralston, Jobyna, 113
Rand, Sally, 115
Randall, Tony, 310
Rapp, Phil, 169, 173, 174, 204
Raskob, John, 125
Rath, Edith R., 122
Rathvon, N. Peter, 250
Ratoff, Gregory, 146, 163, 292
Raymond, Ray, 114
Reader, Ralph, 86
Reagan, Ronald, 312
Reber, John, 147
Red Cross, 217
*Red Skelton Hour, The*, 306, 311
*Red, Hot and Blue*, 174
Reed, Alan. *See* Bergman, Teddy
Reiss, Jacob, 199
Renard, Jacques, 186
Ress, Dr. Irving L., 215
*Restless Jim Mallon*, 102
*Rex*, 166
Rex-British Decca, 169
Reynolds Tobacco Co., R.J., 196, 210, 211, 278
Rhythm Boys, 126
Rhythm Boys, Three, 146
*Rhythm Rhapsody*, Ted Lewis, 196
Rialto Theatre (New York), 112, 145
Rice, Thomas, 29
*Rich Man, Poor Man. See* If You Knew Susie
Richards, Danny, 285
Richards, Vickee, 261
Richman, Arthur, 132
Richman, Harry, 164, 209, 213
Riegelmann, Edward, 67
*Rigoletto*, 176
Riis House (New York), 246
Ringling, John, 80
Rinker, Al, 126
Ritz-Carlton Hotel (Boston), 117
Rivoli Theatre (New York), 138, 162
Roach Studios, Hal, 171

*Road to Rome, The*, 155
Roberti, Lyda, 149, 151, 153
Robinson, Bill (Bojangles), 222, 247
Robinson, Edward G., 301
Robinson, Elmer, 262
Robinson, Hubbell, Jr., 241, 292
Robinson, J. Russel, 82
Rodgers, Richard, 36, 96, 114, 136, 223
Rogers, Betty, 39, 149
Rogers, Sheila, 188–89, 205
Rogers, Will, 38–41, 50, 54, 60–62, 64, 66–
   67, 69, 70, 71, 77, 86, 91, 98, 106, 131,
   143, 145, 149, 161, 173–74, 265, 282, 304
Roland, Gilbert, 111
"Roll, Roll, Rolling Along," 139
Rolling Stones, The, 306, 311
Rolls-Royce, 127–28, 133
*Roman Scandals*, 155–56, 159, 162, 167, 194
Romberg, Sigmund, 103, 272
Roney Plaza Hotel (Miami), 273
Rooney, Mickey, 282
Roosevelt, Eleanor, 266, 301
Roosevelt, Franklin D., 64, 101, 151, 159,
   189, 192, 194–96, 205, 207–9, 225, 230,
   265, 311
Roosevelt Committee, 101
Roosevelt Hotel (New York), 114
Rose, Billy, 181
Rose, Bobby, 175
Rose, Jack, 106
*Rose Marie*, 103
Roseben's Pavilion (Coney Island, N.Y.), 22
Rosen, George, 269
Rosenbaum, Mr., 26
Rosenteur, Phyllis, 296
Rosenthal, Sam, 43
Rosenthal murder, 9
Rosner, Louis, 15, 22, 25
Ross, Joe, 221
Roth, Lillian, 164
*Rotterdam*, 107
Royal Theatre (Brooklyn, N.Y.), 28
Royce, Edward, 96
Ruban Bleu, Le, 247
Rubin, Benny, 141, 145–46
Rubinoff, David, 143, 147, 148, 153, 154,
   163, 173
Ruby, Harry, 63, 71, 148, 245, 285, 306
Ruby (Garson), Toby, 63, 245
Ruggles, Charles, 49
Russell, Connie, 285
Russell, Lillian, 65
Russell's Orchestra, Hank, 261
Ryan, Colletta, 154
Ryan, Police Sgt. Patrick F., 104–5

Safety First Campaign, 251
St. Clair, Margaret, 227
St. Denis, Ruth, 32
St. Germain, Kay, 206–7
*St. Paul*, U.S.S., 43

Sahl, Mort, 174
Sal Hepatica, 219
Salk, Jonas, 299
Salk Foundation Program, 304
*Sally*, 80, 86, 91, 94–97
*Sally, Irene and Mary*, 237
"Saloon of the Future," 72
Salvation Army, 106
*San Francisco*, 184
San Francisco *Chronicle*, 39
San Francisco *Examiner*, 223
San Francisco Opera House, 276
San Remo (New York), 156–59, 169, 176,
   179, 180, 190
"Santa Claus Is Coming to Town," 176
Santa Monica State College, 156
"Santa, Send My Mommie Back to Me," 176
Santley, Joseph, 16
Saphier, Jimmy, 216
*Saratoga Chips*, 192
Sardi's (New York), 159
Sarnoff, David, 142
*Saturday Evening Post*, 123, 172
Sauber, Sunny, 249
Savage, Henry, 80
Savoy, Bert, 58
Savoy, Harry, 188
Savoy, The (London, Eng.), 168
Savoy-Plaza (New York), 258
Savoy Theatre (Atlantic City), 34
Sawyer, Connie, 272
Saxony Hotel (Miami Beach), 278
*Scandals* (generic), 130
*Scandals* of 1919, 74
*Scandals* of 1920, 85
Schader, Fred, 112
Scheff, Fritzi, 47
Schenck, Joe, 78, 113, 165
Schenck, Joseph M., 28, 182
Schenck, Nicholas, 28
Schlessingers, 122
Schmidt, Ruben S., 249
Schoenfeld, Herm, 270
"School Boys and Girls," 34, 39
"School Days," 29, 34
Schulberg, Ben P., 98, 111, 114
Schulberg, Budd, 174, 239
Schwab's (Hollywood), 191
Schwartz, Mrs. Ray, 15, 107
Screen Actors' Guild (SAG), 159–60, 166,
   171, 193, 209, 213, 304, 309
*Screen Guild Players*, 233
*Sealtest Show*, 217
*Sealtest Village Store*, 233, 237, 246
"Search for G.I. Joe," 240
Security Mutual Life Insurance Co., 309
*See Saw*, 76
Seelen, Jerry, 275
Seeley, Blossom, 146
Segal, Dr. Samuel M., 300
Selective Service Act, 225

Selective Service System, 220
Selwyn Theatre (New York), 103
Semple's, Miss, 157
*Service Station*, 114
Shakespeare, William, 132
"Shaking the Blues Away," 117
Shapiro, Dr. Edward, 281
Shapiro, Sol, 264
Shapiro-Bernstein & Co., 106, 170, 254
Shaw, George Bernard, 155
Shea, John F., 84
Shea, Mike, 33
Shea's Theatre (Buffalo, N.Y.), 33, 58
Sheekman, Arthur, 155, 174
"Sheik, The," 89
"Sheik of Araby, The," 89
"She's Wonderful," 123–24
Sherman & Marquette Agency, 272
Sherrill, Jack, 197
Sherry Netherland Hotel (New York), 188, 196, 204
Sherwin, Louis, 67
Sherwood, Bobby, 218
Sherwood, Robert, 155
*Shine On Harvest Moon*, 236
*Shoot the Chutes*. *See* Strike Me Pink
Shore, Dinah, 218, 219, 221–23, 229–32, 236, 237, 248, 257, 258, 261, 284
*Show Boat*, 186
*Show Business*, 235–39, 241, 244
*Show Business Out West*, 250
*Show Business—Then and Now*, 276, 279–80, 283
*Show Goes On, The*, 176
*Show Is On, The*, 186
Shrine Auditorium (Omaha, Neb.), 261
Shrine of the Little Flower (Royal Oak, Mich.), 207
Shriners (A.A.O.N.M.S.), 86, 196
Shubert, Jacob J., 47, 81, 83–87, 88, 90–92, 99, 130, 136, 150
Shubert, Lee, 80, 83–84
Shubert, Messrs., 68, 69, 76, 80–85, 87–92, 98, 122
Shubert, Samuel S., 80
Shubert Advanced Vaudeville, 89
Shubert Theatre (New Haven), 224
Shubert Theatre (Newark, N.J.), 106
Shubert Theatre (Philadelphia), 83
Shutta, Ethel, 107, 124, 125, 126, 137, 227, 236
"Sidewalks of New York, The," 129
Sidman, Sam, 21
*Sidney Shorr*, 310
Siegel, Arthur, 264, 310
Sillman, Leonard, 264
Silver Lake Cemetery (Staten Island, N.Y.), 5
Silverman, Shirley, 296
Silverman, Sid, 114
Silverman, Sime, 61–62, 73, 114

Silvers, Phil, 34
Silvers, Sid, 188
Simon and Schuster, 134
Sinatra, Frank, 241, 285
Sing Sing State Prison (Ossining, N.Y.), 120
*Sing-Song* Program (U.K.), 199
Singer, Stuffy, 276
*Singing Fool, The*, 123
Singleton, Doris, 277
"Sizeman and Son," 292–93
Skelton, Red, 306
*Sketch Book, Earl Carroll's*, 130–31
Skolsky, Estelle, 191
Skolsky, Nina, 191
Skolsky, Sidney, 180, 191, 236, 284, 287, 296
Skolsky, Steffi, 191
Skulnik, Menasha, 292
"Slave Market," 156
Slotzki (Tobias), Rachel, 15, 158–59, 192
*Smartest Girl in Town, The*, 186
Smith, Alfred E., 17, 58, 66, 96, 98, 101, 125, 143, 189, 199, 265
Smith, Gerald L. K., 208
Smith, Kate, 195
Smith, Tom, 55
Smith & Austin, 55
Smith & Dale, 34
Snyder, "Colonel" Moe, 117–18, 125
Snyder, Ted, 23, 28
*So Long Letty*, 47
Social Security, 295
Socony, 113
Sofranski, George, 115
Solomon, Sylvia. *See* Rogers, Sheila
*Somebody Up There Likes Me*, 204
"Something to Remember," 304
Sommerville, Slim, 179
Sondheim, Stephen, 137
Sonneborn, Rudolf G., 276
"Sonny Boy," 123
*Sons o' Fun*, 224, 232
Sothern, Ann, 164, 165
"Soul of the Violin, The," 9, 12
*Special Delivery*, 112–15
Spellman, Francis Cardinal, 261
Spitz, Leo, 181
Sponable, Arthur, 98
"Spring Song," 32
Stallings, Laurence, 103
Stammers, Frank, 49
Standard Club (Chicago), 187
Stander, Artie, 266
Stander, Lionel, 233
Stang, Arnold, 284
Stanley, Eddie, 192
Stanley Theatre (Pittsburgh), 214
Star Theatre (New York), 44
"Star's Double, The," 116
*Star-Spangled Rhythm*, 230
State Theatre (Hartford), 216

Statler, Hotel (Boston), 292
Staudinger, Erv, 258
Steel Pier (Atlantic City), 222
Steele, John, 72, 73
"Step in My Taxi," 89
Stephens, Clarke E., 304
Stephens, Gary, 161
Stephens, Jess E., 249
"Stetson," 125, 137
Stevens Hotel (Chicago), 266
Stewart, Martha, 254
*Stockton, S.S.*, 257
Stoll, Georgie, 175
Stoller, Morris, 291
Stone, Fred, 131
"Story I've Never Told, The," 288
Strand Barber Shop (New York), 76
Strauss, Ambassador, 168
*Strike Me Pink*, 140, 172, 173–76, 192
Stuart, Gloria, 156
*Such a Pretty Face*, 310
Suess, Leonard, 243
Sullivan, Ed, 146, 230, 241, 269, 301
Sullivan, Jack (Twin), 66, 197
Sullivan, Sylvia, 146
Sumac, Yma, 269
*Sun Valley Serenade*, 237
Super Markets Institute, 266
Surprise Lake Camp. *See* Alliance Camp
Surprise Lake Camp All-Star Benefit, 98
Surprise Lake Camp Committee, 98
Susann, Bob, 226
Susann, Jacqueline, 226
Swan Soap, 251
Swartz, Mitchell, 270
Swayne's Rats and Cats," 45
*Sweet Land of Liberty*, 218
"Sweet Sixteen," 72
*Sweet Smell of Success, The*, 204
"Swing Is Here to Sway," 192, 195
Sydenham Hospital (New York), 227
Syria Mosque (Pittsburgh), 274

Taft Hotel (New Haven), 84
*Take It or Leave It*, 233, 259–60, 262, 263, 266
*Take My Life*, 288–89, 291, 292
*Talk of the Town, The*, 19, 285
Tanguay, Eva, 32, 37, 44
Tashman, Lilyan, 45
Taurog, Norman, 174
"Taxi Cab, The." *See* "It Won't Be Long Now—
    A Taxi Ride"
Taylor, Deems, 242
Taylor, Elizabeth, 298
Teasdale, Verree, 156
Technicolor, 149
*Teen Time*, 261
Temple, Shirley, 176, 177, 207
Temple Theatre (Rochester, N.Y.), 46
Temple University (Philadelphia), 274

*Texaco Star Theatre*, 274, 290
*Texaco Town*, 180, 182–84, 186, 193
Texas Oil Company, 180, 186
*Texas Nightingale, The*, 105
Thalia Theatre (New York), 16
*Thank Your Lucky Stars*, 230–32, 244
"That Funny Melody." *See* "It Goes Like This"
"That Mysterious Rag," 28
"That Party in Person," 123
"That's My Daughter—That's My Dad," 293
"That's the Kind of a Baby for Me," 61–63, 67
Theatre Arts Committee, 209
Theatrical Syndicate, 68
"There's No Business Like Show Business,"
    263
"There's Nothing Too Good For My Baby,"
    140
*They Knew What They Wanted*, 103
"They Put on the Victrola and Go Dancing
    Around the Floor," 43
"They're Either Too Young or Too Old," 232
*Thin Ice*, 237
"This Is Broadway," 269
"This Is My New York," 275
*This Is Your Life*, 286
Thomas, Bob, 64, 301, 306
Thomas, Danny, 177, 257, 272, 274, 304
Thomas, Shirl, 223
Thompson, Don, 239
Thompson, Harry, 21, 29
Thompson, W. Robert, 295
Thompson Agency, J. Walter, 140–41, 144,
    147, 182
*Three Brothers, The*, 304
*Three Men on a Horse*, 171–72, 174, 181, 182,
    222–23, 225–26
*Three Smart Girls*, 183, 184
Tibbett, Lawrence, 193, 195
Tibboth, George, 264
*Tickets Please*, 269
Tierney, Harry, 93, 98
*Time to Smile*, 219, 220, 221, 223, 224, 227,
    230–32, 236, 237, 240–44, 247, 250, 254
Tinney, Frank, 39, 54, 62
"To The Ladies," 42
*Toast of the Town*, 269
Tobias, Anna, 15
Tobias, Charlie, 46, 170, 225, 304
Tobias, Clara, 15
Tobias, David, 15, 24, 34, 41, 62–63, 158,
    192–93
Tobias, Harry, 46–47, 157, 304
Tobias, Henry, 46, 304
Tobias (Cantor), Ida, 14–15, 19, 22, 24–27,
    29, 31–34, 37–38, 41–48, 51–55, 58, 62–
    63, 67–68, 72, 73, 77, 79, 86, 90–91, 101,
    107, 110–11, 114, 119–20, 122, 133–35,
    138–40, 147, 151, 155–58, 164, 166, 168–
    69, 172, 173, 176, 180–81, 191–92, 194,
    199, 200, 202–3, 207, 215, 220, 222, 226,

Tobias (Cantor), Ida (*continued*)
    229, 231, 234–39, 243, 245–47, 249, 253–
    54, 257, 258, 260, 262–64, 266–68, 271–
    75, 277–80, 283, 285, 286, 289, 291–95,
    297–304, 309
Tobias, Jenny, 15, 22, 24, 43, 46, 48, 51
Tobias, Max, 46
Tobias, Milton, 15
Tobias, Minnie, 15, 24
Tobias, Nathan, 46
Tobias, Nettie, 15, 158
Tobias, Rachel. *See* Slotzki (Tobias), Rachel
Tobin, Maurice, 247
*Today Show, The,* 299
Tombes, Andrew, 92
Tomlin, Pinky, 193
Tone, Rudy, 269
*Tonight Show,* 274
Tony & Eddy, 273
Torres, H. Z., 97
Touraine Hotel (Boston, Mass.), 63
Townsend, Dr. Francis, 208
Tracy, Arthur, 102
"Traitor's Deathbed, The," 9, 12
Trammel, Niles, 259
"Trans-Atlantic Flight, The," 116
*Treasure Hunt. See* Kid Millions
Treasury Dept., U.S., 231
Tree, Sir Herbert Beerbohm, 85, 126
"Trial of Adolf Hitler, The," 240
Trini, 110
Trix, Helen, 38
Troy, Helen, 193
Truman, Harry, 293–94
Tucker, Lana, 191
Tucker, Sophie, 44, 110, 164, 209–10, 213,
    214, 301
Tuttle, Frank, 111, 155
Twentieth Century-Fox, 182, 192, 194, 200,
    201, 237, 238, 292, 293

United Booking Office. *See* Keith Vaudeville
    Exchange
United Artists, 141, 146, 150, 168, 182, 183,
    221–22
United Jewish Appeal (UJA), 254–55, 257,
    258, 260, 261, 266–68, 277, 278
United Nations Children's Relief Fund, 257
United Services Organization (USO), 154, 273,
    290
Universal, 156, 183–84, 197, 221, 237
Universal-International, 181
University of Arizona, 264
University of California at Los Angeles
    (UCLA), 156, 309
University of Maine, 263–64
University of Newark, 179
University of Pennsylvania, 188
*Up in Arms,* 236

Upton, Frances, 118, 124, 125, 137
Urban, Josef, 59, 124, 125
Utica *Daily Press,* 28

Vague, Vera, 235
Vallee, Rudy, 140, 143–44, 147, 195, 199,
    207, 209, 217, 233, 237
Van, Gus, 78, 113, 165
Van Cortlandt Park (Bronx, N.Y.), 46, 63, 93
Vanderbilt, Gertrude, 227
Vanderbilt, William, 57, 62
Vanderpyle, Jean, 232
*Vanities* (generic), 130, 136
*Variety,* 37, 41, 45, 61–62, 71, 73, 91, 107,
    112, 113, 114, 147, 153, 154, 172, 188,
    193, 194, 196, 199, 201, 213, 214, 216,
    222, 223, 224, 229, 237, 240, 246, 250,
    258, 260, 265, 269, 270, 271–73, 275, 276,
    278–80, 301, 304, 307
*Vaudeville News,* 100
Veiller, Bayard, 173
Verne, Jules, 248
Veterans of Foreign Wars, 299
Victor Talking Machine Co., 63, 123, 134
Victoria Theatre (New York), 30, 31, 37
Victory Bonds, 67, 248
Vincent, Frank, 115
Vincent, Romo, 224
Virginia Minstrels, 29
Vitale, Magistrate, 105
Vitalis, 202
Volstead Act, 94
Von Zell, Harry, 218, 219, 234, 243, 252
"Vote For Honest Abe," 192

Wagner, Dr. Jerome, 121
Wagner, Robert F., 277
"Waiting for the Robert E. Lee," 269, 293
Waldorf-Astoria Hotel (New York), 159, 198,
    207, 236, 243, 248, 263, 267, 274
Walker, Bea, 243
Walker, George, 59
Walker, Herman, 20, 25
Walker, James J., 98, 118, 129, 241
Wall, Lucille, 193
Wallington, James, 143–44, 147, 153, 170,
    177, 186, 193, 287
Walsh, Carey, 22–23
Walter Reed Hospital (Washington, D.C.), 64,
    243
"War in Snyder's Grocery Store, The," 44
War Production Board, 230
Warfield, David, 39
Warfield, William, 273
Warner, Harry, 200
Warner, Jack, 230, 283, 284
Warner Bros., 110, 137, 149, 156, 170–72,
    181, 182, 190, 222, 227, 231, 242, 244,
    283–87

Warwick, Paul, 258
Warwick and Legler, 258
Washburn, Hazel, 73
Washburn, Lillian, 84
Washington, Betty, 37, 40
Washington, George, 253
Waters, Ethel, 109
Watts, Richard, Jr., 153
*Way I See It, The*, 296, 297, 299–300, 304
" 'Way Up North," 232
Wayburn, Ned, 61, 67
WCCO, Television Station (Minneapolis), 268
"We All Like The Medicine 'Doctor' Eddie Cantor Gives," 102
"We Did It Before," 225
"We're Staying Home Tonight," 244
"We're Having a Baby," 225, 242, 244, 269
*We're Not Dressing*, 165
WEAF, Radio Station (New York), 112
Webb, Jimmy, 310
Weber, Joe, 29
Weber & Fields, 29, 68, 307
Wedgwood, Josiah C., 198
Weeks, Anson, 175
Weil, Maurice, 163
Weiner, N. Jeffries, 309
Weir, John C., 25
Weir, J.C. & Co., 25
Weisbord, Sam, 291
Weismuller, Johnny, 123
Weiss, Sammy, 241
Weizmann, Chaim, 267
Welch Wine, 279–80
Welles, Orson, 195
Welsh, Joe, 17
Werba's Brooklyn Theatre, 106
West, Mae, 196
West End Theatre (New York), 28
Western Burlesque Wheel, 21
Western Union, 107
Westinghouse Co., 142
WGY, Radio Station (Schenectady), 143
Whalen, Grover, 129
"What a Perfect Combination," 149
*What Price Glory?*, 103
*What's My Line*, 272
"When I'm Alone I'm Lonesome," 23
"When I'm the President," 144
"Where or When," 273
White, Frances, 54
White, George, 70, 74, 130, 152, 191
White, Pearl, 43
White, Walter, 277
*White Horse Inn*, 186, 200
White House (Washington, D.C.), 65, 195, 209, 218
White Rats, 209
Whitehead, Ralph, 209, 213, 214
Whiteman, Paul, 126, 129, 241, 242

Whiting, Margaret, 252
Whitney, Jock, 222
*Whoopee*, 122–26, 128, 130–34, 136, 148, 220, 225, 236, 299
*Whoopee* (film), 130, 136–38, 140, 215, 223
"Wild Cherries," 23
Will Mastin Trio, 277, 278, 280, 285
Willard, Jess, 65
William and Mary College, 266
William Morris Agency, 122, 149, 152, 180, 182, 186, 214, 219, 264, 291
William Penn Hotel (Pittsburgh), 109
Williams, Bert, 59–62, 66, 68–69, 72–75, 77, 81, 82, 86, 161, 173, 265, 278, 282
Williams and Buttignal, 269
Williamsburg Bridge (New York), 9
Williamsburg Settlement (New York), 274
Willis, Beverly, 237
Willis, Si, 237, 255
Wills, Lou, Jr., 269
Wilson, Andy, 270
Wilson, Don, 217
Wilson, Jack, 44
Wilson, Woodrow, 73
Winchell, Walter, 100, 230, 233, 311
*Wings*, 119
Winslow, Raymond J., 210–11
Winter Garden (New York), 38–39, 47, 80, 81, 82, 89, 90, 130, 232
Witkin, Kate, 226
WJZ, Radio Station (New York), 219
WNBC, Radio Station (New York), 254
Wodehouse, P.G., 52
Wolfit, Sir Donald, 85–86
Wolters, Larry, 270
"Women and Light," 47
*Women, Inc.*, 288
Women's City Club (New York), 120
*Women's Home Companion, The*, 288
Wonder, Tommy, 269
Wood, Helen, 269
Wood, Joe, 27–28, 31
Woods Theatre (Chicago), 107
"Woody Woodpecker Song, The," 264
Works Progress Administration (WPA), 209
World Boy Scout Jamboree, 180
World Series (1917), 64
World's Fair (1939), 207
"Would You Rather Be a Colonel?," 72
"Wreck, The," 122
Wright, Cobina, Jr., 213
Wynn, Ed, 43, 86, 154, 162, 272, 275

Yale University, 84, 140
Yankee Stadium (Bronx, N.Y.), 142, 222
"Yes, My Darling Daughter," 222
"Yes Sir, That's My Baby," 284
"Yes, We Have No Bananas," 91
Y.M.C.A., 106

Y.M.H.A., 199
*Yoo-Hoo, Prosperity!*, 141
York, Dick, 286
Yorkville Court (New York), 105
*You Bet Your Life*, 259, 260
"You Cannot Make Your Shimmy Shake on Tea," 72
"You Don't Need the Wine to Have a Wonderful Time," 74
"You Hit the Spot," 177
"You'd Be Surprised," 72, 73, 284
Youmans, Vincent, 181
Young & Rubicam, 217, 219, 241, 248
Young, Jack, 296
Young, Joe, 109
Young, Robert, 151
Young, Waldemar, 39
"Young Man of Manhattan," 103
*Your Show of Shows*, 306

"You're a Grand Old Flag," 235
Youth *Aliyah*, 200, 267
"You've Got To Have 'It' in Hollywood," 115, 117

Zanuck, Darryl F., 182, 194, 200, 201
Ziegfeld, Florenz, Jr., 49–60, 62–64, 67–68, 70, 73–84, 86, 90–93, 95–100, 103, 106–10, 113–17, 120–31, 135–36, 138–40, 148–50, 152, 168, 207, 225, 226, 265, 272, 289, 299, 306
*Ziegfeld Follies* (NBC), 257
*Ziegfeld the Great Glorifier*, 157
Ziegfeld *Palm Beach Girl, Follies* (1926)
Ziegfeld Theatre (New York), 120
Ziegfeld's *Nine O'Clock Revue*, 87
Ziv Television Programs, 287, 290
Zukor, Adolph, 28, 80, 98, 112, 115